BRITAIN'S SEA-SOLDIERS

Napoleon inspecting the Royal Marine Guard on board H.M.S. "Bellerophon."

BRITAIN'S SEA-SOLDIERS

A HISTORY OF THE ROYAL MARINES AND THEIR PREDECESSORS AND OF THEIR SERVICES IN ACTION, ASHORE AND AFLOAT, AND UPON SUNDRY OTHER OCCASIONS OF MOMENT
BY COLONEL CYRIL FIELD, R.M.L.I.
WITH NUMEROUS ILLUSTRATIONS AND PLANS

FOREWORD BY ADMIRAL OF THE FLEET, EARL BEATTY, G.C.B.,&C

VOLUME II

The Naval & Military Press Ltd

Published by

The Naval & Military Press Ltd
Unit 10 Ridgewood Industrial Park,
Uckfield, East Sussex,
TN22 5QE England

Tel: +44 (0) 1825 749494
Fax: +44 (0) 1825 765701

www.naval-military-press.com
www.nmarchive.com

In reprinting in facsimile from the original, any imperfections are inevitably reproduced and the quality may fall short of modern type and cartographic standards.

CONTENTS
VOL. II

CHAPTER XX.
NAPOLEON BUONAPARTE AND THE ROYAL MARINES.
Page

Story that Buonaparte was once anxious for a Commission in the Corps—Is considered "likely to make a good sea-officer"—Story that he applied for a Commission in the British Navy—Account of Buonaparte's surrender by a Private of Marines—Napoleon and the Marines of H.M.S. *Undaunted*—Inspects the Marine Guard of H.M.S. *Bellerophon*—Various accounts of this incident—"How much might be done with 100,000 soldiers such as these!"—Napoleon wounded at Toulon by a Sergeant of Marines—His conversation with Captain Beatty, R.M. 1

NOTES.
I. Napoleon on Board H.M.S. *Bellerophon* 7
II. The Royal Marines and the Bayonet Exercise 7

CHAPTER XXI.
BOMBARDMENT OF ALGIERS AND THE BATTLE OF NAVARINO.

African Pirate Cities—Their depredations submitted to by the Great Powers—Prayer against the "Turks"—"Much rather Turk than Priest"—News of taking of Buda causes riot in London—Lord Exmouth's negotiations with the Dey of Algiers—Massacre at Bona—British and Dutch Squadrons before Algiers—No reply to Flag of Truce—The Battle begins—Fire of Flagship's Marines repulses gunboats—Officers of R.M.A. sent to fire an Algerine frigate—Excellent practice of the R.M.A. mortars—Lieutenant Bisset's premonition of death and its fulfilment—In action with the gout—Endurance of Captain Wilson, R.M.—Lieutenant Baxter, R.M.A., the first man killed in the action 9

Little information as to doings of Marines at Navarino. Cause of the action—Turkish and Egyptian Fleets—The Fight begins—Destruction of Turkish Fire-ships—Narrow escape of Sir William Codrington—Death of Captain Bell, R.M.—Losses of the Marines on the *Genoa's* poop—Coolness of Private Hill—Another brave fellow—Captain Stevens, R.M., killed—His presentiment of death—Lieutenant Hurdle's account of what happened on board the *Albion*—The *Cambrian* engages the shore batteries 15

NOTES.
I. Supply of Munitions of War to Barbary 21
II. Turks *v.* Roman Catholics 21
III. Uniform of the Royal Marines, 1777-1823 21

CHAPTER XXII.
THE ROYAL MARINE BATTALION IN THE CARLIST WAR, 1836-7.

Origin of the War—The British Legion—Formation of a R.M. Battalion at Santander—Occupation of Portugalette—Battalion at St. Sebastian—Advance over the Urimea—Carlists repulsed at Ametza—The "Ship" Fort at Passages—Carlist attack upon it defeated—Marine Battalion at Passages—Fighting near Fuenterabia—Remarks on the Battalion and on the Legion by a Legionary—Battle of Hernani—Fine practice by the R.M.A. Guns—The Royal Marines preserve the Christinos from disaster at Hernani—"Dash," the Battalion's dog—Another account of the repulse of the Carlists at the "Ship" 27

NOTES.
I. The Royal Marines and the Durango Decree 40
II. The Royal Marines and the Legion 40
III. Change of Uniform, 1829-30 40
IV. Capture of Lieut. White, R.M., by the Carlists 41

CHAPTER XXIII.
OPERATIONS ON THE SYRIAN COAST, 1840.

Ali, Pasha of Egypt, rebels against the Sultan and invades Syria—British Fleet, Turkish and Austrian ships sent to Syrian Coast—Landing at D'Jouni—The Camp at D'Jouni—The Royal Marines formed into two Battalions—Attack on the Castle of Gebail—Sir Charles Napier's "Soldiering" proclivities—Advance on Argentoum—Bombardment of Caiffa—Marines occupy Tyre—Capture of Sidon—Officer of the Royal Marines plants the British Flag on the walls—Bombardment of Acre 42

CONTENTS

CHAPTER XXIV.
THE CHINA WAR OF 1840-1-2.

H.M.Ss. *Hyacinth* and *Volage* defeat war-junks off Macao—Capture of Chusan—Fighting at Macao—Marines of Squadron formed into a Battalion—Storming of the Forts at Chuen-pee—Accounts by Naval and Marine Officers engaged—Defences of the Bocca Tigris—Capture of the Anunghoy Batteries—Heroic death of the Chinese Admiral Kwan—Macao Passage Forts taken—Attack on Canton—Landing of British Forces and capture of Forts overlooking the city—Futile negotiations—Royal Marines rescue company of 37th Madras, N.I.—First use of percussion muskets in action—Attack on Amoy—Capture of Ting-hae—Action at Ching-hae—Tse-kee escaladed—Taking of Cha-poo—Action at Woosung and Pahoshan and occupation of Shanghae—Chin-keang-foo stormed—End of the campaign 54

NOTES.
    I. Chinese "Jingalls" or "Gingalls" 72
    II. Royal Marine Guard and the Chinese 72
    III. Recollections of the fighting near Canton 73
    IV. Uniform of the Royal Marines, 1823 to 1840 73

CHAPTER XXV.
THE WAR WITH RUSSIA IN 1854 AND 1855.

The Baltic Campaign—Difficulty of manning the Fleet—Sir Charles Napier reconnoitres Cronstadt—"I dinna want to visit St. Petersburg!"—Attack on Bomarsund—Troops landed—Hauling up the guns—The British Camp—Fire opened on the Russian Forts—Fort Tzee captured by the French—Bombardment of Fort Nottich—Surrender of Bomarsund—Attack on Domness—Letter from an Officer of Marines——Attack on Viborg—Lieut. Dowell, R.M.A., gains the V.C.—Attack on Sveaborg—The Black Sea and the Crimea—First shot in the War—Landing of the Allies—R.M. Battalion occupies the Heights of Balaklava—Letter from an Officer—Battle of Balaklava as described by a Sergeant of the Royal Marines—Useful work of R.M.A. and R.M. Batteries—Detachment attached to the Light Division at Inkerman—Veteran's account of his experiences in the fighting—Corporal Prettyjohns gains the V.C.—Another Marine's recollections of the Battle—Winter hardships—Hurricane at Balaklava—R.M.A. engage Sebastopol Forts in their Mortar-boats—Expedition to Kinburn—Royal Marines created "Light Infantry" 79

NOTE.
    I. Light Infantry 106

CHAPTER XXVI.
OUR SEA-SOLDIERS IN INDIA.

Defence of Madras in 1758—Capture of Pondicherry—War with Sujah Dowlah—Mutiny of East India Company's European troops—The Squadron lands its Marines—Form small Battalion—March up country—Return to Calcutta—*York* and *Liverpool* sail for Madras taking their Marine Detachments—Remainder of Marines under Captain Wemyss landed and sent to the relief of Patna—Garrison Fort at Manjee—Make prisoners of a revolted Native Regiment—Ringleaders executed—The Company's Army take the field against Sujah Dowlah—The few British regular soldiers form the "King's Battalion" under Captain Wemyss—Battle of Buxar—Share of the "King's Battalion" in the victory—Capture of Trincomalee—Bombardment of Fort Manora—Indian Mutiny—Royal Marines in "Shannon's Brigade"—"Shannon's" Gunners trained by R.M.A. on voyage—Advance up country—Battle of Kajwa—Relief of Lucknow—Battle of Futtehgurh—Lieut. Pym and Detachment in action at Sebanpore—Marine's Diary of the Relief of Bhansi 107

NOTE.
    I. Indian Marine Regiments 124

CHAPTER XXVII.
THE CHINA WAR OF 1856-7-8-9-60.

Immediate cause of the War—Capture of the Barrier Forts—Attack on Canton—A burning expedition—Battle of Escape Creek—Battle of Fatshan Creek—The two Marine Battalions—Marines at the Capture of Canton—"A mine! A mine!"—In garrison at Canton—A night attack—Battle of the White Cloud Mountain—Assault on Nan-tow—Attack on the Royal Marines by the "Braves"—Taking of Shek-tseng—Repulse at Taku—Bravery of Lieut. Evans and Sergt.-Major Wood—Invasion of North China—The Coolie Corps—The Taku Forts—Their storm and capture—Action of Chan-kia-wan 125

NOTES.
    I. Chinese Bows 144
    II. A Chinese Tea Party 144

CONTENTS

Chapter XXVIII.

THE ROYAL MARINES IN JAPAN, 1864-5 AND 1870-5.

Unrest in Japan in the early " 'Sixties "—Attack on the British Legation—Death of Mr. Richardson—Refusal of Satsuma to pay compensation—Bombardment of Kagoshima—Mounted Marines—A Battalion of the Royal Marines sent to Yokohama—Their encampment—Expedition against Simonoseki—Its Bombardment—Royal Marine Battalion and Bluejackets storm a stockade—Battalion returns to England—Another Battalion goes to Japan in 1870—Lieut. A. G. S. Hawes and his work in Japan 145

Chapter XXIX.

THE ASHANTEE WAR, 1873-4.

Origin of the War—Small detachment of the Royal Marines sent from England under Lieut.-Col. F. W. Festing, R.M.A.—Fight at Elmina—Arrival of Sir Garnet Wolseley—Fight at Essaman—Destruction of native villages—The Ashantee forests—Ashantees surprised at Escaibo—Defence of Abrakrampa—Disappearance of the Ashantee Army—Officers sent to drill and organise friendly tribes—A Battalion of Royal Marines and other troops arrive from England—It is left on board with the Welsh Fusileers—Marines only represented in the further fighting by those in the Naval Brigade—Skirmish at Borubassie—Battle of Amoaful and fall of Coomassie 151

Note.
I. Uniform of the Royal Marines, 1840-1880 159

Chapter XXX.

THE MARINE BATTALIONS IN EGYPT, 1882.

Arabi Pasha and his partisans—R.M. Battalion ordered to the Mediterranean—Goes to Malta and Cyprus—Ordered to Alexandria—The Bombardment—The Marines and the restoration of order in the city—Reconnaissance 5th August—Commendation of Sir Archibald Alison—A second R.M. Battalion arrives—Occupation of Suez and Port Said—Base transferred to Ismailia—Fight at El Magfar—R.M.A. relieve R.H.A. at El Mahuta—Fighting at Kassassin Lock—R.M.A. mount and effectively use captured Krupp gun—R.M.L.I. arrive at close of the engagement—Second Battle of Kassassin—R.M.L.I. capture two guns—Night march on Tel-el-Kebir—No Surprise—Egyptian Lines taken by Storm—Rout of the Egyptians—Who were in first ? 165

Note.
I. The Comet at Tel-el-Kebir 176

Chapter XXXI.

THE ROYAL MARINES AND IRELAND.

Ireland never a " Nation "—Recruiting for the Marines in Dublin, 1771—Irish Loyalist Volunteers—Rebellion of 1798—A " Socialist " outbreak—Suppressed by Loyalist Volunteers—Marines at Waterford—Irish Marine Corps—Persecution of Protestants in 1837—The Royal Marines and the Rebellion of 1848—R.M. Battalions sent to Ireland in 1868 and 1880—Ship detachments landed there after recall of the Battalions—Experiences of a Corporal of Marines.—His opinions on " Home Rule "—Plain clothes detachment of R.M. in Dublin after the Phoenix Park murders—Their invaluable services—Thanked by the Lord Lieutenant 177

Chapter XXXII.

THE OPERATIONS NEAR SUAKIN, 1884-5. THE SUDAN, 1884-5.

The Mahdi—Destruction of an Egyptian Force under Hicks Pasha—Marines landed for the defence of Suakin—Battle of El Teb—Battle of Tamai—Failure of the Nile Expedition to relieve Gordon—It is withdrawn to Korti—Royal Marine Battalion despatched to Suakin——Defences of Suakin—Advance on Hasheen—Attack on McNeil's Zareba—Arrival of New South Wales Contingent—Ex-Officers of the Royal Marines serving with the Australians 189

CONTENTS

CHAPTER XXXIII.

THE NILE OPERATIONS, 1884-1898. THE ROYAL MARINE CAMEL CORPS. THE ROYAL MARINE ARTILLERY IN THE NILE GUNBOATS.

Gordon to be rescued—The Camel Corps—The Royal Marine Company of the Guards Camel Regiment—The start—Battle of Abu Klea—Account by an Officer present—Abu Kru—Metemneh—Captain Oldfield and N.C.O's of the Royal Marine Artillery on the Nile in 1896—Action at Hafir—Bombardment of Dongola—Forts at Shendy shelled—Battle of the Atbara—Fall of Omdurman—Royal Marine Officers present—The Mahdi's Tomb blown up by Royal Marines ... 205

NOTE.
I. Services of Major-General C. V. F. Townshend, C.B., D.S.O. ... 219

CHAPTER XXXIV.

ROYAL MARINES AFLOAT. XIXth CENTURY.

"Hints to young Marine Officers," 1842—What to do on going afloat—Clothing and Equipment of Detachments embarked—Allowance of Ammunition—Drill—Precautions on paying off—The C.O. of Royal Marines the head of a Department—Punishments—Gunnery instruction—Improvement in Marines' Kits—Marines no longer required on deck as riflemen—Now man various guns—Reduction in the size of detachments—Mr. Trevelyan's speech in 1882—Periods of service afloat and ashore should be equal to ensure efficiency—"Enforced idleness" of Officers of Marines afloat—Naval Officers opinions on this point—Discussion in the "Army and Navy Gazette"—Improvements sanctioned by the "New Scheme"—No R.M. Officers obtained from Osborne—Separate entry re-introduced ... 220

NOTES.
I. "Crescents" ... 229
II. Marines berthed aft ... 229
III. Uniform White Jackets ... 230
IV. Arms and Appointments, 1842 ... 230
V. Disturbances on Paying Off ... 231
VI. Gunnery in the Royal Marines ... 231
VII. Marine Officers keeping Watch ... 232

CHAPTER XXXV.

THE BATTLE OF GRASPAN AND THE WAR IN SOUTH AFRICA, 1899-1900.

Royal Marine Battalion landed at Simon's Town—Moves up Country—Returns to Simon's Town—Ordered again to the Front—An Officer's account of the advance to Graspan—The Battle of Graspan—Various accounts—Captain Marchant, R.M., brings the Naval Brigade out of action—Naval Brigade Guns in the Free State—In action near Pretoria—On Monument Hill—Captain Leslie Wilson wounded—Naval Brigade broken up—Various services of the Royal Marines ... 233

CHAPTER XXXVI.

THE FIGHTING IN CHINA IN 1900.

The "Boxers"—Foreign Ambassadors wire for protection—Allied forces start from Tien-tsin—Fighting on the railway to Pekin—Trains attacked at Lang-fan—Retreat by railway cut off—Unrest at Tien-tsin—Taku Forts bombarded—Fighting at Tien-tsin—Admiral Seymour's return march—Marines constantly engaged as flank guard—Hsi-ku Arsenal stormed by Major Johnstone, R.M.L.I.—The Expedition besieged in the Arsenal—Captain Doig's attempt to cut his way to Tien-tsin—The Arsenal relieved by Colonel Sherinsky—Tien-tsin—Heavy fighting in and around the city—Assault and capture of the Chinese walled city ... 250

NOTES.
I. Captain Doig's attempt to reach Tien-tsin ... 266
II. Death of Captain Lloyd and attack on native city ... 267
III. Marines at Tien-tsin Railway Station, 1901 ... 267

CONTENTS

CHAPTER XXXVII.
THE DEFENCE OF THE PEKING LEGATIONS, 1900.

Defence must be a Fight to a Finish—Detachments Royal Marines ordered to Peking—Their arrival—The area to be defended—Regular fighting men available—The Boxers in the city—First brush with them—Rescue Expeditions—Murder of Baron von Kettler—Expiration of the Chinese Ultimatum—Sir Claude MacDonald assumes command—Barricade fighting—Destruction of the Han-lin—Captain Halliday wins the V.C—Attacked on all sides—Comradeship of British and American Marines—Loss of the German barricade on the City Wall—Sortie from the American Barricade—Fierce attacks on the Fu—The defenders' artillery—Mines—Sergeant Preston wins the Conspicuous Gallantry Medal—Death of Captain Strouts—Relief at last—Conduct of the Royal Marines ... 268

NOTES.
I. Random Chinese Fire ... 290
II. Guns on the Imperial City Wall ... 291
III. Casualties in the R.M. Detachment at Peking ... 291

CHAPTER XXXVIII.
PRESENT ORGANISATION AND EQUIPMENT OF THE ROYAL MARINES.

Ten years of armed peace—British Navy concentrated in home waters—Strength of the R.M. Corps in 1913—The various R.M. Divisions—H.M. King George V., Colonel-in-Chief—Officers, their duties in general—Advantages of the Royal Marine Service—The Royal Marine Bands—Their efficiency and special Badges of honour—Their uniform—"A Life on the Ocean Wave"—Previous airs played for the "March Past"—The Colours—The Uniforms of the R.M.A. and R.M.L.I.—Deeds and Loyalty of the Corps ... 293

NOTES.
I. His Majesty's Royal Marine Guard in the S.S. *Medina* ... 302
II. Naval Bandsmen ... 302
III. "A Life on the Ocean Wave" ... 303
IV. The Badge of "The Globe" ... 303
V. Peculiarities in Marine Uniforms ... 305
VI. Uniform of the Royal Marines, 1881-1914 ... 306

APPENDIX E.

The "Horse Marines" ... 308

APPENDIX F.

Supplementary Chronological List of the War and other Services of the Royal Marine Corps and its Predecessors 310

ADDITIONAL ADDENDA TO VOL. I.

Chapter II.—Genesis of the Admiral's Regiment ... 341
,, IX.—Sea Kit of Marines in 1702-3 ... 341
,, IX.—Clothing and Duties of Marines when embarked, 1740-46 ... 341
,, XI.—First appearance of the Round Hat ... 342
,, XVII.—Sir James Saumarez' proposal for a R.M. Artillery Corps ... 342
,, XVII.—Further instances of Slow Promotion ... 343

GENERAL INDEX ... 344

LIST OF ILLUSTRATIONS
Vol. II.
PLATES IN COLOUR

Napoleon inspecting the Marine Guard, H.M.S. *Bellerophon* ... Frontispiece	
Drummer, Royal Marine Band, 1826 ... To face page	16
Uniforms, Royal Marines, 1815-1850	28
Officers and Regimental Colour, 1833	46
Field Officers, R.M., 1833	56
Uniforms, Royal Marines, Crimean period	80
Do. do. 1864-1874	150
Do. do. 1880-1900	190
Service and Undress Uniform, various periods	208
Mess Dress, various periods	226
Royal Marine Band Uniforms, various periods	266
Uniforms, Royal Marines, 1914	304

PLATES IN HALF-TONE

Napoleon the Great surrendering himself, 15th July, 1816	4
Buonaparte on board the *Bellerophon* off Plymouth	6
Bombardment of Algiers	14
Battle of Navarino	20
Guns of R.M.A. in Action at Hernani	34
Battle of Hernani. Last Position of the Royal British Marines	36
Capture of Amoy	62
Storming of the Heights of Chusan	62
Capture of Chin-keang-foo	70
Portraits of Lieut.-Col. G. D. Dowell, V.C.; Bombr. Thos. Wilkinson, V.C.; and Sergt. John Prettyjohn, V.C.	84
Bombardment of Sveaborg	88
Relieving a Sentry, 1854	88
Right of the position occupied by R.M. at Balaklava	94
Headquarters of 2nd Battalion Royal Marines at Balaklava	94
Col.-Sergeant, R.M.A.; Private and Drummer, R.M., 1854	96
The Battle of Inkerman	100
The Advance to the Assault of the Secundrabagh	118
The Shah Najif	118
The Battle of Fatshan Creek	127
Attack on the Peiho Forts, 25th June, 1859	140
Camp of the Royal Marines at Yokohama	146
Attack on Simonoseki, 5th September, 1864	146
Storming the Japanese Stockade at Simonoseki	148
Col. Festing repulses the Ashantee attack on Elmina	152
Royal Marines in Reconnaissance towards Kafr-Dawr	168
R.M.A. Working a captured Krupp Gun at Kassassin	168
Capture of two Guns by the R.M.L.I. at Kassassin	172
Tel-el-Kebir, Death of Captain Wardell, R.M.L.I.	172
"Victory!" The R.M.L.I. after storming the Lines of Tel-el-Kebir	174
The Battle of El-Teb	192
The Night before Tamai	192
The Royal Marines at Tofrek (McNeil's Zareba)	202
Halt of the Guards Camel Regiment, Bayuda Desert	212
Sergeant R.M.A. directing the fire of a Nile Gunboat	216
Royal Marines at Upper Deck Guns, H.M.S. *Triumph*, 1892	224
R.M. Detachment of H.M.S. *Royal Sovereign*	228
Royal Marines who fought at Belmont, Graspan, etc.	234
The Royal Marines at Graspan	242
Royal Marines landing at Tong-ku	254
Major Johnstone and the R.M. crossing the Pei-ho to attack the Hsi-ku Arsenal	254
Storming of Hsi-ku Arsenal by the Royal Marines	258
Captain E. Wray, R.M.L.I.	276
Captain B. M. Strouts, R.M.L.I.	276
Non-Commissioned Officers of the Legation Guard	276

LIST OF ILLUSTRATIONS

	Page
Captain L. S. T. Halliday, V.C., R.M.L.I.	280
Captain Halliday wins the V.C.	280
British and American Marines driving the enemy from the Han-lin	282
Sortie of British Marines and Japanese troops	282
Capture of a Boxer Standard by Sergeant Preston, R.M.L.I.	287
Colour Belts and Drum Major's Belt, R.M.L.I.	296
Queen Victoria presenting Colours to the Portsmouth Division	300
A "Horse Marine"	308
The "Knights of the Wave"	310
Contemporary print of the Siege of Gibraltar	313
The Attack on Martinique, 1759	316
The Taking of Havannah	318
Storming of Fort Mulgrave	321
The "Glorious First of June"	322
The Royal Marines at Benin	338

ILLUSTRATIONS IN THE TEXT

N.B.—" I " stands for Initial Letter.

Officers' Belt Locket	viii
Busby Badge, 1860-78, and Valise Badge, 1877-1902	x
Napoleon going on board the *Bellerophon*	1
Head of Napoleon and "those far distant ships" (I)	1
Napoleon's Chair	8
Battle of Navarino	9
Some Turkish Standards (I)	9
Plan of the Bombardment of Algiers	11
Plan of the Battle of Navarino	19
Some Marine Head-Dresses	25
Uniform of the Royal Marines, 1829-30	26
Sketch Map of the Country round St. Sebastian	27
Carlist Soldier, 1836 (I)	27
Rifle Uniform suggested for the Royal Marines	41
Storming of Sidon	42
Officer's Shako, 1832 (I)	42
Shako and Shoulder-Belt Plates, Coatee, Epaulette and Button	53
A Company of the 37th Madras N.I. surrounded near Canton	54
Shako Plate, 1830-45 (I)	54
Plan of Attack on the Heights and Forts of Canton	61
Map of the Canton River	61
Plans of Operations at Ting-hae, Chapoo, Amoy, Shanghae, Ching-hae and Chin-keang-foo	69
Chinese Caricature, English Foraging Party	72
Shoulder-Belt Plate; Colour-Sergt.'s Arm Badge and Brass Shoulder Scale (Sergt.-Major)	78
Fort Nottich, Bomarsund	79
Forage Cap and Shoulder-Scale (I)	79
Lieutenant Dowell, R.M.A., gains the V.C.	89
Officer's Shako and Private's Shako Plate, 1854	90
Plan of the Bombardment of Bomarsund	91
Corporal Prettyjohn wins the V.C.	99
Bombardier Wilkinson wins the V.C.	103
Plan of the Siege of Sebastopol	105
Indian Native Infantry, 1857	107
Field-Officer's Shako, 1856-66 (I)	107
Plan of Lucknow	123
The Storming of Canton	125
Old Chinese Bell, captured at Canton (I)	125
Plan of the Attack and Bombardment of Canton	127
R.M. Officers' Mess, North Wantong	129
Royal Marines landing at Canton, 1857	131
Officers R.M. Bivouacked on the Walls of Canton	134
Battle of the White Cloud Mountain, 2nd June, 1858	137
Chinese drawing of the Fight at Fatshan	144
Royal Marines landing at Yokohama, 1864	145
Japanese Helmet (I)	145
Fighting in the Ashantee Forest	151
The Castle of Elmina in 1721 (I)	151
Forage Cap Badge	164
Plan of the Battle of Tel-el-Kebir	165
Some Egyptian Trophies (I)	165
Badges of Loyal Irish Marine Corps	177

LIST OF ILLUSTRATIONS

	Page
Rebel Pikes made at Carrickmacross, 1848 (I)	177
Officer's Shako Plate, 1854	188
Sketch Plan of the Battle of El-Teb	189
Soudanese Sword and Shield (I)	189
The Battle of Tamai	194
Sphinx Redoubt, Suakin	197
Sandbag Redoubt, Suakin	198
"H" Redoubt, Suakin	198
Right Water Fort Suakin	199
Battle of Hasheen	200
McNeil's Zareba	202
Officers' Shako Plate, 1856-1866	204
The Gunboats at Omdurman	205
"Fuzzy-Wuzzy" (I)	205
Battle of Abu-Klea	207
Battle of Abu-Kru	210
Royal Marines manning a 6-inch Q.F. Gun, 1896	220
Sunset Afloat (I)	220
Royal Marines at Bayonet Exercise, 1908	223
Officer's Shako Plate, R.M.L.I., 1866-1878	232
Sketch Plan of the Battle of Graspan	233
R.M.A. 4.7 Gun in Action (I)	233
Officer's Shako Plate, R.M.L.I., 1878-1905	249
Admiral Seymour's Force before Hsi-Ku Arsenal	250
Chinese Dragon (I)	250
Plan of fighting round Tien-tsin	261
Plan, Railway Station, etc., Tien-tsin	267
R.M. Guard and armed Students at British Legation	268
Chinese Regular Soldier (I)	268
R.M. Guard and Cossacks entering Peking	270
Sketch-plan of Legations during the Siege	272
Plan of Peking in 1900	273
Plan of attack on Chinese Barricade on City Wall	285
Royal Marines manning the "International Gun"	291
The Colours and Officer's Helmet-plate, 1905	292
Variations in the Establishment of the R.M., 1755-1910	292
Forton Barracks	293
Buttons, R.M.A. and R.M.L.I. (I)	293
Special Band Badges	298
Colour-Sergeant's Arm Badge, R.M.L.I.	307
Sabretasches, Mounted Officers, 1872-1902	309
Fort at the New Mole, Gibraltar	312
Plan of the Siege of Louisbourg	315
Plan of the Siege of Quebec	316
Plan of the Siege of Havannah	317
Silver Medal presented to Captain Ewing	319
Major Pitcairn's Pistols	319
Plan of Cutting-out Operations at Corigeou	332
Fight at Obligado	335
R.M. Camp and Blockhouse, San Juan	337
Headpiece to General Index	344

OFFICER'S FULL DRESS BELT LOCKET R.M.L.I.
1868—1902.

NOTES ON THE COLOURED PLATES
Vol. I.
                                                                                                                                    Page

PRINCE GEORGE OF DENMARK'S MARITIME REGIMENT ... ...Facing page 24

    The Hat of the right-hand figure should have been *bound* round the brim with yellow braid, instead of having it laid on below the brim as shewn.

THE TEN REGIMENTS OF MARINES (1740-48). ... ... 74 & 80

    The centre of the Star on the Caps should be white with St. George's Cross, surrounded by a Blue Garter. The Officer's Sash has been omitted by the artist in the first of these two Plates.

THE MARINE CORPS (1755-1770) 112

    The two Privates should have Regimental Lace on the sleeves as well as on the cuffs—arranged similarly to that on the arm of the Officer.

OFFICERS OF THE ROYAL MARINE ARTILLERY 268

    I fancy that the white piping round the edges of the tail pockets is incorrect. I think that there should be no piping. When I made a photograph from the original in the South Kensington Museum, I took it to be white, and it printed white in the photograph. But since then I hear that it has been coloured red in some copies, and on reference to the Keeper of the Museum, I am informed that " it is a narrow line of colour—a paler blue than that of the material of the uniform ; in fact between it (so to speak) and the dead white of the revers." It seems probable, therefore, that Mr. C. H. Martin who coloured the plates in this series, intended to indicate the *edge* of the blue cloth slash only—the light coming from the right in the picture—and not piping at all. The fact that there is no piping elsewhere on the uniform and none on the similar tail-pockets of the Officers of Marine Infantry in the companion pictures, tends to corroborate this idea.

Vol. II.

NAPOLEON INSPECTING THE ROYAL MARINE GUARD ON BOARD H.M.S. *BELLEROPHON*

    From later information I am inclined to think that the tufts, etc., on the Hats of the Marines should have been placed in front and not at the side as drawn, and as I stated to have been most probably correct at the bottom of page 25.

DRUMMER, ROYAL MARINE BAND, 1825, AND BANDSMEN, 1826 16

    There should be two small red plumes curving outwards on either side of the large plume. There should be only one " point " on the bottom edge of the cap—the middle one (*vide* Coloured Plate facing p. 266)..

UNIFORMS, ROYAL MARINES (1815-1850) 28

    The plate on the Hat of the Officer, R.M.A., on the left of the picture should not be oval, but as represented on the page facing the "FOREWORD," in Volume I.

ROYAL MARINES (1854) 80

    The piping on the coatee of the Gunner, R.M.A., is somewhat ambiguous—it should be *white*.

ROYAL MARINES (1864-1874) 150

    The trousers of the Officer and Private of 1864 should be Oxford Grey Cloth and not Blue, which did not become uniform till 1872. Officer's sword rather too curved.
    The blue of the Patrol Jacket is too light, also that of the tunic of the mounted Officer, R.M.A.
    The red lines round the lace on the Saddle-Cloth are too wide.

SERVICE AND UNDRESS UNIFORMS 208

    The trousers of the two Privates R.M.L.I., 1856-66 should be a *darker* grey.

CORRIGENDA, &c.

ADDITIONAL VOL. I.

Page.		Line.	
54		Note 2	Delete final " o " in "Como."
140		26	" 18th April " should be " 12th April."
140		39	" 21st July " should be " 15th July."
141		10	" Sailors " should be " Sailers."
164, Plate facing			Date in last line but two of description should be 1740-8
167		13	" They should be " then."
241		8	" April " should be " July."
271		15	Delete the first " in."
276, Plate facing			Date below should be " 18th August."
296, Plate facing			" Burntfoot " should be " Burnfoot."

VOL. II.

Page		Line	
5		35	Delete inverted comma after " men."
20, Plate facing			" 18th October " should be " 20th October."
21		Note III	" Vol. I " should have been placed after " pages 204-262."
25		16	Delete first " a " in " foaraging."
56		39	" F. S. White " should be " F. J. White."
97, Note 1		1	" R. R." should be " R.A."
108		5	" 1761 " should be inserted after " January."
131		10	" Hecker " should be " Hocker."
138		22	Delete the word " the."
138		27	" 65 " should be " 65th."
140, Plate facing			" W. H. G. Masters " should be " W. G. R. Masters."
141			Note 6. The " 6 " is omitted.
143		2	" Missle " should be " Misile."
146		Note 4	" Appendix F." should be " Appendix E."
147		4	" European " should be " Europeans."
153		31	" Essamen " should be " Essaman."
202, Plate facing			23rd " March " should be " 22nd March."
212		27	" come " should be " some."
217		30	" Pouud " should be " pound."
224		33	" presreve " should be " preserve."
226		13	" Paking " should be " Peking."
228, Plate facing			" 1885 " should be " 1895."
230		18	" H.M.S. *Wellesley*, &c." This line belongs to Note III.
244		15	" had " should be " and."
251		41	" American " should be " Americans."

BAND MASTER'S BUSBY BADGE R.M.A.
1860—1878.

VALISE BADGE R.M.A. & R.M.L.I.
1877—1902.

BRITAIN'S SEA-SOLDIERS

NAPOLEON GOING ON BOARD THE *BELLEROPHON*.

Chapter XX.

NAPOLEON BUONAPARTE AND THE ROYAL MARINES.

"How much might be done with a hundred thousand soldiers such as these."—*Napoleon Buonaparte.*

IN the "Naval Chronicle," for 1803 (page 202), is to be found the following somewhat remarkable statement:— "We have heard it confidently affirmed by persons of great veracity and information, that Buonaparte, at an early period of the French Revolution,[1] solicited a Lieutenancy of Marines on board one of His Majesty's ships." It would be interesting to know who these "persons of great veracity and information" were, for the statement they made or are said to have made, does not, upon the face of it, strike one as very likely to have been true. Were there anything in it Napoleon would very probably have mentioned the matter to the Officers of Marines on board the *Bellerophon* or *Northumberland* with whom he seems to have had a good deal of conversation, and he at least once expressed the greatest admiration for their Corps.

---

[1] About 1790. He left Brienne in 1783.

It is, however, a somewhat curious fact that when at the age of fifteen he was recommended by his masters at the school of Brienne for transference to the Royal Military School at Paris, they reported after various comments on his health, character, conduct and application to his lessons, that he "*would make an excellent sea-officer*, deserves to be transferred to the Military School at Paris."

From this and from the following anecdote taken from a work by Sir William Fraser,[1] it may be that about this period Napoleon's thoughts were turned—like those of many other boys of his age—to the sea and possibly to the British Navy. And if to the Navy, it may have been to the Marines. Napoleon had begun his Military education, and had doubtless heard of the Corps' Exploits at Belleisle, if not elsewhere. The story relates that when at Brienne, "the son of an English peer, who himself became Lord Wenlock, was his schoolfellow. One day the little Corsican came to young Lawley, and said, "Look at this." He shewed him a letter written in remarkably good English; it was addressed to the British Admiralty, and requested permission to enter our Navy. The young Buonaparte said, 'The difficulty, I am afraid, will be my religion.' Lawley said, 'You young rascal, I don't believe you have any religion at all.' Napoleon replied, 'But my family have. My mother's race, the Ramolini, are very rigid. I should be disinherited if I shewed any signs of becoming a heretic.' These facts," says the author, "I had from one who had very good means of knowing. He told me that Buonaparte's letter was sent, and that it still exists in the archives of the Admiralty."

Whether any of these stories are true or not, it would appear to be the fact that until his crowning disaster at Waterloo, the Marines were the only British troops to whom Buonaparte had ever personally been opposed—with the exception of the "Royals," at Toulon, when as a young Artillery Officer he laid the foundation of his military fame. There were Marines, too, who fought with him on that occasion, and it was the Marines, as much as anyone, who baulked him at Acre, and shattered his dream of returning overland to Paris by way of Constantinople, as the monarch of an Empire reaching all the way to Cairo.

"That man" said he, bitterly, when speaking of Sir Sidney Smith, during his exile at St. Helena, "caused me to miss my destiny."

"That man," would have been the first to admit that without Douglas, Oldfield and their Marines, he might not have been able to do so. The story of Napoleon's surrender to the English at Rochfort, his negotiations with the British Government, and his final despatch to St. Helena in H.M.S. *Northumberland*, is too well-known to be repeated here, but the following account, written as it was, by an old Private of Marines who was serving on board H.M.S. *Bellerophon* at the time, is of some interest.[2] It is reproduced just as written in his MS. with all its pre-Board School orthography:—It is headed,

---

[1] "Hic et Ubique."
[2] This M.S. is in the possession of P. R. Overton, Esqre., of Fakenham, who has kindly allowed me to copy it. He writes about Pte. John Sudbury, as follows:—"After he left the Marines he became servant and factotum to my grandfather, Mr. Peter Raven of Liteham, near here, and remained with him till his death which occurred only a few months before that of Mr. R. in 1849. Mr. R. valued him greatly, as a most faithful old friend." Mr. Overton had other MS. of the old Marine giving more detailed accounts of Napoleon's surrender, but he lent them to a Naval Exhibition at the Alexandra Palace, and was never able to recover them.

"John Sudbury, R.M.
His List, of Nepolane
Buonaparte, Surrendred On
15th Day of July, 1815, On Board
His Majestey ship *Bellerophon*
Layin Basque Roads
of Rochford."

Then follows a page of notes on the Emperor's retinue, and a short account of what occurred between Napoleon's coming on board at Rochfort, and his final departure for St. Helena.

"A Correct List of Nepolane Bounapartey Late Emprior of France. The French; Retinue, took on board H.M.S. *Bellerophon* of Rochfort; in Basque Roads in the Morning of the 15th July; 1815. Viz:—

Ltt. Genl. Count Bertrand Grand Marshall of the Palace;
Lt. Genl;—the Duke of Rovigio M.P. Baron Lallemond.
Aid de Camps; to Marshall Count De Montholon; the
Emprior; Count De; Las Casse; Counsellor of Estate; Madame
La Countess Bertrand; Madam La Countess Montholon;
3 Children belongin to Madame Bertrand; 1 to Madame
De Montholon;—M;—D Planet Colonel;—M;—M;—Maigan.
Sergeon, To the Emprior—young De Las Casse Page of Officers on board H.M.S. *Bellerophon*.

On Board the *Myrmirdon*:—Sloop. Lets-Coln Resignue Let-Coln Sheultz Captain Antoine Ponteroche. Lett-Rivicoire et Cathergaine	
Recapticaptalation	
Officers 7	
Servents 10	
Total 17	

Generals	5
Ladies	2
Childrn	4
Officrs	3
Valets	5
Footm	3
Housld Servents	4
Generll Servents	7
Total Encld-Nepolan	34

Despatched to england on Board H.M.S. *Slenay*[1] Marshall Baron Gourgaud—
Surendred on the 15 of July, 1815, at half pst seven O Clock In the Morning.

Madame Bertrand the Daughter of the Late Lord Dillon thats Ladys farther was Count Dillon who was guilon(T)iend at Paris in 1794 for his Adherenc to the Bourbons her Mother was the Countess Latouche of Martinique.

July 17th—1815 of Rochfort.

"We weighed Anchor at one O Clock for England And Arrived at Torbay on the 25 of July at five O Clock in the morning, and Sent Despatches to London and to Plymouth and on the 27 we Weighed Anchor at 4 O Clock in the morning for Plymouth and then We Arrived in Plymouth on the 28 at One O Clock in the Afternoon.

---

1 The *Slaney*.

And there we Remained. Expecting H.M.S. *Northumbling* 74 guns to Recive Nepolane Bounaparty to precied to the Island of St. Helena. But Did not Arived heare—August 4th—Sailed out of Plymouth Sound At Eleven O Clock H.M.S. *Bellerophon* and H.M.S. *Tonnant*, 80 guns Rear Adm of the Red, Lord George Keigh[1] hoisted Red at the Main on board the tonant And Came out side and Creuse between Plymouth And Torbay, Looking out for the *Northumbling* 74 guns On the 5 of August at Five O Clock in the Morning hove in sight H.M.S. *Northumbling* Rear Adm Cockburn Red at Mizzen and at 8 O Clock in the Morning Came On board H.M.S. *Bellerophon* Lord George Keigh[1] Accompaney Nepolane Bounpartey and His Officers and servents. On board the *Northumbling* to Precied to the Island of St. Helena; And Neoplane Bounpartey Left H.M.S. *Bellerophon* at Half Past one O Clock and Went On Board H.M.S. *Northumbling* to Presead to St. Helena at six O Clock at Night, Parted Company With the *Northumbling* and 2 troop ships And Came to Plymouth Sound the Next morning.

JOHN SUDBURY
His List."

Before describing Napoleon's inspection of and remarks on the Marines of H.M.S. *Bellerophon* it may be noted that he had been on board a British Man-of-War before. This was the *Undaunted* frigate, the ship in which he was taken to the Island of Elba in the May of 1814. "He contrived to make himself very agreable to everyone on board and seems to have been somewhat taken with the Marines, for, it is said, that before landing he especially asked that a party of fifty of them might accompany him and remain on shore; but this he afterwards changed to an Officer and two Sergeants, one of whom, O'Goram (one of the bravest and best soldiers I ever met, and to whom the Emperor had taken a great fancy) he selected to sleep on a mattrass outside the door of his bedchamber with his clothes and sword on. A Valet-de-Chambre slept on another mattrass in the same place, and if Napoleon lay down during the day, the Sergeant remained in the ante-chamber."[2]

Captain Maitland of the *Bellerophon* gives the following account of the Emperor's arrival on board :—

"About 10 a.m. the barge was manned, and a Captain's guard turned out. When Buonaparte came on deck he looked at the Marines, who were generally fine looking young men, with much satisfaction, went through their ranks, inspected their arms, and admired their appearance, saying to Bertrand, 'How much might be done with a hundred thousand soldiers such as these.' He asked which had been the longest in the Corps, went up and spoke to him. His questions were put in French, which I interpreted as well as the man's answers. He enquired how many years he had served. On being told upwards of ten, he turned to me and said, 'Is it not customary in your service to give a man who has been in it so long, some mark of distinction.'[3] He was informed that the person in question had been a sergeant, but was reduced to the ranks for some misconduct.

---

[1] Keith.
[2] "Century Magazine," March, 1893.
[3] *Vide* Note I.

Drawn by W. Heath

Published May 1st, 1816, by J. Jenkins, 48 Strand.

Engraved by T. Sutherland.

Napoleon the Great

Surrendering himself to the generosity of the
BRITISH NATION

On board the Bellerophon, July 15th, 1815

Exposed to the factions which divide my Country and to the enmity of the great powers of Europe, I have terminated my political career, and come, like Themistocles, to throw myself upon the hospitality (m'asseoir sur le foyer) of the British People, I claim from Your Royal Highness the protection of the laws, and throw myself upon the most powerful, the most constant, and the most generous of my enemies.
   Vide Napoleon's letter to the Prince Regent.

He then put the guard through part of their exercise, whilst I interpreted to the Captain of Marines, who did not understand French, the manoeuvres he wished to have performed. He made some remarks upon the difference of the charge with the bayonet between our troops and the French, and found fault with our mode of fixing the bayonet to the musket as being more easy to twist if seized by an enemy when in the act of charging."

Admiral William Wolseley, who was a midshipman on board the *Bellerophon*, gives a slightly different account of this incident.[1] According to him, Napoleon did not inspect the Marines when he came on board, but when he was leaving the ship for the *Superb* the next day.

"The Emperor," he wrote in a private letter, "accompanied by Captain Maitland, went on board the *Superb* to breakfast with Sir Henry Hotham, according to the invitation of the previous day. Before the Emperor left the ship the whole body of our Marines were drawn up on the quarter-deck to receive him with all due honour as he came out of the cabin. As he passed the Marines and returned their military salute of arms, ever fond of warlike display, he suddenly stopped, his eye brightened, and crossing the deck, he minutely examined the arms and accoutrements of the Marines—and a fine body of men they were—requested the Captain of Marines (Marshall) to put the men through one or two movements, and when they had performed these, he pointed to him to bring them to the charge. In our army the front rank only charges, but, I believe in the French the second rank keeps poking over the shoulders of the first—as likely to kill their own men as the enemy. Napoleon put aside the bayonet of one of our front rank men, and taking hold of the musket of the second rank man, made a sign to him to point his musket between the two front rank men, asking Captain Marshall at the same time if he did not think that mode of charge superior to ours. To which the Captain replied that it might be so, but it was generally allowed that our mode of charge had been very effectual.[2] Here the Emperor took a most conscious look at the Captain of Marines, as much as to say, 'I know that to my cost,' and smilingly, turned to Bertrand to whom he observed, 'How much might be done with two hundred thousand such fine fellows as these?'"

Buonaparte, it is said, had good reason to know how formidable the bayonet has always proved in British hands for he bore upon his person the irradicable mark of its efficacy. At the siege of Toulon, in 1793, when the Emperor first distinguished himself as a leader of men' "he received three wounds—one in the head, one in the thigh and one in the side," which last he received from the bayonet of an English Sergeant of Marines at the time of the capture of General O'Hara. This last wound, when it healed left a hollow mark behind, which never filled up, and which was visible when he was a corpse, after the lapse of twenty-eight years from the time of its infliction.[3]

Napoleon's inspection of the Royal Marine Guard inspired the French artist Maurice Orange with the theme of a picture which was exhibited in the Paris Salon of 1897. The figures and uniforms are excellent, but the *tout ensemble* is

---

[1] Fr. "A Memoir of William Wolseley, Admiral of the Red." By his grand-daughter.
[2] *Vide* Note II.
[3] "England's Battles by Sea and Land."

somewhat marred by the unreal and inaccurate drawing of the ship and her rigging, etc. The picture was numbered 1282 in the catalogue in which was printed a description of the scene taken from the "Memorial de Sainte Helene." It is worth reproducing here, being so characteristically French and so different from the plain, straightforward accounts already quoted. It agrees with Admiral Wolseley's letter as regards the occasion on which it took place.

Napoleon on the Bellerophon, Sunday, 16th July, 1815. "In the morning, the Emperor, leaving his cabin to go on board the *Admiral Hotham*[1] stopped short on the quarter deck of the *Bellerophon* before the guard drawn up to salute him; he gave them orders for several movements of their arms, making them 'Charge Bayonets,' and, as this last movement was not done quite the same as in the French service, he advanced quickly to the middle of the men, thrusting their bayonets aside. Then a sudden and extreme agitation shewed itself on the faces of the guard, the officers, and all the spectators; they portrayed astonishment at seeing the Emperor placing himself thus in the midst of the English bayonets, some of which were actually touching his chest."

The description does not quite fit the picture as Napoleon appears rather to be testing the firmness of one of the bayonets on the musket as alluded to in Captain Maitland's narrative, rather than going between the bayonets of the front rank to take hold of the musket of a man belonging to the rear rank, as indicated by the other two accounts. In another way it does not agree with either of the English versions according to which there was at least a Captain's guard. In the picture it is only a sergeant's guard. It is a pity that the subject has never been handled by a first-rate English Military artist. It has great possibilities. When Napoleon arrived on board the *Superb*, a Captain's guard was paraded, and Second Lieutenant Robert Smithwick, of the Marines, had the honour of being presented to him, and held a conversation with him. During the passage to Torbay a theatrical performance was arranged for him, under the management of one of the subalterns R.M., who is described as "a fellow of great taste."

On leaving the *Bellerophon* on the 7th August, the Captain's guard presented arms, the drum beating three ruffles—a general officer's salute.

"On this day," says an old M.S. Journal,[2] "came on board (the *Northumberland*) General Napoleon Buonaparte from H.M.S. *Bellerophon*. He was saluted on the quarter-deck by the Marines of the ship, under arms, in the same manner as an English General. He returned the salute by taking off his hat and bowing to all the officers who were present. He then entered into conversation with Captain Beattie of the Marines respecting the length of time he had served, what actions he had been in, and if he had been wounded. Captain Beattie replied, 'that he had served many years, had been wounded, and was at the siege of Acre.' Napoleon took hold of his left ear, and, gently pulling it, said: 'Ah, ah, Vous etes un brave homme! brave homme!' He then expressed a wish to be shown the Admiral's cabin, and afterwards that the officers of the ship should be introduced to him."

---

[1] The writer means of course the *Superb*, the Flagship of Admiral Hotham.
[2] Part of an officer's log or journal in the possession of Lt.-Col. Willis, late R.M.L.I.

BONAPARTE ON BOARD THE BELEROPHON OFF PLYMOUTH.

From an Engraving published 20th January, 1816.

Mr. Warden, Surgeon of H.M.S. *Northumberland*, in a series of articles in the "Hampshire Telegraph," of 1816, giving details of conversations that Napoleon had with various officers, says that one of them—probably the one just described—was with Captain Beatty of the Marines who was a fluent French scholar. He says " he directed his inquiries as to the regulations and discipline of the Marines. Nor could he have chosen an officer better qualified to gratify his military curiosity. Captain Beatty had served with Sir Sidney Smith in the East, and was at the siege of Acre, an event which is not among Buonaparte's most pleasing recollections. When, however, he was informed of the circumstance he treated it with great good humour, and seizing the captain by the ear, exclaimed in a jocular tone, ' Ah, you rogue, you rogue, were you there ? ' "

NOTES.

NOTE I.—NAPOLEON ON BOARD H.M.S. *BELLEROPHON*.

A somewhat different version of this conversation is given by a correspondent of the "United Service Magazine," of January, 1832, who signs himself "Amicus." According to this, which he says he heard whilst in garrison at Plymouth, Napoleon "remarked to the officers commanding the detachment that the men were very fine and well appointed, ' but,' asked the ci-devant Emperor, ' are there none among them who have seen service ? ' ' Nearly the whole of them have seen much service, Sir,' was the reply. ' What,' exclaimed the Emperor, ' and no marks of merit.' The officer explained, as well as the awkwardness of the subject would allow, that it was not the custom of our Government to award such marks of distinction, except to officers of the higher ranks, and Napoleon ended the brief conversation by an expressive gesture, which, had it been interpreted, would have said ' Such is not the way to excite or cherish the military virtues.' "

It will be observed that according to this account Napoleon addressed himself directly to the officer of Marines, though Captain Maitland says he had to interpret as Captain Marshall, R.M., did not understand French. As a matter of fact the gallant Captain must have made a mistake in his recollections as I am informed that Captain Marshall was a fluent speaker of the French language.

NOTE II.—THE ROYAL MARINES AND THEIR BAYONET EXERCISE.

The Royal Marines used to be great exponents of the Bayonet Exercise or " Haymaking Drill," as it was irreverently termed, until it was given up a few years back, and "Bayonet Fighting" introduced. For many years after the invention of the Bayonet there does not seem to have been any special " Exercise " devised for it. In Bland's "Treatise on Military Discipline," first published in 1727, the only drill with this weapon, beyond fixing and unfixing, is in the "Manual Exercise." In Section XL of this the order is given " Charge your bayonet breast-high," with full detail, followed in XLI by " Push your Bayonets." The detail for this is :—" Push your Firelock with both Hands strait forward, without raising or sinking the point of the Bayonet, bringing the Butt-end before the left Breast ; then tell 1, 2 and bring it back to its former place."

It is said that a Captain Gordon of the 67th Regiment invented some kind of a bayonet exercise in 1785. The story goes that having drilled various squads of men in his new exercise, he was ordered to take them from Chatham where he was then quartered, to London, and parade them in order to give an exhibition of his method at the "Queen's Riding House." He drew up his men outside, and while awaiting the appearance of the Military authorities, entered the building by himself and got into conversation with an elderly person dressed in a somewhat shabby cut-velvet coat, wearing a bob-wig and having a broom in his hand. The conversation turned on Irish politics, ever a thorny subject, and both grew rather warm in the discussion. The old fellow tried to change the subject to the occasion of Gordon's presence there to exhibit his new exercise, and pointed out a part of the building which, he considered, would be best for the performance. Gordon, who was still in a contradictory humour, replied brusquely that it was just the very worst spot in the place for it. At this moment in came Sir William Fawcett, Adjutant-General of the Forces, who, taking no notice of Gordon, approached his companion, hat in hand, and apologised to " His Majesty " for having detained him so long. Gordon was paralysed ; the old gentleman whom he had treated in so cavalier a manner was King George III. ! Abashed, confounded, incapable of putting his men through the exercise with his usual precision and energy, he bungled, stammered, failed, and eventually returned to Chatham, cowed and crestfallen, with no further idea of teaching his method of bayonet exercise. It has been stated that the first attempt in this direction was made by the Marines at Portsmouth in "manning ship to repel boarders" before the Duke of Clarence, in 1810, but this is obviously inaccurate as will be seen by the following letter from Lord St. Vincent to Viscount Howick :—

"Near Ushant,
April 8th, 1806.

My dear Lord,

Lieutenant Faden, of the Royal Marines, now serving in the *Hibernia*, had much injustice done him, when I was at the head of the Board of Admiralty, owing to a gross misrepresentation from the Island of Alderney, which I was never informed of until he was placed near me in Essex, with a recruiting party from the Chatham Division. The poor man lost four years and a half rank by this circumstance; being a very meritorious officer, well acquainted with the Bayonet Exercise, in which the Flank Companies of the French Army so much excel other troops, I, at his request, got him embarked on board this ship, and he has brought the Marines forward in the use of that powerful weapon in a very extraordinary manner. His uncle, Major Gaum, now resident at Pimlico, has written a treatise upon the subject, which I hope is known to Mr. Wyndham and General Fitzpatrick, considering as I do that expertness in this exercise may some day or other decide the fate of the country, I beg leave to recommend this officer as a candidate for an Adjutancy in the Royal Marines.

Yours most truly,
ST. VINCENT."

It is apparent from this letter that the Bayonet Exercise had attained a regular place in the French Army at this time, and also that one Marine Detachment, at least, had been drilled in it. Before Napoleon criticised the holding of the bayonet at the "Charge" on board H.M.S. *Bellerophon*, it had been further improved in the Royal Marines. In the Edinburgh Annual Register under date 3rd May, 1811, it is stated that "An experiment of an improved method of charging with the bayonet took place yesterday, by a detachment of the Royal Marines, in presence of the Lords of the Admiralty, and a committee of Marine Officers. The whole plan contains many very superior advantages over the present system, particularly in enabling the rear-rank men to use their muskets at the charge, with similar effect and at the same moment, as the front rank, causing the men to stand in a stronger position and enabling them either to attack or defend, at one instant, both the front and the rear. It appears to be particularly adapted to repel any attack that may be made by an enemy's boarders in a naval engagement. The plan met with entire approbation, and it is reported that it will be adopted."

Napoleon's Chair: now in the Plymouth Mess.

BATTLE OF NAVARINO—DISMASTING OF THE TURKISH AND EGYPTIAN ADMIRALS' SHIPS.

From a small aquatint of the period.

Chapter XXI.

BOMBARDMENT OF ALGIERS, 1816, AND BATTLE OF NAVARINO, 1827.

BOMBARDMENT OF ALGIERS, 1816.

"They bled that Algiers' lawless Dey his piracies should cease,
Fought at famous Navarino to break the chains of Greece,
The storm has sung the *requiem* of thousands 'neath the waves:
Yea, every spot of earth and sea has furnished them with graves."—
Anon, in the "Globe and Laurel."

THE pirate cities on the North Coast of Africa, Salee, Tunis, Algiers, Tripoli and others had for centuries been a thorn in the side of Christian Europe. At first their piracies and depredations were practically confined to the Mediterranean, but in the 17th century they extended their sphere of action, and not only plundered ships in our own narrow waters, but landed and carried off men, women and children into a slavery that was worse than death, from Ireland and even from far-off Iceland. In the times of Charles II and his brother James, a frequent duty imposed on our cruisers was to keep a sharp look-out for "Turks men-of-war" in the Channel. As an instance of the audacity of these "Turks" it is recorded that some years before this—in 1616 to be exact—a Salee Rover was captured in the Thames itself.

The only people who continuously and consistently fought with these marauders were the Knights of Malta. Spain, France and England, from time to time undertook reprisals, which were not invariably attended with success. But as a general rule these great Powers, full of their own quarrels, played into the pirates' hands by ransoming those of their subjects who had been captured, not only with money, but with guns, arms and ammunition, which they must have known would be used on the first opportunity against ships carrying their own flags. The *Speaker* frigate[1] was sent to "Argier in Turkey," in 1652, with the sum of £30,000 to redeem English captives from slavery. Even far off Sweden paid a tribute of munitions of war to the "Turks" well into the 18th century.

There was another reason, which, perhaps, in this country, rather militated against severe measures being taken against the "Turks," though, even as early as the reign of Elizabeth there was a form of prayer in use for special protection against a Turkish invasion.[2]

This reason may be found in the strong national feeling against Roman Catholicism, engendered by the persecutions of "Bloody Mary," and the fear of Spain and the Inquisition. The motto of the Dutch "Gueux"—the "Beggars of the Sea"—who carried on a determined maritime war against the Spanish oppressors of their country about this time, was "much rather Turk than Priest," and there is little doubt that the sentiment was reflected to a very great extent in this country. The Turks—especially the Barbary Corsairs—were recognised not only as "*hostes humani generis*," but as the implacable foes of Spain, from which country their Moorish ancestors and relations had been expelled with much cruelty. This feeling lasted, or at least was in evidence, so late as the time of James II., when the cry of "No Popery" was heard everywhere, in the fear of what the King's expressed adherence to the Roman Catholic religion might bring upon the country. "It is a curious fact that the taking of Buda, this year (1686) from the Turks, by the Christians under the Duke of Lorraine, should have been the cause of both the Foot Guards and Life Guards being called out in London on the night of the 18th September, to quell a disturbance in the streets opposite to the house of Don Pedro Ronquillo, the Spanish ambassador to James II. This functionary had illuminated his house in honour of the occasion, upon which a mob assembled and broke all his windows, declaring it would have been better that Buda had remained in the hands of the Turks than have been taken by the Roman Catholics."[3]

But in the year 1816 the Barbary Corsairs, as they are generally called, emboldened by the immunity they had enjoyed, while the victories and defeats of Napoleon had kept the whole of Europe in a constant state of warfare, went just a little too far.

---
[1] *Vide* Note I.
[2] The following entry occurs in the Churchwardens' Accounts of St. Helens, Abingdon:—"Anno MDLXV, 8 of Queen Elizabeth, payde for two bokes of Common Prayer *agaynst* invading of the Turke, 0—6."— *Vide* "History of Signboards," 1266.
[3] "History of the 1st or Grenadier Guards." Sir T. W. Hamilton. 1874. *Vide* also Note II.

BOMBARDMENT OF ALGIERS, 1816.

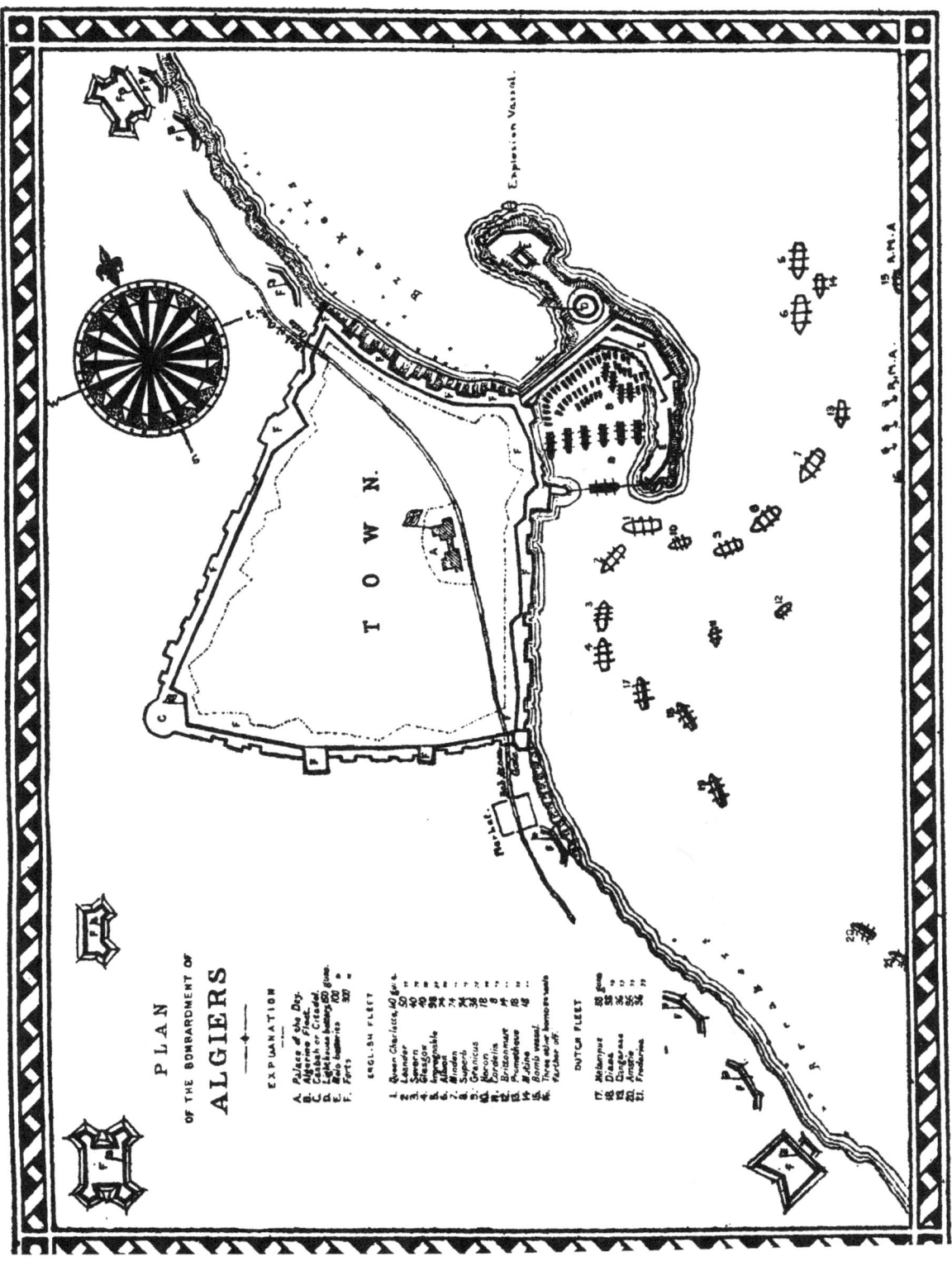

In the early part of that year Lord Exmouth, with a portion of the Mediterranean Fleet, had visited Tunis, Tripoli and Algiers, and proposed treaties to their Deys prohibiting the making of Christian slaves, and stipulating that such prisoners as might be taken in war, should be treated according to the practice of civilised nations. These proposals were accepted by all but the Dey of Algiers. After much negotiation it was finally agreed that three months should be allowed to obtain the approval of the Sultan of Turkey and the *Tagus* frigate was detailed to take the Dey's ambassador to Constantinople. Lord Exmouth returned to England, but scarcely had he arrived, when news came of an outrage that filled the Algerines' cup of iniquity to the brim. Over 300 small fishing vessels belonging to Corsica, Naples and Sicily were lying quietly in the Harbour of Bona, near Algiers, when they were attacked by an Algerine frigate. The Fort on shore joined in with its guns, and a body of cavalry charged along the shore and cut to pieces all the poor wretches who were endeavouring to escape from their sinking and shattered boats.

This outrage was the last straw, and an expedition was fitted out to bring the Algerines to reason.

The command was entrusted to Lord Exmouth and with his flag flying on board H.M.S. *Queen Charlotte*, he left Plymouth on 29th July, 1816, with a fleet of nineteen men-of-war

Having been joined at Gibraltar by a Dutch squadron of five frigates and a corvette under Admiral Van Capellan, the combined armament arrived off Algiers on the 27th August. "On nearer approach," writes an officer on board the *Queen Charlotte*, "the defences became visible, and the batteries were discovered to be studded with artillery, as thickly as space permitted, amounting to several hundred guns. Numerous clear red flags formed a sparkling contrast to the whiteness of the houses. Flags variously striped were also seen on the walls; these were the banners of different Moorish chiefs, assembled to defend the Crescent.

The Dey's Palace, in 1816, was in the middle of the town, or rather lower, towards the sea. A very large crimson flag, the largest I ever saw, waved slowly and majestically over it. It was said to be composed of silk, decorated with silver stars and crescents."[1]

A boat with a flag of truce was sent in to the Dey repeating the demands of England, and of all the civilised world, but when three hours had elapsed without any answer whatever being vouchsafed, the signal was made to "annul the truce," and the *Queen Charlotte* led the fleet into position within close range of the fortifications, so close, that the whites of the eyes of the dark-skinned infidels who crowded the ramparts, and were busily engaged in loading their guns, were clearly visible from the flagship.

Just after half-past two in the afternoon, two shots fired from the Fish Market battery at the British ships were replied to by a tremendous broadside from the *Queen Charlotte*, which killed and wounded no less than 500 of the enemy. The other shore batteries now opened and the action became general and lasted till 10 p.m., by which time the most formidable of the Algerine defences had been demolished and their fire almost completely beaten down.

[1] Naval Yarns, by John Long. 1899.

There are many and most interesting accounts of this great battle between stone walls and wooden ones, but to reproduce any of them or to write a fresh one would be outside the scope of the present work. Unfortunately, as must always be the case in a naval engagement, there is very little specially recorded of the Royal Marines, but a few incidents and anecdotes of the part played by the Corps at Algiers are here set down.

A large force of Royal Marines, Royal Marine Artillery, Sappers and Miners, and the Royal Rocket Corps had been embarked on board the fleet when it left England, and it has been stated that these troops wore for the first time the big-topped shako with brass plate and worsted tuft which was introduced in this year for the infantry, probably in imitation of that worn by the French Army. But as regards the Marines it does not appear that they wore this head-dress till 1821[1], and, as we have seen, *Hats* were specially ordered to be worn by both the Royal Marines and the Royal Marine Artillery in 1816.[2]

At the commencement of the action the Marines on board the flagship were busily engaged in keeping up an incessant discharge of musketry on a flotilla of gunboats, crowded with the enemy, who were futilely attempting to board. Great execution was caused by their fire, and in a short time the boats themselves had been sunk by the gun-fire of the *Leander* and *Queen Charlotte*, and the survivors of the crews were swimming for their lives. About 3 p.m., Lieutenant J. Harvey Stevens, R.M.A., was detached from the *Queen Charlotte* in a boat armed with a 68 pounder carronade, lashed to a stern warp from H.M.S. *Leander*, and was employed in firing carcasses[3] at the dismantled Algerine frigates and vessels lying inside the Mole.

Lieutenant S. A. Rhodes Wolrige, R.M.A., with Lieut. Richards, R.N., and Major Gosset of the Corps of Miners were soon afterwards sent in the flagship's barge to set fire to a large Algerine frigate which was moored across the entrance to the Mole about 100 yards ahead of the *Queen Charlotte*. The *Leander* which lay on the port bow of the flagship with her stern towards the Mole, was ordered to "cease fire," while the barge dashed alongside the Algerine. The work was carried out with the greatest rapidity. The corsair was boarded and captured and in a blaze in less than ten minutes, with a loss of only two men killed among the British. This operation was ordered on the suggestion of Lieut. Wolrige, R.M.A., to Lord Exmouth, and it was only as he prepared to shove off on this service that the other two officers were directed to accompany him. Their companionship turned out most unfortunately for this officer, as while they were both specially promoted for this exploit, Lieut. Wolrige was not even mentioned in Lord Exmouth's despatches.

While the larger ships engaged the batteries almost muzzle to muzzle, the four bomb-vessels, *Beelzebub*, *Fury*, *Hecla* and *Infernal*, were engaged in firing over them from outside. This firing was carried out by the gunners of the R.M.A. under Lieuts. R. Henry, John Maule, F. James and James P. Bisset, all of that Corps. The latter officer was killed. "The shells from the bombs," wrote Lord Exmouth, "were admirably well thrown by the Royal Marine Artillery; and although thrown directly across and over us, not an accident, that I know of, occurred to any ship."

---

[1] *Vide* Note III.   [2] *Vide* page 266.   [3] Incendiary projectiles.

Lieutenant Bisset, of the *Infernal*, had a strong presentiment of death even before the fleet reached Gibraltar, and stated over and over again, that he knew "he should be one of the first." During the action "he seemed calmly waiting for death with the cool yet determined resolution of a gallant spirit who knows his last hour has come," says a writer in the "United Service Magazine," who was apparently present at the time. He was in the act of aiming the fourth or fifth shell when the fatal shot struck him. "I never could imagine," says the above writer, "what sort of missile it was that ended his mortal career. He was cut in three pieces. One leg went forward on the gangway, and the other, and part of his body remained nearly where he had been standing; and his upper works went overboard—certainly on that day the Algerines threw about some queer articles, such as crow-bars, iron bolts, hand-spikes, glass bottles, bags of nails, etc., etc., *ad libitum*. A Lance-Corporal named Polter, fired all the other shots from the *Infernal* during the action."

Captain and Brevet-Major A. Gillespie, the first historian of the Marine Corps, was serving at Algiers on board H.M.S. *Albion*. At the time of the action he was suffering so severely from gout that he was unable to stand. But he refused to remain below, and was carried on deck in a chair and remained sitting there throughout the battle, cheering the detachment by his presence. Unfortunately, although he escaped injury from the enemy's fire, the long exposure[1] produced such a deleterious effect on his constitution that on his return to England at the end of the year, it was found necessary to invalid him.

Lieut. N. C. Holland was quartered during the engagement in the main top of the *Leander* presumably to report the effects of her fire on the batteries, and was specially recommended for gallantry.

Captain J. Wilson, who commanded the *Leander's* detachment, was killed in this engagement, after displaying great courage, by a double-headed shot which crushed both his legs. He bore their amputation with the greatest fortitude, and when one limb was off, turned round, and perceiving Sergeant Brabazon, who had just lost his arm, said, "Ah, Brabazon, are you here? I am sorry to see you thus? There is a glorious work above—we are not unavenged." He remained in the highest spirits till a few minutes before his death.

Lieut. Baxter, his subaltern, was almost the first man killed in the action, having been shot through the head by a musket ball as he was leaning on the hammock rail looking towards the shore, all the men of the detachment being stationed at the heavy guns.

Lord Exmouth, in a letter to Sir Richard Williams, K.C.B., of the R.M.A., wrote of the services of this Corps:—

"I should be very ungrateful my dear friend, if I neglected to thank you for the care you took in selecting for the service I was ordered upon, the best officers and men I ever saw during my service; indeed, my dear Sir Richard, you proved yourself a real and sincere friend to me. Captain Burton, poor fellow, has been wounded; he was a treasure to me in every respect. One very fine fellow

---

[1] A Thunderstorm came on towards the close of the engagement, and rain fell in torrents.

BOMBARDMENT OF ALGIERS, 27th AUGUST, 1816.
From the painting by Geo. Chambers in Greenwich Hospital.

has been killed (Lieut. Bisset, R.M.A.), and I can assure you that all the officers did you full justice—they all knew their duty, and performed it well."

The senior officer of the Corps present was Capt. and Brevet-Major Joseph Vallack, R.M., H.M.S. *Superb*, and he was to have taken command of the R.M. Battalion should it have been landed. He was promoted to Brevet Lieut.-Colonel, but passed over in the selection for C.B., and on remonstrating with Lord Exmouth, was very coolly told that " he was unfortunate in not having served in the flagship."

It was service on board the flagship that secured promotions to Brevet Majorities to Captains Wright, R.M., and Burton, R.M.A., though they were not the senior Captains present.

The senior Sergt.-Major in the fleet, Mr. J. K. Wilson, was specially promoted to the rank of 2nd Lieut. He afterwards was appointed Adjutant at the Portsmouth Division, and became a Brevet-Colonel on half-pay in 1861.

The loss sustained by the Corps in this action amounted to one Captain, four subalterns, one gunner R.M.A., and nineteen privates R.M., killed, and one Captain three subalterns, five gunners R.M.A., and 106 privates R.M. wounded—140 casualties in all.

The immediate result of this victory was the liberation by the Dey of more than 1,200 slaves, of whom eighteen were English, two French, twenty-eight Dutch, and 226 Spaniards; but the great majority were Neapolitans and Silicians. The first clause in the conditions of peace was " The Abolition of Christian Slavery for ever."

BATTLE OF NAVARINO, 1827.

But little information is available as to the special doings of the Royal Marines at the famous Battle of Navarino, but as a large number of the Corps were present it cannot be passed over without some notice. A sanguinary conflict, marked by ruthless cruelty on the part of the Turks, had been going on for some time between the Ottoman Empire and the Grecian Islands and Provinces who were struggling for independence. Great Britain, France and Russia, having in vain tried to bring about a better state of affairs by diplomacy, at length determined to intervene with an armed force, and each despatched a squadron of men-of-war to the scene of hostilities.

Vice-Admiral Sir William Codrington commanded the British contingent, which consisted of three line-of-battle ships, four frigates, and four brigs. The French squadron of four ships of the line, one frigate, and two schooners was under the command of Rear-Admiral H. de Rigny, and the Russian force of four ships of the line and four frigates was commanded by Rear Admiral Count de Heiden.

The Bay of Navarino in which lay the Turko-Egyptian Fleet under Ibrahim Pasha is one of the finest harbours in Europe. The Island of Sphacteria lies across the entrance, the only navigable passage into the harbour being at its southern extremity. This is only 600 yards in width, and is covered by the fire of many heavy guns mounted in the town and Castle of Navarino or Navarin on its southern side, and by that of numerous batteries on the Island opposite.

The Pasha's Fleet, which convoyed a large squadron of transports, was a formidable one, consisting of three line-of-battle ships, each of which in addition to the ordinary armament of her class carried four large 10-inch guns on each side of her lower batteries, firing marble shot weighing 120 pounds apiece—seventeen frigates, thirty corvettes and thirty-nine small craft including six fire-ships.

"About the beginning of October," writes an officer who was present in the British Squadron, "we had returned from our cruise. The men, ever since we had been in commission, had been daily exercised at the guns, and by firing at marks, and they had much improved in their practice. They were frequently overheard expressing their anxious wish for the settlement of the question with the Turks, in one shape or other, that they might have some leave on shore."[1]

On the 18th October, the three Admirals held a conference in which they determined, as being the only possible chance of stopping the daily massacres and the firing of villages that went on in the neighbourhood of Navarino, to enter the Bay and take up a position alongside the Turkish Fleet, trusting that the display of superior force at close quarters would effect what their continued remonstrances had failed to do.

"Before entering the Bay," writes the officer already quoted, "the Ottoman Fleet lay at the distance of ten or twelve miles from the Allies. They appeared numerous, with many small craft. Most of them bore the crimson flag flying at their peak, and on coming closer, a Crescent and Sword were visible on the flags. Their ships looked well, and in tolerable order; the Egyptians were evidently superior to the Turks."

The Egyptian ships were very spick and span, and in excellent condition thanks to the French officers who had shortly before reorganised the Khedive's Navy.

On the 19th, Codrington, who was the senior officer present, made the signal, "Prepare to enter," but on arrival at the mouth of the Harbour he signalled, "No wind within, must wait a more favourable opportunity." The allies had not long to wait for this. Just after 2 p.m., the next day, up went the signal on board the flagship *Asia*, "Enter, prepare to engage the enemy."

As soon as the leading ships cleared the mouth of the harbour, the Turko-Egyptian Fleet came in sight, ranged round from right to left in the form of an extensive crescent in two lines, each ship with springs on her cables.

As soon as she arrived abreast the Turkish flagship, the *Asia* let go her anchor, and before the men aloft had finished furling her sails, the order was passed "Down to your quarters."

Just at this time an exchange of musketry took place between one of the *Dartmouth's* boats and a Turkish fire-ship which she had been sent to request to shift her position. Almost at once the fire-ship burst into a blaze, and the French flag-ship *La Sirene*, which was passing, fired a gun into her. An Egyptian ship returned the fire, and the action became general.

---

[1] "Naval Yarns," by John Long, Portsmouth, 1899.

DRUMMER, ROYAL MARINE BAND, 1826
and Bandsman, 1825.

Two fire-ships were soon in flames, a third blew up, and a fourth was sunk by a broadside from the *Philomel*. The forts at the entrance of the Bay chimed in with their heavy ordnance, and men began to fall fast on both sides.

On board the *Asia* the Admiral had a narrow escape, his watch being knocked out of his pocket and smashed by a musket ball, and Captain Bell of the Marines was killed, "while in the steady performance of his duty."[1]

"The scene of carnage and destruction was most appalling, as the Turkish ships became disabled, they drifted out of the line, and were set on fire by their own crews; and scarcely a quarter of an hour elapsed but a ship was blown into the air, or seen careering wildly about the Bay in flames. Ibrahim Pasha had declared that his ships might be destroyed but would never be captured."[2]

On the poop of the *Genoa*, ten rank and file of the Royal Marine Detachment were killed before that ship fired a shot, the few left with their gallant officer, Lieutenant Miller, on being ordered down to the quarter-deck, could with the greatest difficulty see their way, being literally covered with the blood and brains of their slaughtered comrades. The Captain of Marines—Moore—was mortally wounded, and a Private named Hill who was one of those quartered on the poop, had both his arms shot off almost at the same moment. He at once turned to an officer, who stood near, and said, with the utmost coolness, "I hope you'll allow, Sir, that I have done my duty." The following characteristic anecdote of this brave fellow is worth relating:—After the action, an officer, much fatigued with his exertions in the fight, lay down to rest himself on a chest close to where the mutilated Hill was sitting. Presently he became aware of someone near him singing, and recognising the voice, he exclaimed with surprise, "What, Hill, is that you singing?" "Yes, Sir," answered the Marine, "I'm trying what I can do at ballad-singing, now I've lost my arms." He died, poor fellow, in Stonehouse Naval Hospital, at the early age of 21.

Another of the *Genoa's* detachment had one of his arms shot off in the hottest part of the action; he coolly took up the severed arm, and laid it on the shelf-piece[3] above him, saying, "There's an example for you all!"

Stevens, the Captain of Marines on board the *Albion*, an officer who had served gallantly in many engagements in the French war, had always had a conviction that he would be killed in action, and his premonition was now fulfilled. At the beginning of the battle he shook hands with one of his mess-mates on the poop, said "Good-bye" to him, and asked him to see that his little property should be sent to Canterbury, where they both, at that time, lived. Shortly afterwards a shot came and cut him in two, carrying away one of his hands. A young Marine picked up the hand and put it in his forage-cap, keeping it in security until the action had ceased. Then he took the hand to Lieutenant Anderson, R.M., and holding it up by a finger, asked what he should do with it. The body, had, of course, been thrown overboard at once, and the strange relic of his officer which the young man had preserved, and which he obviously wished to keep as a memento, went over the side also. In recognition of Captain Stevens' services, and death

---

[1] Official despatch.
[2] Nicholas "Historical Records of R.M. Forces."
[3] Straight piece of timber running along the ship's side above the ports close to the beams.

in action, a commission in the Corps of which he had been so conspicuous an ornament was given to his nephew, Mr. Alexander Stevens, by H.R.H. the Lord High Admiral (The Duke of Clarence),[1] who accompanied it with the most flattering expressions as to the conduct of the deceased officer, which, H.R.H. stated, proceeded from information he derived from private accounts.

"The *Albion*," wrote an officer of the Royal Marines[2] who was serving on board her, "passed very close to the ship of the line (the *Genoa's* opponent), and immediately anchored, swinging to the current which soon swept her port quarter to the starboard bow of a very large Turkish frigate whose crew made a most gallant and determined attempt to board. It may be here mentioned that forty Marines were stationed below at the *Albion's* guns, and two or three hours before she entered the harbour, of the seventy-two Privates called "small-arm men," stationed on her poop under the Captain of Marines, forty were taken away and stationed below to carry powder from the magazine to the powder-boys, and twenty more were taken to man four guns on the quarter-deck, leaving only twelve Privates on the poop—a small force to resist the impetuous and resolute attempt to board.

The collision was not at first observed on the quarter-deck—there were no bluejackets or any naval officers on the poop, but Mr. Addington, the boatswain, reached it at the moment of collision, and letting himself down by a rope, quickly cut the frigate's cable with an axe kept on the poop.

The Captain of Marines having been killed, the command had devolved on the senior subaltern who had enough to do to repel the Turks' attempt to board. A sergeant touching his left arm was shot through the head, and a private on his right hand was shot through the shoulder. He himself was obliged to use a double-barrelled pistol twice." The boarders having been called he was about to board with his men when the Captain called to him through his speaking trumpet, 'Don't board!'

On looking along the port side an immense ship, evidently a line-of-battle ship, was seen coming down fast with the current and seemed likely to scrape the *Albion's* side.

She proved to be the Capitana Pasha's ship, which the *Asia* thought she was engaging by directing her guns by a flag at her supposed masthead. The truth is that her cable nearest to the *Asia* was quickly shot away when the strong current soon carried her past her other anchor till it brought her up alongside the *Albion*.

In the meantime an active seaman of the *Albion* ran his boarding-pike through the Turkish Captain's[3] back before he could get to the maindeck; immediately flames rose up ten or twelve feet above her taffrail from materials set on fire on the after part of the frigate's maindeck. The gallant boatswain who had cut the cable, got on the frigate's bowsprit and was in the act of hauling down her Jack when he lost his arm by a musket ball. The Marine Officer[4] although ordered not to board, seeing he was disabled, hastened over to him, took the flag from him and gave it to a sergeant on the poop. He then rushed back to aid Mr. Addington,

---
[1] Afterwards William IV.
[2] Lieut. Thomas Hurdle in an account written privately many years later.
[3] Of the frigate.
[4] Hurdle himself.

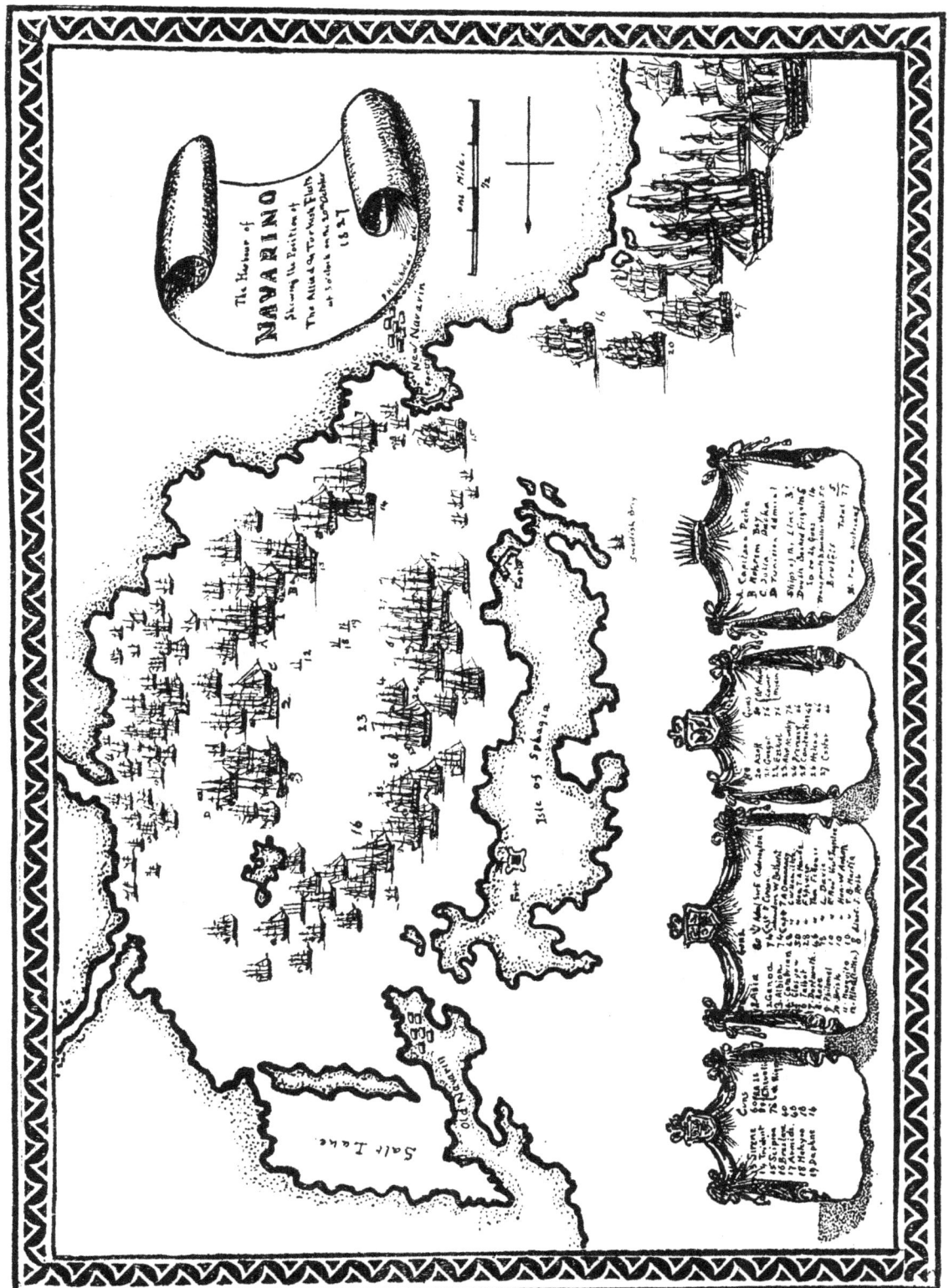

This plan of the Battle of Navarino is from a large coloured drawing in the Royal United Service Institution by "P. H. Nicholas," almost certainly Lieutenant Paul Harris Nicholas, R.M., author of "The Historical Record of the Royal Marine Forces" (1845).

in which he was assisted by a late boarder in getting him over the awkward ropes of the frigate on board the *Albion* again—not any too soon as the current was moving her astern.

As soon as the fire appeared the boarders hurried back to the ship, and some had to make fearful jumps to regain her.

The 86-gun ship now opened fire on the *Albion*, and was for a short time joined on the same (port) side by the 76, she being very much nearer to her, than to her own opponent the *Genoa*. The *Albion* was engaged on her starboard side with the double-banked frigate and a Turkish line-of-battle ship about three or four hundred yards astern also opened a raking fire upon her.

The *Albion* was in excellent fighting order and was closely engaged with her huge opponent more than three hours, when she ceased to fire. At this time the current moved the stern of the 86 nearer so that her broadside looked across the *Albion's* bows towards the *Genoa*, at which she suddenly fired seven or eight of her lower deck guns. A broadside from the *Albion* now silenced her—she was by now a perfect wreck. Her immense fore and main masts each lay in three pieces on her deck, her bowsprit was shot away, also her mizzen top and top-mast. There did not appear to be a square foot in her side that a round shot had not passed through, her quarter deck was encumbered with splinters. On both sides her rigging was hanging down in the water with about sixty dead bodies entangled in it on the port side.

In about fifteen or twenty minutes after the frigate previously mentioned had caught fire, she blew up, at which time one of the large plate glasses in the *Albion's* light room fell out: a man in the magazine promptly replaced it—holding it fast until secured. The accident, which might have been fatal, was attributed to the shock of the blowing up of the frigate."

The 48-gun frigate *Cambrian* seems to have arrived on the scene while the fight was actually in progress. An officer of Marines[1] on board wrote that "On the afternoon of the 20th October, the *Glasgow* came out from Navarino Bay to give us our orders in respect to the battle already raging between the Allies and the Turkish and Egyptian Fleet. We were to engage the batteries on the Island of Sphacteria. Well, we crowded on sail and ran so close in shore that the *Cambrian* was struck by thirty-four shots in her upper works before she could reply with a single gun. Fortunately, the Turkish parapets prevented the cannon being depressed sufficiently to enable our hull to be struck, while only a moderate elevation of our own guns enabled us to play on the battery with so much effect that it was speedily demolished. I had a narrow escape here also. A stray shot struck poor Lieutenant Sturgeon, whose right arm was touching my left, and instantly killed him."

The loss sustained by the Corps in this action, which resulted in the total destruction of the Turko-Egyptian armament, was two Captains, one Subaltern and eighteen Privates killed, one Captain (mortally) and thirty-nine Privates wounded, thirteen very severely.

---

[1] Afterwards Sir A. B. Stransham, G.C.B.

THE BATTLE OF NAVARINO, 18th OCTOBER, 1827.

Captain Moore, who was mortally wounded at the beginning of the action, died on the 30th October, and was buried near Mount Etna in Sicily. His brother officers erected a monument to his memory at Gibraltar. He was the senior officer of the Corps present at the Battle and received the Brevet rank of Major before he died.

H.R.H. the Duke of Clarence[1] ordered that the two senior Lieutenants and the two senior 2nd Lieutenants present should be promoted in the death vacancies, but in consequence of their belonging to a strictly seniority Corps, these commissions were almost at once cancelled.

In the Throne Room of the Royal Palace at Athens there is a picture of the Battle of Navarino, and it is interesting to find that the most prominent feature in it is the boarding of a Turkish ship by half-a-dozen Marines from a man-of-war's boat which is alongside. Muskets in hand with bayonets fixed they are making a desperate attempt to climb the ship's side, while the Greek artist, unacquainted with the spirit which animates all ranks and ratings in the British Navy, has depicted their shipmates the bluejackets of the boats crew, lying quietly on their oars with eyes upturned in full appreciation of the exploit.

NOTES.

NOTE I.—SUPPLY OF MUNITIONS OF WAR TO BARBARY.

The following is taken from the "Annual Register" for 1774:—

"27th October.—Sidi Tahar Fenis, whom the Emperor (of Morocco) some time ago charged with a commission for England. His Britannic Majesty hath, on this occasion, sent to the Moorish Prince a present, which consists of nineteen Mortars, with their carriages, 2850 Bombs, 30 Iron Cannons with their carriages, likewise four Chests of Matches, 3200 bullets, and 25 bales, containing pieces of Silver Plate, Mathematical Instruments, Sabres, Fusees, China, Woolen Cloaths, Linens and divers other effects. Sidi Tahar Fenis hath brought besides, two Brass Cannons, 24 pounders, which were re-cast in England from some old Cannon out of the Emperor's Arsenal."

As far back as the days of Charles II. when the Marine Regiment participated in the fighting against the Moors at Tangier, some Englishmen were found unpatriotic enough to smuggle out 1500 barrels of powder for the use of our opponents. As a journal of the period indignantly remarked: "'Tis too often the custom of our nation to give away their swords and fight with their teeth, and furnish our foes with means to cut our own throats."

NOTE II.—TURKS v. ROMAN CATHOLICS.

As an instance of the "Much rather Turk than Priest" feeling rampant in the British Isles, in the 16th and 17th centuries, the following doggerel couplet used at this time—according to Crofton Croker (Researches in the South of Ireland)—to adorn the principal gate of the town of Bandon:—

"Jew, Turk or Atheist
May enter here
But not a Papist."

The Papists, however, scored heavily over this, so much so that the inscription was withdrawn, for a Roman Catholic perpetrator of this class of poetry replied with the crushing retort:—

"Whoever wrote this, wrote it well,
For the same is written on the gates of Hell."

NOTE III.—UNIFORM OF THE MARINES, 1777-1823. *Vide Coloured Plates facing pages* 204-262.

The following notes on the uniform of this period taken from Divisional Orders, etc., are of interest.

1779.—(PLYMOUTH), April 5. No black Belts to be worn, nor Caps and Jackets, except by Officers of Flank Companies.

(PLYMOUTH), July 1. Officers ordered to wear Laced Uniform Coat and Waistcoat, Breeches, Uniform Swords, and Cross-Belts on all occasions. Officers of Flank Companies, Jackets, Caps, Black Gaiters or Buckled Garters.

---

[1] Afterwards William IV.

1780. (PLYMOUTH), January 6. Officers to get Black Roses for Gorgets.

(PLYMOUTH), Nov. 4. Sergeants to carry Halberds except in Flank Companies when they are to carry Firelocks.

1783. (CHATHAM), Aug. 12. "The following is the dress of the Officers of the Division; when off Duty, Uniform Coat Epaulettes, etc., White Waistcoat and Breeches; Plain Hat with single Silver Looping, one Tassel on each side, and Uniform Button with Silver double Chain Loop, Black Leather Stock, with False Collar to turn over ¼ of an inch, hair to be queued within an Inch of the Head with a Small Rose, and no Curls; the Queue to be 18 inches long. The Sword and Knot to be constantly worn in a Cross-Belt. When on Duty— Uniform Laced Hat, Pouch, Sash and Gorget with Roses. Epaulette to be of Uniform Lace and Pattern on White Cloth, and to have 20 Bullions of Silver Fringe 3 inches long. The lapels of the Coat to be 3 inches and the cuffs 3½ inches wide, Embroidered Anchors on the Skirt. The Sergeants, Corporals, Drummers, Musick and Private Marines are to dress in the following manner:—The Hair clubbed with a Rose, a Cap and Feather. The Old Coat made into a close Jacket; 2 pair of Trousers each; this dress to be worn on common parades and ordinary duties; but when on Guard or when necessary they are to wear their Full Uniforms with Half-Gaiters. The Hats are all to be cocked alike.

1784. (PLYMOUTH), January 7. Officers ordered to wear "Boots with Hessian Tops when mounting Guard."

(PLYMOUTH), April 7. GRENADIER OFFICERS. Coats uniformly cut. Lapels 3 inches broad, Cuffs 3½ inches. Buttons set on "2 and 2," Skirts turned back with single Grenade and Button. Uniform Waistcoat. Hats, Uniformly Cocked, Double Looped, a Tassel on each side the Cock, Uniform Button and Loop, Rose Cockade and White Feather. Uniform Epaulette, Wings decorated like the Privates. Sword-Belt with Buckle and Slides worn across the shoulder; Sword-Knots Crimson and Gold Tassel. Pouch and Belt with a Grenade. Sash and Gorget with Black Roses. Hair in 3 broad Plaits tied close to the head with Ribbands and hooked under the Hat with a Comb. No Curls.

BATTALION OFFICERS. Uniform, Coats, Lapels and Cuffs "to the King's Order," Skirts turned back with a Rose and Button. Waistcoat as for Grenadiers. Half-Gaiters, Hat, Cock and Dimensions as for Grenadiers. Uniform Lace, Button and Loop. Rose Cockade. Belts, etc., etc., as for Grenadiers, but Hair is to be queued 16 inches long, tied with a Rose and one Curl on each side.

LIGHT INFANTRY OFFICERS. Jackets cut and decorated in the manner of the Privates. Also the Waistcoats and Breeches. Half-Gaiters, Cross-Belts, Small Pouches and Ornaments. Gorget and Sash. Hair clubbed close to the head and tied with a Rose. No Curl.

(PLYMOUTH), April 29. Officers are *permitted* to wear a Plate on their Sword-Belts instead of the Buckle, and "a Strap Epaulette in lieu of the one now worn." The men to be provided with Trousers.

1785. (ADMIRALTY REGULATIONS AND INSTRUCTIONS), Aug. 1. "The following articles are to be issued to the Marines on the 1st June every year, or as soon after as possible:—A Red cloth Coat, White Cloth Waistcoat and Breeches, 1 Shirt with 1 Black Stock, 1 Pair of Stockings, 1 Pair of Shoes and a Hat."

1787. (PLYMOUTH). FEATHERS. Grenadiers, White, Top Red. Battalion, White. Lt.-Infty., Green. Those of the Flank Companies to be higher by the tip. OFFICERS, Hackle Feathers, MEN, Common.

1790. (CHATHAM), Dec. 10. "Whenever any Officer finds it necessary to wear a Great-Coat upon the Parade, it is to be of Blue Cloth with a Red Cape and White metal Buttons."

1791. (CHATHAM), March 25. "All the Officers, except those belonging to Flank Companies, are to wear a Black Feather in their Hats upon the Parade."

(PLYMOUTH), April 1. Apparently the same Order as in 1787 as to Feathers, except that the Light Infantry Green Feather is not mentioned and that the Battalion Companies are to wear "Tufts." The Light Infantry are to wear Red Waistcoats and "The Caps now worn." The Officers' Skirts are not to be sewn back.

1792. (PLYMOUTH), Sept. 26. Foraging Caps first issued. No details.

1793. (PLYMOUTH) May 31. Round Hats permitted in summer "as allowed in some other Corps," at the request of the Officers.

1795. (PLYMOUTH), July 23. Powdered Hair abolished, except for Officers. Sept. 10. Trousers ordered for all duties.

1796. (PLYMOUTH), Aug. 29. Powdered Hair again ordered.

Sept. 1. "Taylors to provide themselves with Blue or Grey Pantaloons as they may be procured from the Recruits. To pay 2s. each if good; 1s. if much worn."

"Officers' Servants are forbid to wear them *out of respect to their Masters.*" "Centinels are also forbid to carry their Arms or the Soldiers to touch their Hats to any Marine Officer they meet *in so mean and unmilitary a Dress.*"

(PLYMOUTH), Nov. 15. Soldiers are not to pipeclay their Trousers when on. Attention called to a previous Order.

1797. (PLYMOUTH), April 6. Silver-Laced Hats abolished. Crimson and Gold Ornaments substituted "as used by Officers of the Line."

(CHATHAM), April 6. As above. Also "The Epaulettes for Captains and Subalterns to be conformable to pattern. Majors are to be distinguished by One Gold Star on the Strap, Lieut.-Colonels by Two and Colonels by Three. The Swords are to be the old-established Silver-Hilted cut and thrust Blades, with Crimson and Gold Sword-Knots. The Gorgets to be plain and to have the King's Arms and Anchor as at present. Breast plates are to be Square with the "Lion and Crown."

(PLYMOUTH), Sept. 11. Feathers. Grenadiers, White.
Battalion, White above, Red below.
Light Infty, Green.

"When Officers wear their Regimental Uniforms looped close, or buttoned all the way down to the waist; the Sash to be *over* Coats."

1798. (PLYMOUTH), May 27. GRENADIER OFFICERS to wear a "Fuse" on each Epaulette and No Wings. LIGHT INFANTRY OFFICERS, a "Bugle-Horn" and No Wings.

(PLYMOUTH), June 12. Sashes to be worn outside the Officers' Uniforms. Buttons to be convex.

(PLYMOUTH), Aug. 14. Sashes, of a new pattern, to be worn over the Left Shoulder.

1799. (PLYMOUTH), March 26. Round Hats ordered.
Grenadiers. Bound Black Tape, Band White. Loopings and Tuft White.
Battalion. Bound White Tape, Band White. Loopings Black. Tuft, Red below, White above.
Light Infty. Bound Black Tape Band White. Loopings, White. Tuft, Green.
Officers to wear Red and White Feathers in lieu of Black.

1802. (PLYMOUTH), May 1. "Blue Facings" on becoming "Royal."
May 24. Yellow Gilt Buttons in lieu of White Metal.

1805. (PLYMOUTH), Dec. 3. Officers to wear White Waist-Belts.
White Breeches and Long Boots in Summer and Blue Pantaloons and Half-Boots in Winter. Buttons, Flat set on "2 and 2." Red and White *Spiral* Feather, "to rise 10 inches above Brim of Hat."

1806. (PLYMOUTH), Sept. 30. Men's Shirts to be issued "Frilled," as at other Divisions.

1807. (PLYMOUTH), Sept. 4. Sergeants and Corporals ordered to wear Chevrons on their right arms instead of Shoulder Knots previously worn. (N.B.—This was adopted in the Army 14 Aug., 1802).

(ADMIRALTY), Sept 28. Improvements to Pantaloons and Trousers suggested by General Barclay to be carried out.

Men liable to Foreign Service to have their Hair cropped.

Calling for report as to reason for Plymouth Band not wearing their proper uniform.

1808. (ADMIRALTY), Oct. 10. Circular to Flag Officers that Marines were to have their Hair cropped conformably with the practice of Regiments ordered on Foreign Service.

(ADMIRALTY), Dec. 12. Pantaloons and Trousers to be dyed of a fast Blue instead of being made of Grey cloth.

1810. (PLYMOUTH), April 16. *Badges of Rank.* Colonel, "Crown and Star." Lieut.-Colonel, "Crown." Major, "Star." Captains and Subalterns to wear One Epaulette only, on the Right Shoulder. Bullion Frings except for Subalterns who must have Plain Fringe.

(N.B.—These changes followed on General Army Orders of 19 Feb., 1810).

(PLYMOUTH), Oct. 10. An Officer from the Woolwich Division requests permission to wear Plain Dark Blue Stocking-knit Pantaloons as worn at other Divisions, instead of Blue Cloth.

(PLYMOUTH), Dec. 7. GENERAL OFFICERS AND STAFF. To carry the Sword in a White Belt round the Waist. By all other Officers in a White leather (Shoulder ?) Belt 2¾ inches wide. Belts of Mounted Officers to have suspenders.

1812. (ADMIRALTY), May 27. Experimental issue of "Caps" to be made to see if they are more suitable than Hats for use at sea.

(N.B.—These "Caps" were probably the cylindrical shakos worn by the Infantry in the Peninsula War then generally termed "Caps."

(PLYMOUTH), June 1. OFFICERS to wear same pattern Hats as Privates; also Coats, but with Lapels to button over breadth of body. Drab Great-Coat with Stand-up Collar and Cape. Uniform Buttons.

At Court Officers to wear Long Boots and Cocked Hats. All Epaulettes to be of the same pattern. Badges of Rank as in 1810.

(ADMIRALTY), Aug. 28. Royal Marine Artillery Officers to be allowed to wear Blue Undress Jackets and Caps when employed on Artillery Service.

(PLYMOUTH), Sept. 16. Officers excused from wearing Hair Powder in Town.

1813. (ADMIRALTY), Aug. 8. Commandant ordered to report why Royal Marine Great Coats are Drab instead of a Mixed Colour like the Army.

(ADMIRALTY), Oct. 19. Great Coats are to be the same as the Line.

Oct. 20. Officers' Great Coats to be precisely the same as the Army.

Oct. 28. Permission granted for Ornament in front of Officers' Hats to be removed.

1814. Company Sergeants granted a special badge and 6d. a day in consideration of the meritorious and exemplary conduct of N.C.O's. R.M.

1814. (ROYAL MARINE ARTILLERY), Oct. 7. "In consequence of the men of the R.M.A. being supplied with Grey Trousers by the Navy Board, the Commanding Officer approves of the Officers wearing the same.

1815. (ADMIRALTY), Dec. 14. Men to be supplied with open Trousers and Half-Gaiters of Mixed Cloth similar to the Army, instead of the Blue Pantaloons and Trousers now worn.

(ADMIRALTY), Dec. 26. Barrels of Muskets are in future to be browned instead of being kept bright.

1816. (ADMIRALTY), Oct. 26. The R.M.A. are to be clothed as the Royal Artillery, except for Buttons and Hats. Round Hats are to be worn similar to those worn by the Royal Marines.

(N.B.—Statement of Prices attached includes in each case estimate for Coat and Waistcoat with Sleeves).

(ADMIRALTY), Dec. 9. The Marine Hat to be established for the R.M.A., with "the addition of Plate, Cockade, Tuft and Band agreeably to the Pattern sent herewith."

1817. (ADMIRALTY), Mar. 3. The New Dress Uniform Jacket approved for Officers R.M.A., similar to Jackets for Sergeants.

(ADMIRALTY), Nov. 27. The Marines in the Severn employed in the prevention of Smuggling to be allowed a special issue of Grey Trousers.

1819. (PLYMOUTH), Sept. 3. Non-Commissioned Officers and Men are not to wear Hair Powder, except the Band-Master, Drum and Fife Majors.

1820. (ROYAL MARINE ARTILLERY, FORT MONCKTON), April 14. The Officers will wear White Pantaloons and Hessian Boots. White Overalls may be worn by the Officers and Men at all drills, and at Gun and Mortar practice.

1821. (PLYMOUTH), April 9. "Caps" (i.e., Shakos), and a "Laced Uniform" ordered to be worn by the Royal Marines.

1823. (PLYMOUTH), Feb. 8. OFFICERS, "Coatee, Scarlet, Lapels, Cuffs and Collar Blue. Prussian Collar, full 3 inches deep with a Loop and Small Button at each end; Straight Lapels buttoning back to 10 Large Uniform Buttons, with Loops occupying two thirds of the space from outwards edge of front seam of armhole tapering to 2¼ inches at bottom, closing in front with hooks and eyes: Cuffs 3½ inches deep with 4 Loops and Large Buttons on each. 4 Short Loops on back of Coatee Skirts with Cross Flaps, 4 Loops and Buttons on each, White Kerseymere Backs (?), Uniform Skirt Ornaments.

Lace on Lapels, Cuffs, and Cross Flaps to be in Pairs, preserving the proper distance between Pairs (and a Light of Blue in the centre of each), Laced Backs (?) and Back Skirts.

Epaulettes Gold Lace Straps 2½ inches wide with a Broad and two Narrow Beadings round Edges. Embroidered Crescent, two rows of Bright Bullion 3 inches long. Epaulettes to be worn in pairs by Field Officers only. Adjutant One, and One Strap on each shoulder.

Pantaloons, white Kerseymere, Boots, Hessian. The Shoulder-Belt to be worn over the Coat.

Feather, Red and White upright hackle, 12 inches long with gilt Socket.

UNDRESS. Coatee as in Dress but with Lapels buttoned over. Trousers uniform and the same Colour as the Privates. Boots, Ankle. Great-Coats; Single-breasted, Stand-up Collar and Uniform Buttons. Cloak; Blue, lined Scarlet Shaloon; walking length, Clasp Ornaments at bottom of Collar and Ball Buttons.

(PLYMOUTH), Nov. 24. The Black Glazed Sword-Belt with Rings and Buckles is only to be worn over the Great-Coat.

TROPICAL UNIFORM.

The following extract from the Life of Sir Robert Abercrombie, published in the "Royal Military Chronicle," in 1813, indicates that a White and Blue uniform was sometimes worn by the Marines in hot climates.

Recounting the capture of the Island of Bourbon, in 1810, the writer says :—" In the night a party of Marines joined the Army. In these climates they are usually dressed in White and Blue, and from the obscurity of objects the similitude of their dress caused them to be easily taken for French soldiers. The alarm of surprise spread through the ranks several Corps stood to their arms and some gave fire. By this unfortunate accident some lives were lost and many wounded."

SOME MARINE HEAD-DRESSES.

1   2   3

1.—Marine wearing Hat with feather from a Medal presented by Lord St. Vincent to the Officers, Seamen and Marines of the *Ville de Paris*, in 1800. It is a curious head-dress for that period, but in an old print of the Barracks at Plymouth, in the Sergeants' Mess of that Division, a company—possibly a Light Infantry Company—is shewn at drill wearing what might perhaps be similar hats. The figures are very small.

2.—The two Marines here shewn are taken from the well-known picture of the Death of Captain Faulknor, R.N., of H.M.S. *Blanche*, in the act of boarding the French frigate *Pique*, in 1795. It seems likely that the Caps they are wearing may be either the "Cap and Feather" referred to in the Chatham Orders of 12 August, 1783, or perhaps the "Foaraging Caps" of the Plymouth Orders of 26 September, 1792. The ornament in the right-hand man's cap seems to be in the nature of a feather, but that in the other soldier's looks more like a bunch of silk or ribband.

3.—This hat is copied from the figure of a Marine carved in stone which is one of the supporters of the Arms of Admiral Sir William Hargood, on his Memorial Tablet, in Bath Abbey. As he was created a K.C.B. in 1815, that probably is the date of the grant of supporters to his Arms, and it may be assumed that the uniform of the Marine is that worn at this time. The knob or button on the brim of the hat and the peculiar affair below the tuft were difficult to interpret. On reference to the official drawing of Sir William Hargood's Arms at the College of Heralds, I find that the former is coloured "Gold," and is therefore presumably a regimental button, while the latter is shewn as a narrow white oblong with a red centre, and probably represents an ornament made either of the regimental lace or of red cloth with a white binding. The "stays" on either side of the hat are coloured "Gold." As in several other drawings of a similar nature at the College of Arms, the uniform is very unreliable, these details must be accepted with caution. I should think it unlikely that the tuft, etc., were removed from the side to the front of the hat till rather later, and therefore in the coloured illustration of Napoleon inspecting the Guard on board H.M.S. *Bellerophon* I have had the hat ornaments shewn in their old position, and the "stays" white instead of gold.

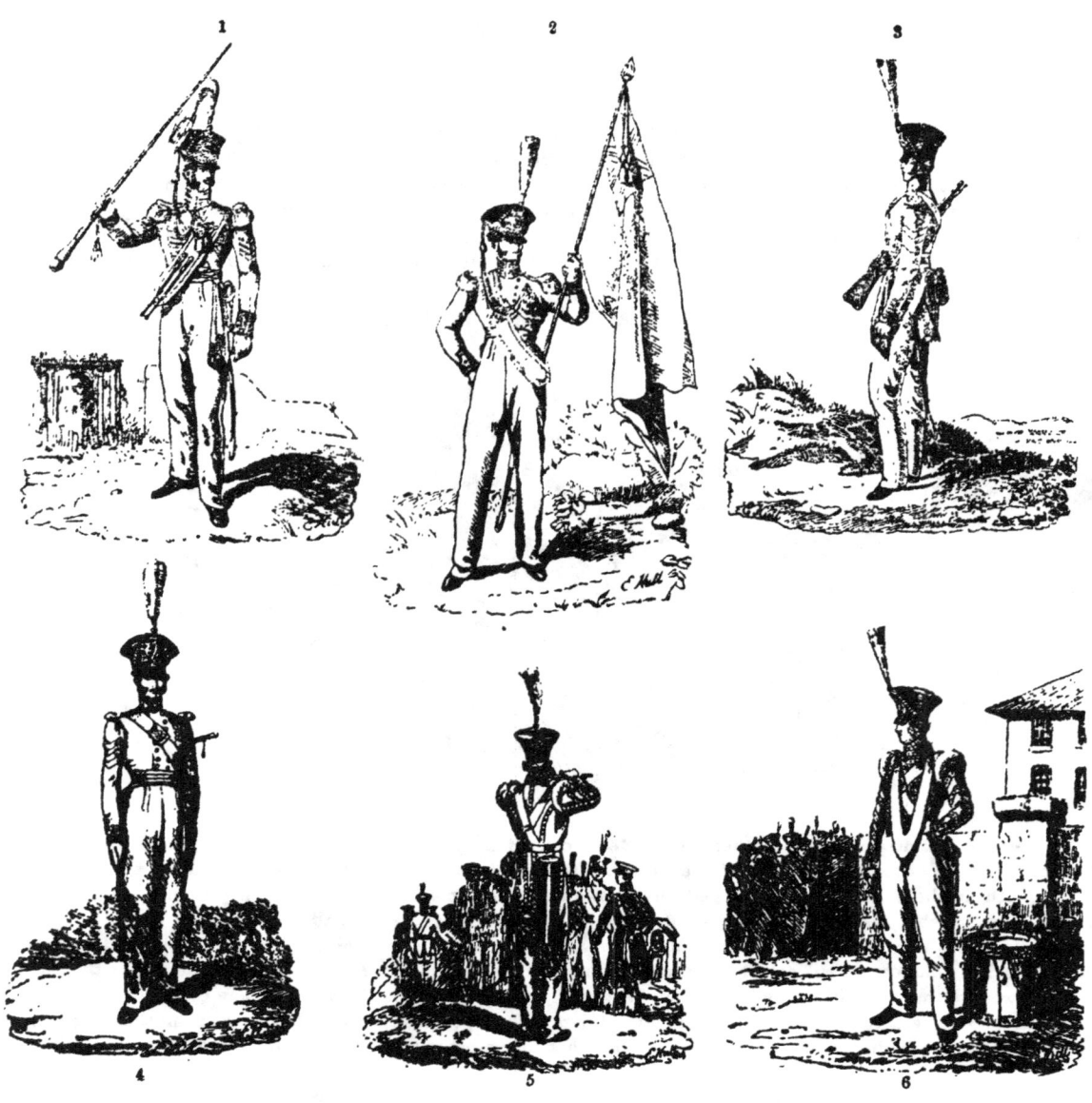

UNIFORM OF THE ROYAL MARINES, 1829-30.

1—*Drum-Major.*   2—*Lieutenant.*   3—*Sergeant.*   4—*Sergeant-Major.*   5—*Fifer.*   6—*Drummer.*

These six figures are from a series of coloured lithographs drawn by E. Hull, and published by Englemann, Graf, Coindet & Co., of 14 Newman Street, London, in 1829-30. There are two others in the series—the "Master of the Band," and "Officer in Undress." These two uniforms have, however, been depicted in the coloured plates in this volume. There are a few points in these figures that call for remark. The Regimental Colour carried by the Ensign is *red*—which seems not likely to be correct, and the "Globe" does not appear in it although we know that new Colours bearing this Badge had been presented to all the Divisions in 1827-8. The Colour belt and the Drum-Major's shoulder-belt are coloured *crimson*, which is also curious. The Ensign, Sergeant-Major and Drum Major are shewn wearing dark grey winter trousers, the other three figures are in white duck trousers. The Plumes are all White, except those of the Drummer and Fifer which have red tips, and that of the Drum-Major which is red.—*Vide* Note III., p. 40.

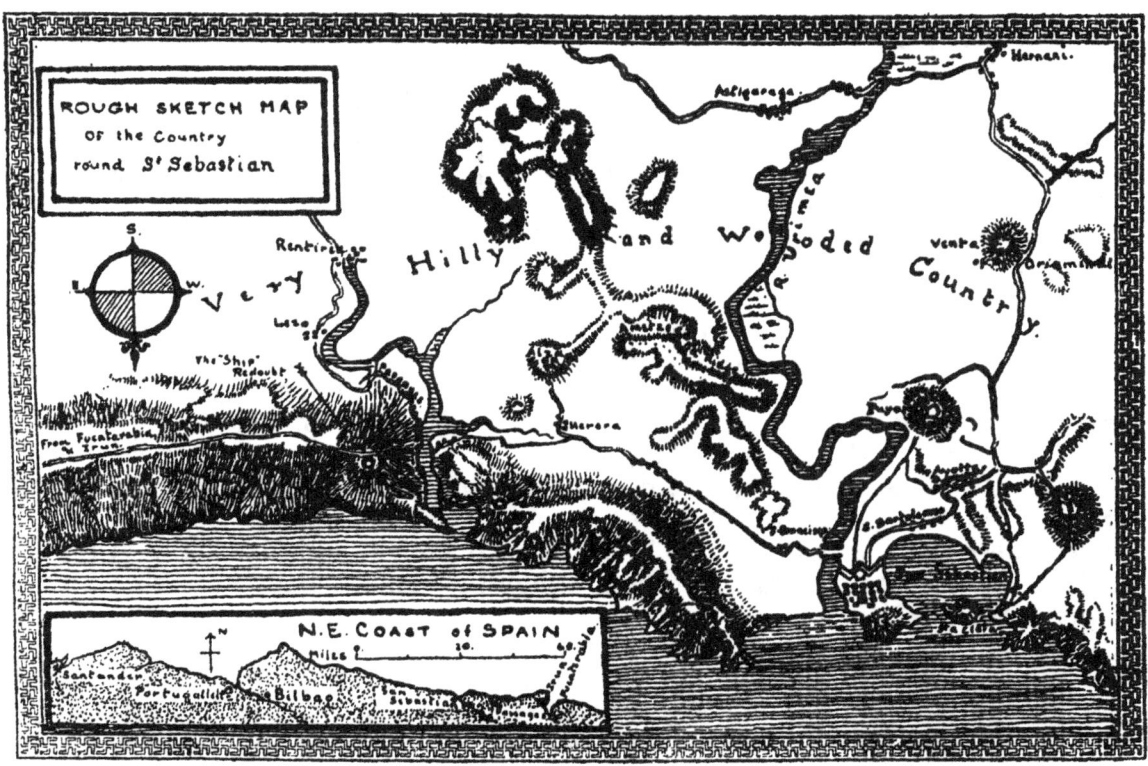

Chapter XXII.

THE ROYAL MARINE BATTALION IN THE CARLIST WAR, 1836-1837.

"Thus much will I venture to anticipate, that whether in union with his gallant brethren of the Fleet, or blended with our disciplined Armies on the shore, the Marine Soldier will never forfeit that distinguished name which he now holds, of Loyalty to his King, Fidelity to his Country, and unshaken Valour against the enemies of both."—
Gillespie, 1803.

THE why and wherefore of the Carlist War of 1833-40 can be explained in a very few words. Philip V of Spain had issued a statute in 1713 limiting the succession to the throne to his male heirs, but in 1830, Ferdinand VII, the then king, cancelled this edict at the instigation it is said, of his fourth wife, Christina of Naples. The result of this was that his infant daughter, Isabel, born the same year, became heir to the crown in the place of his brother, Don Carlos, who up to this time had every reason to consider that he would succeed to the throne, and there is no doubt that both legally and morally he had every right to consider himself as future King of Spain. King Ferdinand died in 1833, and Don Carlos, who had numerous supporters, especially in the North East of the Kingdom, was by no means disposed to abrogate his claims in favour of his infant niece, and determined to fight for his rights. He quickly made himself master of the North of Spain, and would probably have regained his kingdom had not England and France intervened, not to the extent of declaring war against him, but by aiding his opponents with money, and to a certain extent with men. England did, in fact, rather more than this, as in addition to the "British Legion" specially recruited in this country for service with the Spanish Government, she allowed Colonel (afterwards Sir Le Lacy) Evans, an officer on the active list, to command this force with the local rank of Lieut.-General, ordered the squadron on the North Coast of Spain to co-operate against the Carlists, and landed a Battalion of Royal Marines with a proportion of the Royal Marine Artillery, and small detachments of the Royal Artillery and Engineers,[1] who fought beside the Legion and the "Christinos."[2]

A word as to the Legion. It consisted of two regiments of Lancers, known as "Reina Isabel's" and the "Queen's Own Irish," and ten infantry regiments. The 1st, the 2nd "English," the 3rd "Westminster Grenadiers," the 4th "Queen's Own Fusileers," the 5th "Scotch," the 6th "Scotch Grenadiers," the 7th "Irish Light Infantry, the 8th "Highlanders," the 9th "Irish," and the 10th "Munster Light Infantry."

These troops were publicly recruited and wore the national Red except one which was regarded as a rifle regiment, and wore green. The Scottish Corps dressed like the Highland Light Infantry, but wore crimson feathers and ball tufts in their shakos. Many of them were old soldiers, but on the whole they were not of any particular credit to their country. Even if we judge only from the remarks of a writer who served in the Legion,[3] and who throughout his work endeavours, very naturally, to shew it in the most favourable light, it must have contained a very large number of men who cannot be regarded as having been anything else than savage, drunken and mutinous ruffians, ready to desert to the enemy on the slightest pretext, while not a few of the officers seem to have been tyrannical, brutal and in some cases, even cowardly. That they fought as well as they did in the desultory campaign in which they participated, can only be attributed to the national fighting instinct.

The Legion made its first appearance on the 10th July, 1835, when the steamer *Royal Tar* arrived at San Sebastian with the first contingent. After a little fighting leading to no particular result it moved to Vittoria where it spent the winter. Upon the arrival of a Franco-Algerine Legion, in January, 1836, it again took the field, attacked Arlaban, some miles to the North East of Vittoria, and afterwards made its way to St. Sebastian, where it was besieged by a strong force of Carlists. Thanks to the action of the British squadron under Lord John Hay, the "Christinos" kept possession of the coast, and could land men pretty well where they liked, but their jurisdiction in the North East did not reach much

---

[1] Curiously enough these detachments of R.A. and R.E., as well as the Royal Marines, seem to have been under the command of Lord John Hay, the Commodore on that coast. Sir R. Steele, R.M.A., who served in these operations, records that Lieut Vicars, R.E., having applied to Col. Owen commanding the R.M. Battalion for a Court Martial on one of his men, the Commodore intervened, saying that a Court-Martial was superfluous and unnecessary, and ordering Vicars to take his defaulter on board H.M.S. *Tweed* with a letter from him ordering him "a good flogging," which was carried out.
[2] *i.e*, The Government troops, so called after Christina, the Queen Dowager.
[3] Alexander Somerville, author of "History of the British Legion and War in Spain." London, 1839.

Officers R.M.A. and R.M.   Officer R.M.   Trumpeter R.M.A.   Drummer and   Sergeant R.M.   Officer R.M.   Gunner R.M.A.
1810—1815   1823—30   Private R.M.
     1833—1850

UNIFORMS. ROYAL MARINES.
1815—1850

further than the guns of the fleet. The place of assembly for the Royal Marine Battalion was at Santander, where it was formed early in May under the command of Major John Owen,[1] but there was some movement of detachments along the coast in the month previous. On the 15th of that month 100 Marines who had just come from England were despatched from Santander to garrison Portugalette, at the mouth of the Bilbao River. With them went a portion of the detachment of H.M.S. *Castor*, under 2nd Lieut. F. A. Halliday,[2] and on arrival at their destination they were reinforced by others of the same detachment who were on board H.M.S. *Saracen*, then lying in the river, five Marine gunners, and Lieut. C. G. Langley, of H.M.S. *Royalist*. "And here we are," writes Halliday, in his journal, "including officers and five R.M.A. to the tune of 148 valientes, about to fortify an old building situated certainly in a very strong position, and a very romantic spot to boot, but it will require no small amount of labour and skill to convert the convent into a fortress. Our first object was to make out a marching ticket for the two unfortunate old friars, to block up doors and establish apertures in the walls to do duty as loopholes till further orders, besides expending an enormous quantity of soap. How very necessary it is for soldiers to be supplied with two bars of yellow washing. I need not say the convent was in a disgustingly stinking state, or it had not been a Spanish lately inhabited convent." Besides fortifying the building and keeping a sharp look-out for the enemy, Don Carlos having "such a flying army that no one knows where they are," much less where they were not, the little garrison had to work hard in making a battery for a couple of long 32-pounders landed from the fleet, besides a smaller one for two Spanish 9-pounders. On the 19th it received a somewhat embarrassing reinforcement in the shape of 136 Spanish Marines and 25 bluejackets belonging to the same nation. "To prevent unpleasantries which might occur from sentries shooting anyone by mistake from not understanding the different parolles, there is a Spanish sentry placed wherever we have an English one. Both must challenge before either fires."[3] During this time the Carlists frequently appeared in groups and singly on the neighbouring hills, but the guns of the *Royalist* kept them at a respectful distance.

On the 5th May, the Legion attacked the Carlist lines outside San Sebastian, and after a severe fight, in which they were aided by the heavy artillery of H.M.S. *Phoenix* and other British war-vessels, drove off the enemy from their entrenchments and captured half-a-dozen cannon. But as the British were not strong enough to occupy the ground they had won, and had to fall back into San Sebastian again, no very great advantage was gained. Five days later the R.M. Battalion was brought round by sea to Portugalette and proceeded to Bilboa. What it was expected to do there does not appear. In any case it re-embarked in a week's time, and was taken round to San Sebastian. There, men and officers seem to have spent a somewhat unpleasant time, thanks to the town being overcrowded with troops. It is related that "Major Owen, in consequence of a Court-Martial sentence, applied to the authorities for some dark hole where he could place the

---

[1] This officer had served on board H.M.S. *Belleisle*, at Trafalgar, was promoted to Lieut.-Colonel while in Spain, and the end of 1837 was appointed Deputy-Adjutant-General of the Corps.
[2] Francis Augustus Halliday, the grandfather of Colonel L. S. T. Halliday, V.C., R.M.L.I., returned to England in H M S *Castor*, 1837. Captain, 1847, re-appointed to R.M.A., 1848. Retired as Major, 1855. Died, 1873
[3] Lieut. Halliday's Journal.

offenders in solitary confinement. The answer to his request was that his men were already furnished with good quarters, and that there were many Spanish soldiers sleeping in the streets who would jump at a black hole."[1] Despite the defeat of the 5th May, the Carlists still surrounded the city, especially to the eastward along the right bank of the Urimea.

It was the 27th before any movement was made by General Evans, who was in command at San Sebastian. On this day, a feint was made to attract the attention of the enemy by the *Salamander* and *Reyna* steaming to the westward with a small detachment of Marines on their decks to suggest a landing in that direction. On the 28th the R.M. Battalion was ordered to support the 3rd Brigade of the Legion in an advance which was to be made across the Urimea. Supported by the fire of six steamers and a dozen gunboats which enfiladed the Carlist positions from the sea, the guns on the fortifications and the field-pieces of the Royal Marine Artillery which got into action on the right, the British troops forded the river in three places, and after taking up such positions as were necessary to support the Legion bivouacked on a hill near Ametza.

Here they remained peacefully till 3 a.m. on the 6th June, when the Carlists drove in the pickets of the Legion, and followed this up by an attack in some force at 8 a.m., which pressed on both flanks of the Christino position, and eventually, some of the Spanish troops who were engaged, giving way, the Marines had to be called to the rescue. Arriving within musketry range, the three leading companies of the Battalion were deployed into line, and commenced independent firing. Whether it was owing to the deadly effect of their fire, or whether attributable to some other reason, the Carlists fell back and the Marines returned to their bivouac. Three men were wounded, Captain Garmston (severely) and two privates.

On the day that the Battalion left San Sebastian, Lieuts. Langley and Halliday and a detachment of about seventy men from the *Castor* steamed out of the harbour of St. Sebastian on board the *Salamander*, and stood away to the eastward. These Marines were off to play at Passages a somewhat similar role to that which had been theirs at Portugalette. They were to act as a species of advanced guard to the Battalion. "Giving the Legion and Co. time to fight their way along to Passages," writes Lieut. Halliday, "we ships went to breakfast, proceeding slowly along the coast, until, off Passages, we saw the Queen's troops and Carlists popping across the harbour. Three or four shots were fired our way, but did not reach us." After three or four hours' wait outside while the Anglo-Spanish war-steamers entered the harbour, the Marines were landed and marched to the top of "an exceeding high hill from whence one has a bird's-eye view not only of the shipping, but also of the contending forces on the hills around, and a great space of the blue waters to the north."[1] Up here they found thirty Spanish Marines and discovered that their especial duty was to prevent the Carlists finding a position on the hilltop from which they could fire down upon the shipping in the narrow harbour beneath. "The second day we were reinforced by Lieut. Clapperton, R.M.A., and a dozen artillerymen. By dint of hard labour our position became daily more

---

1 Lieut. Halliday's Journal.

strong. Our chief engineer was Lord J. H., whose first object appeared to be to lay down the foundation of a fortification as much like a ship as possible, which piece of ingenuity has repeatedly given rise to the most facetious remarks. This always goes by the name of the "Ship." Here we have the poop aft and forecastle ahead, gangways, ports and all complete; in short, he soon succeeded in getting a ship up the hill, which might have puzzled a more military general. In about seven days we were in a very defensible state, two 6-pounders and two threes, besides a four and twenty pound rocket. Generals from the Legion came up and gazed in wonder at our nautical fortifications. Carlists also appeared to look on with a considerable degree of astonishment, especially when they found that our guns would go off and throw shot to a considerable distance. About 100 sailors now came up, both to make the ship by day, and man her by night, so that we were not easily to be turned out. A company of Marines from the Battalion and their Captain took command."[1] It is only six or seven miles as the crow flies from Passages to St. Sebastian, and the ground about Ametzegana which had been occupied by the Marine Battalion, and the 3rd Brigade of the Legion seems to have been in full view from the 'Ship' redoubt on the eastern heights at Passages, for Lieut. Halliday gives the following account of the fight which took place on the 6th, and which has been already mentioned. June 6th, at about an hour before daybreak our attention was arrested by the sound of many great guns and small arms on the height of Evans' lines and at San Sebastian. Towards daylight the fight was continued all along his lines, and we soon had a charming view of the battle, and 'twas certainly very well worth seeing. From our position we saw more of the Carlists than of the Queen's, but in many places the red and blue cloth was beautifully blended. The Carlists evidently got the best of it at first, but it ended in their being beaten off with considerable loss. This was one of the most bloody fights they have had during the whole war. From about 2 a.m. the firing was kept up without ceasing. Some companies of the Marines were engaged, but not the whole of them."

After sustaining one or two false alarms the little garrison of the "Ship" at Passages was attacked by a body of the enemy estimated to have been at least 400 strong. We cannot do better than to continue to quote from Lieut. Halliday's Journal. "On the morning of the 9th, at about 1-30 a.m., we seized our fighting tools. The sailors were up as usual from the ships to strengthen us, and the picquet had latest orders to retire from the commanding easily-to-be-made-tenable position on the height. Our whole force was about 300 Marines and sailors. About 2 a.m. we were all tired of doing nothing, and all persuaded they would not interrupt our quiet, when the devil of a row saluted our ears. A yell that had not disgraced Hell itself, and a blast of trumpets sounding the charge, accompanied by a pretty considerable roar of musketry. But until we were actually *boarded*, but few of our muskets could come into play. I thought, as a nautical told me, we had better 'fit our men with boarding pikes instead of muskets.' They had been of equal service. After some little time Langley succeeded in being allowed to go outside the walls. Then our fire first began to tell although we could but fire at the flashes.

---

[1] Lieut. Halliday's Journal.

The house in our front, containing thirty-six Spaniards of the 12th, was very hard pressed. At least they could *hardly* hold out any longer, having two dead and three dying, besides fifteen wounded. When daylight enabled us and the guns to amend our aim, the Carlists began to doubt, to retire, or to cease charging. We had then re-occupied our deserted wall in front. The grape and canister fell very thick among them. Also amongst them came Langley with about twenty men, and obliged the Carlists to retire. They say he saved the lives of those within, for the Carlists had already burst open the door and 'twas touch and go work. They would have butchered the whole of them. Langley in front of the house was shot through the thigh, odd enough the only man who was hurt. Several were hit but not hurt. My 'valet de chambre' was hit three times. How singular!

"The Carlists allow to have lost twenty killed, and fifty *hors de combat*. Certes they left eight behind them, and they are not in the habit of leaving their dying or dead. Their attack was beautifully managed. They came so quietly and attacked so gallantly that they deserved a better fate. Langley gained the Order of San Fernando, as well as a hole through his leg, and well did his gallantry deserve the honour. . . . . This is quite an amateur war. All the actors are Volunteers except the Royals, who would nearly all prefer acting on the other side.[1] The men, generally speaking, are of the same opinion, though, like their officers, they obey orders. A frequent remark of theirs is, 'Well, for my part I'd as soon shoot some Spaniard, I don't care whether he's a "Christiner" or "Carlew," but I should not like to go home without shooting some fellow.'"

The defenders of the "Ship" were now from time to time augmented till their force amounted to about six or eight hundred men. Besides the original garrison, there had arrived two Companies from the Marine Battalion, the Marines from the *Pearl*, *Tweed*, *Royalist* and *Castor*, besides some three or four hundred of the 12th de la Linea, Saragossa. The latter were soon relieved by "four companies of the 10th Legion," "Break of day boys."[2]

It was not until the 10th July that the Battalion completed its march to Passages. "That evening," writes Lieut. Halliday, at Passages, "it was very clear there was a move in Evans' lines. Before dark we (and the Carlists) saw the regiments marching. About dusk some of them ascended our hill. Lancers took up a position in front of the Casa Fieurte, so that the enemy could have no doubt with regard to Evans' intentions. Regiments begin crossing the river. Never was such a noise made by soldiers about to *surprise* an enemy. At 10 p.m. Steele[3] received a note from Henderson to tell him that all were to march except the *Castor's* Marines and the R.M.A.—a bore for Joe, and we felt not a little disgusted, but I was not surprised as I am always left behind on every occasion. Some persons are fortunate in that respect. In a short time after hearing our sentence Major Owen and his jolly band came blowing up the hill, damning our elevated situation. I wished them all in heaven that night. Instead of being before the walls of Fuentarabia by daybreak, that night was passed with us expecting all night to march. Sleep for us was out of the question. At 5 a.m. they

---

[1] *Vide* Note I.
[2] The Munster Light Infantry. Surely he means "Peep-o-day-boys."
[3] Capt. Steele, R.M.A.

actually did march to my no small satisfaction. The village of Alza was the only position now occupied by Evans, barring a few houses along the high road from Passages to San Sebastian. At daybreak we saw the Carlists, very busy firing all the huts, etc., which had been occupied by the Marines and the rest of the Legion. (N.B.—They do not like being accused of belonging to the Legion). From our position, there is a high ridge of mountains which runs along the sea to Fuentarabia. This was the route Evans, with about 5,000 men took that morning, July 11th. On these mountains before night they were all routed by about half their number of Carlists. Never was anything so badly managed under the sun. Their departure was worth seeing at any rate. The red coats on the left and white caps[1] in the valley keeping parallel to them—all gone, and Clapperton and I with fifty-two men left in charge of the place. Here was a chance for the Carlists, and we afterwards heard that, had Evans taken Fuentarabia we should have been attacked in the morning. Some of our men took advantage of the coast being clear to go beyond our usual limits and rob potatoes. Towards evening we were reinforced by four Companies of Rifles. At 10 p.m. entered Logan regularly done up, and bringing us the first tidings of their failure and retreat back to our position. Pratt, R.M., also soon came in, and some wounded " Legions " needed our assistance. That night, like the last, was passed with open eye. Having bivouacked that night about a league from us, the troops marched in on the morning of the 12th. But Evans did not think proper to take up his old positions. The Marines remained in Passages and most of the Legion returned to San Sebastian and thereabouts. The Carlists immediately re-occupied their positions around us, and all went on even as before poor Evans' sad disaster, our only pastime being a little practice at over curious gentlemen, some of whom we knocked over now and then to teach them their distance. At the affair of Fuentarabia, two Marines (privates) were killed and ten wounded. Odd enough, the officers never get killed. No promotion ! I think some of the old fellows ought to give us a step or so."

A few further details of this unsuccessful day will not be out of place. The British Force after leaving Passages halted at 8 a.m. at the Monastery of Guadeloupe, from which place General Evans pushed forward the 6th and 10th regiments of the Legion with the Royal Marines in support, with the object of securing a wooden bridge by which it was possible for the Carlists to pour in reinforcements to Irun and Fuentarabia. The operations seem to have been carried out in a halfhearted manner. The Legionaries took the bridge, but were at once attacked by the Carlists, and apparently were not supported till their ammunition was giving out. Then two Companies of the Marines were placed on an embankment near the bridge, and later on two more thrown into a convent hard by, which commanded the bridge, and these four companies contrived to hold the enemy in check till late in the afternoon, when, in accordance with what seems to have been the routine in this campaign—if one can call such operations a campaign—General Evans ordered a retreat to the Isquibel Hills. Two other companies of the Battalion had a skirmish away on the left checking a threatened sortie from Fuentarabia. The next day, as Lieut. Halliday has related, the British fell back to Passages.

---

1 The Carlists, who wore white caps and who marched by a parallel road to the British and "Christinos."

To judge by the account of a member of the Legion,[1] it appears not to have been on the best of terms with the Royal Marines. One grievance was an order issued by General Evans that the Officers of the Royal Marines should have a superior local rank to those of the Legion, Colonels ranking as Generals, Captains with Colonels, and Subalterns with Captains. "It was a foolishly weak and unmanly prostration of dignity in General Evans," writes this Legionary, "thus to succumb to the prejudice of a few persons who snarled at him. One of the officers of the Marines wrote frequently to a London newspaper, complaining of the shocking indignity of their being associated with the Legion. But what to him must have been the indignity, as he was a young fashionable aristocrat, was the obligation he found himself under to wrap himself in his cloak and soil his polished boots by mounting the picquets of the Ametza Hill. His letters are only worth referring to because in England people have been misled by them. The genuine English officers who had seen service in the Marines were never ashamed of being alongside the Legion." If one may hazard a guess, the truth probably was that the Marines were disgusted with the continual aimless attacks on the Carlist positions which always ended in a "withdrawal," which withdrawal they probably —justly or unjustly—laid at the door of the Legion. Anyway there is little doubt that the quality of its men and officers was not of the very first class as regards efficiency.[2] The same writer records a few further opinions about the Corps which are of some interest. "There is not a better drilled Corps," he says, "better appointed in every way, or one that looks better in the British Service, than the Royal Marines do; indeed, for some years past since their uniform has been altered,[3] they have been proverbial as a good-looking Corps; but when they marched where the Legion marched—when they fared—(no, they did not *fare* as the Legion, for the Marines had their tea made for them twice a day whatever went on, and they had their rum regularly, and extra, at such times as that, and rations always of a good quality), but when they were exposed to makeshift quarters, or the toil and tear and wear of the Legion, they looked no better than the Legion did at these times, and when the Legion had nothing to do but mount guard and attend parades, they turned out with as white belts, as clean muskets, and as much under awe of discipline as the Marines did, or as any other Corps do. On the 13th (March, 1837) though it was still wet, and an order to advance expected, yet our regiment was paraded twice with white belts, clean-washed gaiters, polished shoes, buttons and brasses, while the Marines had no dress parade at all, and I believe, their commanding-officer was the wisest, for if the muskets were cleaned at such times, it was enough; only this will shew what kind of military order was observed with us."

With the exception of a Carlist attack on the outposts on the eastern heights of Passages, on 1st October, easily and quickly repulsed, there is nothing further to be recorded of the doings of the R.M. Battalion during the remainder of the year 1836.

In March of the following year, it came in for a certain amount of fighting and acquitted itself with credit, although the general result of the operations undertaken

---

[1] History of the British Legion and War in Spain. Alexander Somerville, 1839.—*Vide* Note II.
[2] Sir Richard Steele, R.M.A., records more than one mutiny among these troops in his private diary.
[3] *Vide* Note III.

THE GUNS OF THE ROYAL MARINE ARTILLERY IN ACTION AT HERNANI.

From a painting in the R.M.A. Officers' Mess, Eastney Barracks

against the Carlists was practically nil. Leaving its quarters at Passages at 3 in the morning of March 10th, the Battalion joined the Legion and a contingent of Spanish troops at Alza. Here the combined force was formed up for an attack on the Ametzegana position then held by the Carlists in some force. While Colonel Lezama of the Spanish Army made a feint against the villages of Lezo and Rentirea, which were so close to Passages that the guns in the redoubt of San Antonio—which had been thrown up by the Marines—were able to cover his advance; the 9th Legion stormed the Ametzegana, while the Spanish "Princessa" Regiment, supported by the Royal Marines, captured the position at Gabara. The whole Carlist position was in the hands of the Christinos before evening, though the enemy held on to their trenches at San Marco for a long time, and were only driven out when the guns of the R.M. Artillery came into action against them with spherical case-shot, which proved very destructive. The next few days the battalion spent crossing and re-crossing the Urimea, and occupying and preparing for defence the village of Loyola on the left bank of that river. It was eventually determined to attack the position held by the enemy near the village of Hernani, seven or eight miles from San Sebastian.

On the morning of the 15th, commanded by Colonel Owen, the Battalion advanced along the Hernani road till it arrived at the "windmill-battery on the Ayette lines." Here the men were halted and cautioned "to keep locked up, to pay strict attention to the directions of their officers, and not to waste their ammunition by a careless fire."

Continuing their forward movement the Marines at 2 p.m. came under artillery fire from the Carlists whom they discovered strongly posted at the Venta of Oriamendi, about 800 yards distant. To reply to this fire the guns of the Royal Marine Artillery were brought up and opened fire with considerable effect. "I had here an opportunity," writes an eyewitness,[1] "of observing closely the excellent practice of the Marine Artillery as they wrought the mountain guns,[2] I believe carrying balls of nine or twelve pounds weight—which in light skirmishing warfare, are by far the most efficient instruments of conflict. Though the enemy's balls came thick among them they continued throwing shells into the opposite entrenchments with as complete regularity in loading, firing and sponging, as if they had been merely at drill practice. At one of the guns, the gunner, who did the duty of elevating (taking aim), was struck on the shoulder with a musket ball; he was looking along the gun when the shot struck him and lodged in his shoulder, but he continued taking his aim until satisfied, only having put his hand to the wound. He then stepped back, straining his eyes as usual to the point where the shell was expected to go, while the man with the match received the order to fire; and the messenger of death being obediently destructive as he desired when it fell among the enemy, the gunner with apparent satisfaction turned his head to his wounded shoulder, and said, 'Well, I have paid them for this more than cent per cent.'"

Meanwhile a flank attack was working round the enemy's right, and at 5 p.m. the Legion drove the enemy from a line of heights which enabled our guns to get within closer range of the Venta. After further bombardment the Venta was

---

[1] Hist. of the British Legion and War in Spain. Alexander Somerville. 1839.
[2] Field guns he must mean.

stormed just before seven o'clock, its defenders being driven out and bolting for the town of Hernani.

By eight the next morning, the Marine Battalion was in position on the plateau of Oriamendi, not more than a mile and a half from Hernani, and covering the movement of the heavy artillery to the right of the Venta Hill. This eminence formed the centre of the Christino position, and close beside it were stationed the Royal Marine Artillery with their 24 pound howitzers under the command of Lieutenant Savage. The field artillery belonging to the Legion moved down the slopes towards Hernani escorted by the Lancers and a regiment of infantry.

With the Marines was the 5th division of Evans' army, while the 2nd Spanish Light Infantry and 6th Legion were pushed forward in extended order over the ground in front of the St. Barbara Heights. As soon as the advance began it came under the fire of three guns which the Carlists had placed in a convent on the left of the town. Lieutenant Castieau, R.M.A., and Lieutenant Dupuis, R.A., who were in charge of the heavy battery at once replied. About 11 o'clock, the Carlist Lancers galloped out of the town and charged down the road upon the advancing infantry, only to be charged in their turn by the Lancers of the Legion whom they had not observed, and who completely routed them. After some heavy firing on the left, four Carlist Battalions suddenly debouched from a gorge in the hills right in front of the Marines, and throwing out a cloud of skirmishers, drove back the 2nd Spanish Light Infantry and the 6th Legion in disorder. It was time for the Marines to take a hand, and Colonel Owen, deploying five companies into line, advanced them to a natural breastwork in his front from which they opened a heavy independent fire upon the advancing Carlists who dropped fast. In vain did their officers urge them to the attack, they wavered and could not be got to close quarters. A flank attack on the right of the position held by the R.M. Battalion met with the same non-success, and finally an attempt to get round on to the San Sebastian road in its rear was defeated by the fire of a company which had been posted by Colonel Owen behind a wall overlooking the line of their advance. The Carlists now fell back from the Marines towards Hernani, but apparently they were still too formidable for the remainder of General Evans' troops, for they continued to gain ground towards the left till it was necessary for the Marines to be ordered back to cover the San Sebastian road. They halted in column at much about the same place at which they had first come under fire the day before, about 800 yards in rear of the Oriamendi plateau. Here they again saved the situation, for about 3-20 the Legionary and Spanish troops were falling back in such disorder that it was uncommonly like a rout, and the Carlists were only checked by the Marines once more deploying into line, and presenting such a formidable front to the enemy, who had already learnt what to expect from them, that they desisted from any further attempt to follow the Christinos, who were enabled to reach the shelter of the fortifications of St. Sebastian. The Battalion afterwards followed them to that place and was quartered for the night in the Church of St. Francis.

Sir Richard Steele, R.M.A., who was present, testifies to the bad behaviour of the Christino Army—British Legion and Spanish troops alike—in his private

HERNANI from the PLATEAU at the VENTA of ORIAMENDI.

Shewing the attack of the Carlists on the position held by Genl. Evans on the 16th March, 1837—and the last position of the Royal British Marines.

Drawn on the spot during the Action by T. L. Hornbrook, Marine Painter to H.R.H. the Duchess of Kent. From a Coloured Lithograph by Day & Haghe.

diary. "The whole Army," he writes, "fell back in the greatest confusion and disorder, abandoning the Oriamendi. The Marine Battalion formed column and also line at different times to restore some order and formation, every effort was made by General Evans and others to get the men together without effect, and even when they reached the protection of the guns at Puyo and the Windmill Battery, force was obliged to be resorted to to stop their flight."

To these unworthy warriors the Royal Marines were held up as an example by General Evans in the following Order of the 21st March:—"The unshaken firmness of the British Royal Marines under Lieut.-Colonel Owen, in repulsing, as they did, four times their number, afforded you a noble example of the irresistible force of military organisation and discipline, which the Lieutenant-General feels confident on future occasions, you will be proud to emulate."

There is not the slightest doubt, that had it not been for the Marines Evans' army would have been completely routed with tremendous loss. An Officer of the Royal Engineers, who was present, has placed this on record in a letter which is well worth transcribing:[1] He writes from San Sebastian:—"Saw ten or twelve battalions file out and extend beyond our right and left; from this time it began to look serious, and about 2 p.m. the Carlists commenced their attack, symptoms of wavering were observed on our left, although they were *not pushed*. On the right they began also to grow troublesome, and Lord John Hay considered it time for the Marines to open their fire: they have hitherto done nothing. It was high time; and it would have done your heart good to have seen the manner in which they did their work. You must know the system of fighting here is regular guerilla —every man for himself—firing as often as you can behind walls, etc., in contrast to this it was beautiful to see the battalion throw in a regular fire, as steady as on parade, and Colonel Owen just as cool as in the barrack yard: it was the admiration of all who saw it, and soon quieted the Carlists. What a fine example of discipline the Marines gave! Had they not acted as they did, our right would have been forced, and the army would have been cut to pieces. They certainly have added another laurel to their many."[2]

"Among the warriors of the Marine Battalion engaged at Hernani was the Regimental dog, "Dash," who was wounded. Dash belonged to Captain Bury's Company, and was always foremost in the fray. Dash was amongst the wounded when the position of Ametzegana was carried by the British Legion assisted by the Marine Battalion on 10th March, 1837, but his wound did not deter him from heading the column which repulsed a Carlist attack on the 16th March. On this occasion Dash was hit in the legs, and after the fight was over, was knighted with a drummer's sword by the Marines, and at the same time invested with a medal made from a Carlist bullet. Sir Dash, we believe, survived the campaign, and returned to England with the Battalion."[3]

On Saturday, 8th July, the R.M. Battalion paraded with reversed arms, this being the day of the Funeral of King William IV, a monarch who had always

---

[1] Quoted in "Historical Record of R.M. Forces." Lieut. H. Nicholas.
[2] "The heavy loss which Evans suffered would have been still greater if it had not been for the gallant conduct of our Marines, who, though not more than 400 or 500 in number, withstood the attack of the whole Carlist Army, and protected his retreat, or more properly speaking, his flight."—Lord Malmesbury's Memoirs.
[3] "Art Journal," July, 1891.

proved himself a good friend to the Corps, and on the day following, " a cloudy and sultry day, the Battalion assembled in full dress, and at 1 o'clock fired a *Feu de Joye* to celebrate the Accession of Her Most Gracious Majesty Victoria to the Throne of Great Britain."[1]

The movements of the Battalion during the remainder of 1837 appear to have consisted almost entirely of marching and countermarching over the same ground over which it had manoeuvred already, though at times a slight skirmish was thrown in. Thus we find it leaving Passages again on 13th May for Hernani, near the Oriamendi plateau the next day, back at Passages the day following, and the day after that taking the same route to Irun and Fuentarabia that it had pursued on the unfortunate 11th July, 1836. This time, however, Irun was captured by assault on the 18th, and Fuentarabia surrendered the same day, after which back marched the Battalion to Passages. On 1st August, Lieutenant White, R.M., was captured by the Carlists. Great fears for his life disturbed the Battalion, but he was eventually exchanged.[2] In September it joined the Spanish Army commanded by Espartero, and was present when Hernani surrendered on the 9th of that month, after which it again returned to its quarters at Passages where it remained till the close of the war in 1840[3] An attack on its outposts alone remains to be recorded. The following account is taken from a work from which several quotations have already been made,[4] and it gives the date of this attack as 9th June, 1837. It seems more than likely that this is a mistake, and that it is the attack for repelling which on the same day in the year previous Lieut. Langley received the Order of San Fernando. The attack according to this account " was on the morning of the 9th before daylight. The Royal Marines and Marine Artillery occupied a height to the eastward of Passages ; a temporary fortification[5] had been erected, for here Lord John Hay had taken up a position as soon as he took the town on the 28th of May.[6] To take this the Carlists ventured to attempt not by cannonade or storm, for they were directed by better judgment than to attempt that. All the forces in Spain put together, would not have taken it by fighting, so inaccessible was the height, but they resolved on trying it by stratagem. The Carlists brought up some columns of their best forces during the night, and after getting them up the steep hillside, and partly under cover of some of the rocks, they were reforming into columns, from having scrambled the best way they were able, and, no doubt, were about to put their plans into execution, though it never became known what those plans were.

It happened that an officer of the Marines' guard was visiting his sentries just at the moment that the first glimpse was got of the enemy, as they gathered under their partial cover. He did not allow the sentry to fire, which, no doubt, the latter would have done ; but ordered him to remain perfectly quiet until they were more distinctly seen. This officer communicated immediately with the commanding officer. The latter directed the sentries to remain without challenging,

---
1 Sir R. Steele's Diary.
2 *Vide* Note IV.
3 Under the command of Lieut.-Colonel Parke, who relieved Colonel Owen on 24th November, 1837, on his being appointed D.A. General.
4 History of the British Legion and War in Spain. Alexander Somerville. 1839.
5 Evidently the "Ship."
6 He here implies the same year 1837—but it was the May previous that Passages was occupied. This points to the probability of the attack recorded being really in 1836.

and the whole force to get under arms. This was silently done, and the guns drawn from the embrasures of the mud fortification, and each loaded with canister shot, then quickly and quietly pointed to the doomed foe. Every Marine, loaded, stood at the 'ready' with his musket through the loopholes of the fortification, and waited for the order which was to be given. In a short while the Carlists began to move from where they had formed, and by their movement, seemed as if intending to surround the place, and devour the sleeping garrison before their sentries could give the alarm, but alas, for them their daring had led them to destruction. The order was given within—Fire!—one whole volley of artillery and musketry was discharged at once, and over the rocks, dead, wounded and living tumbled mingling in confusion. There was not even time to follow them with a second discharge, for they so suddenly disappeared that there was not a living one stood to receive a second shot. Descending down to the lower ground, the Marines followed them, and for a short while kept up a slight engagement as the last of them retired. It could not be ascertained how many were killed, for they carried some of the dead and most of the wounded away; but the Marines got some of them to bury, and some dead bodies lay unburied for six weeks after that time between the lines, no party venturing to put them under earth."

In conclusion, the following letter from Lord John Hay to Colonel Thompson Aslett then commanding the R.M. Battalion may be appropriately quoted:—

"H.M. Ship *North Star*,

Passages, 16th Aug., 1840

Sir,

The Lords Commissioners of the Admiralty having signified to me their intention of gradually withdrawing the Force under my orders from this Coast, have directed me at the same time to convey to yourself, the Officers, Non-Commissioned Officers and Privates of the Royal Marine Battalion under your command, their Lordships' marked approbation of the zeal, gallantry and good conduct which has been displayed by the Battalion on all occasions during the long course of Service in which it has been employed on this Coast.

In communicating this expression of their Lordships' satisfaction, I avail myself of the opportunity of again recording my Thanks to the Officers, Non-Commissioned Officers and Privates of the Battalion, for the zeal and ability with which they have at all times carried my orders into effect, and my admiration of the gallantry they have invariably displayed; more particularly on the 16th of March, 1837; when by their unshaken firmness, they held a position at a moment of extreme difficulty, thus maintaining the characteristic firmness of British Marines.

You will communicate the same to the Officers, Non-Commissioned Officers and Privates of the Battalion under your command.

I am, Sir,

Your obedient Servant,

JOHN HAY,

Commodore.

To Colonel Thompson Aslett, R.M., &c., &c.

NOTES.

NOTE I.—THE ROYAL MARINES AND THE DURANGO DECREE.

Annoyed by the advent of the various Foreign Legions which had been hired by the Christino Government to resist his troops, Don Carlos issued the famous—or infamous—Durango Decree ordering all foreigners taken in arms against him to be shot. It received its name from the place where it was issued. But for the benefit of the British Royal Marines, the following "ROYAL DECREE" was promulgated :—

"The King, our Master, being desirous of drawing a just distinction between the regular foreign troops and the mercenary adventurers, who, in consequence of crimes against society, are obliged to fly to the standard which revolution raises in other countries, and now directs against Spain, and willing to give a proof of his benevolent principles and high sentiments, hath ordered and doth decree as follows :—

"That the officers and men of the Royal English Marines, who, obliged by order of their Government, have come in compliance with their duty, possibly against the dictates of their own consciences and freewill, to the coasts of Guipuscoa and Biscay, and who may fall by the fortune of war into the hands of the troops of his Majesty, shall be respected and held as prisoners of war, the decree of Durango published before the recruitment, applying alone to adventurers who, abandoning their own homes, and renouncing the laws of their country, come voluntarily to extend anarchy, and give a foreign assistance to a cause with which they have no concern.

(Signed) "B. ERRO."
"Villareal, July 15th, 1836."

Don Carlos was probably influenced at least as much by fear of the British Government as by his "benevolent principles and high sentiments."

NOTE II.—THE ROYAL MARINES AND THE "LEGION."

One letter of which Somerville complains is doubtless one written to Lord Palmerston, a copy of which appeared in the "London and Paris Courier," on June 16th, 1836. The writer's principal grievance against the Legion is expressed as follows :—"We see sergeant-majors, who are deserters from our own corps, and a major of a battalion adjoining us, was turned out, only a short time since, as a sergeant from the Woolwich Division of Marines, for drunkenness ! What do you think of the moral contagion of deserters from the Marines acting in brigade as sergeant-majors, with the very corps from which they deserted ? How refreshing to the captains and officers of the Marine Battalion, some of them with 30 years' distinguished service, in all parts of the world, to find themselves brigaded on the Pyrenees with Evans' mercenaries, and liable to be commanded by a man lately drummed out of the Corps for drunkenness."

If the writer's statements were true, and there seems no good cause to doubt his *bona-fides*, especially as he says further, "write to Major Owen, and, my soul on it, he confirms them and more," there certainly were drawbacks in being brigaded with the Legion and General Evans' order giving the Officers of the Royal Marines superior local rank to those of the Legion was fully justified.

NOTE III.—CHANGE OF UNIFORM, 1829-30.

The uniform of the Royal Marines had now for some time been changed from that worn at Trafalgar to one closely resembling that of the Line, with bell-topped shakos, tail coats and white or Oxford grey trousers according to the season. The "Globe" was not yet worn on the shako-plate, but merely a large silver anchor. The following extract from a letter written to the "Naval Chronicle," on 20th May, 1830, is of interest :—

"Mr. Editor,

I had occasion the other day to take a run down to Lewisham, and hearing musket firing, I learned it proceeded from the Woolwich Division of Marines, who were reviewing on Blackheath, when, not having seen this gallant and Royal Corps for some years and thinking perchance I might meet with a face of ' olden time,' I directed my course to the scene of action, and viewed with astonishment and delight this fine and useful body manoeuvring right, left, and athwartships, in a manner fully equal to any regiment of the line I ever beheld : their celerity in throwing themselves into hollow squares was wonderful, and (if a sailor may be allowed to speak of these matters) the firing of the kneeling ranks superior to anything of the kind I ever witnessed, indeed the whole phalanx discharged their pieces as one. The quickness and regularity, too, with which they sprung up again was surely indicative of good drilling. The general appearance also of the men, with their handsome cap-plate and coatees, caused me to ask myself the question, ' Can this really be the same Corps I recollect years ago with round hats, bound and looped up with white tape, and a little black leather cockade and tuft stuck on one side. With short jackets and *tri-coloured* worsted trimmings, etc., but it was so. I confess the sight pleased me exceedingly to see such an improvement in their military appearance. The officers' full dress (established by H.R.H. the Duke of Clarence) is extremely handsome. (*Vide* pages 32 and 53). X.Y.Z."

It may be of interest to mention that in 1835 a pamphlet illustrated by Heath was issued suggesting that the Royal Marines should be formed into a Rifle Corps and dressed in Rifle uniform. Drawings of the actual and suggested uniforms are given in colours. One reason urged for the change is that the conspicuousness of the red coats at Trafalgar occasioned much loss and caused Nelson to order the Marines to be dispersed about the ship instead of drawn up in closed ranks on the poop. The pamphlet is entitled :—

"A few plain and plausible Hints on the Formation of a
ROYAL MARINE RIFLE LEGION. By ' Caleb.' " 1835.

There is a copy in the Royal Marine Library at Plymouth and another in the R.A. Library, Woolwich.

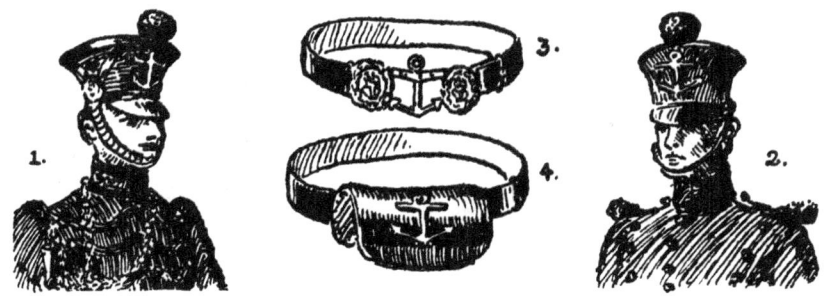

RIFLE UNIFORM AS SUGGESTED FOR THE ROYAL MARINES (*Vide* Note III).
1—Officer. 2—Private. 3—Officer's Belt. 4—Private's Belt and Pouch.
Whistle, Chain and Badges Gilt—Buttons, Braid and Tufts—Black.

NOTE IV.—CAPTURE OF LIEUT. WHITE, R.M., BY THE CARLISTS.

In the United Service Journal of 1841 there is a long account by Lieut. Fred. J. White, of the R.M. Battalion, of his capture by the Carlists and his various adventures while in their hands. The following is a brief summary of the story of his capture and release. On 15th August, 1837, he left Passages to ride to Oyarzum, five miles distant in the direction of Fuentarabia, for the purpose of visiting some brother officers stationed at that place. Half-way there, at Renteria, he stopped to have a shoe replaced which his horse had cast. He says this operation took " some hours," which time he himself spent at an inn or " posada," and he fancies notice of his journey was conveyed to the Carlists by a daughter of the landlord. However, he was able to get on in time to lunch with his friends at Oyarzum. On his way back to Passages he seems to have lost his way, was fired at from a house by Carlists and then attacked by a soldier with a fixed bayonet. His thrust missed White, and the bayonet stuck fast in the saddle. The Marine, after a struggle, possessed himself of the weapon with which he mortally wounded his assailant and rode on. Half a mile further on his way a Carlist started up out of some corn, and presenting his musket at only ten yards distance, ordered White to " Halt." Making his horse rear and swaying his body, he escaped his fire though the ball passed through his cap. In doing this the horse got his foreleg through the rein, and after a short time White had to dismount to free him. The Carlist who had re-loaded his piece, overtook him, and White, trying to mount in a hurry fell over on the off side and being covered at close quarters was compelled to surrender, especially as he had hurt his back in the fall.

As a prisoner in the hands of the Carlists he met with both good and bad treatment, and was moved about a great deal from place to place until June, 1838, when an exchange was arranged for him, and he was handed over to the Spanish Government troops at Alibaron, near Vittoria, on the 21st of that month. Eventually he was sent to Santander from which place he obtained a passage to San Sebastian in H.M. steamer *Phoenix*, whence he made his way on foot to the R.M. Headquarters at Passages, and reported himself to Colonel Parke, who was then in command.

STORMING OF SIDON.

Chapter XXIII.

OPERATIONS ON THE SYRIAN COAST, 1840.

"Our Marines have marched across deserts—have raised batteries—have stormed and taken towns."—
Lord Palmerston (in the House of Commons).

MEHEMET ALI, who had commenced life as a tobacconist, then served as a soldier, and was now Pasha of Egypt, had for some considerable time been a thorn in the side of his Imperial master, the Sultan of Turkey. The Egyptian Fleet and Army had been brought by him to a high state of efficiency, their aid had been of the utmost value to the Sultan in the recent war with the Grecian patriots, and the Pasha began to think that Egypt might well stand alone, and throw off the bonds which united it to Turkey. In pursuance of this idea he commenced hostilities against his suzerain in 1839. His Fleet and Army were devoted to him, and having invaded Syria, which he was desirous of adding to his dominions, he defeated the Turkish army in a pitched battle at Nizib, on the banks of the Euphrates.

But all the time he "had been reckoning without his host." The great European Powers, for many and very various reasons had no idea of allowing the

OPERATIONS ON THE SYRIAN COAST, 1840.

Ottoman Empire to fall to pieces, and though France stood aloof, and was in favour of making an exception to this rule in favour of Mehemet Ali, Russia, England, Austria and Prussia, formally promised to take the Sultan's part against his rebellious vassal. France was terribly aggrieved in having been, as she considered, ignored, and it was felt by the allies that any reverse to their forces would almost certainly bring her very formidable fleet into action.

The brunt of the work fell upon England, though her Mediterranean Fleet, then commanded by Admiral Sir Robert Stopford, was assisted in its operations on the Syrian Coast by a small Austrian squadron, and a few Turkish ships, under Walker Bey, a Captain in the British Navy, but lent to the Turkish Government to take charge of their Fleet. Prussia, now[1] the second Naval Power in Europe, had in these not very far-off days, no Navy at all, while Russia took no part in the war. The British Fleet consisted of the *Princess Charlotte*, 104 guns, the *Rodney*, 92, three 84-gun ships, eight 72 to 80-gun ships, eight frigates and corvettes, three brigs, and half-a-dozen of the new steamships, which had only just made their appearance in the Service.

An ultimatum from the allied powers had been sent to Mehemet Ali requiring him to withdraw his troops from Syria. The defiant answer was returned that " what he had won with the sword he would defend with the sword." Nothing therefore remained for the fleet to do but to take instant action.

On the 9th September, therefore, a landing was effected in D'Jounie Bay, near Beyrout. In consequence of the ill-health of Colonel Sir Charles Smith, of the Royal Engineers, who had been appointed to command the allied troops, the shore operations were confided to Commodore Sir Charles Napier. He it was who suggested the landing at this place, his idea being that the formation of an entrenched camp of Turkish soldiers and British Marines would encourage the mountaineers from the Lebanon to flock down and join the standard of the Sultan.

At nightfall, under cover of the darkness, the Marines o fthe Fleet[2] were embarked on board the *Gorgon*, steam-vessel, while 5,000 Turkish troops, all clad in blue jackets, with scarlet fezzes and white crossbelts, were crowded into other steam vessels, every portion of their decks and even their paddle-boxes being covered with dense masses of soldiery.

At dawn of day the fleet weighed, and followed by the steamers with their cargoes of troops stood towards Beyrout Point. The Egyptian forces at once hastened to the threatened spot, and as their dark-clad columns concentrated in that direction, shot after shot from the ships fell among their ranks. Having succeeded in drawing the greater portion of the enemy in this direction, about noon, when the sea-breeze set in, the steamers were despatched full speed to the other extremity of the Bay, about ten miles distant, followed by the *Castor*, *Pique*, *Dido*, *Wasp*, *Powerful*, and some other ships.

It was impossible for the Egyptian troops to change their position soon enough to oppose a landing so far distant, and the whole of the troops were on shore by 4 o'clock in the afternoon without firing a shot.

---
[1] Written 1912.
[2] Under Lt.-Col. William Walker, R.M.

The heights which commanded the position chosen for the encampment were at once occupied by the Turks, while a Company of the Royal Marines was sent along the beach to the southward, and after crossing the Nahr-el-Kelb, or Dog River,[1] a stream only passable at its mouth, went to reinforce a Turkish detachment which had effected a landing on the further bank, while a second company with about 300 Turkish troops marched to a convent on a hill, three or four miles from the camp, and took up a position covering the road which went to Baelbec by way of Antura. These troops formed the outpost line of the allies behind which all hands set busily to work to entrench and strengthen their position. A good description of the camp at D'Jounie is given by a contemporary writer.[2]

"When I had before seen the eminence on which the encampment had been constructed, it was but a pathless rock, covered with mulberry trees, amongst which were discernable the few houses composing the village of Jounie. At one angle was a small chapel; at another the almost covered ruin of an ancient terrace. Great was the metamorphosis which now presented itself: bristling ramparts extended around it in every direction, surmounted by nearly 100,000 sandbags. It was approached from below by a broad path cut directly across the rock: it had its parade, and its hospital, tents, stables, and magazines; and, in short, every feature of a thoroughly-organised and strongly-fortified military position. From the chapel which was occupied by the commodore, a six pounder peeped from its only window, ranging an adjacent hill. On the raised terrace towards the sea, and elevated above the camp, had been placed a $5\frac{1}{2}$-inch howitzer, protected with sandbags. Within the principal lines were two inner lines, facing the western or weakest portion. Farther on the western side, adjoining the combined English and Austrian divisions, were the Turkish quarters: in front of the latter, a field work had also been thrown up, extending about ninety yards. The artillery in position consisted of nine English field-pieces, three $5\frac{1}{2}$-inch howitzers, and six small Turkish pieces. The camp was slightly commanded from the range of hills skirting it at distances of from 900 to 1,500 yards; but the ascent to these heights would have been very difficult for heavy artillery, and they were at the same time within long-range of the ships. The active force consisted of about 5,000 Turks, 1,500 Marines, 200 Austrians, and a company of artillery, including sappers and miners."

The Marines, immediately upon landing, were formed into two Battalions of eight companies each, and placed under the command of Lieut.-Colonel W. Walker and Captain C. Fegan, but their command was a short-lived one, as shortly afterwards reinforcements arrived from England with orders that Colonel Walker should command the Brigade, and Captain Fegan being required for service afloat. Captains J. Wylock and R. Leonard were appointed Battalion Commanders.

The troops were for some time kept hard at work, night and day, throwing up breastworks, felling trees and in various ways strengthening the defences of the camp at D'Jounie. The Bay of D'Jounie is of considerable extent with a promontory on one side running well out to sea; two roads led from Baelbec to

---

[1] So called from an idol in the form of a dog or wolf which used to be worshipped there. Its body used to be shewn to strangers lying in the sea with its heels upwards. The head was said to be in Venice.
[2] Mr. W. P. Hunter.

Antura, where an excellent position had been taken up by two Battalions of Turks supported by five companies of the Royal Marines.

The Commodore's first move after effecting his landing was to send off the *Dido* and *Carysfort* to open communication with the mountaineers at the little town of Gebail[1] standing on a spur of Mount Lebanon, and washed on three sides by the sea. But, possibly on account of being overawed by the Albanian garrison which held the huge old castle dominating the town, the two ships did not meet with a very friendly reception from the inhabitants, and Sir Charles Napier determined to attempt the capture of the place.

On the 12th September, 220 Marines formed into a small four-company Battalion under the command of Captain Charles Robinson, R.M., and some armed mountaineers came up from D'Jounie in the *Cyclops* which, with the other two ships, anchored abreast of the town.

A bay to the southward of the castle having been selected by Captain Robinson as the most suitable landing place, the troops were sent down into the boats, and about 1 p.m. the ships opened fire on the castle and on those parts of the town where it was supposed Albanian troops were stationed.

As for the huge old fortress which dated from mediaeval times, it might have defied the batteries of the whole Mediterranean Fleet. Its basement for many feet upwards was built of Cyclopean stones generally twenty feet long and twelve feet thick, and behind the massive walls bomb-proof chambers had been excavated, each capable of sheltering 500 men. On the side next the town was a wide fosse of great depth. But after about an hour's cannonade, it was considered that sufficient damage had been done to warrant the disembarkation of the slender force of 200 Marines and 150 Mountaineers who were to take the castle by assault.

The landing on the beach was effected in perfect order, and after the slope leading to the castle which was intersected by breast-high stone walls, and dotted over with mulberry and fig-trees, had been well scoured by the fire of the boats' carronades, the order was given to advance. The Marines, who had formed up in column, extended to the right and at once advanced briskly towards the frowning walls of the castle, taking every advantage of the cover afforded by the walls and fences of the gardens which covered the glacis.

No opposition was experienced until the leading ranks were within thirty yards of the castle, which they began to think must have been abandoned by the garrison in consequence of the heavy bombardment it had sustained from the ships. All at once, just as the men had scrambled over the last garden wall, a tremendous fire of musketry blazed from every corner of the ancient keep, and more especially from a series of loopholes in an outwork which the ground had hitherto masked altogether.

The Albanian musketeers standing in passages excavated in the solid masonry, and firing from loop-holes only just above the ground-line, were able to pick off our men with perfect safety to themselves, and though their fire was returned by the detachment, Captain Robinson, after one or two rounds saw that there was

---

[1] Called by the ancient Greeks "Byblus," once famous for the birth and temple of Adonis.

nothing to be done but to withdraw his men to the shelter of the wall they had just crossed.

He pushed forward a sergeant and four or five men to ascertain whether there was any possibility of getting into the building either by doors or by any breaches which the bombardment might have effected, but the enemy's fire became so severe that he decided that "it was quite hopeless to persevere with any prospect of success,"[1] and ordered a retirement to the beach. The retreat was carried out in excellent order, and by sunset the landing party was again on board.

The loss of the Marines amounted to five men killed, a lieutenant—C. W. Adair—and sixteen men wounded. Lieutenant Gifford, R.N., of the *Cyclops*, who had accompanied them with a gig's crew, was also badly wounded.

Although repulsed, the conduct of the Marines had been such as to gain them the warm approbation of the Admiral, and it was recognised that success would have been absolutely impossible under the circumstances.

"Finding that his men were falling fast," writes Commodore Sir Charles Napier, "that the wall of the castle was impracticable, that there was no gate accessible, and nothing but the muzzles of the enemy's muskets visible through the loopholes, Captain Robinson very judiciously drew his men off."[2]

Moreover, as Admiral Stopford pointed out in his Official Report:—"Although the attack made upon the Castle of Gebail by a party of Marines under Captain Robinson was repulsed, which I deeply regret, yet it was successful in its result, the Castle having been evacuated on the following morning. The possession of that stronghold is of the most material importance, as it commands the main road by which the enemy might advance upon our position from the Northward, and secures a safe point for the mountaineers concentrating and receiving arms. Fully coinciding in the encomiums bestowed by Captain Martin[3] and Captain Austin[4] on the merit of the Officers and men employed on this service, such as must always be conspicuous where danger calls them forth, I beg to recommend them to their Lordships' favourable consideration."

On 22nd September, Sir Charles Napier with a Battalion of the Royal Marines and two Battalions of Turks marched to reconnoitre the Egyptian camp near Marouba.

This officer believed that nature had intended him for a soldier though adverse circumstances had compelled him to become a sailor. He had seen a little land-fighting in the Peninsula, in the company of his cousins who had served under Wellington; and, as an amateur he had contrived to get wounded at Busaco. He was also very proud of the rank of Major-General which had been conferred upon him by the Portuguese Government some ten years before; and he always longed for an opportunity of distinguishing himself at the head of troops.

The advance was made, to quote Napier himself, "by the road of Antura and Argentoun toward Meruba, through the strongest and most difficult country I ever beheld, over roads hardly passable, and under a fiery sun; the Marine Battalion, unaccustomed to marching, were sorely pressed, and arrived with

---
1 His official report.
2 "The War in Syria." By Sir Charles Napier. 1842.
3 Commanding H.M.S. *Carysfort*.
4 Commanding H.M.S. *Cyclops*.

OFFICERS AND COLOURS, ROYAL MARINES.
From "Costume of The Royal Navy and Royal Marines." 1833.

difficulty at Argentoun; there they halted, and I went on with a couple of companies of Turks, who were good marchers, holding a party of Marines, the least fatigued, ready to advance should we be pressed. About two hours before sunset we came in sight of Osman Pasha's camp, and the Albanian standards; they appeared entrenched in a very strong position. The Marines were now ordered to move on and shew themselves, and we continued to advance through a most difficult but beautifully romantic country." After a further reconnaissance a return was made that evening to Argentoun, and on the following morning to the Camp at D'Jounie. The same evening this "soldier and sailor too" was again on the warpath. He intended to attack the left of the Egyptian Army near the heights of Ornagacuan, where he expected to arrive at daybreak on the 24th.

Despatching the Turkish General Jochmus with three Battalions into the deep ravine of the Nahr-el-Kalb, between the camp and Beyrout, he sent another Turkish Battalion over the bridge near its mouth, with orders to occupy the heights on the further side, watch the road leading to Beyrout, and cover the advance of the 2nd Battalion of the Royal Marines under Captain C. Fegan and the Austrian Rocketeers.

"The ground on both sides of the Dog River is very high and precipitous, and offers great advantages to those defending it. The Turkish battalion passed unseen through the deep shady gorge, where the stream runs downwards to the sea, and quietly reached the steep ground it was to occupy.

Our Marines and the Austrians pushed up the riverside by a narrow mountain path overhung by forest verdure, through the openings of which their ranks were seen to glitter at times, until they debouched upon the left of the Albanians."[1] The latter being afraid of being cut off from the road leading to Beharsof, and not relishing the warlike appearance of the Marine battalion, abandoned their entrenchments, moved off to the right, and gained the heights of Ornagacuan,[2] occupying a strong position above the road by which General Jochmus with his three Turkish battalions was advancing.

This force delivered its attack almost at once, and drove the Albanians out of their position, routing them with considerable loss. The Marines had the mortification of seeing this victory won without their further assistance, though, as Napier reported, they "were however most anxious to try their strength, and I hope the opportunity will soon offer."

While these "shore-going" operations had been in progress the fleet had not been idle. The town of Beyrout was bombarded until the 14th of September, and on the 20th an attempt was made on the town of Tortosa, where it was reported that there was a considerable amount of stores intended for the Egyptian troops. The *Benbow*, *Carysfort* and *Zebra*, which had re-embarked their detachments of Marines, were detailed for this operation. The two latter, anchoring within 500 yards of the shore, opened fire on the castle, and effected a breach in its walls. When this had been done, and information received that the enemy had evacuated the place, fifty Marines under Lieutenant R. S. Harrison were put into the boats and preceded by a pioneer party of seamen in a cutter, pulled for the beach.

---

[1] "British Battles." James Grant. Cassell & Co.
[2] Or "Kornet Sherouan."

The town presented on its sea-front a line of wall flanked at each end by a tower, and this wall, in which a bricked-up archway had been battered open, was not more than sixteen yards from the sea.

The cutter, leading some boats' lengths ahead, grated on the beach, and her crew sprang ashore, and had almost reached the archway when a heavy fire of musketry blazed out from every loophole and crevice in the town wall. The heavier boats—a launch, barge, and two pinnaces—with the Marines as they pulled in to the assistance of the cutter's crew, had been suddenly hung up on an underwater ridge supposed to be the remains of ancient walls and buildings; and could get no further. It was for this moment that the enemy had reserved their fire. The stranded boats lay about thirty yards from the shore, and the bullets were splashing into the water on all sides. The fire was returned by the Marines and several ineffectual attempts were made to get ashore, most of their ammunition being wetted and spoiled in the efforts made to do so. Fourteen men, however, were transferred to the cutter, and sent ashore to the assistance of the pioneer party, who had pushed on through the breach and set about breaking open various stores filled with rice, corn and other provisions. At last they came to one whose door being broken down revealed to their astonishment a whole company of Egyptian soldiers. The pioneers, having no arms but their axes, were compelled to beat a retreat, and aided by the arrival of the small reinforcement from the heavier boats, contrived to get back to their cutter. The signal was made recalling the boats and the little expedition returned to their ships having suffered a loss of three Marines and one seaman killed, and eleven seamen and eight Marines wounded, one mortally. The loss would have been still more severe had it not been for the excellent gunnery practice made by the *Zebra* and *Carysfort* in covering the retreat of the boats, and keeping down the enemy's fire. The town of Caiffa had been bombarded by the *Castor*, *Pique* and a Turkish frigate, on the 17th, and its guns and ramparts destroyed by a landing party, and on the following morning the first-mentioned ship took up a position covering the road to Acre, about ten miles from that city. A castle mounting five guns was observed in rear of the town which it commanded, and it was determined to destroy it. The two British ships sailed down, and opened their batteries upon this fortress with such good effect that its garrison were soon scuttling out of it. The Marine detachments and a landing party of seamen were at once put on shore, and although the little force had to march in full sight of a large body of Egyptian troops who were drawn up about a mile outside the town, no opposition was offered to its proceedings. The castle was entered, its guns were hurled over the walls, and after dismantling its fortifications to the best of their ability the raiders returned unmolested to their ships.

Tyre, so often mentioned in Holy Writ, was the next objective of the two frigates. Anchoring off that place, on the 24th, it was summoned to surrender. The civil authorities were ready to do so, but there was a garrison of 500 Egyptian troops who refused to quit the place. A fire was opened by the two ships which soon dislodged the soldiers. At daylight the Marines, with a few seamen, were landed and took possession of the town. Here for some days they were employed in the arduous duty of levelling great sandbanks ten feet high, thrown up by the enemy to cover the approach to the town from the fire of the ships, loading the stores of grain found there into a brig, and manning guard-boats in full sight of 1,500 of the enemy's troops who were in position not more than a couple of miles away.

After Tyre, Sidon.[1] This equally famous city, long fallen from its former high estate, is built on an eminence rising somewhat abruptly from the sea. The area enclosed between the high walls which surround its three landward sides, and the sea, is crammed with closely packed houses, which, along the beach, built as they are of heavy stonework, form practically a line of fortification as formidable as the walls themselves. From a strongly built Barrack on this side of the town a bridge runs out to a castle standing in the sea. There was another and a larger castle situated in the centre of the town, and another smaller fortalice on the south side[2] where the walls crown a small but steep ascent from the level country outside. The principal gate, which at this time was very well defended, was situated on the north side of the town not far from the beach, which here is very smooth and level.

Altogether, Sidon appeared to the allies a formidable fortress, and nothing that prudence or foresight could suggest was omitted in drawing up the plan of attack.

The force detailed for this operation was placed under the immediate command of Commodore Napier, and consisted of the *Thunderer*, 84, the Austrian frigate *Guerriera*, the *Wasp*, 18-gun brig, and the Turkish corvette *Gulsefide*. These were all sailing ships. The two steamers *Cyclops* and *Gorgon* also accompanied the expedition, the former carrying a Battalion of Turks 500 strong, and the latter six Companies of the 1st Battalion of the Royal Marines, a detachment of equal strength to the Turks, and commanded by Captain Arthur Morrison. Off Sidon, the squadron was augmented by the arrival of the steamer *Hydra*, which had come down from Tyre with Walker Bey, the Turkish Admiral, and the *Stromboli* just out from England with a detachment of 284 Marines under Captain Wylock of that Corps.

A brief and peremptory summons to surrender received an equally short refusal, and preparations were at once made by the Commodore to carry out an attack both by land and sea.

Down into the boats which had assembled alongside the *Cyclops* filed the red-fezzed Turkish troops, and from the heavy guns of the *Gorgon* shell after shell crashed into the sea-girt castle and the barracks at the shoreward end of the bridge which connected it with the town. One after the other the broadsides of the bigger ships opened on the walls and houses of the town with the object of driving out and demoralising the dark-skinned Egyptian troops who crowded them, and so preparing the way for the landing parties to deliver their assault.

Captain Morrison's Battalion of Marines had been detailed to land on the beach to the northward of the town, Captain Wylock with his detachment, aided

---

[1] Tyre called the "rock-built," said to have been founded B.C. 2750, Sidon, " the city of fishermen," deriving its origin and name, according to Josephus, from the first-born son of Canaan, was founded about the same year.
[2] Probably the one said to have been built by St. Louis IX of France.

by 100 Austrian Marines under Prince Charles Frederick of Austria,[1] was to get ashore to the south-east, while the Turks had the task of capturing the outlying castle and its connecting bridge.

After half-an-hour's firing a breach was effected in the walls of the latter fortification, and the Turks under the command of Captain Loué, a Prussian Artillery Officer in the Sultan's service, effected a lodgment with some little loss.

But the enemy still occupied the barracks, though the whole of the outer side of the square had been swept away by the *Thunderer's* broadside, and the houses at the shoreward end of the bridge, and the batteries of the war-ships were once more brought into action to dislodge them. Meanwhile the Marine Battalion had effected its landing, and the Austrians and Captain Wylock's Marines got on shore and advanced to attack the small castle on the south side of the town. They carried out the assault with great skill and gallantry, though they suffered somewhat severely from the fire from the windows of a number of houses on a steep acclivity which were strongly held by the enemy. Lieutenant Charles F. Hockin, a young and promising Officer of the Marines, who had recently been decorated with the Order of San Fernando, for his services in the Carlist War, was killed, and several of his men wounded.

But the Egyptians were unable to withstand their determined attack, and the Marines and Austrians, having taken the castle, were ordered to work their way to the main citadel which commanded the town.

While they were engaged in this quarter the Turks, headed by Walker Bey and two British Naval Officers[2] charged over the bridge and attacked the Barrack at the shore end of it, which they captured after a sharp struggle. Simultaneously the Marine Battalion advanced cheering, towards the North Gate. The Commodore who accompanied it gives the following account of its share in the proceedings; "I put myself at the head of the British Marines, and broke into the Barracks.[3] Captain Henderson, R.N., and another party lodged themselves in a house above the Barracks; this done, I marched the Battalion along the line wall to the upper gate, broke it open, and seized the castle.[4] All seemed quiet now below; and leaving a guard in the castle, we descended through several streets, arched over, where occasional skirmishing took place, with detached parties of Egyptian troops, who were easily driven, and finally took refuge in a vaulted barrack, where we found upwards of a thousand men lying ready for a sortie, should occasion offer, or to lay down their arms, should they be discovered; the latter was their fate. A large house near the Barrack still held out, its garrison firing on the assailants, and at last, headed by Hassan Bey, the gallant leader of the Egyptian forces, attempted a sortie. This was met by the British Marines, and this brave man, after firing three times on his enemies, fell with three musket balls in his body. This practically sealed the fate of the place, not one of the garrison of 3,000 men

---

[1] Commanding the *Guerriera*.
[2] Capt. Austin and Arthur Cumming, Mate, both of H.M.S. *Cyclops*.
[3] It does not seem quite clear whether this was the Barracks at the end of the bridge leading to the Sea Castle, or another Barracks near the North Gate.
[4] This is Sir Charles Napier's account. But according to a letter from a Sergeant of Marines, published in the "Morning Herald," about 1853, his memory must have failed him to some extent. "I was orderly to Commodore Napier," he wrote, "on the day of the storming of Sidon, into which he rode on a donkey twenty minutes after it had been stormed and taken by the Royal Marines."

escaped; all were killed, wounded or made prisoners, although the combined landing force was less than half their number. The house belonging to Sulieman Pasha, the Governor, where he resisted to the last, was destroyed by the Marines. He himself, with two Marines' bayonets at his breast, refused quarter, and still showed fight, whereupon they fired their pieces and killed him.

An Officer of Marines, Lieutenant Alexander Anderson, had the honour of first planting the British flag on the walls of Sidon, and one of the enemy's standards was captured by Corporal James Symons, R.M.

The Royal Marines remained in the captured town till the 8th October, when an order was received for their immediate embarkation, and sunset saw them all on board their respective ships. The Commodore, however, was still "soldiering," and on the 9th October, so severely defeated the Egyptian Army under Ibrahim Pasha in the Lebanon Mountains that Beyrout at once surrendered.

The Commodore had been very anxious to have a Marine Battalion with him on this occasion, but Sir Robert Stopford would not allow it, as he said: "it was contrary to his instructions to send them far up country," so the Corps missed the honour of participating in this victory.

Thus the whole line of Egyptian positions on the Syrian coast, with the exception of the town and fortifications of St. Jean D'Acre, the scene of Richard Cœur de Lion's exploits, and of Napoleon's repulse by Sir Sidney Smith, and Majors Douglas and Oldfield of the Marines, had fallen.

The operations of the allied squadron could not achieve finality until this stronghold had also succumbed, but though Commodore Napier and Walker Bey urged an immediate attack, Sir Robert Stopford and Sir Charles Smith, R.E., who by this time had got over his illness, and had assumed charge of the Military part of the campaign, were inclined to hesitate. A powerful French squadron was known to be jealously watching the progress of the Allies, the season of heavy north-westerly gales was at hand, and Sir Charles Smith was not at all sanguine as to the results of an attack from a military point of view.

Luckily, an opportune despatch from Lord Palmerston decided the Admiral to take all risks, and on 31st October the allied Squadron of thirteen British, two Austrian, one Turkish, and one Arabian man-of-war sailed from Beyrout for Acre, anchoring about two miles from the town on the afternoon of the 2nd November.

The night was spent in verifying what information was available as to the localities of the shoals, and in sounding and buoying the channels by which it was intended that the ships should proceed to the stations to which they had been told off for the bombardment which was fixed for the following morning.

There was some misunderstanding as to the exact positions which the various ships were to occupy, so that when fire was opened they were not exactly where the Admiral and Commodore had intended them to be, but as this is an entirely Naval matter no further mention need be made of the incident.

The bombardment began about two in the afternoon, and the cannonade was maintained with such vigour that, to quote from a contemporary writer, "observation was confounded by the continuous roar of canon, and by the masses of smoke, which in many piled-up wreaths began to envelop as well the ships as the fortress. When the smoke at short intervals cleared away, we got a glimpse of one or more of their embrasures; but for the most part the only object seen to mark their locality was the blaze of lurid fire issuing from the pieces at the moment of discharge."

"Thus affairs continued till a little past 4 p.m., when the whole fortress was illumined with an intense blaze of light, which was as suddenly succeeded by a dense cloud of smoke, dust, bursting shells, and large fragments of stone, etc. The principal magazine, supposed to have contained some thousands of barrels of powder, had exploded; believed to have been the effect of a shell thrown by one of the steamships. The cannonade, which for a second had been stayed, was succeeded by a loud and long cheer, which resounded from ship to ship, and the firing was resumed, and continued till near sunset, when not more than twenty guns in the batteries remaining undisabled, the admiral made the signal to "cease firing.' Each ship accordingly left off action, but continued at anchor ready to renew it at a moment's notice; but this was unnecessary, for never was a place more completely torn to pieces."[1] By the explosion, two entire regiments, formed in position on the ramparts, were annihilated, and every living creature within the area of 60,000 square yards ceased to exist. There was a great firing of musketry in the town through the night, which proceeded from the Egyptian troops attacking and plundering the inhabitants before evacuating the place.

On the 4th, in the morning, all the Marines and troops were landed under Sir Charles Smith, and this ancient and far-famed fortress was occupied by the allies without any further opposition whatever. Two thousand of the enemy were seen with grounded arms outside the fortress and were made prisoners by the Marines. Two days later, a second explosion took place among the ruins of the magazine causing a considerable number of casualities, among them a Private of Marines killed and twenty Marines wounded. "In a moment," writes Sir Charles Smith, "we were enveloped in darkness, accompanied by fragments of masonry, with musket balls, shot, and exploding shells of every denomination. The exertions of the Royal Navy and Marines have since been most conspicuous in extinguishing the fire, and in reducing, by precautionary measures, the risk which Turkish evolutions, in the midst of the gunpowder must ever render more or less probable."

The fall of Acre terminated the hostile operations of the allies on the Coast of Syria. Two hundred and fifty of the Marines under Lieut.-Col. Walker were left for a time in garrison, and suffered severely[2] from a raging epidemic of fever which broke out, on account of the Turks throwing the bodies of the dead Egyptians into the sea instead of burying them. As for the share of the Corps in the various operations which had taken place we cannot do better than quote from the speech made by the Marquis of Anglesey, at the banquet, given at Portsmouth to Sir

---

[1] Battles of the British Navy. Allen. 1852.
[2] "It carried off several hundred Turkish soldiers, and sixty of our splendid Marines."
—Rear-Admiral Winnington Ingram.

Robert Stopford on his return to England:[1] "I congratulate the Navy at large on the high and noble proofs which have now lately been given that they have not degenerated; I congratulate that gallant Corps—that useful, that invaluable link in the chain that connects the two services of the Sea and Land, and which unites them in one common band of union, good-fellowship, and interest—I speak as you may well observe, of the Royal Marines—I congratulate them on the splendid share they have had in all these victories. *It is a Corps which never appeared on any occasion or under any circumstances. without doing honour to itself and its country.*"

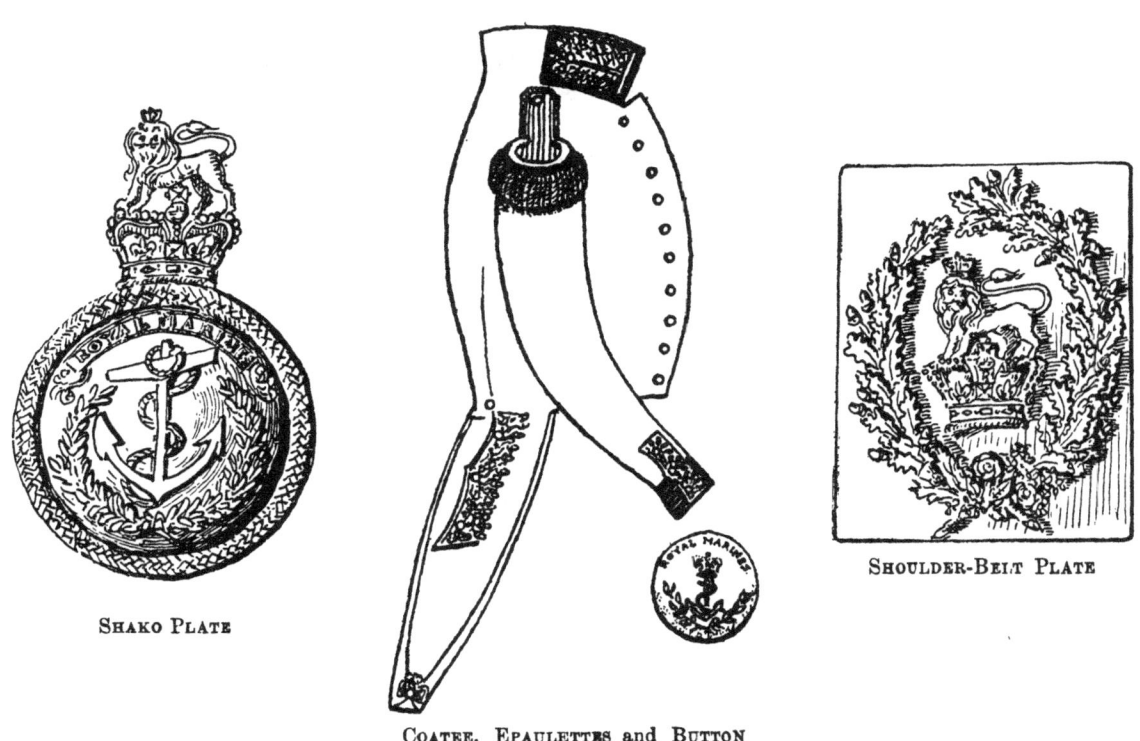

SHAKO PLATE

COATEE, EPAULETTES and BUTTON

SHOULDER-BELT PLATE

UNIFORM OF OFFICERS ROYAL MARINES (circa 1830).

---

[1] 5th August, 1841.

A COMPANY OF THE 37TH MADRAS N.I. SURROUNDED NEAR CANTON.
From a woodcut published in 1846.

Chapter XXIV.

THE CHINA WAR OF 1840-1-2.

> " And ever throughout the ages
> Still shall our vanguards go
> Out to the other peoples
> Out to the lands we know;
> And ever throughout the ages,
> Still shall they bend the knee
> To the first and greatest Regiment,
> To the Regiment of the Sea."
> —Fr. "A Gunroom Ditty-Box."

THE act of hostility which led immediately to the War in China was the advance of a fleet of twenty-nine men-of-war junks under Admiral Kwan, to attack the British merchant shipping in Macao Roads, on 3rd November, 1839. On an appeal for protection being made to Captain Smith, of H.M.S. *Volage*, a 26-gun frigate, that ship and the sloop *Hyacinth* immediately got under way and engaged the junks, sinking three and driving the remainder on shore. On the 4th July, 1840, Commodore J. J. G. Bremer, in the *Wellesley* 74, with the frigates *Conway* and *Alligator*, and a squadron of small craft appeared off the Island of Chusan, and summoned the Chinese Vice-Admiral to surrender the town of

Tinghae. An interview followed on board the *Wellesley*, in which the intentions of the British Government were fully explained to this official. On the 5th the Chinese troops assembled in great numbers; three guns were placed in position, on the Temple Hill, five on a round tower of solid masonry, and twenty-one in line on the different wharves. The war-junks were hauled up on the shore, and their thirty-four cannon and forty-five large gingalls[1] were added to the number of the shore guns. Everywhere the Chinamen could be seen waving their innumerable flags, and making every demonstration of hostility.

At 2 p.m., nothing further having been heard from the Chinese Authorities, the *Wellesley* led off with a shot at the round tower. At once the town cannon thundered in reply, and the whole British squadron began to bombard the Chinese defences. Eight minutes later there was not a Chinaman to be seen. The Custom-House Battery was destroyed, four of the junks had been blown to matchwood, and the Chinese troops had bolted in every direction.

The right wing of the 18th Royal Irish, preceded by the Marines of the squadron, 128 strong, under Captain S. B. Ellis,[2] and three Lieutenants, were at once landed, and were immediately followed by detachments of the 26th and 49th Regiments, Madras Artillery and Sappers, and the residue of the troops; and before three o'clock the Union Jack fluttered out on the first military position of the Chinese Empire ever conquered by the British arms.

At daybreak, on the 6th, eight 9-pounders, two mortars and two howitzers were in battery within four hundred yards of the city wall, but as soon as it was light enough to see, it was discovered that the enemy had decamped and evacuated the city. Both the Commodore and the Officer commanding the troops in their Orders of the Day expressed the highest appreciation of the highly soldier-like appearance, good conduct, sobriety and general regularity of the Marine detachments which had been landed.

Soon afterwards the English residents at Macao having experienced considerable annoyance from a strong force of the Chinese encamped near the barrier,[3] were induced to make application to the British Squadron for assistance. The Marines of the *Druid*, *Larne* and *Hyacinth*, about one hundred strong, under First Lieutenant W. R. Maxwell, and Second Lieutenant James Pickard, landed at about 2 p.m., on the 19th August, accompanied by a party of seamen with a fieldpiece; they were covered by the *Larne* and *Hyacinth*, who directed their fire at one of the principal batteries, as well as upon the Chinese encampment and ten war junks. The Marines moved forward, and on reaching the summit of a hill became exposed to a heavy discharge of round and grape from the fort, and musketry from a considerable body of infantry, who advanced with much determination until they were checked by a well-directed volley, which threw them into confusion, when they immediately gave way, taking with them a number of killed and wounded.

Lieutenant Maxwell was then ordered to retire with his detachment to the beach, to await the arrival of the Bengal Volunteers; and after the lapse of an hour, these troops, commanded by Captain Mee, were landed. That officer, having

---
[1] *Vide* Note I.   [2] *Vide* Note II.
[3] On the narrow neck of land separating Macao from the mainland, there is a barrier consisting of a wall with parapets and ditch running across the isthmus having a gateway with a guard-house over it in the centre.

placed the Marines on the right of the volunteers, and a party of seamen on either flank of the line, with their field-piece, advanced towards the fort, which was entered without opposition, the Chinese having retired to their war junks, and to the Portuguese battery on the Macao side of the "barrier." After a short cannonade the enemy abandoned their guns, and fled in all directions.

Negotiations were carried on by plenipotentiaries appointed for the purpose, and no further hostilities took place until the 7th of January, 1841, when the Marines of the squadron, amounting to three captains, nine subalterns, seventeen serjeants, eleven fifers, four hundred and fifty-eight privates, with six privates of the 18th Regiment, were formed into a battalion, commanded by Captain S. B. Ellis, and were landed without opposition about two miles below Chuenpee-point.[1] In conjunction with this party was a detachment of artillery, having one twenty-four pounder howitzer, and two six-pounder field-guns, aided by a party of seamen, portions of the 26th and 49th Regiments, the 37th Madras Native Infantry, and a detachment of Bengal volunteers, in all, 1,400 men, the whole commanded by Major T. S. Pratt, 26th Cameronians.

Captain Ellis was ordered to advance with two companies, supported by the detachments of the 26th and 49th Regiments, followed in column by the Marine battalion, the 37th Native Infantry, and the Bengal Volunteers.

After advancing a mile and a half, on reaching the ridge of a hill, they came in sight of the upper fort, and of a very strong entrenchment having a deep ditch outside and a breast-work round it, which was prolonged upwards, connecting it with the upper fort; it was also flanked by field-batteries, which had deep trenches in rear of the guns for the purpose of shelter; the whole was strongly lined with Chinese soldiers who, cheering and waving their flags in defiance, opened a fire from their defences. The British guns were quickly placed on the crest of the ridge, and a cannonade continued on both sides for about twenty minutes. Meanwhile the "advance" crossed the shoulder of the hill to the right, driving the Chinese before them. Then descending into the valley they took possession of a field battery there, and moved forward to dislodge a large force of the enemy occupying the crest of a wooded hill in front. Two companies of the 37th had previously gone round the hill to the right of the advance, where they encountered the Chinese, and drove them off with much loss. The advance having cleared the wooded hill in front, the 3rd and 4th Companies of the Marine battalion, under Captain J. Whitcomb, passed by the valley to the left, forced an entrance into the enemy's entrenchment, and proceeded up inside the breast-work to the upper fort, in which there were still a number of men. These were speedily dislodged by two Marines named Bennet and Knight, who first reached it. Thus the fort was captured, and the British Ensign hoisted by Private Knight, R.M. Lieutenant F. S. White, two serjeants, and seven privates of the Marines were wounded, the tota. British loss amounting to thirty wounded. An officer in a letter from H.M.Sl *Nemesis*[2] gives an interesting account of the fighting as seen from the squadron.[3]

---

[1] Chuenpee is a headland on the North side of the estuary of the Bocca Tigris or Canton River. It was heavily fortified forming part of the River defences.
[2] In the "United Service Journal," 1841.
[3] For a general account of the fighting at and below Canton according to the recollections of Pte. Henry Derry, an old Marine veteran—*Vide* Note III.

FIELD OFFICERS OF THE ROYAL MARINES.
From "Costume of The Royal Navy and Royal Marines." 1833.

"Operations were commenced by an attack on some of the forts at the entrance of the Bogue. On 7th January, at 6 a.m., weighed and preceeding the *Minerva* transport, received on board the greater part of the 37th Madras N.I., which, together with the other troops and artillery, were landed by the boats of the squadron in a small sandy bay to the right of Chuenpee upper fort, on the left bank of the river.

No accident occurred, and the troops immediately formed and marched up the hill, to attack Chuenpee upper battery from the land side, while the *Queen* and *Nemesis* should assault it by sea. Beat to quarters and cleared for action; and at 9-55 took up our position in company with the *Queen*, under the upper battery of Chuenpee, preparatory to shelling the Chinese out. At 10 commenced firing shell from the after gun at the fort, and from the foremost gun at a party of Chinese, posted in a hollow to receive our troops as they advanced over the hill: these were soon dispersed and both guns directed at the battery, which was now firing at us in return; but the shot from their guns either fell short, or passed over us, the only well directed shot passing directly over our quarter. By this time the upper battery of Chuenpee was silenced by our shell; and shortly afterwards we observed some of the Marines advancing to the walls. One of them coolly put his musket through one of the embrasures, took deliberate aim and fired, and then coolly stepped back to reload; this he repeated two or three times, and then sprung over the parapet followed by some others. We observed the Chinese colours waving up and down the flagstaff, as if two parties were struggling for the mastership, which indeed was the case. At length they came down and the English jack ascended in their place. At the same time an English officer (Major Pratt) jumped on the parapet, and waved his cap to us, which we returned with three cheers, as did the *Queen*. We had ceased firing from the time we observed the Marines scramble into the fort, nearly 10-25."

His experiences in this action are well told by an officer of the Marines, belonging to H.M.S. *Melville*:—[1]

"The following morning (7th January) we (Marines) were ordered to land, together with part of the 26th Regiment, 37th N.I. and Bengal Volunteers. Five-hundred and sixty-three was the strength of our battalion, which, with parts of the other three regiments and the Royal Artillery, and seamen to drag their guns, made in all about fourteen hundred men. We landed in the morning, at 8 o'clock, in a bay about two miles from the forts, and, as we proceeded inland to attack the forts from the rear, two steamers with two corvettes got under weigh, and commenced battering the sea face of the lower and upper forts: when we arrived within 1,500 yards of their entrenchments we found the hills behind which these works lay defended by a line of Chinese and Tartar troops. Our advance guard and skirmishers very soon engaged them so warmly that they retreated, though not so precipitately as I expected. They, however, only killed one, and wounded three of Captain Ellis' skirmishers. The man killed was shot clean through the breastplate, the ball coming out at his back.

---

[1] "Per Mare, per terram." "United Service Journal," Nov., 1841.

The Artillery with four guns, took up a position on a sudden elevation on our left. As we began to open the forts' batteries and entrenchments, the shot came from these in return, humming and whizzing pretty thickly over our heads; one or two rattled among the bayonets, and caused our men to dip frequently, and I began to bow *myself*, so I ordered their arms the last three or four minutes, when we received the order to advance on the entrenchments. These lay within a well constructed stockade, with a deep ditch in front, and had the Chinese defended the same, it would have surprised and checked us considerably. The main body crossed a hill to the right of this, and scoured the huts or barracks within the entrenchments, whilst my company (the No. 8 or Captain Gillespie's light bobs) went up the hill to the left, crossed the stockade, and peppered the garrison retreating from the upper fort. It was then I first discovered the lower fort, and making for it, got *up second* and *down first*; for no sooner had I climbed the wall than a stone giving way let me down on a flight of steps inside, *down* which I rolled, and up which I ran, and found at the top fourteen or fifteen of our company, peppering some Tartars at the back of some houses below. They started, and so did I, down the steps to the platform, where I found a spear in a wounded man's arms, to which I tied a Union Jack, and waved it to the *Hyacinth* to cease firing, as two shots came into the fort after we were inside the walls. Our attention was now attracted by several shots fired at us from one of the houses We soon dispatched all inside (about thirty), and, proceeding, found every house full of men, some with spears, some matchlocks, and the greater number with bows and arrows. The fronts of these houses were composed of a frame of bamboo, covered with rush mats; and they sent spears, arrows and shot through the same very freely, till our musket balls laid them low. One house, in particular, which it was necessary to pass, was defended by twenty-four men inside, and I endeavoured to get in among them with the idea of saving their lives, or some of them at least; but I got several pokes in the ribs, and blows from their swords (thanks to the Union Jack, which I had twisted round my body, over the shoulder, for keeping me from serious damage). I now got rather hot-headed, which being increased by a fellow sticking his spear into my side, whilst ordering the men not to fire, I ran him through the cheek, when he became hot in return, and stabbed the sergeant through the right arm, for which he received the contents of the sergeant's fusil through his body, and, after one or two encounters of a similar kind, we captured the fort."

On the 25th February, preparations were made for an attack on the formidable batteries at the entrance of the Bocca Tigris river. In advance of the old fort of Anunghoy, and partly surrounding it, was a new, well-built battery of granite, forming a segment of about two-thirds of a circle; on it were mounted forty-two guns. Several strong entrenchments extended to the southward of this battery, and the ridges of the hills were crowded with guns, up to a camp calculated for about 1,200 men. On the North side was a straight work of modern erection, mounting sixty heavy guns; about 150 yards of rocky beach intervened between the ends of this battery and the northern circular battery, on which forty guns were mounted. All these works were protected by a high wall, extending up the hill, on which were steps, or platforms, for firing musketry; and in the interior were the magazines and barracks.

On the east side of the island of North Wangtong was a battery, with a double tier of guns, defending the passage on that side, and also partly flanking a number of rafts, constructed of large masses of timber, moored across the river (about twelve feet apart), with two anchors each, connected by and supporting four parts of a chain cable, the ends of which were secured under masonry work, one on South Wangtong, the other on Anunghoy. On the western end of North Wangtong was a strong battery of forty guns, flanked by a field work of seventeen. In fact, the whole island was a continued fortification.

On the extreme western side of the channel was a battery of twenty-two guns, and a field-work of seventeen, protecting an entrenched camp containing about 1,500 or 2,000 men. South Wangtong was not occupied by the enemy, and being an excellent position, a work was thrown up upon it by the British during the night of the 25th, mounted with two eight-inch iron, and one twenty-four pounder brass howitzer. At daylight on the 26th, this battery was opened with admirable effect by Captain Knowles, of the Royal Artillery, throwing shells and rockets into North Wangtong, and occasionally into Anunghoy.

At 11 a.m. the breeze springing up, the fleet stood in and attacked Anunghoy, and the batteries on the South, South-West and North-West of Wangtong, and the forts on the Western side of the channel. In less than an hour the batteries of Wangtong were silenced, the troops under the command of Major Pratt, of the 26th regiment, which had previously embarked in the *Madagascar* and *Nemesis* steamers, were landed, and in a few minutes became masters of the island, without any loss, and 1,300 Chinese troops surrendered.

The Anunghoy batteries having been silenced, Sir F. Stenhouse landed on the Southern battery at the head of the Marines, under Captains H. Gillespie and J. Whitcomb, with a party of small-arm men; and having driven the Chinese in all directions, before 1 p.m., the British Colours were flying on the whole chain of those celebrated works. To use the words of the commodore,[1] "The individual gallantry displayed by the whole force, convinces me that almost any number of men the Chinese can collect would not be able to stand before them for a moment."

Admiral Kwan died devotedly at his post receiving the bayonet of a Marine in his breast as he defended the gate of Anunghoy.[2]

On the 27th the Chinese works further up the river in Wampoa Reach were stormed by the seamen and Marines who carried all the defences, driving before them upwards of 2,000 of the enemy and killing 300 of them. The officer of the Royal Marines, before quoted, writes :—"The action took place the day before yesterday, the *Blenheim* and ourselves taking the Anung-Hoy forts on this side, the right coming up. The firing was very heavy, and they did not give up for three hours. Our rigging was very much cut up (they mount 261 guns, most 42 pounders), and some shot came through both sides. We were ordered to land (I mean the Marines from both ships) which we did under a heavy fire, but landed

---
[1] Sir Gordon Bremer, R.N.
[2] "When the body was taken away the following day by his relations, minute guns were fired from the *Blenheim* in honour of the bravery of the old man who called himself a descendant of the Chinese Mars."

all safe, and stormed both forts; six Mandarins fell in the assault; of one of whom my sword can tell more than I can, I have got his cap and sword. I did not write yesterday as I was pretty well tired; but to-day I am left in command of the Southern fort, with only fifty-eight men to defend it; and as it requires too great vigilance to sleep, I write. A heavy fire was kept up all last night from the hills at the back, by the Chinese; but when I came here to-day, I made a sortie, and destroyed the camp above, and twenty-two guns, and drove the Tartars off, but they are still annoying the sentries above.

A boat was sent at sunset to tell me to be ready to embark at sunrise, to proceed in steamer to Canton. We have to fight our way up (about twenty-three miles); we have now 593 Marines, and the same force in all as at Chuenpee. The fight was the prettiest sight imaginable. On all sides the river was one roar of cannon. I have been spiking the guns, and heaving them over all day, and destroying the sea-face of the fort. Most of the guns measure seven feet three inches round the breast. I shall finish this on our return to Canton, as I hope."[1]

On the right bank of the river on a point formed by the mouth of a creek, was Howqua's Fort, a square building mounting thirty guns. The river here is about 500 yards wide: in front is a long low island dividing it into two branches, and on its extreme Eastern point was another work mounting thirty-five guns, built to commemorate the death of Lord Napier, from which well constructed and secured rafts, forming a bridge, extended to both sides of the river. Other auxiliary batteries and entrenchments and junks filled with stones and sunk in the channel completed a series of very formidable obstacles to the further advance of the British Forces up the river.

But little or no attempt was made to hold this favourable position On the 5th March, the Royal Marines and a detachment of the 26th under Major-General Sir Hugh Gough, got on shore at a joss-house which projected into the stream near Howqua's Fort, and the ships being seen by the garrison to be standing in to cover the landing party with their batteries, they discharged the whole of their guns and fled incontinently over the rafts and boats.

The way to Canton was now practically open to the British, and the Chinese finding armed resistance of very little use had resort to the tortuous and procrastinating diplomacy at which they are adepts in order to gain time, and cajole the invaders out of the positions they had captured.[2] But as their attempt proved futile, though most of the troops were re-embarked and the ships dropped down to Wantong, operations were resumed on the 13th March when the Macao passage fort having refused to surrender was bombarded by the *Modeste* and *Madagascar*, and stormed by the force of Marines who had been brought up the river in boats for this duty. The Naval Officer in charge of this operation (Captain Herbert) reported that the Marines under Lieutenant Stransham and three other officers " acquitted themselves on the occasion as that gallant Corps is always in the habit of doing."

---

1 "Per Mare, per terram." "United Service Journal," Nov., 1841.
2 " It appears to your Majesty's slave that we are very deficient in means, and have not the shells and rockets used by the barbarians. We must, therefore, adopt other methods to stop them, which will be easy, as they have opened negotiations."—Report sent by Keshen, the Chinese Minister, to the Emperor.

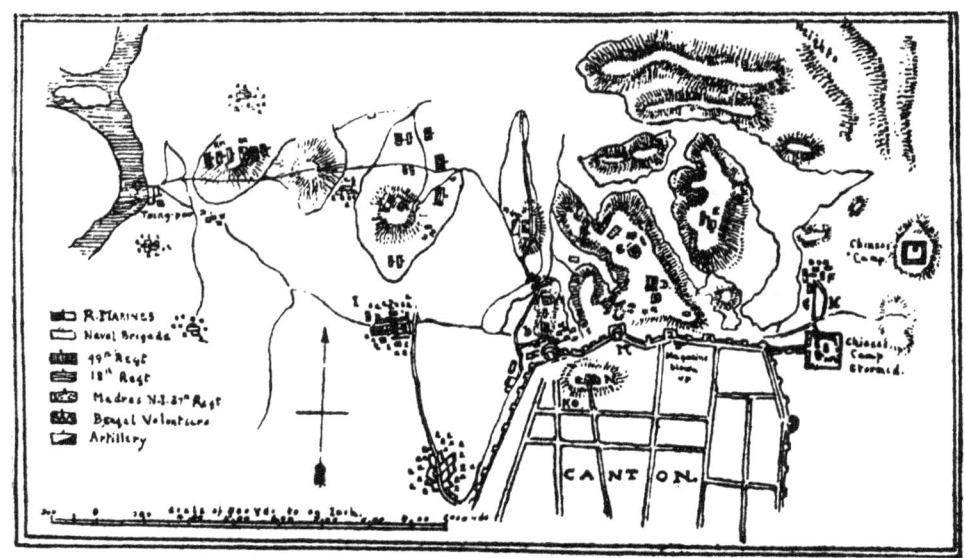

PLAN of ATTACK on the HEIGHTS and FORTS near the CITY of CANTON, 25th MAY, 1841.

REFERENCES.—From a Map in the Admiralty Library, by Lieut. W. S. BIRDWOOD, Assistant Field Engineer.

A—Fort stormed by the Naval Brigade.
B— do. do.
C— do. 49th, 37th N.I. and B.V.
D— do. 18th and 49th. (Occupied as Hd. Qrs.).
E—Temple taken and occupied by 49th.
F—Village captured by 49th.
G—Causeway along which two Companies, 18th and 49th, stormed Entrenched Camp.
H—Causeway (not surveyed) along which the Royal Marines and 18th advanced in support of the attack.
I—Village which the Chinese attempted to occupy, but were repulsed by two Companies of the Naval Brigade.
K—Pagoda within the Tartar City.
M—Five storied Pagoda.
N—Fortified Buildings on the highest ground within the City Walls.

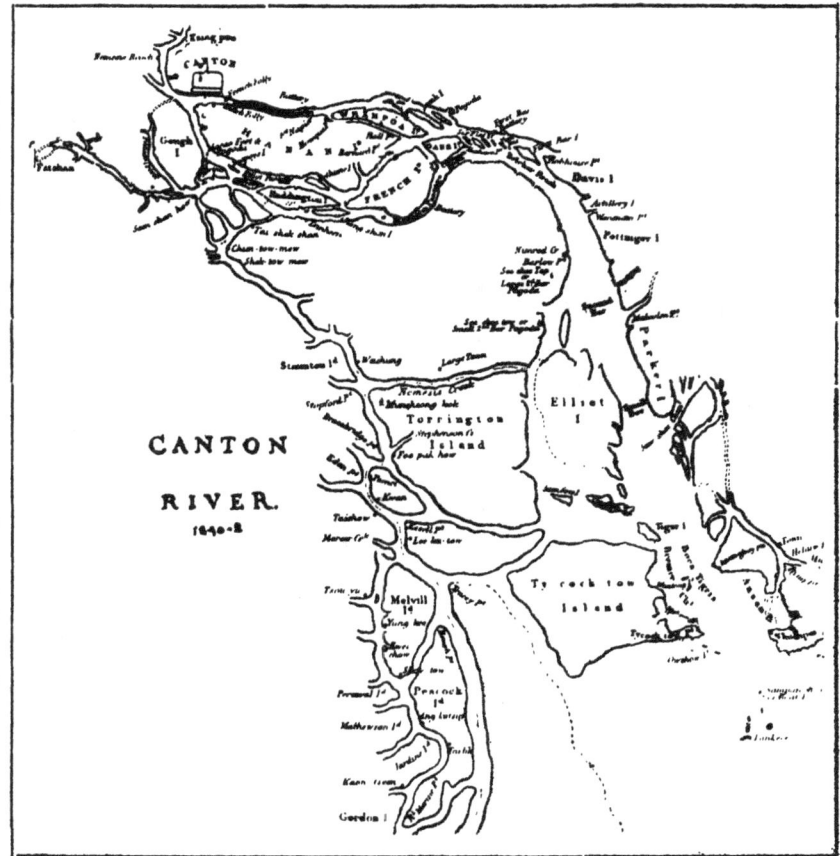

A garrison of the Royal Marines with Lieut. Stransham in command was left in charge of this fort which is comparatively close to Canton, and might prove a valuable *point d'appui* for further operations. These were not long deferred. The Chinese had fired on a flag of truce on the 17th, and Captain Herbert, R.N., having brought up a flotilla of four divisions of boats, embarked six officers and 227 rank and file from the garrison of the fort and set about the capture of the whole of the works which defended the river front of Canton. Some hours operations ashore and afloat resulted in a great destruction of Chinese junks and shipping and the storming and capture of the enemy's defences in the teeth of a most determined resistance on the part of the Tartar troops who garrisoned them.

"The Royal Marines," reports Captain Herbert, ". . . were, as usual, conspicuous for their gallant, steady, soldierly bearing. I have, however, to regret that Lieutenant Stransham, in exerting himself to destroy the works, was suddenly exposed to a heavy explosion, by which he was considerably burnt, but he continues at his post."

Active operations were resumed on the 23rd May, when at 2 p.m., the troops were embarked in various craft which had been commandeered for the purpose of effecting a landing on the North-Western side of the city where numerous fresh entrenchments had been thrown up by the enemy along the river side.

The force landed on the 24th amounted to 134 officers and 2,620 men. The 26th Regiment, under Major Pratt, had the special duty of taking possession of the British factories situated at the South side of the city. The remainder of the troops (including the Naval Brigade) were formed into two brigades. The Left Brigade to which the Bluejackets were attached, landed at the same time, but the Right Brigade of which the Marines, 380 strong, under Captain Ellis, formed part did not land till early the next morning, when they disembarked near the village of Tsing-poo, and moved forward until within reach of the four strong forts crowning the heights at the North and North-west of the city walls. Here a halt was called till the arrival of two mortars, four light field guns, and a rocket battery, which coming into action about eight a.m., poured a well directed fire into the two Westernmost forts. After this artillery preparation the troops advanced to the attack in echellon of columns from the left, the 49th Regiment being detailed to carry a hill on the left of the nearest Eastern Fort, supported by the 37th Madras Native Infantry, and Bengal Volunteers. The 18th Royal Irish, with the Royal Marines in support, were to storm a hill directly in front of them which was strongly occupied, and flanked the approach to the fort just mentioned, and by this movement to cut off the communication between the two Easternmost of the four forts. This being effected, the 49th was to storm the nearest of the two, while the 18th was to assault the other simultaneously. The Naval Brigade was to carry the two Western forts. As it turned out, the 49th, having the advantage of a shorter and perhaps better road, got ahead of the Royal Irish and captured both of the Eastern forts. While these troops were making their attack, the Naval Brigade was exposed to a very heavy fire not only from the forts, but from the city walls, which were much nearer to them than to the other attack. A storm

Queen. Wellesley—72. *Blenheim*—72. *Pylades*—18.
CAPTURE OF AMOY—26th of August, 1841.
From a Sketch by Capt. Crawford, R.N.

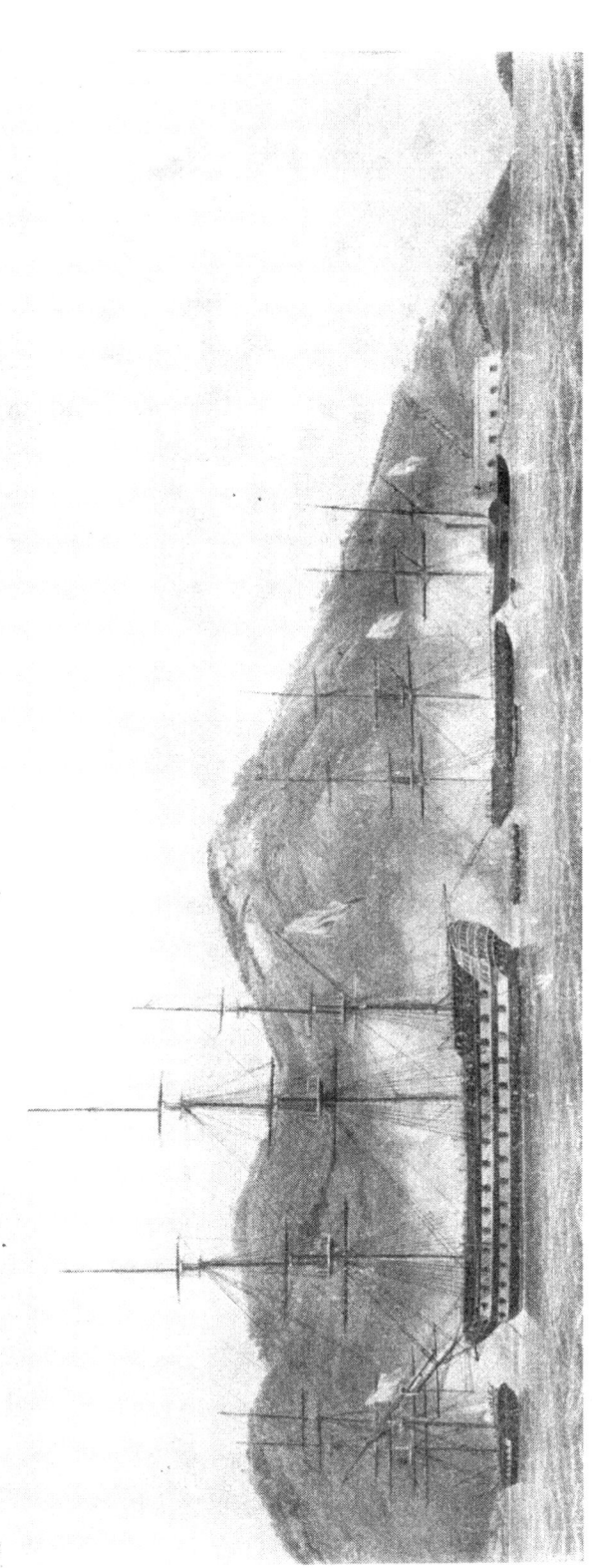

Columbine—16. *Wellesley*—72. H.M. 55th Regt. storming the Heights. *Cruise.*—16—*Phlegethon.* R.M. Forces under Capt. Ellis. 18th R. Irish 49th Regt. Royal & Madras Art. enfilading the 37th N.I., 26th Cameronians, Sea Batteries of and Madras Rifle Corps. Tinghae City.
STORMING OF THE HEIGHTS OF CHUSAN—7th of October, 1841
From a Drawing by Capt. Crawford, R.N.

of balls from matchlock, gingall and wall piece fell among them, causing several casualties. At the same time a strong body of the enemy made such a threatening demonstration on their right flank, that Sir Hugh Gough found it necessary to move off the Marines from their position in support of the 18th to assist the seamen and to cover the right and rear of the columns of attack. In half an hour all the four forts were in the hands of the British, but the Chinese on the city wall and in the neighbouring hilly country kept a constant fire upon them nearly all day, and frequent attacks were made upon the left from a large encampment the Chinese had formed to the North-East of the city. The 49th repulsed these, one after another, up to 3 p.m., when, as preparations appeared to be making for a fresh and stronger attack, the 18th under Brigadier-General Burrell and a company of the Royal Marines under Lieut. W. R. Maxwell reinforced the 49th; and having crossed a narrow causeway, the only means of approach, they gallantly advanced under a heavy fire from the guns and gingalls on the North-East face of the city wall, and repulsed the enemy at all points. The encampment was burnt, the magazines and buildings destroyed, and the troops returned to the heights. On the 26th arrangements were made for an immediate assault of the city itself, and the right column, composed of the Marines under Captain Ellis, was told off to pass through a deserted village to the right of the North Gate, which was to be blown open with powder bags. If this proved impracticable they were to escalade a circular work thrown up as a second defence to that gate.

But once more negotiations put a stop to further operations. The Chinese agreed to pay an indemnity of 6,000,000 dollars and to withdraw all Tartar troops from the city, while the British plenipotentiary, on his part, agreed that all forces on shore should re-embark.

But before all this could be carried out there was some further fighting in the neighbourhood of Canton.

On the 29th large bodies of Chinese, armed with matchlocks, spears and swords, appearing on the heights three or four miles in rear of the British Army, the troops drove them from their position without sustaining any loss, the Chinamen throwing away their arms and flying the moment fire was opened on them. During the dispersion of these masses, a company of the 37th Madras Native Infantry, which had been detached to keep up communication with the 26th Regiment on the left, lost its way in a heavy storm and downpour of rain.

The absence of this company at the conclusion of the operations caused great anxiety as to its fate, since it was feared that it had been cut off by the Chinese. A company of the Royal Marines armed with percussion muskets under Lieut. G. W. Whiting and accompanied by Captain Duff of the 37th, were sent in search of the missing company. Two companies of the 49th were also detached on the same service, but failed to find the missing company. The Marines, having marched several miles through the rain and darkness of the night without coming across any signs of the missing soldiers, Lieut. Whiting ordered a musket to be fired. The explosion was at once answered by three cheers from the Indians, who were discovered in a paddy field formed in square, up to their knees in water, surrounded by thousands of Chinese. Whiting immediately formed line, and opened such a heavy and well-directed fire on the confused crowd that they took to flight, astonished and alarmed at this unexpected discharge of musketry; for it appears that it was the discovery that the rain had prevented the muskets of the Native Infantry from being discharged, that had encouraged the Chinese to attack them so resolutely with their spears that Lieutenant Hadfield, who was in command was compelled to form square. Before the detachment was rescued by the Marines it had sustained the loss of one officer and eight men killed and wounded.

The percussion muskets were supplied to the Marines of the *Blenheim* at the request of Captain Whitcomb, and in consequence of the application the *Blonde's* detachment were equipped with similar weapons; and the first time that the percussion musket was used in the British Army on service was at the capture of Canton.

Pending the carrying out of the provisions of the treaty which had been made, further hostilities were suspended and trade was re-opened, but the Chinese authorities continuing to prevaricate, orders were given to attack Amoy, a principal third class city of the Empire.

The defences of this place were of great strength,[1] every island and headland, whence guns could bear on the harbour, was fortified, and the sea line of defences, after a succession of batteries and bastions in front of the outer town, extended for upwards of a mile in one continuous battery of granite faced with earth, with embrasures covered with large slabs of stone thickly covered with clods of earth and affording perfect shelter to the men working the guns which frowned from the embrasures.

The British squadron anchored off Amoy on the 24th August, and the next day but one the attack commenced. The morning was hot and sultry; but about 1 o'clock, a steady favourable breeze set in, and the ships got under weigh. As they proceeded to their allotted stations occasional shots were fired at them by the Chinese. When all were ready to carry out a simultaneous attack on all the batteries, the British ships opened a heavy bombardment, and for one hour and twenty minutes the roar of the artillery on every side, echoed by the mountains around, was terrific, but by that time the principal batteries on Kolingsoo, an island facing the city, were silenced, and the Marines under Captain Ellis, 172 in number, were put on shore to clear them of their defenders. In this task they were assisted by a small detachment of the 26th under Major Johnstone, which landed just after them. In a very short while the British flag floated from these batteries, and the Marines had taken possession of the heights in their rear.

The *Modeste* and *Blonde* then stood into the inner harbour, and after silencing the town batteries, anchored inside and abreast of the city, capturing twenty-four war junks, with 128 guns on board. About this time the first division of the troops landed, and took possession of the barrier wall. An outwork was also entered and the principal batteries having been battered to pieces by the guns of the *Wellesley* and *Blenheim*, a party of seamen, and the Marines under Captain Whitcomb and Lieut. F. J. White, effected a landing and drove the enemy from their

---

[1] The governor of the province expended 100,000 taels in fortifying Amoy, and then applied for additional sums to surround the whole neighbourhood with stone walls and embrasures of immense thickness. These were the largest works created by the Chinese during the war, and the most useless as it eventually proved. The amount embezzled by the officers of the Government was, however, said to be greater than the actual outlay."—War in China. Davis, 1852.

guns. Every point being now in the hands of the British, they occupied the heights above the town for the night.

After destroying all the Chinese munitions of war that could be found, the troops were re-embarked and the expedition sailed for Chusan on the 5th September.

The plan of operations was to attack Chinghae, and afterwards advance on Ningpo by way of the river Ta-hae.

Since the British forces were withdrawn from Chusan in the February previous, the Chinese had been indefatigable in erecting batteries, and it was almost inconceivable that so much could have been done by them in the time. The whole harbour literally bristled with guns and gingalls.[1] It was intended to have deferred attacking this place until the capture of Chinghae and Ningpo had been effected, but bad and boisterous weather setting in, it was found impossible to carry out the attack on the former place as the ships could not get near enough, and it was therefore determined to begin with Chusan or rather its capital, the city of Ting-hae. The weather delayed this attack for some time, and it was also necessary to prepare for the landing of the troops by the bombardment of the defences. The principal of these was an immense earthwork mounting 95 guns which extended along the whole sea-line in front of the town of Ting-hae, and which had been constructed on the mistaken principle that the assailants would have the extreme complaisance to attack it exactly in front. While therefore a small battery was thrown up by the British on Melville Island, in front of the town, to shell the high mound which marked the left of this long battery, and was known as Joss-House[2] Hill, it was determined to direct the main attack on the right of it which rested on a group of hills on which was a large fortified camp. On the 1st October, the Chinese, who had been expecting a frontal attack, were much and very disagreeably surprised to see the British troops landing beyond the right end of their famous earthwork, and pushing up the hills behind it, driving their soldiers before them. The 55th and 18th led the advance, drove the enemy from the heights and turned the whole line of the Chinese defences, which were enfiladed by the light guns which had been landed; and the 18th, with the Marine Battalion, pushed right along the rear of the long battery to the Joss-House Hill, though the Chinese as they retreated along the narrow road between the battery and a paddy field just behind it, fought with great individual courage, several of the Mandarins boldly rushing forward, sword in hand, to oppose the invaders. Meanwhile the 55th had escaladed the walls of the city and by nightfall the whole place was in the hands of the British.

As soon as the weather conditions permitted the troops were re-embarked, and the expedition proceeded to the attack of Ching-hae. This city is situated at the foot of a very commanding peninsular height, which is crowned by the citadel and forms the entrance to the Ta-hae river on its Northern bank. It is enclosed in a wall thirty-seven feet in thickness, and twenty-seven feet high, nearly four miles in circumference, and armed on the seaward side with twenty-eight guns, and innumerable gingalls. The main body of the Chinese forces was, however,

---

1 "Everything was to be carried by the numerical amount of men and guns. As for the latter, the more powder the more execution; and so it proved to the defenders themselves, when the guns were loaded to the muzzle and burst, as might have been expected." China during the War. Davis, 1852.
2 Or "Pagoda Hill."

stationed on the opposite side of the river in fortified encampments on very commanding and steep hills, field-works and entrenchments being thrown up in every advantageous position, and well equipped with artillery, both light and heavy.

The morning of the 10th October dawned serene and tranquil—an utter contrast to the scene that was to be enacted before night. The water being as smooth as a mirror, without a ripple on its surface, the *Wellesley* and *Blenheim* were towed into their berths in little more than their own draft of water, and remained nearly as steady as batteries on land. It had been determined that while the ships of war dealt with the town and citadel, the troops, in all about 2,200 strong, should be landed on the opposite side of the river to tackle the Chinese military encampments, the steamers which conveyed them thither afterwards returning to assist in the bombardment of the city. The British advance was made in two columns, the first landing about a mile to the right of the spot designed for the disembarkation of the second, and moving along a ridge until it was on the right flank of the Chinese encampments. The second column moved direct on the enemy's front, and although the Chinese troops made a very fair resistance, the combined attack of the British and Indian regiments, under the command of Sir Hugh Gough, drove them out of their strong position and the dark mass of Chinamen wavered, broke up and fled on all sides leaving hundreds of dead and dying on the ground. The main body made for the river where they vainly sought safety in the water.

Meanwhile, the heavy naval guns had poured shot and shell upon the Citadel with such good effect that the Chinese garrison had been driven out of it, and could be seen rushing down the rocky height to the city. It was now the Naval Brigade's turn, and just after 11 a.m., almost at the very moment that the colours of the 49th Regiment had been displayed on the Chinese encampment on the South side of the river, the boats, crowded with seamen and Marines, pushed off for the Citadel Rock. This landing party consisted of 400 seamen, 276 of the Royal Marines under Captain Ellis, twenty-three of the Royal Artillery, and thirty Madras Sappers. The seamen and Marines, disembarking on the rugged rocks at the river mouth, climbed up the nearly precipitous hill and entered the Citadel, the gate of which had been left open by the garrison as it decamped. The Chinese still manned the high walls of the city below, and a couple of batteries down on the river bank. Taking advantage of the general panic among the enemy the Bluejackets and Marines pushed on to attack the city walls. These were soon gained, four private Marines, Robert Beer, George Watts, William Jays, and Thomas Parker, having succeeded with great perseverance and courage, and without the aid of scaling ladders in gaining the entrance of an embrasure whence they let down a rope by which Major Ellis and the rest of their comrades effected an entrance, and aided by the Bluejackets, who had escaladed the walls at another point, drove the enemy before them along the ramparts and out at the East Gate.

No time was lost in following up this success by advancing on Ningpo, where, however, no resistance was attempted. The little force of seamen, Marines and soldiers drew up on the ramparts, while the band of the 18th played "God save the Queen."

On the 11th November, Major Ellis with the Marines quitted Ningpo, and calling at Chinghae, embarked the detachment of 113 men under Captain Whitcomb, who, with a few gunners and sappers, had been left in garrison at that place. Proceeding to Chusan, the Battalion landed there on the 13th. Before Major Ellis[1] and a portion of the *Wellesley's* Marines left for England in February, 1842, there were some changes in the Battalion, the *Blenheim's* detachment going with her to Macao, and a detachment from the *Cornwallis* taking their place.

Just before leaving, Major Ellis, who had commanded the Marines throughout the campaign, received the following communication from General Sir Hugh Gough: "I cannot allow you to leave the expedition without some assurances, on my part, of my regret at losing you, and of my best wishes for your future welfare. As you have been repeatedly placed, by the Naval Commander-in-Chief at my disposal for active operations in the field, I have had occasion to notice the gallantry and steadiness of your little Battalion, as well as the zeal, spirit and judgment with which you exercised the command. The subsequent period of your service in the garrisons at Ningpo and Tinghae, has only tended to increase the satisfaction which I shall always feel at having had you and a portion of the Royal Marines under my orders; and I will beg you to convey the expression of my sentiments to the officers, non-commissioned officers, and men under your command."

Early in March, 1842, the Chinese made surprise attacks both upon Ningpo and Chinghae, which were repulsed, but not without some rather severe fighting, and the defeated Mandarins fell back to a series of entrenched camps near Tse-kee, some way to the N.W. of Ningpo, where they were reinforced from the North by numerous detachments under the renowned General Yang.[2]

To follow up the victory which the garrisons of Ningpo and Chinghae had gained over their assailants, it was decided to at once attack the Chinese Headquarters at Tse-kee, and on the 15th March, 850 troops, assisted by a Naval Brigade of Seamen and Marines, 410 strong, were taken up the river from Ningpo and landed at the nearest point to the town of Tse-kee, behind which, on the Segean Hills, were situated the Chinese encampments. Here they were joined by four guns belonging to the Madras Artillery with an escort, and soon after one o'clock the whole force was marching on Tse-kee, which was to be the first point of attack. After a short cannonade from the field-guns, the walls were escaladed by the seamen and Marines about 4 p.m. Preparatory to a further advance the whole force now concentrated at the North Gate of the town from which the Chinese could be seen in position on the hills to the North and North-west. General Gough's orders were then issued for the attack. The 18th Regiment was to move up a steep ravine on the right, and occupy a hill which quite commanded the Chinese left. As soon as they were in position, the Naval Brigade (who in the meantime, were to occupy two large buildings near the town, a little to its North-west) were to assault a hill on which the Chinese right rested, while simultaneously the 49th

---

[1] Promoted to Brevet-Lt.-Col. in the Army, 26 May, 1841. He was a Brevet-Major throughout the campaign. He is described by the Commodore as a "meritorious old officer," and was in Sir Robert Calder's Action, Trafalgar, the Potomac, and many other engagements. He was awarded a well-merited C.B. for his services in China at the close of 1842.

[2] "When the action commenced, he tied up his beard in two knots, to keep it out of his way; he then posted himself in the rear of his troops. There, armed with a long sabre, he poked his soldiers to the fight, and mercilessly slew all who had the cowardice to retreat. This way of commanding an Army may seem very strange; but those who have lived among the Chinese will be sensible that the military genius of General Yang was based on a knowledge of his troops."—The Abbé Huc.

were to attack the enemy's centre. As the Naval Brigade moved out towards the two houses they were assailed by a galling fire from the Chinese gingalls on the hills which occasioned some casualties.

The 18th, being longer in reaching the Chinese flank than the General had anticipated, he determined to commence the frontal attack without waiting for them, and about 5 p.m. the "Advance" was sounded. After pouring in a heavy fire from the buildings they held, to cover the forward movement of the 49th, the leading companies of the Marines under Lieuts. G. Elliot and A. J. B. Hambly, dashed promptly and gallantly forward, followed by a small party of seamen. As they emerged from the cover of the buildings, the fire of the Chinese was very severe, but seamen and Marines dashed across the paddy field and charged up the hill in front of them, which was steep and rugged, with great spirit. They were boldly met by the Chinese, who did not shrink from the contest but disputed the hill from its base to its crest, and several instances of personal conflict occurred, but the leading companies were not long in gaining the summit, when the Chinese fled in every direction, sustaining severe loss from the fire of the remainder of the Brigade which had pushed round the sides of the hill to intercept their retreat. On the right the soldiers had been equally successful, the Chinese being completely routed with a loss of over 1,000 killed. The Naval Brigade had three killed and fifteen wounded; of that number one sergeant and one private of Marines were killed, Lieutenants Elliot and Hambly and ten privates wounded.

No further operations of importance took place in this district as it had been decided to transfer the theatre of war to the great Yangtze Kiang, and to commence operations by attacking Chapoo, a town situated on the estuary of that river, about sixty miles to the N.N.W. of Ching-hae, and important from being the emporium of the trade with Japan and at the same time the key to Hang-Chow, with which it is connected by a causeway along the shore.

In pursuance of this design Ningpo was evacuated on May 7th, and the garrisons of Ching-hae, Chusan and Keling-soo (Amoy) reduced to the smallest limits in order to augment the striking force which, exclusive of the Naval Brigade, amounted to nearly 2,500 men.

Owing to contrary winds the British force did not reach the neighbourhood of Chapoo till the 17th, and on the following day the attack was commenced. The Chinese troops were found in position on a range of hills parallel to the shore on the left of the town and harbour. The town itself, rectangular in shape and surrounded by a high wall, stands back about half a mile from the harbour, a large suburb lying between. Covered by the fire of the ships, the British troops landed on the left of the Chinese position, while the seamen and Marines were disembarked on the enemy's right near the harbour, the plan being for the former to drive their opponents along the hills towards the town when their retreat would be cut off by the Naval Brigade. After a smart fire of gingalls and matchlocks, the Chinese gave way and fell into the trap laid by the British commanders. A great slaughter ensued. The town was escaladed without difficulty, but in the meanwhile three or four hundred Tartar troops, whose retreat had been cut off, offered a most desperate and gallant defence in a large Joss-House which cost the British the lives of several men and officers, including that of Colonel Tomlinson of the 18th.

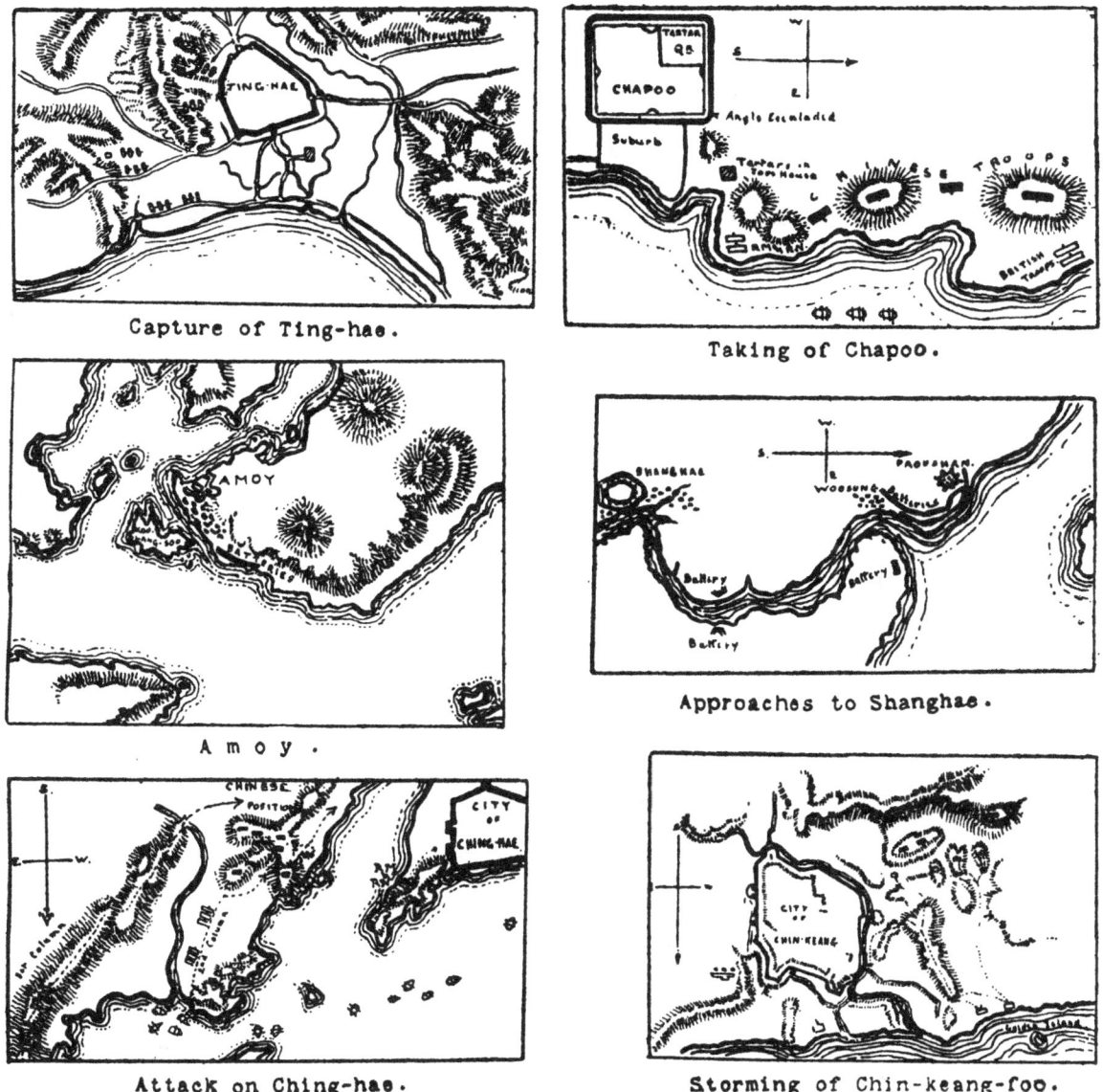

Capture of Ting-hae.

Taking of Chapoo.

Amoy.

Approaches to Shanghae.

Attack on Ching-hae.

Storming of Chin-keang-foo.

As soon as the guns and military stores captured at Chapoo had been destroyed, the expedition sailed for Woosung, where it arrived on the 13th June. This village which stands at the mouth of the river of the same name, which is a tributary of the Yangtze, formed the right of a tremendous series of earthworks and batteries which extended all the way to Paoushan, a walled town on the Yangtze itself.

These defences, which were erected to protect the approach to Shanghae—further up the Woosung—mounted 165 guns, a battery of ten guns being erected on the opposite side of the river.

At six a.m., on the 16th, the ships of the squadron were towed into position along the line of batteries by the steamers, which were lashed alongside for the purpose, and before 8 o'clock the fortifications were in ruins, and the masses of troops which had been collected to oppose a landing were dispersed by the shells and rockets thrown among them. Detachments from the *Modeste, Columbine,* and *Clio* were first on shore, being landed to occupy the ten-gun battery opposite to Woosung, from which the garrison had been driven by the guns and small arms of the first mentioned ship. The remainder of the Naval Brigade were now disembarked near Woosung, and after a sharp tussle with a body of Chinese who attacked them with gingalls, spears and hand grenades, drove them back under cover of some houses and seized the whole line of batteries between Woosung and Paoshan. In the meanwhile the troops had remained on board ship, as most of the steamers having grounded it was found impossible to get them ashore much before 1 p.m. Paoshan was then entered without resistance. The British loss amounted to Lieut. C. C. Hewitt, Royal Marines, of H.M.S. *Blonde*, and one seaman killed, and twenty-five wounded, including one corporal and five privates R.M. On the 19th, the British Forces advanced on Shanghae, a column of about 1,000 men under Lieut. Colonel Montgomerie of the Madras Artillery marching by land and the remainder of the troops going up by river. The Marines of the squadron went up in the steamer *Medusa*. No resistance except a half-hearted one from a battery below the town which was bombarded and captured by the seamen and Marines, was experienced, and like Ningpo, Shanghae passed peaceably into the hands of the British.

On the 23rd June, the expedition returned to Woosung, and having been reinforced by both ships and men, about the beginning of July started up the Yangtze Kiang with the intention of capturing the important city of Nankin, 170 miles up the great river. Little opposition was experienced, one or two batteries fired on the ships on the way up, but were silenced and occupied by the seamen and Marines, and on the 19th July, the *Cornwallis* anchored off the Island of Kinshan, just above the city of Chin-keang-foo. The Island was at once taken possession of by a small party of Marines, and the same evening a favourable breeze brought up the remainder of the fleet.

On the 21st Chin-keang-foo was attacked and captured. As usual, it was surrounded by a high wall. It stood some little way back from the river, and behind and beyond it to the South-westward were about 3,000 Chinese troops encamped on a range of hills. The troops disembarked that morning in three brigades, one to escalade the walls at the N.E. angle, and the other two, after dispersing the Chinese on the hills, were to attack the city on the West side. The first brigade carried the entrenched camps after a short resistance, while the second, covered by the fire of the steamer *Auckland*, escaladed the North-western corner of the city about 10 o'clock, having detached a small force to prevent the Chinese defeated by the 1st Brigade from escaping to the city.

CAPTURE OF CHIN-KEANG FOO

During these proceedings the boats of the *Blonde*, which were employed in landing the guns of the artillery near the West Gate, were suddenly exposed to a very severe fire from the city walls, by which sixteen seamen and eight gunners were wounded in a few minutes. As soon as this was known on board the *Cornwallis* 200 Marines were at once landed at the entrance of the canal, and being joined by 300 of the Madras Native Infantry, they instantly pushed through the suburbs to the city wall, while the whole of the boats of the *Cornwallis* advanced by the canal on their right flank. On reaching the foot of the walls a heap of rubbish was found not far from the West Gate. Upon this the ladders were planted by Captain Richards, R.N., of the *Cornwallis*, and Captain Watson of the *Modeste*, under cover of the fire of the Marines, in face of a large body of Tartar soldiers who lined the wall and appeared determined to defend their post to the last. These two officers, together with Lieutenant Baker of the Madras Artillery, and a private Marine of the *Modeste*, were the first to ascend the ladders. As they got upon the wall (with much difficulty), they were directly opposed to the cross fire from the guard-house, over the inner and outer gateway, by which the Marine was killed, and Captain Watson and Lieutenant Baker wounded. The Marine was killed by several balls passing through his body, and another Marine (also belonging to the *Modeste*) was severely wounded. After about a dozen men had got upon the wall, which was not effected without great difficulty, some rockets were got up, by means of which one of the guard-houses was set on fire, on which the enemy gave way, and just afterwards the outer gate was blown in by the Third Brigade which rushed into the city. Further fighting ensued as the troops advanced along the western ramparts, the Chinese fighting more bravely and desperately than they ever had before. The Bluejackets and Marines, headed by the Admiral in person, marched some way along the walls in the direction in which they had been already cleared by the 55th. The heat was overpowering, and the men, being already much fatigued, several of them died from sun-stroke. Here it was that the gallant Major J. Uniacke,[1] an old and distinguished officer, died from the effects of the sun, as did a private Marine. Having rested something less than an hour in the shade cast by a guard-house, heavy firing was heard within the Tartar portion of the city. The seamen and Marines were instantly fallen in and advanced in the direction of the firing, and for some time were engaged in some severe street fighting, the Tartars opposing them with the most desperate courage and bravery. But it was of no avail, and by night-fall all resistance was at an end and Chin-keang-foo in the possession of the British.

This was the last engagement of the war. After detailing a garrison to hold the captured city the expedition pushed on to Nankin, but the appearance of the now formidable British Naval and Military Force before the city was enough. Proposals of peace were made by the Chinese Government on August 17th, and a preliminary treaty was signed on the 29th of that month.

The Marines,[2] though comparatively few in numbers, had played a by no means unimportant part in the two or three years of warfare which had at length come

---

[1] This officer joined the Corps 28th August, 1804, and at the time of his death 38 years later was only a Captain and Brevet-Major.
[2] Marines—Changes in Uniform, 1823-40. *Vide* Note IV.

to an end. But as we shall see in subsequent chapters, the Corps had by no means finished with the Celestial Empire.

CHINESE CARICATURE—ENGLISH FORAGING PARTY.

From the "Cruise of the *Nemesis*."

The fact that the warriors above are in company with a gentleman, who, by his dress, is apparently intended for a British Bluejacket, gives rise to the suspicion that these marauders are meant to represent Marines!

NOTES.

NOTE I.—CHINESE "JINGALLS" OR "GINGALLS."

These weapons are like enormous breechloading muskets of about one and a half inches calibre, mounted on swivels, and carried by two or three men. Their breech action is practically the same as that of the pateraroes which formed the quick-firing armament of both men-of-war and merchantmen in the 17th and 18th centuries. The breech end of the barrel is prolonged into a kind of trough, in which a short cylinder of thick iron, called a chamber, can be laid. This cylinder is closed at the breech end, and provided with a touch hole. At the other end it is coned so as to fit closely to the rear of the barrel when fixed in position for firing by a wedge or "key." These chambers, fitted with a handle, for lifting in and out, and supplied ready loaded, two or three to each weapon, enable a fairly rapid fire to be kept up for a short time. Two of these Gingalls were brought home from China by the Battalion in 1860, and are now to be seen in the R.M. Officers' Mess, at Plymouth.

NOTE II.—THE ROYAL MARINE GUARD AND THE CHINESE.

After the capture of Chuen-pee, a conference was arranged between Captain Elliott, the British Plenipotentiary, and Keshen, the Chinese High Commissioner, at the Second Bar Pagoda, some way above the Bogue Forts, on the Canton River.

"One hundred Marines, picked men from the *Wellesley*, *Druid*, and *Calliope*, were embarked on board the *Madagascar* steamer, to be carried up as a Guard of Honour for Captain Elliott, at the meeting; they were commanded by Captain, now Lieut.-Colonel, Ellis, C.B., having with him Lieutenants Stransham and Maxwell. The excellent bands of the *Wellesley* and the *Calliope* were also in attendance, and it was expected that the Chinese would be astonished and properly " impressed " by the appearance and manoeuvres of the men, while they would be gratified and put into a good humour by the enlivening tones of the music."

" Early in the morning (of 26th January, 1841), the guard of Marines were landed, together with the bands of the *Wellesley* and *Calliope*. A finer body of men is rarely seen." . . . . " The landing place at the Second Pagoda presented certainly a lively scene. The Guard of Marines drawn up on either side highly astonished the Chinese, but the people were kept from pressing too close by a long line of railing put up for the occasion." . . . . " Keshen could not resist the wish to gratify his curiosity concerning our fine-looking fellows, the Marines, and three of the tallest and finest men were selected for his personal examination. He did not conceal his surprise, and even requested that they might be made to go through some of their evolutions. Keshen also examined their arms and accoutrements minutely, for everything was, of course, perfectly new to him."

—Fr. " Voyages and Services of the *Nemesis*," Pubd. 1844.

NOTE III.—RECOLLECTIONS OF THE FIGHTING NEAR CANTON.

Private Henry Derry, late of the Royal Marines, then about 75 years of age, gave the following account of his experiences in the Chinese War of 1840-1, when on board the *Fox*, to Sergt. W. Turner, another veteran Marine :—

" We did a lot of fighting all over the place ; and we felt it many times, for we had to man-handle Johnnie Chinaman both in his war-junks and on shore. I remember how we went in under close-reefed topsails at Canton, and let drive a broadside from our port guns, and then veered ship, came back and gave them our starboard guns. John Chinaman let us have it fast and furious ; while we put the frigate about down came the main top-mast and yards, then the spanker boom ; and the splinters from the hammock nettings were flying about like hail. We had a good few killed and wounded. Just as we had fired our starboard broadside two shots from the enemy took all the even numbers of our gun, and the captain's right arm while stopping the vent. The trunnion was knocked off, and, flying across the deck, caught the head of sergeant Thorpe, R.M., just as he came up the main hatch ladder, passed on to the port side and killed Corporal Hill, R.M. The two handspikemen were both killed, Frost and Atkins ; thus our gun was disabled and put out of action, but we filled up the numbers of other guns. The pivot gun made good practice, and we saw a big, round line of smoke rise in the middle of the fort, going higher and higher, then a tremendous report, and the ship shook, which some thought was our magazine gone up. Soon after this it was man and arm boats for landing. Our officers were a splendid lot of brave fellows, and although there were quite two hundred to one against us, when you had leaders who said, ' Follow me, lads,' why you felt on fire to get in front of him (they tell me that it won't do now-a-days ; well, I should be sorry to be there then). We had a good deal of fighting at Shanghai and other places ; going about up rivers and into creeks fishing out war-junks. Rather risky work, I can tell you. Many's the time I've had to put up the barrel of my Brown Bess to ward off the down cut of a sword, or the thrust of a spear. Did I ever kill a Johnnie ? I'm afraid I did more than one or two. Long knives into you, or your bayonet into Johnnie. No time to think. What I didn't like was when they bolted out of their war-junks, and blew them up just as we used to pull up alongside. By jove, it was ' look-out,' I can tell you. Splinters, fire-balls, stink-pots, smoke and mud in all directions, and it used to stick to one for weeks after. As for the boat work, we would be away sometimes from the ship for three weeks, creeping up rivers and creeks that no one knew anything about, and we had it hot, and got some ugly knocks, I can tell you. We landed at one place, and just as we got on shore, up went a mine and tons of mud. A piece of a tree knocked me down, and they left me for dead ; for when I came round, I saw the party quite half-a-mile away, so I ran after them, and when I caught up, the sergeant of my company said,' Why, Derry, I have just reported you killed '; so I was called the ' resurrection man.' We had a long spell of it, first one place then another, in open boats exposed to the blazing sun ; and night watches, for the enemy would be on the alert, and try to steal out at night from under the land ; and they used to get out sometimes. Then we had to give chase (we had no steam launches then). It was pull, pull together, boys, pull like mad, or they'll get out to sea, and then it's good-bye."—Fr. " The Globe and Laurel," Nov., 1901.

NOTE IV.—UNIFORM OF THE ROYAL MARINES, 1823 TO 1840.—*Vide* Coloured Plate facing page 46.

There were a great number of changes during this period. In 1823 the Shako was first adopted, the Badge upon it being that shewn on page 53, and the coatees were made to button back so as to show the blue facings handsomely laced with gold. New Colours were presented in 1827-8, the *Globe* and *Gibraltar* then making their first appearance upon them. The eight old colours of the four Divisions were sent to be placed in the Painted Hall, Greenwich Hospital, on 29th August, 1828. " Some of them," says a contemporary account, " were literally in tatters, and were used at the Battle of Bunker's Hill." About this time a new type of shako and new coatees for Officers were introduced (*Vide* Note III, page 40), with handsome embroidery of Oak-leaves and Acorn. (*Vide* pages 26 and 53). The Shako Plate was also altered (*vide* page 54). Upon the Accession of King William IV he introduced the unpopular red facings for Officers of the Royal Navy, and also altered the uniform of the Royal Marines, Naval Lace being substituted for the embroidery on the Officers' Coatees, besides several other changes. According to "Whittaker's Magazine," of 6th October, 1831, very remarkable changes were contemplated in the Royal Marines, and not only in uniform : " We also think that in Naval tailoring," says the writer, " the new taste is by no means an improvement, and that the White Facing which Nelson, Jervis, Howe, and Collingwood made a terror to our enemies, is ill-displaced for the Frenchified Red and Blue of the present fashion.

" Now, too, the British Marines are to have a Frenchified title, and to be called ' Naval Guards ! ' a copy of Napoleon's ' Gardes de Mer.' The ' Naval Guards ' are to be divided into four Corps, with a distinguished appelative to each Division, viz., 1st, King's, or Kent Division ; 2nd, Queen's, or Devon Division ; 3rd, the Lord High Admiral's, or Hants Division ; 4th, Princess Victoria's, or Essex Division ; and that a *third* Colour (the original standard of the Corps) is to be restored and presented to the 3rd Division. This Flag is St. George's Cross, having the rays of the sun diverging from each corner of its centre." The following extracts from Divisional Orders during this period are of interest :—

1823. (CHATHAM), Aug. 10. Lt.-Genl. Sir Henry Bell (D.A.G.) will dine in the Mess Friday next . . . . Officers to appear in White Pantaloons and Boots, with their coats button'd back.

(CHATHAM), Aug. 10. (After order). The Battalion to fall in to-morrow morning to fire a feu-de-joie. . . . . Officers and Men in Dress Caps (i.e., Shakos) and White trousers.

(CHATHAM), Aug. 14. Battalion to be under arms to-morrow. White Trousers and Dress Caps, Officers with facings buttoned back.

(CHATHAM), Aug. 15. Great gun and Sword exercise. All ranks to wear Grey trousers " as usual on Saturdays."

(CHATHAM), Sept. 3. After this date Officers to appear in the morning in Full Dress with coats buttoned over and White Trousers and in the afternoon with Facings buttoned back. No blue Coats or Black Belts to be worn after that period. Men to wear *black* trousers to-morrow.

(CHATHAM), Sept. 5. Officers to appear at dinner to-morrow in White Pantaloons, Hessian Boots and Facings buttoned back.

ADMIRALTY CIRCULAR. Sept. 9. Annual issue of Breeches and Shoes to be discontinued on and after 23 April, 1924, a pair of Blue Woollen trousers and Black Woollen Gaiters to be issued in lieu (These were previously provided at the men's expense). Leggings to be discontinued. White linen Trousers to continue to be issued at the expense of the men.

(CHATHAM), Oct. 7. " During the Winter months the Battalion will on all occasions wear their Caps covered, without scales, except on Sundays when they will wear their Dress Caps."

(CHATHAM), Nov. 3. White Drill Jackets to be discontinued till further orders on account of the cold weather.

(CHATHAM), Nov. 5. " Notwithstanding the C.O's repeated orders relative to Officers wearing their Swords upon all occasions when out of Barracks, he was sorry to observe some yesterday without them."

R.M.O. CIRCULAR.   No. 39 Cadogan Place,
Sir,   21 Nov., 1823.

To preserve uniformity in dress I have to desire, that conformable with the orders issued from the Horse Guards dated 30th Aug., 1823, you will cause the officers under your command to provide themselves with Glazed Black Leather Waist Belts one inch and a half wide, the Suspenders one inch wide. The Rings and Buckles quite plain, the Belt to clasp in front to a Round Plate one inch and three-quarters in diameter corresponding in Device and gilding exactly with the Breast Plate. Upon no occasion or pretext is the Waist Belt permitted to be worn except over the Great Coat.

I am, sir, &c., &c.,

HENRY BELL, Lt.-Genl.

(CHATHAM), Dec. 30. Black Belts never to be worn but with Blue Coats.

1824. (CHATHAM), January 31. Black Belts only to be worn with Great Coats and the Shoulder Belt with a frog (not suspenders) with the Regimental one.

(CHATHAM), April 29. Crape on left arm, above elbow, ordered for a funeral.

1825. (CHATHAM), July 27. "The Feathers to be discontinued to be worn on 31st inst., and from and after 1st Aug. Tufts are to be substituted.

(CHATHAM), July 29. Tufts for Men to be in conformity with pattern from Woolwich. To be made of fine White worsted for 5 inches and one and three-quarters inches of Red. To be One Foot in circumference at the top and Seven Inches at the bottom, close to the tube when the Tuft is fully dress'd and to weigh —exclusive of the tube—2¾ ounces when issued.

(PLYMOUTH), Oct. 2. Officers to discontinue wearing Round Hats and Fancy Capes.

(CHATHAM), Nov. 4. *Horse Furniture for Mounted Officers of Infantry. Saddle Cloth.* Of the same colour as the facing of the Regiment, 2 ft. 10 in. in length and 1 ft. 10 in. in depth, with Gold or Silver Lace, five-eighths of an inch wide and Scarlet edging.

Bridle. Of Black Leather best branch bit with Gilt Bosses having the Rose, Thistle and Shamrock in the centre, encircled with the words "Infantry Mounted Officers," and the Crown above.

Front and Roses to correspond in Colour with the Facings of the Regiment. (*Apparently an Army Order*).

(PLYMOUTH), Nov. 11. *Uniformity of Divisions.* The Brush and Wire to be suspended from the Waistbelt, in the same manner as worn by the R.M.A. The Waistbelt is to have a Brass Slide instead of the Leather Cap. The Frill and Turnover to be abolished. A Leather Strap ⅜ in. wide to be constantly worn under the chin, with the Dress Service and Forage Cap. The two Canteens are to be flat on one side like those worn by the R.M.A. Officers of all ranks to wear Gorgets when on Duty. Staff-Sergeants to have Coatees.

1827. (CHATHAM), April 9. Men's Undress Jackets to be perfectly plain, Sergeants and Corporals, Blue Cloth Chevrons and Shoulder Straps.

R.M.O. ORDER. May 9. Sergeants in future are to embark with *Muskets*, the *Halberts* to be returned at Headquarters.

Aug. 28. Officers ordered to provide themselves with the new uniform Steel-Grey Winter Trousers.

R.M.O. ORDER. Sept. 29. Band Uniform to be changed from Blue to Scarlet at next annual issue of clothing. Boat's Crew to wear a Dark Blue Round Jacket, with Red Cuffs and Collar and Uniform Trousers, i.e., "Oxford Grey."

(PLYMOUTH), Nov. 8. Sergeants to use Muskets instead of Pikes, when doing duty with Arms and Accoutrements, and when Men are under Arms. Other times to wear Swords.

1828. (PLYMOUTH), January 1. Oxford Grey Trousers will come into force in lieu of Blue from this dated order.

(CHATHAM), Feb. 5. Every man to provide himself with a Shell Jacket.

Feb. 24. Pattern of Officers' Undress Cap to be worn with the new Uniform may be seen at the Adjutant's Office.

(CHATHAM), April 29. Officers to appear on Sundays in uniform coats and Dress Caps and *not* in Surtout Caps as heretofore.

May 13. "The Deputy Adjutant Genl. is directed by His Royal Highness the Lord High Admiral to desire that Breeches and Stockings are never to be worn by the Officers except at the King or Queen's Drawing Room, and further that no Officer is ever to appear in uniform without sidearms."

May 31. All men confined to Barracks are to pay the Tailor one penny for sewing a white stripe round the left arm."

R.M.O. GENL. ORDER. July 25. "The Uniform Cap ordered for the Officers for 1829 having a Gold Cord attached to it, I am directed to inform you the said Cord is not to be worn except when Officers are ordered to appear in Full Dress."

July 30. "Guards to mount at all times in Feathers."

Sept. 24. Officers to cease to wear the shirt collar above the Stock.

R.M.O. ORDERS. Nov. 15. "In the new Royal Uniform established for Officers of the Corps to take place next April, the following alterations are to be put in effect. The White edging at present on the Coat being made of Kerseymere is to be a White Silk Cord in future. The Feather at present worn to be reduced (viz.) the wire of the Feather measuring from the commencement of the Feather to the top of the wire to be exactly 13 inches. Dec. 26. R.M. Band. Scarlet trousers with White lace stripes to be continued.

1829. (CHATHAM), Feb. 10. The whole of the Band without distinction to be dressed alike, Cap to be exact shape of those worn by Officers with their new clothing—Ornaments, Plume and Waist-belt as at present. The Master of the Band's coat to be the same pattern as the rest with the addition of two small Gold epaulettes and four Gold Chevrons on each arm. No alteration in Drum Major's Uniform, except Cap.

1829. R.M.O. Order. March 11. Following the change in the Dress and Appointments of the Army, Officers of Marines are to wear Two Epaulettes and as the Rank will now be distinguished by the length and size of the Bullion great attention must be paid that there is no encroachment in this respect but that all adhere to the Regulation strictly. . . . . Black Waist-belt to be totally abolished. The Regimental White Cross-Belt, two Gold Cords to be worn on the shoulders of the Surtout to confine the same, all braided Great Coats totally forbidden. Feather, all White, but as those adopted are made of different feathers from the present one, Officers had better see the Army Regulations. All Officers to wear two Epaulettes argeeable to Army Regulations. Those of the Capts. and Lieuts. to have the straps *striped with Blue*. Field Officers plain. The Forage Cap the same as the Army, the Band round the crown of Royal Marines Red, their facings being Blue. This Cap to be worn with the Great Coat at all times, and no other Cap or Head-Dress allowed except the Chaco. An Oilskin is permitted over the Forage Cap in bad weather.

The option given to Officers to appear at His Majesty's Levees in White Trousers and Boots is cancelled. They are to wear Stockings and Shoes as at Drawing Room.

Box Epaulettes not allowed, the bullion to hang loose as formerly.

R.M.O. Order. March 23. Men to wear White Tufts *with no Red* in their Chaco Caps when issued.

R.M.O. Order. March 25. Staff-Sergeants not to wear braided Cord on their Chaco Caps because the men have no Cord. The Drum Major and Master of the Band to have Gold braided Cords, and the Men of the Band White ones.

R.M.O. Order. March 28. Pattern Straps for Officers' Epaulettes forwarded this day by Coach. "The embroidered Anchor, &c., though not on the pattern sent, to be retained by all ranks, the Field Officers of Marines not having the embroidered 'G.R.' as in the Line."

No. of Bullions.—Lt.-Cols. and Majors: Outside Row, 21; Inside, 20.
Captains: Outside Row, 37; Inside Row, 28.
Lieutenants, Outside Row, 60; Inside Row, 50.

(Chatham), April 9. Tufts to be six inches long, four inches in diameter at the Top, two inches at bottom, and to weigh three ounces. Men to be stopped a penny each for wires for new Shoulder Straps.

(Chatham), April 29. R.M.O. Order *forwarding extract from Horse Guards Order* dated 15 April, 1829: "The adoption of the New Belt, the Dress of the Adjutants, Qr.-Masters, Surgeons and Asst. Surgeons, to take place in the Royal Marines, but the Paymaster to remain, as at present, without uniform."

Horse Guards Memo of above date. New belt in imitation of leather approved to be worn over the Blue Great Coat in lieu of the pipeclayed one. The regimental Breast Plate is to be worn with it. Paymasters, Qr.-Masters, Surgeons, and Asst.-Surgeons, to wear the uniform of their Regiments—Sash excepted—epaulettes of the corresponding ranks and "cocked hats as before." Adjutants to wear the uniform of their Army Ranks "without any particular distinction."

1830. (Chatham), January 26. R.M.O. Order. Officers' Cloaks to be made of Blue Cloth with a stand-up Collar fastened at the neck with an S hook and eye, similar to the new Waist-belt. The Collar to be lined with Scarlet Velvet, the Cloak with Scarlet Shaloon. Button uniform, a walking length, viz., six inches below the knee, no opening behind except for Mounted Officers who require and have it ten inches below the knee and the opening behind the same length. The Horse Guards Order of 15th December, 1829, to be followed except as regards Box Epaulettes. That of the 7th December, 1829 "granting the indulgence of Cap Covers to Officers for the protection of the Ornaments is also to apply to the R.M. Corps."

(Chatham), February 18. "Regimental Buttons" for Officers' Cloaks are to be Army Regulation Buttons, viz., "a plain yellow Bell Button." The Cloak to have a Cape 15 inches in depth.

(Chatham), May 11. Men's Pouches in future to be worn *Square*, not *Slanting*.

(Plymouth), June 7. The Gold Braid on the Surtout Coat is not to be twisted.

(Chatham), June 28th. Admiralty Order. *Death of H.M. King George IV.* Mourning. Officers to wear Black Crape on Left Arm, Hat and Sword-Knot, except on Duty when they are to wear also, Black Gloves, Sash covered with Black Crape, Black Gorget Ribbands and a Black Crape Scarf over the Right Shoulder. The Drums of the R.M. are to be covered with Black" and a Black Crape is to be hung from the Pike of the Division Colour Staff."

(Chatham), Aug. 24. R.M.O. Order. Lace to be put on Officers' Coats in the same manner as in the line, but to be Naval Lace. Time allowed for change.—To Xmas, 1821, at Home, to Xmas, 1832 Abroad. The following being applicable to the R.M. are to be put in force. The Gorget and Cap line worn by Officers to be abolished. The Feathers of both Officers and Men to be shortened as not to shew more than eight inches above the Cap.

1830. The Star upon the Officers' Epaulettes to be of the Order of the Bath instead of the Order of the Garter. The King has been pleased to dispense with Officers of the Army appearing either at Levees or Drawing Rooms in Shoes and Buckles they will accordingly on those occasions appear in the Trousers prescribed by Regulations.
(CHATHAM), August 26. Naval Lace for Coats to be five-eighths of an inch wide instead of half-an-inch.
PLYMOUTH. Oct, 15. The King has been been pleased to grant that Corps and Regiments who wear Embroidery to retain the same.

1831. (PLYMOUTH), July 1. *The Patent Sash.* Net, Crimson Silk with Bullion Fringe, to go twice around the waist and to be tied on the Left Hip. The Pendant to be uniformly one foot in length from the tie and to be worn on all occasions with the Red Coatee. The Black Waist Belt to be worn on all occasions with the Frock Coat, and when Officers are engaged on Duty of any description, the Sash is also to be worn. Epaulettes may be worn either with Pads or Boxed. The Leather Chin Straps on Uniform Caps are abolished, and when required, the Scales to be worn down.
(PLYMOUTH), August 7. Small Buttons to be worn by Officers on the Collar of the new Coatee.
(CHATHAM), December 22. Officers attending the Ball this evening will appear with the Black Belt (and Sword) under the Coat (Sash and Cloth Trousers of course).

1832. (CHATHAM), March 17. R.M.O. ORDERS. White Balls being substituted for Feathers and Tufts, the latter will not be worn on and after 23 April next.
April 18. Pattern of Feather for Officers will be forwarded by this night's Coach.
(CHATHAM), April 25. The pattern Forage Cap herewith forwarded to be established for the Sergeants of the Corps. The Corporals to have two White Chevrons to correspond with the bands on their Caps.
(CHATHAM), November 1. Pouches to be hung full three fingers' breadth below the elbow.

1833. (CHATHAM), December 10. R.M.O. ORDER. Alterations in Shoulder Straps of Frock Coats of Infantry Officers : " Regiments of the Line to wear a Strap of Blue Cloth laced round with three-eighths inch Lace the pattern that worn by the Regiment."
The Officers of the Royal Marines will also conform by 1st January, 1834.

1834. (CHATHAM), March 29. Order as to Shoulder Straps Infantry Frock Coats having been suspended, the Strap in question is to be discontinued by the Officers R.M. till further Orders, and Frock Coat worn as before.
(PLYMOUTH), Sept. 22. His Majesty has commanded that a New Pattern Cap for the Officers of the Royal Marines with the Badge of the Corps (The Globe and Laurel) embroidered on the Band, is to be adopted forthwith and strictly adhered to.

1835. (PLYMOUTH), February 9. At all Courts and occasions when Officers appear in the Red Coatee the Buffalo Waist Belt is to be worn by Regtl. Field Officers and Shoulder Belt by the other Officers.
The Field Officers will wear a Brass Scabbard, except at Levees, Drawing Rooms and in Evening Dress when they will have Black Leather with Gilt Mountings.
(CHATHAM), June 7.—Gloves not to be worn with White Trousers in Summer unless specially ordered, but Sergeants to wear them when under arms and Corporals when in command of Guards.
(CHATHAM), November 5.—The Balls are to be worn close to the flat brass button so as not to permit the piping to be seen (?) The Pouches are to be lowered to the hip-joint and to be square on the swell of the haunch and the Bayonet Belt to be lowered in proportion.

1836. (CHATHAM), August 8.—The Feathers in the Officers' Shacos to be replaced by Balls like those worn by the Sergeants. New pattern tube in which to fit them. Change to be made by 1st September.

1837. (CHATHAM), January 25.—A piece of Scarlet Cloth to be placed under the Brass Ornament on the New pattern Forage Cap. Sergeants' Caps having a Scarlet Band, this will not be required to be done. Brass Chevrons to replace the Scarlet ones at present worn on the N.C.O's Forage Caps.

1838. (CHATHAM). Cloth Half-Gaiters abolished. Duck Frock and Trousers to be issued every two years in lieu. Never to be worn except in H.M. Ships when taking in Ballast or Guns, Painting or Scraping " or such heavy work." The Forage Cap to be invariably worn with them.
(CHATHAM), June 24. " In order to preserve the dress of the Party under Orders to proceed to London and Woolwich, while on board the Steam Vessel, they are to parade to-morrow morning—in the following Dress —Shell Jacket, Grey Trousers and Dress Cap. The Dress Coatee will be packed with the necessaries in the Knapsack."

1838. (CHATHAM), September 14.—Officers serving afloat in Mediterranean, East and West Indies, South America and at the Cape, to be allowed to wear as undress—A Shell Jacket of Scarlet Cloth with Cuffs and Front part of Collar of Plain Blue, with a row of Small Uniform Buttons down the front and Gold plaited Shoulder Straps.

Officers R.M.A. Cos. to wear Sling Belts when on Artillery Service. Corporals and Privates: to wear the Waist Belt when the Pouch Belt is worn, and at no other time.

(CHATHAM), September 18.—The Shell Jacket for Officers "is to be considered quite as an Undress and to be worn only on board ship at such times and in such manner as the Commanding Officer may think fit." (Order by Lds. Comsrs. of the Admlty).

1839. (CHATHAM), November 2.—(A Garrison Order). "No N.C.O. or Soldier shall ever appear out of Barracks otherwise than properly dressed either in Shell Jacket and Forage Cap or Coatee and Chaco, and never if a Sergeant without his Sash and Sword, or if a Corporal, Belt without a Bayonet. Private Soldiers are invariably to appear on week days with Shell Jackets and Forage Caps and Bayonet Belts and on Sundays, and on such Holidays as by the orders of Her Majesty are commemorated by a Salute being fired from the Battery, they will appear in their Coatees and Chacos and Bayonet Belts.

1840. (CHATHAM), July 13.—Worsted Mitts to be supplied instead of leather gloves.

(CHATHAM), October 28.—"In future the Band will wear their Black Trousers at Troop, in wet weather, and their Scarlet ones on the other occasions when fine during the Winter, they are also to be supplied with Balls instead of Plumes during the Winter."—R.M.O. Order.

SHOULDER-BELT PLATE
(Private),
1802—1823 (?)

COLOUR-SERGEANT'S ARM BADGE, 1854.

BRASS SHOULDER SCALE
(Sergt.-Major),
1829-30.

FORT NOTTICH, BOMARSUND.—After Capture by the English

Chapter XXV.

THE WAR WITH RUSSIA IN 1854 AND 1855.

Since Discipline's the strongest cord
That ties the martial Ranks,
Attention be the soldier's word,
To win his country's thanks.
Each cannot be a General,
Nor lead the glorious van :
To be a hero, stand, or fall,
Depend upon the man.
Let all then in their station stand ;
Each point of duty weigh ;
Rememb'ring those can best command,
Who best know to obey.
"*Discipline*," *Dibdin.*

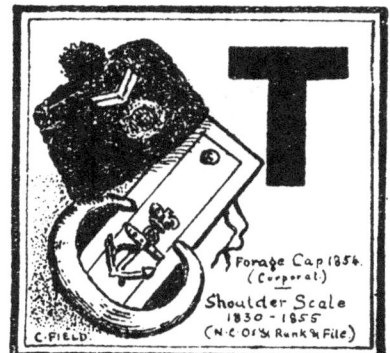

THOUGH there were a considerable number of the Royal Marines employed in the memorable War of 1854-5 against Russia, the chronicle of their doings must necessarily and unfortunately be a somewhat fragmentary one. For though landed in battalions of considerable size at Bomarsund, Balaklava, Eupatoria and Kinburn, these battalions never had the luck or opportunity of distinguishing themselves like their predecessors at Belleisle, Bunker's Hill and other places, or their successors in Egypt and the Soudan. All the same, whenever companies, detachments or individuals got a chance of adding to the laurels of their Corps, they jumped at it, and succeeded in winning no less than three of those little bronze crosses inscribed "For Valour," the proudest distinction which can adorn the breast of a soldier or sailor.

Although the operations of the allied British, French, Turkish and Sardinian forces against Russia are generally known as "the Crimean War," fighting of some sort or another took place wherever the vast Muscovite Empire had a coast-line, and it is proposed—in order to put the story of the part played by the Corps in the most intelligible way—to divide the present Chapter into two parts: 1, The Baltic; 2, The Crimea, including all Black Sea operations. Minor operations also took place in the White Sea and the Pacific, but space forbids their inclusion.

I.—THE BALTIC.

Few more unsatisfactory campaigns are recorded in our history than the Baltic Expedition of 1854-5. The Fleet that, after being reviewed by H.M. Queen Victoria, left Spithead on the 11th March, 1854, was universally admitted to be the finest armament that had ever left our shores. And yet it did little or nothing of consequence. Its failure may be attributed to two causes; the usual British apathy which prevents actual preparation and organisation for any particular war until it breaks out, and the tremendous respect—to put it mildly—in which both the Admiral in command, and the Admiralty of the day held the granite fortifications of Cronstadt and other Russian fortresses. The result of the first was to let the supply of seamen run down to a dangerous ebb, so that this fine fleet was filled with a very large proportion of men who were sailors in name only, anyone who could be collected at the moment, "even to butcher's boys, navvies, cabmen, etc."[1] In fact, had it not been for the coastguard and Royal Marines the fleet would never have got to sea.

"On board the *St. Jean d'Acre*," wrote an officer of the Royal Marines,[2] "we had a splendid crew, thanks to the popularity of 'Harry' Keppel. The work of fitting out from a mere hulk was done by the Royal Marines with a small number of Seamen-gunners from the *Excellent* and some boys. The officers at Portsmouth and other places raised men *who would not join until the hard work was over.*

The four block ships (*Ajax*, *Hogue*, *Edinburgh* and *Blenheim*) were manned almost entirely by the Coastguard, then composed of old men who had never been to sea, boatmen, perhaps; a glance at the Navy Lists of those times will shew that even the Chief Officers were of all kinds; ex-Army men and civilians. These men wore nailed boots, waistcoats and braces, many refusing to go aloft for the first time in their long lives, and the doctors were worried by applications to be invalided; they would tell the doctor he did not understand their case, but if he would write to Dr. Jones at Fowey or some such place, and send 2s. 6d. he would send a box of the pills they always took and which did them good."

A Naval officer[3] who served in the Baltic Fleet fully corroborates these statements:—

"Public opinion resented revival of the Press Gang," he writes, "therefore the only alternative was the offer of a large bounty, and by this means the ships were filled with counter-jumpers and riff-raff of all sorts, and rarely a sailor amongst them. What this meant, only those who had to do the necessary slave-driving

---
[1] History of the Baltic Campaign. By Butler Earp. 1857.
[2] Capt. W. Portlock-Dadson, R.M.L.I.
[3] "Two Admirals," by Admiral John Moresby, R.N.

Colour-Sergeant. Gunner R.M.A. Corporal Private. Officer
Drummer. Privates (Marching Order). (Undress). (Review Order).

ROYAL MARINES, 1854

can tell. In the *Driver* we may have had twenty seamen as a nucleus. The rest were longshore fellows, and when Admiral Berkeley came aboard and told us the Russians were at sea, and probably in a few days we should be in action, there was a strong dash of anxiety in our satisfaction."

As for the second reason for the failure of this grand fleet there is no doubt that the Admiralty were continually warning Sir Chas. Napier to be very careful and not lose his nice ships,[1] and as will be seen from the following extract, the Admiral himself was quite ready to carry out these instructions. Cronstadt to him was a very bugbear.[2] On one occasion he embarked on board the *Driver* with a view of reconnoitring its no doubt formidable defences. "We steamed," writes an officer on board,[3] "across from Reval, with the splendid 50-gun frigate *Imperieuse* on one quarter, and the *Basilisk* on the other—their orders being to keep close and embark the Commander-in-Chief in case of accident, whilst we kept a boat ready at a moment's notice, for the old Admiral was in a state of nervousness, repeating again and again, 'I dinna want to visit St. Petersburg.' As we neared the narrow Sveaborg Channel our consorts had to wait two miles outside. Slowly we approached, and were getting within range, for the forts had dropped some shot not far off. General Harry D. Jones, R.E., was studying the Russian chart of the place, spread out on the capstan, and I was pointing out to him the small island round which we should turn, the Admiral being on the bridge with Captain Sullivan. Suddenly we heard him shouting, 'Hard a starboard, Captain Cochrane. Hard a starboard! I tell ye." 'What's up?' said the General in natural amazement. "It means the Admiral won't go any farther,' I replied. The General rushed on the bridge and joined his persuasions to those of the two Captains, pointing out that a close view of the place ought to be obtained, that it was indeed an absolute necessity. All was of no use. Our chief had a forced journey to St. Petersburg on the brain. He made but one reply, 'Hard a starboard! Hard a starboard, I tell ye!'" The fact is he was broken in both body and mind, and his difficulties were many, for he was not only attacked by the press for not performing impossibilities, but the Admiralty left him unsupported, and many of his Captains held aloof from him."[4]

In the light of all this it is not difficult to understand the abortiveness of the Baltic Campaigns of 1854-5.

After some months barren of results public feeling in England became so strong that the Admiralty had to insist on something being done, and it was decided to attack the Fortress of Bomarsund, in the Aland Islands, though the Admiral had written that "nothing but a superior force of *gunboats* could enter Bomarsund."[5] Gunboats were just what he hadn't got—that is to say in large numbers. But Bomarsund was isolated, and there was an idea in England— an erroneous one as it proved—that its capture would induce the Swedes to join

---

[1] Admiral Berkeley, one of the Lords Commissioners, wrote to Sir Chas. Napier on 27th June, 1854: "We feel—no-one more than myself—*that nothing can be done against such places as Helsingfors and Cronstadt.*"
[2] An officer R.M. who, after the peace, was in 1856 shown over the "terrible" forts at Cronstadt, noted that being built on piles, they were all badly cracked, and was told by a Russian officer who had been in them in 1854, "that if an attack had been made *their own guns would have shaken them to pieces*."
[3] Two Admirals. By Admiral John Moresby, R.N.
[4] He was interviewed almost daily by three particular Captains—Keppel, of the *St. Jean d'Acre*, Lord Clarence Paget, of the *Princess Royal*, and George Elliot, of the *James Watt*—trying to stir him up to do something; at last a signal was made for the three ships to cruise to the rear—"black-listed."
[5] The Baltic Campaign. By G. B. Earp, 1857, p. 326.

in against Russia with their many small craft and a very respectable Army.[1] Bomarsund was not a town of any importance in itself, but merely a fortress protecting an anchorage which would form an excellent advanced base for a Russian fleet in the event of war with Sweden.

"The fortifications of Bomarsund lie on the Eastern point of the largest of the Aland Isles. These islands are mostly rough, irregular heaps of hard red granite rock and boulders, thickly grown over with dark pines, and here and there between the hills, a little green valley, a small fresh lake, or a little Swiss-looking village of bright red wooden cottages may be seen. The land is low, but the shore is all granite; no sand or clay. You would think that an earthquake had forced it up out of the bowels of the earth. Thick forests of small fir or pine trees cover every island, but a mile inland the bare rocks rise to a very great height. The trees grow close to the margin of the sea, and here and there some beautiful little nooks may be found, reminding one of Barnpool and Mount Edgecumbe; but on the whole the scenery is by no means striking. Nearly in the centre of the group is a fine sheltered roadstead called Lumpar Bay, communicating with the sea to the Northward by Bomarsund, a narrow strait between the islands of Bomar and Prasto. This strait was strongly fortified on the Western, or Bomar side. The principal fortress stands at the head of a semi-circular bay; its sombre-looking casemates, like blank eyes, staring over the water, and armed with heavy cannon in two tiers. At the back or northern side of this fort the land rises considerably, and the defence on that side consisted of two round towers, one on the highest ground to the West, the other to the East on a little spit or promontory. These towers with their white perpendicular sides, and their red iron capped roofs, have a bold, martial appearance, but their real strength, as events proved, was entirely overrated. A fourth tower stood on the Island of Prasto, on the other side of the Strait, which was considered to be quite impassable. The British, however, discovered and buoyed out another passage, so narrow and intricate, that the Russians had entirely neglected to fortify or obstruct it."[2]

The main fort was a big semi-circular battery close to the waterside, mounting ninety-two guns in two tiers, and supported by two high round towers of red granite nine feet thick, iron roofed and armed with twenty-four heavy guns apiece. These were Forts Nottich and Tzee. There was a five-gun earthwork near the latter tower.

A preliminary attack had been made on Bomarsund, on June 21st, by the paddle steamers *Hecla*, *Odin* and *Valorous*, but no great harm was done, and it was not till the land forces at the Admiral's disposal had been augmented by the arrival of Brigadier-General Harry D. Jones, R.E., and a company of that Corps, and a large body of French troops under the command of General Baraguay D'Hilliers,[3] that he decided to make a real attack on the fortress. But he still hesitated to pit his line-of-battle ships against its granite walls and made his main

---

[1] They are estimated to have been able to assist with 200 gunboats and 50,000 men.
[2] From "Two Summer Cruises with the Baltic Fleet," and "The Illustrated London News." *Vide* Plan, p. 91.
[3] "Two or three Marines were on some outpost duty, with a like number of the French, when the former, in obedience to orders received, fell to the ground on the firing of a cannon from the fort, but, on observing the Frenchmen to stand up, they decided not to do so in future. Soon after the French General came up the hill; and on a gun being fired, down went the General—likewise one of the Marines, who as he threw himself down, cried out to his comrades—"All right, Bill, Baraguay bobs."—"Illustrated London News," 7th October, 1854.

THE WAR WITH RUSSIA IN 1854 AND 1855.

attack from the shore supporting it by the fire of his small craft. The landing took place on the 8th August, at daylight, without opposition. French troops to the number of some thousands disembarked at Tranvick Bay, four miles to the southward of the fortress, while the British Marines, nearly 700 strong, under Colonel Fortescue Graham, A.D.C., and ninety of the Royal Engineers, effected a landing to the northward near Hulta. This small force was augmented by 2,000 French Marines, under Brigadier General Jones, R.E., who was senior British officer with the Fleet. The advanced guard of one hundred Marines and twenty sappers pushed on over the steep pine-clad slopes of the island, moving with all military precautions[1] till it arrived somewhat to the Northward of Fort Tzee, where a spot for the English encampment was selected. The Russians sat tight within their fortifications, and did not attempt to molest the invaders either on the one side or the other. Since the ships were not to stand in and engage the forts in the same way that they had done a century previous at Cartagena, there was nothing more to be done until the siege batteries could be built and guns landed, a delay that was most distasteful to all hands. " On all sides the greatest disgust was expressed for the modern system of naval warfare; the principle of which seemed to be, to keep out of gun-shot.

" ' None of that d——d nonsense now we're ashore,' said a Marine officer, a sentiment in which all present concurred most heartily."[2]

The French got their guns ashore, four 16-pounders and four mortars, and were able to open fire against Fort Tzee at four in the morning of the 13th, but the British cannon—big 32-pounders—had to be dragged to the top of a steep and thickly wooded height, by the Bluejackets and Marines, while the 5,000 sand-bags required to build the battery had each to be carried separately on men's shoulders to the same spot. The French, too, besides having plenty of horses and necessary appliances made no scruple of helping themselves to any cattle or materials they found on shore in contradistinction to our own system which was thus explained by a Sergeant of Marines at the time, " that's the way we does wherever we goes; we spare the innimey, but we spoil the men."[2] The en certainly had a hard job on this occasion to get the guns up the steep rough and rocky road which had been burnt through the woods for them. And all the ti e the general feeling was " Let five hundred Marines and as many Bluejackets alone, and they'd take the d——d place before dinner-time. What's the use of talking, Sir, 'twas just the same at that other —— place. How do we know the ships can't do nothing if we never tries 'em ? "[3]

The spot fixed on for the British camp " was a little level patch on the spring of the hill on which Fort Tzee was placed. The camp was sheltered from sight by the rising ground, but was well within range of Fort Tzee, and certainly not beyond long bowl practice either of Fort Nottich, or the great half-moon battery below. The hill that intervened was thick with trees, brushwood and irregular rocks. The camp was singularly pretty and picturesque.[4] The most striking thing in

---

[1] Capt. C. O. Hawley's company in front in extended order, Capt. R.K. Caldwell's in two half-companies in support, Lt. W. F. Portlock-Dadson in command of the second half company.
[2] "Two Summer Cruises with the Baltic Fleet." Revd. R. E. Hughes. 1855.
[3] *Ibid.*
[4] It was composed principally of Wig-wams built of short firs and bushes.

the tent-way was the Colonel's. This consisted of a single blanket stretched over a pole, and strained tightly down to the ground; into this the gallant officer crawled on all fours whenever sleep assailed his weary eyes. A number of military accoutrements, and if I remember rightly, a little strip of a flag, gave splendour and dignity to the domicile; and I think, on the whole, the Colonel used to turn out in the morning about the smartest and best shaved man in the camp."[1]

The bluejackets who had been landed to haul up the guns, must evidently have been selected from the small proportion of real seamen in the fleet, for when on the 10th the *Penelope* contrived to get ashore just under the guns of the great battery and the *Hecla*, *Valorus* and *Lightning* had to go to her rescue, the men on shore were sent for on board again. Had the ships been properly manned, two or three hundred bluejackets could have easily been spared from the line-of-battle ships, and the steamers engaged inshore have been left with their full crews. While the English battery, which eventually mounted three guns, was being constructed a perpetual rifle fire was kept up upon the embrasures of Fort Tzee by the French Chasseurs and the English Marines. A night or two after landing about a dozen of the latter "crept close up to Fort Tzee, where in the bright northern light they made out some half-a-hundred Russians standing outside chattering and vociferating after their manner. The Marines let drive into them at about sixty paces, and the yell which followed the discharge was frightful. They saw the Russians afterwards dragging wounded men into the fort."[2] The object of the British battery's attack was to be Fort Nottich which stood low on a small promontory to the Northward of the big battery, but General Jones had, of course, a line of skirmishers all along his front connecting with the French attack,[3] and covering the operations of the working parties at the battery in course of construction. A visit to this advanced line is thus described: "After a time I got permission to move on to the front, where a lot of our Marines were thrown out as skirmishers, two or three together. The two most advanced belonged to that fine Corps, the Marine Artillery; and here we had a splendid view of everything. A few hundred yards in front was Fort Tzee, and we could plainly see them dodging about inside the embrasures; presently out came the gun, and we crouched down as snug as we could. In a moment a shell went roaring by, and then we had five minutes' respite to look about us. To the right the French were firing away merrily, and, near as we were, we could hear the balls strike against the granite with a sharp smack, while the scattering reports of musketry never ceased.

On the left we could just see the chimneys of Fort Nottich peeping over the trees in the valley, from which they occasionally favoured us with a rifle bullet, which came singing dismally overhead.

For about an hour we watched events in security, for the Russians had not got the range, and their fuses being cut too long, the shells did not burst till they reached their home far away in the valley; but at this time a sergeant came round with some grog, the sight of which proved too much for my friends the artillerymen;

---
[1] "Two Summer Cruises with the Baltic Fleet." Nevil Hughes. 1854.
[2] *Ibid.*
[3] The picket covering the working-party in the Battery was under the command of Capt. H. E. Delacombe, who had Lieut. Portlock-Dadson as his subaltern officer.

they jumped up to fill their cans, and the white bands of their caps[1] were not lost upon the foe. The next dose they gave us was spherical case, which rattled right in among us. We heard them come singing along with their ominous tenor voices, and we wriggled ourselves and flinched into our holes as they passed; one took a bit of fir within six inches of my nose, another almost grazed the cap of my friend the Marine.

This was the closest shave— the next time they had lost the range; but it was a shell and seemed to burst close to the picquet. Our men had strict orders not to fire on any account, but if the enemy came out, to receive him with cold steel; but my friend remarked, ' If 1 sees anything gray I think I must have a crack, for I should like to shoot one on 'em, if 'twas only just one, sir! ' "[2]

On the night of the 9th the Russians set the little town behind their half-moon battery on fire, probably to prevent any chance of an assaulting column assembling under cover of its houses. " Whole streets were in a blaze," writes an eyewitness,[3] " Fancy all Greenwich and Deptford on fire, and you will have some idea of this little Moscow. Nearly one quarter of the town was burnt last night. They set fire to their houses at night, and drove the wretched inhabitants into the forest to be devoured by the bears or bayoneted by the soldiers." A night or two later the trees and houses on Prasto Islet also burst into flame, the Russians apprehending a naval attack on the tower there and wishing for light to direct their fire on the bombarding ships.

At 4 a.m. on the 13th (Sunday) the French battery opened on Fort Tzee, but for some time without any perceptible effect, and an officer of Marines volunteered to take up a party of his men after dark, and pledged himself " to get in somehow."[2] This, however, was not allowed, for Fort Tzee had been especially told off to the French. Their battery continued pegging away till about five in the evening, when the Russian garrison hung out a flag of truce. A parley ensued without result, and presently the firing recommenced. About 10 p.m. the other Russian forts opened a heavy fire on a part of the shore where they fancied the British were landing more cannon, but by midnight, the firing had ceased on all sides. Shortly afterwards the French fired four shots at Fort Tzee. No reply was made, and a storming party of their 51st Infantry and the Chasseurs de Vincennes, moved cautiously up to the tower and made their way in through the lower embrasures without a shot being fired at them. " Only one man of the garrison was found faithful to his post. This was the veteran Commandant who was found mounting guard at an embrasure where he received the attacking party at the point of the sword. A thrust from a Frenchman's bayonet sent him to earth, and the place was taken. The cowardly garrison had decamped with the exception of some thirty men and the Medico, who were found drunk and helpless among the *probrosis ruinis* of the fort."[4]

During the 14th a desultory interchange of shots took place between the ships and the three remaining Russian forts and Fort Tzee which was discovered

---

[1] The R.M.A. at this period wore blue forage caps with a white band and a grenade in front.
[2] "Two Summer Cruises in the Baltic."
[3] E. G. Hartley in the "Illustrated London News," 26th August, 1854.
[4] *Ibid.*

to be on fire early in the morning, and at 11-30 a.m., "blew up with a thundering crash, and sent a jet of pitchy smoke and lurid flame high into the air."[1]

It was now (15th August) the turn of the British to tackle Fort Nottich, and the effect of the ships' guns in their battery ought, one would imagine, to have once and for all demolished the bugbear of the impregnability of the "Granite Fortifications" which had held our fleet for so long inactive. "The 32 pounders soon made an impression. Every shot told with full effect, leaving its mark, the next dislodged a fragment, then followed a block of granite, then the whole wall was visibly shaken, and after two or three hours' bombardment a gap had been formed, which a few more salutes increased to a regular breach, obliterating two embrasures in the enemy's upper tier, and opening to view the casemates and inner court."[2] A private letter says: "Three or four shots set the great stones, visibly 'chattering,' as I could mark by a pocket telescope; one block then fell out, then another, then a third, fourth, etc., and these were followed by an avalanche of loose rubbish, just as you see macadamising stones pour out from the back of a cart when the tail-board is removed."

"The fort, being circular, could only bring four of its guns to bear upon the English battery. Two of these had been silenced, and a third speedily followed, but the fourth could not be so easily got at. The fire from Captain Ramsay's battery now began to bring down the wall in masses, and the ruins contributed to shelter the one invincible gun. Its embrasure had become a breach, into which the brave Russians rushed at each fresh blow from the English battery, and deliberately shovelled away the lime and stones from their wonderful gun. So thickly did the ruin accumulate around it, that there was not time to clear away the debris, and the gun was fired from within the heap, so as to blow away the accumulating mass. For some time yet the gun gave shot for shot, but at half-past five[3] in the afternoon, down came the side of the fort, and the noble gun was deeply buried within the ruins.[4] Loud now rose the British cheers, not so much for their success, as for the bravery which had been opposed to it. To resist further was impossible, and the brave defenders of the fort hung out a flag of truce. A hundred British Marines, commanded by Major Ord, at once marched to the fort, and to them the garrison surrendered amidst the eulogies of their captors."[5] The prisoners, three officers and 120 men, were marched off to the *Termagant* under an escort commanded by Captain Sayer, R.M.

While the attack on Fort Nottich was in progress, the ships and a big gun that had been landed and placed in an old Russian earthwork near the shore to the Westward were engaging the half-moon battery, the French battery also chiming in with its mortars with such effect that General Bodisco, the Russian Commander-in-Chief, hoisted the White Flag, and surrendered with about 2,000 men at mid-day on the 16th. Fort Prasto on its islet, which had come in for a share of the allies attention during the bombardment of the big battery, followed

---

[1] "Illustrated London News," August 26th, 1854.
[2] Hist. Baltic Campaign. G. Butler Earp. 1857. An officer R.M. who was present in the Battery, however, contradicts this and says no impression was made for a considerable time.
[3] A mistake, it was not until some time after 6 p.m.
[4] After a while the bluejackets at the guns were relieved by the R.M. Artillery under Lt. Mawbey, who ordered all the guns to be fired simultaneously at one spot instead of independently with the above result.
[5] The Hist. of the Baltic Campaign, by G. Butler Earp. 1857.

suit soon after five in the afternoon, and its commander with his garrison of 149 men and three officers, marched out and surrendered at discretion to Lieut.-Col. De Vassoigné of the French Army and Captain Lowder, R.M. So fell the fortress of Bomarsund after a short siege in which the Royal Marines played a most useful part and escaped with but one casualty—Henry Collins—a Marine belonging to H.M.S. *Duke of Wellington*, who was killed by a stray shot as he lay asleep in his tent, and one Private Thos. Baughan, severely wounded.

The Battalion of Royal Marines paraded the next day and marched down to the principal fort where it formed one side of a lane opposite a Regiment of French Marine Infantry, and the surrendered garrison consisting of 51 officers and 2,235 men was marched down to the waterside for embarkation in various sailing ships, the drums and fifes of the Marines playing "The British Grenadiers," which for very many years had been the recognised "Quick March" of the Corps.[1]

An officer of the Royal Marines who was present wrote in his Journal the following remarks about these Russian prisoners: "A more horrid-looking set of men can scarcely be imagined, nearly half of them, including the Greek priest, were drunk; there were a few fine-looking Guardsmen and Cossacks among them; they carried all their personal effects with them, and some of them seemed to have enough for a dozen. A Russian was brought out with the French soldiers kicking him, and poking him with their bayonets: he had been detected going to the magazine with a lighted match, and we heard they hung him shortly afterwards."

Successful as this, the first operation of any importance, proved, no steps were taken to follow it up by an active campaign in the Baltic. The Fleet fell back into its old routine of doing nothing. One or two isolated coastal batteries were bombarded, a few merchantmen were picked up by our cruisers, and that is about all that took place for nearly twelve months. A Naval Officer[2] gives an amusing account of the attack on Domness, in the Gulf of Riga. "A village in which were only fifteen or twenty Cossack Police, and whose inhabitants had shewed themselves friendly enough to barter eggs, milk, etc. The ships often anchored off there, and were regarded as friends more than enemies. A captain thought he would attack it because of the Cossacks, bombarded it with forty heavy guns, landed 200 seamen and Marines. Cossacks and villagers fled, one man was wounded by one of his shipmates shooting him in the shoulder during the landing. One piece of ordnance was captured. It had long done duty as a lamp-post, and was guiltless of carriage or vent-hole! *These were provided for it on board!* Such were our casualties and such was the victory of Domness."

Eventually the greater portion of the French Fleet and Army withdrew, and Sir Chas. Napier was replaced by Rear-Admiral Dundas.

"That there are cravens in council, and that the war has hitherto been grossly mismanaged," wrote an officer of Marines, in May, 1855,[3] "admits of little doubt. Things appear to be mending in the Black Sea; but the little effected last year in the Baltic seems to have produced an impression that our enemy is unassailable; for we too often hear the question, 'What can we do in the Baltic?'" The

---

[1] *Vide* Note II, page 43, Vol. I. The R.M. "Slow March" was taken from "Norma."
[2] "Two Admirals." By Admiral John Moresby, R.N.
[3] "Illustrated London News," 1855. Letter signed "A Captain, Royal Marines," dated 14th May, 1855.

writer goes on to suggest, what, in his opinion, ought to be done in the way of attacking and bombarding one place after another. He does not think an attack on the Cronstadt Forts is feasible, but he says that "last year it was easily assailable from the North." He hears that 25,000 troops are to be sent to the Baltic, but he considers that number too large for the fleet, and too small to effect a serious landing in the face of the big Russian armies. In lieu he proposes that 2,000 Marines with a couple of hundred sappers and miners should be stationed in the Aland Isles in readiness to embark in a dozen steamers at an hour's notice. He urges that such a force "might effect a great deal in the way of destroying telegraph stations, cutting up roads, and surprises, that would have the effect of harassing the enemy's troops, and keeping the whole of his exposed coast in constant alarm; but this force should never be allowed to remain ten hours in one place, or a strong force of the enemy would be concentrated to crush them."

As summer came on a little more activity was apparent. On June 17 and 18 the forts at the mouth of the River Narva were attacked, and the town of that name bombarded; on the 20th the *Arrogant* destroyed the Fort of Roshensalm; and on the 27th Nystad and Christinestadt were treated in the same way. The Marines in the ships engaged of course shared in these enterprises but their special work is not on record.

We get just a glimpse of them at the time of these little expeditions in "Two Summer Cruises with the Baltic Fleet," from which several quotations have been already made. The writer was on board H.M.S. *Cossack* which, with other ships, was bound to complete the destruction of the barracks and military establishments on the island of Kotka, near Roshensalm, and describes the crew as they appeared on deck as the corvette made for her objective. "Here we had in the narrow limits of a corvette's deck," he writes, "a large assemblage of seamen smoking, for it was the supper hour, and chatting eagerly about the Russians; a butcher in the act of most scientifically slaughtering a bullock; a party of Marines about to land, undergoing inspection on deck, and with their loose serge frocks, dark trousers, and excellent arms and accoutrements, these capital fellows looked soldiers every inch. As we sat in the midst of this scene, up came a tall, but pale and sickly Marine, and, touching his cap to the doctor, begged that he would take him out the sick list, and let him go ashore with his comrades. The doctor somewhat reluctantly consented, and away went the Marine, delighted at the prospect of possibly shooting, or abetting to shoot, a Rooshian or two before supper time. Soon after the Marines had landed, a bright tongue of flame darted out from among the pines, a cloud of smoke followed, then a roar, and a murky glare, and the whole barrack, a huge building concealed behind the woods, was in a blaze."

At Viborg, which was attacked by the *Ruby* and boats detailed from other ships on 13th July, the Marines are mentioned as having been present. Captain Yelverton of the *Arrogant*, who was in command of the Expedition, reported that: "Having anchored the ships as close as I could to the Island of Stralsund, I proceeded in the *Ruby* accompanied by Capt. Vansittart, of the *Magicienne*, and Capt. Lowder, R.M., of this ship, the latter officer having under his command a strong detachment of Marines, towed with us the boats of this ship, and those

BOMBARDMENT OF SWEABORG, AUGUST 9TH AND 10TH, 1855.

Sketch of the Right Attack shewing the Explosion of the principal Magazine containing from 80 to 100 tons of powder and about 25,000 shells, about noon August 9th

Dedicated to the Officers of the Royal Marine Artillery who commanded the Mortar Boats at the Bombardment of Sweaborg.

RELIEVING SENTRIES CHATHAM DOCKYARD, 1854.

Contemporary Water-colour Drawing by Capt. W. G. R. Masters, R.M.

of the *Magicienne*." Opening a bay called Tragsund, a Russian steamboat and other gunboats were sighted and Viborg was in view when the flotilla was brought up by a boom and various obstacles which prevented further progress. At this moment a masked battery, not more than 350 yards distant opened on the boats from the shore with musketry, grape and round shot. The Russian gunboats joined in, and there was nothing for the British but to get out of the trap as best they could, and make their way back to their ships at Stralsund. The *Ruby* could not get through the barrier, but covered the retreat of the boats with her cannon and small arms. An explosion took place on board one of the *Arrogant's* cutters

LIEUT. DOWELL, R.M.A., GAINS THE V.C.

which swamped her. "In endeavouring to save the crew the boat drifted close to the battery, and would have fallen into the hands of the enemy, had not Lieut. Haggard of this ship, and Lieut. Dowell, R.M.A., of the *Magicienne*, in the *Ruby's* gig with a volunteer crew, towed her out under a very heavy fire."[1] It may be added that Lieut. Dowell was accompanied by only three volunteers and pulled " stroke " himself. He received the Victoria Cross for his gallantry on this occasion.

The last important service of the Baltic Fleet was the bombardment of the strong defences of Sveaborg, an Imperial fortress in the Gulf of Finland, three miles south-east of Helsingfors. On the 9th of August, a mortar battery was completed on the Island of Langhorn by the British, and immediately the fleet opened fire

---

[1] Capt. Yelverton's Official Report.

at between 3 and 4,000 yards range. The ships were assisted by a large number of mortar boats, in most of which the mortars were served by the Royal Marine Artillery. Two days' bombardment destroyed the whole of the Government buildings, the barracks, stores and magazines, while no less than twenty-three ships were set on fire. The British loss was one man killed and one wounded!

"In the bombardment of Sveaborg, the duty and conduct of every officer and man was most arduous and meritorious, none more so, perhaps, than those of the Royal Marine Artillery, and after the dreadful and incessant booming of the guns for such a length of time, most of the men in the fleet remained deaf for many hours—even for two days—after it had ceased."[1]

Admiral Dundas did full credit to the excellent work performed by the Royal Marine Artillery in the Baltic in his Official Despatches to the Secretary of the Admiralty, in which he wrote:—"My especial thanks are due to the Officers and Men of the Royal Marine Artillery for the manner in which their important duties have been performed. The cool and steady courage with which they continued to conduct the duties of their stations deserves the highest praise; and I have much pleasure in calling their lordships' attention to the services of Captain Weymss as well as to those of Captains Lawrence and Schomberg of that distinguished Corps."

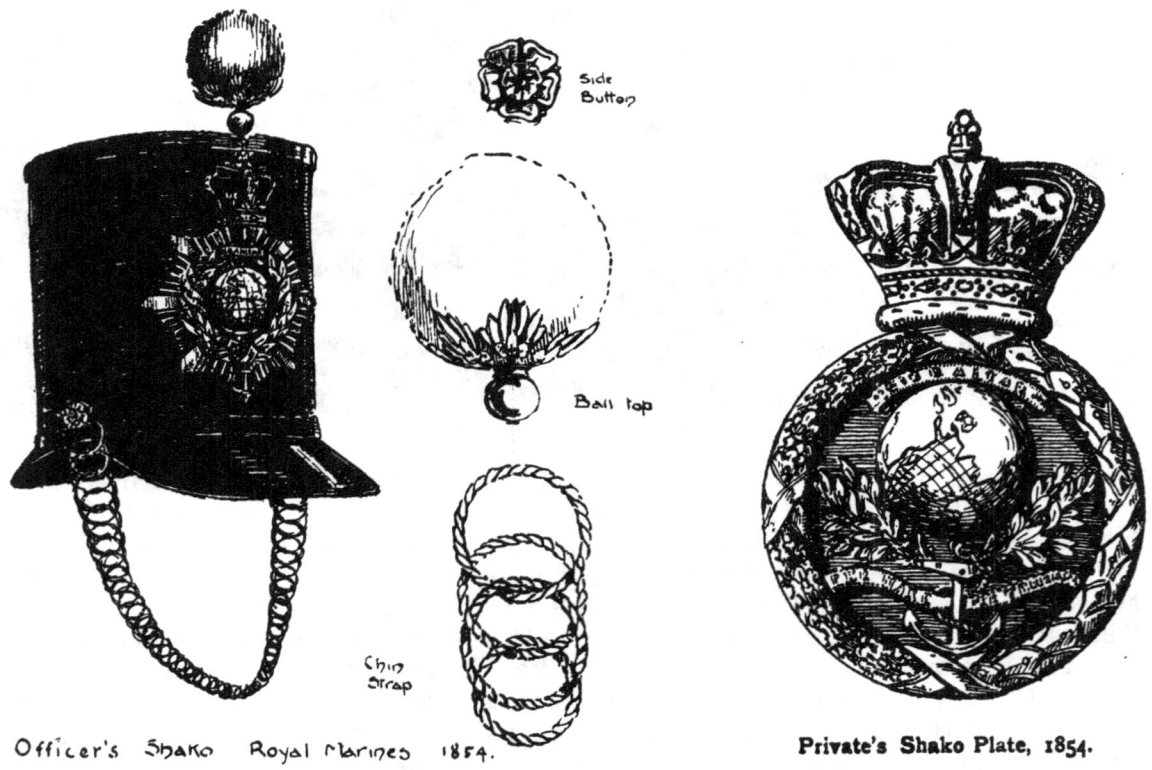

Officer's Shako Royal Marines 1854.　　Private's Shako Plate, 1854.

[1] "British Battles on Land and Sea." James Grant.

BOMBARDMENT OF BOMARSUND.

II.—THE BLACK SEA AND THE CRIMEA.

Jonathan Fisher, an old Marine, who died at New Swindon at the age of eighty, some time in 1898, claimed to have fired the first shot in the Crimean War. He stated that the English residents in Odessa were ordered on board the ship in which he was serving, which must have been the *Furious* since it is on record that she was sent, on 6th April, 1854, to bring off the Consuls and other subjects of the allied nations. He said further that while the last boat-load was pulling between the land and the ship " a shot was fired from some floating object (probably a battery) not far from the shore. The Captain of the ship, seeing this at once ordered :—' The first man that gets on that object—Fire ! ' " Fisher stated that his gun was the first to get on the target and he at once fired. There seems no doubt that the Russians did fire on this boat although under a flag of truce, but accounts do not mention that the *Furious* returned this fire. Still it is more than probable that she did. The bombardment of Odessa took place on the 22nd of April, when the *Samson* is said to have fired the first shot. This bombardment was followed by various attacks on the Russian batteries and guardhouses at the mouth of the Danube, in which the Marine detachments of the *Firebrand* and *Vesuvius* had their share.

The grand debarkation of the allied British, French and Turkish forces took place on the 14th September, at Old Fort, in the Crimea, some miles to the North of the fortress of Sebastopol which was the real object of attack. The French began to land at 8 a.m., and are stated to have put 6,000 men on shore in twenty-two minutes. The British commenced their landing about an hour later, and as the Russians offered no opposition, and with the exception of half-a-dozen Cossacks, did not even put in an appearance, everything was carried out without a hitch and by nightfall practically the whole of the infantry was on shore. The cavalry and artillery landed the day following. According to a contemporary plan of the landing[1] 400 Royal Marines from the Fleet were put on shore as a species of left flank guard to the troops disembarking and were stationed at a point where the road to Eupatoria, which was to the northward, ran along a narrow strip of beach between Kamishlu Lake and the sea.

Whether this detachment actually occupied this position is somewhat doubtful. If used as intended it must have been stationed at the extreme northern end of the strip of beach referred to. For it appears that during the night preceding the disembarkation the French shifted the buoy which had been laid out to mark the division between the portions of the beach selected for the British and their own landings. The result was that when Admiral Lyons and Lord Raglan discovered this unsportsmanlike proceeding, they decided to put the British troops ashore at some distance to the northward of their Allies, and did so on the strip of land between Lake Kamishlu[2] and the sea.

The further movements of the Allied Forces may be briefly summarised. On the morning of the 19th 27,000 British, 30,000 French and 7,000 Turkish troops began their march to the Southward. On the day following the Russian Army, 34,000 strong, was encountered drawn up in a strong position on the heights overlooking the River Alma, and completely barring the invaders' further progress. The Battle of the Alma followed resulting in a victory for the Allies, the Russians retreating upon Sebastopol. Continuing their march the Allies moved round the flank of that fortress by the Eastward, established their base at Balaklava, a rocky harbour a few miles to the South of Sebastopol, and set themselves down to besiege it from the Southward. What part the Royal Marines played in these operations is now to be told.

None of the Corps took part in the fighting at the Alma, but after the battle a considerable number of Marines were landed to assist in carrying down the wounded to the transports, and burying those that succumbed on the beach.

When the Allies established their base at Balaklava, which generally speaking, may be said to have been to the right rear of their lines of investment, it was, of course, necessary to protect it from a possible Russian attack on that flank, and a line of works was put up on the heights on the Eastern side of the harbour,

---
[1] 'Illustrated London News,' 7th October, 1854.
[2] *Vide* "Journal R.U.S.I.," 1905, pp. 353-359.

and overlooking the valley rendered famous by the gallant "Charge of the Light Brigade." This position was in the first instance occupied by the Army, but at the request of Lord Raglan, the British Commander-in-Chief, the troops there were almost at once relieved by a Battalion of 1,000 Marines under the Command of Lieut.-Colonel Hurdle, which was landed from the fleet, and placed on the books of H.M.S. *Agamemnon* which lay in the harbour. It appears that the *Agamemnon's* own detachment under Captain Hayes Marriott and some other details had already landed, bringing up the Royal Marine Force at Balaklava to about 1,200 men.

Rather an amusing story is told of an incident which took place on our taking over this place. Balaklava had been entirely allocated to the British as their base of supplies, the French having the Bays of Kamiesch and Kazatch, but some of their troops taking advantage of the fact that Marshal St. Arnaud happened to be lying sick in the town, entered it and began to pillage and destroy, doing a deal of damage before the British authorities could get rid of them. While there they discovered four mortars in the old Genoese fort above the harbour which had opened fire on our ships on their first entrance. "A large body of Chasseurs, under the command of their officers, proceeded to take them down entirely disregarding the injunctions of the English sentries. Finding expostulation useless, one of our men went and informed Sir Edward Lyons, who immediately landed a body of Marines from H.M.S. *Agamemnon*, and then quietly waited till the French, after no little trouble, arrived with the mortars. He then went up to the officer in command, thanked him most politely for the trouble he had taken, and informed him that he had landed some Marines to take possession of them. The Frenchmen looked astonished, then foolish, but could make no resistance to their being carried at once on board the *Agamemnon*."

The line of entrenchments at this important point extended for "two or three miles in which nature had done so much for defence, that by expending upon it a moderate amount of labour, and arming the works there constructed with a few naval guns of position, our engineers were enabled to place all this portion of the inner line in a fair state of security without drawing from the duties of the siege any very large body of men."[1]

"On the East of the harbour the heights are the commencement of a long range of hills—indeed one may call them mountains—that extend all along the southern coast of the Crimea. Fortunately for the strength of our position, the first hill is almost cut off from the remainder by a deep ravine which runs up from the plain before Balaklava towards the sea, and is only connected by a narrow ridge a few yards in breadth. One of the first works done after our arrival was to construct a battery that would sweep this ridge, and thus render it impracticable for any body of the enemy to force, except at an enormous sacrifice of life. From this point all the way down to the plain a parapet, with occasional small batteries, had been constructed. In these works are several 32-pounder iron howitzers, which for the most part are manned by Marine Artillery, as the entire heights have up to this time been occupied by 1,100 of the Royal Marines from the fleet —as fine a body of men as you could wish to see."[2]

---
[1] Invasion of the Crimea. Kinglake.
[2] Fr. "Letters from Headquarters." By an Officer of the Staff. 1856. *Vide* Plan, p. 105.

Kinglake states that there were twenty-six guns mounted here and manned by the R.M.A., but some of them, at any rate, were handled by the Infantry. The only other troops at first allocated to the defence of these heights—afterwards known as the "Marine Heights," were two companies of the 93rd Regiment, though in the following letter dated 18th October, at a time when a Russian attack was apprehended, it is stated that a reinforcement of 600 Marines had arrived besides other troops:—

"I arrived at this little village about two hours ago, and found that all the troops were fast getting under arms to repulse an attack of the enemy. The fact is, we have been expecting such an attack for some days past; and, for that reason Sir Colin Campbell has been left commanding the garrison. The latter has been further strengthened by the addition of 8,000 Turks,[1] all the English and French cavalry, two additional batteries of artillery, and 600 Marines; altogether, the force to protect this place can be little short of 15,000 men. All the heights which command the approach across the valley to the village of Balaclava have been strongly intrenched, and some of the heaviest ships' guns mounted in redoubts. The enemy would have to storm and capture nearly forty such earthworks before they would be in a position to attack our infantry on the hills; so that I think we are pretty safe. It is a matter of paramount importance to us, not only that Balaclava itself should be retained, but that our communications with it should be perfectly free and uninterrupted. The knowledge of its importance to us will, of course, induce the enemy to attack us; and I believe we shall yet have a bloody battle at Balaclava. While I write, about 12,000 Russians—half of whom are Cossacks—have advanced into the plain towards our batteries. The Turks have opened their fire from the redoubts; but I am certain there will be no close fighting to-day. When the Russians seriously attack this place, they will do it in the night, when their superior local knowledge will give them advantages in skirmishing with the batteries."[2]

"On Wednesday last, the 18th instant," writes an officer of the Royal Marines, "I had scarcely closed the letter to you with the hurried addition, and taken my *al fresco* ablution, and was preparing to breakfast, which the faithful J—— had all ready for us, when our drums beat to arms, the Highland pipes brayed—and all was accoutre and arm. The Russians, in force, were on the plain below—artillery, cavalry and infantry—in all about 10,000. Their cavalry appeared to be their largest arm. Our own cavalry and horse-artillery with some Turkish battalions, who are camped in the plain, advanced, when the Russians retired, without coming to an action. Our field-guns opened on them, but they retired, out of range, across a river and up a ravine, and did not return a shot. It is thought that they were a reconnaissance in force by some; others fancy they wanted to relieve the garrison of Sebastopol, but found our position too strong to attack. They do not, since Alma, like 'the devils in red.' Had we not been here they might have seriously inconvenienced the army before Sebastopol, by taking them

---

[1] The Army was much in need of Turkish interpreters, and it is therefore curious to note that the application of an officer of R.M. (Capt. T. C. C. Moore) to serve in this capacity was refused, though he spoke Turkish so perfectly that Turks sometimes refused to believe he was an Englishman. He was sent to Burmah instead!

[2] From "The Illustrated London News," 11th November, 1854. This letter is apparently, though not certainly, from the same officer as the following one which immediately follows it in the newspaper columns.

H. Bradley Roberts, Lieut. R.M.A. — Dickenson, Lith.

VIEW OF THE RIGHT OF THE POSITION OCCUPIED BY THE ROYAL MARINES AND THE LEFT WING OF THE 2ND BATTALION OF THE RIFLE BRIGADE.—Sketched from the advanced piquet.

H. Bradley Roberts, Lieut, R.M.A. — Dickenson, Lith.

HEADQUARTERS OF 2ND BATTALION BRIGADE OF ROYAL MARINES—THE ORDERLY HUT, THE LIEUT.-COLONEL'S HUT AND THE ADJUTANT'S HUT. (Above are the mud huts of the men).

in the rear, while the garrison might have made a sortie, and placed the Allies between two fires; so, although we have not been ourselves under fire, yet by our presence we have covered the army in the lines. It shows Lord Raglan considers this place of great importance, or he would not have sent Sir Colin Campbell to take the command of this division of the army. We moved off with our second battalion on that morning to the lower part of the heights towards the plain, to keep up a chain of communication with our cavalry and artillery. The Highlanders, one wing between our second and first battalion, held the extreme right of our position, under the command of Captain Hopkins. McLeux commands the second battalion, and moved us off left in front. Captain Timson commands the left company, No. 8 of the 2nd battalion. We remained on the defensive all day, and saw the Russians light their watch-fires, under the cover of which they must have retired, as the next morning they had gone. This was a ruse to persuade us they intended an attack, and also to harass us, in which they partly succeeded; although many officers retired to their tents, and slept uncommonly well after being under arms all day.

"We saw nothing more of them, except a small picket at a great distance, until Friday afternoon, when they again appeared in great force, and Sir Colin ordered the whole of the division to be on the alert, and sent word by Aslett, our Brigade Major, to Lieut.-Colonel Hurdle to have two companies on the plain at the left of these lines, and about the centre of the Allied position. Capt. Timpson commanded this force, but the enemy did not come on, although we had two (alas, false) alarms. The first was the Turkish advanced sentries firing at—perhaps Russians. The second was our own people firing with rockets and great guns on, I think, brushwood (it was a very dark night). I had placed my command in such a low position, and kept them so quiet, that when I was visited and asked where my companies were, I pointed to a hollow. I had them lying down in their ranks with arms in their hands, ready capped and loaded, and gave strict injunctions not a trigger was to be pulled until I gave them the order, which I did not mean to give until I could see, as the black fellows say, 'the whites of their eyes." Being asked what we would do if the Russians came on us before we had time to reload, I replied, 'the bayonet,' in a laconic manner, and added, I had a great opinion of it in English hands. The men were only, like their Captain, too happy to think there was a chance of being the first company to meet the enemy. It was a fearfully cold foggy night, and of course we could have no fires—not even our pipes, until the moon got up, when we smoked away like steam-engines. The men of both companies behaved admirably—quiet, obedient, and steady. I doubt not that, had we had the good fortune to have been attacked, we should have licked three times our number. My men never imagine I am to be shot, as I tell them, when they come asking me to do this, that, and the other, in case they fall. All my suite, lame and lazy, turned out and fell into the ranks on both occasions—so anxious are all to have a fight."[1]

The Russian advance on the 18th, was, as the writer suggests, nothing more than a reconnaissance. But it was a reconnaissance which probably confirmed

---

[1] Letter from an Officer of the Royal Marines, October, 22nd, in "The Illustrated London News," 11th November, 1854.

the Russian general's idea of trying to cut in between the British Army and its base of supplies at Balaklava, a project which from their point of view had a great deal to recommend it.

It must be remembered that the Allies were in a very peculiar position for a besieging army. As a matter of fact they were to a great extent besieged themselves. They had left the Isthmus of Perekop open; which enabled an unlimited number of Russian troops to be poured into the Crimea, while Sebastopol itself was also left perfectly open on the North side. The consequence was that the invaders were confined to that triangular corner of land between Sebastopol and Balaklava. The left attack on the fortress was confided to the French who, with their backs to Cape Chersonese, the apex of the triangle, were comparatively secure, with their base of supplies—Kamiesch Bay—close to it. The British troops forming the right attack, had, on the other hand, their backs at the base of the triangle and were so open to the assault of the whole land forces of Russia. Their extreme right had therefore to be doubled back, as it were, and a line of defence constructed facing eastwards. This ran nearly north and south along a well-marked ridge, but ended three or four miles short of Balaklava, which, as we have seen, had its own line of entrenchments and batteries. The defence of the valley which broke the line of defence and across which all stores for the British Army had to be sent from Balaklava was confined to some scattered redoubts manned by Turks, the cavalry and whatever infantry could be spared when required. It was a weak point which naturally tempted the Russian commanders, and led to the battles of Balaklava and Inkerman.

"It was a crisp sunny autumn day that 25th October," writes an eyewitness of the former battle, who stood in the entrenchments on the Marine Heights,[1] "all nature was in a state of repose, and even the treacherous Black Sea slumbered like an infant, but the spirit of war was in the very air. The Russian General Liprandi, with a strong force some three miles off meant mischief. In front of our battery was a large plain about two miles across, on the edge of which were three mounds, armed with a few guns, manned by a detachment of Turks, with one or two English gunners. They were quite isolated. These redoubts Liprandi attacked, skilfully masking his guns, in a village opposite the largest of them. They pounded away at each other, until the Turks fired their last round, and spiked their guns before they retired."

To relate the magnificent charges of the British Light and Heavy Cavalry Brigades which have been immortalised by both poet and historian is entirely outside the scope of this work, but the part played by the Marines cannot well be more clearly or concisely explained than in the following letter from a sergeant of Marines who was present on that memorable occasion.[2]

"I question very much," he writes, "the happy result of the real engagement at Balaklava but for my corps, and the cool and timely aid given by their guns in No. 1 and No. 2 earth redoubts, known as No. 1 and No. 2 Batteries, on the plain. No. 1 was manned by seventy-eight Blue Marines under the command of Captain Alexander, R.M.A. No. 2 was either under Lieut. Jolliffe or Pym, with

---
[1] "Memoirs of an Old Soldier,' in the "Globe and Laurel," 1904.
[2] Sergt. N. Turner, late R.M.L.I., in the "Army and Navy Gazette," of 22nd November, 1894.

COLOUR-SERGT., R.M.A., PRIVATE AND DRUMMER R.M., 1854.
Contemporary Engraving in the "Illustrated London News."

fifty-six Red Marines; our defences were far from complete, and some of our guns not mounted on the morning of Balaklava; our arms, smooth bores, could not make sure of killing outside 150 yards.[1] The heavy cavalry were drawn up on our left some fifty to sixty yards back, and the light on their left. The Cossacks debouched from four openings, extended across the plain, came on pell-mell in extended order, and closed in opposite to us and the heavy cavalry. We had strict orders not to let the enemy know the range of our guns, but when formed up about 200 yards from us we let them have it, but before we could get our second round ready the bugle sounded 'Cease firing,' to our disgust; we looked over our earthwork and saw the heavy cavalry and Cossacks charging. Our men seemed swallowed up in the mass of Cossacks, who had a squadron drawn up about 200 yards in reserve. The Red Marines in No. 2 Battery opened fire into this reserve, put them into confusion and compelled them to withdraw. This gave our brave handful the chance to wheel round and charge back at the Cossacks, who tumbled over like ninepins. Meanwhile, the Blue Marines planted a few well-directed shell into the Cossacks' right where they were forming up to re-charge the English cavalry. This so upset them that they decamped in groups, during which time several more shell were put into the groups as they made off back across the plain. No. 4 Battery on the heights of Balaklava, under the command of Captain Blyth, R.M.,[2] and manned by Red Marines, did conspicuous service that day from their guns upon the retreating enemy." The writer after mentioning the fact that the R.M.L.I. are never referred to as having been present at this battle in the various histories that have been written about the campaign, goes on to say:—[3] "If you draw a line from the seawall on the heights of Balaklava to the position of the Cavalry it is about two and a half miles as the crow flies; add another half-mile for twistings, and you will have three miles, which were entrusted to the Marines. Two batteries on the plain and four on the heights were manned by Marines, Nos. 1, 2 and 3 Batteries were first and last in action of (sic) the Russian cavalry charge; then took place the light charge, then down came masses of troops and formed line in front of us on the plain, and the battery of artillery on the left of the line engaged the enemy at long ball for a time. About four o'clock the Army moved away and left us to guard Balaklava again, with the support of 250 Highlanders, some French Zouaves, and about 300 Turks."

General Sir Colin Campbell who was in command of the Balaklava defences bears out the efficacy of the fire of the Marines in his official report. "During this period," he says, "our batteries on the hills, manned by the Royal Marine Artillery and the Royal Marines, made most excellent practice on the enemy's cavalry. which came up the hill-ground in front."

Although the Allies held their ground and the Russians retired the result of the action at Balaklava was to render Lord Raglan so doubtful of his ability to keep open his communications with his present base, should, as was practically certain, the enemy return to the attack in increased force, that he made up his

---

[1] Major-General H. T. Arbuthnot, C.B., R.R., at the Royal United Service Institution, on 19th March, 1911, stated. (page 703 of Journal) that, "the guns I had in my battery at the Crimea were actually used at Waterloo!"
[2] Kinglake says that "Lieut. Roberts, R.M.A." commanded "Battery of Position No. 4," if that is the same Battery.
[3] This contention is paralleled by the fact that in the Indices to both Kinglake's "History of the Crimean War" and the "'Times'" "History of the South African War, both voluminous works, "Marines" or "Royal Marines" are not to be found.

mind to abandon Balaklava and share Kamiesch Bay with the French. Admiral Lyons strongly opposed this idea, and when Mr. Filder, the Commissary-General declared, that without the facilities offered by the harbour of Balaklava, "he could not undertake to supply the army,"[1] Lord Raglan had reluctantly to make up his mind to retain it and do the best he could for its defence. The Russians were not long in again putting his defensive arrangements to the test. This time the attack was along the whole line of the British eastern defences, except the Marine Heights which were regarded as impregnable. A sortie in force from Sebastopol was carried out in combination with an advance of other Russian troops from the Northeast and East.

"All the bells in Sebastopol rang a tocsin while the troops composing the sortie, at the early hour of 3 a.m., stole forth under favour of the darkness and a dense mist, and entered the ravines near the Tchernaya which were near the British right. Cautiously and noiselessly the Russian troops stole on, their footsteps hidden by the clanging of the great bells, till 50,000 of them were on the flank as well as in front of our lines, and the first intimation the pickets had of their presence in that unexpected quarter was finding themselves almost surrounded by an overwhelming force."[2] A detachment of Marines was attached to the Light Infantry Division under General Codrington, which was posted near the Lancaster Battery on the Victoria Ridge, not far from the British centre. "This detachment had been brought up to replace a wing of the Rifle Brigade which had been sent down to Balaklava, and fully maintained the reputation of that distinguished Corps." The experiences of this detachment are well told by two veterans who were present, and who have published their recollections in the "Globe and Laurel."

"The 2nd November, 1854, was an active day," wrote Sergeant Turner, R.M.L.I., "312 rank and file marched off from the heights of Balaklava, for the Light Division, under the command of Captain Hopkins, R.M.L.I., the detachment was divided into four companies, taking turn in the trenches. On the morning of the 5th, the relief, which had just returned, were preparing their rude breakfast; the firing from Sebastopol was gradually increased, and then commenced in our rear. Nothing could be distinguished but fog and smoke from where we were. The bugle sounded the "Fall-in" at the double, and officers were flying about giving orders, saying vast columns of the enemy were moving up to our rear. The roll of musketry was terriffic; we were advanced cautiously until bullets began to fall in amongst us, the sergeant-major was the first man killed; order given to lay (sic) down; it was well we did so; a rush of bullets passed over us; then we gave them three rounds, kneeling, into their close columns. At the same time some seamen opened fire from some heavy guns into their left flank, and this drove them back into the fog and smoke. Our Commanding Officer received several orders from mounted officers at this critical time; first it was "advance," then it was "hold your ground and prevent a junction or communication with the town." The Inkermann Caves were occupied by the enemy's sharpshooters, who were picking off our officers and gunners; between us and these men was an open

---
[1] Kinglake.
[2] "British Battles on Land and Sea," Vol. III. Jas. Grant.
[3] Lord Raglan's Official Despatch, 11th November, 1854.

space exposed to the broadside fire of a frigate in the harbour under shelter of the wall, but she had been heeled over so as to clear the muzzles of her guns, when fired, from striking the wall; thus, her fire raked the open part. The Caves were to be cleared, and the Marines ordered to do it; as soon as we showed ourselves in the open, a broadside from the frigate thinned our ranks; Captain March fell wounded.[1] Captain Hopkins ordered his men to lie down under a bit of rising ground, and ordered two privates, Pat Sullivan and another man, to take the Captain back, and there he stood amidst a shower of shot and shell,[2] seeing him removed. A division under Sergeant Richards and Corporal Prettyjohns, was

CORPORAL PRETTYJOHNS, R.M., WINS THE V.C.

then thrown out to clear the caves, what became of the Commanding Officer and the others I never knew, so many statements have been made. We, under Richards and Prettyjohns, soon cleared the caves, but found our ammunition nearly all expended, and a new batch of the foe were creeping up the hillside in single file, at the back. Prettyjohns, a muscular West countryman, said, ' Well, lads, we are just in for a warming, and it will be every man for himself in a few minutes. Look alive, my hearties, and collect all the stones handy, and pile them

---

[1] Severely in the jaw.
[2] " Hopkins' cloak was riddled like a sieve, but though he stood in the thick of the fire, as calm as if on parade, he was unhurt."—(Capt. W. Portlock-Dadson).

on the ridge in front of you. When I grip the front man you let go the biggest stones upon those fellows behind.' As soon as the first man stood on the level, Prettyjohns gripped him and gave him a Westcountry buttock, threw him over upon the men following, and a shower of stones from the others knocked the leaders over. Away they went, tumbling one over the other, down the incline; we gave them a parting volley, and retired out of sight to load; they made off and left us, although there was sufficient to have eaten us up. Later in the day we were recalled, and to keep clear of the frigate's fire had to keep to our left, passing over the field of slaughter. On being mustered, if my memory is not at fault, twenty-one men had been killed and disabled, and we felt proud of our own Commanding Officer, who stood fine, like a hero, helping Captain March. Corporal Prettyjohns received the V.C., Colour-Sergt. Jordan the Medal and £20 for Distinguished Conduct in the Field, Captain Hopkins a C.B., others were recommended."

"Prettyjohns was selected to have the one V.C. for the Marines on that occasion (the clearing out of the Russian sharpshooters from the Inkerman Caves). The Colonel (Hopkins) said, ' Well, boys, there's only one, but you all deserve one each. The men called out, ' Take it yourself Colonel, for you saved all our lives when you ordered us to lie down.' ' No, no, lads, it's for one of you; which shall it be ? Prettyjohns or Jordan ? ' So they said it should be Prettyjohns. ' Then I shall recommend Jordan for the Medal and £20 per annum, for he is in his 21st year of service.' said the Colonel."[1]

"The following morning we went into the trenches," continues Sergeant Turner, "as usual, on short rations and water; about 11-30 my section received a visit from one of the 'hen and chickens,' which squatted down close to us, so we lay down flat on the ground, when up she popped, throwing up an immense quantity of earth, and scattering her fire brood about the place. I was jumped and buried in earth; my memory became a blank until I found myself about half-way to Balaklava, in a waggon which was going to fetch ammunition."[2]

The experiences of another Marine[3] at Inkerman are by no means devoid of interest. "On Sunday morning," he writes, "just before daybreak, we were startled by a scattering fire of musketry, which, before we had time to fall in, became a prolonged roar, and the well-planned surprise of the Russians burst into our camp; our outlying picquets, who were being relieved at the time, and luckily being thus double, disputed the ground bravely, as they were driven in by the immense masses of the enemy. This gave us time to shake ourselves together a bit; the guards away on our right were not so fortunate, being nearest to the enemy, they had to strike their bell tents to make room to fight on.

"The din of artillery now added to the uproar, accompanied by the continued yelling of the Russian army, that could be heard at Balaklava, six miles off. We found out after they were all supplied with Dutch courage in the shape of a drink, something like the arrack in India, maddening stuff; and thus began our Sunday's work. Very soon an aide-de-camp came galloping up to us with the order to

---

[1] " Portsmouth Times," 1911.
[2] Sergt. Turner says in conclusion, " Historians have passed the poor Joeys over, and put some crammers in instead. That yarn about the old Scotch woman stopping the runaway Turks at the Balaklava fight is a *cracker*."
[3] " Memories of an Old Soldier," " Globe and Laurel," 1904.

THE BATTLE OF INKERMAN, 5th November, 1854
"Illustrated London News."

advance at once to a small rising ground where General Codrington was. Here we halted for a few minutes lying down, as the round shot came hopping over us; there was no wonder at the Lancashire recruits' exclamation: 'Naw gi'e o'er, gi'e o'er, throwing them lumps of iron about, somebody 'll be getting hurt.' During this short halt I said my prayers more devoutly than I ever did before or since.

"Whilst sheltering from the storm of shot and shell in rear of this mound of earth a sergeant of the Royal Artillery in charge of two guns was ordered out to the front, but came galloping in again very quick, shouting to the general, 'It's no use, sir, I will only lose the horses.' 'Very well,' said General Codrington, 'go round and join your battery.' When his Aide, Colonel Yeo, came galloping in on his grey horse, saying 'They will never hold it sir, they are ten to one; better send the Marines out.' We marched out accordingly, our appearance in the open being greeted by a tempest of shot and shell from a six-gun battery, and some five hundred yards in our front.

"I was one of eight told off to two stretchers; we had two killed instantly, our drummer having his drum shot away from his arm, and a piece of his trousers from the back part of the legs without getting a scratch; our lot was now in extended order advancing towards the edge of a steep ravine which separated us from the Russians. I got rather confused wandering about with the stretcher in the rear, and, not liking the job, I called to a comrade, 'Come on, Harry, let us join the mob.' The last I saw of the stretcher was one fellow dragging it after him. . . . . As our position was the extreme left, it was a particularly warm quarter, the guns from the Russian shipping in the harbour on our left making a cross fire of artillery. We got what cover we could as we replied to the tempest of bullets that came across that ravine. We saw the plumes of an English battery bobbing above the brushwood on our right, where they unlimbered and opened fire on the six guns in our front, which very soon rid us of their presence. I heard one hurrah on our side, which came from the 88th Connaught Rangers in one of their mad charges against the masses opposed to them. They were very strong in the field, having seven companies engaged. They suffered heavily that day, maintaining one portion of the character that Wellington gave the Regiment in the Peninsula, viz., 'You are the greatest ruffians and the best soldiers that I have.'

"It was getting about nine o'clock when the mist cleared off, and we found our great coats an encumbrance. We had stopped the 'yelling' of the Russians, for they were falling fast and thick before the deadly 'Minie' rifles. I was armed with a Brown Bess, which was now getting clogged, so that I had to hammer my ramrod down with a stone; it kicked dreadfully, and I could not touch the barrel, it was so hot. Towards noon I found myself close to a rifleman whose coolness struck me. He was seated on the ground with his cap by his side loading and firing with the greatest deliberation, laying his ramrod on the ground beside him to save time. Noticing me, he observed casually as he wiped his face, 'It's rather warm,' meaning the weather. I replied, 'I think it's rather hot, myself,' thinking of the fight.

"Towards the afternoon the Russians at length began to retire, sullenly, and at their leisure, leaving the field of battle strewn with six thousand killed alone.

"Whilst still waiting orders to return to camp, we witnessed a fight between a rifleman and a Russian. The former was bringing the latter in a prisoner. The rifleman was a strapping young fellow about 5ft. 10in., but the Russian was a giant, and refusing to give up his sword, they had a scuffle for it, the Russian throwing his adversary away from him as though he were a child, every time he attempted to take it. We could easily have shot the Russian, but an officer of the Rifles shouted, 'Let them fight it out, I'll back my man wins.' The young rifleman changed his tactics, and began to give it to the Russian with his fists, when he had it all his own way, and the Muscovite—who was quite at sea in this mode—was fain to surrender.

"Shortly after we marched back to camp, but before we left the field I and another had a narrow escape. A shell from the shipping buried itself in the earth between us. We thought it a round shot; when it exploded I felt the heat of it on my face. The fragments nearly all went upwards, but one of them struck my companion lightly on the arm. When we got in we had the inevitable roll call; our two companies went into camp 112[1] strong, our loss in killed and wounded amounting to thirty-eight. We had a captain shot through the jaw. Next day I was in the trenches, and we had to keep well under cover for the Russian guns gave us an extra peppering for the defeat of the day before."

Although the Marines did not participate in any more battles such as Inkerman, they shared fully in the strenuous and dangerous work in the trenches and batteries which got heavier and harder as time went on. Although the strength of the Marine Brigade at Balaklava on 13th November, 1854, was 1,950, it so suffered from sickness and the cold of that fearful winter that in January, 1855, "there were strings of stretchers every day going to our graveyard in the ravine; the sergeant in our camp coming round each morning, calling out at each tent, 'Have you any dead?' Our detachment was now getting very small indeed, and the trench duty very heavy. On one occasion I was six consecutive nights in them. We had been reinforced by the Marines of the lately arrived screw liner *Algiers*, all boys more fit to be at home with their mothers. These were dying off so rapidly that we borrowed the French mule ambulance to carry what remained of them back to their ship."[2]

The Marines Camp on the Balaklava heights was perhaps the most exposed of any and suffered severely in the hurricane that wrought such havoc both by sea and land on the 14th November, 1854. "My Company," writes a Marine,[3] "was just leaving the 21-gun battery, where we had been on trench duty the night before. We had the best part of a mile to go to reach camp, and as we had the hurricane full in our teeth, we had the utmost difficulty to get along, a squall of rain making the ground slippery and the task harder. As we neared our encampment all our moveable camp furniture was flying past us—knapsacks, camp kettles, water-bottles, etc., and when we got to where our tents should be, we found them all down fluttering on the ground, and only prevented from taking flight by the tent pegs."

---

[1] There were four companies with the Light Division, but they were not all in the thick of the fight. (Capt. W. Portlock-Dadson).
[2] Memories of an Old Soldier, "Globe and Laurel," 1905
[3] *Ibid*.

"A Colonel of Marines, stationed on the heights,[1] on the extreme right of our Balaklava position, was taken up with his tent, in which he sat, with pillows and bolsters, clothes and weapons, cooking utensils, pots, pans, and kettles, and deposited at the bottom of a deep ravine. He knew not how he got in, and much less did he know how he should get out. When the first confusion in the camp was got over, the gallant Colonel was among the missing. The wind howled and the sea thundered against the cliff and drowned his voice. But at length he made himself heard, and some of his men descending by means of ropes, assisted him in removing to other quarters."[2]

The siege dragged along till 8th September, 1855, without there being any thing of special interest to record as to the doings of the Corps, but the winning of another V.C. by Bombardier Wilkinson, R.M.A., must not be overlooked. He earned this coveted distinction for very gallant conduct in the advanced batteries in placing sandbags to repair the works under a galling fire. The following is an account of Wilkinson's conduct, from an old newspaper:—

BOMBARDIER WILKINSON, R.M.A., WINS THE V.C.

"Bombr. Thomas Wilkinson is one of a group of heroes who won the V.C. in the weary fight for the Redan. The deed for which this brave man won his

---

[1] Hurdle, "Illustrated London News," 16th Dec., 1854.
[2] The wrecks of the vessels driven ashore in this storm provided the Royal Marines with canvas, rope, timber and many things useful; they were all under some cover in a few days, having dragged materials up from the wrecks on the beach below the cliffs.

V.C. is one which shews the wonderful coolness and intrepidity of the British military character. After the British batteries had been for a long time pounding away at the Redan, one of the principal fortresses of Sebastopol, a terriffic fire from the Russian lines, on June 5th, 1855, knocked all to pieces the advance works of the British. The latter were scarcely able to reply, partly in consequence of want of cover, the parapets and embrasures, as Tommy puts it, being hardly distinguishable one from another, being, in trench language, 'all of a heap,' Wilkinson, without an instant's hesitation, saw what was necessary to be done. With the cool head and dauntless courage of the English, this brave member of the Royal Marine Artillery sprang into the very jaws of danger. With the Russian bullets whizzing round him, with cannon belching forth the fearful volleys, with shells whizzing overhead, he sprang to the summit of the earthworks, and calling on his comrades to bring sandbags, began the repair of battery after battery, so that our guns had soon something like a good cover from which to reply to the guns of Sebastopol. He seemed utterly unconscious of the brave act he was doing, although again and again loud and ringing cheers proclaimed the feeling of his comrades towards him. It is quite impossible to say how many lives were saved by his gallant deed, for which Colonel Wesley recommended him for the Victoria Cross, which he obtained, being also decorated with the medal of the French Legion of Honour. This fearless soldier died at York in the year 1887."

On the last day of the siege—the day of the assault on the Malakoff Tower and the Redan—the R.M.A. did good service in the mortar vessels in firing upon the Quarantine Batteries that enfiladed the approach of the assaulting columns. A north-west gale and a heavy sea prevented the big men-of-war from taking up their allotted positions to do this, but the mortar vessels sheltered in Strelitzka Bay, just behind the extreme left of the French attacks, were able to pour in a very effective fire. Captain Digby, R.M.A., was in command and states in his official report that he "opened fire from the mortar vessels at 8-30 a.m. upon the Quarantine Battery and a general and more rapid fire from noon till 7 p.m. upon the Quarantine Battery, and Fort Alexander. The forces of the wind and heavy swell which prevailed were singularly unfavourable to accuracy, and the general satisfactory nature of the firing was due to the ability of the officers of the Royal Marine Artillery who conducted it."

The following day, the Russians blew up their fortifications, set the town on fire, sank their ships in the anchorage, and retreated by a bridge of boats across the harbour to the North Shore—Sebastopol was ours.

In October took place the expedition to Kinburn which occupies a narrow tongue of land at the mouth of the Dneiper. The Royal Marine Battalions, 1,200 strong, formed with some R.E., R.A. and detachment of Cavalry, the 1st Brigade of the British portion of the expeditionary force, and were landed to cut off the retreat of the garrison on the land side. This was on the 15th October. The fort surrendered on 17th October, after a heavy bombardment in which the R.M.A. and their mortar-vessels were again of great service, and which is memorable from the fact of it being the first occasion in which ironclads were in action, some of the then new French armour-plated floating batteries proving very effective.

There were some building in England but none were ready. The Marines on 20th October took part in a short reconnoitring march of twelve miles into the country to Patrouski, but nothing was seen of any Russian troops and the force returned to Kinburn, where it re-embarked on the 30th October and sailed for Sebastopol. Here the Royal Marines were ordered to embark on board the *Jura* for passage home. In conclusion it may be noted that it was during this year—1855—that the present title of "Light Infantry" was bestowed on the Red Marines. Whether this was intended as a reward for their services is not quite apparent.[1]

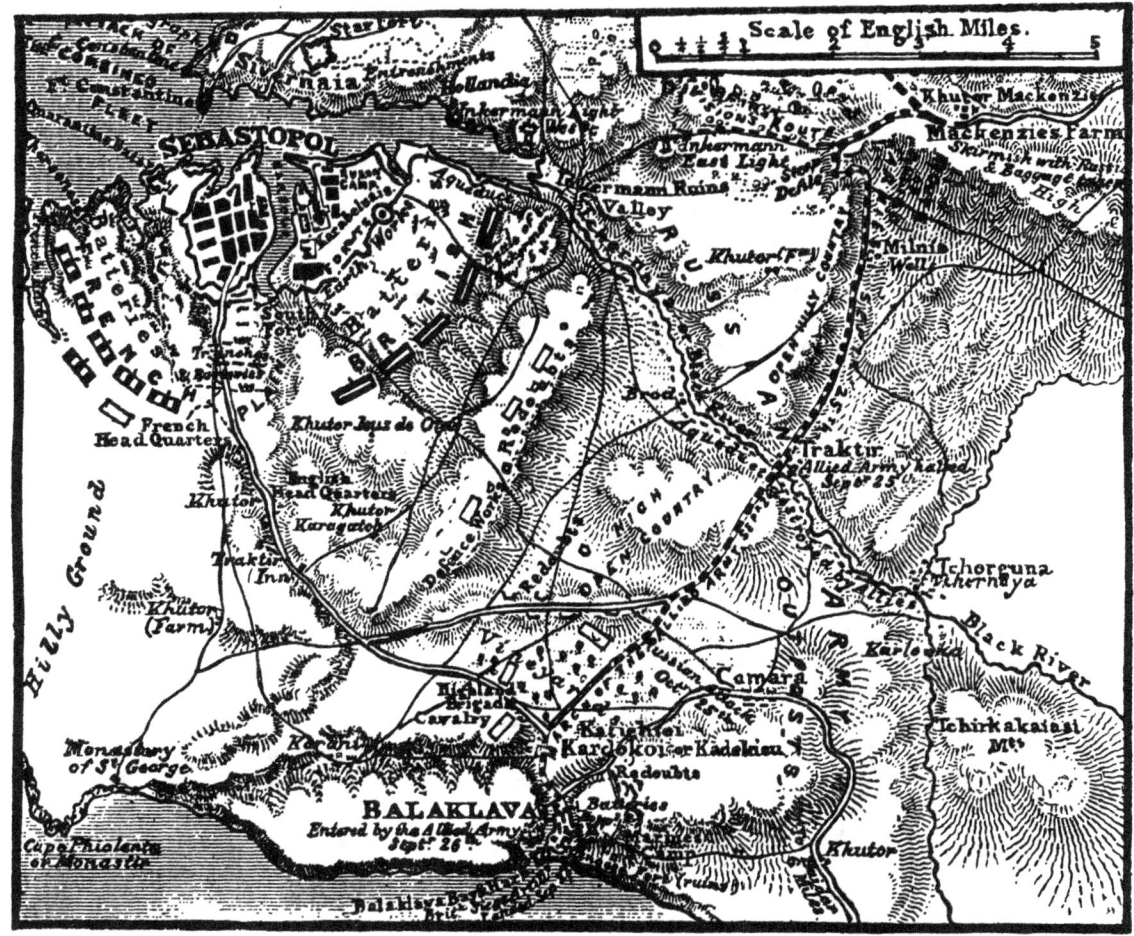

PLAN OF THE SIEGE OF SEBASTOPOL.

---

[1] 2nd February, 1855—"Her Majesty has been pleased to command that the Corps of Royal Marines shall in future be designated 'Corps of Royal Marines, Light Infantry.'"—*Vide* also Note I.

NOTE.

NOTE I.—"LIGHT INFANTRY."

"Light Infantry" was a curious title to bestow on a Corps which is generally composed of men of above average size and height, and was especially so at that time. The official reason given by the Admiralty for the change was that the Light Infantry training was "considered best adapted to the nature of the service which the Corps is generally required to perform when employed on shore." An officer who served on board the *St. Jean d'Acre* in the Baltic says that the detachment were all "big, burly fellows," and states that when he joined at Plymouth, in 1851, he was the shortest man in No. 2 Company, though he himself stood close on 6 feet in his socks. Possibly the fact of the attachment of some companies to the Light Division at Inkerman suggested the distinction. It seems a pity that the Red Marines were not created "Fusileers" instead, since up to the Crimean War the Corps had always been more assimilated to the Fusileer Regiments than to any other. The 'Admiral's Regiment" in 1664 carried no pikes, the Marine Regiments that distinguished themselves at Gibraltar wore something like a Fusileer Cap—so did the ten regiments of 1740-1. The present Corps when instituted in 1775 "wore Caps like those of the Fusileers" according to Grosse, and the white worsted ball on the shakoes adopted in 1832 was also a Fusileer ornament. Again, it appears that the officers always carried fuzees instead of half-pikes—when it was the regulation for officers to carry such weapons—also a Fusileer custom—as was that of never bearing the title of "Ensign" after 1755.

In the writer's humble opinion, the Corps generally has never taken very kindly to the title of "Light Infantry." Certainly the distinctive dress of that portion of the service has never been adopted in its entirety. Thus, at the time of its being created "Light Infantry," although the white pompom on the shako gave place to a green one, the officers—after 1866—were not authorised to wear a green plume as in other Light Infantry Corps. Neither did they wear their sashes in the same way as they did, nor discard their epaulettes for "wings." Nor did the blue cloth of the shako (and its successor, the helmet) nor the forage cap give place to green, as, strictly speaking, it ought to have done. The Drummers certainly were provided with green bugle-cords and the "Bugle" was added to the Corps Badges, but of late years this has disappeared from the helmet plate, as has the "Grenade" from that of the Royal Marine Artillery. "Royal Marine Fusileers" would have been at least as honourable a title as "Royal Marine Light Infantry"—if not a more suitable one. Had that been adopted there would have been no need, when it was decided to gradually assimilate the two branches of the Corps, to deprive the head-dresses of both of their honourable and distinctive badges—the "Grenade" would have been equally suitable for Red and Blue Marines. Possibly, too, the Corps would not be the only one in H.M. Service without a full-dress head-dress, the white helmet which has to play the part being, from a military point of view, merely a secondary head-covering necessitated at various places out of England by the hot climate.

The "March Past," too—up to the time it was exchanged for the music of a song made by an American—was that of the Fusileers—"The British Grenadiers."

It would appear even that the Marine Regiments were, in the early days, not infrequently referred to as "Fusileers." The process of re-armament was naturally very slow in pre-machinery days, and it was not till 1708 that the match-lock was finally superseded by the firelock or "fusil" for the whole army. The first regiments to receive the new weapon would popularly be known as "fusileers," even if that were not their official title, and the Marines were among the first at any rate. Even in official communications, the 30th Regiment (Saunderson's Marines), afterwards commanded by Col. Bissett, were during the War in Spain, as often called "Bissett's Fusileers" as "Bissett's Foot," as I am informed by Col. Neil Bannatyne, the able historian of that regiment. Most probably the same held good in other Marine Regiments of the day. When after the Revolution two new Marine Regiments were formed in 1690 they were ordered to be "all Fusileers without pikes," and again when in 1698 the two were combined into one and three additional Line Regiments turned into Marines it was directed that "the Pykes belonging to the three Regiments be forthwith (sent) into our Stores, to the end that *proper* Fire Armes be deliver'd out of our said Stores in the room of ye Pykes." "Proper" firearms for Marines were without doubt Fusils for the reasons given in Note I, Chapter II. The only British Infantry Battalions at the Battle of St. Estevan in 1707 seem to have been Marines, and in a contemporary account of that battle those companies which were not Grenadiers were spoken of as "Fusileers." These battalions, as we have seen were broken up or transferred to the Line in 1713, and by the time a new force of Marines was organised in 1740 the whole Army was armed alike and the term "Fusileer" had already become the especial property of certain Regiments.

INDIAN NATIVE INFANTRY, 1857.

Chapter XXVI.

OUR SEA-SOLDIERS IN INDIA.

"There is only one method of fighting Asiatics. That mode is to move straight on."
—Col. G. B. Malleson, C.S.I.

BOSCAWEN'S operations on the Coromandel Coast, in 1746, in which 880 Marines participated, have already been mentioned in the Chapter containing the story of Hannah Snell. Since that time few Marines have fought on the battlefields of Hindustan, but there have been two occasions when small detachments of the Corps took part in very momentous events in that important portion of the British Empire. And as accounts by members of the Corps who were present in these stirring episodes have come down to us, the deeds of these detachments, few in numbers though they were, well deserve a Chapter to themselves.[1]

---

[1] Much of the information regarding the events in this chapter is from a little work published in 1817 entitled "An Historical Account of the Rise and Progress of the Bengal Native Infantry," by Captain John Williams, "An old and zealous officer of the Honourable East India Company's Service, etc." But it appears from an editor's note at the bottom of page 33 explanatory of the unexpected use of the word "we" that "the author of this narrative belonged at that period to the Marines." From the fact that the *Argo*, 28, and the *Medway*, 60, were the only two men-of-war from which Captain Wemyss drew his little detachment upon his second disembarkation it may well be assumed that John Williams belonged to the first named ship.

Passing over the defence of Madras in 1758,[1] when the Marines of the *Iris* and *Bridgwater*, which had been driven on shore by the French Fleet, reinforced the small British Garrison, we come to those events which culminated in the decisive Battle of Buxar on 23rd October, 1764. Pondicherry, the principal stronghold of the French in India, had fallen on 16th January, after some months' siege by Colonel Eyre Coote, at the head of a small army of Europeans and Native troops which included 422 Marines landed from the Fleet.

The town was covered by an outer line of entrenchments at an average distance of 1500 yards from the ramparts proper which extended from the sea on the right to the Ariancopang River on the left. At each end was a redoubt and two others at intervals between them. All were strongly fortified and garrisoned and known as the Ariancopang, Villenore, Valdore and Madras redoubts. Two columns were formed for the purpose of breaking this line by the capture of the two central fortifications. Two hundred Marines were in the left column, whose objective was the Valdore Redoubt, together with 150 Highlanders, 1,900 men from Draper's and Coote's Regiments, and 500 Sepoys. They carried the Redoubt after several repulses. The right column was also successful.

Many of the French soldiers after the surrender of the town enlisted in the British forces especially those belonging to Lally's[2] Irish Regiment, but those belonging to the Regiment of Lorraine, and to the Pondicherry Regiment—a French East India Company's Corps—were formed into two independent companies which in 1762 were sent on board Admiral Cornish's Fleet and served in the Siege of Manilla, principally in making gabions, fascines, pickets and similar work. Just as the victorious expedition was leaving at the end of February, 1763, it was discovered that these Companies had conspired with the Spaniards to deliver up the city to them as soon as the Fleet had sailed. They were at once brought on board and landed at Madras. Here the fleet remained till the end of August when news came from Bengal that war had broken out with Cossim Ally, Nabob of Bengal.

After Clive's victory at Plassey in 1757, Surajah Dowlah, the then Nabob, had been deposed by the English and his Commander-in-Chief, Mir Jaffer, created Nabob in his place. Cossim Ally—or as he is more often called—Mir Cossim—was Jaffer's son-in-law. The new Nabob—discovered by the English to be plotting against them—was, in his turn, replaced by Mir Cossim. He, also, quarrelling with the East India Company, finally massacred an English deputation at Moorshebad and fled to Sujah Dowlah, the Nabob of Oudh. The actual assassin of the

---

[1] A somewhat curious incident in connection with this siege is related in "Orme's Hindustan." "Intelligence," he says, "had been received that one of the vessels which had been laden with artillery (for the French) at Alamparva, was detained at anchor off the Point of Conimere, fifteen miles south of Sadras, by contrary winds and currents; and a Dutch snow being in the Road of Madras, it was resolved to equip and employ her to attack the French vessel. Accordingly, twenty sailors belonging to the Squadron, who had been lately exchanged, and forty of the Marines left by Mr. Pocock (the Admiral) were sent on board under the command of a Naval Officer of experience; but just as he was going to weigh, the Sailors refused to come, pretending that they knew the French ship was much too strong for them, on which they were re-landed on the 10th and the attempt was relinquished." It is also a curious coincidence that the total number of Europeans engaged in the successful defence was 1758, the date of that year.

[2] The Count de Lally, son of Captain O'Lally of Tulloch-na-Daly, in Galway, was an Irish soldier of fortune in the French Service and was French Commander-in-Chief in India. He it was who had failed to capture Madras in 1758, and who had defended Pondicherry. The Regiment de Lally had been raised and trained by him and was the 30th of the French Line. Lally met with a cruel fate at the hands of the French Government, being imprisoned for four years, frequently tortured and finally beheaded on 9th May, 1766. The Regiment de Lorraine, sometimes called "Les Gardes Lorraines" was the 119th. There was also a Marine Regiment in the Garrison and Artillery details, etc., These were all made prisoners of war and sent to Bengal where many of them entered the Company's service under Mons. Claude Martine, formerly of the Lorraine Regiment, and who died a Major General in the Honourable Company's Army.

forty-nine English gentlemen and one child who were massacred was Cossim's German Commandant, Somers or "Sumroo." This fine specimen of a Hun invited the Mission to supper and as soon as his guests were at table the butchery commenced. But the Englishmen fought so stoutly with plates and bottles that the murderers were withdrawn to the roof, whence they fired down upon their victims till all were slaughtered. The soldiers who had accompanied them were despatched in batches of sixty at a time. Their blood cried for vengeance, and since Cossim refused to surrender the German assassin there was nothing for it but the arbitrament of the sword.

After a short campaign the town of Patna was taken by storm by the British forces under Major Adams, and its defenders pursued as far as the River Carumnassa which separated the dominions of the Nabob Sujah Dowlah of Oudh, from those of the British East India Company. Major Adams then encamped at Sant, a village about four miles from the river. He himself went down to Calcutta, probably on account of ill-health, since he died there in the January following. Major Jennings of the Artillery succeeded to the command of the mixed force of natives and Europeans of various nationalities, which seems to have been in anything but a satisfactory state of discipline, the men considering themselves aggrieved by the non-fulfilment of some promises of extra pay which, on taking the field, they had understood they were to receive. On a certain day the whole force got under arms and threatened to march at once into Sujah Dowlah's country and enlist in his armies if their demands were not acceded to at once. The Europeans actually set out, but by the persuasions of their Officers and non-commissioned Officers all the British and a few of the German soldiers were brought back. A sergeant Delamar formerly of the 84th Regiment, born in London of French parents, was, on account of his speaking the language, sent after the deserters to induce the Frenchmen to return. However, as soon as he came up with them, he placed himself at their head saying, "Now is the time to make your fortunes, and if you will follow me, I will lead you to riches and honour!" They gave him three cheers and pushed on to the Carumnassa, where more of the Germans decided to return to their colours at Sant. Meanwhile the Sepoy battalions, who were about to follow the Europeans, were induced by liberal promises and the distribution of all the money available, to return to their duty.

As soon as the tidings of the outbreak of war had reached Madras it was determined to send reinforcements to Bengal. H.M.S. *Argo*—the fastest ship in the squadron—was sent off post haste on 1st September to Old Fort (Calcutta), arriving on the 9th and immediately landing her Marines. A week or so later Commodore Tinker with the *York* and *Medway*, 60 gun ships, and the *Liverpool*, a 28 gun frigate, followed and also landed their Marine detachments. The Marines from the four ships mustered nearly 200 men, and were formed into a small battalion under Captains Maurice Wemyss[1] and Frederick Thomas Smith,[2] but as there were only a couple of Marine subalterns in the four ships, "the Commodore commissioned a few of the midshipmen."

---

[1] Afterwards Major General of Marines and Commandant.
[2] Joined the Company's Service, was a Major in 1768. Town-Major of Fort William, and died at Patna in 1770 whilst in command of the Purgunnah Battalion.—*Vide* Note I.

The little battalion marched in the first place to Ghyretty, thence in October to Burdwan, where it came under the command of Major Carnac with a Sepoy battalion and a troop of the Company's Hussars, and early in November was joined by 300 European trooops from Madras, which included the two unreliable French Companies they had had to remove from Manilla. Major Carnac's force was intended to look out for a threatened move by the Maharattas, but on the way towards Ramgur on the Maharatta frontier, he heard that danger from that quarter was at an end and proceeded with all the Company's troops to join Major Adam's force at Sant, where it is probable that the two French companies were the prime instigators of the mutiny which has been mentioned above. The Marines, on their part, marched back to Calcutta where they rejoined their respective ships. The *York* and *Liverpool* shortly afterwards sailed for Madras. Hardly had these two ships made an offing when Calcutta was thoroughly alarmed by the news of the mutinous proceedings at Sant. Commodore Tinker was at once appealed to and asked to send off his Marines to join the army. Only 100 were available from the two ships left at Calcutta, but they were at once fitted out with camp equipage, and after a terrible march in the hottest season of the year, joined the army on the 9th May. Captain Wemyss was in command.

In the interim the Rajah Sujah Dowlah and the Emperor Shah Allum[1] had declared war upon the Company in order to assist the defeated Cossim Ally, and on 25th April had laid siege to Patna. Hearing of the advance of the small, but to him formidable, body of Marines, Sujah Dowlah determined to capture Patna before their arrival, at the same time detaching a force of cavalry to cut off the expected reinforcement. What happened to this detachment does not appear, but when Patna was assaulted on the 3rd May, the garrison made things so hot for its assailants, that the attack was abandoned and the besiegers seem to have been so disconcerted that when the Marines reached the city from the opposite side of the Ganges, they were able to enter without opposition and to take up their position in the entrenchments.

On May the 30th the roll of the drums beating to arms denoted a movement on the part of the enemy, who were discovered to be marching off to their own left. The Marines with some European Grenadiers and four companies of Sepoy Grenadiers under the command of Captain Wemyss sallied out to harass the rear of the retiring enemy, but were in insufficient force to make very much impression. The enemy continuing his retreat, the day following the Marines, the Company's Grenadiers and the 6th, 9th and 15th Native battalions with eight guns were sent by water to Hadjepore, with the object of clearing the Sircar Sarum district of any scattered troops of Sujah Dowlah. After several days march this little force which was commanded by Major Champion, arrived at Sewan on the banks of the Gogra, the boundary of the Company's territories, finding the whole countryside clear of the enemy. The rainy season approaching Champion set out to march back, and on arriving at Manjee the Marines were ordered to garrison the fort at that place, the 9th N.I. being left in the town. The remainder of the expedition continued its way to Choprah where it was to be cantoned during the rains, with

---
[1] Titular Great Mogul.

the exception of the Grenadiers who marched to join Army headquarters at Bankypore. At the beginning of August, the Marines also were ordered to Choprah, where temporary barracks had been prepared for them. But they had not seen the last of Manjee, for three or four weeks after the Marines had left, the 9th battalion mutinied and marched out of the town. As soon as this was known at Choprah, Captain Wemyss with the Marines and the 6th N.I. was sent in pursuit of the mutineers and after two days very fatiguing marching, most of the way knee deep in water, discovered them in a mango tope on an eminence surrounded with water of considerable depth. "However, we moved down and drew up facing them," says the author of the work from which the above details are derived, thereby disclosing that he at that time was a Marine himself, " and after a little conversation they agreed to surrender." The appearance of " 'is Majesty's Jollies " was too much for the nerves of the mutineers. They feebly decided not to fight although they had a good position, and the surrounding water was so deep that rafts had to be improvised to bring them over as prisoners. In four days after starting Wemyss had the mutineers back at Choprah in custody and there met Major Munro who was in supreme command of the Company's army and who had come over especially to see the Marines. " Hearing of what had passed at Sant and the misbehaviour of this battalion upon the present occasion, he thought it right to make a severe example "; says our narrator, " and a severe, although necessary example it undoubtedly was. He ordered eight and twenty of the most culpable to be picked out, and tried by a drum-head General Court Martial, when the whole were sentenced to suffer death. The eight guns with the detachment, being brought out, the first eight were fixed to their muzzles and blown away. Here it was, that three of the grenadiers entreated to be fastened to the guns on the right, declaring that as they had always fought on the right, they hoped their last request would be complied with, by being suffered to die in the post of honour. Their petition was granted and they were the first executed. I am sure there was not a dry eye amongst the Marines who witnessed this execution, although they had long been accustomed to hard service; and two of them had actually been on the execution party which shot Admiral Byng, in the year 1757. The other twenty were ordered to the several stations of the army, where they all suffered death in the same manner."

Early in October, the whole of the available forces were concentrated near Arrah with the object of attacking Sujah Dowlah who had cantoned his troops at Buxar during the rains. The Company's army consisted of eight complete Sepoy battalions, two Companies of European Grenadiers, 857 Europeans of various kinds, and 1100 irregular cavalry—about 8000 men in all, with 22 guns. The only representatives of the King's troops were the Marines and small parties of the 84th, 89th and 90th Regiments,[1] barely 200 in all, which were formed into a battalion known as the " King's," and placed under the command of Captain Wemyss.

At 5 in the morning of the 13th October, the Army commenced its march on Arrah, arriving at the Bridge crossing a nullah near that place just as day began to break. Here the advanced Guard of the Company's Hussars, some irregular

---

[1] Not the Regiments now known by these numbers. The 84th was raised 1758 and disbanded 1764. The 89th, a Corps of Gordon Highlanders raised at Badenoch, in 1759, was disbanded in 1765, whilst the 90th, Irish Light Infantry, was raised in 1759 and disbanded in 1763. All ephemeral Regiments.

horse and two companies of Sepoy grenadiers, which was evidently moving without sufficient precaution, was ambushed by a body of the enemy's cavalry, which allowing the head of the column to pass the bridge, suddenly charged its centre and cut up the whole advance. Some got back over the bridge, others swam across covered by the fire of the grenadiers, who had not yet crossed. At the sound of the firing the King's Battalion was pushed forward, but the whole affair was over by the time it arrived on the scene of action. It was evidently necessary to move with increased precaution and a fresh Advanced Guard was detailed consisting of the European Grenadiers, four Companies of Sepoy Grenadiers, with the King's Battalion in immediate support. Harassed by continual skirmishing with the enemy the advance was continued till the 22nd, when the Advanced Guard debouched upon the plain of Buxar where it discovered Sujah Dowlah's whole army drawn up in line of battle three miles ahead of it. The Advanced Guard and the King's battalion inclined to the right while the remainder of the army prolonged the line to the left as each battalion arrived. The hostile armies looked at each other for over an hour, and Sujah Dowlah's gunners fired a few rounds which fell short, after which the enemy fell back on his lines at Buxar, and the British forces pitched their tents, the troops being strictly ordered not to remove their accoutrements. A Sepoy battalion was sent forward to occupy a village which lay about a thousand yards to the front to observe the enemy and protect the encampment from surprise. A Council of War was held which decided to defer further operations till the morning of the 24th in order to give the troops a much needed rest, but early on the 23rd Major Munro, riding out to reconnoitre Sujah Dowlah's position, saw that the enemy were already under arms and that if he did not attack at once his little army would very likely be surrounded. The guards and outposts were at once called in, the drums beat to arms, and in no more than twenty minutes the army was in battle formation. Wemyss, with his little battalion of Royal troops, was near the right of the front line. On its right was a Sepoy Battalion. On the left of the " King's " was another battalion of Sepoys, and the Bombay contingent of rather over a hundred Europeans and Topasses, " this is native Portuguese dressed as Europeans, who formed the centre and rear ranks." Another Sepoy battalion formed the left of the front line. At either flank of the line and between each battalion were placed a couple of field-guns—a dispersion of the artillery arm not at all in accordance with modern ideas. This line formed the front face of a square, each side face being composed of a Sepoy battalion, that on the left having two guns attached to it; while three more Sepoy battalions and the Company's European battalion formed the rear face. " By this time Sujah Dowlah's line had advanced within about 500 yards of us, where they seemed to halt, and then we had a distinct view of them, and a grand sight it was: their left was close to the river and their right extended into the country almost as far as the eye could carry, but bending a little inwards so as to bring their guns to bear on the left face of our square. About 9 o'clock we began to advance upon the enemy, and then, for the first time, our fire opened, which we could clearly see had a fine effect. After moving about one hundred yards, a jeel[1]

---

[1] A swamp or morass.

in front of the left wing, obliged us to incline to the right in order to clear it. This took us up nearly an hour, the enemy's cannon and rockets playing upon us the whole time, but their guns were not well served, otherwise, from the number they had in the field, they must have torn us to pieces.

"The left having cleared the jeel, orders came along the line to move forward; but at that instant, a large body of cavalry appearing in the rear, obliged us to halt, and the rear line to go to the rightabout. The enemy's horse having been thrown into some disorder in coming through a village about a thousand yards in our rear, it took them a few minutes to close, and then they made a furious charge on the rear line; but they met with so warm a reception, both of grape and small arms, that they fled, and never after returned to the field. They took care, however, to carry off our baggage and all the tents which had been left standing.

Whilst the rear line was engaged, the right wing of the enemy bent round, so as nearly to enclose our left, and then the action in that quarter became warm. It was now about noon, when Major Munro rode to the right, and finding it much annoyed by a battery in a tope or grove of trees, in front of the King's Battalion, he ordered Major Stibbert's (1st N.I.) Battalion from the right of the line, to advance and attack in flank. The battalion accordingly moved forward in excellent order; but receiving the fire of a battalion of Nejeebs,[1] and being attacked at the same time by a body of horse on each flank, they were thrown into disorder and retired towards the line. Major Munro having gone to the left, Major Champion ordered the right wing to advance, but not to give their fire until they could push bayonets; they accordingly moved on with recovered arms, and when they got in a line with the disordered battalion, it instantly formed, and went on with them. On entering the tope they received a heavy fire from the Nejeebs, which, however, did little execution. They pushed on, and on getting clear of the trees, perceiving the Nejeebs had retreated, they gave them their fire, which obliged them to quicken their pace. At the back of the tope they found twenty-seven pieces of cannon, some of which had been taken from us at the unfortunate affair at Manjee the year before. As soon as the guns were taken possession of, and the wing had reloaded, they faced to the left, in order to support the left wing and flank, still closely engaged; but the enemy seeing them moving down, fled in disorder, so that at one o'clock we were complete masters of the field. The wing immediately halted and then Major Munro came in front of the line, and returned thanks to the whole army for their steadiness and bravery during the action; after which, taking off his hat, he gave three cheers for the victory which was returned by the troops with hearty goodwill." The casualties on the British side amounted to 101 Europeans killed and wounded, including seven or eight officers, 773 Sepoys and 150 irregular cavalry, besides a considerable number of camp followers.

The enemies losses were immense. Their army was 50,000 to 70,000 strong, and besides heavy casualties in the battle, an enormous number of soldiers and camp followers crowded each other into a muddy nullah in their panic flight and perished miserably. 126 guns were taken, and seven more brought in the next morning by one of the foreigners who had deserted at Sant, and who received his

---
[1] Infantry armed with matchlocks and sabres.

pardon in consequence. Several others were found dead on the field, and "two who had been wounded, and could not get off with their army, were hung up to a tree in front of the line, by the provost serjeant."

The political results of this battle are outside the scope of our history, but it is evident that the little force of Marines and Linesmen under Captain Wemyss had a considerable share in the victory. The actual attack was made by the right of the front line, and on the 1st N.I. being checked at the tope, it would appear that it was the "King's Battalion" which rallied it and captured the grove and the twenty-seven guns behind it, and it was the threatened advance from this position upon the enemy's left which brought about the collapse of Sujah Dowlah's army. Major Munro's despatch reporting the "Victory of Buxar over the King of Indoostan with 600 Europeans and 6000 Sepoys over an enemy of 70,000 men," was sent home by Commodore Tinker on 29th November, 1764, and in his covering letter he adds, "The Marines are specially commended and also Captain Wemyss *who commanded the King's troops.*"[1]

The next important service of the Corps in this portion of the "Shiney East" was at the capture of Trincomalee in 1782.

Early in the morning of the 4th January the Marines belonging to Sir Edward Hughes' squadron with two 6-pounders, were landed with a detachment of Artillery and Sepoy pioneers at about three miles from Trincomalee Fort. During the day 800 seamen and a force of Sepoys were put on shore. The same night the whole force advanced under cover of the darkness, and the Grenadier Companies of the Marines, led by Lieutenant Orr, made themselves masters of the Fort by pushing resolutely on through the gateway, while the governor was writing down the terms of capitulation which he intended to propose. After garrisoning this Fort and landing their siege guns and stores the British turned their attention to Fort Ostenburgh situated on a high hill which completely commanded the Harbour. This fort was in turn commanded by a rather higher hill upon which the enemy had posted an Officer's Guard, which was driven from its position by a night attack of the Seamen and Marines. This point was only 200 yards from Fort Ostenburgh, the Governor of which was at once summoned to surrender. He refused to do so, and preparations were made to take the Fort by assault. On the 11th the storming party consisting of 450 seamen and Marines advanced at daylight, its flanks covered by pioneers and seamen with scaling ladders, and supported by three Companies of Marines and the same number of Companies of Seamen. A Sergeant's party of Marines led the attack, and got through the embrasures, the remainder of the stormers followed and soon made themselves masters of the Fort with the loss of twenty-one killed and forty-one wounded, including Lieutenant Orr, who was acting as Brigade-Major.

With the exception of the presence of Captain S. B. Ellis with two subalterns and a detachment at the bombardment and reduction of Fort Manora by the Reserve of the Army of the Indus in 1839,[2] we have no further record of any services of the Corps in India until the outbreak of the Great Mutiny of the Native Troops

---

[1] Collection of Home Office papers, 1760-65, page 565.
[2] The Marines probably belonged to H.M.S. *Wellesley* and *Algerine*, which bombarded Fort Munora (or Mulhara) at the entrance of Kurachee Harbour on 2nd February, 1839. The 40th Regiment and 2nd Native Grenadiers were also present.

in 1857. On this occasion there were a certain number of Marines, though not a very large one, who saw very considerable service in the fighting which accompanied its suppression. But very few people are aware of this, even in the Army.

"Bah," said a Highlander to a Marine veteran[1] who had served in the famous "Shannon's Brigade," through the Indian Mutiny, "Marines at Lucknow! I never saw one there. There was one sailor called Peel there."

"Sometimes it makes me mad," exclaimed this old Marine, "to hear so much about the Mutiny, and not a word about the old Joeys. Why, if we had not taken up those guns and made a hole in the wall for those bare-legged johnnies to get through, I'm thinking a different story would have been told."

It is not every one who is quite so ignorant of the Mutiny Campaign as the Highlander quoted above, but there are very few people who are aware that the Royal Marines shared in the toils and glories of the Naval Brigade from H.M.S. *Shannon* and *Pearl* which, under the command of that brilliant sailor Captain W. Peel, R.N., bore such an important part in the suppression of the dreadful Indian Mutiny of 1857 and 1858.

To the general public the words "Naval Brigade" do not convey the slightest hint of the presence of the Marines. Who has ever seen a picture in a popular journal representing a Naval Brigade in close action in which the artist has depicted a single Marine? Even in a Service publication—which might reasonably have been expected to have known better—a picture was published depicting the *Shannon's* Brigade at Lucknow, in which one may look in vain for any indication of a Royal Marine.

It is rather hard luck on the Royal Corps, and it is not to be wondered at that at times it feels just a little bit sore like the old soldier who has been quoted.

The *Shannon*, a steam frigate of fifty-one guns, when commissioned on 13th September, 1856, was considered the finest ship of her class afloat. How it was that such a ship commanded by such a Captain as William Peel was not able to get the pick of the seamen who had been through the Russian War, does not appear, but according to an Officer of the R.M.A.[2] who took passage in her when she left England for Hong Kong in 1857, her crew, splendid fellows as they soon afterwards proved themselves, were not considered up to the average. "There was no reason," says this officer, "why, in 1857, a ship bearing the name of the *Shannon* ought not to have been manned by the *élite* of the seamen in the service. But what was the fact? A telegram came down from the Commanding Officer directing a detachment of Marines and Artillery Officers to embark. In four hours we were on board the *Shannon*. During the passage to China it was discovered that we had a most inferior crew as far as the seamen were concerned, and that it consisted of much of the refuse that had been hanging about the "Hard" and elsewhere. Fortunately the ship was commanded by Captain William Peel, a name that can never be mentioned before Naval or Marine Officers without a feeling of sorrow at his untimely end, and a feeling of pride in such a man. Fortunately she was commanded by him, and a most efficient class of officers, and the men with

---

[1] Henry Derry, Pte., R.M.L.I., The quotations are from an interview which Sergt. W. Turner, late R.M.L.I., had with him, and which was published in the "Globe and Laurel," Feb. 7th, 1902.
[2] Captain Studdert, late R.M.A., speaking at the Royal United Service Institution, 24 April, 1871.

the greatest care and attention during a long voyage were brought to a state of discipline and to some degree of knowledge in their duties. I was embarked as a supernumerary R.M.A. Officer, and I was called upon during the voyage to assist in carrying on the gunnery duties of the ship. Also the N.C.O's that I had with me of the supernumerary detachment who were competent to do so, were employed in giving instruction to the crew." "Captain Peel placed the utmost confidence in them (the Marines), and on leaving the *Shannon* at Hong Kong, he thanked the detachment on the quarter-deck for the example it had shewn the ship's company, and for the assistance the N.C.O's had given the gunnery staff on board. He had all hands on deck, and they heartily cheered us as with heavy hearts we left the old ship for the gunboat alongside."[1]

The news of the Mutiny met the *Shannon* on her arrival at Singapore on 11th June, but she had to continue her voyage to Hong Kong where she dropped anchor on the 2nd July. Although, as we have seen, she disembarked the supernumerary Marines she had brought out for service in the Chinese War, she very soon afterwards took on board a considerable number under the command of Lieut.-Col. Lemon who were destined to garrison Fort William, Calcutta. Here it may be said in passing, they remained till November when, having been disappointed in seeing service in India, they were only too glad to be ordered back to China where they had plenty of opportunities of smelling powder. The *Shannon* and the *Pearl* arrived in the Hooghly at 5 p.m. on the 5th August, much to the relief of the European inhabitants of Calcutta, who felt greatly reassured under the formidable batteries of the two war-ships. But Captain William Peel was by no means content to lie off Calcutta doing Guard duty. He at once organised a Naval Brigade consisting of 450 men from his own ship, and 155 from the *Pearl*. The author of "The Shannon's Brigade in India,"[2] from which these figures are taken does not specify how many Marines were included in these numbers, though he mentions their two Officers, Captain Gray and Lieutenant Stirling. The old Marine who has been already quoted gives their numbers as "140 Reds, and 15 Blues," which is probably correct, being just about what the aggregate of the two ships' detachments might be expected to amount to. He also says that Lieutenant Byam landed with them. "We had to land a siege train and 68 pounders,"[3] he goes on, "and it was no joke to move about with rafts, but, by Jove, they were stubborn customers over soft ground. We had to be our own horses and bullocks, and face the fiddle and the enemy too, I can tell you, in a blazing sun. There was no galloping away with our guns, like the soldiers did. We had to stick to them under all conditions. We went up the river until the ship[4] bumped, then we anchored head and stern, made a raft of barrels, booms, and planks, hoisted out guns, took four days' provisions then manned boats, and started again, cheering. But we soon had to save our breath and pull for dear life. I don't quite remember how long we were going up, but it was night and day.[5] As we approached the narrows, there were

---

[1] The R.M.A. may therefore justly claim a share in the fine gunnery developed by the *Shannon's* men during the Mutiny.
[2] Lt. E. H. Verney, R.N. The *Pearls* did not leave for some time after the *Shannons*. They and a second contingent from the *Shannon*, 120 strong, joined Peel at Allahabad, on 25th October. The first *Shannon's* Brigade left Calcutta 18th Aug., 1857.
[3] Ten 8-inch guns and two brass field-pieces.—"Shannon's Brigade in India." 1862.
[4] The River Steamer *Chunar*.
[5] The distance by river from Calcutta to Allahabad is 809 miles.

constant delays; the rafts kept going aground on the mud banks, which were infested with alligators, and the stench was awful. No, I don't recollect any of the Sepoys showing up on our way up, and we didn't know where we were going. All that we understood was the anxiety of Captain Peel to get on as fast as possible; he used to say, 'Hurry up, lads, or we shall be too late.' However we landed all right, and started inland. When we had gone about two miles, our right flank was fired into from some rifle pits, and the order to halt was given.[1] Then Captain Peel led the way to the pits, and in among them he went pell-mell, slashing to right and left. I was in disgrace, and was right hand man of the Red Marines. I left the ranks and went after Peel, followed by Corporal Head, who had orders to bring me back. He said that I had one black chiel in my mouth, and one in each hand, banging their heads together. However they soon cleared out, and Corporal Head and I helped Captain Peel, who was quite faint from loss of blood, out of a rifle-pit. I was threatened with a Court Martial for leaving the ranks without orders. While the above was taking place, the guns had been used freely, and several men were badly hurt."

It is not at all clear what action the old Marine is describing. The Naval Brigade took part in an action at Kajwa, on November 1st, marching with their guns from Allahabad to Cawnpore. A portion of it under Captain Peel himself formed part of a force under the command of Colonel Powell, C.B., of the 53rd. On arrival at the latter place information was received that a body of mutineers, about 3000 strong, was occupying a strong position at Kajwa, twenty-four miles to the North West. An attack was at once planned and successfully carried out. Powell was killed early in the fighting, and Peel assuming command, as next senior officer, manoeuvred the little force of 500 men with so much skill that he cut the enemy completely in two, drove them from their position, and captured their guns. The British paid for their victory with a casualty list of 95 killed and wounded. Among the latter was Lieutenant Stirling, R.M., who was severely wounded in the calf of the leg.[2]

The great object which the British generals had set themselves to carry out was the relief of the little European garrison of the Residency at Lucknow, which had long been closely beleaguered by an immense host of Mutineers. On November 13th, the Naval Brigade, with eight heavy guns, was before the city of Lucknow.[3] The whole relieving army under Sir Colin Campbell did not amount to more than 5000 men of all arms and, after capturing a position taken up by the enemy at the high ground about Dilkusha[4] Park to the S.E. of the City, had to fight its way round its Eastern end before it could advance in the direction of the Residency which was situated to the North West of it. The heavy Naval guns were of great use in "crushing" the Sepoys out of their position on the flank of the advance, and early on the morning of the 16th the British columns were marching straight for the Residency. But the Sikandarbagh, a high-walled enclosure, about 150

---

[1] I have been unable to find any corroborative account of this skirmish, and of Capt. Peel's wound.—C.F.
[2] This officer must have been hors-de-combat for a considerable time, as he does not seem to have received the Medal for the Relief of Lucknow, as did Captain Gray. He was present when the Brigade left Cawnpore, April 7th, 1858, to return to Calcutta.
[3] Now only 250 strong. Other portions of it had been detached to various quarters where heavy guns were required.
[4] Dilkusha—"Heart's Delight." "A strangely fantastic looking domicile it is too, built apparently of nothing but domes and arches, and points and peaks and cupolas in endless variety."—"Up Among the Pandis."

yards square with towers at each angle—suddenly barred their way. Not much further on the Shah Najif, a Mosque in a garden surrounded by a high loopholed wall presented another formidable obstacle, while to its right rear a large masonry building formerly used as an Officers' Mess, defended by a ditch twelve feet wide with a high loopholed wall on the further side was also crammed with our mutinous Indian soldiery. Hesitation would have been fatal. The Horse Artillery guns and a heavy battery of 18-pounders were rushed into action against the towering Sikandarbagh at close quarters, and after a small hole had been breached in a bricked up doorway, the 93rd and the Sikhs got in.

A Sikh of the 4th Rifles was the first to reach the opening, but was shot dead even as he sprang through it; he was followed by an officer of the 93rd who, literally flying through the breach with the force of his rush, landed unscathed on the other side. Eight or nine men followed this gallant officer. They succeeded in holding their own against overwhelming odds until the main gate was burst open and their comrades dashed in to their aid, and after a desperate resistance left nothing inside but 2000 Sepoy corpses. It was a "murder grim and great," but our men, maddened by the atrocities committed by the mutineers on helpless women and children, seized every opportunity of giving them " a Cawnpore dinner "— six inches of cold steel. Meanwhile, the Naval Brigade guns had pushed on and devoted their attention to the Shah Najif upon which for some time no impression was made. "The enemy, about 4 o'clock, got a heavy gun to bear upon us, from the opposite bank of the river, and their very first shot blew up one of Peel's tumbrils, whilst their deadly musketry obliged him to withdraw the men from one of his pieces and diminished the fire of the others. The men were falling fast. Even Peel's usually bright face became grave and anxious. Sir Colin sat on his white horse, exposed to the whole storm of shot, looking intently on the Shah Najif, which was wreathed in volumes of smoke from the burning buildings in its front, but sparkled all over with the bright flash of small arms. It was now apparent that the crisis of the battle had come. Our heavy artillery could not subdue the fire of the Shah Najif; we could not even hold permanently our present advanced position under it. But retreat to us there was none."[1] The advance had been made by a narrow lane now crowded by camp followers, baggage animals, and various impedimenta. To fall back that way, which was the only way, would spell disaster. Nor could the women and children in the Residency, anxiously expecting relief, be abandoned. There was nothing for it but to persevere in defiance of all odds and all obstacles. More guns were brought up. Peel shoved forward two of his guns to within a few feet of the walls. His gunners redoubled their efforts while the Marines and the 93rd Highlanders endeavoured with their rifles to keep down the fire which rained on the bluejackets. But the walls were impenetrable. Evening was fast coming on. A couple of rocket tubes were brought up and their fiery projectiles, skimming over the high walls, descended in a blazing deluge inside. Under cover of this the guns were drawn off. Meanwhile fifty men, under Colonel Adrian Hope of the 93rd, crept round to a fissure that had been discovered in the wall some way to the right by Sergeant Paton[2] of that Regiment. An entry

---
[1] Blackwood's Magazine, Oct., 1858.
[2] Sergeant Paton received the V.C. for this service.

Sir Colin Campbell.   Capt. Hope Johnstone.

Lieut.-Col. Metcalfe.   Major Norman.   Capt. Allison.
Capt. Allgood.   Major-Gen. Sir W. Mansfield.
Sir David Baird.

THE ADVANCE TO THE ASSAULT OF THE SECUNDRABAGH.
From a Contemporary Sketch by Capt. W. Hope Crealock, 90th Regt.

THE SHAH NAJIF.   From a Contemporary Photograph.

was made without discovery by the garrison, the opening was enlarged by the sappers, the troops poured in and the Shah Najif was won.

Our Marine veteran gives the following account of this incident, though he seems to have forgotten the exact locality where it occurred. "About 4 o'clock our battery opened fire, and continued till dark, commencing again next morning. The Marines were detailed for outpost duty and rifle pits, picking off the gunners from the batteries, to save Captain Peel's men, who were within close range, and suffered very much. 'It's no use unless we are close up,' he said, 'we must bring the whole place about our ears, and then get to close quarters.' There was a Scotch sergeant who came with a message. 'Ah mon,' he said, 'ye are the very de'ils to fight. Who's yon with the glass ? He's a grand chiel with a charmed life. Peel did ye say,' I've a message for him. Sure I'll be killed dead with all these marbles flying about.' Just then a gunner's mate asked, 'What will ye give me if I just take that weather-cock off yon mosque' ? 'Oh, ye'll nae do it.' Next shot, down it came. 'Ah, laddie, ye can shoot, take a wet out of my bottle, and then take me to your Captain.' 'Just dodge the bullets, for Sir Colin awaits my return, and don't forget the bairns at Cawnpore, and their mithers, boys.' It turned out afterwards that the Scotch sergeant was only spying about for an opening, for later on he came back with a party of men and entered a breach in the wall near the river, which the Naval Brigade, who were ordered to turn their guns on another part of the town, had made. The sappers soon made the hole bigger, and General Hope Grant (*sic*) led the 93rd through and opened the big gates. The place was then supposed to have been taken, so that night we had a rest. Well, some of us did, and others did not, for there was sniping all night in all directions. In the morning we were astonished to find that the city was still held by thousands of Sepoys, and they gave us a warm reception Captain Peel, during the night, had put all his guns in working order, and opened fire at the first streak of light, directing his gunners to shell a large building they called the Mess, and for about three hours our 68 pounders did make a mess of it, I can tell you. About 3 p.m. an officer was seen on the highest part of the city waving a Union Jack, and then we Joeys got mixed up. The question was, 'Who are we to obey, Captain Peel or General Outram ? ' This was soon settled, for said Captain Peel, ' I want a guard for my guns.' We then had orders to retire, and our work was cut out to get our guns back to the river." It is to be feared that the narrator of the above account was somewhat confused in his recollections, but as he was over 75 years of age at the time he recounted his reminiscences, his errors are excusable, especially as in most battles, the man in the ranks gets but a partial idea of what is going on. Thus it is evident that he is inclined to mix up the city of Lucknow itself with the various fortified buildings that were successively attacked by the relieving force. The " officer waving a Union Jack on the highest part of the city " must have been Captain Wolseley[1] planting the British Flag on the roof of the Mess House, which, it would appear, he and his comrades thought a signal to advance. So, too, when he speaks of Hope Grant he evidently means Adrian Hope. The Scotch Sergeant must have been Sergt. Paton of the 93rd, although he had forgotten the Regiment

---

1 Afterwards Field-Marshal Lord Wolseley.

and thought it was the 42nd. But this story, coming from a Marine actually present is none the less very interesting.

During the withdrawal of the hard-pressed garrison of the Residency, the Naval guns were of the greatest service in distracting the attention of the enemy by their bombardment of the Kaisar Bagh, their principal stronghold. As breaches began to appear in its walls the rebels busied themselves in preparing for the assault that they expected would follow, instead of attacking the somewhat extended and weak screen of troops which protected the flank of the retiring garrison. Some days later the Naval Brigade with Sir Colin Campbell's relieving force was back at Cawnpore, where it repulsed the Sepoy artillery with its heavy guns and prevented the destruction of the great bridge of boats over the Ganges which secured our communication with Allahabad. A week later, one of its guns was mainly instrumental in the capture of a bridge over a canal which proved the key of the enemy's position. The enemy made one stand after this behind an entrenchment from which they were quickly driven by the bayonets of the Marines under Captain Gray, and of 162 men of the 53rd Regiment. In the "round-up" of various rebel forces which followed the defeat of Tantia Topi's[1] army at Cawnpore, the guns of the Naval Brigade were of great use at the battle of Futtehgurh. The entrance to this place, in which a considerable body of rebels had congregated, was barred by the River Kali Naddi. As the British approached, the rebels set themselves to work to destroy the suspension bridge which would enable the avenging Europeans to cross the river. They began the work on 31st December, 1857, but with so little energy that an advanced force pushed forward by Sir Colin to prevent its destruction, and which included three guns belonging to the Naval Brigade, was able to drive them back early on the morning of New Year's Day, 1858. By 7 o'clock, the bridge was in a fit state for the Army to cross. In the battle that followed the Naval guns dismounted one of the enemy's cannon which was concealed behind the corner of a house and was annoying the British very much indeed, and followed this up by blowing up its tumbrill. The infantry advanced, panic seized the enemy, who streamed out of Futthegurh only to be met and cut to pieces in their flight by the cavalry.

According to the old Marine who has been so often quoted, the Naval Brigade on this occasion came up the river in boats. He says "One night, about December, 1857, Captain Peel gave orders to up anchor, man the boats, and take the rafts in tow, and up the river we went again till we came to a suspension bridge which the black devils were pulling down as fast as they could. There was a General[2] on shore, keeping in touch with our boats etc., so despite the warm reception we received, we drove the Sepoys off between us, and helped the sappers to repair the bridge. Then we had a fog, under cover of which some rebel battalions brought down some guns, one of which, a 24-pounder, they sandbagged in a shed. However we cleared away the 68 pounder on the raft, soon put that out of action, and blew up the whole concern. There was a lot of fighting going on on shore, one regiment, partly under cover by the bank, got dreadfully mauled, but charged the guns,

---

[1] A Mahrattra chief, who under the orders of the infamous Nana Sahib had superintended the massacre at Cawnpore. He was the only native among the rebels who shewed any great qualities of generalship. On this occasion he commanded the mutinous Gwalior Contingent, the best of the rebel army.

[2] He evidently means Col. Adrian Hope, whose Brigade had been pushed forward to secure the bridge.

taking several, and then our turn came again, for as the cavalry and Sikhs put them to flight, we simply mowed them down by hundreds."

Some of the Naval Brigade, with their big guns, took part in the final capture of Lucknow in March, 1858, but no information is forthcoming as to any special services of the Royal Marines. After the fall of that city its work was regarded as completed and it started for Cawnpore on its way back to Calcutta and its ships. At Cawnpore it had to mourn the loss of its splendid leader, Captain William Peel, R.N. Wounded in the thigh by a musket ball when selecting a position for his guns at the final attack on Lucknow, he became convalescent and was brought down to Cawnpore, where on 20th April, he was struck down by confluent small-pox. Too weak to withstand the progress of the disease he succumbed seven days later.

The Naval Brigade had left Cawnpore on 7th April in three detachments, the first to leave being its 1st Bluejacket Company and the Royal Marines with whom went their two Officers, Captain Gray and Lieutenant Stirling. We need not follow them to describe their welcome in Calcutta, but in conclusion have to record some of the doings of a small detachment of thirty Marines under the command of Lieutenant Pym,[1] who with 130 of the Naval Brigade, under Captain Sotheby, R.N., formed part of a column under Colonel Rowcroft which, with two others had been organised to clear the rebels out of the districts North of Benares and East of Oude. Rowcroft's column, which besides the Bluejackets and Marines, comprised fifty Bengal Police, and 350 Nepaulese troops with four 12-pounder Howitzers, marched from its entrenched camp at Mirwa, about forty-nine miles from Chapra, to attack a rebel Army estimated at 1200 regular Sepoys and 4000 armed adventurers which lay at Sebanpore. This was on 26th December, 1857. "The enemy's position was strong. They occupied a village, covered in front by a tank with high banks, and on the right by a tope of trees. Rowcroft halted within half-a-mile of the place and rode forward to reconnoitre. He resolved to render useless the enemy's strong positions in the centre and on the right by turning his left. He did this with great coolness and success. The Nepaul troops behaved splendidly under fire. Sotheby of the Naval Brigade managed the artillery with great skill. The Minie rifles of the Royal Marines, directed by Lieutenant Pym, produced a striking effect. The result was that the enemy, attacked a little after 10 o'clock, were completely beaten by half-past one, forced back from Sebanpore, and followed six miles further to Majaoli, and thence driven across the Gandak, with the loss of one large iron gun. Rowcroft followed up his victory the next day by crossing the river and destroying the homesteads of the leading rebels."[2]

In the Autumn of 1858 the *Pearl's* Naval Brigade took part in the Relief of Bhansi, and its experiences are well told in the Diary of Quartermaster F. Butler, late R.M.L.I., who was present during the operations:—

"6th September, 1858:—News reached our Camp at Bustee that 200 Sikhs who were protecting a friendly Rajah at that place (Bhansi) were besieged by the enemy.

---

[1] This officer was sent with a detachment to garrison Patna.
[2] "History of the Indian Mutiny." Col. G. B. Malleson, C.S.I. 1879.

"At 4 p.m. one troop of Bengal Yeomanry Cavalry and one troop of Madras Cavalry marched, and at 6 p.m. a detachment consisting of twenty Marines, fifty-eight Seamen (with two Naval guns and a rocket tube), and seventy-two Officers and men of the 13th Regiment marched to support the Cavalry, the roads were covered with water, and in some places up to our knees in mud. On account of the bad state of the roads bullock-carts were sent to assist us to-night. Guns and provisions were carried on elephants, it being impossible to drag them through the water and mud. Often someone would slip off the muddy road into deep water and have to be pulled up again, and Jack often remarked that we wanted our boats with us. We kept on our journey till midnight when we reached a dry spot, we then halted for our party to close up, the elephants were unloaded, a dram of rum served out, and we rested till daylight, when the bullock carts were sent back to camp, elephants loaded and we started again. The roads were worse this morning than last night, but having daylight we got along better, the sun was very hot, and knocked up several of our party. We kept on till noon when we came to a nullah (river) which was not fordable, but a boat was found by the natives and we commenced to cross, halting on the opposite bank till all had crossed. The elephants were unloaded and they swam across. After a meal and sharing our grog with the 13th, who had none, we pushed on again; the first four miles was fairly good road, we then forded a nullah and it was as bad as ever, sometimes up to the waist in water, at other times up to your knees in mud. The Marines under Sergt. Butler were now hurried forward to join the Cavalry, whom they found at 9 p.m. encamped, the remainder of the force arrived at 10 p.m., all very tired and wet; we pitched tents alongside the Cavalry, made some tea and laid down on the damp ground for the night.

8th September.—The Cavalry marched at 3 a.m., leaving twenty Sowars[1] for our rearguard, we struck tents and marched at daylight; the roads were very bad, and the sun very hot; several of our party were knocked up and had to have a ride on the elephants, and the dhoolies[2] were all occupied. We halted several times to close up; at noon we arrived on the opposite bank of the river to Bhansi, the enemy on the approach of the Cavalry retreated, and the Sikhs sent some boats over for us to cross the river Raptee, which we found as wide as the Medway. The Marines were left as rearguard until the Infantry and guns had crossed; the cavalry did not cross but moved a few miles along the bank of the river. Having had nothing to eat all day, we looked about us and found a field of Indian corn, in a green state, which washed down with water from the river, did duty as breakfast and dinner. The Marines crossed at 4 p.m., and marched about a mile to the town and found shelter from the sun in some mud huts. As we had out-marched our provisions the Sikhs made some chupatties (a sort of thin cake, baked on a hot iron plate), they eat something like sawdust, and require plenty of water to wash them down with. We found the green Indian corn a little better.

9th.—We were to re-cross the river this morning and follow the enemy, but we were so fatigued that we had to rest till 3 p.m., when we crossed, being reinforced by 100 Sikhs. We had, however, to leave at Bhansi twelve Seamen and Marines,

[1] Native Cavalry troopers.
[2] A species of litter for the wounded.

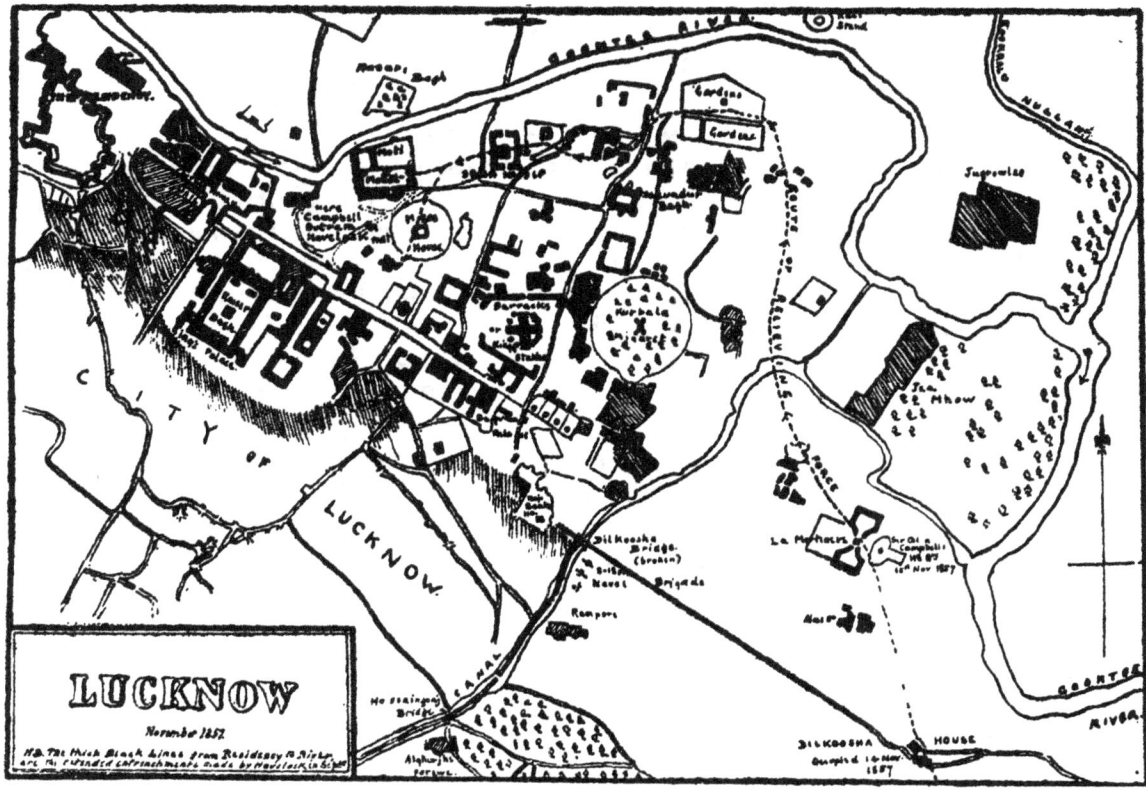

and twelve of the 13th, who were quite knocked up. After a march of four miles along the bank of the river we came upon the enemy's rearguard as they were retreating. The cavalry and guns were pushed forward, and succeeded in cutting down forty-two of the rebels, our loss being three horses killed and one wounded; the ground was too wet for the Infantry to take an active part. We returned to Bhansi at 9 p.m,, greatly fatigued and wet through.

10th.—Brigadier Fisher, of the Madras Army, arrived on the opposite bank of the river with reinforcements from Gorrockpore. At 3 p.m. we again crossed and joined the Brigadier. Sun very hot.

11th.—Rested to-day. Reinforcements very tired.

Sunday, 12th.—Marched at 5 a.m. to follow up the enemy, who appear to stop when we stop. About six miles from Bhansi we came upon the ground where the cavalry charged last Thursday, the dead bodies and horses were lying about in all directions, and the vultures were enjoying their morning meal. We halted at 11 a.m. and encamped. Sun very hot.

Monday, 13th.—Marched at 2 a.m. to Dumooreahgunge (12 miles). On nearing the place the advanced guard was fired on from some entrenchments, the cavalry was sent to the front, guns got off the elephants, mounted and hurried forward, and the Marines and Seamen doubled up to support the guns; the Infantry formed line and marched steadily to the front; we doubled across paddy-fields and through the water for about three miles, when we found that we were chasing the enemy's rearguard, who were retreating to Intwa. The ground being so bad we marched back to Dumooreahgunge and encamped.

Tuesday, 14th.—The cavalry and 13th crossed the river at 1 a.m.; Naval Brigade and Staff at 2 a.m., intending to attack the Fort at Intwa. We marched about a mile along the road when the cavalry rode back and reported the road impassable for guns and Infantry; there being no dry ground to encamp we returned to the ground we left in the morning; the Madras Cavalry and Infantry were sent to Bhansi to reinforce the Sikhs, and the remainder of the force marched to Bustee, where we arrived at 7 a.m., on the 17th, glad to get back to our huts after ten days harassing work during the rainy season in Bengal."[1]

Here we must leave this attempt to follow the services of the Royal Marines in the Great Mutiny. The numbers employed were but small, yet the occasion was great. Further particulars of the work of the Naval Brigade may be found in the writings of many authors, but as the Marine veteran who has been so frequently quoted says: "You see, chum, I can't separate we Joeys from the Jacks, nor the Jacks from we Joeys, so we get lost in the Naval Brigade."

NOTE.

NOTE I.—INDIAN MARINE REGIMENTS.

It may be of interest to note that there are still two Native Indian Regiments which may claim to have a Marine origin—the 69th Punjabis and the 121st Pioneers, raised originally in 1795 as "The Marine Battalion," and still, I believe, sometimes called by that name. Both the above regiments bear the motto "Khooshke Wu Turee "— "By Sea and Land." The badge of the 69th is a Galley with the motto above it in Persian characters, that of the 121st "An Anchor and Laurel Wreath." Neither, however, appears to have been raised to perform the actual Sea-Service which is the principal *raison-d'etre* of the Royal Marines. The 69th was raised between 1762-5 as "the 10th Battalion of Coast Sepoys," which may have entailed a certain amount of coastal work afloat. The duties of the 121st seem to have been more on the lines of those now carried out by the French *Infanterie de Marine*, for it was raised for the purpose of duty in the Islands of Sumatra, Penang, etc. It consisted of twelve companies of 100 Privates each, commanded by Captains, with seven Lieutenants to command the detached portions of the Corps. These officers were to be borrowed from the regiments of the Line, from which they were to be occasionally relieved, when they would rejoin their own Corps. In 1801 the Marine Corps was formed into a regiment on the same establishment as those of the line and denominated the "20th, or Marine Regiment." In 1809 it was augmented to 16 N.C.O's, and 130 Privates a Company, to enable its two Battalions to completely relieve each other for duty in the islands. In the operations attending the conquest of Java in 1811, the 2nd Battalion, augmented by volunteers from other Native Infantry Corps, "nobly maintained and enhanced the reputation of the Bengal Infantry, having by their steadiness and gallantry in action, and by their discipline and good conduct in all situations, excited general admiration and esteem."

---

[1] From "The Globe and Laurel," September, 1893

THE STORMING OF CANTON, 28th DECEMBER, 1857.

From a Lithograph.

CHAPTER XXVII.

THE CHINA WAR OF 1856-7-8-9-60.

" The bursting shell, the gateway wrenched asunder,
The rattling musketry, the flashing blade,
And ever and on, in tone of thunder
The diapason of the cannonade."—*Longfellow.*

ON the 8th October, 1856, the lorcha[1] *Arrow*, under British colours, was boarded by a Chinese Officer and men, and twelve of the native crew carried off, whilst she lay at anchor off Canton. The remonstrances of Sir John Bowering, the British Consul, proving ineffectual, the Admiral on the China Station, Sir Michael Seymour, was called upon to take action, and it was determined to seize the defences of that important city. On the 23rd and 24th October, the four Barrier Forts were captured and their guns disabled, and Blenheim Fort and Macao Fort mounting 86 guns, and situated on an island in the middle of the Canton River, a little below the city, and three or four smaller fortifications were occupied. On the morning of the 24th the small detachments of Royal Marines, which were already in Canton for the protection of the British factory, were reinforced, and later on the remainder of the Marines were landed under Captain Penrose, R.M.L.I., bringing up the total on shore to 199 men. The next day the important Fort known as "Dutch Folly," close to the city, was occupied. About mid-day the British quarter was attacked by a body of Chinese troops supported

---

[1] A Chinese Native Craft.

by a much larger force which occupied the streets in rear, but they were promptly repulsed by the Marines, who killed fourteen of them.

On the 27th and 28th the ships aided by a detachment of the Royal Artillery which had come up from Hong Kong, and manned two 32-pounders in "Dutch Folly" fort, opened fire on the Compound of Yeh, the High Commissioner, and on the troops on the hills behind the city, near Gough's Fort,[1] and on the suburbs between the river and the city wall, the object being to clear a way to the wall itself. This suburb was seen in flames, and the bombardment having been continued till 2 p.m. on the 29th, the Seamen and Royal Marines advanced under a heavy fire to a breach which the cannonade had made in the city wall, stormed it and diverging to the right and left, in ten minutes were in complete possession of the defences between two of the Gates with the field-pieces in the breach. At this time the Marines were considerably harassed by the fire of a party of Chinese who were well sheltered by an angle of the wall. Lieut. Swale, with Acting Lance-Corporal Lyne and six men, was sent to dislodge them. Having effected his object and having in the heat of the moment pursued them too far, they discharged a gingall with fatal effect, killing two men, mortally wounding one, and severely wounding two others. Lieut. Swale was also slightly wounded. Finding himself with but half his original detachment and at least 500 yards from any support he was on the point of retreating when Corporal Lyne said, "No, sir, we must not leave these bodies," and at once advanced to the place from which the gingall had been fired, and discharged his musket into the enemy. Captain Boyle, R.M., now arrived with a reinforcement, and the detachment fell back with their killed and wounded. Corporal Lyne was especially mentioned for his gallant conduct on this occasion. At sunset the bluejackets re-embarked, and the Marines returned to their quarters. The casualties sustained by the Marines in this affair amounted to three killed and ten wounded.

On the 3rd November the bombardment was resumed, and on the 5th and 6th French Folly Fort mounting twenty-six heavy guns and a fleet of twenty-three war junks which lay under its protection, were attacked, the fort captured, and the junks burnt. On the 12th the two Wantong Island Forts were attacked and taken possession of by the boats and the Royal Marines after a considerable, though ill-directed resistance of about an hour. They were fully manned, and had 200 guns in position. The Chinese stood to their guns till the British were actually in the embrasures. The day following the Anmunghoy Forts on the opposite side of the Bogue entrance to those already taken and mounting 210 heavy guns were also captured without any casualty. The Chinese retaliated on the 14th December by burning the British factories, but the Admiral was not to be driven from his foothold in the city, and determined to hold on to the gardens with the Church and Club-house, which were at once put into a state of defence, and surrounded with an entrenchment. The garrison at this time consisted of two Companies of the 59th Regiment, some Artillery, and the Royal Marine detachment from H.M.S. *Calcutta*. The detachment from H.M.S. *Sybille* was sent to Dutch Folly Fort, and that of the *Nankin* to Macao Fort. The Chinese during the Naval operations

---

[1] *Vide* Plan.

BATTLE OF FATSHAN CREEK, 1st JUNE, 1857.   From a painting in possession of Genl. R. C. Boyle.

had frequently endeavoured to destroy the British men-of-war by means of fire-rafts and floating mines, but without the least success. Possibly in reprisal for this the Admiral set fire to portions of the city. "This afternoon," writes a Naval officer, on the 11th January, 1857,[1] "we went on a burning expedition; each ship had her work laid out for her by the Admiral. The First Lieutenant and myself had charge of the party from this ship (H.M.S. *Encounter*). Many thousands of pounds worth were burned—even the market-place full of live fish, geese, pigs, etc., etc., on an extensive scale. The Chinese were maddened by the loss of property and life; manned the house-tops to hurl bricks and stones down on our heads, and the Chinese soldiers who were very thick, tried hard to cut us off; but as they had only spears we knocked them down like ninepins. Our party lost two men killed and one mortally wounded, and one officer of the 59th from a brick on his head. The Chinese got the bodies, and cut off their heads for the reward. One poor fellow, wounded, saw them cut the heads off, and, as soon as he could get a chance, he ran for the party, but got mortally wounded in his run. We were obliged to make such a sharp retreat that we could not recover their bodies although the Marines offered to go and try. These Marines are the finest fellows I have ever been with; the more danger we get into the firmer and more determined they are."

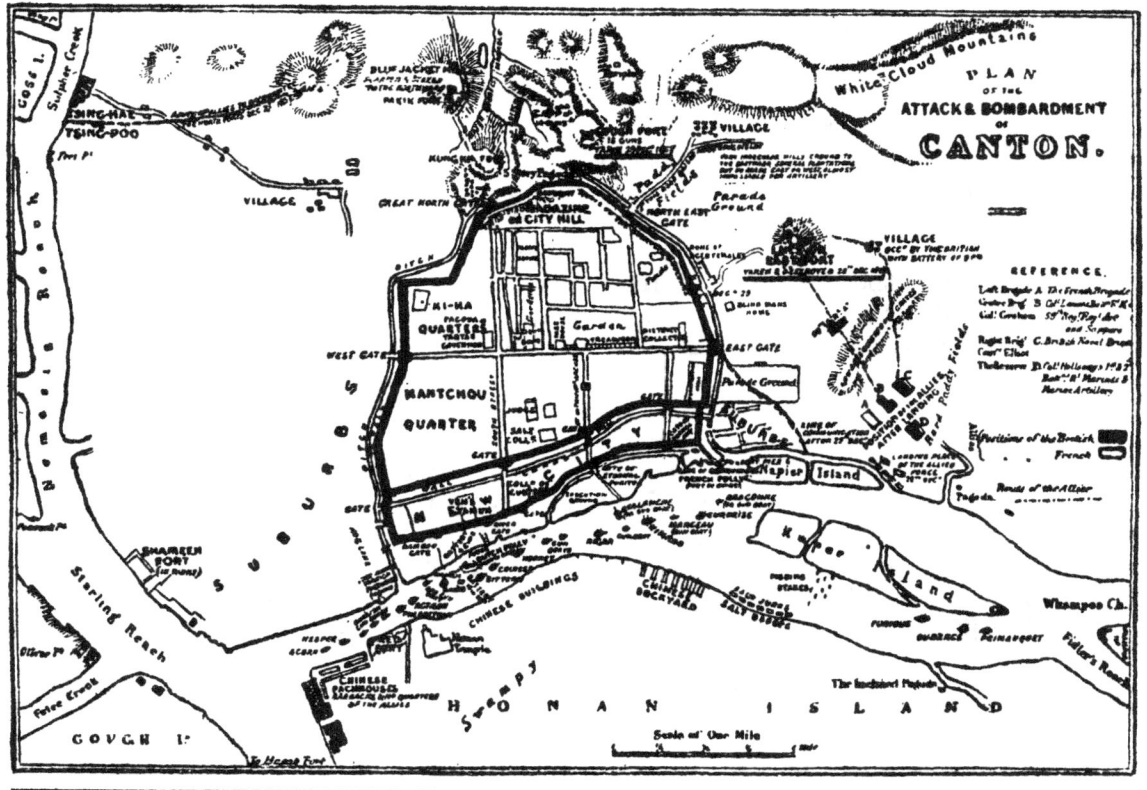

[1] Published in the "Illustrated London News."

From time to time more war junks were destroyed, and on the 25th and 27th May an attack was made on a large force of those vessels in Escape Creek, off the Canton River, and in the midst of the City of Tung-Chow, about twelve miles up the creek. At the latter place the crews of the junks took refuge in the houses, and opened a heavy fire with gingalls on the boats' crews as they were endeavouring to tow off the biggest junk, and destroy the rest. The only thing to be done was to land the Marines who created a diversion by charging into the streets of the city. It was a perilous duty, and they were lucky to escape with only nine men wounded A similar expedition was undertaken against a fleet of junks in Fatshan Creek on 1st June. The Marines present on this occasion amounted to 250 men with twelve officers and twenty-two N.C.Os. They went up either in the *Coromandel* with the Admiral, the *Haughty*, or in the boats which were towing behind. The junks, which were heavily armed, were in a position to sweep the channel as the British flotilla advanced and were supported by the fire of a fort perched on a hill on the left of the attack, and a six gun battery on the opposite side. Arrived at this point the Marines were landed and attacked the fort while the gunboats engaged the junks. The hill was steep, which proved a protection to the stormers as the volleys of grape shot discharged by the Chinese guns swept over their heads as the gunners were unable to give their pieces sufficient depression. Finding their fire unavailing, the Chinese rolled down 32 pound shot, and threw showers of stink-pots, and three-pronged spears. Commodore Elliott who had also landed, a midshipman, and Captain Boyle, who was in command of the Marines, ran a neck and neck race for the fort. When close up Captain Boyle fired his revolver at a Chinaman who he noticed aiming his matchlock at him. Panting from his run up hill, he missed him, whereupon the Chinaman rolled down two huge shot at him, and hurled a trident at the midshipman. But it was his last effort, a bullet from the Commodore finished his career. The Chinese gunners stuck to their posts till the Marines were within fifty paces of the embrasures; then they made a bolt down the back of the hill. The gunboats having gone on up the creek, the Marines descended that side of the hill which looked in the direction of the junks and stood in the paddy fields up to their waists in water, opened fire on the Chinamen, who, after abandoning their junks, were retreating across the country. In a short time the whole of the junks at this point (72 in number) were captured or blown up. Meanwhile, Commodore Keppel with seven boats, after running the gauntlet of the junks had gone on up another branch of the creek. Four miles further on he found twenty more large junks which he pursued almost into the City of Fatshan, after a chase of six miles. The Chinese turned out of the city in martial array, and came down to attack the boats. Keppel at once landed the few Marines he had with him who formed up and poured such a volley of Minie balls into the Fatshan Militia, that they went tumbling over one another into the town fosse. Several more junks were secured or destroyed, and the expedition returned to Canton. The casualties sustained by the Royal Marines were one sergeant and two privates killed, a bombardier and five privates wounded.

Operations lagged for a time. Canton was a city of 3,000,000 inhabitants, and no reinforcements except the 59th Regiment had reached the Admiral.

THE CHINA WAR OF 1856-7-8-9-60

Troops were detailed to proceed to China in 1857, but the outbreak of the Indian Mutiny had diverted them to Hindustan. Towards the end of the summer, however, orders were issued for the formation of a Brigade of Royal Marines for service in China. Colonel Holloway, R.M.A., was appointed Brigadier, his Brigade, consisted of two Battalions R.M.L.I. and about 100 R.M.A. The 1st Battalion formed from the Woolwich and Chatham Divisions was under the command of Lieut.-Col. Walsh, Lieut.-Col. Hocker commanded the 2nd, whose men came from Portsmouth and Plymouth. Major Schomberg was in charge of the R.M.A., and Major Travers, R.M.L.I., was appointed Brigade Major.

R.M. OFFICERS' MESS, NORTH WANTONG.

"The Marines are the boys for making themselves comfortable; they have turned this old joss-house into as neat a mess-room as you would wish to see.—"Illustrated London News."

The Brigade left England in August in the *Imperador* and *Imperatrice*, belonging to the Brazilian Steam Navigation Co., and the *Adelaide*, a big four-master, and arrived in the Canton River about the end of November. The North Wantong and Macao Forts were at once occupied by companies from the Brigade.

The Marines, about this time, were strengthened by the arrival of another Battalion under Colonel Lemon (generally referred to as the Provisional Battalion) which had left England some time before the other two, to take part in the suppression of the Indian Mutiny, but arriving at a time when the British forces had broken the back of the rebellion had remained doing garrison duty in Calcutta until it could be spared to go on to the new theatre of hostilities in the Celestial Empire. "The force now collected," wrote a newspaper[1] correspondent, "amounts

---

[1] "Illustrated London News."

to one Colonel, three Lieut.-Colonels, twenty-four Captains, seventy Subalterns, and 3000 rank and file, a noble body of men, acknowledged to be the finest Corps in the world. They are all in excellent health and spirits; at the time I write, not a man in hospital."

But the Expedition was going to be a bigger one than could be carried out by the Admiralty Forces alone. A considerable body of troops, both British and French, were to participate in bringing Mr. Commissioner Yeh to reason. General Van Straubenzee, C.B., was in command of the former, which besides the Marine Battalions, comprised detachments of the R.A., R.E., a Volunteer Company of Sappers, the 59th Regiment, and the 38th Madras Native Infantry. The French naval force was commanded by Admiral Rignault de Genouilly.

Due warning having been given, a slow bombardment was opened on Canton upon the 28th December. From the moment that a yellow flag, the signal to commence, floated out upon H.M.S. *Plegethon*, a steady and carefully directed fire was concentrated upon the walls both from the ships, from the captured fort known as Dutch Folly, and from the guns of the R.A. and R.M.A. "All night the city was girt with a line of flame. The approach of morning was indicated by a suspension of the rocket practice, and by the re-opening of the mortar battery with redoubled energy. As the day broke, the flames sank down and the sun rose upon a perfectly smokeless city."[1]

Meanwhile, the European forces had been effecting their landing close to the city, and formed up in the following order:—British Naval Brigade on the right. Next came the R.M. Provisional Battalion, with the 59th Regiment, R.A. and R.E. French Naval Brigade on the left. Col. Holloway's Royal Marine Brigade and the R.M.A. were in reserve.

Directly the ships detailed to enfilade the eastern wall of the city ceased fire the troops moved forward to the assault, and for the next two hours nothing was visible to the spectators in the ships and the captured forts but smoke and nothing heard but the rattle of musketry and loud cheering. A young officer of the 2nd Battalion R.M.[2] gives the following account of his experiences in a letter written home after the capture of the city walls.

"The troops were all conveyed up the river in gunboats, and landed at the furthest point beyond the city. Our battalion was the last to disembark, so that on coming up to the scene of action we found we were behindhand, as the French, the 59th Regiment, and Colonel Lemon's Battalion of Marines had taken Lynn's Fort,[3] with only a few men wounded. However, it could not be helped, so we piled arms about a mile from the work, and set about our dinner. . . . The 1st Battalion was sent up to the front about 6 o'clock that evening, and took up a position under Lynn's Fort, the guns of which, as well as some which the Royal Artillery and Royal Marine Artillery had with them, were turned against the town. The Chinese threw a great many rockets, but luckily did little damage with them; they also fired some shot and shell where our Battalion lay. You must know that a Chinese rocket is not at all like an English one, although fired in the same way.

---
1 "Times" correspondent.
2 Lt. W. H. Poyntz, afterwards Major and Chief Constable of Nottingham and of Essex.
3 This was the day previous.

ROYAL MARINES ABOUT TO LAND AT CANTON, 28TH DEC., 1857.—"Illustrated London News."

It is a thick arrow, with a heavy iron barbed head, which causes it to descend with great force, it is said to be poisoned, so that the wound is exceedingly dangerous. They make capital practice with it. I think I may say it is about their best weapon. You can see these rockets quite plainly; but from their zig-zag flight they are fearfully deceptive. It was with one of these young Thomson of the Naval Brigade was wounded, he is, poor fellow, since dead. We had not any tents with us, so we slept that night and next in the open. My company, under command of Captain Spratt, first of all escorted reserve ammunition from the landing place to the front, and at 8 o'clock the remainder of the 2nd Battalion were ordered forward under Colonel Hecker. When we got there the French and Naval Brigade had advanced to the attack; we followed. Just after we had passed Lynn's Fort, an order came from the General for the 1st Battalion to draw the Chinese from a very strong position where they were congregated in great numbers behind a wall, with sandbags and straw thrown up in front of it. They made almost their best stand here, as they held it for nearly two hours. Colonel Holloway was for driving them from their position at the point of the bayonet; but the General ordered the 1st Battalion to throw themselves into skirmishing order, and to dislodge them. The Chinese had also a small battery in a copse to the left of this, from which they annoyed us considerably with rockets and shell. There was splendid cover for skirmishing for about half-a-mile in the vicinity of this wall, so we were able to take advantage of it, and that accounts for the small loss here. The only wounded were Colonel Holloway, both his orderlies, and Lieut. Dadson[1] of ours; the latter, I am sorry to hear, is getting on unfavourably. Eight men were also wounded at this spot, two of them dangerously. . . . While this was going on the others were not idle. Two companies of our Battalion had been detached with scaling ladders, and placed them under cover of the French, the 59th, and Provisional Battalion. As soon as these were set up, the Naval Brigade mounted the breach in one place, and Cook's and Blake's Companies in another; the two latter were first within the walls. It is most extraordinary that the Chinese made so little opposition when the men were scaling the ramparts. They let our people get inside before they offered much resistance. Blake's Company met with a good deal, however; he had rather a hard fight for it, as it was ordered on by itself. He had to force one gate, where he had one man killed and eight wounded. Blake cut down three Chinamen with his own hand, and was complimented by the General for the splendid way he brought his men up, and his gallantry in leading them. . . . . As you may suppose, once having got inside the walls, it was short work with the Chinese. By dusk Canton was ours to all intents and purposes. The men were quartered on the walls. We are now in a large "joss-house," or temple filled with gods, with the exception of Colonel Holloway, our Brigadier, who resides in the yamun or palace of Governor Yeh. Of course ere this you will have read of the capture of this ruffian and the Tartar General. I was amongst those present when we bagged them. We took prisoners a lot of Tartar soldiers; they were taken by surprise, and had no arms, so we let the poor devils loose. On the same day that we bottled all these swells, the 59th and part of the 1st Battalion seized the Treasury, and got, it is said, an immensity of money. . . . Captain Bates was killed while superintending the placing of the scaling ladders, and Lord Gifford wounded in the arm."

One or two other incidents in the experiences of the Marines in the attack on Canton may be mentioned.

The attacking force, after the fall of Fort Lynn on 28th January, was distributed out of fire from the city walls along the whole eastern and north-eastern front, where they lay in the open, or in the shelter of such bamboo groves as were handy. An hour before daylight they fell in quietly and moved off to the attack. By some oversight the men of the Provisional Battalion of Marines had slung their small tin pannikins with the handles run on to the straps of their water-bottles. Moving off in the dusk and stumbling over unknown ground, now jumping from a bank, and anon attempting to double over roughly ploughed paddy fields, or dropping into a wet ditch to scramble up the other side, it can be well understood that the noise made by the ever clashing of the tin pannikin against the wooden water-bottle in the stillness of the early morning was like the jingling of the bells of a large flock of bell-wethers. If this had been in the face of an European enemy the result might have been disastrous, and even as it was there can be no doubt

---

[1] Lt. W. Portlock-Dadson, afterwards a Captain in the Royal Bodyguard.

the sound was wafted to the city walls, as when the day broke the Chinese were not caught napping, but were found at their guns along the walls from whence they lost no time in opening fire upon the advancing force."[1] "We had scaled the walls of Canton," says another writer, "and while driving the enemy along the ramparts, a company of the Provisional Battalion, Royal Marines, was ordered to seize and open the N.E. Gate in the Archway below the ramparts. This was done, but as the massive gates were thrown open and the Company rushed into the outwork or spur, a large open tub of loose gunpowder was tilted through an embrasure above. It came down the twenty-five feet with a crash, and left a heap of fully a cwt. of gunpowder piled at the base of the wall. The question was what to do with it as the Gate had to be held, and a serious explosion might at any moment occur while replying to and keeping down the fire from the street leading to the gate. There were no means then at hand for safely transporting such a mass, and it was decided that each man should take a little in the tin cover of his canteen and scatter it thinly among the grass in the open square of the gate. This was quickly done, and then, when the outer gate was also forced and a small stream of water discovered, the water was scattered over the powder and all twas thought safe. The rest of the Battalion now marched in after their fight on the N.E. Parade Ground, and piling arms in quarter column in the enclosure, fell out and sat down by their arms to await events. By this time the sun had gained power, had evaporated the water and dried the powder, and in one moment the whole surface of the ground was ablaze. All rose to their feet and those who knew nothing of the cause made a rush through the piles of arms, shouting 'A mine! a mine!' Down went the rifles in rows as the men made for the outer gate, but the panic was of short duration, as the fizz of the gunpowder left but a little smouldering grass. It is a marvel that no more harm was done than a few men somewhat scorched, for the rifles were all loaded, and although the stocks of some of them were charred not one exploded; nor did the ammunition in any of the pouches of the men although many of them were actually sitting in the blaze before they had time to rise. To have avoided such a possible catastrophe it would have been better to have laid a train from the mass, withdrawn the men for a few moments and got rid of it by an explosion, but mistakes are made ever day, and all's well that ends well."[1]

The Allied Force now settled down to garrison the captured city, and though the picket and patrol duties were naturally pretty arduous, both officers and men seem to have, on the whole, made themselves very fairly comfortable, and an officer of the Royal Marines[2] records in his memoirs that Canton "was allowed by all branches of the Service to have been about the happiest garrison that ever anyone had ever been stationed in; all pulled together, and no jealousy existed between the regiments composing it."

The garrison had a moderately peaceful time during the seventeen or eighteen months it held the big Chinese city, but for many weeks there was a nightly bombardment of rockets from the country outside the city, usually commencing at midnight, though but little damage resulted from this pyrotechnical display. As

---
[1] From "Globe and Laurel."
[2] "Per Mare, per Terram," Major Poyntz, R.M., 1892.

OFFICERS OF THE ROYAL MARINES BIVOUACKED ON THE WALLS OF CANTON.
—"Illustrated London News."

may be supposed, the Marines had the knack of making themselves at home in their new quarters at least as much as anyone else. "On New Year's Day," writes a correspondent, "I walked along the walls and was delighted with the 'coup d'œil.' It was a very hot day indeed, and to see the various arrangements of the Marines on the walls in making themselves comfortable was highly amusing. Some were reclining on luxurious Chinese chairs under an impromptu awning; others had erected a kind of tent with Celestial mosquito curtains. In one curious domicile a party of three, with Mandarin hats, and those enormous spectacles, were reading the "Illustrated London News," much to the amusement of passers-by; at another was a magnificent bearded Marine in full Mandarin toggery. His Highness was occupied in chopping wood. There could not be a better country for campaigning, as you find all you want handy."[1]

Early in 1858 reinforcements began to arrive in the shape of the 65th and 70th Bengal Native Infantry, and in the summer one or two expeditions were made into the surrounding country to let the Chinese know that we had not finished with them. The first of these was directed against the Chinese Headquarter Camp in the White Cloud Mountains, a few miles to the North of Canton, and was undertaken as a return for an absurd attack on the city which is thus described by an eyewitness.

---

[1] From "Illustrated London News."

"One very lovely night a curious spectacle was to be observed from the city walls, truly characteristic of the Celestial Empire. A considerable army came on to attack us, and as in many places the country was hilly, the path or track by which they advanced was cut into steps, shewing that discretion was considered the better part of valour. Nearly every soldier carried a lighted lantern, on the principle of, I presume, 'taking care of number one, and no light how can see.' They kept, however, at a respectful distance, and a few well-directed rockets and shell from the city walls soon doused their glims. It certainly was a novel, picturesque sight indeed, and would have been highly appreciated at Cremorne or Vauxhall Gardens."[1]

On the 2nd of June General Van Straubenzee with 100 men went out to reconnoitre in the direction of the White Cloud Mountains, and at a distance of five miles made out a large encampment which he estimated from the number of tents would probably contain a couple of thousand men. He sent back at once for reinforcements, and by 7 p.m. a force of 1400 men (including 80 Frenchmen) and eight guns had started. Half this force, consisting of the Royal Marines and a portion of the 59th with four guns, under Colonel Holloway, R.M., and Major Travers, R.M., proceeded to join the General. The other half, comprising a Battery of the R.A., twenty-five of the 70th N.I., and about 300 of the Naval Brigade, embarked in gunboats, and went down the river in order to land the next morning, at a point from which they could take the enemy in flank. When the advance began at daybreak the country was found impracticable for cannon, which had accordingly to be sent back, and the only thing in the nature of artillery which could be taken were a couple of rocket tubes manned by the R.M.A. About 11 a.m. the advanced guard sighted the enemy's camp and the General pushed on with it to reconnoitre, in doing which three officers and eight men were wounded. Owing to the intense heat a halt was ordered and the force remained in the shelter of a wood and village until the evening. This village had been held for a short while by some of the enemy and with the thermometer 90 deg. in the shade the Marines had attacked it, moving in three single files along the narrow ridges between the paddy fields which, themselves, were nothing but mud and slush. Major Travers led this advance, which was covered by the rocket tubes and supported by the 59th and the Naval Brigade. The Bluejackets had rigged themselves out in all sorts of extraordinary head-gear to keep off the sun. Many of them carried fans, and with their Union Jack surmounted by a Mandarin's hat the Brigade presented a sufficiently bizarre appearance.

The "Braves" who held the village did not wait for the Marines and their bayonets, but cleared out and took to the hills.

About 5 p.m. the force again advanced and crossed a mountain 1200 feet high, but on arrival at the site of the enemy's camp found that it had totally disappeared, tents and all. The force returned to Canton on the morning of the 4th having burnt three villages—a poor result considering the casualties sustained. Col. Wynne, R.E., and Major Travers, R.M., were slightly wounded by spent balls, Lieut. Rokeby, R.M., was dangerously wounded, twenty-six men were wounded,

---

[1] "Per Mare, per Terram," Major Poyntz.

three died from sun-stroke, and 200 of the 600 Marines engaged were laid up from the effects of the great heat. In August another expedition was despatched to attack the walled town of Nantow in retaliation for having fired on a flag of truce sent there with a message from the Governor of Hong-Kong. The expedition had to go by water in the gunboats, and although the General had made up his mind that it was best to attack it on the S.W., it was found impossible to effect a landing in that quarter on account of the rocks and very shoal water. The disembarkation was accordingly made on the S.E. of the city which entailed the advance to the walls being made through the streets of a populous suburb.

The advanced party consisted of the Naval Brigade, which was very soon engaged, a heavy fire of matchlocks and gingalls being opened from the front and the cross streets. The attack was made in two parallel lines, one advancing along a canal which intersected the suburb, the other close to the sea, the boats following just in rear of the heads of the two columns.

The inner line, moving along the canal, was composed of the 59th Regiment with the Royal Marines under Major Foote in reserve. But though in rear of the column the latter were constantly under fire from the right flank. The heat was terrible, necessitating frequent halts whenever shady trees or sheds could be found where the men would not be too exposed to the fire of the enemy.

It was 1 p.m. before the ladders were put in position against the walls of the city. The escalade was carried out by the Naval Brigade covered by the 59th, and supported by the 12th Madras N.I. The Royal Marines were engaged in protecting the right flank while the assault was going on, and by 2 o'clock the British were in possession of the city. Having set it on fire and blown in the gates the expedition returned to Canton the next morning. The casualities occasioned by the enemy's fire were but slight, but there were two most untoward deaths among the officers. Captain Lambert, R.E., was mortally wounded by the accidental discharge of a musket by one of the bluejackets who were crowding up a scaling ladder behind him, while Lieut. Danvers, 70th N.I., attached to the Military train, was killed by accident from the discharge of his carbine by one of the Gun Lascars during the re-embarkation.

Before the end of the year the Provisional Battalion was broken up[1] and the officers distributed between the 1st and 2nd Battalions R.M., Col. Lemon taking command of the former vice Col. Walsh, who had been invalided home.

Early in 1859[2] the Chinese commenced operations by an attack on Col. Holloway's Brigade as it was out for its usual weekly route march. The aggressors were a party of Quantung "Braves." They were speedily put to flight by the advance of two companies and sustained some loss, and with the exception of Lieut. O'Grady, R.M., who was slightly wounded by a war rocket which passed between his arm and his body, no harm was done by the attack. There were some remarkably narrow escapes however. One man had the strap of his water-bottle cut from his back, another the sole shot from beneath his foot, while a bugler trying

---

[1] In November, the Royal Marine Brigade was further reduced by the despatch of two Captains, five Subalterns, and 200 men who were sent to British Columbia. Col. W. Delacombe, R.M., was in command of this detachment during most of the time (some years), Vancouver Island was conjointly and (most harmoniously) occupied by British and American Marines. It was eventually handed over to the United States by the decision of the late German Emperor, William I., who was acting as arbitrator.
[2] January 4th.

BATTLE OF THE WHITE CLOUD MOUNTAIN, 2ND JUNE, 1858.
m m m—Royal Marines crossing paddy fields in single file.

"Illustrated London News."

to sound the "Alert" had his call cut short by a bullet which smashed his bugle and sent it spinning from his hand.

Four days later it was the turn of the Canton garrison to take the offensive, an expedition of 1700 picked men marching on the town of Shek-Tseng, nine miles distant. It was a city of 40,000 inhabitants, boasted of as an impregnable fortress, and no European had ever crossed over its beautiful bridge which was defended by twenty guns of heavy calibre. At the same time that the troops left Canton, a Naval Brigade 400 strong under Captain M'Cleverty, R.N., went round by water, and arrived at the mouth of the river that runs by the town just as the soldiers reached a village 1000 yards from its walls. The enemy had got the range of this village and of the mouth of the river. They opened a well-directed fire which for a time they kept up with vigour. Two of the gunboats were hulled and the leaves began to fall from the trees in the village, and the old walls to tumble and crumble so fast under the cannonade that it was evident that the protection it afforded to the attacking force was worse than nothing. Yet there across the deep, unfordable river stood Shek-Tseng unassailable except by way of a narrow wooden causeway leading to an island on which the beautiful bridge abutted; and the bridge itself. On the island were a dozen Chinese guns, well manned and making very decent shooting.

But the place had to be taken and the fighting line with 200 French on the right, 150 of the 1st Royals in the centre, and the same number of R.E. on the left, moved forward in skirmishing order with the Col. Lemon's Battalion of Royal Marines in support. The remainder of the troops were kept in reserve.

Impetuous as ever the Frenchmen rushed boldly past a group of houses with a thick hedge in front of them. From this hedge suddenly banged out a volley of gingalls which caused them momentarily to recoil. But General Van Straubenzee was quick to note the check, and at once pushed forward the 65 Bengal N.I. in support of the Frenchmen. Meanwhile, covered by the fire of eight howitzers and the rocket tubes, the Royals and Sappers worked close up to the river, their accurate fire doing great execution among the gunners on the island. At this moment down came the Naval Brigade who had landed on the Shek-tseng side of the river, on the Chinese flank. A panic set in among the Chinamen, and over the bridge rushed the Royals and Sappers closely followed by the Marine Battalion. Shek-Tseng was won, and with it tons of the Chinese munitions of war, even down to waterproof coats and hats for the Braves in the summer. When the expedition started on its return march to Canton, the flames of the vaunted impregnable city were rising to heaven behind it. It is said that the fall and destruction of this city made more impression on the Chinese than the capture of Canton itself.

There is little more to be recorded of the operations at Canton. The Marine force in that city continued to dwindle until at the end of the year 1859 it was reduced so much that the Brigade was formed into a single battalion, and Colonel Sir Thos. Holloway, C.B., A.D.C., the Brigadier, returned to England.[1]

---

[1] A strong body of volunteers came on to China from regiments in India, many being undersized men, nicknamed "Dumpies." Fifty of these from a light Cavalry Regiment elected to join the Marines where they looked perfectly ridiculous among their big comrades. However, they behaved very well. On return of the Marines to England they were discharged.

But although nothing of moment happened in the south of China, there had been a somewhat disastrous move made in the north, in which 400 Marines from Canton, under Colonel Lemon, and the same number from the ships' detachments had taken part. In order to bring additional pressure to bear on the procrastinating Chinese Government, which had not yet been brought to its knees, it was determined to capture and occupy the forts at the mouth of the river Peiho, sometimes known as the Taku or Peiho Forts, which barred the water-way to Pekin. These forts had been attacked in May, 1858, and after a bombardment by the British and French war vessels, were occupied by a landing force of seamen and Marines without any resistance worthy of the name. But their occupation was but a temporary one, and since that time the Chinese had been busily engaged in strengthening them in every way. Whether or not this was known to the Allied Commanders, it was common knowledge among the Chinese at Canton, for when rumours of the intended operation were "mentioned to John Chinaman in the course of conversation, he usually knowingly and smilingly remarked on the impossibility of success in his curt fashion, 'No can do.' "[1]

But unfortunately Admiral Sir James Hope, K.C.B., the Naval Commander-in-Chief on the Station thought otherwise, probably influenced by the easy capture of the forts the year previous. When therefore the Chinese Authorities refused to remove various booms and floating obstructions they had placed in the river, he attacked the very formidable series of batteries which lay on both sides of the entrance with eleven gunboats. After a heavy artillery duel which lasted from 3.30 p.m. till 6, and which entailed the sinking of three of his vessels, he considered that he had sufficiently beaten down the fire of the Chinese to warrant him landing his small force of seamen and Marines, sixty French sailors from the *Duchayla*, and a party of sappers with scaling ladders with orders to assault and capture the big fort on the south side of the river. Colonel Lemon, the senior Military Officer present, expressed himself strongly against the proposed attack on the river face of this stronghold, and events proved the wisdom of his view. For to reach their objective the little storming party had to wade over an expanse of soft mud—in which many of them sank never to rise again—and cross three deep wet ditches, the last of them close under the ramparts of the forts. Formidable abbatis and sharp-pointed bamboo stakes surrounded the works which had been recently strengthened with flanking batteries. The Mongol troops who defended the Forts belonged to the Imperial Guard, considered the best soldiers in the Empire, and having in their ranks the pick of the Chinese gunners and bowmen. In the hands of the Mongols the bow[2] becomes a wondrous instrument, and several of the Royal Marines were killed under the walls of the fort by men armed with bows and arrows.

"As the boats pulled in to the shore the fire from the North Fort had ceased, and only an occasional shot was fired from the long rampart of the South Fort; the landing place was 500 yards in front of the right bastion of this fort. The tide had fallen so far that it was not possible to get any nearer, and the column had to make its way across the five hundred yards of mud covered with weeds

---

[1] "Per Mare, per Terram." Major Poyntz, R.M.
[2] *Vide* Note I.

and cut up with ditches and pools, the ground being so soft in places that men sank up to their waists in it. And as the first boat's crew landed on this mudbank, suddenly, to the surprise of every one, the whole front of the South Fort burst into flames.

The silence of its guns was only a clever ruse to lure the British to closer attack. Now every gun opened fire again, while the Chinese, regardless of the covering fire from the gunboats, crowded on to the crest of the parapet, and opened fire with small arms upon the landing party. As they struggled onwards to the river bank, round shot and grape, balls from swivels and muskets, rockets and even arrows fell among them in showers."[1] Not 150 men reached the second ditch, and only fifty the third, at the foot of the ramparts. Their cartridges had been soaked in crossing the previous ditches, and the men were unable to use their rifles. Only one scaling ladder had been got up, but a gallant attempt was made to use it. Ten men were climbing up it to measure their strength against the hordes in the Fort, when a volley from above killed three and wounded five of them. As they fell the ladder was thrown down after them and broken. Captain Shadwell, R.N., who had been in command, Col. Lemon and Capt. Vansittart, R.N., had been incapacitated by wounds. Commander Commerell after consultation with Major Parker, R.M., Major Fisher, R.E., and Commandant Tricault of the French Navy reported to the wounded leader of the attack that further progress was impossible with the attenuated forces at their disposal, and received the order to withdraw and re-embark. It was now dark and the Chinese sent up fireballs and rockets, lighting up the beach with the ghastly glare of blue lights that they might see to fire on their retreating enemies. The wounded were first sent back in twos and threes, and after waiting no less than two hours to enable them to get off the small advanced party retreated in good order from ditch to ditch examining the ground in their retreat for any wounded who might have been overlooked. It was 1 in the morning before the last man had left the shore. In this disastrous and ill-conceived attempt on the Peiho Forts, sixty-four officers and men were killed, and 252 wounded. Out of the 400 men belonging to the R.M. Battalion from Canton, and the small detachment of R.M.A., two officers, Lieuts. Inglis and Wolridge, with thirteen rank and file were killed, while fifteen of the latter were missing, many having been lost in the mud; fifteen officers and 142 men were wounded.

Among the many acts of bravery performed on this extremely disastrous occasion may be mentioned the conduct of Lieutenant and Acting Adjutant H. L. Evans, R.M.L.I., who being amongst the foremost to advance to the forts, and one of the last in retiring to the boats, returned three times in the face of a murderous fire, and on each occasion brought back with him a wounded or disabled man, thus rescuing three valuable lives at the imminent peril of his own.

A private letter from an officer of high rank at Canton, referring to Lieutenant Evans' bravery said, "Many a man has got the Victoria Cross for a great deal less."

Sergeant-Major Wood also displayed gallantry on this occasion which in the opinion of the writer of a letter to the "Army and Navy Gazette," at the time of

---
[1] Battles of the XIX Century. Cassell & Co.

ATTACK ON THE PEIHO FORTS BY THE ROYAL MARINES AND SEAMEN, 25TH JUNE, 1859.
From a Contemporary Drawing by Captain W. H. G. Masters, R.M.L.I.

the engagement, rendered his also a case for the coveted Cross "For Valour." No crosses were however bestowed upon these brave fellows; possibly on account of the highly unsatisfactory result of the operation.

The Chinese were not given much time to congratulate themselves on the repulse they had inflicted on Admiral Hope's forces at the Peiho. Both the British and French Governments had made up their minds not to be further trifled with by the Chinese, and a year later troops from England, France and India began to pour into China. When in August, 1860, the Allies invaded North China the British Forces were 11,000 strong, consisting of a Cavalry Brigade, two Infantry Divisions, a Battalion of Royal Marines[1] and a Reserve of Artillery and Engineers. General Sir Hope Grant was in command. The French troops under General de Montauban amounted to nearly 7000 men.

As a place of assembly the Island of Chusan about half-way up the Chinese coast was occupied, and on the 21st April, Sir Hope Grant and the French and English Admirals entered the city of Tinghae, its capital, escorted by a guard of the Royal Marines. The Right Wing[2] of this Corps was left to form part of the garrison of this place, while the left went on to Shanghaie, as the Taepings, or rebels, were threatening that settlement. A Corps of Cantonese coolies for the transport of Military Stores was embodied and mainly officered from the Marines.[3] Those coolies who could speak a little English, were appointed Sergeants and Corporals, and although the men of this Corps did not enjoy the highest reputation,[4] it performed yeoman service and great heroism was displayed by these, to our ideas, somewhat unpatriotic Chinamen.

When the allied Forces arrived off the Peiho the forts gave no sign of life but a solitary Tartar flag which waved over the biggest battery. Sullen and threatening they looked, with their embrasures masked and not a man in sight. But the allies had no intention of repeating the mistake of the year previous. About eight miles to the northward was the town of Peh-tang, at the mouth of a river of the same name. Here an unopposed landing was effected. A wide plain of mud and swamp lay between Peh-tang and the Taku Forts, but there was a road or causeway leading to the village of Sin-ho, not far from the Peiho River, and some way above the entrance. Marching down on this place the allies defeated the Chinese garrison and drove them from their entrenchments. Thence, turning down the river, they moved on Tang-ku, and having captured this place, found themselves in position just three miles above the Forts and in rear of them.

These forts " are all constructed on the same plan, being redoubts with a thick rampart heavily armed with guns and wall-pieces, and having a high cavalier[5] facing seawards, the guns of which were all turned towards us. They have two unfordable wet ditches, between which and the parapet sharp bamboo stakes were thickly planted, forming two belts each about fifteen feet wide, round the fort, an abbatis encircling the whole, and further covered by pieces of water, which force an advance to be made only on a narrow front."[6]

---

[1] The Royal Marines appear to have been attached to the 2nd Division.
[2] Col. Travers commanded this wing, and Col. March the other.
[3] Major H. Evans, R.M.L.I., was second in command.
[4] "After the departure of the Coolie Corps with the expedition, robbery became a thing almost unknown in the Island of Hong Kong."—Swinhoe, " N. China Campaign." 1861.
[5] A raised work overlooking the other fortifications, and mounted with guns having a higher command.
[6] Sir Hope Grant's Despatches.

For this reason it was found necessary to limit the force told off for the assault of the smaller North Fort, which it had been decided to attack first, to 2900 men, of whom only 400 were French. General Montauban wanted to begin with the great South Fort, but being over-ruled only contributed this small detachment, and came to look on himself without his sword, as it were to take no responsibility in the operation. But events proved Sir Hope Grant's theory that the capture of the smaller of the two Northern Forts meant the capture of all, since it commanded the other three, was correct. On the 21st August, at 5 o'clock in the morning, the storming party left Tang-ku, and at the same hour the allied guns opened on the Small North Fort, while Admiral Hope's squadron down at the mouth of the river chimed in with the object of keeping the remaining forts busy in looking after themselves.

The troops employed in the assault consisted of the 44th and 67th Regiments, the Marine Battalion under Col. Gascoigne, a detachment of which, under Col. Travers, carried a pontoon bridge for the passage of the wet ditches, and a Company of the Royal Engineers. On the right of the British advance was the French detachment, belonging to the 102nd Regiment.

The Chinese were not slow in replying to the bombardment by opening fire from the big guns perched up on their cavaliers, but after an hour's artillery duel a magazine in the upper North Fort blew up with a stunning report, the flat, muddy ground around trembling as if from an earthquake, and a few minutes later a similar shock and detonation told that a magazine in the other North Fort had followed suit.

Now was the time to press the attack. The field guns were rushed on to the close range of 500 yards, and their shell rattled and banged on the Fort with redoubled energy. A breach began to yawn beside the gate and French and British detachments were pushed to within thirty yards of it to clear the way for the stormers by a rapid rifle-fire. But this was somewhat premature. The British guns had to cease fire, and at once the Chinese, whom the bombardment had kept well down under cover, sprang up and replied by an equally heavy roll of musketry. The French troops instantly dashed forward and established themselves on the berm[1] of the salient next the river. They were enabled to get there by the gallantry of their Chinese coolies who jumped into the ditches and standing up to their necks in water held up the light bamboo ladders which they were carrying so as to form bridges over which the French crossed. But they were unable to escalade the ramparts—the resistance of the Mongols was too strenuous.

The British followed suit, the Royal Marines carrying the pontoon equipment in front. But so severe was the enemy's fire that sixteen of the men carrying it were bowled over in an instant, one of the pontoons was destroyed and the Engineers found themselves quite unable to bridge the ditches. But the British meant to take the fort this time, and were not to be denied. Some jumped into the ditches and swam or struggled over somehow, others utilised the French ladders, and eventually Major Anson of the Staff, having got across himself, cut loose the ropes of a drawbridge over which the men crowded as fast as they could. The stormers were now all huddled together on the berm. The Chinese could not

---

[1] A ledge left at the foot of the outside slope of the ramparts to prevent the earth slipping down into the ditch.

reach them with their muskets, but showered down bombs, jars of lime, cannon shot, and their favourite missle " stink-pots." For a long time the stormers could get no farther. Their ladders were hurled down or pulled up into the fort. At last a Frenchman got to the top of the parapet and fired rifle after rifle into the enemy's ranks, as they were handed up to him. But he fell back at last with a spear through his eye. Lieut. Rogers, of the 67th, was first man in, climbing up by means of a sword which Lieut. Lemon of the same regiment drove into the mud wall, and supported by the hilt. Rogers pulled Lemon up after him. Captain Prynne of the Royal Marines was close after them, and sitting on the parapet, shot the Mandarin in command of the Fort with his revolver. Simultaneously Jean Fauchard, drummer of the French 102nd Regiment, got over the right angle of the Fort, closely followed by Lieut. Pritchard, R.E. Lt. Chaplain of the 67th, with the Regimental Colour, raced the colours of the French 102nd, won, and placed the British flag on the highest point of the Fort. All was now over with the Mongols. They had fought a good fight, but in vain, and now that they were bolting from their fort many of them came to grief over their own bamboo stakes and other obstacles, to say nothing of those who fell under the fire of the victors. The garrison lost 400 out of their total of 500 men. The British loss was 21 killed and 184 wounded. Of the Royal Marines one man was killed, one dangerously, fifteen severely, and eight slightly wounded—a total of 25 casualties. An hour later the other forts hauled down their flags and were occupied by the allied troops without further opposition. The river way to Tien-tsin was open.

Very little is to be gleaned of the adventures of the Royal Marines in the advance on and capture of Pekin which followed the storming of the Taku Forts. As soon as the obstacles were removed from the mouth of the river the Admiral in the *Coromandel* with five gunboats behind him, steamed up to Tien-tsin, landing small parties of Marines at each of the Forts below the town on the Eastern Gate on which the colours of the Allies were hoisted by a detachment of the same Corps.

The Marine Battalion was present at the action of Chan-kia-wan where they formed a portion of the reserve and also at the battle of Kaowle, where they were placed with the 2nd Queen's on the extreme left of the line, and at the fighting at Pa-li-chian, but unfortunately no further information as to their doings in these engagements is available.

On the arrival of the Allies at Tung-chow, the small suburb just outside the North Gate was occupied by 400 Marines and an equal number of French soldiers, but the city gates remained closed, and the walls manned by numbers of " braves " armed with spears and matchlocks. Two of our Chinese coolies having been murdered by these gentry, the General ordered the Marines to occupy the Gate. They hustled out the Chinese Guard without a blow. The Marine Battalion was left in charge of this town under the command of Colonel Travers until the 12th November, when with a half-battery of Artillery, Probyn's Horse and the 99th Regiment, the whole under the command of Colonel Gascoigne, R.M.L.I., they marched down to Tien-tsin, and not long afterwards were embarked on transports and returned home.[1]

---

[1] *Vide* Note II.

NOTES.

NOTE I.—CHINESE BOWS.

The Chinese bows here referred to are most powerful weapons. Two or three were brought home and are now in the R.M. Officers' Mess at Plymouth. They appear to be made of a species of horn spliced together, and when unstrung spring back and curve in exactly the opposite way to when ready strung for use. It must take a powerful man with considerable skill to use them effectively.

NOTE II.—"A CHINESE TEA PARTY."

While not bearing directly on the story of the Campaign in China which terminated in 1860, the following anecdote by a Naval Officer of a small detachment of the Royal Marines who were serving on the Chinese coast a year or so later is worth recording:—

"In 1862 the *Snake* was ordered to search the coast of China from Macao to Hainan, to rescue, if possible, the survivors of the crew of the *Lord of the Isles*, a Scottish barque which had been attacked by pirates and captured.

"When visiting the Mandarin of Tieu Pach (he with his blue button, I with our paymaster, gunner, and a guard of ten Marines and a Sergeant), tea was offered us, and accepted as a matter of course. Then, in an excess of politeness, the attendant proceeded with the tea to the guard stiffly drawn up in the court-yard, the men with rifles 'shouldered.' The Sergeant looked round for guidance, he had no precedent for a tea party on duty. The men stared with cold contempt at the spoonful of acid tea. Fearing lest a refusal might be an affront, I hastily said, 'Sergeant, let the men take it.' He looked at me with a face of remonstrance and disgust, then, stepping to the front, he gave the word, 'Order Arms—Ground Arms—Take the cups—Drink the Tea.' This was done in two motions. Next came the stern command 'Return the cups—Take up Arms—Shoulder Arms.' It was such men that made it possible to march our little handful through sinister crowds, in festering streets, where the least want of self-confidence would have meant our destruction."—Fr. "Two Admirals," by Admiral John Moresby, R.N. 1909.

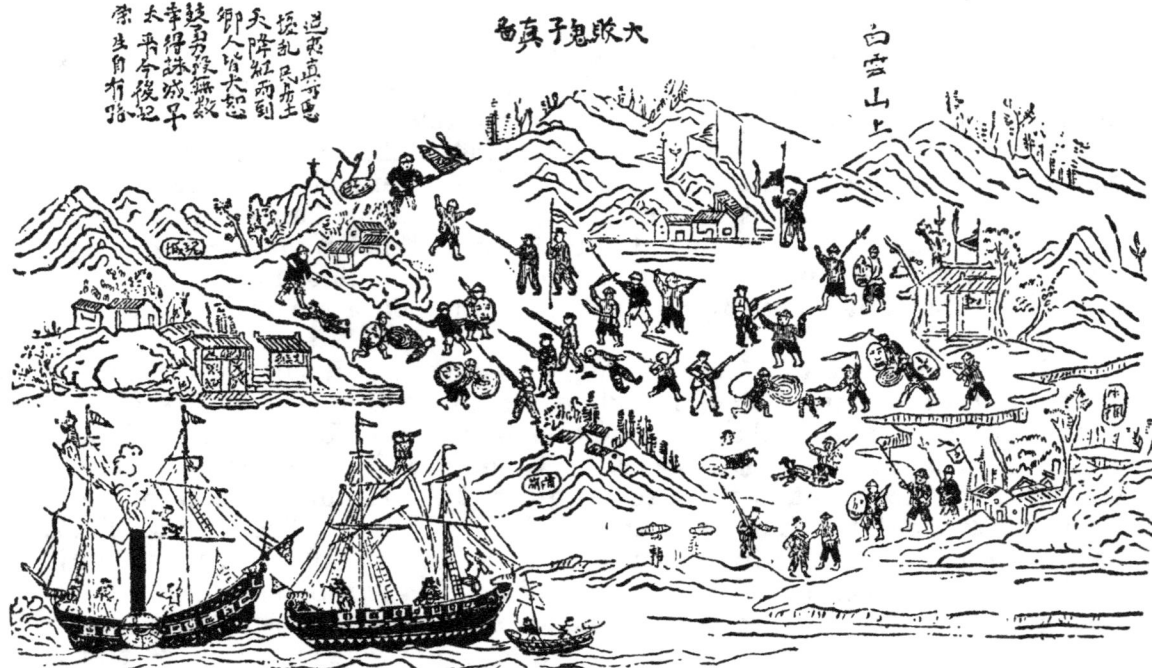

CONTEMPORARY CHINESE DRAWING OF THE FIGHT AT FATSHAN.

Marines in red coats, blue trousers. Sailors—blue coats, red trousers. Officers—green coats.

ROYAL MARINES LANDING AT YOKOHAMA, 1864.   "Illus. London News."

Chapter XXVIII.

THE ROYAL MARINES IN JAPAN, 1864-5 and 1870-5.

> "Pass not unmarked the island in that sea,
> Where Nature claims the most celebrity,
> Half hidden, stretching in a lengthened line
> In front of China, which its guide shall be,
> Japan abounds in mines of silver fine
> And shall enlighten'd be by holy faith divine."—Camoens. *The Lusiad.*

AFTER 1860 there was a period of great unrest in Japan. Since 1850 treaty after treaty had been signed with different foreign nations, opening ports to their commerce, and gradually admitting their subjects to privileges which up to that time had been jealously restricted. The Government and Customs of the Japanese had been of a distinctly Mediaeval type, from which they were only now beginning to emerge, and it is only natural that there should have been a strong party in the Island Kingdom which resented any concessions made to Europeans or Americans. This being the state of affairs, it is not surprising that more than one of the hated interlopers were murdered by infuriated native fanatics, animated, without doubt, by motives of mistaken patriotism.

On 5th July, 1861, a band of these "Ronins" as they were called, had the temerity to attack the British Legation in Yedo, and though the Minister—Mr. Alcock[1]—escaped, Mr. Oliphant, the Secretary of Legation, and several of the Guards were killed, while Mr. Morrison, the British Consul at Nagasaki, who happened to be at the Legation, was everely wounded. Appeal for redress was, of course, at once made to the Japanese Government, but at that time it was afraid to take the drastic steps necessary to punish the perpetrators of the deed and to prevent further outrages. In June, 1862, there was a second attack on the Legation resulting in the slaughter of two of the Legation Guards. Colonel Neale, then chargé d'affaires, fortunately escaped. Later on, in September, Mr. Richardson, a merchant of Shanghai, when riding with some friends, met Satsuma,[2] a powerful noble with his train and escort on the highway. Contrary to all etiquette, he refused to stand on one side during his passage, but rode right into his guards, one of whom instantly cut him down and slew him. The general opinion—and not only among the Japanese—was that the victim had brought his fate upon himself. Would a foreigner in the 15th Century who had treated Warwick the Kingmaker, for instance, in a similar disrespectful way, have got off any more cheaply?

And Japan in 1862 might be fairly compared with England at that period of her history. Satsuma refused to give up the assassin or to pay the indemnity demanded by the British Government. The result proved unpleasant to this powerful Daimio.[3] On 11th August, 1863, Admiral Kuper with a small squadron of men-of-war appeared off Kagoshima, his principal city, and in the course of a few days, attacked and burnt it, dismantled its batteries, and destroyed three new war-steamers which Satsuma had just purchased.

The disturbed state of the country had now reached such a pitch that Colonel Neale considered it necessary to apply for a Military Guard strong enough to protect British interests in Yokohama. His predecessor, Sir Rutherford Alcock, had had a small mounted guard formed from men belonging to the Military Train, but later on this duty was undertaken by a detachment of the Royal Marines, specially sent out from England for the purpose.[4]

This, however, did not appear to Colonel Neale to be sufficient, and in accordance with his request a Battalion of the Royal Marines, eight Companies strong—two from each Division—was despatched from England. Colonel Suther, C.B., of the R.M.A., was selected to command the Battalion which left Plymouth on 19th December, 1863, on board H.M.S. *Conqueror*, a fine line-of-battle ship with her main deck guns taken out to make room for the troops. After touching at Hong Kong, orders were received to proceed at once to Japan, and before long the Marines were gazing at the settlement of Yokohama from the beautiful bay which fronts the picturesque island on which it stands, backed in the distance by the snow-capped cone of Fuji-yama. A site had been selected for the encampment of the Battalion on a high bluff overlooking the harbour, which is at the present time covered with pretty villa residences.

---

[1] Afterwards Sir Rutherford Alcock.
[2] *i.e.*, The Prince of Satsuma.
[3] *i.e.*, Noble.
[4] *Vide* Appendix F, "Horse Marines."

CAMP OF THE ROYAL MARINES AT YOKOHAMA.

Semiramis.   Euryalus.   15-Gun Battery.   Amsterdam.   Conqueror.

ATTACK ON SIMONOSEKI, 5TH SEPT., 1864.

"As we were the first body of troops to be stationed in Japan," writes an officer belonging to this Battalion,[1] " we may to some extent consider ourselves 'pioneers of civilisation.' The landing was witnessed with great curiosity, and as we marched up to our future camp, headed by the drum and fife band, a large crowd of European, and Japs, including many dear little musmees,[2] accompanied us, many of them afterwards to become good friends of the 'danizans.' "[3] . . . "The situation of the camp was splendid, overlooking the European Settlement and the native town and Bay of Kanagawa; while further along the sea coast, thirty miles off, lay Yeddo, the Capital of Japan, but shut out from view by an intervening promontory. The surrounding country was picturesque, undulating, and fertile; beautiful woods dotted about, interspersed with fields of wheat, millet, rye and rice."

The Marines were not long left sole representatives of the British red coat, for the 2nd Battalion 20th Regiment, two Companies of the 67th, and detachments of Belcochees, Royal Engineers and Royal Artillery were successively added to the strength of the Force at Yokohama. The camp of the Royal Marine Battalion was on one side of a deep ravine, while on the opposite the 20th Regiment and remainder of the troops were quartered. The space between formed an excellent drill-ground and was further utilised for cricket, races, and regimental sports. The stay of the Marine Battalion in Japan would appear, from all the accounts of its officers, to have been a most enjoyable one in every way, but any account of its amusements and interesting experiences of Japanese life and customs would be out of place here. It was once, and once only, in action, and the officer who has been already quoted[4] has given us a vivid account of its proceedings on this occasion.

The "Daimios," or powerful Feudal Nobles of Japan, have already been mentioned, and the lesson received by Satsuma, one of the most important of all. This lesson does not appear to have been taken to heart by Prince Chosiu, another very powerful Daimio, whose territory was situated at the entrance of the inland sea. Following the methods of the old robber barons of the Rhine, this nobleman had erected batteries along the shore to prevent all traffic by sea, and had fired on the vessels of more than one European nation. An allied expedition in which English, French, Dutch and Americans were all represented, was therefore assembled in the Inland Sea to punish Chosiu for his high-handed proceedings. The Marine Battalion was embarked on board their former floating home—the *Conqueror*—on the 29th October, 1864, and accompanied the allied squadrons to the intended scene of action, but the 20th Regiment was left to safeguard the Europeans at Yokohama.

"For the attack the allied fleet rendezvoused and anchored in the Straits on the side nearest to Simonoseki.[5] The surrounding hills were very high, and clothed with verdure almost down to the water's edge. Along the shore were several redoubts, with heavy guns mounted, and later on masked batteries hidden among the thick foliage of the trees, half-way up the hillsides, disclosed themselves on opening fire.

---

[1] Major W. H. Poyntz, R.M.L.I., in "Per Mare, per Terram." 1892.
[2] *i.e.*, "Girls."
[3] *i.e.*, "Masters."
[4] Major W. H. Poyntz, R.M.L.I.
[5] From "Per Mare, per Terram." Major W. H. Poyntz, R.M.L.I. 1892.

The bombardment commenced on the 5th September, 1864, with the fire of the combined fleet, which was formed into two lines, the larger ships lying outside those of lighter draught, which were closer in shore, and nearer the enemy's works. H.M.S. *Conqueror*, our floating barrack *pro tem*, was anchored some distance beyond all the other vessels, and well out of range of the Japanese fire. I have never seen a more soul-stirring sight than when H.M.'s corvette *Perseus*, commanded by Captain Kingston, a well-liked and gallant officer, passed close under our stern, cleared for action. The guns' crews fallen in at their proper stations on the upper deck, sponges, rammers, and trigger-lines in hand, heads, necks, and feet bare, clothed only in flannel shirts and trousers, looked a workmanlike lot, as they were—fit for anything. This ship and a Dutch corvette led the inshore squadron. Most people imagined the Japanese would not show fight; but almost simultaneously with the first shot from the flag-ship their batteries returned the fire. It was a beautiful sight to see the flashes and puffs of smoke darting forth from the wooded sides of the hills, and very well indeed for a time were their guns served; many of the allied vessels were hulled, and several men were killed and wounded; but Armstrongs and Krupps, of heavy Naval calibre, belching a hail of shot, shell and rockets, were too effective, so by degrees the enemy's fire slackened, and eventually ceased. Our gallant old ship was not going to be left out in the cold, so the Armstrong pivot gun, manned by Lieutenant Lye and gunners of the Royal Marine Artillery, fired over the heads of all at long range, and made some excellent shell practice. It was easy to see through the glasses that the works were much knocked about, so the order was given for the landing next morning, 6th of September, to destroy the batteries, spike the guns, and occupy the town of Simonoseki.

The British landing force was under command of Colonel Suther, and consisted of our Battalion (Col. C. Penrose), another Battalion of Royal Marines from the fleet, Colonel C. W. Adair, Major Wolridge, Brigade-Major, a Naval Brigade under Captain Alexander, R.N., Flag Captain, also a Dutch Battalion of Sailors and Marines. The landing was covered by the guns of the ships, and by men-of-war boats with howitzers in the bows. Captain Luard, R.N., H.M.S. *Conqueror*, was in command of the latter, and performed the duty of beach-master. The enemy had evidently had enough through the bombardment, so the attacking force disembarked without opposition, and formed on the shore. Skirmishers and flanking parties were thrown out, and an advance was made along the line of deserted batteries towards the town, which was found evacuated, so we halted outside, as it was understood Prince Chosiu had informed Sir Augustus Kuper and the foreign representatives that a large ransom would be forthcoming to spare Simonoseki. . . . .

"A more desolate-looking place than Simonoseki can hardly be imagined; very different, no doubt, from its every-day aspect. It looked a clean, well-built town. As we retired towards the fall of the evening to the spot from which we had started in the morning, all thoughts of a skirmish had quite subsided, so our astonishment can be imagined when our Brigade and the British Naval Brigade were unexpectedly fired into, when passing across the foot of a ravine, densely wooded on either side with a marshy valley in the centre. Colonel Suther gave the order

ROYAL MARINES AND BLUEJACKETS STORMING THE JAPANESE STOCKADE AT SIMONOSEKI, 6TH SEPT., 1864.

"Illustrated London News."

to throw out skirmishers and attack. After taking advantage of all possible cover in our advance, a large well-built stockade opened straight in front of us, with two field-pieces at the entrance, which evidently had commenced the game. The Marines took the right,[1] and the Naval Brigade the left attack; shot and arrows whizzed about pretty freely, and a few of our fellows began to drop. Almost the first person I saw wounded was Colonel Adair;[2] he had been struck by a spent ball, which only knocked the breath out of him *pro tem*. A few men remained behind with him, and he was able to proceed forward again in a few minutes. I don't know how often I did not fall down myself while endeavouring to make my way too quickly through the thick cover and brushwood towards the stockade. This was built of very strong wooden stakes, having barrack buildings inside, and a large entrance gate in front. However, eventually I found myself, with many others over the obstruction, after a terrific scramble; while the yaconins[3] had an easy exit from the rear of the work by rushing out into the woods which clothed the hill directly behind it. The sailors, as usual, poured in with impetuosity. A good many Japanese lay dead; but they had managed to carry most of their wounded away with them. Several were clad in armour, and I have now a couple of suits taken off two defunct men, one chain and the other plate. After setting fire to the barracks, and laying a train to ignite the magazine (which went up grandly when we were some little way off), we retired unmolested to the beach, and the whole force re-embarked, under the supervision of Captain Luard, R.N. It was a pity the gallant Dutchmen were out of it, but they appeared to have taken a different route to ourselves; the whole affair only took a very few minutes, but was sharp while it lasted, and had it not been for the grand cover, which we made the most of, the casualties would have been considerably greater. We had two officers severely wounded, Captain Nevinson de Courcy and Lieutenant Inglis, together with some men killed and wounded. The Naval Brigade had other casualties also. On the mornings of the 7th, 8th, 9th and 10th of September, covering and working parties were landed for the purpose of spiking the guns in the batteries, blowing up the magazines, and bringing on board several brass field-pieces, two of which were handed over to our Battalion, the object being to leave everything as useless as possible for Prince Choisu and his followers. . . . . . Only one sad duty remained before leaving this lovely spot, and that was to pay our last tribute of respect to those poor fellows whose lives had ended in their country's service on the far-off shore of the Inland Sea, and whose comrades rejoice to know it would be impossible to wish for, or find, a more beautiful and peaceful spot to rest in. I quite believe our men's graves will never be disturbed, for no nation has a greater reverence for the dead than the Japanese, and I have a high opinion of their honour and civilised ideas."

A Naval officer[4] who was present gives the following account of this affair. "The French and Dutch contingent re-embarked, and I had returned to my ship,

---

[1] I think the writer is mistaken since Colonel Suther, in his Official Despatch says, "I directed the two Battalions of Royal Marines to storm the building upon *its* right approach, whilst the Battalion of Sailors stormed *its* left." This makes the positions of the Royal Marines and Sailors in the contemporary picture in the "Illustrated London News," which is here re-produced, quite correct.
[2] Afterwards Deputy-Adjutant-General R.M.
[3] *i.e.*, "Warriors."
[4] Admiral John Moresby in "Two Admirals."

thinking all was over, when a really stiff bit of fighting occurred. Captain Alexander advanced his men to dismantle the hidden battery on the bluff, and on his return was fired on by Japanese concealed in the thick bush. Our men deployed in open order, and, with some loss, pushed them back, and immediately afterwards came upon a really well fortified stockade at the head of the valley defended by field guns. Just then the *Perseus* grounded under the captured batteries, and remained fast, and it was therefore necessary to take the stockade and drive the Japanese back before night. To effect this purpose, Colonel Suther led the Marine Battalion up one side of the valley, and Captain Alexander the Naval Brigade on the other. They were met by an exceedingly hot fire from the parapet of the ditch and the top of an eight foot wall protecting the front of the palisade, and in a few minutes seven of our seamen were killed, and twenty-six wounded, besides several casualties among the Marines. Captain Alexander was disabled by a musket-ball through the ankle. But our men were never checked, and, rushing on, swarmed over the wall, and won the stockade, the enemy disappearing in the bush."

The Royal Marine Battalion remained at Yokohama till it was ordered home in September, 1865, and returned to England in H.M.S. *Conqueror*, the same ship which brought it out. Another Battalion, under the command of Lieut.-Col. Richards, went out to Japan in 1870. It was quartered in what is now known as the R.N. Hospital at Yokohama. "This Battalion was withdrawn in February, 1875, when the relations of the Treaty Powers with Japan were considered to have become friendly. Even if it could have been withdrawn earlier, it appears that at any rate its presence saved the Japanese Government trouble and expense. It served as a sort of military model for the re-organised Japanese forces, and in 'The Life of Sir H. Parkes,' we read that the Japanese officers eagerly availed themselves of such an excellent opportunity of obtaining a practical knowledge of their profession. In this volume occurs the following passage:—

'Every honour was paid to the battalion on its departure. The Commandant, Colonel Richards, and his officers were presented to the Mikado by Sir Harry Parkes,[1] and entertained by the officers of the Imperial Marines, whose organisation was the work of Lieut. Hawes, R.M.L.I., afterwards H.M.'s Consul at Tahiti. The foreign residents gave a ball, and as the Battalion marched down—drums beating and colours flying—to the pier, every man, woman and child in the place, Japanese and foreign, turned out to bid them farewell. It was long before the settlement recovered from the loss of so considerable and genial an element in its society.'"

How many people to-day recollect or know of the connection of the Royal Marines with Japan, and of the debt that our allies' forces owe to Lieutenant A. G. S. Hawes, R.M.L.I., and to other officers and men belonging to the British Navy? Probably but very few. Hawes "died a disappointed man fully sensible of the value of the work he had performed, a firm believer in the future of Japan as a great Naval Power, but disgusted with the non-recognition of his labours."[2] All he seems to have received in the way of reward was a decoration from the Mikado and the small Consular appointment at Tahiti from the British Government.

---

[1] The British Ambassador.
[2] "United Service Magazine," Oct., 1903.

Private   Lieutenant   Major   Capt. & Adjt.   Private   Gunner   Lieut. R.M.L.I.
R.M.L.I.   R.M.A.   R.M.L.I.   R.M.L.I.   R.M.A.   Patrol Jacket.
1864   1874

UNIFORMS. ROYAL MARINES.

FIGHTING IN THE ASHANTEE FOREST. "Illus. London News."

Chapter XXIX.

THE ASHANTEE WAR, 1873-4.

"It's a dreary kind of region, where the river mists arising
Roll slowly out to seaward, dropping poison in their track,
And, accordingly, few gentlemen will find the fact surprising
That a rather small proportion of our garrison comes back."—"Fun," 1863.

FOR the nine years following the action at Simonoseki there was practically "nothing doing" in the way of active service so far as the British Navy, Marines and Army were concerned. Abroad there was the great Civil War in America, the conflict between Prussia and Austria, the German invasion of France in 1870, and fighting in Spain, Italy and Mexico. Except for some small affairs in New Zealand, and the more or less unopposed promenade to Magdala, the British Forces lived in profound peace. But about the middle of 1873 a small war broke out with the fierce savages of the Kingdom of Ashantee on the Gold Coast. The quarrel originally arose in connection with the sale of the Castle of Elmina by the Dutch to the British Government. King Koffee of Ashantee maintained that it was not theirs to sell, having only been leased to them by his ancestors. This and other matters of dispute eventually led to an invasion of the territory under British protection by an Ashantee army 12,000 strong. The few Houssa[1] troops, volunteers, and native levies that represented the British forces were not strong enough to cope with so powerful an enemy even with the assistance of the natives living in the protected territory. After two days' fighting the invaders reached Dunquah, only five and twenty miles from Cape Coast Castle. There were a few small craft and the corvette *Druid* on the coast, and their Seamen and Marines were landed to garrison Elmina, Fort William, and a position on Connor's Hill, which defended the approach to Cape Coast Castle.

The news of the outbreak of hostilities reached England about the middle of May. It was evident that assistance must be sent at once. As usual in these cases, the Government turned to the Royal Marines, for no other regiment or corps can send off a detachment fully equipped for active service at a few hours' notice.

The first contingent was not a large one. It consisted of 110 Royal Marines, partly artillery and partly infantry. Lieut.-Col. F. W. Festing, R.M.A., went in command and took out with him two mountain guns with ammunition, and 200 war-rockets. The detachment was sent out in H.M.S. *Barracouta*, which in herself, was a useful reinforcement to the meagre British force on the Gold Coast.

The *Barracouta* arrived at her destination on 7th June, and as it had been discovered that the population of "King's Town"—a portion of Elmina separated from the commercial part of the town by a river, were in league with the enemy, and supplying them with arms and stores, Martial Law was proclaimed as a preliminary to disarming the natives of this part of the place.

On the night of the 12th, Col. Festing, at the head of 300 men composed of Marines, Houssas, West Indian soldiers and Cape Coast Volunteers, occupied the land side of the town. Between 2 and 4-30 a.m., the same number of men from the *Barracouta, Druid, Decoy, Seagull* and *Argus* were embarked in twenty-one ships' boats and towed into the river by the *Decoy*. By daybreak they were moored in a double line, with their guns and rocket-tubes laid on the disaffected quarter. An ultimatum was sent to its inhabitants requiring them to surrender the arms and ammunition they were keeping for the Ashantees. They did not comply with the British demand, and at 12 noon, the boats and the Castle opened fire. The natives were soon seen scurrying out of the town and making for the bush, whither they were pursued by Colonel Festing and his little detachment. Captain Fremantle, R.N., with a number of bluejackets followed in support. A running fight ensued, the natives being driven several miles away, while their quarter of the town was burnt down by landing parties from the squadron.

In the afternoon, having given up further pursuit, the troops under Colonel Festing had just got back to Elmina, and the seamen, bringing with them a trophy in the shape of a captured flag, were going off to their ships, when the Dutch Vice-Consul came running to the Castle with the news that 2,000 Ashantees had rushed out of the forest and were advancing on the loyal part of the town. Away doubled

---

[1] Men of an African tribe living inland to the North of Lagos. They are Mahomedans. They had been trained and uniformed in blue serge with red facings, and proved first-rate fighting men.

COLONEL FESTING REPULSES THE ASHANTEE ATTACK ON ELMINA. "Illustrated London News."

the Marines and Houssas to tackle the new enemy, followed by the seamen of the *Barracouta* who had not yet reached their boats. The fire of the Marines and their dusky allies checked the advance of the Ashantees, and the "Barracoutas" attacking them in flank, they were driven off with the loss of a large part of their force. Col. Festing followed them up for two miles, and punished them severely.

For two or three months there was no more shore fighting, though the squadron was engaged in chastising disaffection in the coastal villages. But the deadly West Coast climate so decimated Colonel Festing's Marines that nearly all had to be sent home, and 150 others were sent out to replace them. In the end, one only was left, who received from the new-comers the nickname of the "Fossil."

A pause in hostilities, which lasted for three months, followed the fighting at Elmina. The Ashantees seem to have lost much of their assurance as the result of the handling they had received from Colonel Festing, while the British forces were not yet strong to assume the offensive and advance on Coomassie, the capital of the Ashantee nation. But a general and extended reconnaissance of the route to that native city was carried out by Lieut. Gordon of the 98th Regiment, who not only located the enemy's principal camps and made himself acquainted with the country, but constructed roads, bridges and redoubts. He built one of the latter at Abbaye, to the north of Elmina, and another at Napoleon, to the N.W. of Cape Coast Castle. But the British Government had made up its mind to give the Ashantees a severe lesson, and to send out an expedition strong enough to brush aside any opposition it might encounter on the road to Coomassie. The officer selected to command the expeditionary force was General Sir Garnet Wolseley, who had made a name for himself in the Canadian Red River Expedition, in 1870. Accompanied by a large staff of specially selected officers, Sir Garnet left England in the s.s. *Ambriz* on 12th September, and landed at Cape Coast Castle on 4th October, 1873.

His first step, after ordering all the Fantee[1] Chiefs under British protection to assemble their fighting men, was to punish the villages on and near the coast to the Westward of Elmina which had been assisting a large Ashantee Army encamped at Essamen, about six miles north of Elmina, with stores and provisions. The chiefs of these villages were summoned to meet the General at Elmina, but they returned evasive or impertinent messages. "I have small-pox to-day," said the Chief of Amquana, "but will come to-morrow."

At 4 a.m. on 14th October, Sir Garnet Wolseley with his Staff and a small body of white and black troops landed at Elmina, and an hour later, reinforced by some of the garrison, a start was made for Essaman, the nearest of the contumacious villages. The force consisted of 29 Royal Marine Artillery, 129 Royal Marine Light Infantry, 29 Bluejackets, 205 men of the 2nd West India Regiment, 126 Houssas, 40 armed natives, and 270 carriers. There was one 7-pounder gun and a rocket tube. The path through the bush, which scattered at first, gradually became denser, was only eight inches wide, so that the whole column was tailed out in single file. Although the greatest precautions had been taken to keep the expedition secret, the enemy were found to be on the alert, and

---

[1] The Fantees are a large local tribe, who had been in subjection to the Ashantees, and were quite valueless in action.

when about 7 a.m. the head of the column was pretty close to Essaman a sudden volley from musket and blunderbus banged out from the woods. The Houssas were thrown forward in extended order, the 7-pounder, which was carried slung on a pole, was put on its carriage, and forming up where a hillock partially clear of scrub gave the troops a chance to deploy, the little British force returned the fire of its invisible enemies. The bush on all sides seemed to be full of them, and a smart little engagement went on for half-an-hour before a further advance could be made. Then the column pushed forward with great rapidity. The village soon came in sight, and was set on fire by the shells from the 7-pounder, the Houssas moved round the right flank of the houses, while the Royal Marines rushed into the middle of them. It proved to be deserted. After an hour's halt the column fell in and left the village in the direction of Amquana, four or five miles further on. The Royal Marines led in extended order. Suddenly there was heard a single shot, followed by a heavy fire of musketry, mingled with wild yells on one side and cheers on the other.

"Steady, Marines," cried their commander; "don't throw away a shot my lads, and don't fire at random. Take ground to the left, get the steel gun on its carriage, and bring it to the front."[1]

All this time a wild and continuous fire was flashing on all sides. On our left was a grassy plateau, with a thick wood distant 300 yards. In our front the ground fell, and was covered with low bush, breast high. Along the front of the plateau, which was now our position, the Houssas and 2nd West India advanced guard pushed on, shouting and yelling as negroes alone can yell and shout, and keeping up the while a tremendous but almost random fire, which the officers in vain ordered them to cease.

"The din was deafening. Not one in ten took aim, and half the muskets were fired in the air; in fact, so that they fired, they did not seem to care in the slightest in which direction the rifles were directed, and often as I have been under fire," wrote an eyewitness, "I do not know that I ever felt more uncomfortable than I did here for a few moments. At length the efforts of Sir Garnet Wolseley and the whole of the officers put a stop to this reckless waste of ammunition. The wood to the left was now attacked on one side by Captain Crease, with the R.M.A., and on the other side by the seamen, supported by the fire of the gun and rocket tube. The main body of the column continued to push forward and without any further opposition being encountered, the village of Amquana, down on the sea-beach, was reached after two hours' further march. It was found to have been abandoned and was destroyed. It was now 12 noon, and the heat was intense, and when Captain Luxmore, R.N., of the *Decoy*, which lay off the village, landed with his seamen and Marines to reinforce the column, and brought with him a case of claret for the thirsty Marines who had marched from Elmina, those who say the British soldier will not drink claret should have seen the pleasure with which these men drank their allowance."[2]

At 2 o'clock, 30 white men and 250 black soldiers moved on to the neighbouring coastal villages of Akimfoo and Ampenee, both of which were given to the flames, after a bombardment by the *Argus* and *Decoy*.

---
[1] "British Battles" by James Grant. [2] "Daily Telegraph."

The loss sustained by the column, which had marched no less than twenty-two miles since daybreak, amounted to two men killed and twenty-three officers and men wounded. The fighting had not been of a very severe nature, but the moral effect of this well organised raid was very great, especially along the coast. As for the Ashantees at Essaman, they began to fall back slowly towards the north.

" From this time the operations were carried on in dense forests of gigantic trees, often 200 feet high, laced together with creepers supporting foliage so thick as to shut out the sun. There were few flowers, but, except around villages, the undergrowth was not so thick as near the coast. It was, however, close to villages that most of the fighting occurred, where the system of African cultivation afforded good cover to our enemies. Clearing the ground by fire, they sow in the ashes, and when the soil is exhausted they abandon the spot for another clearing. On these deserted fields there rises lofty vegetation, impenetrable save to naked savages, who crawl through it on their faces."[1]

After the successful termination of the expedition to Essaman, and the coastal villages West of Elmina, Colonel Festing was despatched to hold Dunquah, a station about fifteen miles North of Cape Coast Castle, on the direct route from that place to Coomassie, and on the 27th of October, aided by an opportune thunderstorm, he surprised Escaibo a short distance to the Westward. Here he fell upon the encampment of the right of an Ashantee Army which had its headquarters at Asianchi, further to the South-West. The enemy were surprised when cooking and fled incontinently into the bush, whence they opened fire which, however, did not prevent the total destruction of the village and encampment.

Sir Garnet Wolseley was at this time at Abrakrampa, to the South of Asianchi, and the day after the affair at Escaibo he marched to join Colonel Festing at Dunquah, at the head of 100 Marines under Captain Alnutt, R.M.L.I., 158 seamen, a detachment of Houssas, and some native levies. To defend Abrakrampa, which was an important strategic point, he left a garrison under Major Baker Russell of the 13th Hussars, consisting of fifty Marines and a number of friendly natives. who were in charge of about half-a-dozen English officers from various regiments. The whole force, black and white, amounted to about 1000 men. Abrakrampa, situated on a hill-top, is the capital of the native kingdom of Abra, and is larger and better built than the majority of such places. It was hastily placed in a state of defence, as it lay on the route by which the main Ashantee army, which had been baffled in its designs on Elmina, would naturally fall back towards Coomassie. The bush had been cleared for 100 yards round, shelter trenches had been dug, the houses were loopholed, and the angles of the town protected by abbatis. The Mission Church formed the citadel. Its thatched roof had been removed lest it should be fired by the enemy, and the ceiling formed what was termed by the Marines, the " upper deck," upon which were mounted a rocket trough and a Dutch brass field piece on which the name " Nelly " had been engraved.

After all these preparations, Sir Garnet Wolseley—who had returned from Dunquah to Cape Coast Castle—came to the conclusion that Abrakrampa was

---

[1] The Ashantee Expedition of 1873-4. Col. Evelyn Wood, V.C., in Journal of the United Service Institution, 15th May 1874.

not likely to be attacked after all, and ordered Major Russell to send back the Marines. This was on 5th November. The order placed Baker Russell in a difficult position. He had good reason to differ from Sir Garnet's opinion, as for the last day or two he had been aware that the surrounding bush was alive with the enemy, the deep booming of whose drums could be heard in every direction. But "orders are orders," and reluctant as he was to send away the only Europeans he had with him, he gave the necessary directions for them to return to Cape Coast Castle. Luckily the very moment of their falling in to march off was selected by the Ashantees to open the ball. A heavy fire of musketry suddenly burst out on the left and the pickets came rushing in with the news that the whole Ashantee army was closing down on the town. There was no further idea of sending off the Marines even if it were now possible to do so. Every one of them was instantly required at his station, and no time was lost in replying to the fire of the Ashantees who were estimated to be at least 10,000 strong.

"When I reached the church roof," writes the correspondent of the "Daily Telegraph," "the volleys of our men had been stopped, but the Ashantee muskets alone, booming and full-voiced as small artillery, made a deafening fusilade. Our foes were still in the bush, but quite upon its edge. Columns of smoke arose amongst the trees as volley after volley was fired by the thousands of savages congregated in one spot or another. They were evidently working down towards the valley lying along our left flank. Suddenly, as we looked out through the bamboo rafters—for our church had been unthatched for fear of fire—a myriad voices struck up the Ashantee war-song. Very fine and stirring it is sounding quite unlike any savage music I had heard hitherto. With ten thousand voices chanting in chorus, for there was all that number, the effect was so fine that no wonder Fantee hearts fail them at the sound. Scores of horns, modulated in tone, played a wild accompaniment, and even the tom-toms came in harmoniously. When the song was finished, the fusilade recommenced more furiously than ever. Inspirited by their own noise, and stirred, as we hear, by the encouragement of their women, posted behind, the enemy rushed into sight."

"They were met, however, by a fire too crushing for savages to stand, and again they fell back, to sing again, drum a little, and madly fire and advance again. I could not have believed that troops armed with muzzle-loaders, for the most part, could have kept up such a thundering roar. The sunny landscape was so draped in smoke, lurid and yellow in the declining rays, that we could not see a foot distant from the church top. Through the dense cloud, now and again a line of leaping flame close to the ground told that our troops were firing. At longer intervals the Sniders made an angry crackle borne above the din. In the thick of the fight, just as a warning, Lieutenant Wells gave the order for a volley from "both decks.' On the port side issued a sheet of flame that stilled the uproar for a moment, to recommence immediately. The church became silent again, though every sailor[1] lay expectant and eager behind his breastwork of rolled tents or boxes of earth. Every Marine stood at the 'ready' by window and loophole. What a contrast on the two sides of the building. To starboard all

---

[1] Lieutenant Wells was a Naval Officer, but according to Sir Garnet Wolseley's despatch (*vide* page 13) the Royal Marines were the only Europeans present except officers.

was green and sunny, the higher trees alone were dimmed at top by a thin wreath of smoke, the grass-green of the lower bush, endless in variety of tone and shape of leaf, stood out in all the brilliant clearness of tropical light. To port, heaven and earth were hidden in smoke, impenetrable yellow in mid-sky, grey-blue in the eddies and puffs near earth.

Towards 5 p.m., after an hour-and-a-half of hideous uproar, the enemy's fire began to slacken, and a rocket from the church, well directed, reduced them to silence."

The attack was over for that day, but the next morning the Ashantee army, reinforced during the night to a strength of 15,000 men renewed the attack, advancing on three sides at once. The garrison had also received a small addition in the shape of fifty men of the West Indian Regiment, which had managed to make its way in under Captain Brett. But the enemy seemed to have lost heart, and when, in response to an urgent message for assistance, Sir Garnet Wolseley arrived about 6 p.m. at the head of fifty Marines and Bluejackets, ninety-six West Indians, seventy-five Houssas and thirty Cape Coast natives, the fight was all but over.

The arrival of the small British reinforcement was the finishing touch. The Ashantees had enough for the time being, and started off in full retreat for Coomassie which, by the way, it took them no less than six weeks to reach. The successful result of the fighting at Abrakrampa, reported Sir Garnet Wolseley, was "solely attributable to the admirable conduct of Major Russell and the officers under his orders, who, with only fifty Marines in addition to native levies, held the town against numbers, at least twenty-fold, during the two most fatiguing days and nights, throughout which time none of them could rest for a moment."

For the next three weeks the enemy made themselves so scarce that practically nothing was seen of them. There were not enough British troops on the spot to follow up their retreating army with vigour, and the native levies, who had a wholesome dread of the Ashantees, were careful not to tread on their heels. There was a skirmish on the 26th November at Faisoo on the road to the River Prah and Coomassie, which was occasioned by Amanquatsia, the Ashantee general, having reinforced his rearguard of 4000 men with 5000 additional warriors with orders to resume the offensive. Our advanced force consisted of 300 men, Houssas, West Indians and Wood's Native levies, and on being fired on by an Ashantee picket at once drove it off. The most trustworthy of the native levies were extended into the bush on either hand "whence they fired into an immense camp . . . . with considerable effect. Several rockets also were well aimed by the three Marine Artillerymen, whose cool, courageous bearing it was a pleasure to witness."[1] Though some confusion followed, occasioned by the native baggage bearers throwing down their loads and bolting, which rather unsteadied some of our sable allies, Sir Garnet reported that "This attack caused the whole of the Ashantee army to retreat in the utmost haste and confusion, leaving their dead and dying everywhere along the path."

In the meanwhile the British Government had been making considerable preparations for eventualities. A number of British officers, specially selected

---
[1] Col. Evelyn Wood, in R.U.S.I. Journal.

for the work, were detailed to attach themselves to various friendly kings and chiefs in order to see that they supplied their proper quota of warriors to augment the British troops and to bring these levies into some sort of order and discipline. Among these commissioners, one, Lieutenant Parkins Hearle, was chosen from the Royal Marines under Colonel Festing. The particular sable potentate to whom he was accredited was the King of Denkerah—Aquassie Kay by name.

From England considerable reinforcements were despatched, most of whom landed at Cape Coast Castle on New Year's Day, 1874. There were the 42nd, "The Black Watch," the 23rd Royal Welsh Fusiliers, the 2nd Rifle Brigade, and a Battalion of the Royal Marines—consisting of two Companies R.M.A., and four of R.M.L.I., with a Rocket Battery, under the command of Colonel De Courcy, and a proportion of Royal Engineers and Artillery. The Marines and the greater part of the 23rd were, to their bitter disappointment, kept in reserve on board H.M.S. *Himalaya* off Cape Coast Castle. For some reason or another the authorities chose to consider that their health would not stand the climate of the bush so well as that of the " Black Watch " and the Riflemen. It may be said here, that as the forces now arrayed against the Ashantees proved sufficient to bring the campaign to a successful termination without further reinforcement, the Marines and the greater part of the Welsh Fusiliers remained at Cape Coast Castle till the end of the war when they were sent home in H.M.S. *Tamar*.

The Corps was, however, represented in the further fighting that took place, though in a much smaller way than had been expected and hoped. Sixty Marines, R.M.A. and R.M.L.l., under Lieutenants Crosbie and Deane formed part of a Naval Brigade about 250 strong which accompanied the Army on its advance to Coomassie.

Arriving at the Prah early on the 3rd January, the Naval Brigade crossed the river on the 6th, and marched for some distance into the enemy's country. The object of this advance was to impress two envoys of the King of Ashantee, who were in the British Camp at Prahsu, and who, passing the Brigade on the far side of the river on their return journey, were expected to carry the news of an immediate advance of the white troops. As soon as they had gone on the Seamen and Marines turned about and re-crossed the Prah.

On the 29th of January, the Naval Brigade took part in a sharp skirmish at Borubassie, and on the 31st participated in the victory gained at Amoaful. On this occasion the head of both the right and left flanking columns between which the main body of Sir Garnet Wolseley's little army deployed for the attack of the Ashantee position, was composed of Royal Marines and Seamen, half the Brigade being allotted to each. The rear of each flank column was formed of auxiliaries. A detachment of the Royal Engineers and Artillery with rocket troughs accompanied each column.

At 8 in the morning, the main advance of the British passed through the village of Eginassie, and after advancing three or four hundred yards was assailed by a tremendous roll of musketry from an invisible foe hidden in the bush in front. The Left Column, headed by men of the Naval Brigade, was fiercely attacked before it had got a hundred yards from the main track, but pushed its way on till it came to rather more open ground where it was able to drive off its assailants. The Marines and Seamen heading the Right Column were also heavily engaged, and especially by some of the enemy who were hidden in a particularly dense bit of bush between them and the right of the British main body. The Marines were unable to return this fire for fear of hitting the men of the 42nd or the detachment of the 23rd who were advancing on the further side of this thick patch of wood. Sir Garnet Wolseley, on being informed of their predicament, ordered the right column to work its way more to the right and prolonged the main attack in that direction to fill in the gap. Fighting of this nature went on for four hours without any great advantage being gained till about noon, when the left column, which had lost touch with the left of the main advance was ordered to cut its way in a North-Easterly direction through the bush in order to resume its original position. Cutting rather more to the East than had been intended the Marines and Seamen of this column arrived at this time on the right of the Black Watch, just when reinforcement was most needed. Their advent enabled the Highlanders to carry the big Ashantee camp right ahead of it. This was the turning point of the battle, for though the enemy made a determined attempt to turn our right flank, and attacked an intrenched post which had been established at Quarman, some way to our rear, his resistance was broken and, though desultory firing went on till nightfall, the day was ours. The day following the Naval Brigade was at the capture of the adjacent village of Becquah, and a day or two later, at the fight at Ordahsu, six miles from Coomassie, where it ambushed one of the enemy's attacks, and inflicted terrible loss upon them. Its last duty was the clearing of the streets of Coomassie before that bloodstained capital was committed to the flames.

NOTES.

NOTE I.—UNIFORM OF THE ROYAL MARINES, 1840-1880. *Vide* Coloured Plates facing pages 16, 28, 46, 56.

1841. (CHATHAM), February 5.—Decision to arm the R.M. with "Percussion Firelocks."

1842. (CHATHAM), November 21.—Officers reminded that at Balls, Dances, or Evening Parties they must wear Sword and Sash as laid down in Regulations for Full Dress. The Sword may be removed at Dinner but under no other circumstances.

(CHATHAM), December 23.—Adjutant to wear uniform of his rank and Sword suspended by slings to shoulder belt and in Field Steel Scabbard. Paymaster, or Qr. Masters, Surgeons and Asst.-Surgeons to wear uniform of their Corps, with Epaulettes of their respective Ranks excepting that they are to wear Cocked Hats and Black Waist-Belts with Slings under the Coatee. The hat of Paymaster and Quarter-Master to have Regulation Laced Loop and Bullion Tassels, the former without a Feather. That of the Surgeon and Asst.-Surgeon, plain, with Black Button and Loop, no Feather. Sash not to be worn.

1845. (PLYMOUTH), April 23.—New Pattern Cap. The Lords Commissioners of the Admiralty have approved of a New Pattern Cap for the Corps of R.M's which is to be adopted from this date.

(CHATHAM), June 5.—Officers dining at the Mess this evening to wear their Sword Belts.

1846. (CHATHAM), November 14.—"An innovation having been observed in the Dress of the Officers' Servants, the attention of Officers is requested to the Regulations on that subject and in future no Servants will be allowed to pass the Gate wearing Shooting Jackets."

1849. (PLYMOUTH), 8th February.—The Blue Chevrons on Shell Jackets to be replaced by White ones.

(PLYMOUTH), 21st February.—FORAGE CAP.—The Lords Commissioners of the Admiralty have approved of a new pattern Forage Cap for Officers, N.C.O's and Men of the Royal Marines.

A sealed pattern of the Black Oak Leaf Lace to be in future worn as bands to Officers' Caps, also a pattern band for Sergeants, has been received. No further alteration is to take place, the expense trifling, and only a short period to be given.

(PLYMOUTH), 4th July.—The Lords Commissioners of the Admiralty are pleased to direct that the Uniform of Royal Marines shall be in every respect the same as the present, except the skirt of the Coatee is to be without Lace, and a Red Stripe is to be introduced in the outer seam of the Cloth Trousers, the same as the Infantry of the Line.

Officers hereafter joining on first appointment, or arriving from foreign stations, will be allowed to wear the uniform with the alterations which is to be adopted by the Corps on the 23rd April, 1850.

(PLYMOUTH), 4th September.—The Lords Commissioners of the Admiralty are pleased to approve of Colonel Commandants of Royal Marine Divisions wearing the Cocked Hat and Short Plumes of the regulated staff pattern, their present Chacos being discontinued.

(PLYMOUTH), 26th November.—Muzzle stoppers are to be issued to N.C.O's and Men.

1850. (CHATHAM), July 13.—The Frog of the Black Leather Belt now worn with the Undress Uniform of the Officers R.M. is to be changed for Flat Slings, and the Officers are to adopt Sleeves to the present Uniform Cloak.

1851. (PLYMOUTH), 3rd November.—New Pattern Accoutrements. The Lords Commissioners of the Admiralty have been pleased to signify that the New Pattern Accoutrements recently adopted for the Infantry of the Line are to be introduced into the Corps of Royal Marines. Measures have been taken for the substitute of a Waist Belt for present Side Arms, etc.

1852. (CHATHAM), February 21.—Garrison Order.—Plain Clothes.—"Officers are permitted to wear Plain Clothes for walks into the country and field amusements, and when they wish to go in plain clothes to the other side of Rochester they are to proceed by the Military Road, the New Road, Gravel Walk, Troy Town, through the Vines and by the Riverside of the Castle to Rochester Bridge. When they ride or drive through any of the neighbouring towns in Plain Clothes they are not to stop, loiter, or get off their horses nor out of their carriages in the streets, but to go at once into the country or to Barracks."

(CHATHAM), July 26.—Whenever men have been awarded Confinement to Barracks as a punishment—they are to be marched up to the Tailor's Shop by a N.C.O. of the Company to which they belong, for the purpose of having the *Defaulters' Ring* sewed on their Fatigue Frocks and Jackets.

(CHATHAM), September 22.—Funeral of the Duke of Wellington. Mourning dress the same as directed in Order of 28 June, 1830.

1854. (CHATHAM), October 4.—Moustaches allowed, after Admiralty's consideration of Horse Guards' Memo. of 21 July, 1854, notifying Her Majesty's permission for the Army to wear them.

1855. (CHATHAM). Double-breasted Tunics introduced; Coatees abolished.

(CHATHAM), November 29.—"The Adjutant General during his visit to Chatham yesterday noticed the inordinate length of the skirts of the Tunic as worn by most of the Officers of the Garrison and remarked that they had converted a Military Dress into an English Hunting Frock. As a general rule the Skirt of the Tunic should never reach below the end of the thumb when the arm hangs loosely down the side of the coat. Some Officers were also observed to have confined the Sash by the Belt. The Sash should always be worn over the Waistbelt."

1856. (CHATHAM). Single-breasted Tunic for Officers.

(PLYMOUTH), 22nd January.—The Bugle Ornaments will be worn instead of Brass Chevrons.

1856. (PLYMOUTH), 12th April.—Her Majesty has been pleased to approve of a single-breasted Tunic same as the Army for the Royal Marines. All Officers will provide themselves with one, to be taken as from the 25th April, 1857 : Tunic—Scarlet single-breasted with nine buttons in front, at equal distance with fly 1¼ inches wide on inside, to button well over with collar. Lappels and Cuffs of the regimental facings. The Collar to be round in front. Waist long. The Cuff round 2¾ inches deep, and 10½ inches wide, a slashed flap on the sleeve, of regimental facing 6 inches with 3 loops of ½ inch lace, and regimental buttons. The Skirt 12 inches in height, with a variation ½ inch longer or shorter for every inch of difference in the height of the wearer. Scarlet slashed flaps on the skirt behind, 10 inches deep, two buttons on slash, and one on waist, the two waist buttons standing 3 inches apart with 3 loops of ½ inch lace. The Coat Collar, Cuffs and Slashes edged with a white Cloth ¼ inch wide, and the skirt lined with white. On the left shoulder a crimson silk cord to retain the Sash with a regimental button.

The Field Officers to be distinguished by Lace round the top and bottom of the Collar, down the edge of the Skirt behind, also on the edge of the Skirt flaps, and edge of sleeve flaps. Two rows of lace around the top of the Cuffs, and the following badge being embroidered in silver at the end of each side of the Collar, viz :—

    Colonel.—A Crown and Star
    Lt.-Col.—A Crown   } Of the size prescribed for General Officers.
    Major.—A Star

The other Officers to have lace on the top only of the Collar, one row round the top of the Cuffs, none on the edge of the Skirt, the loops only on the Skirt flaps and sleeve flaps, and the following badges at each end of the Collar :—

    Captain.—A Crown and Star.
    Lieut.—A Crown.
    Ensign.—A Star.

Lace Gold according to pattern established for each regiment, but in no case to exceed the breadth of ½ inch. Buttons Gilt with the number of the regiment surmounted by a Crown of uniform size throughout, except that on the shoulder which is to be small.

1857. (PLYMOUTH), 4th February.—Grenades and Bugles on Forage Caps or Collars of Officers and Men of the Flank Companies are to be discontinued. Chevrons are not allowed on the Forage Caps of N.C.O's nor on both arms, nor of Gold unless by Authority. Plumes are not to be worn in the Chacos of the Band. Officers are not to wear any Badges on their Forage Cap unless due authority has been given. Shell Jackets are not to be worn by Officers of Infantry at any time.

(CHATHAM), August 27.—The Sergt. Schoolmaster to rank next below the Staff-Sergeants, and to wear : Blue Frock Coat with Red Collar, Trousers, Oxford Mixture, Boots, Shoulder Knots, Gold Cord, Forage Cap. Staff Sergts. pattern with oilskin Clover, Silk Sash, Sword and Sword Belt, the same as the Staff Sergeants.

(CHATHAM). Enfield Rifle issued : Short for N.C.O's ; Long for Privates.

(CHATHAM), September 20.—New Uniform for Officers.—Col. 2nd Commandant to have 3 rows of Regimental Lace (shewing a light of ¼ of an inch between), round the top of the Cap (Shako). Lieut.-Cols.: Two Rows and Major One Row. *Plumes.*—For the Lt. Infty.: Companies, Green Horse Hair with Gilt Ball Socket. For the Arty. Companies: White Horse Hair with Gilt Grenade Socket. *Sword Knot* : Crimson and Gold Strap with Acorn Head. *Pouch.*—For Arty : Companies only :—Black Patent Leather with Gilt Grenade on the leaf. The Pouch to be 6¾ inches long, 2¾ inches deep, 1½ inch wide, to contain Scale, Compasses and Pencil. *Pouch Belt.*—White Patent Leather 2 inches wide.

(CHATHAM), November 7.—ALTERATIONS IN OFFICERS' UNIFORM.—In accordance with Army Regulations of 1st April, 1857.

Trousers.—1st October to 30th April : Oxford mixture Cloth with Scarlet Welt ¼ inch broad down the outward seam.

    1st May to 30th September :—White Linen.

Shell Jacket.—(When permitted to be worn). Scarlet edged with White with rounded Collar and pointed Cuffs 5 inches in height of Regimental facing, and 10 Small Regimental Buttons down the front at equal distances, and 2 on each Sleeve.

Field Officers distinguished by Crown or Star in Gold on Collar.

Forage Cap.—As at present with Black Button and trimming on the top.

1860. (PLYMOUTH), 2nd June.—Blue Cloth Chevrons will in future be worn on Great Coats by all N.C.O's.
(PLYMOUTH), 9th July.—BLUE CLOTH CAP Officers' Servants. Officers to obtain permission to get these from the Master Tailor. The charge is 4s. each, to be worn week-days instead of (tall) Hat and Cockade.
(CHATHAM), August 27.—Leather Leggings sanctioned.

1861. November 9th.—Blue Serge Tunics first issued.

1862. (PLYMOUTH), 29th January.—CHACO.—A White Cover to be worn in warm climates, to be issued free with first new Cloth Chaco.
(PLYMOUTH), 19th September.—CR. SERGEANTS TO WEAR GOLD LACE CHEVRONS.—The Lords Commissioners of the Admiralty have been pleased to approve of clothing issued to Colour Sergeants to be distinguished by Chevrons of Gold Lace, instead of worsted as heretofore.

1863. (CHATHAM), 5th November.—The Lords Commissioners of the Admiralty have been pleased to signify that a *Scarlet* Shell Jacket to each Sergeant and a *Red* Shell Jacket to each of the drummers and Rank and file of the Light Infantry shall be issued biennially instead of the White Jackets hitherto supplied annually. Duck Tunics first issued.

1865. (PLYMOUTH), 10th April.—The Lords Commissioners of the Admiralty have been pleased to signify that Half-Boots may in future be substituted for shoes in Free Clothing Issues to Royal Marines in *Steamships*.
(PLYMOUTH), 6th June.—Officers wearing old pattern Cloaks with Collars are to have the alteration made. To be lined with red.

1866. 10th May.—Green Ball supersedes Green Plume on Officers' Shakos.
(CHATHAM), 15th June. The Lords Commissioners of the Admiralty have been pleased to signify that they approve of the Sergeant Instructors of Gunnery and Musketry of the 2nd Class being placed on the same footing as Colour Sergeants as regards wearing Gold Lace Chevrons.

1867. 19th January.—Snider-Enfield Rifle adopted.
(CHATHAM), 1st April. The Lords Commissioners of the Admiralty have been pleased to signify that a Blue Patrol Jacket of the pattern and under the regulations prescribed by the Horse Guards General Order shall be substituted for the double-breasted Blue Frock Coat of the Officers, Royal Marines Light Infantry. Steel Scabbards replace Leather ones.

(CHATHAM), 26th April.—Officers going into Society in the evenings either to Dinner or Evening Parties may wear the dress in which they dine at Mess, viz.: Shell Jacket unless going beyond the limits of Chatham or Rochester in which case they are permitted to wear plain clothes.

1868. 11th April.—"The Band of the Portsmouth Division of Royal Marines appeared at the Church Parade on Sunday morning last at Forton, adorned with the new Head-dress which has just been served out to them. It is a Black Sealskin Cap, somewhat less heavy in appearance than the ordinary Grenadier headgear, and in shape, a modification between those Caps and the French pattern."—Fr. *Army and Navy Gazette.*

(PLYMOUTH), 1st July.—"Forty New Sets of Equipment have been received and will be issued to the same number of selected N.C.O's and Men, who will drill and march out into the country to test the New Equipment."
(CHATHAM), 15th July.—"Shell dress for Mess."
(CHATHAM), 17th October.—The following alterations to be made in the uniform at present worn by the Royal Marine Light Infantry.
Officers.—The Gold Lace as hitherto worn on the tunics of the Officers is to be discontinued, the collars, sleeves and cuffs are to be of, and laced etc. in accordance with the pattern approved of for the Infantry of the Line, drawings of which are attached to Horse Guards Circular, 1st September, 1868.
The Lace to be of the same pattern and description as that now worn and is not to exceed half-an-inch in width, the braid to be of the Army pattern.
The relative Rank of Officers to be distinguished by the Lace and Braiding, etc., on the cuffs and collars as shewn in the drawings above referred to.

1868. The skirt to be of the present shape and pattern for officers of all ranks. The collars, sleeves and cuffs of the non-commissioned officers and men are to be altered and in shape assimilated to those of the officers sealed patterns which are lodged at the Dept of the Deputy Adjutant-General, Royal Marines. The skirt to be of the same pattern as that now is use.

(CHATHAM), 14th November.—The Lords Commissioners of the Admiralty have been pleased to approve of Officers of the Royal Marines being permitted at Levees, Balls, etc., to wear the Gold Lace Sash and Sword Belt, together with the double stripe of half-inch Gold Lace down the seams of the Trousers under the same regulations as those issued recently to the Infantry of the Line by H.R.H. The Field Marshal Commander-in-Chief.

1869. (CHATHAM), 13th April.—The dress of all Officers' Servants living at the Mess is Knee Breeches and not Trousers.

(PLYMOUTH), 18th November.—The New Pattern Chaco with curb chain recently adopted for the Army has been approved for the Royal Marines. The Plate and Ball of the present pattern will be worn with the new. Officers will not be required to provide themselves until 23rd *April*, 1871.

1870. 17th January.—Staff Uniform approved for Commandants. Valise equipment supersedes Knapsacks.
24th January.—Glengarry supersedes round Forage Cap for Rank and File.

1871. (PLYMOUTH).—The following regulations are substituted for those in present use. Pouch belts are to be worn over the left shoulder, without reference to the tunic buttons. Pouch to be horizontal and at such length (not less than three inches) below the waist-belt, so that when the pack is worn, the Pouch may be opened and ammunition withdrawn without inconvenience.

1872. (CHATHAM), 30th January.—In compliance with instructions received from the Deputy Adjutant General the Non-commissioned Officers and Men named below will on the 1st proximo take into wear a pair of *Blue Tweed Trousers* which will be issued by the Quartermaster.

The Field Adjutant in the case of the Non-commissioned Officers and the Captain of the Private Soldiers' Company are requested to report to the Colonel Commandant at the expiration of three months whether the Tweed is in their opinion better adapted than the present *Oxford Grey Cloth* for general wear by the Sergts. and the Rank and File.

(CHATHAM), 17th May.—Pantaloons of the colours authorized for Trousers and High Boots are to be worn by Staff Officers of the Corps on all mounted duties, on all other occasions Trousers will be the regulation dress.

A Sabretache is also to be worn on Field duties by all Staff or Mounted Officers.

When the new boot is on the upper edge should be one inch below the Knee Cap and sloped off to the rear so as not to interfere with the bend of the Knee.

(CHATHAM), 6th April.—A new pattern Mess Jacket (Scarlet) and Waistcoat (Blue) have been approved for Officers of the Royal Marines Light Infantry to which all officers on joining or requiring new articles of this description will conform.

(CHATHAM), 4th October.—A new pattern Scarlet Patrol Jacket has been approved for Officers, Royal Marine Light Infantry.

It is to be worn without the Sash at drill and on parade when the men are dressed in Frocks.
Field Officers are to wear Gold Embroidered Collar Badges. The Blue Patrol Jacket may be worn at present on Regimental Boards and on Fatigue or Orderly duty, but not on parade.

Officers are not obliged to provide themselves with Blue Patrol Jackets but may wear the Scarlet Jacket on all occasions when the Blue Patrol Jacket is permitted to be worn.

1873. (CHATHAM), 15th May.—The Lords Commissioners of the Admiralty have been pleased to approve of *Scarlet* Cloth Tunics being issued to Royal Marines Light Infantry so soon as the present stocks of *Red Cloth* and *Red Tunics* are exhausted.

1874. (CHATHAM), 8th December.—The Lords Commissioners of the Admiralty have been pleased to decide that :—
  1.—The Scarlet Patrol Jacket for Officers is to be discontinued, but those now in possession may be continued in use as laid down in existing regulations until worn out.
  2.—Subject to the above exceptions Tunics must be worn on all occasions, but in order to save expense Officers may furnish themselves with a second Tunic of serge or light cloth. . . . .

1875. 22nd April.—Martini-Henry Rifle adopted.
  10th August.—White Drill Tunics made Uniform for hot climates.

1876. (CHATHAM), 5th July.—In pursuance of the commands of H.M. the Queen, the band of the Portsmouth Division of Royal Marines are to wear the *Prince of Wales plumes* in their caps to commemorate their attendance upon His Royal Highness during his voyage to India and back.

1877. (CHATHAM), 16th August.—The Lords Commissioners of the Admiralty have been pleased to approve of a Brass Device (*the Lion and Crown, the old breastplate ornament of the Corps*) being worn on the centre strap of the valise (Artillery and Infantry). The Device is to be worn as follows :—
  1.—When the canteen is carried, the foot of the ornament should rest on the Buckle of the centre valise strap.
  2.—When the canteen is not carried the Crown should be in the centre of the valise.
  (CHATHAM), 7th November.—The Lords Commissioners of the Admiralty have been pleased to direct that Officers on appointment to the Royal Marines, should provide themselves with *Chacos* and *Busbies*, but if the *new Helmets* are supplied generally to the Marines within twelve months from 5th November, 1877, My Lords will approve of *Helmets being supplied free of charge* to the Officers who have now on first appointment to provide themselves with Chacos and Busbies.

1878. (CHATHAM), 24th July.—Non-commissioned Officers and Men who have not been fitted with Blue Cloth Helmets will be furnished with the same to-morrow. . . . .
  (CHATHAM), 5th August.—A Fresh supply of Helmets having been received from the Royal Army Clothing Depot, all non-commissioned Officers and Men who have not been supplied with them will attend at D4 Barrack Room on Wednesday the 7th inst.

1879. (CHATHAM), 3rd July.—The Lords Commissioners of the Admiralty have been pleased to direct that white *Helmets* shall be issued to all future detachments—instead of Blue—before embarking on H.M. Ships except those for service at Home Ports and in the Channel Squadron, Officers at the same time conforming.

1880. (CHATHAM), 13th May.—The attention of Field Officers of the Division is again called to page 53 of Dress Regulations of the Army, 1874, which provide that the Collar Badges of Rank on Shell Jackets are to be embroidered in silver.
  (CHATHAM), 9th July.—The Lords Commissioners of the Admiralty have been pleased to approve Officers of Royal Marine Light Infantry a new pattern Forage Cap, and a Glengarry for Active Service and Peace manoeuvres made in accordance with the patterns approved by Her Majesty for Officers of Infantry Regiments, with a Red Band to the Forage Cap (the Marines being a Royal Corps), and preserving on both caps the distinctive badges of the Corps.

FORAGE CAP BADGE. Globe—Silver. Laurels—Gold embroidery. (*Actual size*).
Crossed Guns above for R.M.A. Bugle for R.M.L.I.

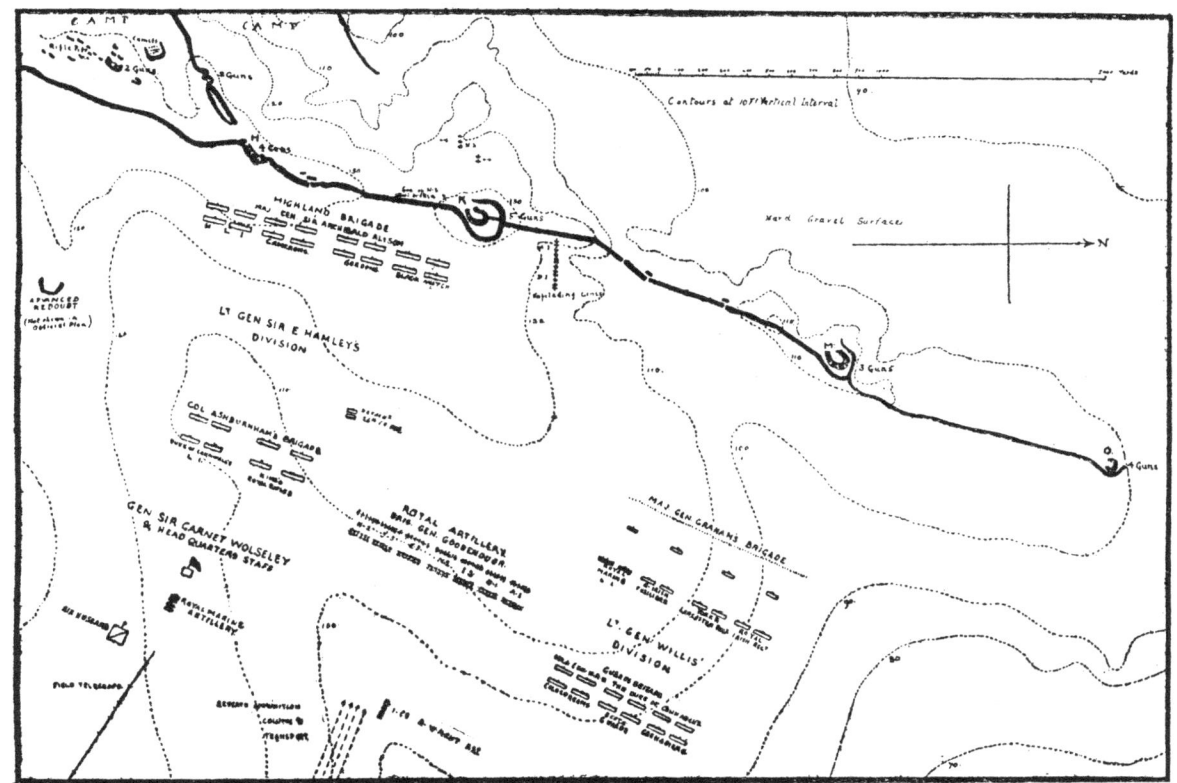

PLAN OF THE BATTLE OF TEL-EL-KEBIR, 13TH SEPT., 1882. Fr. Official Report.

CHAPTER XXX.

THE MARINE BATTALIONS IN EGYPT, 1882.

"Portentous Egypt, now with discord riven,
  The avenging fire and hostile spear affright,
And smoke, slow mounting to the light of heaven,
  O'erclouds her cities in its pall of night."—*Fernando de Herrera.*

THE ambition of Arabi Pasha, a Colonel in the Egyptian Army who sought popularity and advancement by exploiting the cry of a part of his fellow-countrymen of "Egypt for the Egyptians"[1] was the immediate cause of the Anglo-Egyptian War of 1882. But he only voiced the impatience with which those Egyptians who loved and profited by the old order of things, saw the growing influence of England and France, who at this time had immense financial interests at stake, and were not disposed to sacrifice these to the forces of reaction. By the summer of 1882 Arabi was practically Military Dictator of Egypt, and Mehmet Tewfik, the Khedive, a non-entity. Alexandria was teeming with anti-European

[1] It has been left to our latter-day futile politicians to surrender to this parrot-cry—"Englishmen often let carelessly go what they have won," says a 14th Century writer in the "Polychronicon."

feeling, and the British and French Mediterranean Fleets were lying in the harbour watching the progress of events. On June 11th, there was a riot and massacre of Europeans, the victims being principally Greeks. Arabi and his partisans became more and more truculent and self-confident, and openly menaced the Foreign warships by arming and strengthening the fortifications on the sea-front of the city. Anything might now preciptate a collision, and it was determined to prepare for eventualities by despatching a force of Marines to the Mediterranean to be at the disposal of Admiral Seymour, the British Commander-in-Chief on that Station. Orders were therefore given for the formation of a provisional Battalion, which was composed of 300 R.M.A. and 500 R.M.L.I., of which number 250 came from the Chatham Division, 150 from Portsmouth, and 100 from Plymouth. They were embarked on H.M.S. *Orontes*, and left Plymouth on 30th June. The Battalion was dressed for service in the blue serge jackets worn as undress at this time, with low standing collar having a bugle—or grenade—worked in red worsted on either side, and a shoulder cord of crimson twisted worsted. One small patch pocket only was provided. The pipeclay was washed out of belts and accoutrements, which were stained with strong tea boiled in a big copper in the yard of the store in which they first bivouacked in Alexandria. Tropical helmets were treated in the same manner. Valises were not worn, but folded coats took their place on the back, while the two ammunition pouches in front were balanced by the removal of the " ball-bag " from below the right-hand side one, to the back, where it was hung below the coat by a strap passing over the intersection of the valise braces. No leggings were taken. The exact destination of the battalion does not seem to have been decided on. It pursued a somewhat leisurely course, spending a day at Gibraltar, where for some undiscovered reason, it was ordered to turn over bag and baggage to H.M.S. *Tamar*,[1] which lay alongside the New Mole, and even to tranship the coal in the bunkers. The best part of three days were also expended at Malta. Even then no orders were received to go to Egypt, though they were daily expected, and when the *Tamar* put to sea again on 11th July, amid the cheers of the men of the Flying Squadron, which had recently come into harbour, it was with orders to proceed to Limasol in Cyprus. Arriving there about midnight on the 15th, the Battalion found the news of the Bombardment of Alexandria awaiting it with orders to the *Tamar* to push on at once for that place. Turning round without anchoring the old trooper started off again on her way and arrived off Alexandria at 4 in the morning of the 17th. The long line of the city lay black below the kaleidoscopic colours of the dawn, clearly silhouetted against which stood up the heavy masts and spars of the British ironclads with their top-masts struck and still in battle array. Here and there dark columns of smoke rose up from the town, tokens of the fiery ordeal through which it had just passed.

Matters had come to a crisis on the 10th. When the search lights had been turned on the fortifications round the Ras-el-Tin Lighthouse and Palace on the night of the 6th they discovered hundreds of Arabi's soldiers busy with pick and shovel. Failure to comply with a request that such work should discontinue caused the British Admiral on the 9th to issue an ultimatum to the effect that

---

[1] The *Orontes* followed the *Tamar* to Alexandria, where she arrived " empty " a few days later, to the disgust of every one, as reinforcements were sorely needed.

unless certain of the fortifications were dismantled within twenty-four hours, he would open fire upon them.

No satisfactory reply being forthcoming the British ironclads steamed out of the harbour on the day following and took up their positions opposite the forts they had been detailed to engage. The French had declined to co-operate, and their fleet sailed westward. At 7 a.m. on the 11th the *Alexandra* fired the first shot which evoked an immediate reply from many quarters. The Egyptians had evidently made up their minds to fight. Both sides went at it hammer and tongs all day long, the Marines in the fleet amply playing their part at the big guns to which they were allotted. About 5 in the afternoon the shore batteries had been silenced and a white flag floated out over Ras-el-Tin. But far worse things than the bombardment were going on in Alexandria, and continued for the best part of two days. A wholesale slaughter of Christians was in progress. The European quarter was lurid with the flames ignited by fanatic incendiaries, and murder and pillage reigned supreme. Had a landing force been on the spot, possibly some of these horrors might have been prevented. But as we have seen the Marine Battalion, the first troops on their way to the East, had just missed the news of the bombardment at Malta, and had lost time in being sent out of its way to Cyprus. However, two days after the bombardment, Arabi and his army having fallen back on Kafr-ed-Dawr, fourteen miles to the southward, the Admiral landed 450 Marines[1] and 150 seamen from the Fleet to do what they could towards restoring order. They were assisted by sixty American Marines from a United States Frigate then in harbour, and for two or three days very stern measures were taken with the roaming bands of looters and incendiaries. The machine guns of the Bluejackets and the rifles of the Marine patrols accounted for many of these ruffians caught red-handed in their evil deeds, while others, almost without number, were haled before the court of summary jurisdiction established in the Tribunal—almost the only building left standing in the once fine Square of Mehemet Ali—where a rough, ready and wholesome justice was meted out to them by the officer detailed for the purpose of investigating such cases. In addition to these duties a series of pickets had to be established at Rosetta Gate, Ramleh and other points at which an attack might be looked for from the vastly superior forces of Egyptians which were in the neighbourhood of the city. The arrival of the Marine Battalion was very welcome to the hardly worked Bluejackets and Marines landed from the Fleet, who had hardly had a moment's rest since the opening of the bombardment nearly a week before. No time was lost in relieving as many as possible of the almost worn out pickets and patrols, and the acquisition of force was considered to be sufficient to warrant the withdrawal of the detachment of United States Marines who had established themselves in the Club Building at the corner of the Great Square. With the view of facilitating and encouraging a "scrap" these warriors had left the large portals of the club quite open and undefended, arranging their first barricade and their Gatling gun on the staircase at the back of the hall, ready to deal with any desperadoes who might be tempted to enter in search of plunder and so lay themselves open to a charge of making

---

[1] "*Tell that to the Marines.*" From Mr. Punch to Sir Beacham Seymour. "Although not mentioned in despatches they have done their work bravely in Alexandria." "Punch," 12th Aug., 1882.

an attack upon the Club premises. Beyond an occasional rumour of an impending attack, things went on quietly in Alexandria till the beginning of August. Picket duty was incessant, and the collection of arms and the special arrangements made for the watching of the streets still went on. The 1st Battalion Staffordshire Regiment and a Company R.E. had landed about the same time as the Marine Battalion and the King's Royal Rifles a day or so later. Sir Archibald Alison had come with the Staffords and had assumed command of the whole Garrison, which after the arrival of the Duke of Cornwall's Light Infantry and half a battalion of the Sussex Regiment amounted to something like 4000 men.

On the 5th August it was determined to push a strong reconnaissance in the direction of the enemy's position in order to carry out the orders which had been received from England to "Keep Arabi alarmed." The advance was made in two columns. The left column under the command of Lieut.-Col. Thackwell moved out from Ramleh to the N.E. of the City, along the banks of the Mamudiyh Canal, and consisted of half a battalion each of the D.C.L.I. and Staffords, the K.R.R., some Mounted Infantry and a couple of 9-pounder guns manned by Bluejackets. This column was ordered to push on as far as a certain white house on the Canal. Unfortunately there was another and a nearer white house near the Canal which was understood to be the one referred to, and so the operation was not so entirely satisfactory as it might have been, for at the further white house both columns would have joined hands and probably captured a considerable number of the enemy. The right column—preceded by the armoured train mounting a 40-pounder Armstrong gun which was commanded by Captain Fisher,[1] and had already done excellent service—went out by train from Alexandria to Mallaha Junction where the line met the branch from Ramleh. It consisted of the R.M.A. and R.M.L.I. and was under the personal direction of Sir Archibald Alison. The armoured train carried two naval 9-pounders and their crews and some machine guns. The Marines[2] detrained some way beyond the junction and formed up in column of sections under shelter of the high embankment. To the right was a sandy, muddy waste stretching away to Lake Mareotis. Over the embankment could be seen grass, trees and a range of low hills. After moving along below the embankment for a few hundred yards, the Marines were ordered to extend behind it, and in this order continued to move in file. The Egyptian guns beyond the railway now opened fire, which was replied to by the big gun in the train, and the two bluejacket guns, which having been lifted out by a crane carried for the purpose, were now run up on the embankment and opened fire. The R.M.A. were pushed over the railway line while the R.M.L.I. lined the embankment and opened fire by sections. The first volley[3] directed upon one of the Egyptian field-pieces dropped the whole gun's crew. This was replied to by rifle fire from two or three directions, and a portion of the Marines was extended to the right. The fire from a house surrounded by trenches a little way ahead on the railway line was particularly annoying as it deprived the Battalion of the cover afforded by the embankment which it took in flank. The three guns were served magnificently and made excellent practice at this house. The fighting went on till about

---
[1] Afterwards Admiral Sir John A. Fisher, G.C.B., Senior Naval Lord.
[2] Under the command of Major H. H. Strong.
[3] Fired by a section of the Author's Company.

THE ROYAL MARINE BATTALION IN THE RECONNAISSANCE TOWARDS KAFR-ED-DAWR,
5TH AUG., 1882. *From a Sketch by the Author.*

THE R.M.A. WORKING A CAPTURED KRUPP GUN AT KASSASSIN,
28TH AUG., 1882. By permission of the "Graphic."

7-30 p.m. when it began to grow dark, and the order was given for a retirement, which was carried out by alternate companies by the Marines who were covered by the Naval guns till they were able to re-embark in the train of coal trucks which had been waiting for them. Sir Archibald Alison was particularly pleased with their conduct and expressed himself in the following way:—[1]

"Colonel Tuson, Officers, N.C.O's and men of the Battalion Royal Marines; I thank you for your steadiness under fire, your perfect discipline, and the obedience displayed by all under the severe fire of yesterday, and what struck me most was the perfect silence in the ranks. I heard nothing but the crack of your rifles and the words of command from your officers. A reconnaissance in force is a very difficult operation, and a great test of good troops; you had to engage the enemy just sufficiently to make him shew his hand, at the same time not enough to commit yourselves to a general engagement. That reconnaissance was necessarily followed by a retreat and the battalion retired in such a manner as to elicit my admiration."

Reinforcements were now coming in daily from England, among them another Battalion of Marines, Artillery and Light Infantry under the command of Col. S. J. Graham, about 570 strong in all, which arrived in the s.s. *Dacca*, on August 8th. There was also a Marine Battalion formed from the detachments belonging to the Mediterranean and Channel Fleets. The latter had come in after the bombardment. This Battalion, which was placed under the command of Major Le Grand, was principally employed in garrison duty at Alexandria.

But the plan of campaign which had been drawn up by no means contemplated an attack on the formidable lines of Kafr-ed-Dawr which daily grew in strength under the shovels of hundreds of hard-working fellaheen, although it suited the purpose of Sir Garnet Wolseley, the Commander-in-Chief, who had now arrived, to make Arabi think so. His plan was to suddenly transfer his base to Ismailia on the Suez Canal, and advance on Cairo by way of the Sweet-water Canal. To account for the sudden re-embarkation of troops which took place on the 17th and 18th August, it was given out that the Forts defending Aboukir Bay were to be bombarded by the Fleet under cover of which the Army was to effect a landing and thus turn the position at Kafr-ed-Dawr. The scheme was well carried out. The men-of-war weighed and moved off in the direction of Aboukir, and the transports, crowded with troops, anchored in long lines off the Bay. Meanwhile the Canal had been secured at both ends. At Port Said before the attacking parties left the ships, the sentries were surprised and seized by Lieut.-Col. Tulloch who landed from an open boat with six Marines. While Companies of seamen from the *Iris* and *Monarch* cut off all retreat from the town by occupying the narrow isthmus between Lake Menzaleh and the sea, two companies of Marines[2] surrounded the barracks and made prisoners of their occupants without firing a shot. At Ismailia, covered by the fire of the *Orion* and *Carysfort*, much the same thing occurred and a wire was sent to Cairo in the name of the Railway Traffic Manager to the effect that 5000 British troops had already landed. This " terminological inexactitude " prevented an attack by a force of Egyptians at Nefiche Junction, only two or three miles off. Early the next morning Shaluf, an important point on the Canal between

---

[1] When he visited the Marine Quarters at Gabarrie, the day after the fight.
Under Capts. R. P. Coffin and F. Eden.

Ismailia and Suez, had been attacked and captured by the Seaforth Highlanders (who had come from India) and the Seamen and Marines from the *Seagull* and *Mosquito*, and the whole Canal was in British hands. In the meanwhile the Fleet and Transports anchored off Aboukir slipped away after nightfall on the 19th, and made for Port Said. The *Roshina*, a collier, which had been rendered more filthy than ordinary by having been used as a hulk for a number of European refugees at the time of the massacre and bombardment, carried 570 Marines and a quantity of forage, and did not anchor with the rest of the transports being a terribly slow craft. As it was, she was passed by several of those ships which sailed much later, including the *Nerissa* with 380 R.M.A. and some Engineers, and which had broken down, and was in tow of H.M.S. *Alexandra*. The *Euphrates* attempted to assist the *Roshina* in the same way, but after getting a hawser on board it parted and she was then left to crawl along on her own. The ironclad *Penelope* also carried 500 of the Marine Battalion. By the 21st, on which day the *Roshina* arrived at Ismailia, about 10 a.m., landing there was in full swing, and Sir Garnet Wolseley the Commander-in-Chief also arrived on the scene. An advanced post having been established at Nefiche Junction, out of which the enemy had been driven by the high-angle fire of the big guns on board the *Orion*, directed from the tops of the *Carysfort*—from which elevation only could their target be observed—no time was lost in organizing the Army for a further advance along the banks of the Sweet-water Canal towards Tel-el-Kebir. As the Army depended for its supply of drinking water upon the muddy liquid which filled this mis-named canal, an immediate advance became imperative early on the 24th as news arrived that the enemy were erecting a dam across it at El Magfar, and the water was already beginning to fall low at Ismailia. At daybreak, therefore, the Household Cavalry, the R.M.A., the 2nd York and Lancaster, and two guns R.H.A., were pushed forward to capture and destroy the dam. The Marine Artillery which had come out in the *Tamar* and *Dacca* had by this time been formed into a single Battalion, and the same process had amalgamated the two drafts of R.M.L.I. which had come out with them. The former were placed among the Corps troops as a special body-guard to the Commander-in-Chief, while the latter were brigaded with the 2nd Royal Irish, the 1st West Kent, the 2nd York and Lancaster and the 1st Royal Irish Fusiliers to form the 2nd Brigade under Major-General G. Graham, V.C., C.B. It was not till 4-30 p.m. on the 24th that the Marines (L.I.) left Ismailia. Their route for the first few miles lay over deep sand in which the light Maltese carts with their narrow tyred wheels which had been specially purchased for their regimental transport, sank nearly up to their axles and had finally to be abandoned. After a somewhat trying march on account of the bad ground and the great heat a halt was ordered about 2-30 a.m., and the Battalion lay down in rather a marshy spot close to the Ismailia and Cairo Railway embankment. During the past day the advanced troops having arrived without much opposition at the dam at El Magfar, found the enemy strongly holding a position at El Mahuta—some way further along the Canal—where they had constructed another dam. An engagement took place which lasted all day, the British acting on the defensive against a considerably superior force. So exhausted did the Horse Artillery gunners become after some hours of hard work at their two guns in the broiling heat, that they had to be relieved by guns' crews from the Marine Artillery, who made excellent practice with their 12-pounders, their first shot striking one of the enemy's guns full on the muzzle and disabling it. By nightfall the Guards and other troops had come up.

Early the next morning the whole of General Willis' Division and the Cavalry Brigade had arrived, and a forward movement began. The 60th Rifles and the Royal Marines who had risen up from their short slumbers about 4-30 a.m., were held in reserve while the enemy was being driven from his positions, or rather was evacuating them as very little fighting went on, so hastily was his retirement carried out. It was a very hot day, and after marching down to the Canal to fill water-bottles the Marine Battalion was ordered to pile arms till 4 o'clock. The men fell in at this hour, and the battalion was about to move off when orders were given to postpone its departure till 5, so that they could enjoy a meal of tinned beef and ships' biscuits which were provided by the Guards; the Marine transport, as we have seen, having completely broken down. The Battalion arrived at Masameh, whence the enemy had been driven by the Cavalry and Mounted Infantry, towards evening and established itself in the camp which the Egyptians had left behind them, and where the sandflies were most unpleasant. Here it remained, clearing up and burying horses and doing other fatigue work till the 28th. About 7 a.m. on that day, just after coffee had been served out, heavy firing was heard to the front, and the Battalion stood to its arms. After a short time it was dismissed. This happened two or three times in the course of the day, but no forward movement took place till 5 in the evening, at which time also the Household Cavalry and some guns set out, but bore away towards the North-West under orders, as it afterwards appeared, to attack the left flank of an Egyptian force which after making several half-hearted movements against our advanced troops at Kassassin Lock, had settled down to attack them in real earnest at half-past four in the afternoon. The British force consisted of the Royal Marine Artillery, who were at the Lock itself, and formed the extreme left of our line facing about South-West, the York and Lancaster, and the Duke of Cornwall's Light Infantry. There were two, and later on four, R.H.A. guns, and in addition, a Krupp gun which had been captured from the enemy and mounted on a railway truck by Captain Tucker of the Royal Marine Artillery, who with a detachment of his men fought it against several of the Egyptian batteries throughout the engagement. Most of the time it was single-handed as the ammunition for the other guns ran out, and they were ordered back to Masameh to replenish their limbers. But by constantly pushing the truck backwards and forwards upon the railway line the Marines managed to throw out the enemy's range just when he thought he had got it, and so escaped with very little injury. "The detachment seemed to bear a charmed life. In front of it, beside it, and behind it, fell shrapnel bullets and ragged morsels of shell fired in salvoes by the Egyptian guns. But not a single man was hit during the engagement."[1] The Egyptians, who seem to have been aware of the weakness of the British force, pushed their attack now on the left where it was repulsed by the Marines, now on the right

---

[1] "The Times."

where it was held in check by the two line regiments formed in echelon, and by the fire of Tucker's gun. As dusk fell the attack slackened somewhat and General Graham, who was in command, ordered a general advance. Just at this moment the Marine Battalion from Masameh came up on the extreme right. For some time it had been watching the long line of rifle flashes through the twilight without apparently being observed itself—though several shell burst in its neighbourhood. In the growing darkness the advance company came suddenly upon an Egyptian battalion in quarter column or some equally close formation, and delivered a volley at close quarters which caused its instant dispersal. But as it was absolutely dark very soon afterwards, the British advance was countermanded and the troops passed the night in their well-defended position. Rumours flew about of a great cavalry charge and the capture of a battery of guns, and at dawn the Royal Marines (L.I.) were sent out to find it, but without success. No traces could they find of the sanguinary struggle which had, it was said, taken place at the close of the action of the previous evening. Either the search was prosecuted in a wrong direction or the Egyptians had, during the night, removed all traces of the fighting.

At Kassassin there was a long pause in the forward movement. A large camp was formed, gun-pits dug, and a railway siding made. The greater part of the Army was encamped upon the strip of ground lying between the Railway embankment and the Sweet Water Canal. Day after day it was augmented by reinforcements including an Indian Contingent under General MacPherson, and day after day rumour magnified the extent and formidable nature of Arabi's entrenchments at Tel-el-Kebir only a few miles further on. But nothing of any interest happened till early on the morning of Saturday, the 9th September, when just after the Marine Battalion had been dismissed from parade about 6-15, and had sat down to its kettles of coffee, the 'Assembly' followed instantly by the 'Double' rang out through the camp. All hands rushed to their arms and fell in again. The Marines (L.I.) were marched due north over the railway, and in about a quarter of an hour found themselves engaged with the enemy's infantry supported by several guns. The Marine Artillery were formed on the South side of the Canal near the lock, supported by five companies of the West Kent. According to the stories that went round the camp after the fighting, the Indian Cavalry who had furnished the outposts during the night had been in touch with the enemy for some time, but being anxious to defeat them 'off their own bat,' had delayed sending in word of their advance until their guns had actually got within range of the British camp, and even bowled over several tents. Certainly the Egyptian Infantry were within easy rifle range directly the Marines came into action to the North of the Railway, and were advancing in extended order. Most of the enemy had come from Tel-el-Kebir, but others had moved down from Salahiyeh, a place just fifteen miles due North of Kassassin, situated at the boundary line between the desert and the cultivated portion of the country. Here Arabi had established a small force which threatened the flank of any advance from Kassassin towards Tel-el-Kebir. To meet the Northern attack the York and Lancaster, who were on the right of the Marines, had their right somewhat thrown back, and echelloned in their rear were the Royal Irish and the Duke of Cornwall's regiments. Between

SECOND BATTLE OF KASSASSIN, 9TH SEPT., 1882.   Capture of two Guns by the R.M.L.I.
From a Sketch by the Author.
By permission of the "Graphic."

TEL-EL-KEBIR.—DEATH OF CAPTAIN WARDELL, R.M.L.I.
From the "Pictorial World."

the left of the Marines and the Canal were the King's Royal Rifles, while on the railway Captain Tucker's gun was again in action. The Egyptian attack very soon changed to a retirement, and a general advance was ordered at 7-45 a.m., which was continued till 10-30.[1] "The Marines," says the official account, "had one opportunity of coming to close quarters with the enemy, which they seized so effectually by taking very clever advantage of some under features of the ground in order to cut off a portion of the enemy, that they captured two of the enemy's guns."[2] From the spot where the Marines were finally halted the lines of Tel-el-Kebir could just be distinguished, and they were even fired upon by the guns in position there whose prejectiles, however, fell short and failed to reach them. The order to fall back and return to camp was not a very welcome one, as the general idea was " now that we have got the Egyptians on the run, we have a good opportunity of driving them out of their famous lines." But Sir Garnet Wolesley, as it came out afterwards, did not wish to attack under such conditions. He wished to encourage the enemy to stick close to their fortifications till he had got up all his reinforcements and so arranged matters that when he did attack, he would be able to utterly "smash" their army and leave no-one to oppose his advance on Cairo. The event proved the wisdom of his views. The delay, moreover, was but a short one, for at dusk on the 12th, the whole Army was quietly fallen in and orders issued for the assault of Tel-el-Kebir at daybreak. The following are the Author's personal recollections of the night march and battle:—

"At about a quarter past six tents were struck and piled close to the railway embankment. The Royal Marine Battalion then fell in, and after a minute inspection by its officers was marched over the railway and halted in quarter column on the further side. Presently several mounted shapes loomed up out of the obscurity, who turned out to be the General commanding and his Staff. He spoke a few words to us, telling us what part he intended the Army to play, and finished by telling us that 'the Highlanders said that they would be in first.' This remark was received with a murmur between a suppressed cheer and a chuckle which, however, was stifled at once, but it raised the spirit of emulation to the highest pitch. After some time the assembled brigade moved off in columns of half-battalions at deploying interval. My recollections of the march itself are very like those of the monotonous and unending journeys one takes in dreamland. We halted more than once, but there was nothing to differentiate one halt from the other, always the same shadowy battalions to our right and left, the gravelly ground underfoot, and the enclosing night. I slept at most of these halts, and I believe for rather a longer period than I imagined at the time. But at last, just as the stars were beginning to pale, the whole of the leading battalions were formed into line and then everyone woke up, and pulled himself together as he knew that the end was at hand. But after some time the order to advance in fours from the right of companies was given as it was difficult to avoid crowding and the ends of the line had a slight tendency to converge.

" Just as the approach of dawn made the nearest rise or wave of the brown desert visible against the still darkling sky, line was again formed.[3] About this

---
[1] According to the official account. The Author's recollection is that it was considerably later than this before the advance was stopped. [2] Capt. C. Frampton and Capt. Wardell and his Company were the actual capters.
[3] *Vide* Note I—The Comet at Tel-el-Kebir.

time the battalion next on our right seemed to be thrown into some confusion by the sudden appearance of an Arab horseman slowly coming over the rise in front of us. A cry or two were raised, and I saw some of its men bring their rifles to the 'ready,' but they were prevented from firing. As the newcomer approached I could distinguish that he was mounted on a wretched pony, and was half crazy with fear at so unexpectedly happening on a hostile army which extended beyond his vision to the right and left, and was topped with a glittering line of bayonets.[1] Powerless to turn and fly, he dropped his reins and wrung his hands as he was carried towards us on his Rosinante, who on his part did not seem in the least put out by the rencontre. He passed through the line close to me calling out as he came 'Me Christian, me Christian.' He was pulled off by the supernumerary rank, and that was the last I ever saw of this warrior.[2] Suddenly away to our left front cracked a single rifle-shot, then two or three others. Then a trumpet rang out clearly in the same direction succeeded at once by a loud outburst of cheering. The whole line pricked up its ears. Three or four rifle flashes sparkled out in our immediate front, but at some distance, followed by a vivid and continuous blaze all along our horizon from right to left as the enemy opened on us with a most rapid and well-sustained rifle fire. The ceaseless roll of musketry was accompanied by the buzzing and hissing of the bullets that flew in thousands between us, over our heads, or rebounded from the hard ground in front and men began to drop fast. There was to be no surprise visit on our part. The way in which fire had been opened proved that every man in the enemy's entrenchments was ready at his post. Now, too, the lower edges of the clouds were momentarilly outlined by the ruddy reflections of the flashes from the Krupp guns in the redoubts, which crashed out in a general salvo. Luckily for us they seem to have been laid for a point which we had already passed, as their shells screamed through the air high over our heads, a dozen together. Some, I believe, fell close to the Brigade of Guards under the Duke of Connaught which formed a second line to our Brigade. It seemed to me that the Egyptian lines were 800 to 1000 yards distant, and this being the case, we were ordered to lie down and unfix bayonets. Four companies were then extended as a firing line, followed by the remaining four as supports. We advanced by rushes, lying down to fire. The enemy's bullets were still falling thickly and the entrenchments and our own firing line still blurred with smoke when the bugles—to the relief, I think, of everybody—sounded the 'Charge.' The whole line, every man burning to get at the Egyptians, rushed forward at the double with a continuous shout or roar rather than a cheer. As we caught a misty outline of the parapet at a few yards distance there was a slackening of fire—our firing line had at that moment rushed it, followed closely by the supports. and after a minute or two's play 'with the baynit and the butt' that part of the works was ours. But we had paid for our success, Major Strong was shot dead just as he was dismounting from his horse when near the entrenchments, Captain Wardell was killed as he crossed the parapet, but was at once avenged by his subaltern,

---

[1] The "Times" correspondent remarked "There was no moon and thus almost within cannon shot the two armies were resting peacefully, the one side dreaming probably little of the terrible scene of the awakening, when, their rest at length rudely disturbed, they awoke to see swiftly advancing upon every side an endless line of the dreaded red-coats, broken by the even *more fearful blue* of the Marines."

[2] The official account. "Rumours spread that the movement had been watched throughout the night by Bedouin horsemen, who retired before us and carried notice of the coming force into the lines of the Egyptians. We now know for certain that nothing of the kind happened." Yet was our Arab out "on his own?"

"VICTORY!"—THE R.M.L.I. AFTER STORMING THE LINES OF TEL-EL-KEBIR, 13TH SEPT., 1882.

From a Sketch by the Author.
By permission of the "Graphic."

Luke, who almost decapitated the man who had fired at him. McCausland,[1] another subaltern, was severely wounded, one or two others more slightly, and altogether our losses amounted to five killed and fifty-four wounded. But the white clad Egyptians and Soudanese lay about in heaps, and soon a huge disorganised crowd of fugitives came running diagonally across our front from the left where the Highlanders had made themselves masters of their entrenchments, and upon these fugitives we at once opened a heavy independent fire, and we could see them falling by twos and threes as they ran. At last the " Cease fire ' sounded, and I set myself to get my men into some kind of order. As I was forming them up about fifty yards in rear of the works, a staff officer, who had lost his helmet, came galloping up and said, ' Will you take your company up to that redoubt behind you, there are still some Egyptians in it ! ' This proved to be a false alarm, as the occupants of the redoubt turned out to be some of our own troops. The day was now fast lightening, and looking back we could see the earthworks we had won standing darkly up against the orange dawn. Smoke and dust hung around them in ragged strands, and here and there rose heavenward in slender columns. All the brown gravelly soil between us and the trenches was scattered thickly with white-clad bodies, the once snowy linen of their uniforms now disfigured by ugly patches matching the hue of their fezzes, while rifles, ammunition boxes, and every kind of military debris lay in all directions. As I looked, the Artillery were driving over the fortifications, and forming up inside, and presently the Guards' Brigade with H.R.H. the Duke of Connaught at the head of it, appeared marching in column from our right rear, and saluted us with a rousing cheer. This was returned with enthusiasm by our men, who raising their helmets on their bayonets, shouted to the echo. Away to the North-West the fugitive Egyptians could still be seen suffering heavily, as, though a long distance off, the Indian Cavalry (who had circled round the left flank of the lines) could be plainly distinguished galloping in close ranks through the scattered crowd and plying lance and tulwar with deadly effect."

There was some little controversy at the time as to whether the Highlanders or the Royal Marines were the first to penetrate the enemy's lines. Colonel H. S. Jones who commanded the latter claimed that honour for his battalion, but after the passage of a letter or two he was ordered by higher authority to " shut up." It is, however, quite on the cards that his contention was justified. There had doubtless been some loss of alignment during the advance through the darkness, and when fire was opened the Highland Brigade was much nearer the works than was General Graham's Brigade. But on the other hand, reading between the lines of the official account, and from my own observation a day or two after the battle, they struck a tougher and more formidable section of the entrenchments than that where the battalions of Graham's Brigade crossed. Indeed, on the extreme right the Royal Irish had only to step over a low shelter trench, if they did not overlap the unfinished works in this quarter altogether. So that while the Highland Brigade was checked for a considerable time at the entrenchments, the Royal Marines and the other Battalions on the right—though they had further to go—were over the trenches almost as soon as they arrived there, and " carried,

---

[1] Afterwards Commandant Chatham Division, and General.

almost in a rush, the line of works opposed to them "—to quote the words of the official account. According to this the Highlanders were at this moment " beginning to push on to the interior entrenchments." "Perhaps—p'raps not." The official plan is certainly misleading since, unless the 2nd Brigade had altered its direction half-left or half-right after fire had been opened, the Royal Marines could not well have crossed where they did, *i.e.*, immediately to the North of either K or M Redoubts. It is noteworthy, that Arabi Pasha, according to the official account, maintained " firmly that the attack on the Egyptian left was delivered before the Highland attack on their centre." This the writer of the account endeavours to explain away, but his explanation comes very near to my own idea which is that while the Highlanders were still fighting on the entrenchments, the Royal Marines were over and clear of them altogether and driving the enemy before them. What Arabi probably meant was that it was his left which was first defeated and driven in and not that in point of time the attack here *began* first.

The official account is not quite accurate in other respects. " The Royal Marines," it says, " advanced without firing a shot up to within 100 yards of the parapet," and they " seized and held the parapet, but the enemy stubbornly kept their ground in a formed body, fifty feet distant." My recollection is that though not extended as shewn in the Official Plan at the first moment of attack when the Highland Brigade charged; fire was opened as soon as the advance in extended order began, and that though our opponents—a Soudanese regiment —stood their ground, they were annihilated at once, few, if any, escaping.

After the battle the Marines spent about a week encamped near the Tel-el-Kebir Railway station busily employed in the not too congenial task of burying the dead and destroying ammunition and stores of which an immense quantity had been accumulated by the Egyptians. At the expiration of this time a train of luggage trucks carried them to Cairo, where they were quartered for a day or two in the Kasr-el-Nil Barracks, but were soon moved out of the city to be encamped with other troops on the island of Gezireh Bulak. They took part in the Review held in front of the Abdin Palace in honour of the return of the Khedive to his capital when their march past in their red tunics, and spotless white duck trousers aroused the enthusiasm of the German Military Attache. Soon afterwards came the order to return to England which—except for the services of a small battalion soon afterwards quartered in the Dutch House at Port Said to guard the canal and keep order in that not too puritanical town—closed the connection of the Royal Marines with the Country of the Pharoahs, but for a time only. For two years later they were again " on the warpath " in the Soudan.

NOTE.

NOTE I.—THE COMET AT TEL-EL-KEBIR.

What I and others took to be the first glimpse of sunrise seems to have been the light of a Comet. "About 4·50," says the Official Account, " a shaft of light shewed itself in the East, as Sir Garnet was still waiting for the sound of the first shots. It was still nearly an hour before sunrise. It was impossible to see watches. This streak of light therefore apparently the harbinger of coming dawn, caused no small anxiety. If it meant that day would be immediately upon us, the attack was clearly too late. It is now as certain as anything can be that the shaft of light so seen was the Comet, which on that day was for the first time reported in Europe."

THE SHANNON SEA FENCIBLES MEDALLION
for "SKILL AT GUN PRACTICE," 1796.

SHOULDER-BELT PLATE, 1803
(Gilt and engraved).

BADGES OF LOYAL IRISH MARINE CORPS.

CHAPTER XXXI.

THE ROYAL MARINES AND IRELAND.

"The Devil was the first o' th' name
From whom the race of Rebels came."—*Samuel Butler.*

AMONG the many and varied services which the Royal Marine Corps has rendered to its country, the keeping of law and order, and the suppression of disturbances and incipient rebellion in Ireland, though unattended by the "pomp and circumstance of glorious war," and barren of a harvest of honours and rewards, are among those which are too important to be passed over without mention. The Marines have been selected for this duty more than once, and a very unpleasant and unwelcome duty it has always been. Those ordered on this service could only console themselves by realising that their selection for it was a tribute to the steadfastness and loyalty of their Corps.

Whether it is due to the air or the great intermixture of races in its inhabitants, discord, murder, and unsettlement seem to have been perennial in Ireland, century after century. The fable that the Irish are a conquered and downtrodden nation only desirous of recapturing an imaginary independence, which it has never been sufficiently a nation to have enjoyed, is one of a very modern origin.

When Strongbow landed in 1169 the inhabitants were divided into independent tribes, without any common government; fighting, confederating and dissolving, and in no sense a nation. Round the coast trading settlements had been established by various continental aliens which were at this time occupied by a mixed population of Danes and Frenchmen who supplied the native tribes with groceries and Poitou wine. The Anglo-Normans " coming in the name of the Pope—and with a superior national organisation, which the Irish easily recognised, were accepted by the Irish. Neither King Henry II nor King John ever fought a battle in Ireland."[1]

The Irish had no national dynasty, capital or flag, they never contemplated independence or separation. Like the Saxons in England, they generally submitted to the feudal Norman conquerors, and although there was doubtless—on account of the tribal system, or rather want of system—more restiveness, here and there, now and again—they amalgamated with the newcomers even more rapidly than was the case in England, so that " the Fitzgeralds and Butlers soon became to them as much their natural leaders as the O'Briens, the McCarthys and the O'Neills."

In the centuries that followed the quarrels and warfare between the Anglo-Norman chiefs and barons were not directed against English sovereignty in particular, but were due to foreign influences and to such events as the Wars of the Roses—when they were not private and inter-tribal feuds.

The Civil War between Charles I and his Parliament naturally spread to Ireland, and from this time the rabid antagonism between the Roman Catholic and the Protestant religions served to embitter all future hostilities. That those who are now referred to as foreign conquerors had become one with the descendants and representatives of the tribes is shewn by a memorial from the officers of Cromwell's Army demanding a more drastic enforcement of the scheme of transplanting the Southern Irish "en masse" to Connaught. "For," said they, " the first purpose of the transplantation is to prevent those of natural principles (*i.e.*, affections) becoming one with the Irish, as well in affinity as in idolatry as many thousands did, who came over in Queen Elizabeth's time, many of which have had a deep hand in all the late murthers and massacres."

This extraordinary absorption still went on. " Seven years after the Battle of the Boyne the following was written : 'We cannot so much wonder at this—(the quick ' degenerating ' of the English of Ireland)—when we consider how many there are of the children of Oliver's soldiers in Ireland who cannot speak one word of English. And (which is strange) the same may be said of some of the children of King William's soldiers who came but t'other day into the country.' "[2] At this time it was religion more than anything else which tended to create a breach between British subjects in England and in Ireland. It may be remembered that the Irish in 1690 were eager to fight for the man whom they considered the rightful King both of England and Ireland. They quite accepted his sovereignty, and thousands went into exile with him.

---

[1] " The Cromwellian Settlement of Ireland."—Prendergast, 1865. As this is an anti-English work, these views may be considered as quite unbiassed.
[2] " The Cromwellian Settlement of Ireland."

The first appearance of the Marines in Ireland seems to have been at the siege of Cork, in 1690.[1] Thenceforward, up to the establishment of the present Corps, they apparently saw nothing of the sister island. But soon after the outbreak of the Seven Years War the Admiralty turned its attention to Ireland as a recruiting ground, and 1,200 Marines were raised there in 1758, although the Army—except possibly in the case of certain regiments—would not accept Irish recruits till some time later. They were not objected to as Irish, but as Papists. After the advent of William of Orange a recruit was called upon to make oath that he was a Protestant. There were, however, a number of Irish Papists in the Marine Regiment raised in America in 1740 for service at Cartagena.[2]

Whether the Corps continued to recruit in Ireland cannot be said, but Colonel A. T. Collins was sent to Dublin on recruiting service in September, 1771, and the fact that he very soon afterwards purchased a map of the country at a cost of £1 6s. 10d. may, perhaps, be taken as an indication that recruiting there was a new departure. He does not seem to have found his work very easy, for he writes to the Admiralty on 16th December following:—

"Sir,

I am sorry to acquaint you that the men I have approved of begin to desert; if the tender or some ship does not arrive soon, I shall be glad of their Lordships' Directions whether it wouldn't be better to stop recruiting for a time rather than accumulate a large body, which becomes the envy of the Priests who have a yearly tribute from ev'ry Roman Catholic in the Kingdom, and of course will use ev'ry method to make them desert."

At this time there were plenty of loyalists in Ireland, even if there were a certain number of discontented people. The loyalists, too, were well organised, strong and influential. When France intervened in our contest with the rebellious Americans, these loyalists, mainly Protestants, instead of utilising England's difficulty as an opportunity for extracting concessions, which as regards commerce at any rate, were certainly overdue, formed associations for Imperial Defence all over the country. Enthusiastic Companies of Volunteers were armed and drilled, and these were aided by liberal subscriptions from the Catholics, who were themselves forbidden by law to carry arms. Every town, every hamlet almost, had its little Volunteer Company, and when we find corps with such titles as "The Cork True Blues," and the "Cork Boyne Volunteers," we can at once judge how different a spirit prevailed in Ireland to that which overspread the country at a later date. Had the British Government encouraged these loyalists and recognised their loyalty, things might have been very different in the next century, but it required the Volunteers' "united action, when brigaded in Dublin to secure from an unwilling Parliament not only a measure of reform, but also a free trade that opened English ports previously closed against Irish manufactured goods."[3] There can be little doubt that the usual sequence of the refusal of reasonable demands, discontent, insurrection, outrage and repression, followed by concessions to those lately in rebellion, combined with the discouragement and

---
[1] *Vide* Chapter II.
[2] *Vide* Chapter VI, pp. 73 and 89.
[3] "Medals and Mottoes of the Irish Volunteers," by Robt. Day, F.S.A., in the Journal of the Royal Society of Antiquaries of Ireland.

abandonment of loyalists, gradually increased the numbers of those ready to rebel and reduced the numbers of loyal folk. What else could be expected ? But for this policy, or want of policy, in all probability there would have been no "Irish question" in the twentieth century.

The great rebellion which broke out in 1798, and was attended by the atrocities usual in Ireland, was in no sense a revolt against British rule. It was a Socialist, or as it was then termed, Jacobin, outbreak not directed against King George in particular, but against all kings and established governments, and was inspired without doubt by the French Revolution. The only mention of the Marines in Ireland at this crisis is that Captain Richard Williams and a detachment were sent in a gunboat on 19th June, 1798, to dislodge the rebels from a position they had taken up on the banks of the river close to Waterford, in order to secure a landing for a body of troops expected from Portsmouth. But as a matter of fact the rebellion was practically suppressed by the loyal Irish Yeomanry and Volunteers. Out of about 90,000 troops engaged against the rebels only about 10,000 belonged to the regular British Army.

There is little doubt that the same influences which brought about this insurrection inspired the Mutinies in the British Fleet in 1797 and later, as well as the abortive outbreak at the Marine Barracks at Plymouth. In connection with the latter affair it may be noted that although all the ringleaders belonged to the United Irishmen, there were many loyal Irish in the Corps if we may judge from the signatures to the manifesto issued by one of its Light Infantry Companies which is reproduced in facsimile on another page. Though no place or date is appended it is supposed to have been issued in May, 1797, in reply to a seditious circular inculcating discontent (based on the usual Socialist perversion of the Tenth Commandment) which was addressed "To the British Army," and found in various Marine and other Barracks.

It may be remarked that the local forces raised about the time of the Rebellion of '98 were not the same organisations that have been previously mentioned, which had then ceased to exist. The later ones were generally known as "Yeomanry." They were not regimented as a rule but consisted of small corps of various strengths raised locally by Loyalists and landowners for protection and keeping the country free from rebels. Some were raised as late as 1803.

Among these Corps it is interesting to note that there were some with a more extended scope which may claim to be considered Marines. These were the Sea Fencibles, of which some, at any rate, dated from 1792. They "were a Marine Force that could be either used ashore or afloat, and who gave volunteers to the Royal Navy. The first monument to commemorate the victory of Trafalgar was erected by the Sea Fencibles who were ever ready for action, and whose triumphal arch, after resisting the south-west gales of one hundred years, still stands as a monument of their patriotism and zeal upon the summit of the hill on the demesne lands of Castle Townshend."[1]

Their particular "raison d'étre" was the defence of the coast against foreign invasion. They learnt how to handle boats and to man the harbour fortifications,

---

[1] "Some Mementoes of the Irish Volunteers and Yeomanry," by Robt. Day, F.S.A. in the Journal of the Royal Society of Antiquaries of Ireland.

MARINE CORPS.

WE the Non-commissioned Officers and Private Men, belonging to the *Light Company*, finding, to our great Astonishment, that evil-disposed Men have said the Discontent about Pay had arisen with Us, and by that Means throwing on us the BASE *Stigma of Disloyalty* to our *King* and *Constitution :* We hereby come forth to declare, and most solemnly Swear we are true to the Oath we have already taken, to serve our *King* and *Country*; that so far from taking any other Oath to betray that Service we have voluntarily entered into, We here publicly declare, *we are Individually most grateful for the Bounty we receive from Government*; that we neither *know* any *Person* or *Persons* in the Barracks, who are *Disaffected*, and also pledge ourselves to bring to our Officers, any Person or Persons who may endeavour to use any Means to make us swerve from that Duty it is here our Glory to avow.

SERJEANTS.
Robert Dalley
Francis Murphy
Richard Frodsham
H. H. W. Bray
Charles Old

CORPORALS.
Richard Lavis
James Dalby

PRIVATES.
Arthur Hutchinson
James Mulhollan
Thomas M'Ellory
Owen Connor
Peter Healey
John Brenan
William Olliver
Thomas Connoll
Thomas Shaw
Benjamin Allport
Thomas Murray

Edward Sinnott
Robert Glass
Samuel Officer
Patrick Carroll
Michael Carr
Dennis Donoghue
James Doyle
Andrew Larson
Soloman Perry
David Dixon
Daniel Woodward
Patrick Commiskey
James Ryan
James M'Guire
William Jenks
Thomas Forster
John Holmes
Patrick M'Donough
Henry Blundell
Daniel Coffey

Michael Cavanaugh
John Kennedy
Charles Gorman
Neil Gelaspie
John Davis
Dennis M'Carty
Patrick Farley
William Anderson
John Marks
Patrick Shea
Michael Breman
Thomas Harvey
Edward Roberts
Isaac Simons
Thomas Smith
Robert Knight
Joshua Gregory
Thomas Lloyd
John Rabjohns
Joseph Garrison

GOD SAVE THE KING.

and naturally, therefore, gunnery formed an important part of their curriculum. The oval medallion illustrated is one that was given to the Shannon Sea Fencibles in 1796, as "A reward for skill at Gun Practice," by a General Smith, who on 30th March, 1792, had been appointed Colonel Commandant " of the Marine Forces." The Mermaid on a Ducal Coronet was probably the badge of the Shannon Marines, since neither crest nor motto belong to any of the numerous branches of the Smith family.

The " Loyal Marine Volunteers " of 1803 was another " Yeomanry " Corps. This does not imply that they were " Horse Marines," but probably another Sea Fencible association belonging to the Yeomanry volunteer organisation. They were a Dublin Corps and under the command of Captain-Commandant John Fish, who had under him five Captains, five Subalterns, and an Adjutant.[1]

The Irish Roman Catholics were "emancipated" in 1829, and as usual, concession was the signal for disturbance. According to a clergyman whose parish was in the South of Ireland in 1837, many of the 2,000 Protestants who formed his congregation were "invariably assaulted on their way to church, the men frightfully beaten, and cows turned into their gardens whenever they absent themselves from home." This was in County Cork. In Tipperary, he said, it was worse, " the priests putting direct premiums upon murder, and no man venturing out of his house after dark." The same clergyman stated that he had been informed by Judge Crampton, Attorney General, in Lord Grey's administration, " that any man might be murdered in Tipperary for 2s. 6d. and a pint of whisky ! " " This is the boasted tranquility which we enjoy under Radical domination," he adds bitterly.[2]

Next came the abortive attempt at revolution in 1848. As in 1798, this synchronised with revolutionary outbreaks on the Continent of Europe, and is generally referred to as the "Smith O'Brien" disturbances. It was soon suppressed, and its leader transported to Port Arthur in Tasmania. It is referred to here on account of a Battalion of Royal Marines having been sent over to Ireland to assist in the restoration of law and order. It was not a large one, only 300 rank and file. Landing in Dublin in July, it marched to Waterford, where it was stationed until February, 1849. Part of this time it was under canvas, and for the remainder it was hulked on board the *Rhadamanthus*, where both officers and men suffered a good deal from the crowded state of the vessel. This Battalion was present at the attack made on the Portland Barracks, and the attempted destruction of Granagh Bridge, over the Suir, on 12th September, 1848.

The possibility of an outbreak had evidently been foreseen some months before it actually occurred, since on 1st March the complements of Marines on board the men-of-war stationed on the Irish coast were ordered to be strengthened, and on the 8th the troopship *Resistance* sailed from Plymouth for Cork with 100 Portsmouth and 200 Plymouth Marines as reinforcements. In July, Admiral Sir Charles Napier wrote from Cork to Lord Auckland : " Steamers I have none, and I will pause before I move the Marines ; but I suppose I am entering into your views and the views of the Government in doing all I can to prevent an insurrection ? "

---

[1] This is stated to have been a "Supplementary Corps" to a similar one in England, but I can find no trace of the latter.—C.F.
[2] From a contemporary Diary, Sept., 1837.

Whether he refers to the battalion or to the Marines belonging to his squadron is doubtful, but it is evident that he had no particular confidence in the loyalty of the Government to the country generally, or why is he not sure as to his duty in the crisis?

Twenty years later, in 1868, another and a larger Battalion of the Royal Marines was despatched to Ireland under the command of Lieut.-Col. John H. Stewart, and again in 1880-1 another Battalion commanded successively by Lieut.-Col. Maskery and Lieut.-Col. Howard S. Jones, was quartered in the South of Ireland. It was distributed in detachments over a considerable district. Some of these were in the forts at Queenstown Harbour, others at Skibbereen, Skull, Bantry and other places. Their general duty was to assist the police evictions by presenting themselves as targets for abuse and stone-throwing without being allowed to retaliate. Some slight collision did take place at Bantry between a detachment of the Royal Marines and the populace on the 3rd August, 1881, which occasioned an adverse question to be asked in the House by a Nationalist Member. Mr. Childers,[1] in reply, said that the matter had arisen from most unprovoked and brutal attacks being made upon the Marines, and that the Bantry magistrates had forwarded to him a resolution expressing their general testimony to the exemplary good behaviour of the detachment at Bantry, and their regret at its removal.

What the rank and file thought of duty of this kind is evident from the following conversation which a correspondent of the "Globe"[2] had with a Corporal of Marines at a later date. No Battalion had been sent to Ireland after the return of the one quartered there in 1881-2, but there, as everywhere else, H.M. ships are always prepared to land men in cases of emergency.

"He was a Corporal of Marines, a great massive fellow of four or five and twenty, with a keen, intelligent face and a hearty voice. One day we were talking of his recent experiences in Ireland. 'You were stationed at Bantry for some time'?' I said.

'Yes, Sir, I've been there about three years altogether, off and on. I was on the old S—— (? *Shannon*).

"'Seen much of the country'?

"'Why, yes, Sir, plenty. Too much in fact. We Marines were always on shore what with one row and another. You see, sir, the soldiers who live among the people get to know them and chum with them, and don't like to do the dirty work of eviction and riots; so the authorities like to send us, who are strangers. .... There certainly have been fewer evictions in the last two or three years. Awful things they were, especially for us. We used to go out with our rifles and bayonets, and an oak sword-stick. Not to use it as a sword, but as a cudgel. When we had to turn anybody out of doors the people crowded round with sticks and pitchforks, and old guns. We had strict orders not to hurt anyone if it could be helped. I have stood for more than an hour with stones whistling about me, and many of them hitting me, and never struck a blow. The men were pretty bad, but the women were lots worse. They were like savages with hair flying

---

[1] Then Secretary of State for War.
[2] The "Globe," 5th July, 1892.

loose, and generally without shoes and stockings. They knew uncommonly well that we shouldn't touch them, whatever they did, and they took advantage of it to any extent. Ugh! I don't want any more evictions."

"'You were at the Cork election?'

"He laughed a great round laugh.

"'I should think I was. You never saw such a business in your life. There was one lot called themselves Parnelites, and another Anti-Parnelites. I didn't know what they wanted, and I don't believe they did themselves. We had to parade the town all day and all night to keep them from a free fight. One day a chap called Healy or Davitt, or something, made speeches and both parties went raving mad. We stood for three mortal hours with fixed bayonets keeping them from one another's throats. I believe but for us Marines there wouldn't have been one of the blessed fools left alive. I got a crack over the head with a brickbat that day which nearly stunned me, and my mate got a pitchfork through his arm. I marked the man that did that, and let him have the oak stick over his head. The stick split all to bits; I don't know about the man's head. I didn't ask.'

"'What do you think of Home Rule?' I asked.

"'Just ridiculous. They ain't fit for it. If some of these politicians I read of in the papers had seen what I have they wouldn't dream of it. Of course there are sensible men among them, but the crowd are just children. They laugh one minute, cry the next, and fight like ten thousand cats the next.'"

Though, as we have said, the Battalion of 1881 was the last sent to Ireland by the Royal Marines, a strong detachment of 300 picked men was quietly despatched to Dublin to assist the police in that City in the troubled times immediately succeeding the infamous Phoenix Park murders.[1] These amateur policemen were all fitted up with plain clothes, and were in charge of three selected officers—Major Noble, R.M.A., and Captains Morgan and Boyd-Hamilton, R.M.L.I. Many rôles have been played by the Royal Marines, but this was an entirely new one. The idea of employing them originated with Mr. Jenkinson, the head of the Dublin Criminal Department, and the event fully justified any anticipations he may have formed with regard to the assistance they would be to the Police. The method of their employment was ingenious and great credit is due to their officers for the organisation and arrangement of a system of patrolling the streets which proved most efficacious. Instead of being told off to various "beats" like policemen, which would probably have rendered them known and marked men to the "Invincibles" and their allies, a series of intersecting routes was planned out, the length of which was such that the two men who formed a patrol—the detachment always worked in couples—would necessarily take the whole morning or afternoon to complete the one for which they had been detailed. The points of intersection being known and arranged so that they would be passed by two or more different patrols at approximately the same time, each patrol knew when and where reinforcements could be met with.

---

[1] Lord Frederick Cavendish, Chief Secretary for Ireland, and Thos. H. Burke, Under Secretary were assassinated on 6th May, 1882, in the Phoenix Park, Dublin, near the Viceregal Lodge. The murderers were members of a secret society composed of some of the most desperate Fenians whose object was the assassination of public officials. This band of criminals were known as the "Invincibles."

The officers, too, were constantly on patrol duty. "The work was very hard," said one of them, "for we had to patrol the streets from about 4 p.m. until sometimes 4 a.m., and this in winter was not all joy; the worse the weather the more we had to be about to look after the men. We knew exactly where each patrol should be every half hour, and of course the places of meeting the patrols were changed every day. We knew where to find assistance from each other, and we could assemble about 250 men at half-an-hour's notice in any part of the city. The arrest of the Invincibles was effected by the police at about 9 p.m., but we had to surround the houses where they were known to be, to prevent ingress or egress. During their trial, as the Court House was in my district, I had to be there with about forty men who sat amongst the audience. The men were, of course, all armed with revolvers. The behaviour of the men was excellent, for with so many public houses which they had to pass during the weary cold hours at night it was a wonder that we had not many cases of drunkenness. I believe that there were under ten."

Besides patrol work there was a system under which whenever Lord Spencer's[1] movements were known beforehand, Marines were posted in pairs all along his route. An officer and a party of men were also on duty whenever there was an execution at Kilmainham Jail.

The three officers in the prosecution of their unwonted duties were exposed to constant risk of assasination, and by the order of the Lord Lieutenant given personally to each of them never walked out without an escort of two men. It may be noted in passing that the "Invincibles," whose apprehension was due in a great measure to the Marines, were, after conviction, quietly shipped off to England on board H.M.S. *Valorous*—the last of the paddle frigates. She sailed for Chatham where her arrival was totally unexpected. She was reported coming up the Medway about 9 on a Sunday morning, and on board H.M.S. *Pembroke*, which then flew the Flag of the Admiral Superintendent of the Dockyard, there was great speculation as to the why and wherefore of her arrival, especially when she signalled for a strong guard of Marines to be sent to meet her as she came alongside the Yard.

A subaltern and about thirty men left the *Pembroke* at once, and on reaching the *Valorous* the "Invincibles" were handed over to them, and marched by a narrow path bounded by high wooden fences, which then traversed the Dockyard, but which has since been removed, to the Convict Prison in St. Mary's Vale. This has also disappeared, its site being now occupied by the Royal Naval Barracks.

The "Irish Times," when the "Plain Clothes Detachment" of the Royal Marines was leaving Dublin, published the following account of their work and behaviour, which may well be quoted:

"It is at all times difficult for men who have undergone a purely military training to suddenly undertake civilian duties, but the nature of the task imposed upon the Marines was of exceptional difficulty, requiring considerable tact, keen observation, constant attention and the careful avoidance of public notice. They came to Dublin at a period when the mind of the citizens was disturbed by painful apprehensions consequent upon the perpetration of frightful murders and daring

---

[1] The Lord Lieutenant.

attempts at assassination in the business thoroughfares of the metropolis. Their advent gave the citizens confidence, while their 'unseen presence' proved a terror to the evil-doer whether he was the implacable 'Invincible' or the ruffianly corner boy who invariably chose the time for his attack when the helmet of the uniformed constable was not within view. In no instance could the assassin or lawbreaker be certain of escape, for the attempted outrage would in all probability be nipped in the bud by a couple of "constables-in-aid." It is but justice to the Royal Marines to say that the onerous duties they had to perform were discharged with marked moderation and great judgment during a term of unprecedented excitement. When it is remembered that they were strangers to the country, that they had not been accustomed to police duties, and that their assistance was procured very much in the nature of an experiment, the highest praise must be given, not only to the privates, but to the officers, for the great common sense they displayed, and the unobtrusive but disciplined and effective manner in which they acquitted themselves of the responsible task entrusted to them. The Metropolitan Police were over-weighted and unable to meet all the demands suddenly cast upon their shoulders. A certain amount of justifiable panic prevailed. As a matter of fact the city was in a state of alarm owing to the presence of an undetected murderous organisation in our midst, that seemed to confidently laugh at the efforts of justice to overtake them or the law to hinder them in their designs; and there was a feeling abroad that no one was safe in the streets of the Irish capital who had the courage to perform his duties to the State or to the public. The arrival of the Marines in their new capacity as auxilliaries to the Police at once restored confidence. The Marines fell into their new duties with alacrity. The great value of their support and assistance was speedily recognised by the police. It became evident by the tranquillised conditions of things brought about by the presence of the Marines that their coming to Dublin was in the highest sense a boon to the citizens. The safety of life was secured and the property of the public protected. While the Marines patrolled the principal highways of the Metropolis the strain was taken off the police and due attention was permitted to be paid to the suburbs. The ubiquity of the Marines was so well understood that conspirators dared not try to accomplish any of their murderous intents, and the class of loungers who had been in the habit of congregating after nightfall at corners to the great danger of pedestrians, found it necessary to quit their accustomed haunts and avoid their brutal assaults on passers by.

"To their credit it must be said that no section of the body of Marines committed any excess in the way of interfering with the just liberties of any class of the people. As a detached patrolling force they were invaluable. They seemed to suddenly spring into existence when required, and the moment their work was finished they seemed to mysteriously disappear. The first detachment of Marines for this special service landed in Dublin on the 3rd December last, and the men arrived daily from that date in small numbers, till three hundred were stationed in the city. They were in charge of three officers, viz., Major Noble, Captain Morgan and Captain Hamilton, and no three gentlemen ever better deserved the thanks of the inhabitants for their unvarying zeal in the performance of new and difficult duties and the constant attention they bestowed upon securing that the men under them gave the most effective aid. Hard work they had, no doubt, in completing their arrangements and establishing a system of organisation that enabled them to give the best possible assistance to the authorities without attracting the slightest public attention. The men were located in five houses in different parts of the city. One hundred and sixty were lodged in the Bilton Hotel, Sackville Street, forty were located in Hood's Hotel, Great Brunswick Street, thirty-five had their abode in Holles Street, thirty-seven occupied premises in Merchants' Quay, and in La Touche's Bank, adjacent to the Castle, there were twenty-eight. Each of these places was connected by telephone with the Castle, so that orders could be rapidly carried out. The officers had no easy task at the outset. It was found necessary to divide the city into districts, beats had to be devised, patrols established, the reliefs provided for, and certain points fixed upon where some of their men could be found upon any emergency. The work was harassing because it was irregular. A good portion of the work fell upon the men at night, and sudden calls were made for assistance without previous warning. Yet all the arrangements proved satisfactory, and no demand was ever made upon the officers that they were not able to immediately comply with.

"The Detective Department in their uphill and dangerous investigations of the 'Invincible' conspiracy, the ramifications of the 'Vigilance Committee,' and other frequent raids for arms, never interfered with the duties of the ordinary Metropolitan police by seeking their aid and escort. They invariably relied for assistance on the Marines, who accompanied them on all their expeditions with warrants, whether for apprehension or search, and in the most approved manner occupied the posts allotted to them. The memorable arrests in January of twenty-three Invincibles, including the Phoenix Park assassins, were made by members of the G Division, with the sole assistance of the Marines, all the arrangements to secure the prisoners and provide against any attempt at rescue being made under the responsibility of the three officers named. During the many investigations at Kilmainham, the police courts and the Castle, the Marines were constantly brought into requisition. They were specially detailed to guard the Court-House in Green Street during the trials of the Park assassins, and a variety of other duties kept them constantly employed. Often singular ingenuity was displayed by members of the body in their 'get-up' to hide their identity and calling, and an amusing instance is recorded where this was so successfully carried out that a brother Marine was deceived. The Marines began to return to England on the 1st June, and the last detachment of two officers and eleven men left yesterday."

In conclusion, the remarks made by the Lord Lieutenant in 1883 on the occasion of a banquet given in Dublin to Lord Wolseley are worth recording. In his speech referring to the Army and Marines, he said :—

"The Army in this country has many most arduous and difficult duties—duties not ordinarily connected with the Service. But the service on detachments during the last year (1882) has had to undertake still more arduous duties. They had to aid the police in many districts and assist in patrolling the country in order to put down outrage and crime. They had still further to devote themselves to the personal protection of men who were in danger. All these unusual services the Army and Marines performed most admirably. They shewed a spirit of discipline, a spirit of forbearance, of energy and activity, which does the highest credit to them, and I feel that I am only right in referring to these matters in this assembly where we are met as we are on this occasion to do honour to one of the greatest soldiers that belongs to our Queen. . . . While speaking of this I must specially refer to the force that has been in Dublin now so many months. It was a time of most unusual danger, even of panic, when the highest officials were threatened, their lives were threatened, and when there was considerable panic in the city when we called upon one of Her Majesty's Forces to assist the police in keeping order, and the Marines in considerable force came to Dublin. (Cheers). Nobody could have behaved with more admirable discipline, more admirable tact, or more admirable ability than the officers and men of that noble force during their stay in Dublin. I think the Government, the citizens of Dublin, and the country at large, owe a great debt of gratitude to that force for the manner in which they have performed their duties here."

OFFICER'S SHAKO PLATE—ROYAL MARINES, 1854. Gilt. Globe and Anchor, Silver.
(*N.B.—Observe the spelling of "Gibraltar."*) (*Actual Size*).

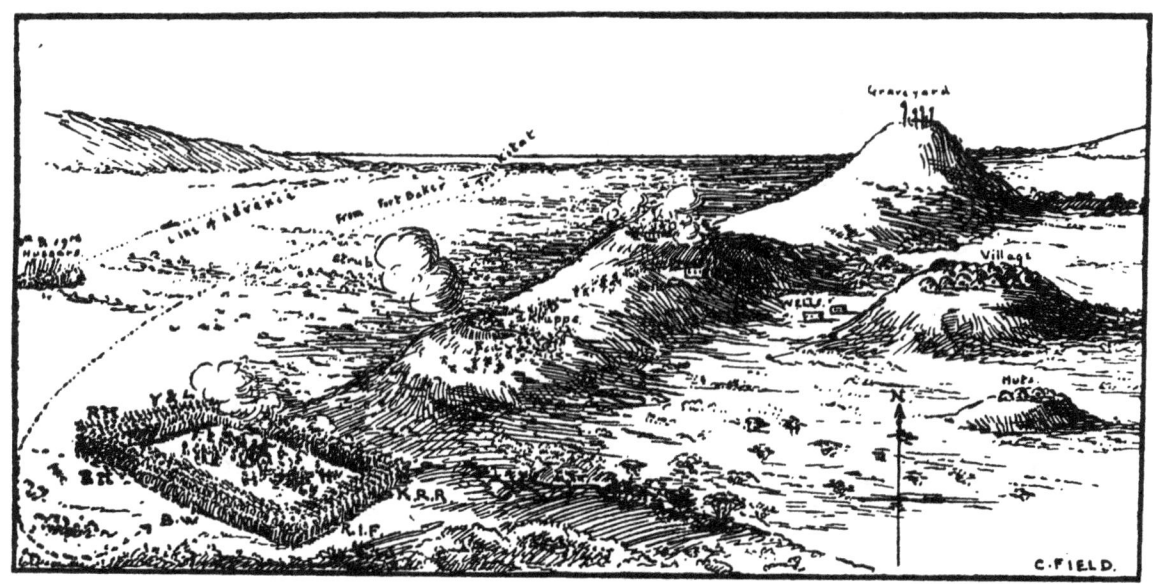

SKETCH PLAN OF THE BATTLE OF EL TEB, FEBRUARY 29TH, 1884.

CHAPTER XXXII.

THE OPERATIONS NEAR SUAKIN, 1884-5.

THE SUDAN, 1884-5.

> "Always ready for the front,
>   Always game to bear the brunt
>   When and wheresoever;
>   Always handy, and at hand—
> Much we owe that plucky band,
>   Courage-fired, and clever!
>
> Bravo, boys! Let lubbers chaff,
> On them you have turned the laugh
>   In a hundred scenes;
> England has her eyes upon you,
> Seals the praise your pluck has won *you*,
> Tell *that* to the MARINES!"
>   —*Punch*, 9th May, 1885.

Soudanese Sword & Shield.

WHILE the British troops were engaged in the short but successful campaign which culminated in the victory of Tel-el-Kebir, events were in progress in that big "hinterland" of Egypt known as the Soudan, which before very long committed them to a whole series of warlike operations which did not attain finality until our generals had reconquered the whole province and firmly established British authority in Khartoum, its capital city. But this was not until 1898. Early in 1882 a sheik named Mohammed Ahmed —the son of a Dongola carpenter—proclaimed himself as the prophet, foretold by Mohammed, who was to regenerate and gather together the forces of Islam. Nor did he rely alone on what religious enthusiasm he could arouse among those who were inclined to believe in his mission. He was cunning enough to proclaim his adherence to the modern Socialistic doctrines of universal equality and community of goods, though as events afterwards proved, he had about as much intention of "sharing alike" with his dupes as had other leaders of the communistic and revolutionary movements which have from time to time deluged the earth with blood and tears.

But his programme appealed with exceptional force to the natives of the Soudan at a time when the veniality of the Egyptian officials, the oppressive manner of collecting the taxes and the suppression of the slave trade—to which the most powerful of the tribes owed their wealth—made them welcome anything by way of a change. If not for the better, it could hardly be for the worse they argued. All attention and most of the Egyptian troops had been concentrated on Egypt proper. After the Army had been beaten and broken up by the British invaders, it seemed to the Mahdi—as the latest of the False Prophets was generally designated—and to his lieutenants, that they had everything in their favour.

The movement gathered force, and the revolt spread rapidly. In November, 1883, an Egyptian force under an English officer—Hicks Pasha—was attacked and annihilated near El Obeid, the capital of Khordofan, and on the coast of the Red Sea, Osman Digna—Osman the Ugly—one of the most able of the Mahdi's commanders, had reduced the garrisons of Tokar and Sinkat to the greatest straits, and was threatening Suakin, the principal port on the Red Sea for all merchandise from the Nile Provinces. It was time for the British Government, which had made itself responsible for Egypt, to intervene, but as has often been the case, it moved feebly at first. Starting from Suakin, which had been secured as a base by Admiral Hewett and a British squadron, an Egyptian force of over 4000 men with several British officers, under the command of Baker Pasha,[1] landed at Trinkitat with the object of relieving Sinkat. After advancing about three miles it encountered the Mahdists near El-Teb, and was totally routed with the loss of nearly 3000 men and all its guns. The fall of Sinkat and Tokar followed almost at once. Osman Digna, ex-merchant and slave dealer of Suakin, was victorious all along the line. It was necessary to tackle the rebellion more firmly, and, as usual, the Navy and Marines led off as an advanced guard.

In reply to a request from Admiral Hewett, the British Government, on 6th February, 1884, decided to undertake the defence of Suakin itself, and informed him that they were reinforcing him with 500 Royal Marines at once. 140 of these were on their way home from China and the East Indies, and others had been ordered to be sent immediately from the ships of the Mediterranean Fleet. The whole were to be under the command of Major Colwell[2] of the Flagship *Alexandra*. From Cairo came detachments of the "Black Watch," the "Gordons," 60th Rifles, Royal Irish Fusiliers, York and Lancasters, Artillery and Engineers. The little army was completed by detachments of the 10th and 19th Hussars. Sir Gerald Graham, the same officer who had commanded the Brigade in which the R.M.L.I. had served at Tel-el-Kebir, was put in charge of the whole force, which, concentrating at Trinkitat on the 28th February, marched out the same afternoon and bivouacked at Fort Baker.

---

[1] Colonel Valentine Baker, previously of the 10th Hussars.
[2] Afterwards General G. H. T. Colwell, C.B.

Private   Drum Major   Captain R.M.L.I.   Lieut. R.M.A.   Capt. R.M.L.I.   Private R.M.L.I.   Col. Sgt. & Drum Major R.M.A.
(Review Order).   (Review Order).   (Full Dress).   (Full Dress).   (Review Order).   (Marching Order).   (Review Order).
Drummer
(Marching Order).

UNIFORMS, ROYAL MARINES.
1880—1900.

On the 29th—it was Leap Year—the troops moved out in a square formation, its interior measurements being about 200 yards by 150. In front marched the 1st Battalion Gordon Highlanders, on the right the 2nd Battalion Irish Fusileers and the King's Royal Rifles. The "Black Watch" formed the rear face of the square, and its left was composed of the 1st Battalion York and Lancaster and 380 R.M.A. and R.M.L.I. At the corners of the square in front were detachments of Bluejackets with machine guns, and at the rear corners field guns manned by the Royal Artillery. In the centre were the transport animals with reserve ammunition and surgical appliances.

"As the huge square continued its advance over the barren sandy soil, it came upon ghastly vestiges of the butchery of Baker Pasha's Egyptian force. The corpses studded the route to Teb, lying about in hundreds and polluting the air. 'Swarms of carrion birds,' said an eye-witness, 'flew off on our approach.' By half-past ten we had marched three miles from Fort Baker, and here we could plainly see that the enemy had built some sort of earthworks, in which they had mounted guns and set up standards. Their outpost fire had almost ceased, only a few shots were popping off on our extreme right and left, and these were aimed at our scouts. It was a fine sight to see our fellows step out as if on holiday parade. It gave a grand idea of the power and pride of physical strength. The bagpipes played gaily, and the Highlanders, instinctively cocking their caps and swinging their shoulders, footed the way cheerily."[1] The enemy's main position faced North-west and ran along a low range of hills that rose above the scrub covered plain. On their left they had placed a couple of the Krupp guns captured from Baker's force behind a species of breastwork or epaulment. Near their centre were three unroofed brick houses, the relics of an old sugar mill, and near them lay the old boiler belonging to its engine. In front of the houses on a knoll the "Fuzzy-wuzzies"[2] had dug a number of short trenches and rifle pits, and immediately behind this knoll rose another on which stood a native village of reed huts. Between the two knolls were situated the wells belonging to the village.

The ridge was crowded with the black faces and dirty white 'gibbahs'[3] of the enemy, full of fight, and armed with their formidable cross-hilted Crusader swords, and lead-weighted spears, to say nothing of the numbers of rifles they had captured in their recent victories. Hundreds of others skulked in the scrub on the plain below continually skirmishing with the Cavalry and Mounted Infantry who were hard at work clearing the way for the advance of the main body.

A halt was made when the square arrived opposite the enemy's right, but as soon as General Graham had decided on his plan of action, which was to move along the enemy's front and attack on their left flank, the word was given to advance. As the square again started on its way, inclining a little to its right in order to make a longer detour, the enemy's trenches blazed with musketry fire, and their Krupp guns, manned by the gunners they had captured at Tokar, opened with shrapnel. Several men were hit, especially among the York and Lancasters

---

[1] Cassell's "Battles of the XIX Century."
[2] So called from the bushy way they trained their hair.
[3] Smocks of native woven cotton with distinctive coloured patches, usually blue.

and the Royal Marines who were on the side nearest to the enemy during this march. After advancing about 1000 yards without firing a shot the men were ordered to halt and lie down, while the Field and Machine Guns came into action against the enemy's cannon at a range of about 900 yards. This was about noon, and very shortly afterwards the enemy's guns were completely silenced by the accurate fire of the R.A. and the torrents of bullets from the machine guns.

The square now rose up and with bugles and pipes sounding, it wheeled to the left and advanced steadily on the enemy's position. The black fellows kept up a hot fire on the advancing British until they arrived within a couple of hundred yards of them, and then suddenly ceased firing and charged down on the square in their thousands, shouting, yelling and brandishing their formidable swords and spears. The stream of Martini bullets that rushed to meet them brought them down in scores, but the survivors hurled themselves upon the bayonets and steel clashed on steel. Many gallant soldiers bit the dust but the long triangular bayonet[1] did deadly work, and when the Gardner guns at the corners began to pump lead into the already decimated ranks of the enemy, they gave way. The British followed up the repulse with a rapid advance on the left of the enemy's position where they carried all before them. It was during this advance that Captain Knyvet Wilson,[2] R.N., gained the V.C. in engaging single-handed no less than six of the enemy who, with several others, had sallied out on a Gardner gun as it was being pulled up the hill.

But the enemy were not beaten yet. They stood firm in their central position and crowded the ruined mill buildings, from which they had to be evicted at the point of the bayonet, as the British field guns were not able to cope with the massive brick-work.

The last stand of the Arabs was made round the wells of El Teb itself. Here they had made a barricade of barrels and sand-bags and mounted two guns, but two companies of the Gordons worked round and charged the position from the rear, driving its defenders helter-skelter into the desert. During the infantry fighting on the ridge the cavalry had not been idle. Wheeling still further round the Arab left flank they charged a large mass of the enemy they found in rear of the main position. As the "Fuzzies" saw line after line of mounted men galloping down on them at top speed, they scattered among the low mimosa bushes, and proved very nasty foes to tackle. Crouching in the scrub in order to hamstring the horses and slaughter their riders as they fell, it was found very difficult to get at them with the sword and the cavalry suffered many casualties. To cope with such tactics in the future General Graham afterwards equipped his mounted troops with spears captured from the enemy, which they made good use of on subsequent occasions.

This victory, which cost the Mahdists something like 3000 men out of the 6000 which they are considered to have had engaged, was accounted for by Osman Digna to his followers, by saying that he had inadvertently given them the wrong "fetish" against steel and lead! The British, in the three hours that the action

---

[1] The bayonet used on the Martini-Henry rifle was of the old socket type, quite straight, with three channelled out sides and 1 ft. 10 in. long. Sergts., R.M.A. and Rifles had long sword bayonets.
[2] Afterwards Admiral of the Fleet, Sir A. K. Wilson, V.C., G.C.B., G.C.V.O.

THE BATTLE OF EL TEB.
By permission of the "Illustrated London News."

THE NIGHT BEFORE THE BATTLE OF TAMAI.
By permission of the "Graphic."

had lasted, had to mourn the loss of thirty-four killed and 155 wounded, including one gunner, R.M.A., and three privates R.M.L.I. killed, and twenty wounded.

The morning following the British advanced to Tokar, brought away those of the loyal inhabitants who had survived the siege, re-embarked on the 4th March at Trinkitat, and returned to Suakin.

Hoping that the Arabs had been taught a salutary lesson, Admiral Hewett issued proclamations denouncing Osman the Ugly as a rebel, and calling upon the tribes to submit to the Egyptian Government.

Meanwhile the Arabs had formed a large camp at Tamai, and when having received no offers of submission, General Graham sent them word of his intention of advancing against them, he received a defiant reply signed by a number of the sheiks. There was nothing for it but another fight. Accordingly, the British Forces, which by now totalled 116 officers and 3216 N.C.O's and men—not including Cavalry—moved out of Suakin on the 10th and 11th to a zareba, known as "Baker's Zareba," about eight miles to the Southward. Here concentration and strengthening of its defences went on till the 13th, when an early start was made for Tamai.

While this was going on the enemy from time to time fired a few long range shots at the zareba, especially at 1 a.m. on the 13th when they succeeded in killing a man belonging to the 65th and Major Colwell's horse. One officer, four men and two camel-drivers were wounded as well as several horses.

The Royal Marine Battalion now totalled 14 officers and 464 N.C.O's and men. It was divided into six companies and placed under the command of Colonel Tuson, R.M.A. When the advance was made on Tamai, 100 Marines under Lieut. Brittan, R.M.A., were left in Fort Euryalus[1] at Suakin, to protect the town and the sick men left in Camp. About 7-30 a.m. the Mounted Infantry were pushed forward to get in touch with the enemy, information having been received from a native spy that the bulk of Osman Digna's forces would be in a deep khor or watercourse in front of the village of Tamai, the sides of which would answer the purpose of an entrenchment.

The British Infantry were formed in two brigades, the 1st under Brigadier-General Buller, consisting of the 60th Rifles, the 75th, the 89th and a Camel Battery, moved echeloned to the right rear of the 2nd Brigade commanded by General Davis, which advanced in the following formation. On the left flank four companies of the "Black Watch" in open columns of companies; on the front face, three companies of the same regiment, and at an interval of thirty paces three companies of the 65th, on the right flank three companies of the 65th. The Royal Marines formed the rear face of the square. Inside the square were the guns of the Naval Brigade and a 9-pounder Mule Battery.

The rear battalions and the half-battalions on either flank of each Brigade marched at wheeling distances, so that on the word to form outwards being given, two complete squares could be formed. The two Brigades were thus placed so as to form two independent oblongs, the front face or line of each Brigade being about 200 yards in length, the sides about 100 yards. The main body of the

---

[1] This fort mounted five guns.

Cavalry was echeloned on the left rear of the 2nd Brigade. The morning was bright and clear, but there was no wind to carry off the smoke.

When the leading 2nd Brigade square got within 200 yards of the ravine, a series of broken and irregular rushes was made by the Soudanese on the front and right, but none of them reached within twenty yards of the British line.

THE BATTLE OF TAMAI, 13th MARCH, 1884.[2]

Then apparently an order was given to charge, and the front rank of the square charged up to within thirty yards from the edge of the ravine; the enemy were now swarming on the ridges on the opposite side of the ravine, and the Naval machine guns, which had been run out a few yards in front of the right corner of the square, were turned upon them. Many of the enemy were observed running down the slopes, and disappearing among the rocks in the little valley intervening. Under cover of the smoke hundreds of the Soudanese crept up the near side of the ravine, and threw themselves upon the right front and the right flank of the square."[1] "And now, as the pressure increased, the weak points of a square formation became visible," says an eye-witness. "The companies of the 'York and Lancasters' and 'Black Watch,' forming the front face, swept forward against the foe; but the remaining companies of these regiments, which formed the sides of the square, and were also expecting an attack, did not keep up with the rapid movement of those in front, the consequence being that many gaps appeared in

---

[1] Major E. Brittan, R.M.A., in "The Globe and Laurel."
[2] This and the four following illustrations are re-produced from the "Illustrated Naval and Military Magazine," 1885.—By permission of the "Illustrated London News."

what should have been a solid wall of men."[1] "The 65th, unable to resist the onslaught, were forced back upon the Marines in the rear, the right wing of the 42nd became exposed, and the enemy rushing in were among the Highlanders on their flank and rear, cutting and spearing in every direction. The men were so huddled together, that many of them were unable to use their rifles or bayonets. The Marines in rear of the Brigade were wheeled up to support the 65th, and close the gaps in the formation, but it was too late, and they too were thrown back, and borne away on the line of retreat. As the Marines were being swept away, Major Colwell, R.M.L.I., shouted in stentorian tones, "Men of the Portsmouth Division, rally," which they did, 150 of them closing together in a compact little body, forming a small square. The Highlanders and 65th also formed one or two such groups, and materially assisted in bringing about the general rally, which soon followed.

In spite of every effort, however, it appears that the whole force fell back about 800 yards. The Naval Brigade, which had been sent to the front with their machine guns, during the rush lost three of their officers, and many of their men, and the guns had to be abandoned.

It is due to the soldiers of the 2nd Brigade to say that although driven back, there was no such thing as a stampede; they retreated backwards, face to the foe, loading and firing all the time they were not engaged in meeting the attack with thrusts of the bayonet. The rally took place in about twenty minutes. This was greatly assisted by the cross fire of the First Brigade, from its position at some 400 or 500 yards from the ravine, and by the fire from the Cavalry, who were dismounted for the purpose, and fired volleys into the enemy's right flank. Covered by this fire, the retreating troops were halted and reformed, this time in "line" with the Marines on the right, the 65th in the centre, and the 42nd, with the Naval Brigade in their rear, on the left. After a quarter of an hour's halt, while a fresh supply of ammunition was being served out to each man, the 2nd Brigade once more moved forward to the attack.

The 1st Brigade had now moved up 200 yards closer to the ravine, and halted, pouring a raking fire into the enemy, preventing any attempt to again rush the flank of the 2nd Brigade. In ten minutes the lost ground had been regained, and the guns recaptured."[2]

Referring to this dangerous crisis of the engagement, General Graham says in his official despatch, " In rear of the square were the Royal Marines, than whom there can be no finer troops, and on whom I had counted as a reserve in the last emergency. Such, however, was the sudden nature of the disorder, and the impetuosity of the rush, that the Royal Marines were for a few minutes swept back, and mixed up in the general confusion. Yet, I submit, there was no panic among the men; they had been surprised, attacked suddenly, and driven back by a fanatical and determined enemy, who came on utterly regardless of loss, and who were, as I have since learned, led by their bravest chiefs. As soon as the men had had time to think, they rallied and reformed."

---

[1] Cassell's "Battles of the XIXth Century."
[2] Major E. Brittan, R.M.A., in "The Globe and Laurel."

It was now the turn of the 1st Brigade, which, still in square formation, was sent to take a second intervening ridge, some 800 yards off. The Soudanese, disheartened, kept up a feeble fire, retreating as the Brigade advanced, and the second ridge was carried without difficulty. From the top of this ridge, Tamai could be seen in the valley below, with the tents and huts of Osman Digna's camp. By 11-40 a.m. these were in the possession of the British Forces.

The British losses were five officers and 86 N.C.O's and men killed, eight officers and 100 men wounded, nineteen missing. Out of these numbers the Royal Marines lost three killed and fifteen wounded, including Surgeon Cross, R.N., the Medical Officer attached to the Battalion. To these numbers must be added two privates wounded in camp the night previous.

The force returned to Suakin the next day leaving Osman Digna's camp blazing behind it.

Three days later Captain Baldwin, R.M.L.I.,[1] and his detachment re-joined H.M.S. *Euryalus*, and the men belonging to H.M.S. *Briton* also went on board their ship. On March 27th, Tamanieb was taken and burned, but slight resistance being encountered. This closed the operations for the time being, all the British troops returning to Cairo with the exception of the 60th Rifles and the residue of the Royal Marines[2] who remained as garrison of Suakin till the 14th April, on which date the latter 371 strong embarked on board the s.s. *Utopia* for passage to their ships in the Mediterranean Fleet.

In the meanwhile, although the British Government had punished Osman Digna and occupied Suakin, it had made up its mind all along that the Soudan should be abandoned, and advised the Khedive to withdraw his garrisons. It was a difficult matter to do this in the disturbed state of the country, and when General Gordon, who was well acquainted with Khartoum and the surrounding country, having administered it for several years, volunteered to superintend the evacuation, the Government jumped at the idea. He arrived at Khartoum on February 18th, just ten days before the battle of El Teb, and by the beginning of March had sent no less than 2500 men down the Nile. He was then gradually being hemmed in by the forces of the Mahdi, and after April 16th, when the telegraph wires were cut by the Arabs, had no communication with the outer world. The Nile Expedition of 1884-5 followed, in which a detachment of the R.M.L.I. took part as a Company of the Guards Camel Regiment. How the expedition arrived too late to rescue the devoted Gordon from his fate, and how the Royal Marines acquitted themselves in the novel rôle of a Camel Corps is related in the next Chapter.

Although this Expedition had been unable to prevent the death of the heroic Gordon, and the fall of Khartoum, public feeling in England had been so thoroughly aroused that the idea of the evacuation of the Soudan had been altogether displaced by the determination to let the Mahdi see that he was dealing now with the British nation, and to make him learn to his cost that he could not ' twist the lion's tail " with impunity. The Nile Expedition withdrew temporarily to Korti, and prepared to go into summer quarters along the Nile, but it was

---

[1] Afterwards Commandant Plymouth Division and General.
[2] The Marines who had been detained on their way home from the paid-off ships on the China and East India Stations had left for England on 29th March.

decided to send a second and stronger expedition to Suakin, again under the command of Sir Gerald Graham, with a view not only to settling Osman Digna once and for all, but of building a railway to Berber on the Nile, so that when completed, a converging advance might be made on Khartoum, by both river and railway.

SPHINX REDOUBT, SUAKIN.
1 Gun.   2 Gatlings.   Garrison—Royal Marines.

A Battalion of the Royal Marines had left England[1] on the 10th February, 1884, to assist in the holding of Suakin and in the proposed operations in that quarter, and it did yeoman service against the attacks of Osman Digna and his savage levies. The feeble and out-of-date Egyptian defences of the town had been improved, and a number of improvised blockhouses and redoubts constructed until it was surrounded by a complete cordon of works, which while not capable of offering much resistance to modern artillery, were yet quite good enough to present formidable obstacles to the Arab besiegers. On Quarantine Island—connected with the mainland portion of the town by a railway embankment or causeway—were two redoubts. On the land side of Suakin, beginning at the Northeast, was the Tabiat-el-Yemin Redoubt garrisoned by one company of Egyptians and four guns. This was connected to the westward with the Tabiat-el-Ansari with a similar garrison, two guns and a Gatling. Next, going in a southerly direction came Tabiat-el-Wustanieh, with one company of Egyptians. This work consisted of a coral stone house surrounded by a mud wall and ditch. Forts "Carysfort" and "Euryalus," of somewhat similar construction came next, and were manned by a detachment of the Royal Marines, and a company of Egyptians with one French gun, one Krupp, a mountain gun and two Gatlings. Here, too, was an electric searchlight. Then came "Sphinx" fort, Camel Post and Left Redoubt, the first held by the Royal Marines with two Gatlings and a Krupp, the others by Egyptians with a gun in each. Fort Foulah, a coral stone tower

---

1 According to a story current in the Corps, when the Plymouth Contingent of this Battalion cn tajked a man was heard to say, "Who's this Mahdi we're going to fight?" "Oh, he's a sort of Salvation Army Captain, that's what he is," replied a comrade.

surrounded with earthworks mounting a couple of guns and held by Egyptian troops completed this line of defences. Away to the extreme North-west, for the protection of the railway, was the Sandbag Redoubt. This was made of sandbags, and railway iron, covered in with a canvas tent as roof and surrounded by a ditch

SANDBAG REDOUBT, SUAKIN.
2 Guns.　　1 Mountain Gun.　　1 Gatling,　　Garrison—Royal Marines.

and zareba of mimosa bushes. It was built by the native working parties in twelve hours and manned by the Royal Marines with three cannon and a Gatling gun. Another work for the defence of the railway, but not so far out, was known as "H" Redoubt. It was built of solid cement and railway iron with an earthwork in front for the guns. It also had a garrison of the Royal Marines. Finally, to the westward of the town, were the Right and Left Water Forts connected by a covered way. Each had two guns and a Gatling. The former had a garrison of fifty Marines, and the latter was manned by Egyptians.

"H" REDOUBT, SUAKIN.
2 Guns.　　1 Gatling.　　Garrison—Royal Marines.

RIGHT WATER FORT, SUAKIN.
2 Guns.   1 Gatling.   Garrison—50 Royal Marines.

At the beginning of 1885 the new expeditionary force began to assemble at the little Red Sea Port. A Guards Brigade—Grenadiers, Coldstreams and Scots—the East Surrey, Shropshires and Berkshire Regiments, a Battalion of Mounted Infantry, Engineers and Artillery, and a small Cavalry Brigade consisting of two squadrons of the 5th Lancers, and the same contingent from the 15th Hussars. From India came the 15th Sikhs, 17th and 28th Native Infantry, some Madras Sappers and the 9th Bengal Cavalry. On 8th March a reinforcement of 153 Marines arrived from Suez, and on this day a small reconnaissance was made towards Tamai and Hasheen. The rebels, though not making an open attack at this time, crept now and again inside the defences and murdered those they could take unawares. Thus on the 9th March two men were stabbed in the camp of the "Surreys," and on the day following, lurking Dervishes stabbed a couple of Sikhs. A few casualties were occasioned by long range firing at night, and the Arabs getting bolder attacked the Ordnance Store near H.M.S. *Dolphin*, killed two men of the Guard, and a coolie, and wounded nine of the Berkshires. These small night attacks and sniping went on from day to day, and made things somewhat uncomfortable for the expeditionary force. Sir Gerald Graham arrived to take command on the 12th, the Marines, who had twice before served under him, turning out and cheering him most enthusiastically. We cannot do better than quote from the diary of an Officer of Marines who was present:—[1]

"March 14th.—Preparations taking place for a reconnaisance. Sikhs last night killed three dogs, a donkey and a rebel. Osman Digna sent in letter asking for the body of the man killed the other night, and saying also will be peaceful if the General turns Mussulman. Several shots fired during the day from forts and *Dolphin* at enemy at a long range.

"March 19th.—All troops paraded on left of West Redoubt. After having been inspected by Sir Gerald Graham, he told us the Marines looked well on parade. Cavalry went out towards Hasheen followed by the Indian Infantry. Remainder

---

[1] Lieut. Marchant, afterwards Major-General A. E. Marchant, C.B., A.D.C.

of troops in rear to support if necessary. At 12-30 we march off for our new bivouac. The advanced troops came on the enemy at Hasheen, but did not do very much. A few killed and wounded. Orders came for march on Hasheen tomorrow.

"March 20th (Friday), Reveille at 4-30. At 5-15 we paraded and marched to West Redoubt. Here all but 53rd Regiment (the 'Shropshires' who were left behind to garrison Suakin) were drawn up in two Brigades. The General told us that the Marines were to be where they wanted to be, viz., in the front. At 6-30 a move was made. Cavalry threw out their scouts, and the two Infantry Brigades advanced in fours over very difficult ground thickly covered with mimosa bush. After going some distance we deployed into line. The cavalry having thoroughly searched the country also halted. On arrival at the entrance to a valley, the Staff took up their position on a small hill. The Berkshires advanced in a line of skirmishers, right half battalion Royal Marines in their rear. We advanced rapidly up a hill over the brow of which was our enemy, who opened a heavy fire all round, slightly wounding three men of the Berkshires." This advance is somewhat vividly described by another eyewitness.[1]

"The bushes seemed alive with riflemen," he writes, "they crowded on the Hasheen Hill; they swarmed through the underwood, and nothing could be seen but little puffs of smoke rising over the mimosa trees. Here and there a shriek, a groan, a gap in the ranks—instantly filled up—showed that some of the

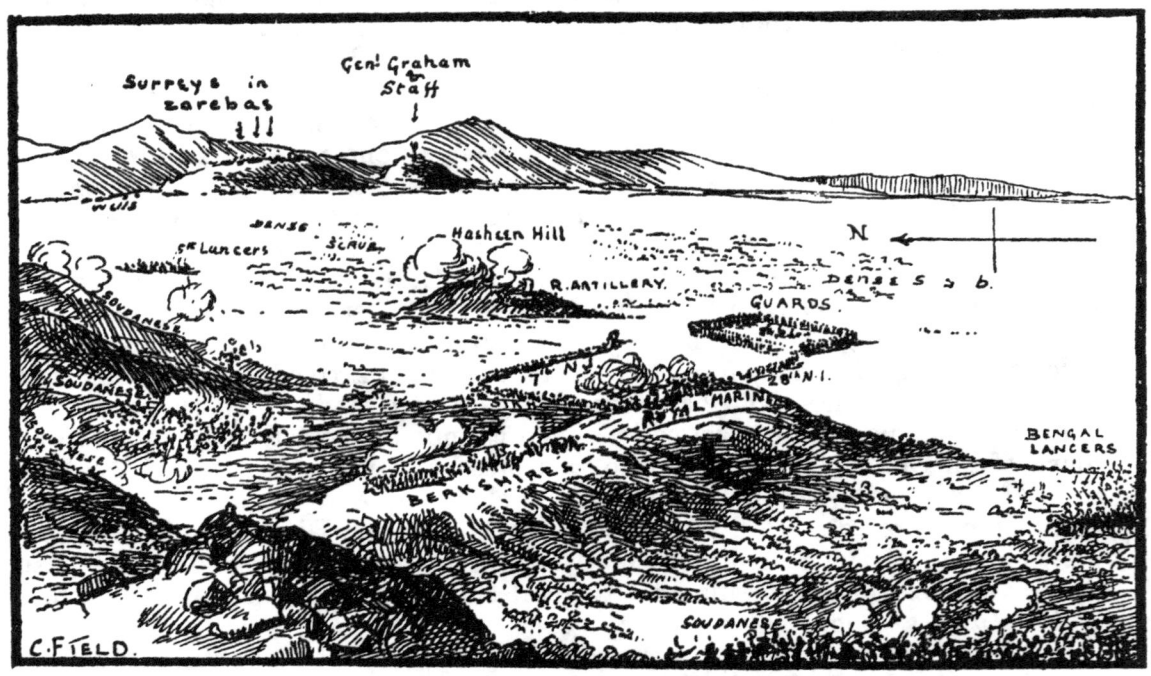

SKETCH PLAN OF THE BATTLE OF HASHEEN, 20TH MARCH, 1885.

---

[1] Quoted in Cassell's "Battles of the XIXth Century."

enemy's bullets had found a billet. But for one hit a thousand whistled harmlessly over us. The 'Berkshires' and the Marines were first sent forward to assault the enemy's position; this they did in the most gallant style, making it look like a race between the two Corps to reach some hillocks on the right of the ridge occupied by the foe. The Marines were the first to reach the crests of these earth-waves, from which they covered the advance of the 'Berkshires' by well-directed fire, the rolling volleys of musketry re-echoing among the surrounding hills."[1]

"The Guards Brigade had formed square at entrance of valley," writes the officer before quoted. "The Indian Infantry and the other Royal Marines half-battalion and the 70th Regiment advanced up this valley. From the hill we were able to get a splendid bird's-eye view. The Indian cavalry on the left behaved splendidly. The enemy who had been driven off the hill by the "Berkshires," went for the cavalry in gallant fashion, in many cases lying hidden and then ham-stringing the horses, bringing them to a standstill, and then dealing with the riders. Several on both sides were killed. The Rebel horsemen retired, and we on the hill fired volleys at them and emptied a good many saddles. The English Cavalry and Mounted Infantry on the right had a pretty hard time of it. The enemy in large numbers attacked, but were beaten off. A water-cart fell into their hands, but was recaptured. Some of the enemy, not seeing the square behind the knoll, rushed on to it, and were pretty badly handled by the right face firing volleys into them. One gallant man, apparently a shiek, riding a splendid white camel, advanced quite close and was wounded. The whole army admired and almost applauded this superb individual act of gallantry—perhaps fanaticism. He was brought into the square struggling hard. The beautiful camel was killed. The Guards, who remained stationary, lost pretty heavily, losing Captain Dallison, shot through the heart, a surgeon (Lane) dangerously wounded, and several men killed or wounded. The Indian cavalry suffered pretty considerably as well. From our post on the hill we witnessed several actions of individual gallantry on both sides. Our casualties were about sixty-five killed and wounded, and the enemy about 500. After we had withdrawn for some distance the enemy came on again, and were shelled from a hill. The first shot was fired, I should say, at about 9-15 a.m., and we marched back to camp at 4-15 p.m., eventually reaching it, thoroughly done up, about 7 p.m., but happy in having been in action and having had a thoroughly exciting sporting day, if somewhat hot. We occupied this position, and fortified two hills, and the 70th Regiment remained there. Sir Gerald Graham's object was attained, for he established a post at the Hasheen Wells, an important fact in this hot and waterless tract of country."

Having cleared Hasheen and obtained possession of the Wells the General's next object was to march on Tamai which was practically Osman Digna's headquarters, but before doing this he considered it advisable to establish an intermediate station or zareba in the desert as a depot for supplies. Sir John McNeill was sent in charge of the force detailed for this purpose.

---

[1] "The second range of hills was held by the enemy in some force, but was cleared by the Marines in splendid style, the rocks and precipitous slopes being rapidly scaled and the Arabs driven off at the point of the bayonet."—"Illustrated Naval and Military Magazine," June, 1885.

"On Sunday, 22nd," writes an officer of Marines[1] who was present on this occasion, "having struck our camp we marched at 4 o'clock in the morning to make a zareba on the road to Tamai. Off we went in two squares, one consisting of Berks and R.M.L.I., the other of Indians. We had to march through awfully thick scrub, so that what with the heat and sand and the snail's pace at which we went we had scarcely done seven miles by 12 o'clock. This was mainly owing to the frequent halts so as to regain formation and keep up the camels of which we had a large number. On arriving at our ground we commenced to form a zareba, though the majority were lying about in bushes or eating and drinking what they could get. The zareba was formed in three squares in echelon, and was to be occupied as shewn below.[2] The zareba being partly made, most of the troops

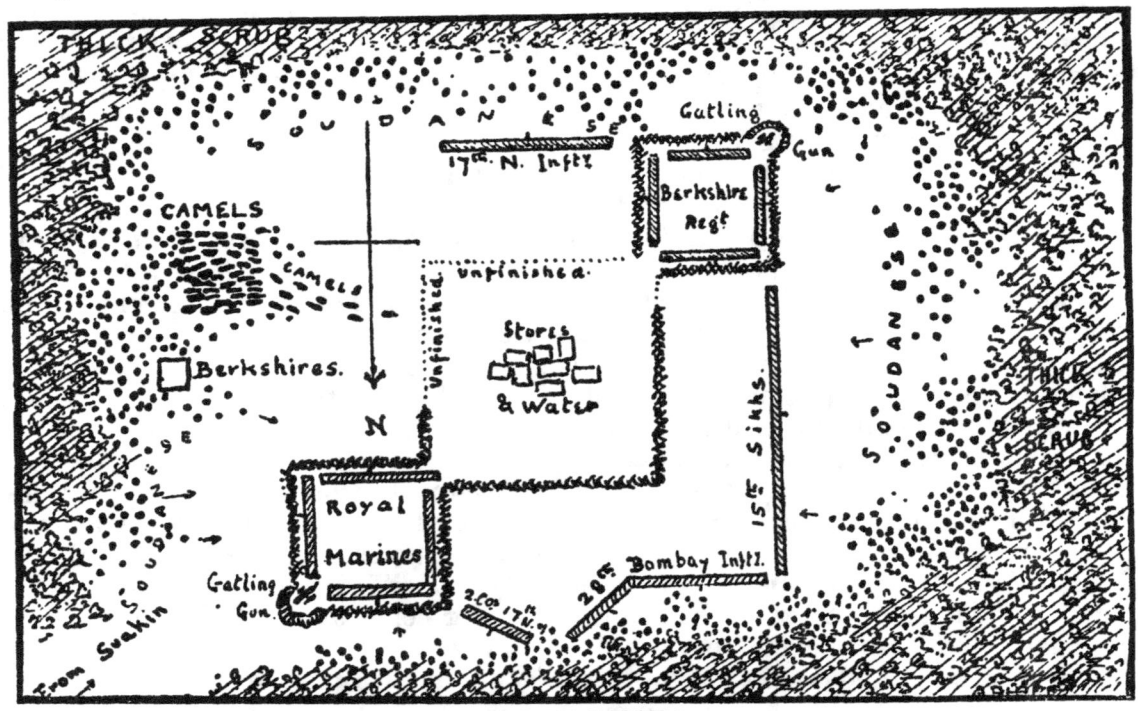

McNEILL'S ZAREBA.

were moved in, though some working parties were left outside cutting bush. The R.M.L.I. having piled arms, all round their square, were employed drawing water, rations, etc. Most had taken off their accoutrements and jackets. About 800 camels that had been unloaded inside, had been placed temporarily outside just South of the R.M. square. While thus employed, we were all suddenly startled by a roaring noise just like the sea would make in a squall. A cry of 'They're upon us,' and 'Stand to your arms' was raised. This all came from the South. The Cavalry scouts came galloping in immediately followed by a mass of Arabs. Some of them at once got into the Berks' square, killing those around their Gardner

---
[1] Lieut. afterwards Major-General Cotter.
[2] *Vide* plan.

THE ROYAL MARINES AT TOFREK (McNeil's Zareba), 23RD MARCH, 1885.

gun before they could fire, but the Berks, rallying, killed those who got in—about a hundred—and prevented any more from entering. Those who came in front of the Marines and Indians, set to work hamstringing the unloaded camels, the result being a general stampede of the camels and drivers—mostly Aden men—towards the Royal Marine square, sweeping away the feeble zareba, they darted through our square, carrying everything with them that was in their way including about fifty Marines, some Berkshire men, some Sappers, and a host of camp followers, also A—— and K——. Hard after the camels the enemy came and about twenty of them penetrated our square, but our men, closing up, killed those who got in and drove back the remainder. All the camels were ruthlessly shot. About 150 of the Berks, who were clearing the ground near-by, and had their arms with them formed a rallying square just about 400 yards to our South-east. These fellows drew off a large number of our assailants, killing over a hundred round their little square. The attack of the Arabs was well planned, but they did not understand the formation of the three squares for mutual defence, and evidently reckoned on but one. They were puzzled. Our loss was heavy. The Berkshire Regiment behaved, I think, splendidly. It is a fine battalion, all heavy bearded, long-service men. For that matter so are all the other Regiments here. In fact the Marines are the youngest body of men—as a whole—out here."

The officer from whose diary we have already quoted says with regard to this surprise: "Some officer raised a great cheer, and this, no doubt, greatly assisted to restore order again. Sergeants Mitchell and Stanton (a volunteer from the Mediterranean Squadron), both in my Company, were killed, the former having his arm cut off—probably by one of the splendid swords these niggers carried. My own opinion, formed quietly after this affair, is that if this determined rush had taken place a few minutes earlier, there would have been a grave disaster, for the enemy came on with great determination, and appeared to rise almost from under our feet, and were in amongst us as soon as our cavalry were. It was known that the enemy was about, but apparently no notice was taken."

The next day was spent in burying the dead and strengthening the zareba, and on March 24th, the day following, the morning was spent in the same way, but always in constant readiness to meet an attack of the Arabs who hovered on all sides. In the afternoon the Marines and Guards Battalion marched back towards Suakin to meet a large convoy which was coming to the zareba. During this march there was constant firing on both sides, and Lieuts. Marchant and Maclurcan were wounded, the former severely, as well as Dalrymple, the Brigade Major of the Guards, and several men.

"We halted and fired away," writes another officer,[1] "the enemy coming right up to the square singly and in groups of from four to a dozen. They never think of turning, but come right on till killed. There were two horsemen carrying banners, one of whom was knocked over, the other disappeared. It is really wonderful the way these fellows come on, they fear nothing. On Sunday I saw one fellow who had forced his way into the zareba, going along at a sort of jog-trot, brandishing his sword, receive three bullets in his body, and then it took another before he fell."

---

[1] Anonymous, in the "Globe and Laurel."

There is little more to be said about the Suakin operations. An advance in considerable force, nearly 3,000 strong, was made on Tamai on the 3rd April, in which the Marines took part. But it turned out to be a wild goose chase. The village was found to be deserted and the wells filled up and dry, so that there was nothing for it but to turn round and march back again. The only interesting point in this day's proceedings is the fact that one of the units which participated in them was the New South Wales contingent of Infantry and Artillery which had just arrived from Australia. The soldiers of the Colony, which the Marines had taken such a leading part in founding, were now for the first time standing shoulder to shoulder with the troops of the Mother Country. It may be noted, too, that among their officers were no less than three who had borne commissions in the Royal Marines.[1] The General made further reconnaisances to Handoub and Otao, but nothing but insignificant skirmishes resulted, and the Suakin-Berber Railway was pushed on as far as the last mentioned place, about fifteen miles from Suakin. But once more the Government, having put its hand to the plough, turned back. Orders were given to evacuate the Soudan altogether except Suakin, where a small garrison was left, and the expedition was broken up and returned to England.

OFFICER'S SHAKO-PLATE (R.M.L.I.), 1856-1866.
Gilt. Globe, Anchor and Bugle Silver. (*Actual size*).

---

[1] Lieut.-Col. Spalding and Major Airey, N.S.W. Permanent Artillery, Major Jekyll, Infantry. The two former retired from the Royal Marines on 1st May, 1869, and 1st April, 1879 respectively.

THE GUNBOATS AT OMDURMAN.

Chapter XXXIII.

THE NILE OPERATIONS, 1884-1898.
THE ROYAL MARINE CAMEL CORPS, 1884-5.
ROYAL MARINE ARTILLERY AND THE GUNBOATS, 1896-8.

"I've rode in a ship, I've rode in a boat,
  I've rode in a railway train,
I've rode in a coach and I've rode on a moke,
  And hope to ride one again;

But I'm riding now an animal
  A Marine never rode before,
Rigg'd up in spurs and pantaloons
  As one of the Camel Corps."
—*Sergt. Eagles, R.M.*

THE circumstances that led to the isolation of General Gordon at Khartoum have already been explained. Far from being able to complete the evacuation of the Sudan, he found himself, with a small remnant of Egyptian troops, closely besieged by ever growing hordes of fanatical Dervishes. "As the year wore on, the difficulties that environed him increased, and it became evident that the task he had undertaken was beyond his powers. His position was perilous in the extreme, and called for speedy relief from home. Neither Gordon nor the Government which allowed him to start on a perilous adventure had contemplated this contingency, but the public voice called indignantly for a rescue, and slowly and unwillingly Mr. Gladstone's Government yielded to the pressure. Unfortunately this tardy resolve was not carried into execution till success had become problematical from considerations of time and distance."[1] Eventually a relief expedition under the command of Lord Wolseley left England for Egypt and the progress of each detachment, as it slowly worked its way up the Nile, was eagerly watched in the papers. Arrived at Korti, on the upper Nile, Wolseley acquired the certitude that Gordon's position had become desperate. He therefore pushed on a flying column composed of the Mounted Infantry, the Guards Camel Regiment (Grenadiers, Coldstreams, Scots and Royal Marines), the Heavy Cavalry Camel Regiment (formed from the three Household and seven other cavalry regiments), the Mounted Infantry Camel Regiment (from various Infantry battalions), a squadron of the 19th Hussars, and various other details including the First Division of the Naval Brigade with their guns under Lord Charles Beresford. Most of the bluejackets were also mounted on camels. This very mobile force which was commanded by Sir Herbert Stewart, was to cut across the great loop made by the Nile between Korti and Metemneh, while the remainder of the expedition continued its progress up the river.

"A little before 3 a.m., on the 29th December, the cavalry scouts under Major Kitchener, with some Arab guides, moved off, and then Lord Wolseley gave his orders for the column to get into motion, and strike straight across the pebble-strewn desert, towards the distant horizon, which was indicated only by a dark, opaque and undulating line, against which a mimosa tuft stood up, and above which the rays of the yet unrisen sun were faintly crimsoning the then hazy sky, which otherwise as yet was totally dark." . . . . "It was a strange sight to watch the departing camels with their long slender necks stretched out like those of ostriches, and their legs, four thousand pairs in number, gliding along in military order, silently, softly, noiselessly, like a mighty column of phantoms, beasts and riders, until the light, rising, dust of the desert blended all, soldiers, camels, convoy, artillery and baggage, into one grey uniform mass, which, ere long, seemed to fade out, to pass away from the eyes of those who remained behind in the camp."[2]

"After a halt of about a week at the Jakdul Wells," writes an officer of the Marine Company of the Guards Camel Corps,[3] "a fresh start was made, and on the afternoon of the 16th January, 1885, the column, numbering about 1800 British troops (of whom four officers[4] and ninety-five men were Royal Marines), 350 natives, and 3000 camels, arrived at the valley of Abu Klea, and caught their first sight of the enemy. Seeing that it would be folly to go straight along the caravan track, which was completely commanded by the enemy on the hills, Sir Herbert ordered his force to diverge to the right and march up a stony slope on to a flat piece of ground at the entrance of the defile. The Arabs were evidently determined to make the column fight for the water, but, it being too late to attack them that evening, it was decided to pass the night where they were. All hands were at once employed, officers and men alike, in building a zareba wall with

---

[1] "Epochs of the British Army."—Spalding,
[2] "Playing with Fire," by James Grant.
[3] Lieut., now General H. S. Neville-White. M.V.O.
[4] Major Poe. Capt, Pearson, Lieut. C. V. F. Townshend, Lieut. H. S. Neville-White.

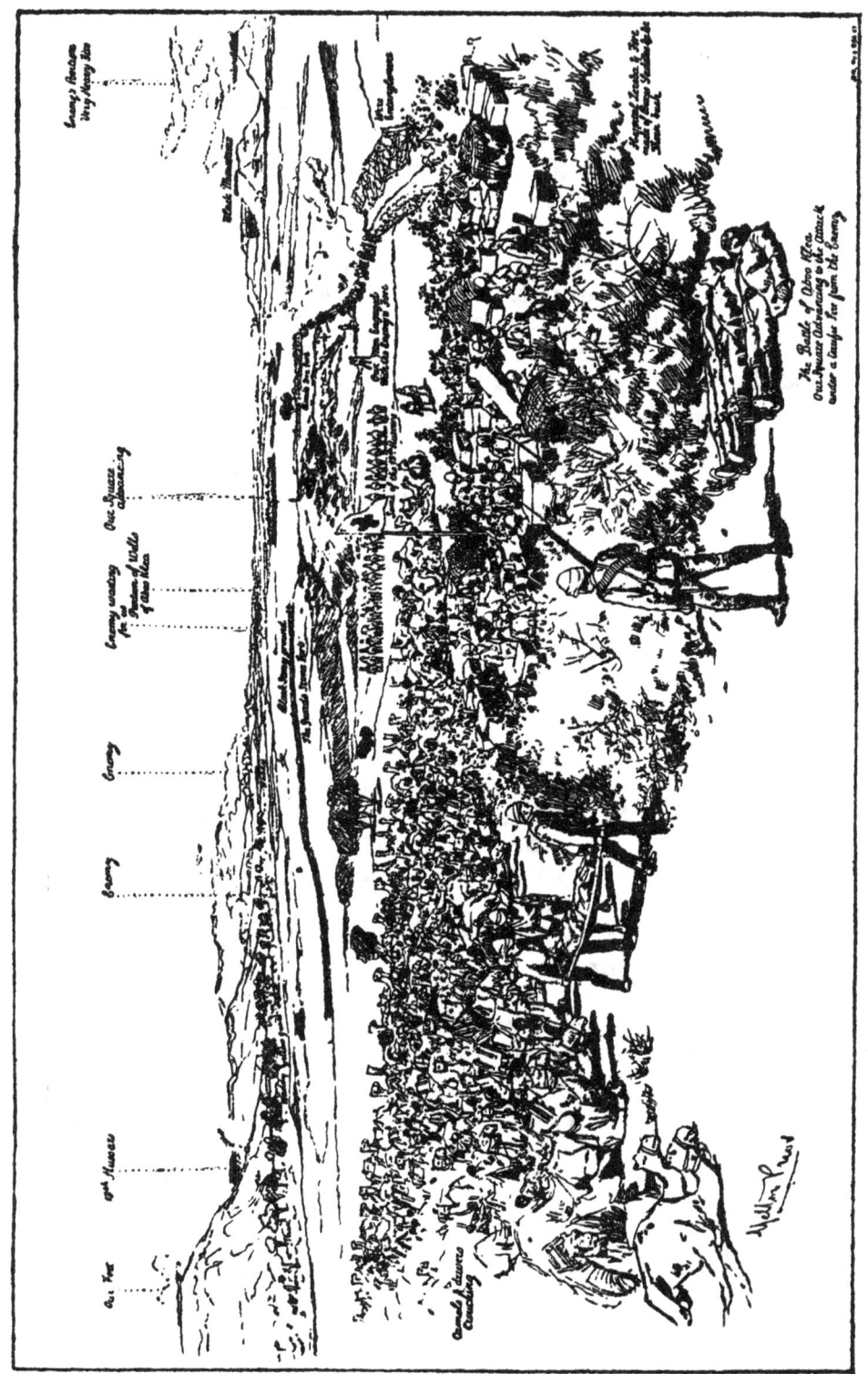

BATTLE OF ABU KLEA.

By permission of the "Illustrated London News."

such stones as could be procured from the rough surrounding ground. As the evening came on, several of the enemy occupied a hill some 1200 yards to the right, and started a dropping long range fire. A couple of field guns were brought to bear on them, which, though afterwards found to have done considerable damage, did not materially check the fire, which went on, more or less, all night, without, however, doing very much damage.

At daybreak the fire from the hill became heavier, and the men were glad to avail themselves of any cover procurable. After waiting some time in the hope that the enemy would be induced to attack, Sir Herbert Stewart prepared to advance, intending to fight his way to the wells at any cost, leaving a small garrison to protect the baggage and camels in the zareba. Having captured the wells, he could send back for the baggage, feed and water the column, and push on for Metemneh at once. The ground being too rough for rapid manoeuvring, and the enemy being in vastly greater numbers, he decided to advance in square, with camels inside to carry water, ammunition and cacolets for the wounded. At 10 o'clock the square started, keeping on the higher ground on the right of the valley, the caravan track being on the left. The Arabs redoubled their fire, and men fell right and left. The pace was very slow, the ground being too hilly, and too intersected and broken with deep water courses for rapid progress, while the camels and guns could move but slowly. Frequent halts were necessary to attend to the wounded, and the camels, unable to keep up, were constantly throwing the rear face into great confusion. The formation of the square was as follows:— Guards Camel Regiment on part of the front and on the right face, the Marines (who formed part of the regiment) being near the right rear corner, Mounted Infantry on the remainder of the front and greater part of the left face, Heavy Camel Regiment on the remainder of the left face and greater part of the rear face, in the centre of which was the Naval Brigade. A detachment of the Sussex Regiment reached from the right of the Marines to the "Heavies" and formed the right rear corner. The Royal Artillery, with their guns, were in the centre of the front face. The total fighting force was about 1300, with 150 details in the centre.

After an hour's marching some green and white flags were observed some way off to the left, which were at first taken for a burial ground, but proved to be the headquarters of the enemy, though the main attack was expected from the right, the ground being more favourable for attack and the fire being heavier from that side.

Just as their position was being turned by the square, a small forest of flags suddenly appeared and the valley became alive with vast masses of Arabs who had apparently sprung from the ground. The skirmishers, who had been sent out to check the enemy's fire were at once called in, and the square was moved to the top of the knoll some thirty yards back. The Arabs with loud yells moved across the left front, and charged the left and left rear faces of the square, intuitively selecting the weakest part, and running with incredible swiftness, so that the skirmishers had barely time to get into the square, and, indeed seriously masked the fire of the left face.

The Gardner gun, belonging to the Naval Brigade, had been moved outside the rear face to fire, but jammed after six or eight turns of the handle, and the

R.M.L.I.   R.M.L.I.   R.M.L.I.   R.M.L.I.   R.M.A.   R.M.A.   Boats Crew   R.M.A.
1856–66   1872–4   1854–66   Egypt, 1882   Soudan, 1884   1900   1854–1872   Drill Order, 1880

R.M.L.I.   R.M.L.I.
1914   1904

ROYAL MARINES. DRILL ORDER AND SERVICE KIT.
1856–1914.

Arabs, charging at that moment, nearly captured it. After a severe hand-to-hand struggle, in which two Naval officers lost their lives, and many Bluejackets were killed and wounded, the gun was dragged back into the square and saved. Meanwhile a terrific fire from the left and rear faces was opened on the Arabs, apparently with not much effect (as the enemy were charging uphill, probably most of the shots were too high), for amid shouts and yells the left rear corner was forced back by sheer weight of numbers, and the square was broken, the left and rear faces, pressing with tremendous force against the right and front faces. They, however, were still intact, and held firm, with their rear ranks faced about, or the whole square could have been swept away.

Desperate hand-to-hand fighting ensued, and the ground became literally heaped with dead and dying. It was too hot to last, and the enemy at length, almost annihilated, wavered, turned and retreated, our men shooting them down in scores as they fled. A small squadron of Arab horsemen charged the left rear corner, but were easily repulsed, and many brave Arabs turned and charged the square singly, but of course never reached it. The discomfiture of the enemy was further advanced by the fire of the front and right faces, whose rear ranks had turned about, and, being on higher ground, were able to deliver a fire over the heads of the other faces. Expecting another charge, the order was given to close up, but no charge was made and the Arabs contented themselves with a long range fire, which eventually ceased, and the enemy disappeared.

Various causes have been assigned for the breaking of the square, the fact being that owing to the dragging of the camels, it was never properly closed at the time of the charge, while the skirmishers masked the fire of the left face until the charging Arabs were within about 200 yards of the square. It is also stated that the Heavies on the left face had closed a little to the right to touch the Mounted Infantry, and thereby left a gap at the left rear corner, while the employment of cavalry in a square, and their use of a weapon to which they were not accustomed, and which, moreover, often jammed, no doubt, had some share in the catastrophe. The camels, however, which had been the main cause of the imperfect square, ultimately assisted greatly in its preservation, as they formed a solid rampart, which the Arabs could not penetrate.

The square was now moved on to a clear space of ground, and the gaps were closed up. Our losses were found to be very severe, nine officers and sixty-five men being killed, and nine officers (of whom two afterwards died) and eighty-five men wounded. The Marines suffered but little, losing only two men killed and two wounded. Over 1000 Arabs were counted dead on the ground, and fatigue parties were sent to collect and bury the arms and ammunition which were scattered about in great quantities.

The square was then moved slowly onwards to the wells, most of the men suffering greatly from thirst, but there was no water to give them. The wounded were carried on stretchers by their comrades, who were unwounded, but dead-beat from fatigue and thirst. At five o'clock the news came that the Hussars had found the wells, and the wounded were at once carried there, the remainder of the force halting a short distance off until water could be apportioned to them.

A bitterly cold and sleepless night, without food or blankets, followed the battle, during which a party of volunteers marched back to the zareba and brought up the baggage next morning, and about 10 o'clock the force got their first square meal for nearly two days.

At 4 p.m. the column paraded for a fresh start, and by half-past they were well under weigh, a small garrison being left to guard the Wells and the wounded. It was expected, when clear of the defile, that the column would halt for the night, but it soon became apparent that Sir Herbert intended by a forced night march, to cover the twenty-four miles between Abu Klea and the Nile. Strict silence was kept, the orders being passed in whispers, and at nightfall two companies of the Guards Camel Regiment (one being the Marine Company) and two of the Mounted Infantry, were dismounted to act as advance guards. As night wore on, the camel drivers fell asleep, and the starving and worn-out camels lagging behind and wandering about in an uncontrollable state, threw the whole column into confusion. Badly secured loads fell off, and in the darkness were put on again in a still more insecure manner; many of the men fell fast asleep, and orders passed from the rear to "Halt in front" never reached the head of the column. The confusion reached a climax as the force entered the Shebacat bush, and in spite of frequent halts to allow the rear to come up, the column straggled more than ever, while the worn-out soldiers fell fast asleep. At 1 o'clock the edge of the

BATTLE OF ABU KRU (from the Zareba).
By permission of the "Illustrated London News."

bush was cleared, and a more lengthened halt took place, which, however, was not sufficiently long to completely reorganise the column. This was not effectually done till dawn (about 6 o'clock) when daybreak seemed to act as a stimulus to both men and animals, and the column assumed some sort of control and formation. This spot was subsequently found to be eighteen miles from Abu Klea, and about five from the river. The time taken to traverse those eighteen miles had been fourteen hours, out of which the head of the column had been halted four and a half hours, and the rear one hour. At 7-30 a.m. the Nile and Metemneh were in sight, from which place crowds of Arabs were seen streaming out, while a force was already in position between the column and the river. Seeing he would have to fight before reaching it, Sir Herbert Stewart decided to leave the baggage in a zareba and march straight to the river with his fighting force. Accordingly, a halt was made, and a square was formed round the camels on some open ground, about four miles from the river. At 8 o'clock the enemy's sharpshooters commenced a heavy fire on the square, and Sir Herbert Stewart ordered the formation of a zareba of saddles and provision boxes to give some little protection to the men. At 10-15 Sir Herbert Stewart received his mortal wound, and the command devolved upon Sir Charles Wilson who determined, after strengthening the position, to march to the Nile. A small redoubt was accordingly constructed by volunteers, under a heavy fire, on a knoll to the right front of the zareba to prevent its occupation by the enemy, and it was not until 2-30 that the square was formed up in rear of the zareba to make for the river. The fire of the enemy's skirmishers, concealed in the long grass had, meanwhile, been incessant for six or seven hours, and the casualties were numerous.

The strength of the square was about 900 men, the Mounted Infantry being on the left face and the Guards on the front and right faces, the Marines forming the left of the front face, and thus coming in for the full brunt of the attack, which was mainly made from the direction of the left front.

At 3 o'clock the square marched off under a heavy fire, the executive orders being given by Colonel the Hon. E. E. T. Boscawen, Coldstream Guards, commanding the Guards Camel Regiment. Skirmishers were dispensed with, and the square advanced slowly, halting and firing volleys whenever the fire became very hot. The constant firing of the enemy, which, however, was to some extent checked by several well-pitched shells from the zareba, was exceptionally trying to the men, besides causing many casualties, and it was with cheers of relief, on nearing a raised gravel ridge, that they saw the Arabs preparing to charge. At the commencement of the charge a very heavy fire was brought to bear on them from the square, but the "cease firing" was then sounded, and, when the enemy was within about 300 yards, the order for volley fire was given. The regular and systematic volleys of the front face and of the Mounted Infantry were irresistible. The enemy were mown down, and not an Arab reached within thirty yards of the square. In five minutes the whole scene was changed. The yelling mass of fanatics who had headed the charge was now a heap of lifeless bodies, their comrades in rear melted away in the distance, and the road to the Nile was free, while, as was afterwards learnt, a force which was threatening the zareba also disappeared.

No further opposition was encountered, and the square reached the Nile half-an-hour after dark. In spite of the parching thirst from which the men were suffering, the most perfect discipline was maintained. The men were marched down to the river by companies, the Foot Guards and the Marines being first. On the following day, the force returned to the zareba, and brought away the wounded and the baggage without opposition, and by the evening of the 20th the whole column was encamped on the bank of the river.

In this, as in the previous engagement, the rifles frequently jammed, and many officers carried cleaning rods with jags on them.[1] When any rifle jammed, the owner fell to the rear, extracted the cartridge with the cleaning rod, and took his place in the ranks again.

The British losses on the 19th were one officer and twenty-two men killed, and eight officers and ninety men wounded. The Marines suffered heavily, losing five men killed and thirteen wounded.

The officers of Marines who were present at these engagements were Major W. H. Pöe, Captain A. C. Pearson, Lieutenant C. V. F. Townshend, and Lieutenant H. S. N. White.

Two days after Abu Kru was fought a reconnaisance was made to Metemneh, a considerable town on the Nile bank, which was not carried out without some severe fighting, in the course of which Major W. H. Pöe, of the Royal Marines, received a most severe wound in the thigh which necessitated amputation. He was hit while standing up in the open talking to his men who were lying down. Ever since the expedition had left Korti he had worn a red jacket, almost the only one in the force, which rendered him a too conspicuous target for the Mahdi's riflemen.

How Gordon's steamers were met at Metemneh and how on their returning to Khartoum with come of the expeditionary force, it was found to have fallen into the hands of the enemy, and that the gallant Gordon had been murdered, are matters of history which do not require enlarging upon here. The expedition had arrived too late, and was forthwith ordered back to Wady Halfa, and eventually broken up. But the following short account of the Royal Marine portion of the Guards' Camel Corps, written by one of its units, is of interest:—

"The Company was formed from the Battalions who were garrisoning Suakin and Suez, after General Graham's operations in the Eastern Soudan in 1884, and consisted of four officers and 102 N.C.O's and men. We left Suakin on the 10th, and Suez on the 17th October, 1884, for Cairo, where the equipment for men and beasts was obtained. After being inspected (in our new rig) and addressed by Lord Northbrook, then First Lord of the Admiralty, on the 23rd, we left Cairo on the 25th by train for Assiout, arriving there the next day and embarking on board covered barges for conveyance up the river. Leaving Assiout in company with the 19th Hussars under Colonel Barrow, and the Southern Division of R.A. under Major Hunter, we arrived safely at Assouan on November 6th. A stay of four days was made here, during which time we had lessons in mounting, dismounting and harnessing camels, under Major Marriott, R.M.A., who commanded

---

[1] A "jag" is a piece of gun-metal round which a rag can be twisted and screws on the end of the cleaning rod. The cartridges were not "solid-drawn" so the base was constantly pulled off by the extractor and the case stuck in the rifle.

A HALT AT SUNSET OF THE GUARDS' CAMEL REGIMENT, BAYUDA DESERT, RIVER NILE, 1885.

From the painting presented by the Officers of the Brigade of Guards to the Officers of the Royal Marines who served with them in the Camel Regiment.

the Egyptian Camel Corps there, and we left again for Wady Halfa arriving about the 24th. Here our camels were served out, numbered, the same as a rifle might be, on one side of the neck, the Broad Arrow being on the other side. Wady Halfa was left ten days later, in company with the R.A. and their guns, the Marine Camel Corps forming the escort to Korti, at which place we arrived on December 27th. We were inspected on arrival by Lord Wolseley, who complimented us on our clean and soldierly appearance, and were at once attached to the Guards Camel Regiment, of which we became No. 4 Company, and remained so until our arrival in England."[1]

The author of "Too Late for Gordon and Khartoum,"[2] gives us an interesting peep at the Marine Camel men at Wady Halfa:

"No part of the expeditionary force," he writes, "made themselves more comfortable under existing circumstances at Wady Halfa than did the detachment of Royal Marines forming part of the Guards Camel Regiment. When they landed here on the 20th and 21st from the barge on which they came up from Assouan, what with their pipe-clayed sun helmets and polished boots, they looked as trim as when I saw them inspected by the First Lord of the Admiralty at the Egyptian capital. Much of this trimness must of course be referred to the strict, if not rigid, discipline maintained by the officers. It was, however, largely due to the habit of theirs of being quite at home when most abroad, as they certainly were on this occasion. When under canvas on this dusty plain the same order and regularity was observed. During one of my daily strolls through the camp I noticed a tent labelled 'Rose Cottage.' The whole surroundings were so foreign to a flower garden, as to make the designation suggestive of something quite out of the common so far as its occupants were concerned. It suggested a poetical tendency and such in fact I found was the case. One of the Marines, Sergeant Eagles, was a poet! He had written some verses on the present position of this detachment of Marines in the Camel Corps, of which his comrades seemed very proud. Falling in with their humour, I accepted an invitation for sunset to hear it sung. Seated round the tent, accompanied by a banjo, they sang the song of which I here give the first verse and chorus:

> When years ago I listed, lads,
> To serve our gracious Queen,
> The sergeant made me understand
> I was a Royal Marine.
> He said sometimes they served in ships
> And sometimes served on shore,
> But never said I should wear spurs
> And be in the Camel Corps.
> I've rode in a ship, I've rode in a boat,
> I've rode in a railway train,
> I've rode in a coach and I've rode a moke,
> And hope to ride one again;

---

[1] Staff-Sergeant W. H. Martin, R.M.L.I., in the "Globe and Laurel."
[2] Mr. Alexr. MacDonald.

> But I'm riding now an animal
> A Marine never rode before,
> Rigg'd up in spurs and pantaloons
> As one of the Camel Corps.

The allusion to spurs was specially emphasised, as this part of their equipment excited peculiar interest among the men. 'Surely,' I asked, 'you have not been supplied with spurs for camel riding ?' 'Yes, indeed, sir, we have,' was the answer, 'we were served out with them at Cairo, and wore them when Lord Northbrook reviewed us.' The spurs found their way back to the Ordnance Department at Wady Halfa, but the men carried away with them the kind words of Lord Northbrook on that occasion, and his hearty recognition of their deeds and sufferings at Kassassin and Suakin, whence the detachment had been brought to join this expedition."

Here ends the story of the Marine Camel Corps, but no record of the services of the Royal Marines on the Nile would be complete without some mention of the excellent work put in by the few selected officers and men who were fortunate enough to participate in the final recapture of Khartoum in 1898.

When the British Forces were withdrawn to Wady Halfa and Suakin thirteen years previously, the Soudan had been left to the tender mercies of the Mahdi and his followers. The false prophet did not live long after this, as he died before the end of the year, but the evil he had sown lived after him. He was buried at Khartoum, or rather Omdurman, and his tomb there became a sanctuary, and the centre of the new Mahdist empire. His successor, the Khalifa Abdullhi, had been one of his best lieutenants, and for the next ten years, though the Soudan became a land of bloodshed and extortion, he consolidated his power, and carried on a continual warfare with his neighbours including the British and Egyptian frontier posts. In 1889 the Dervishes were severely defeated at Toski, and near Suakin, Tokar was recaptured from them. In March, 1896, the total defeat of an Italian Army by the Abysinnians at Adowa produced great excitement among the Mahdists, whose raison d'étre, be it remembered, was war against the " infidel." News came from Cairo that the Dervishes were about to descend on the frontier.

At this time Egypt was by no means so defenceless as in the days of Gordon. Under the careful training and toning of British officers, a really formidable and efficient native Army had come into being, and when the British Government decided that it was time to put an end to the anachronism of a cruel and mediaeval despotism which continually threatened the borders of its protectorate, it had on the spot a most valuable auxiliary to any forces it might send out.

In order to assist the expedition which it was now decided to send up the Nile, a flotilla of shallow draught gunboats was provided armed with 12-pounder and 6-pounder quick-firing guns, and Maxim machine guns. To train the Egyptian crews in the use of these weapons, Captain H. Oldfield, R.M.A., and nine corporals and bombardiers were sent out to Egypt in June, 1896. Arriving at Cairo early the following month they went through a short course of instruction in the use of the Krupp guns which still formed a considerable part of the armament of the Egyptian Army in order that, if necessity arose, they would be able to handle these weapons as well as those to which they were accustomed, such as were mounted in the latest gunboats on the Nile. A special correspondent[1] wrote at the end of the year:—"In a letter written immediately after the siege of Hafir, where gunners had their great opportunity, and made the most of it, I paid a tribute to the services rendered by N.C. officers of the Royal Marine Artillery under Captain Humphrey Oldfield. That letter went to the bottom of the Nile when the nuggar carrying mails was wrecked near Hannek Cataract, but happily the record of good work was not blotted out there. It remains indelibly impressed on the memories of all who saw what the small detachment of Royal Marine Artillerymen did from the moment of their arrival at Wady Halfa, where day after day Captain Oldfield and his nine sergeants (sic) laboured zealously at the hottest season of the year towards the completion of the task that had been entrusted to them. But for their efforts it would have been impossible to get the new gunboat put together and fitted with her armament in time to take part in the final scene at Dongola. After landing the troopers and sections of the vessel at Wady Halfa they went on to finish the work at Kosheh, where their duties as artificers ceased only on the eve of a general advance. Then they resumed their proper character as gunners, being told off by detachments to man the batteries afloat, or rather to direct the practice of the Egyptian guns' crews. Under the strain of mental and physical toil while exposed to blazing sunshine, Captain Oldfield nearly broke down for a time, but if nominally on the sick list, he managed, nevertheless, to get through a great deal of routine work, and he reported himself fit for full duty before the Nile flotilla was ready to steam away for Kosheh, under the broad pennant of Commodore Colville. Captain Oldfield was then given command of the gunboat *Metemmeh*, and took her into action at Hafir where he had two narrow escapes of being hit by shells from the Dervish battery, to say nothing of rifle bullets which buzzed around him like a swarm of bees, where he stood on the unprotected upper deck directing the movements of his ship, and correcting the aim of her gunners. One shell, without exploding, passed clean through his cabin just as he was leaving it, and another struck a gun-shield close to him, scattering iron fragments in all directions, but leaving him and the gun's crew unscathed. When Captain Colville had to leave Dongola invalided, as the result of a wound received at Hafir, Captain Oldfield was transferred to the *Tamai* in command of which he has since been patrolling the Nile."

One of the little R.M.A. detachment[2] who served in the *Zafir*, one of the newest of the river gunboats, gives the following account of the bombardment of Dongola on 23rd September, 1896:—

"We weighed anchor at 4-30 a.m., and having had a splendid view of the whole army, 15,000 strong, marching across the desert, reached the outskirts of Dongola at 5-30.

"Scarcely were we in sight of the town when the enemy opened fire on us from a brass gun throwing a 20 lb. shot. However, we were out of range; Commander Robinson immediately ordered us to our quarters—" range 4,000 yards, common shell, load "—with directions to aim at two mosques in the centre of the town—

---

[1] Of the "Daily Graphic."
[2] Corpl. G. T. Marley, R.M.A.

"commence"! The first two shells dropped right alongside the mosques, and the Dervishes immediately commenced streaming out of the town on horses, donkeys, and camels up the hills behind. Range 4,500 yards, and the fight continued. Shell after shell, common and shrapnel, dropped right into the thick of them, and made large gaps in the mass. We eventually drove the enemy over the hill into the desert where the Cavalry and Egyptian Artillery had a hot set-to, completely crushing the Dervishes, who fled in all directions. The 12-pounder fired fourteen rounds, and the 6-pounder fifty-six rounds (twenty-nine common and twenty-seven shrapnel). The other gunboats were out of range most of the time, and only fired a few rounds from their 9-pounders, which dropped short. Immediately the firing ceased, two of the gunboats proceeded up the river to Debbeh where the Dervishes had a fort. It was deserted, though the peasants near declared there were 5,000 Dervishes a few miles off in the desert."

After a few days' patrolling firing an occasional shot at parties of Arabs, the gunboats anchored off Dongola.[1] During the following year, 1897, the gunboats did not have much fighting until the bombardment of Metemneh on the 16th and 17th of October. But their presence on the river in many ways facilitated the gradual progress of the Egyptian troops up the Nile, Abu Hamed being captured on the 7th of August, and Berber occupied early in September. Driven out of Metemneh, the Dervishes crossed the river and occupied Shendy which they fortified, but were again pursued by the gunboats.

A Marine on board the *Zafir*[2] writes on 14th March, 1898:—

"For the last fortnight two gunboats have been on patrol duty, one being stationed off Shebaligah Island, where, by the way, a look-out post has been rigged up. It consists of an "angarib" (native bedstead) lashed on the top of two poles at a height of twenty-five feet above the ground. One of us British N.C.O's is always on sentry-go with a pair of field-glasses, watch, paper and pencil to observe and note the numbers of any enemy passing. The other boat has been running up to Shendy to find out if the last party of the enemy has yet left that place, and then steams back here to telegraph the latest information to the Sirdar. On Thursday, 10th inst., the gunboat *Fatteh*, Lieut. Beatty, R.N.,[3] in command, brought down news that Sergeant Russell was wounded. He was on watch, standing on an elevated platform, recently erected on deck to enable us to overlook the banks, and when steaming past Kitiab, where the stream shears close in to the right bank, some of the enemy's snipers suddenly opened fire from the thick bush at that spot, and Sergeant Russell was hit in the right leg, just below the knee, fracturing the bone. He is doing very well, and has every comfort and attention; all the officers are much concerned, and most of them have been to see him, General Hunter sent him his own tent from Berber."

"On February 25th, the *Nasir* and this boat steamed up river to shell the Forts at Shendy, and had some fun. Just after passing we observed six nuggars full of household effects, said to belong to Mahmud himself. These boats were alongside the bank, with an escort of 200 picked riflemen. These men were posted

---

[1] It was difficult to distinguish the Dervish warriors on these occasions as on the approach of a gunboat they would turn their uniforms, "gibbahs," with their distinctive coloured patches inside out, and appear as peasants in plain white only.
[2] Corpl. G. T. Marley, R.M.A., in the "Globe and Laurel."
[3] Now Admiral of the Fleet—Earl Beatty, G.C.B., O.M., G.C.V.O., D.S.O., D.C.L.

A SERGEANT OF THE R.M.A. SUPERINTENDING THE FIRE OF A NILE GUNBOAT.
By permission of the "Graphic."

in shelter trenches on top of the bank and they opened a rapid independent fire on us as we approached. You may be sure we were not many seconds getting the Maxims to bear, and very quickly silenced their fire, and whenever the muzzle of a rifle shewed afterwards it was promptly knocked away by a six-pound shell. Still we had had a lively ten minutes or so whilst the sailors were making the nuggars fast alongside us. We should have much enjoyed hearing Mahmud's comments on our capture of his furniture, etc."

Shortly after this, the Emir Mahmud, in pursuance of orders received from the Khalifa, marched northwards with 18,000 men and ten guns to attack Berber. But his march was so harrassed by the attentions of the gunboats and their R.M.A. gunners that at El Aliab, about eight miles north of Shendy, he left the river bank and struck away to the North-east to Nakheila on the Atbara River, a tributary of the Nile, where he established himself in a fortified camp.

Meanwhile the Egyptian Army, about 10,000 strong, had been reinforced by a British Brigade under General Gatacre, consisting of the Camerons, Seaforths, Lincolns and Warwicks, with a battery of four Maxims—about 3,500 men in all.

The Sirdar, General Kitchener, concentrated these troops at Kenur, just below the mouth of the Atbara, and afterwards advanced to Hudi on the North bank of that river, where he encamped.

Although the gunboats could not take part in the battle which ensued one of the R.M.A. Sergeants[1] was present. He writes:—

"Several days were employed in trying to coax the enemy out into the open, but without success; so the Sirdar determined to attack, and finding by reconnaissance that they had constructed numbers of huts of dry grass in their camp, sent word to Captain Keppel, R.N., for a rocket party from the gunboats. I was fortunate enough to be selected from our small detachment, and at 10-30 p.m., on the 5th inst., the party consisting of fourteen native gunners and myself, under the charge of Lieut. Beatty, R.N., with one rocket tube and a good supply of 24-pouud Hale's war rockets, left for Atbara camp, probably the smallest Naval Brigade on record. Camels carried the gear, and we marched. Moving all night we reached the Sirdar's camp—thirty miles—next day at 11 a.m.—Dervish camp eight miles distant."

After describing the night march which brought the Anglo-Egyptian Army within one mile of Mahmud's entrenched camp, and the opening of fire by the Artillery and rocket tubes, the narrator goes on:—

"On account of the distance and nature of the ground, I was unable to get in any good work with the rockets, so the General gave us permission to move to the right of the artillery, and we took up a good position at 500 yards range, where I was able to get in some good shots, setting their camp on fire in several places.

"By 7-30 a.m., our artillery had made it so warm for them that the Sirdar determined to assault the position, and the 'Advance' was sounded. All the bands and the pipes of the Highlanders struck up their liveliest airs, and in quick

---
[1] Colour Sergeant Jenvey, R.M.A.

time they started on their journey, passing through us and the artillery, who ceased firing. I had fired all my rockets, so we followed in rear of the firing line. The sight was truly magnificent, and one I am never likely to forget. The enemy now shewed us what stuff he was made of, pouring in a hot rifle fire, and our fellows began to drop. At about 300 yards our line halted, fired two volleys and again advanced. At 150 yards the ground sloped gently down to their position: here we were met by a perfect hail of fire, and many were hit. A halt was called and 'independent fire' ordered for two or three minutes, when the 'Advance' again sounded, and on we moved up to the zareba, and with a charge and cheer were at the enemy with the bayonet. The result was never for a moment in the balance, from trench to trench our men fought their way in grand style and the position was ours."

There would appear to have been other N.C.O's of the Royal Marine Artillery present as five were specially mentioned in the Sirdar's despatches "for their good services during the recent operations on the Atbara." Captain G. E. Matthews, R.M.L.I., was also at the battle in command of the 14th Soudanese Battalion. Gordon Bey of the Royal Engineers, a former subaltern in the R.M.A., and Captain H. Slessor, R.M.A., and Lieut.-Col. E. F. David, R.M.L.I., were also employed on the Nile at this time with the Egyptian Army.

The end of the campaign was not far off, and the Anglo-Egyptian armies slowly but surely drew nearer to Omdurman, the last stronghold of the Khalifa. A description of the great battle which finally broke the Khalifa's power and destroyed the savage empire set up by the Mahdi would be out of place in this record of the services of the Royal Marines, but we may quote from a letter of Captain H. Oldfield's,[1] a few paragraphs describing the action of the gunboats in which he and his N.C.O's superintended and directed the guns.

"Early on the morning of September 1st, the Anglo-Egyptian Army arrived at Kerri Heights, the gunboats having already gone up the river to shell Omdurman, accompanied by an Arabic rabble of various local tribes, marching abreast of them along the east bank. The gun-boats were away all that day, and did a good deal of execution, putting out of action most of the forts by the simple method of placing a shell just above an embrasure, bringing down a heap of earth, thus masking the guns; any attempt to clear away the debris being rendered dangerous and futile by Maxim fire. The boats towed down the Howitzer battery which was placed on Tutti Island, opposite the town for bombarding purposes."

The writer, after describing how the Dervish Army moved out of the town and came into collision with the Sirdar's Forces, the charge of the 21st Lancers, and the fierce attack on MacDonald's Brigade, says:—"This was, I think, the only tight place in the battle, as had the Dervishes pierced the line they would have got among the animals inside the square and stampeded them. The gun-boats on the right made good practice during this attack, and must have assisted materially in driving back the Dervishes. The Khalifa's flag was very prominent, moving slowly about on the crest of the hill until a shell burst in its immediate vicinity, when it disappeared down the lee-side rapidly."

---

[1] In the "Globe and Laurel."

THE NILE OPERATIONS, 1884-1898

The officers present who belonged or had belonged to the Marines were Gordon Bey, R.E., commanding the *Melik*, Captain Hobbs, R.M.L.I., commanding the *Fatteh*, Captain Oldfield, R.M.A., commanding the *Kailar*[1] and Water Transport Officer. Besides these there were present Captain Slessor, R.M.A., commanding the 1st Egyptian Battalion, Captain Matthews, R.M.L.I., in command of the 14th Soudanese, and Lieut.-Colonel Townshend,[2] formerly of the R.M.L.I., who commanded the 12th Battalion of the Egyptian Army. A letter from an N.C.O. Royal Marine Artillery[3] describing the destruction of the Mahdi's Tomb forms a fitting termination to the story of the services of the Corps on the Nile.

"The Dervishes believed that this tomb was indestructible, and always regarded it with most superstitious respect and veneration. On hearing this, the authorities gave instructions to Sergeant Lambert and Corporal Maynard, R.M.A., under the orders of Gordon Bey, R.E., to destroy the tomb with the assistance of a few friendlies. Three hundred pounds of gun-cotton, and about 400 yards of wire were procured together with a No. 13 detonator. The party retired to the distance of the wire's length from where the detonator was placed. When the current was put on, the tomb was entirely annihilated together with a few of the faithful."

NOTE.

NOTE I.—SERVICES OF COLONEL (AFTERWARDS MAJOR-GENERAL) CHARLES VERE FERRERS TOWNSHEND C.B., D.S.O.

This officer, one of those who, from time to time, have left the Royal Marines in search of a less circumscribed career, has a distinguished record. He is in possession of no less than nine decorations all won since 1881, in the February of which year he joined the Royal Marines. He first saw service in the Marine Company of the Guards Camel Corps in the Nile Expedition of 1884-5, shortly after which, in 1886, he applied to be transferred to the Indian Staff Corps. He took part in the Expedition against the Hunna-Nagars in 1891-2, and when a Captain in the Central Indian Horse, greatly distinguished himself in the defence of Chitral in 1895, as commander of the garrison. For his conduct on this occasion he received the C.B., the Brevet rank of Major, and the thanks of the Indian Government. In the following year he served in the Dongola Expedition in command of the 12th Soudanese Battalion, and in 1898 took part in the Expedition to Shendy and the Battles of Atbara and Khartoum. He was re-transferred to the British Service and served in the 7th Royal Fusileers whence he was promoted to 2nd in command of the Shropshire Light Infantry, and appointed Colonel on the Staff at Fyzabad. He served in the South African War, was Acting Military Attaché in Paris in 1903, and was, on 19th June, 1911, A.A.G., 9th Division of the Indian Army, 1907-9. In the latter year he was Brigadier-General in command of the Orange Free State District. Promoted to Major-General he was appointed to the command of the Home Counties, Territorial Division in 1911.

. . . . .

Since the above was written General Sir C. V. F. Townshend, K.C.B., D.S.O., has become well-known as the defender of Kut.

---

1 A Post Boat.
2 *Vide* Note 1.
3 In the A. and N. Gazette.

ROYAL MARINES MANNING A 6-in. Q.F. GUN (1896).

Chapter XXXIV.

ROYAL MARINES AFLOAT, XIXth CENTURY.

"When you wish success to all who sail in Her Majesty's Ships, you do not forget that splendid force, the Marines. (Cheers). Always to the fore when hard knocks are expected; men who march with the perfect precision of soldiers on shore, and command equally the movement of their legs at sea. Side by side with the sailors they take their place at the ships' guns."—*Mr. Goschen, 1st Lord of the Admiralty, at the Mansion House Banquet,* 1896.

SOME account of the position and duties of Marines when embarked in the 18th Century has already been given, principally from the writings of two of their officers between 1760 and 1770. The Naval Service is naturally conservative in its manners and customs, though these are necessarily modified by the successive improvements in naval architecture, armament and the general trend of civilisation. But the quotations which we are now about to make from a little book[1] published in 1842, will make it evident to our readers that as regards Detachments of Marines when embarked, very little change had taken place in the first half of

---

[1] "Hints to Young Marine Officers on their Duties Afloat," by Lieut. J. Urquhart, R.M.

the 19th Century. There is the same contriving and scheming to make both ends meet in a military sense, the same complaint of the inferiority of their equipment to that supplied to the Line—though it was evidently not so bad as it was a century earlier—the same reflections as to anomalies of command. But it must be remembered that the ships of 1842 were much more like those of 1760 than those of 1860, when steam had "arrived" and the battle between rifled guns and armour-plating had begun. The writer of the little work referred to above, begins in the approved "Early Victorian" style: "As very young officers are not unfrequently embarked in small frigates, in command of Detachments of their Corps, with no other experience in their Duties afloat than that which a Tour[1] in a Guardship can give them (and not always that); and as no Code of Instructions is issued either by the Admiralty or from Headquarters for their guidance, the few following Hints from one who has been thus circumstanced, may not be unacceptable to his juvenile Brethren in Arms." After mentioning the adverse effects of "the duties Marines are called upon to perform on board of Ship," upon Military discipline, our author goes on: "Many experienced Professional Friends whose opinions, though I differ from, I value, maintain that if a Commanding Marine officer keep his men *serviceable* while belonging to a small craft, it is as much as he can accomplish; but be that as it may, mere efficiency is *not all* that the young and zealous Commander should, at least, *attempt*; nor is it, I conceive, *all* that he may, *nay, will,* ultimately effect by attention, activity, perseverance, and gentlemanly bearing on his own part. There are few, if indeed any, Captains of the Royal Navy, who, seeing an officer desirous of doing his duty, will not gladly assist him in it, and cheerfully yield to any reasonable suggestions that he (the Commanding Marine Officer) may have to offer for the good of the Service, or the convenience and comfort of his men." This paragraph is very reminiscent of the "Marine Volunteer" of 1766, as is the following suggestion for providing for deficiencies afloat before leaving Barracks. "As Marine Cap-mountings, Shoulder-straps, strap-badges, Crescents,[2] etc., cannot be procured anywhere abroad, and are often lost at sea, notwithstanding the care that may be taken of them, the Sergeants and Corporals should be instructed to collect as many of these Ornaments about the Barracks (and there are always numbers of old ones to be had) previously to leaving, as they can. A few spare chacos should also be procured and the whole made up into a parcel, and placed in the Marine Store-Room on going on board, to be issued as required." We now come to the actual embarkation.. "Supposing the officer and his party now fairly on board, he will apply, before he dismiss his men from the Quarter Deck, to the Commanding Officer, to be shewn the Berths set apart for them; which in an Eight-and-Twenty Gun Ship are generally the two aftermost ones on the Larboard side of the Lower Deck.[3] He will then tell off his men into as many Messes as there are Berths, and appoint a Non-Commissioned Officer, or steady old soldier, to the charge of each." ... "During the period of fitting out the men will have little Military duty to perform (a Cabin-door Sentry is all that is required at first) being chiefly employed in assisting the Sailors in rigging, cleaning and provisioning the Ship, and getting the Guns,

---
[1] *i.e.,* A turn of Embarkation Duty.
[2] *Vide* Note I.
[3] *Vide* Note II.

Ammunition and other Stores on board. These are Duties which destroy the Men's Clothing in a very short time; and the only means an officer has of correcting the evil, is to set the Tailor immediately to make every Private Man (the Non-Commissioned Officers have no occasion for them), a loose Duck Frock (commonly called a Jumper, and worn over all), and pair of Trousers, the latter large enough to draw on over old Cloth ones in the Winter season. The Duck is to be had from the Purser, on a Demand being made out for it. This Document must be signed by the Marine Officer, and countersigned by the Captain." ... "When the Ship is nearly ready for Sea, and the Men are about to receive their two months' advance of Pay, the Officer will direct the Sergeant to make out a List of such things as the Men require to take abroad with them, such as Pipe-clay, Pumice-stone, Prussian Blue, Heel-balls, Blacking, Bath-brick, Copperas, Nut-galls, Bees-wax, and Rotten stone and Oil; and when the quantity of each article is determined on, and the lowest price ascertained, the Officer will cause a Subscription to be entered into among the Men (it will only amount to a couple or three shillings each) for the purchase of these requisites."

To the Marine of to-day who has little to do with pipe-clay[1]—though in the opinion of the writer the patent materials he uses in lieu have a most deleterious effect on his waist-belt and white helmet—this list of "Cleaning Gear" is Greek or Double-Dutch. Probably the older hands will remember the use of heel-ball and Bees' wax for the black pouches that used to be worn, and for the bayonet scabbards, which not long ago were required to present an appearance akin to that of patent leather, but the other articles—with the exception of Bath-brick, the use of which is only too familiar on board ship—require a little explanation. The Pumice-stone, of course, was to rub down rough and uneven pieces of buff, and the Rotten-stone and Oil to put a fine polish on bayonets etc. The Nut-galls and Copperas were for mixing a solution to be rubbed into the Pouches—which were to be previously scraped with glass and "immersed in Urine for four-and-twenty hours"—to the end that the application of Heel-ball and Bees-wax should produce the very best results in the way of blackness and polish. Additional uniform was also to be provided out of the detachment's pockets. The men were to be "induced" to provide themselves, "from some respectable tradesman, with a good white Cloth Jacket (and Materials for a second), with Blue Cuff and Collar, and small Uniform Buttons (and a spare Foraging Cap and Chinstay), the Military Undress that obtains in most ships on Foreign Stations, and which has been sanctioned and ordered by several Naval Commanders-in-Chief,[2] as being indispensable to the health and comfort of the men in hot latitudes. The coarse Flannel Waistcoats supplied with the Annual Clothing may be converted, at leisure, by the addition of Sleeves, Facings, and Uniform Buttons into comfortable Jackets for Night Duty, but all should be of one Uniform pattern." Further economy in clothing was to be made by converting the old coatees into "Uniform Shell Jackets" for wear in cold weather as soon as the new ones arrived with the Annual Clothing. There were difficulties about Boots, too, and it is

---

[1] His equipment is now made of thick khaki-coloured webbing and he has only to pipe-clay his helmet and pouch and waistbelt worn with the full-dress red-coat.
[2] *Vide* Note III.

suggested that when none were to be had, "and the Men are compelled, in consequence, to wear Purser's Shoes, which are light, and low in the quarter, and as the thick woollen Stockings with which they are supplied, cannot be worn within the Tropics, and as nothing is more offensive to the eye of an Officer than a bare instep, and ankle of a Soldier in uniform, every Man in such a case should be required to have two pair of neat well-fitted Duck Gaiters, which the Officer should insist on being worn on all occasions, both *on* and *off* Duty." We pass over various details as to the wearing and fitting of the heavy marching Order Equipment of the day, and the schemes for carrying out the inspections of various articles of clothing equipment and piecemeal, the reason for which is disclosed in the following remarks. "Thus, without interfering with the duties of the Ship, or coming into collision with the Naval Officers, for everything relating to Soldiering is done by sufferance in a Man-of-War, a Marine Officer may carry out his views quietly and effectively, and the result cannot fail to answer his expectations, and afford him satisfaction." We learn, incidentally, that the number of rounds of ball cartridges carried in "Heavy Marching Order" was 60, and from another source that the amount allowed at this time for "exercise on board," and supplied on commissioning, was "as many as will furnish one-half the Seamen and all the Marines

ROYAL MARINES AT BAYONET EXERCISE, 1908.
By permission of Messrs. Wm. Walker & Sons, Otley & London.

with 60 rounds each—half blank and half ball—for every six months."[1] The equipment to be worn when landing "abroad on Service, with the prospect of remaining on shore for any considerable or indefinite period," was to be "Red Shell Jackets, Cloth Trousers, and Blue Foraging Caps, and in Heavy Marching Order, with Mess and Water Canteens, and a Blanket rolled and carried on the

---

[1] "An Epitome of the Royal Naval Service," 1841.

top of the Knapsack, the Great Coat being folded square on the outside of the Pack, and the Mess Tin carried on the outer face of the Pack." The Knapsacks in use do not seem to have met with the approval of the author, for he says, "The new pattern Knapsack, complete with Mess-tin and Cover, Straps and Slings, which has been approved by the Consolidated Board of General Officers for the service of the Infantry of the Army, costs from 14s. 6d. to 16s. The Packs with which Marines are furnished are of a very inferior quality, but do not cost more than half that sum; they are, however, the dearest in the end."[1] Very little is said about Drill and Exercises, far less than in the two 18th Century books quoted in a previous Chapter. The author of "Hints to Young Marine Officers" considers that "Nothing but the Extension Motions, Club Drill, the Dumb Bell, and the Manual and Platoon Exercises, the Formation of Threes and Fours, and the Changing Front by ranks and files, and proving a Company should be attempted in a Ship," and who shall say that he is not right? But he goes further, and says that even when landed for Exercise nothing should be done but the Manual and Platoon, and Squad-Drill, occasionally Ball-practice."

The arrangements as to leave, Sentries, etc., upon all ordinary occasions do not call for comments as they do not differ in any important particular from those of to-day, but the special precautions to be taken when a ship manned by the non-continuous service seamen of that day was paying off[2] are worth quoting if only to make us realise the improvement which has been brought about by enlisting seamen for a fixed period instead of for a commission.

"In Harbour," says our author, "while the Ship is being got ready for 'Paying off,' the Marines are all usually employed as a Guard throughout the Ship, to check the excesses that unavoidably arise in most Ships out of the indulgences which the custom of the Service permits to the Ship's Company on such occasions. . . . The laxity of discipline, of which I speak, induces all sorts of irregularities in the Ship, and circumstances over which the Officers have but feeble control, afford every facility for the introduction of spirituous liquors among the men. Intemperance follows as a matter of course, and the safety of the Ship would be in imminent danger every hour of the day, were not the delirium of the drunkard restrained by the active exertions of that branch of the Service whose peculiar duty it is to presreve decorum among the Ship's Company under every temptation, and to maintain subordination and obedience to command despite of every disadvantage."[3]

Like his predecessors who wrote in the 18th Century, the author makes various comments on the position of the Officer of Marines and the administration of punishment to his men. He points out that the Commanding Marine Officer is equally with the Surgeon, Master and Purser, the head of a distinct, separate and responsible Department, and ought, like these Officers, to have direct intercourse with the Captain, on all matters concerning the detachment, and he admits that this is a point which "in all well regulated Ships,

---

[1] The author gives a list of the arms and appointments supplied to Marines, for which, vide Note IV.
[2] Even the continuous service Marines sometimes lost their heads when paying off. The "Illustrated London News," of 11th February, 1847, records that when the *Pluto* paid off at Woolwich that year, two privates R.M. "for a trifling wager commenced eating several £5 Bank of England notes with bread, cheese and onions; but were stopped by some of their more sensible comrades who came up at the time and compelled them to desist. Fortunately the numbers of the notes remained unmutilated."
[3] *Vide* Note V.

ROYAL MARINES MANNING THE UPPER DECK GUNS OF H.M.S. *TRIUMPH*, 1892.

Photo by the Author.

Captains will not hesitate to concede." "As a general rule," he continues, "that admits of but few exceptions, the punishment of all minor offences among the Marines should be in the hands of the Marine Officer, and he and the Captain are the only Officers who should have the power of ordering punishments of any severity to be inflicted upon the Marines." But he goes on to complain that "some Captains delegate a considerable part of their authority on this head to the First Lieutenant."[1] This has always been considered a grievance among Officers of Marines, but it is only brought forward here for the purpose of pointing out that in the previous century this question does not seem to have arisen. Whatever grievances the Officers of Marines had, and there were many, this was not one of them. Neither O'Loghlan nor McIntyre make any reference to it, and to judge from contemporary Naval History the Senior Officer of Marines was considered by his Captain to be as much the head of one part of his command, as the First Lieutenant was of the other—next to himself in both cases.

It is rather strange to find that the writer of "Hints to young Marine Officers" makes no allusion whatever to Gunnery instruction. And yet we know from Captain Glascock, R.N., that by 1826 the Royal Marines had "regular instruction and acquaintance with the management of Great Guns." Gunnery indeed has been more and more insisted upon in the curriculum of a Marine's training and instruction as time has gone on, and at present takes the precedence of all other drills and exercises, the Marine of the present day being at least the equal, in this respect, of the Seaman Gunner.

With the progress of time, too, the clothing and equipment supplied to the rank and file improved in quantity and quality. The "Hints" which have been quoted so freely, say in a note that the necessity of converting the men's waist-coats into "comfortable Jackets for night duty" had already passed since "Jackets of this description are now supplied with the Annual Clothing." In 1861 the blue serge Jacket or "Jumper" was introduced, which, slightly modified, now forms the neat and serviceable field service dress of the Corps.[2] It proved a most useful garment afloat for work for which the red coats and white cloth jackets were entirely unsuited.

With the advent of the machine and quick-firing gun of small calibre in the late "seventies," the Marines with their rifles were no longer required to provide what the old writers would have called "Small shot." Moreover, at anything like effective musketry range they would have been swept away by machine-gun fire if drawn up on deck in the fashion of the "good old days." This and the reduction in the numbers both of Blue-jackets and Marines on board our men-of-war occasioned by the increasing numbers of Stokers needed to attend to the more powerful main engines and the dozens of auxiliary engines and machines with which the progress of Naval Engineering Science equipped them in an ever increasing ratio, brought all Marines to the Guns. From being riflemen in action afloat they became gunners, and their increased training in this portion of their duty, fully qualified the Infantry as well as the Artillery for the work.[3] Some manned the machine guns, some the light quick-firers, others the heavier natures

---

[1] Who then occupied the position now held by the "Commander," *i.e.*, next in command to the Captain of a man-of-war.
[2] Until the use of khaki became almost universal on actual service.
[3] *Vide* Note VI.

of cannon. Nothing was exactly laid down, except that the R.M.A. only could be stationed at the very heaviest pieces such as those carried in turrets. In each man-of-war they served or assisted at those guns which the Captain and Gunnery Lieutenant considered most advisable.[1] In the "eighties" the time-honoured custom of placing a number of Royal Marines in the sternsheets of each boat when "Man and arm Boats" was piped was done away with, the Marines merely assisting to equip the boats with their armament, ammunition, stores, etc. One would have imagined that the splendid record of the Corps in boat work would have prevented such an order. Towards the end of the century, too, there were other and somewhat unsatisfactory changes introduced.

The detachments embarked became smaller and smaller and the numbers of the Corps being reduced on this pretext, it did not benefit by its officers and men having longer on shore between their embarkations to keep up their training as soldiers. For it must be borne in mind that the duties of a Marine being—as set forth in the motto of his Corps—"Per Mare, per Terram"—perfection in these is best attained by his serving an equal portion of his time ashore and afloat. Moreover, the longer time a recruit is under training on shore as a soldier and gunner, the better he is able to benefit by what he learns on board ship. The reduction in the numbers of Marine detachments was summarised in Mr. Trevelyan's speech introducing the Naval Estimates in March, 1882, as follows:—"I have taken the complements of specimen ships twenty years ago, and at the present date. A first-rate man-of-war in 1862 carried four Marine Officers and 156 men. The *Thunderer* and *Devastation*[2] in 1882 carry one Marine Officer and 39 men; while the largest of our vessels, and those very few indeed, carry three Officers and 130 men. A second-rate in 1862 carried 150 Marines, and a third-rate 122. There is not a second-rate now in the Navy that carries 100 Marines. But perhaps the best comparison is afforded by a 40-gun frigate and a modern corvette. The 40-gun frigate of 1862 carried 59 Marines, men and Officers. The *Comus* and her consorts, in 1882, carried only some 35. In 1862 the total force of Marines afloat was 8,500 men. In 1882, the force afloat has fallen by the force of circumstances which cannot be controlled, to 6,200 men; and as the Admiralty is fully persuaded that, in order to preserve the efficiency of the Corps as a sea-going force, there should be at least one man afloat for every man on shore, they feel themselves bound to place the establishment of the Corps at the figure at which it appears on the present estimates, about 12,400 men."

Omitting the words "at least," few Marines will be found who will not endorse the speaker's views as to the maintenance of "sea-going efficiency," always provided that the periods of embarkation and disembarkation are, neither of them, unduly short or unduly long. But though since 1882 the Corps has been somewhat increased it has not been augmented "pari passu" with the enormous increases which have necessarily been made in the number of our large men-of-war, so that of recent years the Marines' shore experience, after having been once embarked, is confined to flying visits of a few months at a time. As regards the Officers,

---

[1] In three ships in which the writer served the Marines were stationed—(1) at the two after 10-inch guns on main deck, after quickfirers on upper deck; (2) all guns (including central box batteries of 9-inch guns) on upper deck; (3) the four after 6-inch guns on main deck.

[2] Ships of exceptionally low freeboard carrying four heavy guns in two turrets. The type did not last.

R.M.A. 1859 R.M.L.I. 1867 Livery Ply. Div. 1893 R.M.A. 1914 R.M.L.I. 1869 R.M.L.I. 1914 Mess Waiter Ch. Div. 1910 R.M.A. 1914 R.M.A. 1879 R.M.L.I. 1881-1900.

ROYAL MARINES. MESS DRESS, &c.
1859—1914.

when embarked, considerable changes crept in during the latter half of the 19th Century. We have seen how in the old sailing-ship days they were constantly given charge of boats, and were even now and then in charge of a ship which had been captured. One would have imagined as the days of handling ships and boats under sail passed away and mechanical propulsion took its place, that their sphere of usefulness in this direction would have been increased. But the contrary was the case. Their activities were more and more limited and restricted, and in the discussion on a lecture on the Royal Marine Corps, given by Major-General Schomberg, R.M.A., at the Royal United Service institution in 1871, we find Commodore Goodenough saying, "There can be no doubt whatever that the *enforced idleness* of Marine Officers afloat is most prejudicial to both services, and we should ask ourselves, can we, in ships of the present day, afford to have officers afloat who have no defined duties. It is a very remarkable point, one of the most curious things in the whole of our Naval Discipline, that the "Queen's Regulations and the Admiralty Instructions" contain no instructions on that head at all." In 1884 in the Naval Prize Essay[1] Captain Charles Johnstone, R.N., remarks on this point: "Such a Corps as the Marines deserves to have its Officers made of more use in the Navy than is now the case. The Officers are in a false position on board ship; occasionally they are employed, but generally they have nothing of the least importance to do. It is much to be desired that this should be changed; the Marine Officer should, in all cases when he is competent, take charge of the work in hand; take command according to his relative rank. Thus a mixed party on shore of seamen and Marines should be commanded jointly by the Senior Officer present."

The outcome of these gradual changes was that, not being allowed to have the same interest in the ship and her doings that he used to have in the old days, and being at the same time reproached for not being of more assistance in her general work, a feeling of disgust with the Naval portion of their duty was aroused in the more ambitious and energetic of the Officers of the Royal Marines. They felt they had no scope for their talents and industry in the Navy while they saw those of their comrades who had entered the Indian Staff Corps and other branches of H.M. Service working and gaining reputation as component parts of the military machine. Such a feeling was only natural but to be deprecated from the point of view of the Naval Service generally. In 1894 it found expression in a series of letters in the "Army and Navy Gazette," under the heading " The Future of the Royal Marines." This correspondence was aroused by a paragraph in an interesting brochure entitled " The Next Naval War," written by Captain Eardley Wilmot, R.N. It ran as follows:—

"I may remark in passing that as a result of the war the Marines became more firmly knitted to the Navy. Certain excrescences were removed. They were placed entirely under the admirals at the different ports, and their principal training was in gunnery afloat, rather than in taking part in field-days under the general of the district. Their uniform was assimilated more to their connection with the sea, and blue became its predominant colour. The officers lost

---

[1] Of the Royal United Service Institution.

all desire to be considered part of the land forces, and took up their new duties afloat with enthusiasm. The only difference between them and the Naval Executive was that they represented a later entry into the Service."

This paragraph proved a veritable apple of discord. Some officer of Marines wrote to " the Army and Navy Gazette " commenting very adversely on the idea conveyed to him by the paragraph[1]—he was answered by a virulent letter from a Naval " Lieutenant (G)," and one person after another rushed into the pen and ink fray which went on week after week, and found an echo in other journals. The only reason it is mentioned here is that the controversy would appear to have eventually borne fruit, for many of the innovations which were suggested by one side or the other were to be found in the famous " New Scheme " of Naval Training issued by Lord Selbourne, 22nd December, 1902. "A plain Sailor" wrote, " If a proposal is afoot to solve the difficulty by officering the Marines from the Navy with Lieutenants (M), and Commanders (M), just as we have lieutenants (G) and Commanders (N), then, why not out with it and let us discuss the matter on its merits ? " Another writer suggested that " the *Britannia* should supply all officers to the Navy except Doctors and Chaplains."

A Marine (R.M.L.I.) wrote, " We ardently desire to be of more use on board ship, for instance, in taking turns with the lieutenants on watch in harbour, or by being employed as gunnery officers." There were suggestions from various quarters that the two Corps of R.M.A. and R.M.L.I. should gradually be merged into one, opinions expressed that Blue should be the universal colour of their uniform, though as a matter of sentiment—never to be ignored in fighting organisations—red might be retained for full dress parades.

This last has now been a *fait accompli* for several years. Under the " New Scheme " it was decided, " that henceforth all Officers for the Executive and Engineer branches and for the Royal Marines shall enter the Service as Naval Cadets under exactly the same conditions between the ages of 12 and 13." " Lieutenants (M) " became an official title though up-to-date there has been " no such person." The Marine who hankered after keeping watch in harbour[2] must have been gratified by seeing the modern officer of Marines doing what he suggested, possibly not the less in that his wish is gratified vicariously—unless at the time he wrote he had not been more than a few days in the Service. Finally, though the Admiralty hesitated to abolish such a splendid unit as the Royal Marine Artillery by merging it into the rest of the Marine Corps the scheme ordained that : " For the purposes of promotion and seniority in the Corps all these Officers, *i.e.*, the Lieutenants (M) from Osborne will be on one list, and not divided into two lists as is now the case with the Officers of the Royal Marine Artillery and the Royal Marine Light Infantry."

Though the latter part of this Chapter may seem to be somewhat of a digression from its general subject, it must be observed that all the discussions referred to and their result are closely connected with the question of the Duties of the Royal Marines Afloat and led to two very important innovations, Watch-keeping

---

[1] Captain Eardley Wilmot afterwards wrote to the "Army and Navy Gazette" to explain what he really meant by the paragraph in question. But his explanation was somewhat vague.
[2] *Vide* Note VII.

Lieut. St. G. B. Armstrong, R.M.L.I.   Lieut. E. Henderson, Maj. F. Newington,   By permission of the "Sketch."
R.M.A.   R.M.L.I.
ROYAL MARINE DETACHMENT PARADING IN MARCHING ORDER ON THE QUARTER-DECK OF H.M.S. *ROYAL SOVEREIGN*, 1885.

in Harbour, which has been already referred to, and the following still more weighty pronouncement in the " New Scheme " : " On shore, when employed with landing parties and with Naval Brigades, etc., Naval and Marine Officers will take command over one another according to their seniority in their corresponding ranks. It will also be arranged that one of the special duties of Officers of the Royal Marines will be to advise in respect of the organisation, equipment, and training of landing parties and work on shore." If the reader will refer to Captain Johnstone's remarks some pages back, he will see that this regulation exactly realises the proposition he made in 1884.

It only remains to add that so far as the Royal Marines were concerned, the "New Scheme" did not work, and in 1912 it was decided to revert to the old arrangements under which Officers passed an examination for direct entry held by the Civil Service Commissioners, but on passing, instead of joining Headquarters at once, underwent a course of study at Greenwich, before finally receiving their commissions. The weak point of the common entry scheme was that, unlike the system at the Royal Military Academy, Woolwich, under which successful candidates were placed in the order of merit attained in the entrance examination, and given the choice of the Royal Artillery or Royal Engineers in accordance with their places in the passing out examination, the candidate for the Naval Service had no idea where he was or to what branch he might be allocated. The names of successful candidates were published in an *alphabetical* list on passing in and no position on the passing out list gave a boy the right of selecting the particular branch of the Navy in which he would prefer to serve. No young man would appreciate being " told off " in this way, and after becoming thoroughly imbued with Naval ideas at Osborne it was only natural that nearly all the cadets made up their minds that the Executive Branch was the only one they wanted. That under these circumstances those selected for other branches should feel that they had not " had a square deal " cannot be wondered at, since the regulations indicated above obviously gave every opening for " partiality favour and affection." The upshot of it all was that the Admiralty announced that it had found that insufficient boys had been entered at Osborne in the earlier batches of candidates to supply officers for any branch but the Executive, and re-introduced separate entry for the Royal Marines as already stated.

NOTES.

NOTE I.—" CRESCENTS."

The " Crescents " referred to are the crescent-shaped pieces of brass which formed the ends of the shoulder scales which the Royal Marines wore from about 1820 up to and including the Crimean War. The shoulder scale and strap was of white cloth, from the button to which it was fastened two parallel blue cords ran down to the Brass Crescent. On the strap was a Brass Anchor and Crown.

NOTE II.—MARINES BERTHED AFT.

The custom of berthing the Marines aft, between the Officers' quarters and the Seamen and Stokers, which still exists, is generally considered to be due to Lord St. Vincent, who on 14th June, 1800, wrote to Sir J. B. Warren: " I lose no time—that timely precautions may be taken to defeat any machinations that may be carrying on on board—I am preparing to issue a general secret order—which will recommend that the Marines be berthed close aft to the Gunroom—(*now called the Ward Room*)—netting, without any seamen mixed with them." But as a matter of fact it would appear probable that the idea is of much older date, although it may have fallen into abeyance at the time of the Great Mutinies, for in a pamphlet published in 1699, entitled "A Short Vindication of Marine Regiments," we find the following :—" I believe it possible to prove in one instance that the Mariners (*i.e.*, Marines) have been instrumental in preventing Mutinies at Sea, and very many reasons why they may be useful that way, constant Discipline leaving deeper impressions of Duty, and the highest Regard to good Officers, and I am told *that is* the Reason their Arms are always lodged in the aftermost part of the Ship." The writer does not say definitely that the Marines were themselves berthed right aft, but it is not likely that they would have been far separated from their arms.

In this connection the following order issued by Sir H. Hotham when in command of H.M.S. *Defiance* in 1803 is of some interest.

"The Marines being a military body of men embarked for the performance of a duty similar to that in a garrison for the maintenance of good order, discipline, and subordination ; it is expected that their conduct will be an example for the seamen to follow, and that in the deportment of the officers and men they will study to preserve a soldier-like appearance and a respect in the ship, and that they may be the better able to fulfil the several duties of their office, their officers are directed to discourage as much as possible all intercourse and intimacy between them and the seamen. The Captain of Marines will be present at Guard mounting every morning to receive the report from the Officer of the Guard of the men being properly dressed, their arms clean, and he will enquire whether I have any particular orders."

H.M.S. *Wellesley*, at Trincomalee, 5th August, 1839.

NOTE III.—UNIFORM WHITE JACKETS WITH BLUE FACINGS.

"White woollen Cloth Jacket, single-breasted, with twelve small uniform buttons at equal distances down the front, blue Collar and Cuff (the latter slashed the same as scarlet Shell Jacket), the Collar to have a small button on each side, above the Shoulder Strap, which is to be of blue Cloth, lined underneath with white, and of the same size and pattern as that on the red Shell. A White Cloth Cap, eleven inches in diameter in the crown, White Band two inches wide with a narrow Blue Cloth edging or cord, Globe and Laurel on a Scarlet ground (as per regulation for blue Foraging Cap), and black patent Leather Peak and Chinstay.

This Dress, however, is only to be worn by the Royal Marines of the Squadron when they may not be required to appear in the established FULL or UNDRESS (both of which are to be taken every care of), and on all occasions when landing for exercise, unless otherwise ordered."—F. J. MAITLAND,

Rear-Admiral and Commander-in-Chief.

NOTE IV.—ARMS AND APPOINTMENTS, 1842.

	Price.			Weight.	
	£	s.	d.	lbs.	ozs.
Musket, Musket Sling and Bayonet	3	0	0	13	0
Cross Belts and Pouch (containing 60 rounds of Ball Cartridges), Breast Plate, Cap	0	11	0	11	2
Pouch, Tin Magazine, and Bayonet Scabbard, Nipple Wrench or Turnscrew	0	1	1½	0	5
Haversack (containing 3 days' Provisions)	0	1	0	5	12
Water Canteen (filled with Water)	0	3	6	5	5
Chaco	0	5	1	1	12
Coatee	0	13	0	2	12
Duck Frock and Trousers	0	5	0	3	0
White Flannel Fatigue Jacket	0	4	6	1	13
Two Pairs Cloth Trousers (one pair supplied by the Government annually ; deducted in the Total)	0	17	0	4	2
Three pairs linen ditto	0	8	9	2	12½
Knapsack and Slings	0	8	5	5	1½
Great Coat	0	13	4	6	12
Blanket (in the field)	0	8	0	4	8
Mess Canteen, Cover and Strap	0	2	6	1	9
Knee Cap	0	0	8	0	1½
Three linen Shirts	0	8	9	3	9
Three pairs Worsted Stockings	0	6	9	1	8
Two Flannel Body Belts	0	2	0	0	9
Red Shell Jacket	0	9	6	2	0
Stock and Clasp	0	0	8	0	1½

	£	s.	d.	lbs.	ozs.
Two pairs Half Boots	0	16	0	6	0
Blue Foraging Cap, Badge, Peak and Chin-Stay	0	2	3	0	10
Pair of Gloves	0	1	1	0	2½
Set of Shoe-Brushes (3 in number)	0	1	9	0	12½
Clothes Brush	0	0	10	0	3
Two Towels	0	1	0	0	12
Housewife, containing—					
Case-Knife, Fork and Spoon	0	1	4		
Pair of Hair Combs	0	0	8		
Button Stick	0	0	1		
Button Brush	0	0	5	1	2¼
Sponge	0	0	6		
Box of Blacking	0	0	10		
Set of Types (Name, Company, etc.)	0	0	6		
	5	5	1		

NOTE V.—DISTURBANCES ON PAYING OFF.

Even as late as 1859 and 60 the Marines were required to enforce discipline in one or two cases of disturbances such as are here referred to. When the *Princess Royal* was paying off in Portsmouth Dockyard, in November, 1859, a large number of liberty-men who were not allowed to pass the Dockyard Gates on account of having no officer with them, returned on board and broke up and destroyed the mess traps and tables on the lower deck, and created such a disturbance that "Marines were sent for from all the ships in harbour, and over one hundred of the crew taken prisoners on board the *Victory* and placed in irons."[1]

Similarly in March, 1860, whilst the *Diadem* was paying off at Plymouth, there were so many desertions that leave privileges were very much reduced. It would appear, too, that pay was temporarily withheld, probably with the view of making it harder for deserters to get away. The dissatisfied ship's company thereupon refused to fall in when ordered, darkened the scuttles, and put out the lights on the lower deck, raising a shout of "Money and Leave!" The Marines were drawn up under arms and the crew piped on deck. The crew obeyed the pipe and the Captain having lectured them on their conduct, promised that their grievances should be inquired into, upon which, with some reluctance they returned to their duty. "The Captain was so pleased with the conduct of the Marine Detachment that he ordered the officer in command to remit all punishments then in progress."[1]

NOTE VI.—GUNNERY IN THE ROYAL MARINES.

While it is impossible to give anything like a complete and tabulated record of the Gunnery efficiency attained by the Royal Marines — both Artillery and Infantry — of late years, a few out of a great number of meritorious achievements in this direction may be quoted. While no comparison is made with the Gunnery records of the Blue-jacket branch of the Navy, it must be pointed out that as a rule the detachment of Royal Marines on board a man-of-War does not number more than a third of her complement of Seamen. Beginning with the year 1904, we find that in the Gunlayers' Competition for that year the best shot in 19 Battleships and Cruisers was a Marine. In H.M.S. *Caesar*, which stood at the head of the list in gunnery, the group of three 6-inch guns manned by Marine Artillerymen made a World's Record of 62 rounds with 42 hits in two minutes. The best of the three guns fired 21 rounds and made 18 hits in this time.

In 1905 a Gunner, R.M.A., of H.M.S. *Euryalus*, made a "possible" with his 6-inch gun firing eight rounds, each of which scored a hit, in one minute. Sergt. Maton, R.M.A., did the same on board H.M.S. *Goliath*. Sergt. Boyce, R.M.A., of H.M.S. *Illustrious*, also made the magnificent total of 10 hits out of 11 rounds in one minute, with a 6-inch Q.F. Gun. The same year in the Gunlayers' Test on board H.M.S. *Hindustan*, Bombardier E. J. Nicol, R.M.A., made record shooting with a 9.2 gun, scoring 10 hits out of the same number of rounds fired in the space of two minutes. Between 1900 and 1906 the Marines won four times out of the seven annual 12-inch Gun Competitions in the Mediterranean Fleet. In 1908 Gunner S. Coleman, R.M.A., in the 12-pounder Competition tied with Able-Seaman F. Turtle, with twelve hits out of a dozen shots in a minute. These two men were the best 12-*pr.* gun shots in the Navy for that year.

Coming to 1909 we find the Royal Marines of H.M.S. *Magnificent* win the Quick Loading Competition, and Sergt. Lye, R.M.A., adjudged the best shot in the ship. In the *Victorious* the Marines also won the Loading Competition, and their group of 6-inch guns proved the best in the ship. The group of similar guns on board the *King Alfred* which were manned by her Marines scored 37 hits out of 41 rounds, the best gun, captained by Gunner

---

[1] *Illustrated London News*, 19th November, 1859, and 10th March, 1860.

Jeffries, R.M.A., making 8 hits out of 9 rounds. The same year Bombardier W. H. Rann, R.M.A., of the *Indomitable* firing one of her big 12-inch guns made five consecutive hits at the rate of 1.82 a minute. In the *King Alfred* Gunner R. Scutchings, at a 6-inch gun fired 11 rounds in a minute, hitting the target with every one. In 1910, in the *Temeraire*, Acting Bombardier H. A. Oliver, R.M.A., made 4 hits with a 12-inch gun at the rate of 3.29 a minute, while with a similar weapon on board H.M.S. *Bellerophon*, Sergt. G. H. Field, R.M.L.I., made the same number of hits at the rate of 2.22 a minute. Sergt. F. G. Spicer, R.M.L.I., of the *Lord Nelson*, made 3 hits at the rate of 3.14 a minute with a 9.2 gun, while Lance-Corporal R. W. Windsor, R.M.L.I., with a 12-pounder, got in 6 hits at the rate of 16.36 a minute. The year following Sergt. W. Beaumont, R.M.L.I., was adjudged the best shot in the Home Fleet, having with a 4-inch gun made 13.33 hits per minute on board H.M.S. *Topaze*. Finally, we may mention that Acting Bombardier J. E. Ward, of the *Commonwealth*, made 6 hits with a 9.2 inch gun at the rate of 6.10 a minute, and Gunner B. W. Clarke, R.M.A., of the *Exmouth*, the same number of hits in even better time, viz., 10.91 a minute.

NOTE VII.—MARINE OFFICERS KEEPING WATCH.

Even in sailing-ship days it would appear that Officers of the Royal Marines were considered by some Naval Officers to be qualified to take charge of the ship as Officer of the Watch, if we may believe the following anecdote published in the "Naval Chronicle" (Vol. XII, p. 14): "When Lord Howe commanded on the American Station, it was a regulation in the Fleet for Marine Officers to keep watch with the Lieutenants in the Navy. His Lordship once remarking at his table that Pursers, Surgeons, and even Chaplains might occasionally be employed on that duty; a son of the Church who was present, opposed that doctrine: 'What,' cries his Lordship, 'cannot ye Watch as well as Pray?'"

It does not say whether the Officers of Marines only kept watch in harbour or not, but as no reference to harbour is made, it seems probable that they kept it under any ordinary circumstances.

OFFICER'S SHAKO-PLATE (R.M.L.I.), 1866-1878.
Gilt. Garter pierced to shew Blue Enamel.
Silver Globe and Bugle. (*Actual size*).

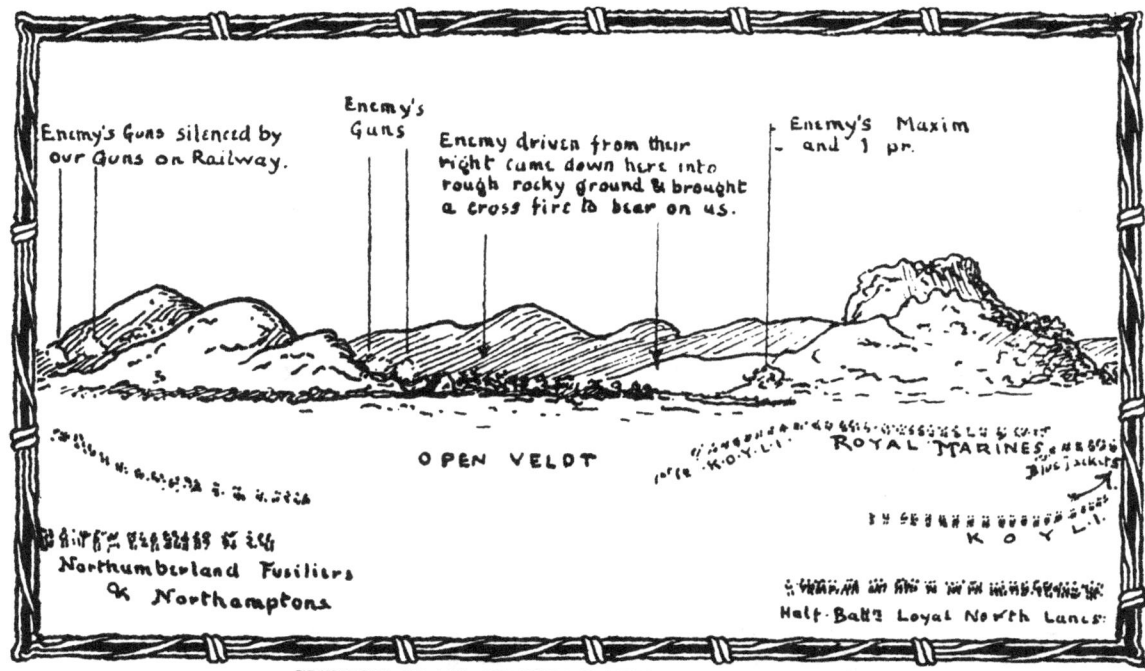

SKETCH PLAN OF THE BATTLE OF GRASPAN.
By *Lieut. W. T. C. Jones, R.M.L.I.*

Chapter XXXV

THE BATTLE OF GRASPAN

AND

THE WAR IN SOUTH AFRICA, 1899-1900

"Graspan! thy worn sides bear a fresher hue,
 Deep thy scant herbage drank thy costly dew!
 Guard well the treasure Britain gives to keep
 Watch o'er her sons, who in thy bosom sleep.
 Let no rude hand profane the lustrous green,
 That waves above a hero—a Marine!"—*John W. F. Rowe.*

THE task of writing of the doings of the Royal Marines in the South African War is a somewhat difficult one. There were but a mere handful present, all belonging to Naval Brigades with the exception of a few officers who were lent to the Army for staff duties or general service, and who had in most cases little or no opportunity for earning distinction on active service. The fact was that the greater part of the Corps was doing useful service on board the various ships of the Royal Navy, whose duty it was at this critical time to make absolutely sure the line of communication between Great Britain and her Armies engaged in South Africa. Those left at headquarters were "standing by" to go afloat in case of a fall in the European political barometer rendering a further mobilisation of the Fleet imperative.

Under these circumstances, we cannot but call the Admiralty well-advised in not sending any battalions of Royal Marines to the assistance of the Army in South Africa, useful as they would have been, and anxious as were all hands from Drummer to Colonel, to participate in the campaign as they had done in Egypt in 1882 and 1884, and in numerous other warlike operations which have been recorded in these pages. Nevertheless, although the Corps was so poorly represented in point of numbers in what turned out to be the biggest war in which we had been engaged for many decades, yet its few representatives upheld its reputation to the very utmost, especially at the Battle of Graspan, and no record of the services of the Corps would be complete which did not give some account of their work in this momentous campaign.

But so scattered were its units that any continuous and connected account of their performances is practically out of the question. Fortunately several of those engaged have written of their personal experiences, and a liberal quotation from this source of information appears to be the best way of dealing with the matter.

On Friday, 20th October, a Marine Battalion about 260 strong, was landed at Simons Town from H.M.S. *Doris, Terrible, Powerful* and *Monarch*, as escort to two 12-pounder guns manned by bluejackets.

Major Plumbe[1] was in command of the Battalion with Capt. Marchant[1] as Adjutant, and Commander Ethelston, R.N., was in command of the whole force which constituted the Naval Brigade. The following letter from a Marine[2] gives a good account of the proceedings of the Brigade.[3]

"We left our respective ships on October 19th, 1899, and reached Stormberg on Sunday, the 21st, at 4 p.m. We were met by the Royal Berkshire Regiment who had hot tea, biscuits and cheese waiting for us, and they pitched our tents, and made us as comfortable as they could. We made a stay of a fortnight. We had plenty of drill to do, also plenty of hard work in the way of building redoubts, etc., so there were not many idle moments for us. Every morning at 4 a.m. till 5 a.m., we stood to arms, that hour being passed away in practising the attack or scaling hills. We were surprised one forenoon with a false alarm. We were called to arms by the bugle sounding the " alarm.' Of course, everyone thought we were going to be engaged, but as we were climbing the hills to take up our positions, the 'retire' was sounded, much to the surprise and disappointment of everyone. We found out afterwards that it was only done to see how smartly it could be done, and it gave much satisfaction to the officer commanding troops. On Wednesday, November 1st, we suddenly received news to the effect that Stormberg had to be evacuated, and we had to pack up everything and leave at once. Nobody knew where we were going until we were in the train ready to leave, and we knew it was to Queenstown, as General Buller had made that his base, vice Stormberg. The time taken from when received the news about leaving till everyone, things and all, were in the train ready to leave was one hour and a half, and Commander Ethelston complimented the men on their smart work. Our journey to Queenstown was none too pleasant, as we had to ride in coal trucks, cattle and fruit vans,

---

[1] R.M.L.I.
[2] Bugler Lionel Ranner, R.M.L.I., in the "Globe and Laurel," February 7th, 1900.
[3] Both Royal Marines and Bluejackets wore khaki uniforms, as supplied to the Army, in this campaign.

ROYAL MARINES WHO FOUGHT AT BELMONT, GRASPAN, MODDER RIVER, MAGERSFONTEIN AND LADYSMITH.

all well exposed to the sun, which was very powerful. We reached Queenstown at 5 p.m., and were gladly welcomed by the residents. The Cape Mounted Rifles were there to play us to our camping ground, but as darkness had set in they could not play. When we left Stormberg, the Royal Berks remained behind to destroy everything, and followed on two days afterwards. At Queenstown there was little to do, because it is 100 miles from the Free State border, and there was no fear of an attack being made, so we had easier times, which we wanted badly. After a stay of ten days, we got news to the effect that we had to return to our ships. This was taken to heart by everyone, as we had not fired a single shot, but Major Plumbe and Commander Ethelston told us to take it all in good part, as we had done our best. We left Queenstown at 9 p.m. for East London, and as we were leaving camp we were cheered by the Berks, who were sorry to lose us, and their band played us to the station, and as the train went out of the station, the residents cheered and cheered, and the band played 'Auld Lang Syne.' During our run to East London, we passed the Royal Irish Rifles, with General Gatacre, and when we reached Komgha Station, there were three train-loads of them waiting to go on to Queenstown. Our train stopped opposite theirs, and they wanted to know who we were. On telling them we were the Naval Brigade, they said, ' Oh, you're the Navy. Have you brought your ships with you, as they are just the thing to fight those Boers in,' which, of course, caused great laughter amongst us.

And then they asked us if we had seen any fighting, and wanted to know if we were all wounded, and we had to reply in the negative. We reached East London at 3 p.m. The men of H.M.S. *Powerful, Monarch* and *Doris* embarked on board the *Roslin Castle* for Simonstown, and the *Terrible's* men on board the Union liner *Moor* for Durban. We got into Simonstown on Sunday, 19th, at 2 p.m., and just before the liner anchored the Flagship made a signal to prepare to entrain at 4 p.m. for another up-country trip, and this news was received with loud cheering. We left the *Roslin Castle* just at three, and went to the Dockyard, and were marched to Rear-Admiral Harris' House, where we met another party of bluejackets with four 12-pounders (12 cwt.) guns, with Captain Protheroe, R.N., in command. The Admiral inspected us, and gave us a little speech, also saying he was sorry he could not accompany us. We left Simonstown amidst cheers and strains of music to join Lord Methuen's force at Orange River."

We will let an officer who was wounded at Graspan[1] take up the story at this point.

" November 22nd.—The brigade left De Aar at 4 a.m. for Orange River, but we found on arriving there the column was at Witteputs, a place twelve miles north ; so we started off again, and with some difficulty joined the columns at 6-30 p.m., who were expected to arrive at 1-30. Wagons were then loaded and everything got ready for a forward movement. At about 8 p.m. everything was ready to advance. Senior's[2] Company was leading, then the guns, my company next, followed by the wagons, the rear being brought up by Saunders'[3] Company. It was very dark, so our advance was slow, though steady. After about three

---

[1] Lieut., now Col., W. T. C. Jones, C.B., D.S.O., R.M.L.I., in the " Globe and Laurel," March, 1900.
[2] Captain, R.M.A., killed at Graspan.
[3] Lieut. F. J. Saunders, D.S.O., R.M.L.I., killed at Beaumont-Hamel, Nov., 1916, in command of the *Anson* Battalion of the Royal Naval Division.

miles two of the wagons had to be left on the road ; the mules, which had been working all day, being done up. Marchant,[1] and Saunders, with his company, remained behind with them. We saw lights right ahead, but could not tell how far they were, we knew them to be our force which was bivouacing near Thomas' Farm, about 4,000 yards from enemy's position. On we went, halting now and then to allow the mule wagons to close up, and at last the lights, which were always in view, seemed to get much more distinct. At 11-15 p.m. we halted on the road and awaited orders, which soon came. We remained on the road at some little distance in rear of the main body, threw out piquets round the guns and wagons, forming a ring round them. I had three out-lying piquets of one section each, and an inlying piquet on the road of one section. After going round piquets and sentries giving orders and seeing that they knew what was wanted of them, I went back to the inlying piquet and lay down, about 12-15 a.m., with the Sergeant-Major and my servant alongside me. Our orders were to withdraw piquets at 2-30 and then advance. I dozed, and found the rest refreshing after a long day, but sleep was not possible as reports from piquets kept coming in."

"November 23rd.—We advanced at 2-45 a.m. about one mile, and halted opposite Thomas' Farm, and luckily my company was near the farm well, so we all had a good drink of most beautiful water, I think the best we had had since we left our ships. We now knew that there was to be a general engagement, and the division was to attack the enemy about 6,000 strong, in an entrenched position. Here was a halt of half-an-hour, during which time there was a continual stream of men passing, mostly guns, lancers, and mounted infantry. It was really marvellous how quiet everything was, except the muffled sound of the horses' hoofs on the dusty ground, and the low rumble of guns. If we had had anything to eat in the shape of tinned beef and biscuits, we had ample time to eat it and wash it down with good water, but we had nothing, except our emergency rations, which, of course, could not be thought of. One-pound tins of corned beef, which are easily opened by a patent key, are very handy on these occasions: they are good things to have with your own quartermaster's stores (if it is possible to carry them), quite independent of any Army Service Corps rations, and of course, a reserve store of ships' biscuits. To return, I have said we halted for half-an-hour, which would make the time about 3-45 a.m. Suddenly, three miles to our right front there was a rattle of musketry, which broke out while yet dark all along the line of kopjes, some of which were 400 or 500 feet high. This was the enemy firing from his position which, as the fire developed, had the effect of showing us the exact delineation of the enemy's position, which would have been impossible to see in the daylight. In a few minutes, our infantry, which had advanced under cover of darkness right across the open plain, opened fire in return and so formed a lower tier of flame. This reminds me of grounds at home illuminated with numerous fairy lamps. After about a quarter-of-an-hour of this it grew light, the rifle flashes faded, the Field Artillery Guns galloped out, and here I must follow the movements of the Naval Brigade alone, as any attempt to describe what went on elsewhere would be hopeless as far as accuracy is concerned. There seemed to be a

---

[1] Afterwards General A. E. Marchant, C.B.

great hurry to get the guns into action, as it had grown light, and the main positions had not been carried, there were also some Boer guns to be tackled, which had opened as soon as there was sufficient light. Thus the guns had a double duty, to silence the enemy's guns and also to support the infantry attack, which had reached its decisive stage. The Naval Brigade guns were pushed along as fast as possible, trying to join our F.A. Battery which had galloped out to the left front, At 3,000 yards we commenced firing, but as the F.A. Battery advanced over the railway, we had to limber up and get on. Our formation was the four 12 pounders 'in line abreast,' at twenty paces interval, supported on either flank, by my company on the right, and Senior's Company on the left. We crossed the railway in good style, the wire railing being pulled down by the Marines extended along it and pulling together. I should have mentioned that when we fired the first shot, the gun mules which were the riff raff of the mules of the whole Division, became unmanageable, so we had to drag the guns ourselves, Marines and bluejackets manning the drag ropes. After we had crossed the railway, we came under a slight fire, but no-one was hit. A few bullets passed over us, the majority going into the ground 100 to 300 yards short. We seemed to be walking right into them, but just at this time we saw that the first position was taken by the Guards Brigade on the right, and 9th Brigade on the left (Northumberland Fusiliers, K.O.Y.L.I., and Northamptons, with detachments). While we were advancing we had a beautiful view of the whole fight, the most interesting incident being a duel between the Boer battery posted in the kopjes on their left and our F.A. Battery on our right. They shelled each other for an hour, until one by one the Boer guns dropped out of the fight. By 5-30 the enemy had been driven out of their first position, when we moved to our right front, towards a valley about 800 yards broad, which divided the Boer right from their left. The difficulties of dragging the guns were very great as the ground was rough and in some places cut up by miniature nullahs but the mules were inspanned again and we got on better. Senior had taken his company back to get the gun ammunition over the railway and to bring it up. After he had got the wagons over, he was given a chance of joining the Grenadiers in the attack of the second position, but he loyally refused to leave the wagons and so brought them up to us. He lost a chance which none of us ever expected to get, but he did what he was told to do and his loyalty and unselfishness was very gratifying to all of us. At last about 8-30 a.m. we came into action in support of an infantry attack against the third position. The infantry, I think Northamptons, were right up under the kopje, heavy firing being kept up on both sides. Our guns shelled the hill, which luckily was a flat-topped one, and so easily searched by shell fire bursting over the crest. Here again, we came under a slight fire about 1,500 or 1,600 yards, but it was going very short. If the enemy had directed their fire on us seriously we should have been obliged to retire a few hundred yards, as we were offering a splendid target within a reasonable range. However, about two dozen shells, mostly 'common,' silenced the enemy's rifle fire, and the kopje and third position was taken.

This was practically the end of the day's fighting, but we still advanced and endeavoured to get the guns up a ridge or nek to our right front, but this was not possible as the ground was very bad, and we had got amongst boulders. So we went as far as we could and halted, my company being 700 yards in advance, and lying down just under the ridge. It was now 10 o'clock. Senior's company was with the wagons; Saunders' company had brought the two wagons up which had been left on the road the previous night; Marchant had come up with them. We lay down here for an hour, and although resting, felt the heat of the sun, no shelter being available. It was most interesting watching detachments, companies, half-battalions and regiments collecting and passing us from all parts of the field. There was nothing whatever about them to show that they had been through a stiff fight, except perhaps an occasional blood-stained stretcher, and one or two men who had been scratched and had tied themselves up with handkerchiefs. Otherwise it was for all the world just the same as an Aldershot field-day, especially that one which usually takes place when you suppose an army is advancing on Pirbright and Farnboro, and a force opposes him at the southern end of the Fox Hills, Woking, towards the Hog's Back. Some Scots Guards were coming down over the nek, when they caught sight of the Naval Guns, with the bluejackets standing round them wearing their khaki-covered straw hats, I heard one of them say, 'Gawd, Towny, there's them —— Boer guns we've took.' These hats are deceptive at a distance. At 11 a.m. we commenced our return to bivouac, my company doing rear guard, being relieved by Senior after about two miles. It was a hard day and our men stuck it well, they had full kit on, which was a mistake on our part, but all took it cheerfully with one exception.

"I have two cases of sunstroke in my company which happened 1½ miles from bivouac, just after we had all had a long drink of water. One or two more men fell out after this drink. We bivouaced at Thomas' Farm. When we got into camp the men were very done, but a rest and good dinner set them up, and they were soon as cheery as ever. That night we had no outpost, and went to sleep with a pipe and most excellent tot of rum. The cavalry did not come on until 4 p.m., but they were not successful in cutting up the retreating enemy, owing chiefly to the exhausted condition of the horses. There were too few of them, three regiments instead of one would have been far more to the point. We had a thorough rest and plenty to eat and drink until 2 a.m., the next day we moved northwards.

"November 24th, Friday.—We sent the guns on by rail in rear of the armoured train. The Naval Brigade was now split up, fifty bluejackets and 190 Marines advancing with the main column, the four guns manned by the remainder of the bluejackets going on by train. Lieut. Dean, R.N., was put in charge of guns, Flag-Captain in command of blues and Marines with column, Commander Ethelston and Major Plumbe commanding blues and Marines respectively. I believe the reason our guns were sent by rail was that the F.A. horses were much exhausted by the previous days' work, so they took our gun mules and gave their own horses a rest. This turned out very satisfactorily. Our bivouac that night was to be about a seven miles march from Belmont. It was rather off the real line of advance and to the right of the railway. Here we were to find water and were not at all sure that we should not have to fight for it.

Our advance was slow, owing to the very careful scouting going on in front. But we were glad to hear that the enemy had left the water and retired, so we halted just at dark, and bivouacked where we halted. At 8 p.m. Saunders took half his company up to a nek on our right rear to watch the country on the other side, or rather to give us good warning should the enemy—especially snipers—try to occupy the nek. I took the other one-and-a-half companies for water, going over the nek, Senior had already been. It was about as rough a journey as I ever hope to do. It was not very dark, there being a quarter moon, but that only made things worse, as the rocks lying in the long grass appeared to be but ground, and level ground appeared to be rock. I walked ahead and so got on fairly well, but the men who had to keep closed up had a very rocky time. Once over and down the slope of the kopje we found the water, which was really only a mile from our bivouac, but took us nearly an hour and a half to cover. The water we found was a farm dam, very shallow, so that we had to get into it to fill our water-bottles; we had a good drink, rather muddy, but beautifully cool. Coming back, I went round the kopje and got back in half-an-hour without difficulty; some men who were not with us, having gone astray in the dark, went back the same way and arrived back an hour after us. About 9-30 p.m. the A.D.C. came to the skipper to give him orders for the next day. The enemy were supposed to have occupied a strong hill about two miles out. Their strength was about 400, we were to be the firing line in an attempt to drive them out, when they were to be cut up by cavalry. The K.O.Y.L.I. were to support us, also a battery of artillery. I heard him say that the general thought it would be a nice job for us, and that we should like it. The Captain read the orders by the light of a candle produced by poor Senior, he and I both had candles in our haversacks. Ship's candles are beauties, they last so long. 1 had given him one of mine in exchange for a pencil, two or three days before. Everyone was delighted with this chance, a chance we never expected to get. . . . ."

"November 25th.—At 2-30 a.m. we withdrew picquet, fell in, charged magazines (a beastly operation at night as someone seems quite bound to let off his rifle), and marched down to the place of assembly, where we were joined by cavalry, mounted infantry, and K.O.Y.L.I., the remainder of the 9th Brigade moving after us, the Guards' Brigade with baggage. At 3-45 we advanced in mass of quarter columns opening out the space between the companies slightly. We could just distinguish our hill in the dark, or rather growing daylight; we went on slowly, the mounted men bearing away on the flanks. We saw some men on the hill as we approached, but imagine our disappointment when we found them to be our own men. The whole division then advanced, parallel to and at about 1,000 yards from the railway, in much the same order, except that the two batteries R.F.A. went to the front, with the cavalry well out. It was beautiful marching over the veldt, the pace was steady with occasional halts, and the air delightful, bracing and cool, the sun just appearing over the horizon. At 5-45 a.m., or a little before, the cavalry found the enemy strongly posted in a position which was almost identical with Belmont, except that the line of kopjes was rather broken on their left centre, and they did not run quite so high. The position extended about three miles or a bit under. The flanks were beautifully drawn back, and the field of fire was, if anything, more approaching the ideal than at Belmont; there were no commanding positions for our artillery, while the enemy had theirs beautifully posted. There was not the slightest cover for the attacking force, the flat veldt extending some thousands of yards round the positions; the grass on the veldt was about 18 inches high, with an occasional anthill here and there. On our right a F.A. battery was shelling the enemy's left at 2,000 yards; on our left the other battery and also the Naval guns which had come up by rail from Belmont behind the armoured train, were in action against the enemy's right and centre. They were opposed to the Boer guns and were subjected to a well directed shrapnel fire, but they worked the guns beautifully, silenced the enemy's artillery, and drove them from their right which was found by them to be untenable. I think the reason of this was that the kopjes on the enemy's right were of a rather round shape than conical, there was also less cover afforded by large rocks, the ground being smoother than on most kopjes. At 7 a.m. the positions were: Naval Brigade leading extended to single rank with one company K.O.Y.L.I. and the 9th Brigade also extended to single rank, supporting, were opposite the right centre of the enemy's position at 3,000 yards. The Guards' Brigade were on the main line of advance near railway with baggage. The two F.A. Batteries were on the flanks, the Naval guns being with the one on our left. The mounted troops were mostly hovering round the enemy's left flank. We now received the order to incline to our right so as to bring our firing line opposite the extreme left of the enemy's position, which the guns on our right were shelling. The brigade for the attack of this portion was made up of (1) Firing line—one company Bluejackets, fifty strong; three companies of Marines, 190 strong; one company K.O.Y.L.I., 85 strong; (2) Supports—seven companies K.O.Y.L.I.; (3) Reserves—half battalion L.N. Lancashire Regiment. There were also detachments of Northumberland Fusiliers and Northamptons, but how the latter were distributed I do not know. We now extended to four paces, and did a very difficult diagonal march for nearly two miles, keeping our left shoulders well up. The men must have found it very difficult to keep their intervals, as the point of direction kept on changing, and even the directing file was not clearly pointed out, and when this happened with a line nearly a thousand yards long the diagonal march is somewhat difficult. Our great object in doing it seemed to be to get in front of their position without exposing our left flank to attack. The sun was getting very hot and the men were a bit droopy, none of them having had breakfast before starting. Dr. Porter,[1] Marchant, Senior, Saunders, myself, and my servant had shared a 1-lb. tin of beef and a bit of bread I had brought from Belmont. I may mention that there was no such thing as a second and third line, the Northamptons and Northumberland Fusiliers, who belonged to the 9th Brigade, were separated from us. At 7-45 a.m. we were 700 yards from the base of the principal kopje, the guns ceased firing, and almost immediately the kopjes, which a moment before had seemed quite clear of the enemy, opened a regular storm of fire. (Now I am obliged to say what happened close round me, and what one sees outside one's own immediate neighbourhood seems to be very little). Bang went the guns again, firing over our heads from our right rear; our firing line was even now doing diagonal march to the right, but as this rifle fire opened on us, without any order that I heard, we instinctively turned our front towards the kopje. In places the line seemed a bit crowded, but from what I could see, the accurate extension was four paces.

---

[1] R.N., afterwards Surgeon Vice-Admiral Sir James Porter, K.C.B., K.C.M.G.

We advanced at the quick without halting. Captain Protheroe, R.N., was on the right of my company, Ethelston,[1] Boyle,[2] Midshipmen Huddart and Sillem, with blues, Plumbe, Marchant, and Sergt.-Major Dyson were with Saunders' company. The enemy's rifle fire seemed to grow in intensity, but no one was hit, when suddenly three of my men went down, falling forward. I saw one was hit by our own shrapnel bursting prematurely, so were the other two. Johnson, who was hit in the back of the head, got up, but I told him to go back, as he looked dazed and badly hit. Baddeley, signalman, who with my servant, Rice, always remained near me, gave me his rifle when he (Johnson) lay down. He afterwards told me that he remembers nothing of what I said to him, but remembers his rifle being taken; he got hold of another rifle, and went on firing over our heads. He suffered two days' concussion of the brain afterwards, but has the honour of being the first man shot, and the first man out of hospital, and is also in possession of the shrapnel bullet which had lodged in the back of his head. At about 600 yards we halted, lay down, and opened fire. First, volleys were tried, but with the noise and distance apart of the men, this was almost impossible. These rushes were continued with halts for firing, until the base of the kopje was reached. At 350 yards the enemy's firing was hottest and continued so until we got to within 100 yards of base of kopje when it seemed to slack off a bit, or perhaps it was dead space to some to the enemy. At about 300 yards I saw Captain Protheroe was hit, he was bleeding badly, so he got up, looked about him, and walked back as if nothing was going on. Why he was not hit again is an absolute marvel. At 250 yards I was hit, but it did not disable me; here I saw that Colonel Money, Northumberland Fusiliers, our Brigadier, had come up into the firing line. He, I noticed, carried a stick, and did not leave the knee, while we lay down, which also made him conspicuous to the enemy, but he was not hit. There was something very fine about the men, they did not want leading in the rushes, but only wanted someone to give them the tip as to whether it was time to get on, if you did get up a bit before time then all seemed to follow you like clockwork, there was no hesitation with them. They drilled beautifully, and this was their nature, as there was no cover, so when the line was halted to fire, you could distinctly see that wave of men closing up into line, and so keeping the line firm.

Private H. Freeman, who was near me all the time, was wounded at about 300 yards—hit through the leg—he told me it was nothing, and went on with the line as if nothing was wrong. Private Rigsby, too, was most cool and humorous, licking his bullets as he put them in as if he was using a Martini, which he told me he had a great liking for—he was Marchant's servant, and a very fine old soldier of twenty years' service. My servant Rice, and Baddeley, signalman, were very good in looking after me, not taking the slightest care of themselves. When we reached the base of the kopje, there was a pause for breath, and it was lucky that the steepness of the hill itself was to a great extent a shelter from the enemy's fire, both frontal and cross, which mostly went over us. From here we reached the top, with two halts. It was difficult climbing, the rocks being large. About twenty-five yards from the top the firing from the ridge ceased, and we knew that

---

[1] Commander R.N. (killed).   [2] Lieut. R. N., now Capt. the Hon. E. S. H. Boyle (retired).

the enemy thought that it was time to go. We at once gained the ridge. By this time the supports had all closed up to us. We had to keep under cover, as the enemy were still firing at us from the front from some small kopjes a hundred yards or so to the rear of the position they had just vacated, and also enfilading us from our left, but this was soon stopped by about two companies of supports bringing their right shoulders up and manning the left edge of the kopje, which was rather thrown forward, when they had the advantage of firing down on to the enemy who had annoyed us so much from our left. Now, the only thing left for infantry to do was to turn the few Boers who remained out of the kopje 100 yards or so in front, so Marchant took some men of various corps over and did it; it was most encouraging to watch his coolness and presence of mind, and to hear him directing the men to keep down and fire into the retreating enemy, who, luckily for them, were partially screened in their retreat by the smaller kopjes. My servant told me afterwards, that they got into them fairly well, and soon turned out those who remained to annoy us. From the main ridge it was a wonderful but tantalizing sight to see all the wagons trekking away northwards as hard as they could go. Would that our few cavalry (we were very badly off for mobile mounted troops) could have got amongst them, as wagons and all went away right across miles of open plain and had we had some really fresh lancers we might have got the whole lot. Our guns did gallop round the right and put some shrapnel amongst them, but they had not time to do much damage. Before Marchant left me he dressed me with the 1st field dressing, and Private Baddeley helped me down the hill, and got me a good billet under our own water cart, where I found one of my company and one of Senior's, both wounded. After a bit Dr. Porter came along and had a look at us, put bandages right, gave us a little brandy, and went on. It was hard to realise at first, the accounts given of our losses.[1] Poor Plumbe, Ethelston, and Senior and other men we knew so well. Stretcher bearers soon came up and took us down to a collecting place where there were some 70 or 80 wounded being looked to. There was no shelter, and the sun must have been very trying to the more serious cases. Two of our men died next to me, but they seemed wonderfully free from pain. We were gradually all taken to the first Field Hospital, where we got some tea and bovril and some shelter; about 7 p.m. we were taken in wagons to the Base Hospital, a distance of some five miles over the veldt, this was really trying. We, i.e., three K.O.Y.L.I. officers and self shared a tent for the night, and were moved the next morning into a hut by the railway. I wish they had left us in the tent as the hut was full of bugs which went for me properly, both large and small, and in trying to rid myself of them I burnt my legs with neat carbolic which we thought was diluted."

Another officer of the Battalion,[2] adds a few further details of the fight:—

"The men fell quickly after the first rush, Captain Senior, R.M.A., being killed in the second rush, and Major Plumbe in the last rush before reaching the foot of the kopje, just as he had stood up to give the signal to advance. When we reached the foot of the kopje we were in comparative safety, out of sight of

---

[1] Out of the five officers and 185 other ranks, Royal Marines engaged in the storming of the Graspan Kopjes, two officers and six men were killed and one officer and eighty-two men wounded.
[2] Lieut. now the Rt. Hon. Sir Leslie O. Wilson, D.S.O., G.C.I.E., Governor of Bombay, Lt.-Col. R.M.L.I. (retired), in "Globe and Laurel," February, 1900.

THE ROYAL MARINES AT GRASPAN.

By permission of the "Illustrated London News."

the enemy. Our men then rushed the position with fixed bayonets, but by the time they reached the top of the kopje, all the Boers had fled in carts or on horseback carrying their dead and wounded with them; only three dead Boers and one wounded were found on the top. In addition to Major Plumbe and Captain Senior being killed, Lieut. Jones was wounded in the hip, but got up again and went right up to the top—bullet and all. Captain Marchant and Lieut. Saunders were the only two Marine officers not wounded; though Saunders had three very narrow escapes, one bullet striking his pocket book, one his revolver ammunition pouch, and one the magazine of his rifle.

"The loss amongst our men was terrible, out of about 180 Marines who started in the firing line, 87 were killed and wounded—8 killed, 79 wounded. Some of the wounded I am sorry to say, died of their wounds, and a good many of them have returned to duty.[1] The Sergt.-Major, Colour-Sergt. Dyson, R.M.A., was wounded in the foot, but we hear he is doing well. Of the Naval Company Captain Protheroe was wounded in the shoulder, and Commander Ethelston killed; Midshipman Huddart was wounded in two places, but still went on till a third bullet stopped him, and he died of his wounds that night. Two bluejackets were killed, and many wounded. The officers and men at the guns were having a very warm time, too; as they got up to within 2,800 yards of the enemy, the Boers managed to get the range and burst shrapnel all round them wounding a great many of the guns' crew. Lieut. Jones, R.M.L.I., has been recommended for conspicuous gallantry."

Lord Methuen in his despatch reporting the battle of Graspan or "Enslin" as it is sometimes called, wrote as follows:—

"The fire from here was very heavy, and the Naval Brigade suffered severely, keeping in too close a formation. The officers, P.O's and N.C.O's led their men with great gallantry, and I have great pleasure in bringing to your notice the plucky conduct of Lieut. W. F. C. Jones, R.M.L.I., who, although he had a bullet in the thigh, led his men to the top of the kopje, and only had his wound dressed at the conclusion of the action. The command of the Naval Brigade devolved on Captain A. E. Marchant, R.M.L.I., when his senior officers were killed or wounded, and he led the remnant of the Naval Brigade up the kopje with great coolness and ability."

Captain Marchant as senior officer present, after the many casualties, took command of the Naval Brigade and led it out of action.

On hearing of the circumstance, the Naval Commander-in-Chief at Simonstown wired: "You are hereby promoted to Acting Major, Royal Marines, pending Admiralty instructions, and you are to take command of the Naval Brigade until the arrival of a senior officer."

Although this was a departure from general precedent, which gave a Naval officer of any commissioned rank precedence of a R.M. officer, the order was received with great satisfaction and applause by all members of the Naval Brigade. It is interesting to note that when the famous Cawdor "New Scheme" was promulgated in December, 1902, it was laid down that whenever the work in hand—on shore— permitted, the senior officer should take charge whether Naval or Marine.

---

[1] "It was on these gallant Marines, the men who are ready to fight anywhere and any how, moist or dry, that the heaviest losses fell."—Sir Conan Doyle, "Great Boer War," p. 126.

The Naval and Marine Brigade accompanied the further advance of General Methuen's command, the guns several times coming into action under the protection of their Marine escorts. On 20th November, reinforcements of fifty Marines under Captain Morgan[1] and Lieut. Wilson, and forty Bluejackets under Commander De Horsey arrived, the latter officer superseding Major Marchant in command of the Brigade.

On 3rd December, Commander De Horsey was replaced in command by Captain Bearcroft, R.N., of H.M.S. *Philomel*, and on the same day Major Urmston[2] came up and took command of the Marines vice Marchant. On this day, too, a 4.7 gun on the mounting designed by Captain Percy Scott, R.N., and a Naval engineer officer arrived, and a week later took part in the battle of Magesfontein. During this time the Royal Marines were constantly on outpost duty, watching the rear of the position at Modder River. Here the Brigade remained till on the 16th February, 1900, the news of Cronje's sudden flight from his position resulted in the movement of the Guards to occupy the ground he had vacated, had a sudden order from Lord Roberts to the Naval Brigade to move on to Jacobsdaal.

On the morning of the 17th, four 12-pounder guns, under Captain Bearcroft, R.N., with Major Urmston and Lieut. Saunders in command of the escort R.M., moved into the Free State, and at about 6 p.m. on the same day the remainder of the Brigade, under Commander De Horsey, with Major Marchant, Captain Morgan, Lieutenants Raikes,[3] and Pöe,[4] moved across the Modder River—Lieut. Raikes being in charge of the advance guard, and Lieut. Pöe the rearguard, and entered the Free State en route for Jacobsdaal, bivouacing for the night on the main road.

Thence the Brigade moved successively to Klip Kraal Drift, Stockfontein and Paardeberg. Here the three 4.7 guns and four 12-pounders which now formed the Naval Artillery train were placed in position to fire on the Boer laager, and the escorts entrenched themselves. A week was spent here under continuous "sniping" from the Boers, luckily without much result in the way of casualties.

On 1st March a move was made to Kitchener's Kop. An exchange of shots between the 12-pounders and a Boer gun took place at New Kop two days later, and shortly afterwards the 4.7 guns were in action at Osfontein Farm with considerable effect. On the 8th the whole Brigade was assembled at Poplar Grove where it was joined by Major Peile,[5] who had come up to take command of the Marines in place of Major Urmston, who had been appointed Provost Marshal to the 9th Division.

The Brigade missed the fighting before Bloemfontein, but arrived at Feriera Siding, four miles south-east of that city, after four days' hard marching. This march, tabulated, reads as follows:—

```
            10th March ... 18 miles
            11th    „   ... 15  „
            12th    „   ... 16  „
            13th    „   ... 15  „
```

---

[1] Now Colonel R. H. Morgan, C.B.E., R.M.L.I.
[2] Now Colonel A. G. B. Urmston, D.S.O., R.M.L.I. (retired).
[3] Now Lt.-Col. G. L. Raikes, D.S.O., R.M.A.   [4] Now Major and Bvt. Lt.-Col. W. S. Pöe, R.M.A.
[5] Now Col. S. P. Peile, C.B., R.M.L.I. (retired).

Altogether sixty-four miles in seventy-two hours. Not bad going—and that without a single man falling out.

On the 15th the Brigade moved into Bloemfontein and encamped on the southern slope of Monument Hill near the Free State Artillery Barracks. While at this place the Brigade was reduced by the departure of the *Powerful's* seamen, who were ordered back to their ship. Here, too, one of the 4.7 guns was handed over to a R.M.A. crew under Lieutenant Raikes; the seamen who had hitherto manned it being required to fill up the gaps which had occurred in the crews of the other Naval guns. It would be altogether too long a business to follow the wanderings of these guns and their escorts in the Free State and the Transvaal, during which they covered about 1,000 miles of all kinds of country, but here and there we find an account of their performances in action which is worth setting down.

Leaving Kroonstadt on the 22nd of May, and marching through Johannesburg the two 4.7s came into action against Louis Botha near Pretoria, on June 4th. At this time the Marines' gun was in charge of Major Peile, R.M.L.I., Lieutenant Raikes having gone to hospital with enteric.

"We advanced under cover of a ridge," writes an officer,[1] "but no sooner had we appeared on the crest than we were greeted with some heavy firing from our left front. Our commander, De Horsey, was severely wounded in the ankle while placing the guns, but luckily, that was our only casualty, in spite of the bits of shell and rock that were flying about all round us. We got the guns into action, and started firing, the enemy replying with a battery of 15-pounders. Fortunately for us, nearly all their shells went over our heads, and landed in the midst of all the infantry, hospitals, and baggage which were in our rear. Some of the enemy got on a ridge about 2,000 yards to our front and sniped at us, but once having located them, we quickly drove them away with shrapnel. We continued firing until about 3-30 p.m., when the infantry advanced, our fire being principally directed at one of their forts and the railway station, which was some 2,000 yards behind their nearest fort. At sunset all firing ceased, the troops encamping for the night on the field, and, at daylight, next morning, we heard that Pretoria had surrendered to Lord Roberts, at 10 p.m. on the night before. We started off for another procession at 10 a.m., and at 1 p.m. marched past Lord Roberts, who had taken up his position in the very fine church square, opposite the Grand Hotel, the balconies and front of which were filled with an immense crowd, which was principally composed of released prisoners, who were, naturally, delighted to see us.

We were all pretty well done up, and I think our friends at home would have been at a loss to recognise as members of the Royal Marine Corps the seventy dusty, dirty men dressed in khaki that had certainly seen its best day, and with greasy, out-of-shape 'smasher' hats on their heads. However, we were cheerful enough, as with Pretoria reached at last, we thought that most of our troubles were over, but it was sad to think that out of the 300 or so Marine Officers and Men who have been with the Naval Brigade since it left Orange River that only three Officers and forty-one Royal Marine Light Infantry and twenty-two Royal

---

[1] Lieut. L. O. Wilson, R.M.L.I., in the "Globe and Laurel," August, 1900.

Marine Artillery should be present at Pretoria on the day it was captured, which numbers, of course, exclude Major Marchant and twenty-five men who had been left at Bloemfontein, and were following up behind."

After remaining in the neighbourhood of Pretoria till 22nd July the guns went on "trek" again, and after some weeks' pilgrimage found themselves again in action under General Pole Carew near Belfast.

An officer writes:—[1] "On Sunday, 26th, we were able to take up our position on Monument Hill or Steynsplaatz, as it is shewn on the map—early in the morning. Here we found an unpleasant amount of 'stuff' flying about. The Bluejackets' gun came into action almost immediately, and made some excellent practice against a Boer gun which was shelling General French's Division, which was working round the right flank of the enemy's position. About 4-30 p.m., Wilson's gun came into action on the north-east corner of Monument Hill, against a Creusot gun, and also, later, against some snipers who were annoying us from a farm house on the left of the Boer line. After having made them each a small offering of lyddite, we sat down under cover of the gun to await fresh events, and to watch a very pretty 'pom-pom' display which was taking place uncomfortably near our camp. Then it was that Wilson was hit by a Mauser bullet. The wound was within an ace of being extremely dangerous, but we were all very glad to hear that the bullet had come out, hitting his left foot on the way. No serious trouble is anticipated for him, in fact, we have just heard that he has been able to leave his bed for a lounge chair already. We were very lucky not to have had any more casualties. Sergeant Burroughs, R.M.A., had his puttee cut by a bullet, which also grazed the captain's boot, and that was all the damage done to us.

The following day the two guns were separated, the Bluejackets being sent into position on a hill commanding the railway station, and Wilson's or rather Major Marchant's gun as it is now, remaining on Monument Hill, while Lieut. Beck, R.N., and his 12-pounder guns were ordered to be ready to proceed with the Army as soon as the advance commenced. On Monday, 27th, we were in action all day, our first object being a Long Tom (probably a 6-in. 94-pounder) which was shelling some field batteries on our left. We eventually put it out of action, having to sink the trail to do so, as the range was 10,500 yards or 500 yards beyond our sighting. We next engaged a gun which was most probably a 15-pounder Krupp, but which we never managed to hit, as the Boers changed the position immediately after each shot, to judge by the puff of white smoke, which was the only target we had to range on. The Bluejackets from their position on Station Hill were able to be of great use to General Buller's advance against the left flank of the enemy's position. This gun dropped a lyddite shell among a body of twelve or fourteen Boers, who were seen galloping away from a farm at Bugandal, only three of whom survived to tell the tale.

The following morning found the Boer position deserted, and we heard to our great grief that the field marshal who had arrived on the Saturday had decided that the country beyond Belfast was too 'alpine' for us to hope to keep up with the Army over it. General Pole-Carew wrote an exceedingly nice letter to Captain

---

[1] Lieut. A. H. French, R.M.L.I., now Lt.-Col. D.S.O., Royal Corps of Signals.

Bearcroft, saying how sorry he and the Eleventh Division were to have to part with their Naval guns, and we were very sorry to say good-bye to him."

On September 5th, the Naval Brigade was split up, and although Major Marchant and forty Marines remained for five weeks at Belfast, we may here take leave of the Seamen and Marines that landed at Simons Bay nearly a year previously. Elsewhere the Corps was represented, though in small numbers. An armoured train which formed part of the defences of Durban was manned by Captain Mullins, R.M.L.I.[1] and thirty men from H.M.S. *Terrible's* detachment, and these Marines afterwards garrisoned a redoubt protecting the waterworks of that place, having been relieved in the train by thirty other Marines landed from their ship. One of the 12-pounder guns that went up with the Ladysmith Relief Column was manned by Marines and took part in the Battle of Colenso, in which it fired 163 rounds, and in a good deal of other fighting during the relief operations.

Captain Robertson, R.M.L.I., of H.M.S. *Katoomba*, stationed at Sydney, N.S.W., went to South Africa as Instructor to the N.S.W. "Bushmen," and was in command of the B. Squadron of this Corps when killed in action at Selous River, 22nd July, 1900. Major F. White,[2] who was serving as Administration Commissioner at Ladybrand, assumed command of the company of the Worcestershire Regiment, and forty-three rank and file of the Wiltshire Yeomanry, which formed its garrison when attacked by a Boer force no less than 3,000 strong, and contrived to hold this formidable commando at bay until relieved by Lord Roberts. For this service he received the Distinguished Service Order.

Major—now General—A. F. Gatliff was present at the operations on the Modder River, Jacobsdaal and Paardeberg. This officer was on the spot at the very beginning of hostilities, was a graduate of the Staff College, and moreover, had made a careful study of the probabilities of warfare under South African conditions. Had the Naval contingent of Bluejackets and Marines which fought at Graspan been placed under his command it seems possible that Lord Methuen's criticism attributing the heavy losses of the Naval Brigade to a too close formation, would not have been called for.

Captain—now Major-General—A. R. H. Hutchinson, C.B., C.M.G., D.S.O., A.O.C.[3] —too, who was in charge of the transport of various columns, was engaged at Wittebergen, while Captain J. A. M. A. Clark and Lieutenant F. A. Nelson, both of the R.M.L.I. each commanded companies in the Royal Dublin Fusiliers, with which Regiment they were present at all the operations and engagements in the Western Transvaal under Generals Hart and French, while Major Aston, R.M.A.,[4] as D.A.A.G. (for Intelligence) to the 8th Division was present upon all occasions upon which it was engaged with the enemy. Lieutenant C. H. Hood, R.M.L.I., who was afterwards transferred to the "Buffs," was many times in action as A.D.C. to Brigadier General Smith-Dorrien.

Major—now Major-General Sir Archibald Paris, K.C.B., of the R.M.A., had a very roving and checquered experience in this war. Landed for special service at Beira, on 2nd May, 1900, he set to work to train and organise No. 2 Battery of the Rhodesian Field Force. The guns were supplied by Armstrongs, a fine

---
[1] Now Col.-Commandant G. J. H. Mullins, C.B., R.M.L.I.
[2] Now Lieut.-Col. F. White, D.S.O. (Retired).
[3] And Adjt.-General Royal Marines.
[4] Now Major-General Sir Geo. Aston.

selection of horses by the London General Omnibus Company, while the men, except a few N.C.O's and Gunners, R.A., were volunteers from the Yeomanry and the New Zealand Contingent. The original idea was that this Force under General Sir F. Carrington, was to endeavour to effect the relief of Mafeking, but this had been effected before its arrival as it had to march all the way from Buluwayo. After some column work with Lord Methuen, Major Paris, his battery having been broken up, was left at Mafeking with one section. Later on he joined the " Kimberley Column " as 2nd in Command, and in charge of a section F.A. and a section of " pom-poms." The principal work of this column was to feed and supply a number of isolated garrisons from Boshof and Koffyfontein in the East to Griquatown and other places out west. Major Paris after a short time succeeded to the command of the column which had a strength of from 600 to 1,000 men with four to six guns, and operated continuously in the Western Transvaal, Western Orange River Colony and Bechuanaland, including various chases after the elusive De Wet. The personnel of the Column was constantly changing, and generally speaking, was of a very irregular and dubious description.

Strengthened by 300 men from the 1st Northumberland Fusileers and the 1st Loyal North Lancashires, Major Paris, under the immediate command of Lord Methuen, who accompanied the column in person, left Vryberg on the 2nd March, 1902, for Rootrantjesfontein, in order to prevent the Boer General De la Rey from moving northwards between Lichtenberg and Mafeking. It was a combined operation as Colonel Kekewich with another column had been ordered to meet Lord Methuen at the above place. Progress was slow owing to being hampered by a long supply column of ox and mule wagons, and eventually, before connection could be made with Colonel Kekewich, Lord Methuen's force was attacked in the rear near Tweebosch by 1,500 Boers under several of their best Commandants. The attack developed towards the right also, resulting in the rout of the British irregular cavalry. Major Paris with forty men established himself in a kraal situated upon a knoll and endeavoured to check the advance of the enemy, who were now pressing their attack home. The Artillery and Infantry detachments also put up a good fight. But they were out-numbered and overpowered, Lord Methuen was wounded in the thigh and the final surrender was inevitable.

The Boers were not in a position to hamper themselves with prisoners so that after disarming their late opponents they set them at liberty, and after a long and harassing march, short of both food and water, they arrived at Kraaipan. The " Kimberley Column " had ceased to exist. Major Paris was exonerated from all blame by a Court of Enquiry, and was particularly mentioned by Lord Methuen for the good work which he did upon the disastrous day at Tweebosch.

Finally, the work carried out by the detachments of some of the men-of-war upon the coast must not be passed over without notice. Captain J. A. Tupman[1] and Lieutenant H. H. F. Stockley with sixty-five N.C.O's and Men of the R.M.L.I. were landed from H.M.S. *Niobe* with about the same number of Bluejackets, a 12-pounder gun and two Maxims, on 10th February, 1900, in order to protect the

---
[1] Now Colonel (Retired List).

colonists at Walfisch Bay. After three or four days of strenuous work in trench digging, patrols and outpost work the Bluejackets were re-embarked. The Marines remained to defend the place until they were relieved by the Cape Garrison Artillery some days afterwards.

Similarly the Marines of H.M.S. *Terpsichore* landed with some of their Bluejacket shipmates and entrenched themselves at Lambert's Bay. Early in the war Mossel Bay was occupied in the same way by the Marines of H.M.S. *Barracouta*, while those of H.M.S. *Naiad* were landed in Saldanha Bay for duty at Piquetberg.

A small party of Marines belonging to the Island of Ascension proved of great use in quelling a mutiny of the men in charge of the mules and horses which the s.s. *Milwanhee* was bringing from New Orleans for the use of the Army. They adopted effective and drastic measures with the mutineers, and brought the ship in safety to Durban.

Certainly in the South African War, as upon other occasions, for "doing all kinds of things," as Kipling has it, the Royal Marine proved himself bad to beat.

Gilt—
Garter Blue
Enamel,
Globe
and
Bugle Silver.

The Meridians, &c., on the Globe are raised instead of sunk as in previous Badges.

OFFICER'S HELMET PLATE, R.M.L.I., 1878-1905. (*Actual size*).

ADMIRAL SEYMOUR'S FORCE BEFORE HSI-KU ARSENAL.
By permission of the "Daily Graphic."

Chapter XXXVI

THE FIGHTING IN CHINA IN 1900

"To-day we ask vengeance, to-day we ask blood;
We ask it; we're coming to make our word good;
The storm flinches not, though the woods choke its path;
We ask it; we're coming—beware of our wrath!"—*Burger.*

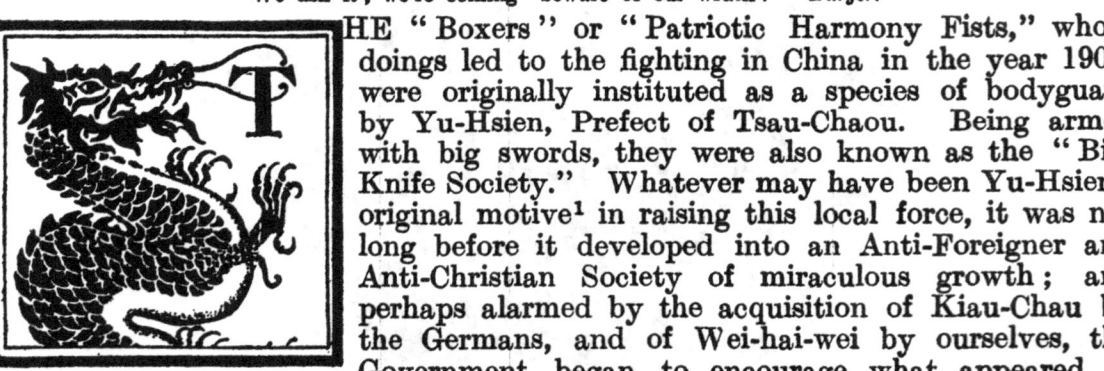

THE "Boxers" or "Patriotic Harmony Fists," whose doings led to the fighting in China in the year 1900, were originally instituted as a species of bodyguard by Yu-Hsien, Prefect of Tsau-Chaou. Being armed with big swords, they were also known as the "Big-Knife Society." Whatever may have been Yu-Hsien's original motive[1] in raising this local force, it was not long before it developed into an Anti-Foreigner and Anti-Christian Society of miraculous growth; and perhaps alarmed by the acquisition of Kiau-Chau by the Germans, and of Wei-hai-wei by ourselves, the Government began to encourage what appeared to be a powerful popular movement. It seemed to offer a chance, if properly directed, of ousting the hated "Foreign Devils," and in any case the Chinese ministers thought it was better to turn the energies of this sudden ebulition of patriotism, such as it was, in that direction, rather than perhaps be swept away by it

---

[1] Almost certainly a reform movement against the Manchu dynasty afterwards craftily turned by the Manchu Government against the foreigners.

themselves. The Imperial Court, led by the Empress Dowager, began to foster the movement, and Prince Tuan, the father of the heir apparent, placed himself at the head of it. Space does not permit reference to the internal disorders and persecution of the Missionaries that accompanied the "Boxer" movement, but it is to be observed that those who led it contrived to import a religious fervour into their misguided followers. No one has ever accused a Chinaman of being a religious fanatic in any circumstances. We know that not only among Mohammedans, but among Christians, religion has served as a pretext for the most dreadful atrocities, but those responsible for them have generally been so imbued with misdirected religious zeal, that they have really thought that they "were doing God service." But a Chinaman is "not built that way." He can and does commit fearful acts of barbarism, but these cannot in any way be put down to religious feeling. But the leaders of the Boxer movement were clever enough to provide something of the kind for their followers. Thus they contrived to make them believe that their hatred of the "Foreign Devils" was inspired by religion and was of such sanctity that it rendered them invulnerable to lead and steel.[1]

By the end of May things were so bad that the Foreign Ministers in Peking considered it necessary to telegraph to the Naval Representatives of their nations in Chinese waters for protection in the shape of an armed guard. This, though, as it turned out, much fewer in numbers than it ought to have been, was sent up by rail with as little delay as possible, since any day might see the line destroyed by the Boxers and communication severed.

On 1st June, 1900, the battleship *Centurion* flying the flag of Admiral Sir Edward Seymour, arrived off Taku at the mouth of the Peiho River, the scene of so much fighting in 1859 and 60. The cruisers *Endymion* and *Orlando* were already there as well as a considerable number of warships of other nationalities.

Stories of rapine and massacre came in day after day, and on the 6th, Admiral Seymour, as senior Naval Officer on the spot, convened a meeting of the senior officers of all nationalities with a view of forming some plan of procedure should matters continue to go from bad to worse. Affairs were brought to a head on the 9th, when an urgent telegram was received from Sir Claude Macdonald, the British Ambassador in Peking, saying that if a relief force could not be sent at once, it would be too late.

No time was lost in putting a force on shore. Preparations were carried on well into the night, and in the "wee sma' hours" of the morning a flotilla of destroyers, torpedo-boats and tugs slipped past the big forts at the river mouth and landed their cargoes of armed seamen and Marines at Tong-ku. Here the little army entrained and steamed off to Tien-tsin, thirty miles up the river. After a hasty breakfast, Admiral Seymour, now in command of a combined international force of about 2,000 men, including 915 British Seamen and Marines, started again by train for Peking. The British, American, Austrians and Italians were in the first train which left about 10 a.m. It carried in addition a quantity of railroad repairing material, some English engineers and seventy Chinese coolies. More of the British, the Russians, French and Japanese followed as soon as trains could

---

[1] According to an officer who took part in the defence of the Legations, some of the Boxers captured by the Marines were undoubtedly under some hypnotic influence and acted as if in a trance.

be assembled to carry them; the Germans, who arrived late, not being able to start till some hours after the first train had left.

"The parching heat of a North China summer was now at its zenith," writes one who participated in the expedition, "and we steamed off into the sunshine with the hot dusty plain spreading away before us into haze, and the smart new station behind, lined with our European comrades, and packed with the glowering native crowd. We looked forward to a journey of a few hours perhaps, at the most of a day, and then to an easy and successful march into the Tartar City and the resumption of diplomacy. Little did we think that we should never get to Peking and that when we struggled back to Tien-tsin with a seventh of our force killed and wounded, the station, the settlement, and the many signs of civilisation that we now saw and took pride in would be burnt and desolated ruins, riddled with shot and shell and disfigured by rotting corpses."[1]

"The country through which we were moving," says the same writer, "was the flat loess plain that constitutes the seaboard of most of Northern China. It is watered by the insignificant streams of the Red and White Rivers, which, descending from the Shansi Mountains to the west and east of Peking, unite with the Grand Canal near Tien-tsin. Cultivation as soon as the Taku marshes are left behind is general, corn, millet and maize being the general crops. The trees, with the exception of those that cluster round the villages, have all been cut down, and the landscape, unrelieved by hills, forests, or lakes, presents a monotonous and uninteresting aspect. The climate at that season of the year, a month or more before the earliest rains, was intensely dry and hot, the sun at mid-day striking down with tremendous heat on the arid lowlands, while every two or three days a dust-storm enveloped earth and sky in a burning sandy whirlwind which robbed us of sight, sound and almost of sense."

The leading train travelled without incident past Yang-tsun, at which place the Peking Railway crosses the Pei-ho, but a short distance further on it was found necessary to pull up, as the line had been torn up for some little distance. This was about half-past three in the afternoon, and though work on the damaged track was taken in hand without delay, it was evident that many hours must elapse before further progress could be made. Under these circumstances it was determined to bivouac for the night and await the arrival of the other trains. One reason for this was—probably—the discovery that the Chinese General Neih with 4,000 Imperial troops was encamped at no great distance, and though as yet the latter had given no indications of sympathy with the Boxers, in China "one never knows."

And yet there was no doubt that General Nieh had recently been operating against the Boxers as the headless bodies and innumerable empty cartridge cases scattered along the route bore witness.

However when the trains reached Lofa, the next station, it was considered wise to leave a guard there consisting of an officer and thirty men, and not long afterwards it was decided to double this little force. The whole countryside wore a deserted aspect. Most of the villages had apparently been deserted by their inhabitants, who had very probably donned the red turban of the Boxers and gone off to join that pleasant fraternity.

---
[1] Clive Bigham, "A Year in China."

The expedition left Lofa at 11-30 a.m., but progress was slow. The operations of the Boxers had been conducted on an extensive scale. In some places several hundred feet of the line had been torn up, the sleepers burned, the telegraph poles cut down, and the wire removed. Small bands of Boxers hovered in the distance but shewed no desire to come to closer quarters. During the afternoon, while working parties were engaged in repairing the line, a patrol of sixteen Marines under the command of Major Johnstone[1] of H.M.S. *Centurion*, was sent forward to examine the line. Some way ahead of the train, at a distance of eight miles from Lofa, parties of Boxers were seen breaking up and destroying the railway, but they disappeared as the patrol advanced.

When about two miles ahead of the trains, a considerable force of Boxers, some of them mounted, estimated at about 2,000 men, suddenly poured out of a village lying on the left of the track, and from the direction they took it was evident that they had designs of cutting off the little party of Marines. The horsemen crossed the railway and made ready to attack from that side while the footmen made for a partially burnt bridge and a village which commanded the line. The magazine rifles of the Marines began to crack as they fell back towards the trains, and the Boxers began to bite the dust. But they must have been " bad " Boxers, or they would have been invulnerable, thought their comrades, who, each one confident in his own virtue, continued to charge down on the railway line waving their spears and swords and firing their rifles.

For a mile the running fight went on till the Marine patrol sighted a strong reinforcement of their shipmates coming up from the trains to their assistance. Major Johnstone then halted and opened a heavy fire on his assailants, driving them across the front of the reinforcing troops, who got to work with rifle and Maxim to such purpose that the Boxers turned tail and sought shelter in the nearest villages. The Bluejackets and Marines pursued them, stormed the villages and drove them out again in headlong rout. There were no casualties on the British side but the Chinese are estimated to have lost about forty men.

Meanwhile the line had been repaired, and by 6 p.m. the trains carrying the expedition had arrived within three miles of Lang-fan, which, as it turned out, was the furthest point they ever reached. On the day following, 12th June, Lieut. Smith, R.N., with three officers and forty-four men was ordered to push on to An-tung, the next station, but met with considerable opposition, and was compelled to fall back.

The whole of the trains had now come up, but no further advance was made. Not only were the enemy found to be numerous in front, but disquieting rumours filtered up from the rear. On the 13th there was more mending of the railway, and Major Johnstone and sixty men were advanced to An-tung to prevent further interference with it. But the danger was thickening. On the 14th the line was cut behind the expedition at Yang-tsun, and in the morning of that day a determined attack was made on the trains at Lang-fan which, however, was repulsed with heavy loss. The expedition had five casualties, all Italians. Hardly had the victors time to look round before news arrived that the post at Lofa was attacked and the Admiral at once went down with reinforcements. The blue-jacket guard

---

[1] Now Major-General Johnstone, C.B.

contrived to drive off the Boxers just before the Admiral's train arrived, but the reinforcements were not too late to give them a taste of their Maxim guns. Major Johnstone rejoined the main body from An-tung in the evening.

But no further progress was made. Two trains were at Lang-fan while more repairing work was taken in hand, but on the 15th word came up from Lofa that the line between it and Tien-tsin had been again badly broken. An attempt was made at 4 a.m. the next day to get a train through, but it was found that the railway had been rendered impassable. On the evening of this day the expedition was distributed as follows. The Admiral in No. 1 train had gone back to Lofa; trains No. 2 and 3 were still at Lang-fan, where Captain von Usedom of the Imperial German Navy was left in command, No. 4 train was at Lofa. All night long the working parties toiled on the line below Lofa and to such good purpose that a train got through to Yangtsun.

But here not only was the station a total ruin, but the bridge by which the Peking railway crossed the Peiho was a complete wreck. There was no possible chance of the Expedition getting back by the way it had come.

Worse was to follow. On the following afternoon the force left at Langfang was attacked by 7,000 Imperial troops armed with modern rifles. These soldiers, who hitherto had shewn themselves rather friendly than the reverse, were only repulsed after severe fighting and heavy loss. The allies, on their side, had a good many casualties—about 5 killed and 50 wounded.

What had occasioned this unforeseen attack?

To explain the situation which had now arisen, it will be necessary to see what had been occurring lower down the river since the departure of the Admiral's relief expedition.

At Tien-tsin, the twenty-five Marines who had been left behind when the Legation Guards left for Peking, were joined on the 11th by the same number of Marines from H.M.S. *Barfleur* under Major Luke and Lieut. Armstrong. Four companies of Bluejackets from the *Aurora*, *Barfleur* and *Orlando* also arrived. The European settlement was naturally in a state of considerable alarm and other troops were dribbling in. There were German Marines from Kiao-chaou, and on the 13th no less than 1,700 Russians and six guns turned up. The Tien-tsin Volunteers were called out. All this while the unrest among the native population and its hostility to the " Foreign Devils " was increasingly apparent.

On the 15th there was a great concentration of Chinese Imperial troops at the Taku Forts at the mouth of the river, and fires were seen on that night blazing up in every direction round the city of Tien-tsin. Communication was kept up with Tong-ku by means of armoured trains which patrolled the line all night, but the telegraph wires were cut notwithstanding.

At 1 a.m., on the 16th, there was a Boxer attack on the Tien-tsin Railway Station, which was driven off, but between 2 and 3 in the afternoon there was another attack made on the north side of the concessions supported by the fire of artillery. The French troops who were present repulsed the attack and set fire to the Chinese suburbs.

More momentous events were in progress down at Taku. Seeing the big reinforcements of Chinese troops pouring into the forts guarding the entrance of the

THE ROYAL MARINES LANDING AT TONG-KU, 10TH JUNE, 1900.

MAJOR JOHNSTONE AND THE ROYAL MARINES CROSSING THE PEI-HO
TO ATTACK THE HSI-KU ARSENAL.

By permission of the "Graphic."

River Peiho, the Commanders of the Allied Fleets issued an ultimatum demanding their withdrawal under threat of bombardment. No answer was returned, but at 1 a.m. on the 17th the Chinese took upon themselves to open fire on the fleet. The Allied war-vessels replied at once, and their landing parties, having been stationed in readiness near Tongku, advanced, and after some fighting made themselves masters of the forts.

It was this that more than anything else precipitated matters. News of the capture of the Taku Forts seem to have been conveyed almost instantaneously to Peking where it produced an ultimatum to the Ambassadors to leave the city in twenty-four hours, to the Imperial troops near Lang-fan, resulting in the attack on the allies at that place the same afternoon, and to the troops in the neighbourhood of Tien-tsin. Thenceforward the allies had not only to contend with the Boxers, but with the whole available strength of the Imperial Chinese Army, which proved itself much more formidable both in its armament and courage than had been expected.

The bombardment of Tien-tsin grew heavier and as soon as the news arrived from Taku the little garrison of the European Concessions sallied out to attack the Chinese guns which were firing on them from the Military college. A Marine[1] gives the following account of this sortie:—" On Sunday, 17th, we heard that Taku Forts had been taken and in the afternoon were fallen in, and being joined by a party of Germans were ordered to take the Military College. We crossed the river and approached the College, which was built in the shape of a hollow square, surrounded by a mud wall about five feet high. This we scrambled over as best we could, and forcing the doors, were met by a heavy rifle fire by which Private Robinson of the *Orlando* was killed, and five more wounded. We then drove the Chinese students from room to room, killing at least fifty of them, and set fire to the building. The Germans in the meantime had destroyed some eight or nine B.L. Krupp guns, and the whole force then returned to their quarters, the Germans' loss being one killed and five or six wounded.

" On the next day, the 18th, the Chinese made a determined attack on the railway station, which was defended by the Russians, who were supported by the *Orlando's* company of bluejackets, and who lost very heavily. At this time we were on the left flank and were not engaged till the afternoon, when the Chinese attacked from the N.W. Arsenal, shewing considerable pluck, especially in the manner in which their banners were kept flying, one bearer being no sooner killed than another took his place. We managed to keep them off till we were reinforced by some Germans and Tien-tsin Volunteers, when we finally succeeded in driving them back. It being our turn for outpost duty, we then threw out our sentries, and about 8 o'clock our 'dinner' was sent out, accompanied by a tot of rum, which, as we had had nothing since 6 that morning, was found most acceptable, especially as during the night it came on to rain very heavily. As we were the only troops supplied with any covering, and that simply a blanket apiece, one could frequently see Germans and Austrians, who were working with us, walking arm in arm with a 'Royal' all getting as much shelter as possible under one blanket. Nothing of any importance happened during the remainder of the week, the Chinese having apparently received a good lesson, except constant sniping and bombarding, especially at night.

---

[1] Corpl. Hicks, in the "Globe and Laurel."

"One incident may, however, be worth chronicling; Corporal Lye and five privates manning a 6-pounder Hotchkiss, mounted on a railway truck at the station, and doing excellent work until all the ammunition was expended. Pte. Marr was unfortunately wounded, and has since been invalided with a paralysed right arm, the result of his wound. On Saturday, 23rd, the relief column from Taku[1] arrived, the British contingent being under the command of Commander Craddock of the *Alacrity*, whereupon the Chinese all retired behind the walls of the city."

Our story must now return to Admiral Seymour's Expedition which we left in a very tight place at Yang-tsun, with a regular army of Chinese following close behind, and the railway bridge over the Peiho broken down at their feet, cutting off all retreat by the way they had come.

There was only one thing to be done, and that was to get back by the road running along the left bank of the river. Some junks were obtained, and after the whole force had crossed the river the wounded and what supplies were left were put into them, and they were towed along by captive Boxers.

It was a terrible march. "Starting at 4 a.m.," writes one who participated in it, "and not halting for the night till 7 o'clock in the evening, we barely averaged six miles a day. The junks which had to be tracked or towed, were continually grounding owing to the shallow water, and the march of the column had to be regulated by their pace. At every half mile or so along the banks are situated straggling wooded villages, surrounded by ploughed fields and irrigation ditches, through which lay our only road. Nearly every one of these villages was held by the Boxers in more or less force, but always sufficient to make us halt the junks. deploy and form firing line. These positions, with their high mud-walled houses, clusters of timber and treeless zone outside, were easy to hold, and the first lesson we learnt was that the attack must always be prepared to lose four or five times as much as the defence. We had to bring our machine and light field guns into action as the Boxers had three and six pounders, pom poms and large native jingalls, and were frequently entrenched. We were also continually being harassed on our left flank by masses of Imperial cavalry accompanied by Horse Artillery (12 and 15 pounders), with which they regularly shelled us from the railway embankment as soon as we had again got into column."

It fell to the Marines, as the most experienced soldiers, to perform the very difficult and important duty of Flank Guard on the exposed flank. They were therefore constantly engaged with the Imperial troops and unable, from the peculiar nature of their task, to take much advantage of what little cover was available, this little force, which was most skilfully handled by Major Johnstone, suffered severely.

A N.C.O. who was present[2] says of this harassing march, "We left the train in the evening and camped out at night. In the morning, early, we started again, and came to a place where the enemy was strongly entrenched, and had a regular pitched battle, and a lively time of it we had, we killed upwards of 500 Chinese,

---

[1] 50 Royal Marines from *Terrible* (Capt. Mullins and Lt. Lawrie.)
    50 Bluejackets   ,,   ,,   100 Bluejackets (various ships).   1,200 Russians.
    1 12-pr. gun   ,,   ,,   300 Royal Welsh Fusiliers.   30 Italian Bluejackets.
    50 Royal Marines   ,,   *Barfleur*.   150 American Marines.
[2] Sergt. Cooper, R.M.L.I., in the "Globe and Laurel."

gained the day, and resumed our march. . . . The next day we were shelled from a fort all day. It was then decided to abandon the guns, and put the lightest of them in junks, and march by night, which we thought a good move, as we had found that the Chinese were rather averse to night-fighting, but with our usual ill-luck, we were spotted by another fort, and as we now had no artillery with us, we were in a pretty predicament, but managed to get out of this scrape. The *Aurora's* seamen and Marines charged a village close handy, hooting, yelling and cheering, and I think we frightened them, for there was no more firing, and so we got out of that."

The writer probably refers to the capture of the considerable town of Pei-Tsang which was taken on the 21st after some hours heavy fighting. By this time the casualties among the Europeans amounted to 150 including the Admiral's Flag Captain,[1] who was badly hit in the chest, and though the little expedition had now arrived within ten miles of Tien-tsin, there was yet worse to be encountered.

After a halt for three or four hours, during which the constant booming of Artillery from the direction of Tien-tsin beat ominously on the ears of the wearied Europeans, the march was resumed at midnight. Whether comparative safety would be reached at Tien-tsin, or whether the desperate pilgrimage would have to struggle yet further to the sea-coast no one knew, but it was known that its route lay close under the walls of the fortified Arsenal of Hsi-Ku. Whether the garrison had, like other Imperial troops, thrown in its lot with the Boxers, was uncertain, but in any case it was as well to pass it, undiscovered if possible, under the shelter of the darkness. Villages again blocked the way along the river bank. "The first village was captured by a charge of Marines in column of fours, deployment in the darkness being found too slow. Its glare, for it had caught fire, lighted up the sky and the black waters of the river, and gave a weird effect to a scene that few who saw it will ever forget. We hurried on. Half a mile further down we found ourselves in another and apparently deserted village, the narrow towing path leading between the dead walls of the houses and the high precipitous bank. Below us came the junks, slowly floating down the current, and on the opposite shore ran a long embrasured parapet—the river face of the Hsi-ku Arsenal.

Almost before we knew it we were abreast of it, Americans and Germans in front, British and Russians in rear. In the semi-darkness two figures could be seen advancing from the postern gate to the glacis, dressed in the red turbans, sashes and stockings, which formed the regular Boxer uniform. But they carried no arms. They hailed us across the water: "Who are you and whither go you?" We answered that we were foreign troops making our way to Tien-tsin, and the reply came back, "It is well." Hardly had the words sounded before the stillness was broken by a roar of musketry, and the whole line of parapet flashed into a sheet of flame. We were caught in a sort of death-trap, and for an instant all was confusion. Final disaster seemed upon us, and indeed had we had trained troops against us instead of Boxers, not a man would have escaped alive. As it was their first few volleys were luckily too high, and we were able, somehow, to take what cover there was, to lie down, and so to return the fire. But the junks lay below us, almost defenceless and absolutely exposed. I remember seeing a

---

[1] Captain, now Admiral of the Fleet, Viscount Jellicoe of Scapa, G.C.B., O.M., G.C.V.O.

wounded German officer emerge on the deck of the leading barge, calmly adjust the Maxim gun that had been placed on its poop, and slewing it round, sit down behind it, and begin methodically to press the button and defend his ship. He sat there all through the action under a withering fire, and was not once hit, but I regret that I have forgotten his name."[1]

The crisis was desperate. Some action must be taken on the instant or the little force would be annihilated. Once more the Marines were able to show what they were made of. Major Johnstone, strengthening his detachment with half a company of bluejackets, hurried back up the river bank for about a quarter of a mile, got across by making a rough bridge of a couple of junks, and advancing against the flank wall of the Arsenal, fixed bayonets and stormed it with a tremendous rush, his men driving the garrison before them and turning their own guns upon the flying Boxers. Almost simultaneously the Germans at the front of the column crossed the river on an improvised raft, and made things warm for the enemy as they streamed out of the arsenal. The Admiral and all hands now came over and the expedition established itself in the big walled enclosure without further opposition. The enemy made a half-hearted attempt on an angle of the work while this was in progress, but were instantly repulsed by Major Johnstone and his Marines.

The arsenal proved to be rectangular and no less than forty acres in extent. It contained several stone buildings, a Buddist Temple and a number of huts. One of the buildings, situated on a knoll near the centre of the enclosure, was appropriated for the wounded as a hospital. At the end nearest to Tien-tsin the ground was overgrown with high reeds. The whole was surrounded by a high wall with a banquette on the inner side, and having the exterior slope very steep. Inside were found a great quantity of modern up-to-date field guns, rifles and ammunition, mostly brand new, and in addition medical stores and provisions. Here it was considered that the little force would be able to hold out some considerable time, and as soon as it was daylight Seamen and Marines set to work to mount as many guns as they could man. But they were not long left undisturbed in their task. General Nieh having heard of the way his present friends, the Boxers, had lost the Arsenal with all its valuable munitions of war, sent no less than eight thousand regular troops to recapture it, together with three batteries of field artillery. The attack was delivered with great fury about 3 in the afternoon, and was only repulsed after hard fighting and heavy loss.

When there was leisure to make arrangements for the night it was decided —against the advice of Major Johnstone—to make no attempt to occupy the whole circuit of the walls on account of their great extent, and the small number of men available. Instead, the little force, after throwing out a few sentries, bivouaced around the knoll in the centre of the enclosure. The unfortunate result of this decision was that after having stormed the ramparts of the Arsenal from the outside, the Marines had, before daylight, to storm them again from the inside !

It came about in this way. Finding the walls unguarded, the Boxers and their military allies crept stealthily over them without being discovered until a considerable number of them were concealed among the high reeds which covered

---

[1] Clive Bigham, "A Year in China."

THE STORMING OF HSI-KU ARSENAL BY THE ROYAL MARINES. By permission of the "Sphere."

one end of the enclosure. Then, when a patrol stumbled up against some of them, a desperate fight began at close quarters, the Marines having to clear them out and re-occupy the walls.

In this surprise attack, which ought never to have had an opportunity of taking place, the Marines lost Captain Beyts of the R.M.A., and several men. The bluejackets also sustained losses.

It was pretty evident that further movement of the " Relief Column " either forward or backward had been rendered impossible. Its only course was to make the best preparations it could to stand a siege in the comparatively strong position in which, by an unforeseen turn of events, it now found itself. One attempt was made by a hundred of the Royal Marines under the command of Captain Doig, R.M.L.I.,[1] to cut their way through to the European Concession at Tien-tsin, but although, to quote Admiral Seymour's report, the attempt was "made with skill and credit," the enemy were in such overpowering strength that the party had to fall back on the arsenal with the loss of four men. Several Chinese messengers also tried to get through the enemy's lines to Tien-tsin, but with the exception of the last one, who with much pluck, ingenuity and resource, succeeded in carrying the news of the expedition's investment in Hsi-Ku Arsenal to the British Consulate, all were killed by the Boxers.

Although the relief forces from Taku had only entered Tien-tsin on the 23rd inst., no time was lost in assembling a force of Russians and British, under the command of Colonel Sherinsky, to extricate Admiral Seymour and his command from their perilous position.

Sherinsky arrived at Hsi-Ku early on the morning of the 25th, and found that the garrison had suffered severely during the past day from the fire of heavy siege guns which the Chinese had mounted on the outskirts of Tien-tsin, so that in addition to there being 66 killed outright, there were no less than 230 wounded men to be carried back to Tien-tsin. Sherinsky's force, which consisted of 1,000 Russians, and 900 men of other nationalities, included two companies of the Royal Welsh Fusiliers, and a Naval Brigade 400 strong, under Commander Craddock, the Marines being commanded by Major Luke. It had started at 11-30 p.m., on the 24th, crossed the river and marched off in the supposed direction of the Arsenal. But either by accident or design, its guides lost their way, and at daybreak were miles out of their course. The column plodded on, sniped at from time to time, and eventually sighted the garrison of Hsi-Ku standing on its ramparts waving and cheering for all they were worth. The relieving force remained bivouacked on the far side of the river, opposite the Arsenal, all day, the snipers occasionally honouring it with their attentions. The sniping got so bad at one time that a detachment had to advance to drive them out of the space between the railway and the river. On the other side of the line Chinese cavalry were observed at some distance. The wounded having been brought over the river, the whole force, relievers and relieved, set out on its return journey to the Tien-tsin Concessions at 4 a.m., on the 26th, after having spent a bitterly cold night down by the river. The retreat was unmolested by the enemy, thanks it is claimed, to the excellent practice of one of the *Terrible's* 12-pounder guns which during the absence of the relieving

---
1. *Vide* Note I.

column had been giving the Chinese a sample of what it could do. In and around Tien-tsin, that usually busy city, hostilities were in full swing, and it was far from an ideal haven of refuge. But the European seamen and soldiers were daily increasing in numbers and becoming more and more able to assume the offensive.

The native city of Tien-tsin is a huge oblong block entirely enclosed in high massive walls, and is 2,000 yards long by 1,400 broad. It stands on the right bank of the Pei-ho at the point at which the Grand Canal runs into the river.

About two miles to the S.E., on the same bank of the river and situated in one of its banks, are the various European Concessions grouped together. The Railway Station is on the opposite bank. From a point on the river bank just below the Concessions, a mud wall runs away nearly six miles to the N.W., meets the Grand Canal some way beyond the Native City, runs roughly east and west till it is again crossed by the Canal on the further side of the Pei-ho, after which, at a point two miles east of the river, it turns south and finishes just opposite to where we began to trace it on the right bank. All this immense enclosure is filled with Chinese houses and gardens except certain marshy ground to the south of the Native City. The houses are naturally closest together just outside this city and between it and the river. Almost due south of the Native City, just inside the mud-wall is the walled Arsenal of Hai-kwang-su, while the Pei-Tsang or Eastern Arsenal is about two and a half miles north east of the Concessions on the left bank of the river. Another mud wall branches off, opposite to the Concessions, from the encircling one already described, and runs away to the neighbourhood of this Arsenal. The Native City, these two walled Arsenals and forts and batteries on the river bank just north east of the Native City and others at the point where the Grand Canal passes through the mud-wall further in this direction on the opposite side of the river, constituted the main Chinese positions. They also held one or two villages to the south of the mud-wall, and here, too, they were provided with artillery. All their guns were of the very latest type.

It was in this arm that the Allies found themselves most deficient. To oppose the up-to-date weapons possessed by the Chinese, the French and Japanese had only little 7-pounder guns, the Russians a 15 pounder battery dating from more than twenty years previous. The British had no heavier metal than the 12-pounder quick-firing guns landed from the *Terrible* as well as some 6-pounder quick-firing guns, but these being mostly mounted on improvised carriages were wanting in mobility.

The Allies by this time began to feel themselves strong enough to assume the offensive. The first objective was the Pei-Tsang Arsenal. The Russians and Germans started out to attack this place at 10 a.m., on the 27th—the day after the return from Hsi-Ku—but before very long they found it was a tougher nut to crack than they had expected, and sent back for reinforcements. In hot haste six companies of the Royal Marines under Major Johnstone, and the same number of bluejacket companies under Commander Craddock were fallen in and hurried over a bridge, which the Russians had constructed, to the scene of action. The British prolonged the Russian line to the left, the Marines taking the extreme left, and the advance against the Arsenal was resumed, under a heavy shell and rifle fire under which, wrote an officer of the Corps who was present, " the men behaved magnificently." Meanwhile the *Terrible's* ubiquitous 12-pounder kept up an incessant and splendidly directed fire on the arsenal, and about 11 a.m. hit the main magazine which exploded with great violence, shells and debris being hurled in all directions. The attack was now pushed on with more determination than ever, the Naval Brigade, as it neared the buildings, wheeling to the right so that its attack was made nearly at right angles to that of the Russians and Germans. As the fighting line got nearer and bayonets were fixed, the rattle of the enemy's musketry seemed to redouble in volume. But the fire did not double in intensity,

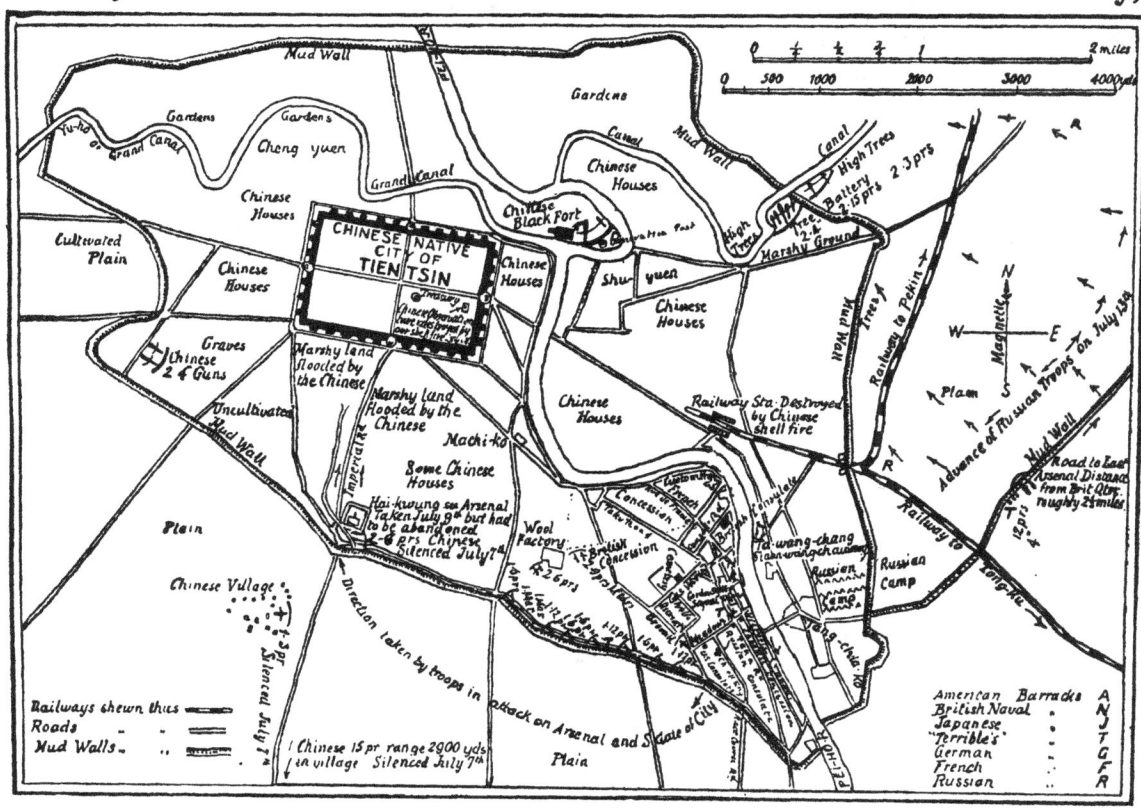

PLAN ILLUSTRATING THE FIGHTING IN AND AROUND TIEN-TSIN.
From "*The Commission of H.M.S. Terrible*," 1899-1902.
By George Crowe.
By permission of the Author.

as the greater part of the noise was made by the Chinese letting off innumerable crackers as a preliminary to bolting from their position. Presently out they rushed. Unfortunately for them, the change of direction just made by the British had brought the Marines almost parallel to their line of retreat, and their magazine fire punished the fugitives most severely. Meanwhile the Arsenal was taken with a rush, and remained in the hands of the Russians, the British picking up their wounded and returning to the Concessions. The Marines lost two privates killed and a sergeant and a private wounded. Their bluejacket comrades suffered more severely, their casualty list being five killed and nineteen wounded.

On the day following a native runner got through from Peking with a message from Sir Robert Hart. "The foreign colony is besieged in the Legations. The situation is desperate. Hasten." The British and Russian commanders, however, decided that it would be useless to attempt to relieve Peking with the forces at present available. For the next few days things were fairly quiet, except for a certain amount of sniping. Reinforcements continued to arrive from Taku for the Europeans, and more Chinese troops and Boxers collected in the surrounding country and increased the strength of the enemy in and around the native city. When on 1st July, the British and Russians made a strong reconnaisance in this direction it was found that they had got additional guns in position as well. Several recently mounted cannon were unmasked, and the Russians suffered somewhat severely from their fire. As a kind of return visit the Chinese suddenly attacked the Railway Station but were driven off by the Russian troops on guard there. The famous 12-pounder was brought into action, and a Japanese battery and a French gun also engaged the enemy, whose artillery fire was of the most accurate and deadly description. The Russians after this declined to hold the station any longer, and it was occupied by a mixed force consisting of the Marines of H.M.S. *Terrible*, under Captain Mullins, R.M.L.I., fifty of the Hong Kong Regiment (Sikhs), some Japanese, and detachments of French Marines and Bluejackets. These relieved the Russians at 8 a.m. on the 4th July. About 2-30 p.m., after a comparatively quiet morning, a considerable body of the enemy was observed coming out of the Native City and crossing the river, after which they disappeared into the ruins of a village which had been burnt and which lay some way to the left front of the station. The station Guards at once manned their defences. The French Bluejackets occupied a trench on the left. Their Maxims took cover behind the platform, while our Marines held the enginehouse in the centre, and the Sikhs were posted in a trench dug in front of the water-tower on the right of the station. The Japanese held more buildings between the station and the river. The Chinese extended to other ruined villages in front of the station, and then pushed on to a couple of houses not more than 250 yards from the French trench. They had not developed this attack without losing several men from the rifle fire which had been opened upon them as soon as they began to extend, but their return fire was so heavy, supported as it was by their guns which were placed in various surrounding positions, that a reinforcement of Bluejackets and men of the Chinese regiment was sent up from the Concessions. From Commander Granville, who commanded the seamen, Captain Mullins borrowed a Maxim gun which he placed in the left corner of the enginehouse. Unfortunately it fired cartridges loaded with black powder, and the smoke gave its position away at once to the Chinese gunners who put seven shells into the engine-house in three minutes, all bursting near the gun, severely wounding Sergeant Peek and two privates, who were working it. There was nothing for it but to remove it and withdraw from the building, which had become a mere shell-trap, and share the shelter afforded to the French Marines by the Station platform. For half-an-hour the Chinese shells continued to fall with the greatest precision after which the fire slackened. The detachment re-entered the engine-house and took shelter in the pits made for getting underneath the engines to clean them. The enemy had by this time been driven off, and their shell fire which latterly had been directed over the engine house in the town, ceased about 7-30 p.m. On the 6th the Allies set to work to bombard the Native City and its forts with every available gun. Two additional 12-pounders had now come up for the British seamen, and to assist these useful little weapons, a couple of 15-pounder Krupps, which had been captured at Taku, were brought into action. They were manned by the *Terrible's* Marines under Captain Mullins and Lieut. Lawrie, R.M. But after four or five rounds had been fired a serious accident occurred at one of them, a shell bursting prematurely as it was being rammed home. The base flew back, blew off a Blue Marine's right forearm, slightly wounded a private and severely bruised and cut Captain Mullins' left side. Fire from these guns was at once suspended, and orders were received to withdraw them from the engagement. In the evening a couple of 4-inch guns and four 6-pounders came up, a welcome addition to the Naval Artillery park, especially the two former. All day on the 7th, an Artillery duel went on, the "Heathen Chinee" proving a real good gunner. "His artillery practice is marvellous," wrote an officer, "directly he has found his object, and it is only the sand-bags that have saved our blues up to date." Even on ordinary days something like a hundred shell would fall in and about the European lines. All this time the Chinese were working round the Allies' left towards the river below the concessions, with the evident design of cutting their line of communications with Taku. It was necessary to nip this movement in the bud. On the 9th, therefore, General Dorward, who was in command of the British troops, moved out of the South Gate of the Concession at the head of a mixed force of 950 British, including the Naval Brigade of 400 Bluejackets and Marines, 1,000 Japanese, 400 Russians and 200 Americans.

Starting at 2-30 in the morning, this force marched about three miles in a southerly direction, and then wheeled to the north-west. This manoeuvre brought it in front of the Chinese positions, and was effected without being discovered by the enemy. A small body of Japanese Cavalry circled away towards the left front, and the infantry deployed for attack, the British on the right, Japanese on the left. The remainder acted as a reserve which was formed close up to the fighting line.

By this time the Chinese had become aware of what was going on and opened a heavy shrapnel fire, which was immediately returned by the Japanese and Hong Kong Artillery. Suddenly the Japanese horsemen galloped furiously down on the Chinese flank. The infantry at once advanced, but the cavalry charge had been enough for the enemy, who broke and fled in the direction of the Hai-kwang-su or Western Arsenal, the Japanese horse, in hot pursuit, cutting them down as they ran. Six guns were taken together with a great quantity of small arms and ammunition. The allied troops now pushed on to the Arsenal, a party of 300 Americans and Japanese co-operating by moving along the mud wall from the Concessions. It was rushed from both quarters almost simultaneously, and the Japanese troops tried to improve the occasion by advancing towards the south gate of the Native City itself. But though this attack was seconded by a heavy artillery fire from several guns, principally Naval, that were now mounted on the mud wall to the west of the Concessions, the fire from the City walls and the Chinese supporting batteries was too severe to be faced with any prospect of success by such a small force, and the attempt was, for the time, abandoned.

The next day, the 10th, was comparatively quiet. The 9th American Regiment, about 600 strong, and 2,500 Russian and French troops arrived from Taku. It had been intended to make a night attack in force on the Chinese "Tree Battery" situated astride the mud wall to the north east of the Concessions, but the failure of a pontoon bridge over the river led to the operation being abandoned. The Chinese, who had plenty of spies about—some Europeans, even, were caught in the act of signalling information to the Native City—are supposed to have heard of the proposed move, and thinking that a large portion of the allied troops would be out of the way near the "Tree Battery" tried again to rush the railway station. Captain Mullins and the *Terrible's* Marines were again on duty there, as were the French and Japanese and a party of the Hong Kong Sikhs. About 3-15 a.m. the enemy had crept close up under cover of the darkness and got among the station outbuildings and the railway trucks on the sidings, and made a sudden charge on the pickets. But the blaze of rifle fire that greeted them was too much for them and they fell back behind the trucks and sheds where they hung on for some time until the relief company of the Sikhs arrived on the scene who, with the Japanese, ferreted them from their lurking places at the bayonet's point.

With daylight the Chinese shell-fire on the station became tremendous. At one time it and their rifle-fire was so intense that doubts were entertained of the possibility of maintaining the position. It was not till strong reinforcements had been sent over that the enemy were finally driven off with a loss of something like 500 men.

At noon, the Allied guns retaliated by a heavy bombardment of the Native City, the 4-inch guns introducing John Chinaman to the uses of lyddite projectiles. The Chinese replied with vigour, but their fire was eventually beaten down, after which the *Terrible's* 12-pounders were turned on a pagoda in the city which had served as a watch tower, and carried away the upper half of it.

About this time, as there were now plenty of troops available, Admiral Sir Edward Seymour and the Seamen and Marines of his ship, left to rejoin the *Centurion* off Taku, leaving Captain Bayly as Senior Naval Officer at Tien-tsin.

The 12th was another quiet day, but heavy fighting was impending, the allied commanders having decided to assault the Native City on the day following, and at the same time to attack the Chinese Batteries to the east of it. The latter task was allocated to the Russians. The remainder of the Allied troops paraded at 3 a.m., and, except the French, left the Concessions by the Southern Gates, wheeled to the right and advanced on the Hai-kwang-su Arsenal in two parallel columns, with about 500 yards interval between them. The Japanese 1,500 strong under General Fukushima formed the right column, and moved parallel to the mud wall at about 500 yards from it. The French force, numbering 900 men, were to get over the mud wall and advance under its cover, while two companies were to advance independently from the French settlement to clear the houses between it and the City of Chinese snipers. Neither of the French columns effected very much at the outset, the main one being checked by the enemy's fire at a bridge in the mud wall about a quarter of a mile from the Arsenal.

The Left Column, consisting of the British Naval Brigade (which included three companies of the Royal Marines), 500 British and 900 American troops, together with 30 Austrian bluejackets, had a longer detour to make than the others, and had also to clear some villages of lurking Chinamen, so that by the time it arrived at the mud wall, the Arsenal had already been captured by the Japanese, who with the French, were now engaged with the Chinese troops on and about the City wall. The Royal Welsh Fusileers and the American Marines were pushed forward to fire from the cover afforded by the mud wall, with the 9th Americans in close support. The Naval Brigade and the Chinese Regiment (two Companies) lay down in the open as a reserve and got all the bullets that were aimed at the Arsenal and the mud wall and went over. It was here that Captain Lloyd of the R.M.L.I. was mortally wounded.[1] Here, too, a bluejacket was killed, another mortally wounded, and three Marines and seventeen Seamen wounded. The Naval Brigade was now advanced to the cover afforded by the mud wall, and here it remained for three or four hours. When it arrived at this point it found that the Japanese and the French had got within 300 yards of the City Wall. All this time the allied field artillery, massed to the south of the mud wall, and every gun mounted in or near the Concessions, had kept up a heavy bombardment of the Native City.

The Welsh Fusileers and the Americans had by this time crossed the mud wall and were heavily engaged with a considerable force of Chinese to the south and south-west of the City. They were supported by a detachment of the Hong Kong Regiment, which, with a couple of Maxims, was stationed on the mud wall 2,500 yards away to the left, but exposed as they were to the fire of a fort mounting seven or eight guns to the west of the City, and enfilade rifle fire from the suburbs, they suffered very severely, particularly the 9th Americans, who lost their Colonel and most of their officers. Eventually the Japanese General, hearing that his troops had entered the city, sent a note to General Dorward to that effect; and asked him to cease fire. The necessary orders were given, and the Royal Marines sent forward towards the south gate to support the Japanese. Unfortunately the Japanese General had been misinformed. So far his men had not effected an entrance, and with the cessation of the Allies' fire the Chinamen redoubled theirs. "We moved in quick time," writes an officer of Marines, "for some 300 yards under cover along the road, then we got on to a causeway with water on each side and no cover. We ran our hardest for about 300 yards and then found a little cover to get our breath under. The whole of the south wall was blazing at us and it was real warm. After getting our breath we went on another 300 yards and reached a large mud hut which we found full of Japs and French. The enemy started shelling us so we got down into a ditch and stood in the water. Our guns soon afterwards stopped that amusement and we got out and took cover in the house. This was about 11-30 a.m. Then we found that the Japs were not in the City, so there was nothing to do but to sit tight. We sat in that house till 3-30 p.m. Whilst daylight lasted bullets kept whizzing all over the place. Luckily the mud walls proved sound and stopped everything. After dark all fire stopped except a little sniping, and we got the wounded back and some grub and water up. About 2-30 a.m. the Japs blew in the south gate, and about 3-40 we entered the City through

---
1 *Vide* Note II.

the south gate. We did not go into the city, but marched along the wall to the west gate where we stopped some time. About 11 we moved along to the north gate and joined up with some of our bluejackets; there we stopped till ordered to march in about 3 p.m."

All fighting at Tien-tsin was now at an end. The Native City, the main stronghold of the Chinese had fallen, and the Russians aided by two British Naval guns, a 4-in. and a 12-pounder, had captured the Chinese Batteries to the east of the City and routed their defenders.

Little now remains to be recorded of the doings of the Royal Marines employed with the Peking Relief Expedition.[1] Three hundred of them formed into a Battalion under the command of Major Luke, R.M.L.I., took part in the advance of the Allied Army of 19,000 men and 96 guns, which, on 3rd August, started to relieve the hard pressed Legations in Paking. It was present at the action of Peit-sang, then and afterwards acting as escort to the guns of the Naval Brigade. Owing to the difficulties experienced in getting these guns along, the Naval Brigade and the Marine Battalion did not arrive in Peking until the day after the first relief was effected. How the Royal Marines of the Legation Guard acquitted themselves in the long Siege will be related in the next Chapter.

NOTES.

Note I.—CAPTAIN DOIG'S ATTEMPT TO REACH TIEN-TSIN.

"We left the Arsenal at 9 p.m., with a hundred Marines, under the command of Capt. Doig, R.M.L.I., with Capt. Lloyd, R.M.L.I. Crossing the river by boat, we were ordered to fix bayonets and form fours.

"Before leaving the Arsenal, Capt. Doig explained to us that we were to try our utmost to reach Tien-tsin, or get somebody through safely, as it was thought that only by this sacrifice could the remainder of the force be saved. Also we were informed that anyone wounded would be counted as dead, as we could not be hampered with wounded. Captain Doig also informed us where to find the dispatches (in his left breast pocket), and should anything happen to him they were to be passed on one to the other and taken to Tien-tsin if possible. So after a few cheery words and congratulations from all concerned, we left the Arsenal, and crossed, as explained above, finding that our guide was a Mr. Corrie, a railway official. After taking us about a mile, he found out that we were going in the wrong direction, so we returned to the river again, when we were fired at by the Russian sentries, which fortunately went over our heads.

"We very soon made another start, and got about three miles when we were fired upon by the Chinese. We had orders at once to lie down flat, but as they continued firing at us, we rose and fired company volleys into them, finally taking the position at the point of the bayonet. Some of us received nasty falls, owing to the earth being entrenched. We came up to the railway, and dashing up the bank, formed a square and continued to fire in the direction of the flashes from the rifles. All at once the firing ceased, and then we could hear the bugles blowing the 'Cease fire.' Capt. Doig at once gave orders to 'Cease fire,' and told our bugler to sound our Division Call, followed by 'Cease fire.' The 'Cease fire' was answered, our bugler remarking that it was sounded from a trumpet, and by that we found out that we were right in the midst of General Neih's army which we tried to force. We could see Tien-tsin railway station about 1½ miles distant from us, so Capt. Doig gave the order 'Towards Tien-tsin Advance.' We had only advanced a few paces when we were fired upon all round, so an order was given to halt and lie down when we returned their fire. Capt. Doig then thought it advisable to retire, as it was useless trying to get to Tien-tsin as the odds were (as we learnt afterwards) about 100 to 1. We retired in square, being fired at all the way; luckily none were hit. Unfortunately we had to leave five casualties on the railway line. We reached the Arsenal about 2·20, being taken across by the Germans, who brought over junks. Capt. Doig at once reported the impossibility of reaching Tien-tsin, on which the Admiral said he did quite right in retiring, so saving the lives of 95 men out of 100."—Fr. "The Globe and Laurel," Oct., 1902.

---

[1] *Vide* Note III.

BAND UNIFORMS—ROYAL MARINES.

1825 Drummer. 1826 Musicians. 1825 Musicians. 1826 Drummer. 1830 Master of the Band. 1874 R.M.A. Musicians. 1900 Master of the Band. 1854 Drummer. Band Sergeant.

NOTE II.—DEATH OF CAPTAIN LLOYD, AND ATTACK ON NATIVE CITY.

A Non-Commissioned Officer of Marines who took part in the attack writes as follows :—

"About 2 p.m., on the 14th, we were ordered to fall in, and set out to capture the Native City, the allied forces having captured all the surrounding forts on the previous day. At about 4 p.m., when the bombardment commenced, we were acting as supports to the Japanese, the Americans being just behind us in reserve, and it was here that we lost so heavily, for as the Chinese were firing at the advancing Japanese, all their bullets were falling where we and the Americans were lying. We had absolutely no cover except what we could construct with our bayonets. Captain Lloyd was right in front of our company, and as he was getting up to have a look round, he was struck in the jaw by a bullet which passed clean through his head. We were then ordered to get under cover of the Arsenal, where we remained for some hours, when we were ordered to do something or other, I forget just what it was, but at any rate we had to double down a lane 600 yards long in face of a terrific fire from the Chinese on the City Wall, and I think I can safely say that we covered that 600 yards in record time. At the end of the lane we came to some mud huts and being unable to go any further we remained there till dark when we sent the wounded back, and waiting till the morning, entered the city and hoisted the British Flag, which was, I believe, the second to be run up. We remained in the Native City till night, when we marched back to our quarters, our first duty on arrival being the melancholy one of burying Captain Lloyd and the remainder of our killed."

NOTE III.—MARINES AGAIN AT TIEN-TSIN RAILWAY STATION, 1901.

" On 16th March we (at N.W. Fort, Taku) received a wire from Tien-tsin : ' Rioting in Tien-tsin, 100 Marines to be held in readiness to proceed to Tien-tsin at any moment.' We fell the men in at once (about 4-30 p.m.), and issued biscuits, etc., and 100 or 150 rounds of ammunition per man. Capt. Dyer, R.M.A., and Lieut. Lawrie, R.M.L.I., were the officers detailed. We heard no more till 10 p.m. that night, and the men had turned in, when another telegram arrived ordering us to go to Tien-tsin at once. We marched out of the Fort at 10-0 p.m., and arrived at Tong-ku about 10-45 p.m., nearly two miles, and a bad road. All this time we thought we were going to assist in policing the streets of Tien-tsin, as the French had had a bit of a down on the Indian troops and several rows had taken place ; but at Tong-Ku we heard that there was a dispute with the Russians over a railway siding which the British were making on land which the Russians claimed had become theirs by right of conquest or some reason of that sort. It was a bluff of De Wogack's, but Colonel Barrow was not taking any. We arrived at Tien-tsin about 3 a.m., on 17th, and found it pitch dark, and as cold as charity. A staff-officer met us, and led us to a railway truck on a siding about 200 or 300 yards south of the station. We were told it was to be our guard-house. Then we relieved the Sepoy guard, and posted sentries at the disputed points. After the day dawned we were able to see more or less the position of affairs. This I have tried to shew in the sketch I enclose. All the land between the road AB and the siding was waste, where the houses of Chinese railway employés had been, but which had been destroyed during the siege of Tien-tsin as they gave cover to snipers. That morning we got orders to prevent the Russian road AC, which was being made, from touching our siding BC, which was within thirty yards of the river bank. The road was being made so as to cut the siding. The Russians hurried up with the road and got so close that we marched down to stop them if necessary. Our magazines were charged and bayonets fixed, and the Russian officer then fell his men in and made them load. We waited for about twenty minutes like this, standing at ease and trying to look stolid, and then De Wogack came along with Captain McSweeney (who was Russian interpreter). De Wogack, looking very disgusted, came along and gave some order. McSweeney said, ' That's all right ; he's ordered them not to interfere with the siding.' So we marched back and spent the remainder of the day trying to get away from the dust—a bad dust storm was blowing the whole time. Next morning at dawn we relieved the sentries, presented arms to the Russian guard, and withdrew, they also presenting arms and withdrawing. We caught the 7-15 a.m. train to Tong-Ku and marched to Taku, here we arrived about dinner-time (12 noon). Total strength of Russian guard was 20 men. Royal Marine guard 30 men, afterwards increased to 60."

Fr. letter in " Globe and Laurel," 7th Dec., 1901.

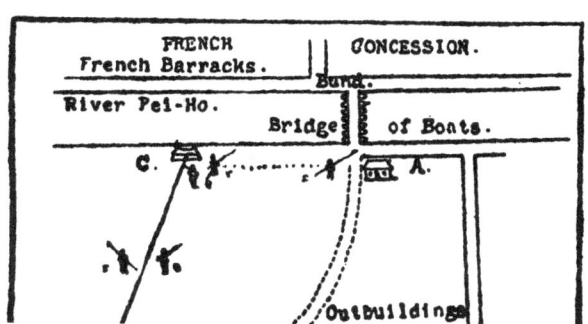

A—House occupied by Marines.
B—Railway truck for Marine Guard.
C—Tent for Russian Guard.
e—English Sentry. (Royal Marine).
r—Russian Sentry. (Cossack with sword and rifle).

THE ROYAL MARINE GUARD AND THE ARMED STUDENT INTERPRETERS
IN THE BRITISH LEGATION.—By permission of the "Daily Graphic."

Chapter XXXVII.
THE DEFENCE OF THE PEKING LEGATIONS, 1900.

"Tell the stout lions of our race,
   Lions alike on shore or sea,
We hold them in the pride of place
   Of freemen fighting to be free !
Fighting for all that men hold dear.

Their honour, Britain's, and their Queen's.
From land to land, from sea to sea,
The 'Joey' guard with three times three,
The empire gives this great, glad cheer,
Tell THAT to the Marines."
—Fr. "Punch," 29th April, 1900.

Chinese Regular Soldier.

We have now followed the doings of the Marines, "Soldiers and Sailors too," through more than two centuries, and have seen how they acquitted themselves —by sea and by land—in battle, siege, and assault on shore and in all kinds of fighting afloat. But it is no belittling of our fore-bears to say that never were their all-round qualities as fighting men better displayed than by the small detachment which took a leading part in the Defence of the Peking Legations in the summer of the year 1900. They not only fought stoutly and valorously as ever, but "cannily" as well. It is recorded that the German and Japanese Marines who fought beside them displayed the utmost bravery, but that they so recklessly exposed themselves to fire that their losses were heavier than they need have been. There is of course a time for all things, and such defiance of danger is an invaluable asset to any fighting force, and every true soldier must be prepared to exhibit it when called for, as it constantly is and must be in the course of all warfare. In the case of the Marines we have to go no further back than a few pages to find an exhibition of this kind of courage at the Battle of Graspan, not to speak of innumerable earlier instances.

But in the Defence of the Peking Legations against hordes of barbarians armed with the deadly weapons of civilised warfare, it was more than ever necessary to "fight to win."

The only possible way of winning, under the circumstances, was to gain time for a relieving force to assemble and fight its way through to the rescue of the helpless women, children and wounded men, between whom and the horrors of torture and death at the hands of an infuriated mob of the worst type of Chinese, nothing intervened but the stout hearts and ready hands of a little band of less than 500 men of various nationalities.

The defence had therefore to be a "fight to a finish." Surrender was unthinkable. The lesson of Cawnpore had not been forgotten. The life of every fighting man, and every round of ammunition had therefore to be husbanded to the last moment possible. It used to be laid down that to properly occupy a defensive position a force amounting to six men per yard of front was requisite, though where good field entrenchments had been provided this figure might be reduced to three or even two-and-a-half. This too, presupposes a position selected as the best available, and of course a more or less clear field of fire over which the enemy would have to advance to the attack.

In Peking, on the other hand, the area to be held was roughly about 1,000 yards square, so that allowing for irregularities in the perimeter, the line to be defended may well be assumed to have been 4,000 yards, so that instead of even two-and-a-half men to the yard, there were at the very least eight yards to each man. The loss of a single man, then, meant an additional eight yards of front to be guarded by the diminished band of survivors.

At Wei-Hai-Wei, where there was a small garrison of Royal Marines, a telegraphic order was received at 9 p.m., on the 28th May, for a detachment to proceed at once to Tien-tsin. Captain Wray, R.M.L.I. and twenty-five N.C.O's and men with a five-barrelled Nordenfeldt machine gun left the following morning in H.M.S. *Algerine*. They arrived about 9 p.m. on the 30th, having performed the last part of their journey in a river boat into which they had been trans-shipped at Taku. Here they joined Captain Strouts with his "Winter Guard" of twenty-five men, and early the next morning (May 31st), Captain Halliday and fifty more Marines arrived from H.M.S. *Orlando*. That day the combined Legation Guards, except the Germans and Austrians, left by the 2 p.m. train for Peking. Unfortunately, twenty-five of the one hundred Marines were left behind in order that the British Guard should not be larger than that of any other nationality. As events proved they would have been invaluable in Peking, though they found plenty of fighting to do later on at Tien-tsin.

Peking was reached at 7 p.m., and with the exception of Captain Halliday, a Corporal, and seventeen men who remained at the station till the following morning guarding their baggage till carts could be sent for it, the Guards marched to their destination.

Their five miles march was enlivened by the conversation of a Chinese convert employed at the Legations, who seemed to think that the Marines required cheering up. One remark of his, however, was not of a particularly cheering nature. He had stated that he did not think the Guard would return by the same route as the one they came by. "Which way will that be then?"

THE ROYAL MARINE GUARD AND COSSACKS ENTERING PEKING.
By permission of the "Daily Graphic."

asked someone. Shaking his head the Chinaman replied, "You no come back this way, no, no," and lifting his eyes upwards, "You go up top!"

"We got to the Legations shortly after 9 p.m.," writes Corporal Gregory,[1] "the distance being five miles from the station. We were almost suffocated with the dust and stench, marching through the Chinese city, the streets being crammed with Chinese all the way. But we got through safely. A cheer went up from the Legation people as we entered the gates."

"The next day, June 1st, the German and Austrian Guards arrived, bringing up the total force to 464 men.

"Waking up next morning, the 1st of June, we felt rather stiff, and looked rather dirty, as some of us could not get a wash overnight. Our baggage soon arrived, so we shifted into our clean white suits, and were soon fit to appear before Sir Claude and Lady McDonald. The first thing was to mount a guard at the gate, so we soon settled down a bit; one-half stationed at the small theatre, the other half in the bowling alley. There did not seem to be any immediate danger in

---

[1] In the "Daily Malta Chronicle."

Peking just then, so a small routine of drill was carried out for the first week. We had only been there a few days, when Sir Claude thought it was safe to send his children with the lady and the nurse[1] to their summer residence in the hills about twelve miles off; so Corporal Sheppard and twelve privates were sent with them as guard. They got there all right and stayed the night, but early next morning the Boxers could be seen not far off at drill in large numbers, so, of course, it was soon reported to Sir Claude, and you may guess he soon had his family and the small guard safe back in the Legation again. The same beautiful residence was totally destroyed by fire the following day. This was then our first notice of approaching danger. The next day everything in the shape of buildings at the European racecourse was destroyed. That was only about three miles off, so they were gradually working their way into Peking from the surrounding villages.

On the 5th, thirty French and eleven Italian bluejackets were detached to guard the French Roman Catholic Pei-Tang Cathedral, about three miles off, in the N.W. part of the city.

"The next few days were comparatively quiet, but provisions were collected and preparations for defence taken in hand. On the 6th, all available Marines, Seamen and volunteers were posted in the positions they had been told off to occupy in case of attack, and a general Council of War composed of all foreign ministers, secretaries and the Commanding Officers of the Legation Guards was held in the British Legation. It was then and there decided to hold all the Legations and to make the British Legation the final line of defence should the outlying ones be driven in, as it was considered to be the best situated and most capable of defence. Captain Strouts, R.M.L.I., in virtue of being the military commander of the largest Legation directed the general military arrangements.

"The Palace and grounds of Prince Su (generally referred to as the 'Fu'[2] opposite the British Legation were to be held for the Christian refugees, and an area was to be defended some half a mile long by half a mile broad, bounded by the Austrian and Italian Legations on the east, the street running over the north bridge of the canal to the north, the British, Russian and American Legations to the west, while the southern boundary was to be the street running at the foot of the great city wall from the American Legation on the west, past the German Legation on the east, to the lane running from the wall north past the French Legation, the buildings of the Inspectorate General of Customs, and the Austrian Legation. All women, children and non-combatants were to come into the British Legation."[3]

A glance at the map of Peking will show that it consists of a large square—the Tartar City—which is surrounded by an enormous wall sixty to seventy feet high, sixty-five to seventy feet wide at the top, with battlemented parapets three feet high at the sides, and square bastions at intervals of 100 yards on the outside face. At wide intervals along the inside face were pairs of ramps or inclined ways for mounting the wall, the ramps being about eight feet wide. In the centre of

---

[1] This party which consisted of Sir Claude Macdonald's two children, Miss Armstrong (Lady Macdonald's sister), and their nurse, went to the Summer Legation in charge of Capt. Wray, R.M.L.I., and Rose, a Consular student. Capt. Wray returned the same evening, and on his report of the state of the country, he was sent back the next day to bring them into Peking.
[2] The "Fu" "consisted of an enclosure of some twelve to fourteen acres, surrounded by walls twenty feet high. Inside were some thirty buildings of various sizes, beautiful gardens, houses, pavilions, rockeries, summer-houses, etc." Col. Shiba who commanded here designed no less than nine successive lines of defence.
[3] "Times" correspondent.

the Tartar City is the Imperial City, also enclosed in high walls, while the Chinese City, oblong in shape, adjoins the southern wall of the city proper, and extends rather beyond it to the east and west. The walls of the two latter cities are not so massive as the Tartar City wall, that of the Chinese City being thirty feet high and thirty feet thick, that of the Imperial City twenty-eight feet high and six feet thick. The Imperial City, though practically a square, pushes out a species of promontory towards the "Chien Men," the Central gate on the south side of the Tartar City, and which is surmounted by an immense tower. The Legation quarter lies between the south-eastern corner of the Imperial City and the southern wall of the Tartar City between the Chien Men and the Ha-Ta Men—another big gate—tower half-way between the Chien Men and the south-east corner of the Tartar City.

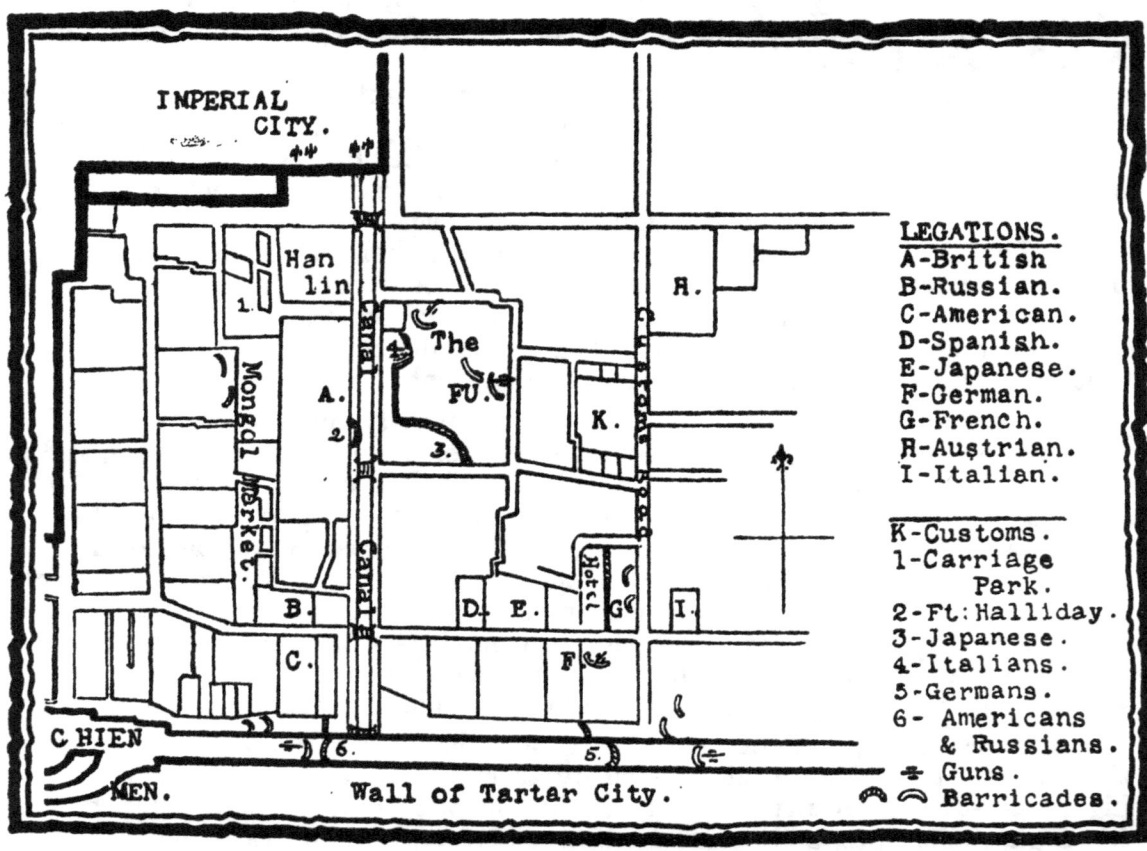

SKETCH PLAN OF THE PEKING LEGATIONS DURING THE SIEGE.

The British Legation was surrounded by a wall ten feet high and contained no less than five wells of good sweet water—a rarity in Peking, besides two other large wells of water, which though not drinkable, were very useful for washing or for use in case of fire. It contained eleven houses occupied by Europeans, a chapel, a theatre, a covered bowling alley, a fives court, and two large pavilions

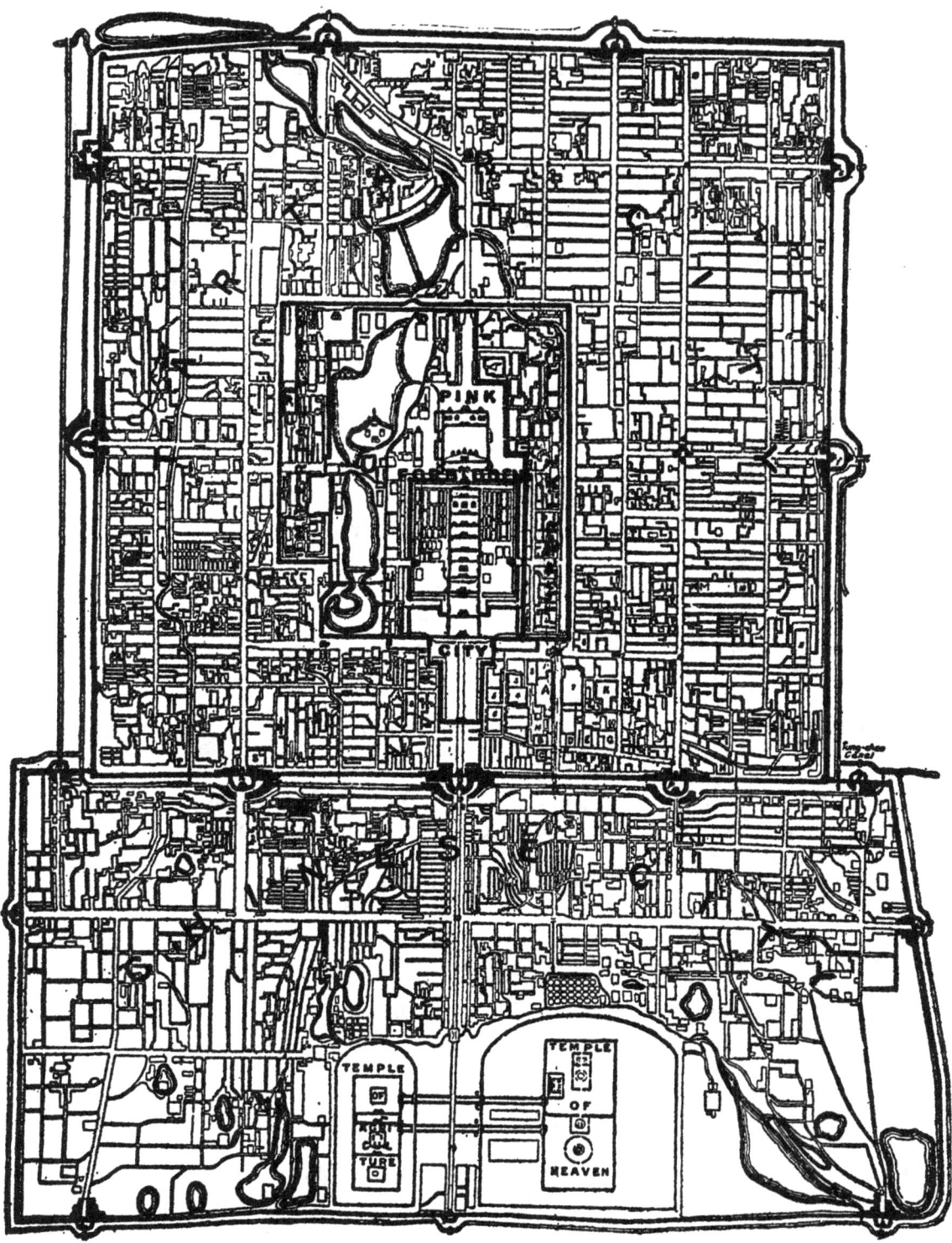

PLAN OF PEKING IN 1900. *By permission of "The Times."*

N.B.—The Legations are to the South-East of the Imperial City, between it and the outer wall of the Tartar City. The Tartar City is just over four miles square.

A—British Legation.	E—Japanese Legation.	I—Italian Legation.
B—Russian ,,	F—German ,,	J—Belgian ,,
C—American ,,	G—French ,,	R—Pei-tang Cathedral.
D—Spanish ,,	H—Austrian ,,	

Gates:
O—Chien Men.
P—Ha-Ta Men.

called "Tingerhs"[1] in front of the Minister's House. The other Legation enclosures were smaller and without so much open space. The north wall of the British Legation adjoined the Hanlin University Library, a large tree-shaded enclosure containing several halls in which was a priceless collection of books and manuscripts. On the west side the wall overlooked the Imperial Carriage Park, and to the south of that an open square known as the Mongol Market.

Between the Hanlin and the wall of the Imperial City nothing intervened but the width of the road which ran along the north side of the Legation Quarter. Similarly the huge wall of the Tartar City towered even higher above this quarter from which it was only separated by the breadth of the roadway at its foot. Here then was a weak point in the Europeans' defences, as from the wall the Chinese could command the whole quarter. It was therefore necessary to hold the top of the wall at the south-east and south-west corners of the quarter.

The force available to man the two miles of walls, barricades and other improvised defences at the opening of the siege may be estimated as follows:—

REGULAR FIGHTING MEN.

BRITISH.—79 R.M.L.I., 3 Officers (Captains B. M. Strouts, L.S.T. Halliday, and E. Wray). 3 Seamen (Leading Signalman H. Swannell, Armourer's Mate Thomas, and Sick Berth Steward Fuller).

AMERICAN.—53 Marines. 3 Officers (Captains Myers and Hall, and Surgeon Lippett).

GERMAN.—51 Marines (3rd Batt.), 1 Officer, Lieut. Count Sodon.

JAPANESE.—24 Marines. 1 Officer (Lieut. Hara).

RUSSIAN.—72 Seamen. 2 Officers (Lieut. Baron Von Rahden and Lieut. Von Dehn). 7 Legation Cossacks.

FRENCH.—45 Seamen. 2 Officers (Captain Darcy and Midshipman Herbert).

AUSTRIAN.—30 Seamen. 5 Officers (Capt. Thomann, Lieut. Von Winterhalter, Lieut. Kollar and two Midshipmen).

ITALIAN.—28 Seamen. 1 Officer (Lieut. Paolini).

To the above may be added the following Regular Officers:—

BRITISH.—Captain F. G. Poole of the East Yorkshire Regiment; Capt. Percy Smith, South Staffordshire Regiment (retired), Nigel Oliphant of the Scots Greys (retired).

JAPANESE.—Lieut.-Col. G. Shiba (Military Attaché), Captain Morita, Captain Ando.

RUSSIAN.—Lieut. Vroublevsky, 9th Eastern Siberian Rifles.

GERMAN.—Lieut. Von Strauch, Imperial Guard (retired).

FRENCH.—Captain Labrousse, Marine Infantry.

These officers were in Peking on business, political duty or on leave. A Volunteer Force of 75 men including Japanese, which proved a very useful and efficient auxiliary, and an irregular body of 50 gentlemen known as "Thornhill's Roughs," or the "Carving Knife Brigade" made the sum total of the little Army which therefore amounted to 392 regular Marines, Seamen and Cossacks, with 27 Officers (including those on the retired list), and 125 Volunteer Civilians, a grand total of 543 men of various sorts and kinds.

---
[1] Open reception halls.

Their available guns were not very formidable. There was an Italian one-pounder with but 120 rounds of ammunition, an American colt gun with 25,000 rounds, the British five-barrelled Nordenfeldt brought from Wei-Hai-Wei, which distinguished itself by "jamming" every few rounds, and an Austrian machine gun. The British[1] and other Guards had not more than 300 rounds of rifle ammunition apiece, while the Japanese, Russians and Italians had only 100, 145 and 120 respectively. The little garrison was in a tight place if a determined attack should be made.

Up to the twelfth there were but mutterings of the coming storm and indeed there was a gleam of light on the darkening horizon when on the 10th it was announced that reinforcements were on their way from Tien-tsin under Admiral Seymour. Indeed a large party under Captain Halliday went out on the day following to meet and welcome the expected troops. Thirty carts were sent to the railway station outside the Chinese City to the south-west to bring in their baggage. But it was a delusive hope. The relief column had certainly started but far from getting to Peking it had all it could do to get back to Tien-tsin. The depression created by this disappointment was increased by the murder of a Japanese Legation Secretary who was set upon and slain on his way to the station in a cart on which he was flying the Japanese colours. Thenceforward the outlook became momentarily blacker. Continual reports flew about of the growing influx of Boxers into the city, and of fighting on the railway line between Peking and Tien-tsin. News came that the summer Legation buildings near Fengtai had been burnt to the ground and the keeper and his family massacred.

A Boxer Proclamation was posted in the West City about this time stating that some Boxers at prayer had heard a terrible voice saying: "I am none other than the Great Yu Ti (God of the Unseen World) come down in person. Well knowing that ye are all of devout mind, I have just now descended to make known to you that these are times of trouble in the world, and that it is impossible to set aside the decrees of Fate. Disturbances are to be dreaded from the Foreign Devils; everywhere they are starting missions, erecting telegraphs and building railways; they do not believe in the sacred doctrine and speak evil of the gods. Their sins are numberless as the hairs of the head. . . . . The will of Heaven is that the telegraph wires be first cut, then the railways taken up, and then shall the Foreign Devils be decapitated. In that day shall the hour of their calamities come. The time for rain to fall is yet afar off, and all on account of the devils. . . . . If my tidings are false, may I be destroyed by the Five Thunderbolts!"

On the evening of the 13th, fires were seen blazing on all sides, 300 Boxers rushed in by the Ha-Ta Men Gate and fell upon the Methodist Chapel near by. They succeeded on setting it on fire, but were driven off with some loss by a party of French Volunteers.

The crackle of musketry reached the Legations, the Guards stood to their arms. "The Marines doubled through the gate in the greatest excitement," writes an eyewitness, "'I 'ope they let us get at 'em with the bayonet,' one of

---

[1] The British Marine Guard had 240 rounds a man. Captain Wray in his report to the Senior Naval Officer at Taku after the relief says of his men—"As a proof of their steadiness and coolness, I beg to state that out of 18,000 rounds of Lee-Metford ammunition brought from Tien-tsin, some 9,000 remain."

them was heard to say, 'it soothes your feelin's more like.'"[1] A guard was placed on the bridge at the north end of Customs Road, with orders to allow no Chinaman across without a pass. The road across this bridge was a very important thoroughfare, as with the Legation Street closed to traffic, it connected the east and west sides of the Tartar City. With the passage over this bridge held by the Europeans would-be passers had to go either right round the Imperial City or round through the Chinese City by the Chien Men and Ha-Ta Men gates. No actual fighting took place in the British zone, but the machine gun at the Austrian Legation appeared to be busy, though as far as could be ascertained its only effect was to cut away all the electric light wires which overhung the road to the north. Some apprehension was aroused by the discovery of a mysterious light burning at the sluice-gate under the Tartar Wall at the end of the Canal. A patrol was sent to investigate. Somewhat to their surprise they found it proceeded from the lantern of a small picket of Chinese Regular troops who stated that they had been placed there to prevent anyone getting into the Legations by that way. The soldiers appeared to be perfectly friendly. It seems curious that this opening in the Wall had not been already occupied by the defenders of the Legations. By this time the whole city was in an uproar and it was recognised that a crisis was at hand. The Guards were ordered to remain at their posts day and night, the men taking their blankets with them to snatch a nap at any odd time possible. Captain Halliday was sent to patrol the Mongol Market. There was little sleep for anybody that night.

"As darkness came on," writes Dr. Morrison, the "Times" correspondent, in his magnificent account of the Siege, "the most awful cries were heard in the city, most demoniacal and unforgettable, the cries of the Boxers, 'Sha kweitze,' 'Kill the devils'—mingled with the shrieks of the victims and the groans of the dying. For the Boxers were sweeping through the city massacreing the native Christians and burning them alive in their homes." On all sides the skies were crimson with the glowing of the fires kindled by these incendiaries.

Day dawned on the 14th. The Boxers' track was marked by fresh columns of smoke in various quarters of the Tartar City wherein were located all the missionary stations and foreigners' dwellings. The inhabitants of the Legations worked hard at improving their barricades and preparing for the worst. No direct attempt was made on the Legations before late in the evening, when a party of Boxers tried to rush the north bridge. Captain Halliday has written in his diary of this first brush with the enemy:—

"Thursday, 14th June. I was on duty at the picket 10-30 p.m. Boxers came down road from the north (a dusty lane). I retired on the bridge and got Oliphant's brother (Nigel) to challenge in Chinese; as they were waving torches in a silly way and shouting, I thought they might be an innocent religious prosession. They answered 'Sha, sha' (kill, kill), and came on. I fired a volley which stopped them, except one who dashed on the bridge flourishing an enormous sort of pike, and was shot by Sergeant Preston when within four feet. Strouts came up with reinforcements and told me to watch the road on our left, while he went up road on right. He was charged by a Boxer who suddenly appeared (it was a dark

---
[1] Rev. Roland Allen in "Siege of the Peking Legations."

CAPTAIN E. WRAY, R.M.L.I.

CAPTAIN B. M. STROUTS, R.M.L.I.

Left to right—1 Cpl. GOWNEY; 2 Cpl. SHEPHERD; 3 Sergt. SAUNDERS; 4 Sergt. MURPHY; 5 Cpl. GREGORY (wounded right foot); 6 Sergt. PRESTON; 7 Cpl. JOHNSON; 8 Signalman SWANNELL, R.N.
NON-COMMISSIONED OFFICERS OF THE LEGATION GUARD.

night), but shot him. Found we had shot four and wounded two (they probably carried away several). Dr. Poole came out with missionaries and stretchers and took in the wounded. Strouts then went in. Another Boxer came down the road and was shot, and I took his sword. We decided to leave the bodies there as a lesson, as they had on Boxer uniform, and it might help dispel the idea that they were invulnerable."

The next day was a day spent in expeditions into various parts of the city to rescue the Christians from the clutches of the savage Boxer gangs.[1] Everywhere these parties came across horrid exhibitions of the demoniacal fury of the Boxers, men, women and even children killed, cut and mutilated out of all recognition. The Boxers they fell in with received short shrift. The Americans and Russians went out in the morning, and in the afternoon twenty British Marines and the same number of Germans went out under Captain Halliday, and succeeded in rescuing about a couple of hundred Christians. They had the satisfaction of wiping out a considerable number of their persecutors. More rescue work went on on the 16th. A detachment of twenty British, nine Americans and five Japanese Marines under Captain Wray went out and caught a number of Boxers in the very act of torturing and murdering Christians in sacrifice to their gods in a Taoist temple to the accompaniments of incense and incantations.

"We had not marched for more than fifteen minutes," writes a Marine, "when we noticed a number of them (Boxers) run across a street just ahead of us. They were in full Boxer uniform, there was no mistaking them, so we broke into the charge after them. They took shelter in a temple and commenced to bombard us with stones and bricks over the wall, but we soon managed to burst open the strong doors, and it was all up with them, but they made several attempts to rush at us with their swords, and they went down before our rifles without any mercy. Their yells for mercy were awful to hear, but our men had heard and seen too much of their barbarous work to give them a chance. Forty-seven of them were laid out dead in that small place; they were piled up on top of each other as they tried to take shelter behind the gods of the temple; it was a ghastly sight indeed. We collected all the arms and had a splendid collection of swords. We left the bodies lying as an example to others."[2]

That afternoon a fire broke out in the huge Chien Men and destroyed a considerable portion of the edifice, and in the evening there was some desultory skirmishing near the north bridge. The Americans spent the night in firing periodical volleys down the street at the back of their Legation to keep it clear of Boxers. This system may have effected a saving in patrol work but under the circumstances would seem to have been an extravagant expenditure of ammunition.

The next two days were spent in constant watchfulness and preparation. The missionaries were set to work to build a barricade across the road leading to the bridge, and at night every man slept at his post with 140 rounds of ammunition in his pouches. The top of the city wall was occupied on the west by the Americans and Russians, and on the east by the German Marines. Elsewhere, however, events

---

[1] "The road to the Nantung Missionary Station," writes an Officer who was present, "lay along the foot of the high Tartar City wall, which was lined by Chinese Imperial troops, who were fully armed, but who did nothing to molest the foreign troops or to hinder the Boxers."
[2] Corporal Wm. Gregory, R.M.L.I., in the "Daily Malta Chronicle."

were occurring which brought matters to an acute crisis. On the 17th the Allied squadrons bombarded and captured the Taku Forts at the entrance of the Peiho River, the immediate result in Peking being that at 4 p.m., on the 19th, the Chinese Government ordered the European Ambassadors and everybody belonging to them to clear out in twenty-four hours. After much discussion all the Ministers with the exception of Baron Von Kettler, the German Ambassador, were inclined to accept the ultimatum and endeavour to make their way to the coast, at the same time a request was sent to the Tsung-li-Yamen[1] asking for an audience in order to arrange for transport and protection during the journey. A rumour of this possible decision was received with astonishment and alarm by the greater number of the European population, who were very loath to leave their defences and expose themselves to the tender mercies of Prince Tuan and the Boxers in the open. When on the morning of the 20th no reply had been vouchsafed by the Tsung-li-Yamen another meeting of the Ministers was held. Things were looking very ugly indeed and Baron Von Kettler, who spoke Chinese with considerable fluency, stated his determination of proceeding forthwith to the Yamen. Attended only by his secretary and a couple of Chinese servants he set out at 9 a.m. on the 20th, but never reached his destination. One of his escort of three Imperial Chinese soldiers wearing full uniform with a Mandarin's hat and button stepped up to the chair in which he was being carried, and deliberately shot him through the head.[2] This atrocious murder at once put an end to any idea of leaving the shelter of the Legations. The position of the Europeans in their precincts was by no means a safe one, but such as it was it was too good to be abandoned.

Further preparations for defence were pushed on with desperate energy. The mouths to be fed were augmented by the arrival of 1,700 more native Christians from the American Mission who came in with the guard of Marines whom it was necessary now to withdraw to the Legations.

According to the terms of the Chinese Government's ultimatum the foreigners were to have departed by 4 p.m. The order had been disregarded. What would happen next ? "In the British Legation," writes the Rev. Roland Allen, "a small group of men gathered on the lawn, watch in hand to await the expected moment. It reminded one of the Eights at Oxford. Five minutes more, three minutes more, two minutes more, and then firing was heard on the east. One Frenchman was shot dead, an Austrian wounded. Very soon we joined in. Captain Strouts was standing on the lawn. Sergeant Murphy rushed up and saluted. 'Firing has begun, sir,' he said. The real siege had begun."[3]

From this time forth the little garrison of the Legations had not only to deal with the fanatical but ill-armed Boxers but with the comparatively well-equipped Imperial regular troops, who, up to this time, had shewn themselves rather more friendly than otherwise.

The Boxer rabble were distinguished by their blue jean jackets and loose trousers tied at the ankle with red strings, red sashes and waistbands, and in some cases

---
[1] The Chinese Government House.
[2] His secretary, Herr Cordes, who was also being carried in a chair in rear, stood up when he heard the shot and saw the carriers of his Minister's Chair drop it and run away. His standing up saved his life for he was also fired at and wounded in the hip instead of being struck in the head as he would have been had he not done so.
[3] Rev. Roland Allen, in " Siege of the Pekin Legations."

red caps. Their leaders wore yellow instead of blue, and were also denoted by numerous black flags ornamented with various devices, and mottoes. Most of them carried murderous looking 7-foot halberds, others swords and spears of all kinds. The regular Chinese Infantry, who from this time forward reinforced the Boxers, were a very different and more formidable proposition. Their uniform was usually dark blue, grey, or black, with white, yellow, black or red facings. Their coats were made very loose and in the centre of both back and front was affixed a large circular piece of parchment upon which was inscribed the wearer's regiment, army and all other necessary particulars of his identity. These placards formed excellent " bulls-eyes " for the Marines, so that eventually John Chinaman found it advisable to " take his coat off " when going into action. These troops had had the advantage in most cases of having been trained by European instructors —they were well armed with Mauser and Manlicher rifles, and had it not been for the contemptible quality of their officers, the defence of the Legations would have been almost hopeless.

The new phase of the siege had an ill-omened beginning. At about 8 a.m. the next morning—the 22nd—all the Legation guards except the Japanese, who were garrisoning the Fu, fell back into the British Legation, in accordance with the previous arrangement in the case of necessity. This mistake was owing to a false report reaching the Austrian Legation that the Russians and Americans had been driven from their posts. All was confusion for the moment, and had the Chinese chosen to make a real attack, disaster must almost certainly have supervened. But fortunately nothing of the kind happened. The French and other detachments were able to re-occupy their former positions, but the Austrian Legation which formed the north east corner of the rectangle to be defended was lost and a new line of defence had to be formed running diagonally across the grounds of the Fu[1] towards the French Legation.

It was now decided that the chief military command should be vested in Sir Claude MacDonald, the British Ambassador, who had served some years in the Highland Light Infantry, and was still in the Reserve of Officers. It appears that the abandonment of the original line of defence had been due to the ill-considered action of Captain Thomann, the Austrian commander, who in virtue of being the senior militant officer on the spot, had assumed chief command. His supercession was urgent, and the assumption of command by Sir Claude MacDonald at the earnest solicitation of the French, Russian, and other Ministers offered the best way out of the difficulty.[2] The Chinese idea seems about now to have been to destroy the Legations by fire and burn or slaughter their defenders when driven out by the flames. They began operations on the south-west side where a mass of small buildings and stables were contiguous to the British Legation Wall. But by the determined efforts of the Europeans—even the ladies assisting to pass along the buckets of water—the fire was got under. All this time it must be remembered, the Chinese bullets were flying in every direction,[3] and one of them found a billet in Private Scadding, R.M., who was on watch on a stable roof, and was the first Englishman to lose his life in the defence.

---
[1] The " Su Wang Fu "—the " Palace of Prince Su, opposite the British Legation on the east side of the Canal.
[2] Up to this time Capt. Strouts had directed military operations as already recorded.
[3] *Vide* Note I.

"At the commencement of the siege," said Sir Claude MacDonald,[1] " our men had not learnt the art of barricade fighting, and exposed themselves needlessly; as time wore on the deadly fire from our loopholes would have done credit to the crack shots who figure in the novels of Fenimore Cooper. I had observed this particular Marine on the west wall, and had cautioned him only half an hour before. Some days afterwards the Sergeant of the Marines on the north stable picket shot a man through the head who was peering round a wall some 100 yards distant, as he fell two of his comrades jumped out to pick him up, but were instantly shot down by the same sergeant."

Foiled in this quarter the Chinese next set fire to the Hanlin Academy adjoining the north-west corner of the British Legation. No one had dreamt that such a deed was possible, even those who knew the Chinese best could not conceive that they would not spare this museum of the most priceless manuscripts and documents. But no European *does* understand the Chinese mind, and those who at this time could legitimately claim to know it best were the most often mistaken. Nor was this the work of the fanatical Boxers. The buildings were ignited by the Imperial soldiers who were in occupation of them.

The wind, high and gusty, blew volumes of flame in the direction of the British Legation and the danger was imminent. Its defenders proved equal to the emergency. A hole was knocked in the wall, and out sallied a party of Marines and volunteers under Captain Poole. A hurried rush through the Courts of the Hanlin resulted in a considerable " bag " of flying Chinamen, after which the fires had to be extinguished and much of the buildings pulled down to prevent the recurrence of such an attempt. A timely change of wind relieved the danger of the fire spreading to the defences. Elsewhere the Russians, Japanese and Americans were also contending with the efforts of the incendiaries.

About this time, too, the enemy brought a Krupp gun into action from the Chien Men Gate, which set all hands to work digging bomb-proofs. The Americans and Germans advanced along the wall to try and capture the gun, but as they had not sent word of their intention, they were not supported and found the task too heavy for their strength. More attempts at incendiarism were persisted in on the 24th, and it was in the sortie that their extinction necessitated, that Captain Halliday gained the Victoria Cross. Let him tell his own modest tale:—

"Sunday, 24th June.—Next morning I had the 2 a.m. to 4 a.m. watch, and found that Wray, who had the 12 to 2 a.m., had put a man with a loaded gun on the alarm bell, as he had found a French official was just going to ring it for a fire which was beyond the American Legation. Just as I was turning in, a Frenchman, whom I presumed to be the same man, came to where we were camping out (we had all given up our quarters and the Chancery Mess to the refugees), and said: ' Zere is fire in ze house of ze American missionaries.' I was very annoyed and told him to ' allez,' whereupon he went to turn out Sir Claude. I found it was the muleteers cooking their breakfast! I soon turned out again to make a sandbag bullet-proof place near the stables, and then was sent with six Marines and six civilians to help the Japs, who, however, said they were able to hold their own: so came back to find a bad attack on the south-west stable. Lead sortie among

---
[1] In his lecture at the R.U.S.I., 25th March, 1914, on the Defence of the Legations.

CAPTAIN L. S. T. HALLIDAY, V.C., R.M.L.I.

CAPTAIN HALLIDAY, R.M.L.I., WINS THE V.C.

some ruined houses. Went down a narrow alley and came upon five men with rifles round the corner of a house. One immediately plugged me in the shoulder cutting the left brace of my Sam Browne belt in half. I then began to empty my revolver into them, as they were only a yard away there was no question of missing. I finished four and the fifth bolted round another corner. The men had then come up and I told them to go on. I found my way back to the hole in the wall through which I was helped. Poole helped me to the hospital and dressed me there. Had no pain to speak of. That finished my active share in the siege which was rather hard luck."

Sir Claude MacDonald reported this incident as follows:—

"On the 24th June, the enemy consisting of Boxers and Imperial troops made a fierce attack on the west wall of the British Legation, setting fire to the west gate of the south stable quarters, and taking cover in the building which adjoined the wall. The fire, which spread to part of the stables, and through which and the smoke a galling fire was kept up by the Imperial troops, was with difficulty extinguished, and as the presence of the enemy in the adjoining buildings was a grave danger to the Legation, Captain Strouts, with my sanction, organized a sortie to drive them out. A hole was made in the Legation wall, and Captain Halliday, in command of twenty Marines, led the way into the buildings and almost immediately engaged a party of the enemy. Before he could use his revolver, however, he was shot through the left shoulder at point blank range, the bullet fracturing the shoulder and carrying away part of the lung; notwithstanding the extremely severe nature of the wound, Captain Halliday killed three[1] of his assailants, and telling his men to 'carry on, and not mind him,' walked back unaided to the hospital, refusing escort and aid so as not to diminish the number of men engaged in the sortie. For some days the surgeons feared the wound was mortal, but I am happy to say that, though still in the convalescent hospital, Captain Halliday is out of danger."

Meanwhile, to quote the account of a Marine who was present:—[2] "Captain Strouts then took charge and led his little handful of men forward; they would not stand before our bayonets, but we got many of them cornered in the houses, and had some hand to hand fights;[3] it was a case of our lives or theirs. Captain Strouts was grazed in the neck by a bullet;[4] it stunned him a little but he jumped up and went forward again as brave a young officer as ever led men. Private Sawyer was most seriously wounded in this affair, and others had marvellous escapes. Private Layton had his serge and trousers both shot through without the bullet touching his skin. I got my bayonet smashed by a bullet; it is wonderful that none of us were killed in this affair."

Fire having failed, treachery was resorted to. A placard was shewn under a flag of truce on the north bridge inscribed: "Imperial command to protect Ministers and to stop firing. A despatch will be sent to the Bridge of the Imperial Canal." Apparently it was either a trap to induce some of the Europeans to quit the shelter of their defences, or it was to prevent an attack being made on the

---

[1] A mistake. The number should be 4.
[2] Corporal Wm. Gregory, R.M.L.I., in "The Daily Malta Chronicle."
[3] Thirty-four of the enemy were killed in one house.—Sir C. McDonald's report.
[4] This Officer had an extraordinarily narrow escape, the bullet passing close to the carotid artery.

Chinese barricade builders, who were very busy till midnight, when suddenly a most furious fusilade was opened, most of the bullets passing well overhead.[1]

The clamour of this intensive rifle fire was increased by the use of a kind of explosive bullet which made a loud report on impact. The Marines and the rest of the garrison "sat tight" behind their barricades as there was no target worth expending ammunition on, and no harm was being done by the fire. Possibly this was what the Chinese were playing for. The fusilade may have been intended to keep the defenders of the Legations under cover while they still further strengthened and advanced their barricades. Certainly they had surrounded the Legations on all sides with these entrenchments by the day following. On this day Corporal Allen was wounded at the American barricade. It may be remarked in passing, that our men, very naturally, much preferred to fight alongside the United States Marines. "A splendid feeling of affection existed between our men and the Americans at this period," wrote Sergeant Gowney, R.M.L.I., 'quite in contrast to the feeling shewn by two other nationalities, alongside whom we have to fight."

The date, too, is noteworthy on account of the first issue of horseflesh to the garrison, which was the only meat eaten until the relief. The next few days passed in the usual wild indiscriminate firing on the part of the besiegers and "sniping" between their best shots and the Marines. The latter in order to save their valuable ammunition generally used a Martini-Henry[2] rifle for this purpose. Moreover, if the big leaden bullet did hit a man, that man was spoiled for further fighting.

The Royal Marine Guard did not find their regulation uniform and equipment all that could be desired for this "sniping" work. They had already dyed their white tunics khaki in a mixture of Condy's Fluid and coffee, and now found both helmet and cap "utterly useless." The helmet "always seemed to give the enemy a good four to six inches sight—when looking over or round our barricades and trenches. One had to risk a sunstroke by removing it, and a bullet by keeping it on. Our field-service caps were far worse than the helmet when in the open."[3] The ordinary cloth caps which they were able to borrow from the civilians in the Legations proved far more serviceable. The pouches were not only more or less ungetatable when firing lying down, but their weight, unbalanced by valise or greatcoat at the back, tended when worn, as they were almost continuously, to produce pains in the stomach. The bandolier equipment, as worn by some of the foreigners, seems to have been much more comfortable and serviceable. The Chinese varied the proceedings on the 28th by getting a Krupp gun to work in the Mongol Market, and did considerable damage to buildings at the south end of the British Legations. As this piece was not more than 300 yards distant a combined sortie of several nationalities was organised to capture it. The attack proved a fiasco, the mixed force losing its way in the confused turnings of the Chinese alleys, but the attempt was sufficient to induce the enemy to withdraw the gun. There were no casualties. More buildings were burnt which increased the field of fire which the Boxers incendiarism had already gained for the garrison.

---

[1] *Vide* Note I.
[2] These M.H. rifles belonged to the Legation for police purposes when no regular soldiers were present and were now issued to the volunteers.
[3] Q.M.S. Gowney, R.M.L.I., in the "Globe and Laurel."

BRITISH AND AMERICAN MARINES DRIVING THE ENEMY FROM THE HAN LIN.
By permission of the "Graphic."

BRITISH MARINES AND JAPANESE TROOPS MAKING A SORTIE FROM THE LEGATIONS. By permission of the "Graphic."

Indeed they seemed to have decided to try their fortune more particularly in other quarters. On the 29th the French at the south-east corner of the defences were subjected to a fierce attack and the Germans and Russians were hard put to it to hold their barricades on the city wall.

On the 30th, Corporal Gregory, R.M., was sent with seven men to the assistance of the Germans who, thirty in number under Major Von Soden, manned a barricade on the Tartar Wall facing eastwards. The Chinese had just made two attempts to rush the position but had been repulsed with heavy loss. "Many of their dead and wounded lay outside the barricade, but no-one could afford to venture out to assist them.[1] The Germans, who had been many hours in action, now retired to their Legation for a rest, with the exception of a N.C.O. and a Private. Corporal Gregory with these two and his seven Marines was left in charge. In about half-an-hour's time the barricade was suddenly attacked by shell-fire. The third shell carried away a considerable portion of the breastwork and seriously wounded Private Horne, who had to be carried below by three of the party, leaving Gregory with but five men, all told. A fourth shell brought down more of the barricade, which fell on Private Tickner, who was looking through a loophole with a pair of field glasses. He was also badly hit in both legs. But plucky fellow that he was, he refused any assistance in order not to further weaken the party, and crawled and rolled himself down the ramp towards the Legation. The German Private was the next to be knocked out by an injury to his face, and was assisted below by his corporal. Two of the Royals were now alone left to 'hold the fort.'"

Luckily the Chinese did not attack, and Von Soden seeing so many wounded men coming down, returned with his men and the barricade was re-built. He then returned below leaving a German Corporal and six men with Gregory. "This Corporal and his men," wrote Sergeant Gowney, "were most reckless in exposing themselves to the enemy. One of the privates recklessly leaned over the left of his position and fired down upon the enemy, who were in some strength in the houses below the wall. This naturally drew their fire upon the whole party, the private eventually receiving a bullet through the chin which passed out at the right side of his forehead. . . . . During the afternoon the corporal was also shot dead through carelessly exposing himself.

These incidents were always taken advantage of by the N.C.O's and men of our Guard to point out how useless such methods were, as we could ill afford to lose men, for, without doubt, many lives were carelessly thrown away."

The Germans relieved Gregory and his men early in the evening, and at daylight on the 1st July found the muzzles of three field-guns grinning at them over the Chinese barricade facing their's at not more than a hundred yards distance. There were only eight Germans and three British, and the Chinese making a sudden attack the German N.C.O. in charge ordered a retirement. The Americans, seeing the Chinese climbing over the German barricade and its defenders retreating down the ramp from the wall, leaving their own rear entirely open to attack, also abandoned the wall with much precipitation. The key of the whole position was now in the hands of the enemy, but the absence of co-operation and system in their attacks, enabled it to be re-occupied. The departure of the Americans had

---
[1] Q.M.S. Gowney R.M.L.I., in the "Globe and Laurel."

not been observed from the Chinese barricade opposed to them on the wall, so that when they were immediately reinforced by twelve British Marines under Captain Wray, they were able to re-occupy their former position without much difficulty. Captain Wray was, however, wounded in the shoulder during the operation. This officer had been ordered to attempt to build a barricade on the wall 200 yards east of the Russo-American position to cover its rear and to replace that lost by the Germans. This spot was exposed to a severe cross-fire from the Ha-Ta Men and Chien Men Gates, the Mauser bullets from the latter just clearing the American barricade in rear of the little party and ricochetting along the wall. After four hours work the enemy's fire became so heavy that further construction was impossible and a retreat was ordered," which was carried out with most exemplary coolness under a severe fire."[1]

The German barricade was not recaptured and the Americans had therefore to build a second barricade parallel to their original one to protect their backs and to sweep the wall to the eastward, now that the Germans were not in a position to do so. Meanwhile a strong attack was being pressed against the Japanese in the grounds of the Fu. A Krupp gun was brought into action and proved so dangerous to the defence that another sortie composed of British, Austrians, Frenchmen and Italians was sent across the canal to try and capture it. The Italian officer in command was Lieutenant Paolini. As in the case of the sortie of mixed nationalities into the Mongol Market, a wrong turning was taken and it proved entirely ineffective. Unfortunately, too, it cost the garrison three men killed, and an officer, four men and one volunteer wounded.

The next day the pestilent Krupp was at work again and the gallant little Japs with their auxiliaries, a corps of Chinese Christian refugees, organised by Colonel Shiba, were driven further back, though they clung to each position to the last, and succeeded in ambushing a number of Chinese soldiers.

Nor were the Chinese idle elsewhere. The American barricade on the City Wall was built at a point where a big square bastion jutted out from it, but unfortunately did not command the ramp leading up the wall from the enemy's side. The Chinese had erected theirs at the opposite side of the bastion, from the top of this ramp, and prolonging it a little way into the bastion itself they were enabled to push a line of wall across it towards the Americans at such an angle that they could not enfilade it. When close to the American barricade they erected a small tower from which they intended to fire down into the space between the Americans breastworks thereby rendering their position untenable.[2] It was an ingenious and well planned piece of engineering work, but neglecting to occupy the advanced approaches during the hours of darkness, the Europeans were able to capture the whole construction by a night attack. The force detailed for this operation consisted of twenty-six British Marines under Sergeant Murphy and Corporal Gregory, with Mr. Nigel Oliphant as a Volunteer, fifteen Americans, and the same number of Russians under Captain Vroublesky, Captain Myers of the U.S. Marines being in command of the whole.[3]

On the word "go" the British and Americans jumped over the left end of their barricade, scrambled through a gap between the Chinese tower and the wall

---
[1] Sir C. MacDonald's Report.   [2] Vide Plan.
[3] It is this sortie which is depicted in one of the tableaux on the Royal Marine Memorial near the Admiralty. The officer leading can be recognised as an American by his felt hat. The Royal Marines are wearing helmets.

leading up to it, and finding no-one behind it pressed on for the main Chinese barricade. The Russians at the same time got over the right of the American barricade and attacked it on the left. The Chinese opened fire, but were evidently taken by surprise and were driven from their position with the loss of fifteen killed and many wounded. No time was lost in strengthening the Chinese barricade and turning it against its late holders who had another one across the wall some way further along. On the 5th a new class of attack was directed against the British Legation. A number of smooth-bore 14 and 7-pounders were mounted up on the wall of the Imperial City directly to the northward,[1] and round shot fired at a close range came crashing into the crowded Legation Buildings in all directions. Fortunately but little damage was done.

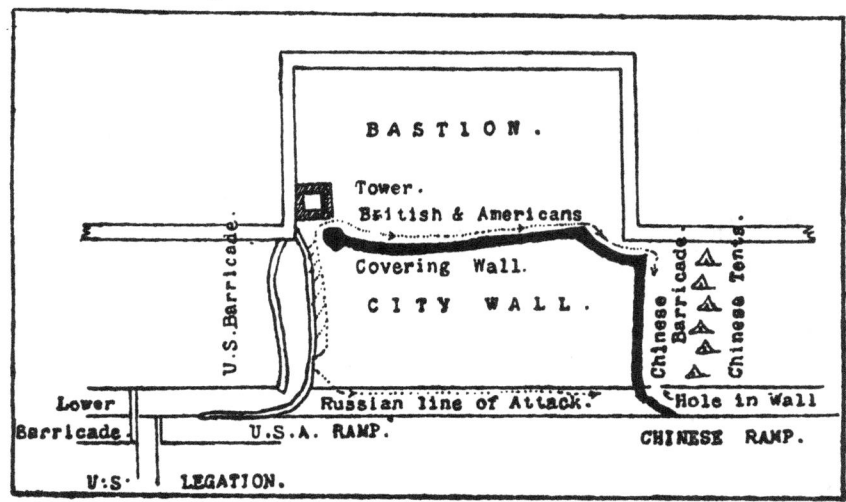

Plan of Combined Attack on Chinese Barricade on City Wall, 3rd July, 1900.

Fr. "A Diary of the Siege of the Peking Legations," by Nigel Oliphant.
By permission of Messrs. Longmans, Green & Co.

One entered the big dining room through the north wall of the British Minister's House, and passing behind a large picture of Queen Victoria, without injuring it any way, pierced the south wall of the room, and fell into the little central garden, where Sir Claude MacDonald's children were playing at "Boxers, barricades, sorties and mimic warfare generally."

These Chinese guns enfiladed the canal, but thanks to the prevision of the defenders, a covered way across it to the Fu had already been constructed. In the Fu itself the attack was pushed with more intensity and determination than in any other quarter, probably owing to the burning desire of the Boxers and their allies to get at and slaughter the Chinese Christians. The Japanese on the 8th were reduced to thirteen Marines and fourteen Volunteers. The next day the front they held was prolonged by fifteen Italian and five Austrian sailors who had become nervous since the loss of their officer, Lieutenant Paolini, and were with difficulty dissuaded from relinquishing their somewhat isolated corner during the night.

---

[1] *Vide* Note II.

The want of anything in the nature of artillery to reply to the Chinese guns became more felt every day, and on the 7th July, Mitchell, an American gunner, and Thomas, the British armourer, were trying to fabricate something like a cannon out of brass piping and copper wire from which some shell which the Russians had brought up[1] could be fired. While they were deliberating on how to close the breech of the tube, some Chinese brought in an old gun[2] which had been found in a shop on Legation Street. Poor weapon as it was, it was a Godsend under the circumstances. On experiment it was found that the Russian shells could not only be got into it, but discharged without disaster, and mounted on a spare gun-carriage belonging to the Italians, fired by an American gunner, and discharging ammunition made by the British Naval Armourer, it proved of considerable use against the Chinese barricades. The Italian 1-pounder had at this time expended all its projectiles, but the happy idea of re-filling the empty brass cartridge cases and fitting them with a leaden bullet was found to be a practicable one. So that the garrison now rejoiced in the possession of an artillery train—of sorts. As for gunners, the British and American Marines, and at any rate the bluejackets, among the foreigners, were of course accustomed to the handling of all kinds of cannon and were able to make the best possible use of the two feeble pieces of artillery. The resuscitated weapon received several " soubriquets," —the " International," " Long Claude," " Boxer Bill," the " Empress Dowager," were some of them, but finally it was generally known as " Betsy," at any rate among the British Marines.

The fighting in the Fu continued to be most strenuous, and on the 10th Captain Wray was sent over to permanently command the British and Italians holding the left portion of the entrenchments within that enclosure. An artillery attack on the American barricade on the wall by a gun, which the Chinese suddenly unmasked within fifty yards, bid fair to become a formidable one, but luckily at the fifth round some mishap befel the weapon and its fire ceased altogether. The ten British Marines, who with two Russians, were behind the portion of the barricade that was attacked behaved with the resourcefulness of the well trained soldiers which they were.[3] Lying flat till the Chinese shell struck and burst they instantly sprang up and poured a volley on the gun. But had not the gun been silenced the barricade must have been destroyed piecemeal.

The French, too, at the south-east corner of the defences had been having a very warm time, and the Germans as well. On the 13th the Chinese sprung a mine under the French Legation burying two seamen up to their necks in the debris[4] thrown up and opening a way for the attackers. The French and Austrians who were defending it were driven back to an inner line of entrenchment from which the enemy were unable to oust them. Simultaneously the Chinese effected an entrance into the Club, next the German Legation, but collected on the tennis court, they were charged with the bayonet by the German Marines and pitchforked out again. It was afterwards found that another mine had been driven under the

---

[1] They had had a gun with them, but it was left behind at Tientsin.
[2] This was an old gun of British manufacture, rifled, and with the Government cipher upon it. Both trunnions had been knocked off. It was probably a relic of the allied operations in 1860.
[3] "I consider the British Marine is the best all-round fighting man in the world."—*Kaiser Wilhelm II. at Eastney Barracks, in August,* 1890.
[4] Curiously enough the explosion of a second mine just afterwards released them unharmed.

CAPTURE OF A BOXER STANDARD BY SERGEANT PRESTON, R.M.L.I.
From "The Regiment."

wall of the British Legation. Sentries had frequently reported curious noises but the idea of a mine was for a time scouted, but in the digging of a countermine the Chinese could be distinctly heard at work. Subsequent investigations after the relief exposed the mine fully laid. But the workers were evidently disturbed by our diggers, as it hereabouts turned away from our defences to go under the carriage park.[1] On the 14th July, Sergeant Preston, R.M.L.I., earned the Conspicuous Gallantry Medal by the following act of bravery:—"After the enemy had been driven from their barricade on the Imperial Carriage Park Wall, near the West Hanlin, by shell fire, this N.C.O. climbed on the wall, some twelve feet high, with the intention of capturing a banner left on the barricade by the enemy. Finding that he could not reach it, he called for his rifle to be given to him, and pushing down part of the barricade kept the enemy, some fifty in number, at bay, while an American gunner named Mitchell, was enabled to lay hold of the flag. Sergt. Preston then jumped down and assisted Mitchell in drawing the flag over with difficulty, as the enemy had laid hold of the other end. He was struck on the head at the same time by a brick which partially stunned him."[2]

The 16th July was a black day for the defence, for on it fell Captain Strouts, who had so ably maintained the reputation of his Corps by the way he had carried out his duties as Commander of the British portion of the defenders of the Legations. "Throughout the siege," writes Dr. Morrison, "he had acted in a way that won the admiration of all. He was always cool and self-reliant, and never spared himself, while always considerate for his men." Sir Claude MacDonald spoke equally highly of this fine young officer: "I have no hesitation in saying," said he,[3] "that I have never met an officer who combined cool and fearless daring with judgment and skill to such an extent as did this young officer of Royal Marines —the death of Captain Strouts was little short of a calamity."

During the 15th the enemy had been "making a strong attack upon the north-west corner of the Fu, in the hope of cutting the communication between the east and west sides of the canal. Their gun had battered down the barricade, and at 10 p.m. their fire drove back the coolies who were then trying to restore it, but they were soon able to return, and after the first fusilade were only annoyed by occasional shots. About 7 a.m. on the 16th July, Captain Strouts, Dr. Morrison and Colonel Shiba were making a round of inspection. There was one place in the Fu which it was always dangerous to cross. After passing the Italian Guard-house, the way lay under the shelter of a low range of artificial hills. The enemy built high barricades on the other side of the hills and kept up a continual fire across this little piece of open ground. . . . It was a standing order to double across this open space. Here Captain Strouts and his fellows were caught in a storm of bullets. Strouts was hit in the thigh; the large artery was cut, and he died of shock and fatigue in the hospital very soon after. Dr. Morrison, in turning to help him, was wounded in the leg; Colonel Shiba received a bullet through his coat.

---

1 After the Relief another mine driven under the American barricade on the City Wall was also discovered, as well as one in Legation Street nearing the Russian barricade there, and others directed against the French and Japanese defences.

2 Official Report.—The flag was a black silk one with the Chinese character for "Artillery" inscribed thereon. The same day the French captured a white silk flag with a red inscription to the effect that it had been presented by the Dowager-Empress to General Ma.

3 In his lecture at the R.U.S.I. on 25th March, 1914.

It was a terrible loss." .... "Captain Strouts was buried with Mr. Warren (a student who had been killed the day previous) in the afternoon. The scene in the little cemetery behind the 1st Secretary's House was a striking one. The whole world turned out to follow these two to the grave—Ministers, Officers, Marines, missionaries, ladies, children, all who were not on duty were there. At the moment there was a furious attack going on and bullets were whistling through the trees."[1]

Poor Strouts fell just as a more peaceful period arrived. From the day on which he was shot on till the 4th August the Chinese, with the exception of a certain number of "snipers," desisted from their attacks and the Yamen seemed inclined to be conciliatory. Space does not admit of a description of their curious[2] and tortuous negotiations and proceedings. Meanwhile, on July 18th, the beleagured garrison received certain news of the advance of a relieving army, and were looking every day for the end of their hardships and trials.

In the afternoon of July 29th, the Chinese began to throw out heaps of bricks and stones at the corner of some ruined houses on the east end of the north bridge over the canal. This bridge was commanded by the north stable picket and by the caponier in front of the main gate of the Legation, called by the Marines "Fort Halliday." It soon became evident that the heap of bricks and stones was the commencement of a barricade, and a lively interchange of sniping took place between the Chinese sharpshooters and the Marines, the men of the north stable picket having many narrow escapes. "Having been musketry instructor of my old regiment, the 74th Highlanders," said Sir Claude MacDonald,[3] "I could not resist the temptation of trying my luck and, borrowing a Marine's rifle, at the third shot carried away a large brick which was being placed on the top of the barricade by visible hands belonging to invisible workers. With the brick went, I think, portions of a human hand; recollecting that I was breaking one of my own regulations regarding the waste of ammunition, I 'ceased fire' and handed the rifle back to its owner. As I did so, a bullet flicked viciously through my loophole, the only comment my friend the Marine made was 'nearly had you that time, Sir!'"

Both sides, however, continued to improve their barricades and defences, and it was well for the garrison that they had not neglected to do so. For about the 5th August the "sniping" increased very considerably, especially from the Mongol Market, and a new fortified position which had been built there by Lieut. Von Strauch proved most valuable. On the 8th, 9th and two following days the firing from the Chinese barricades was fast and furious. In their eagerness to press forward, the enemy overthrew one of their own barricades. Instantly our sharpshooters opened a deadly fire; and the Nordenfeldt was brought to bear. Before they could escape this hail of bullets, twenty-seven including their leader fell in a riddled heap. On the 13th there was regular bombardment. It was however silenced after seven rounds by the Italian and Austrian machine guns, and a Krupp

---

[1] Rev. Roland Allen in "Siege of the Peking Legations."
[2] There were several "curious" things connected with this siege, besides the conduct of the Chinese authorities. Heavy gun fire was heard at times to the west or south-west of the city, and electric flashlights to the south-east. These things have never been explained.
[3] At the R.U.S.I.

quick-firing gun made an attack from the Imperial City Wall. Fortunately there were but few casualties, and at 8 a.m. on the 14th, the shells fired by the relieving force were seen bursting over the Chin-Hua Men[1] and everyone was overjoyed to find that the long-expected succour was at hand. In the afternoon General Gaselee and his Staff made a sudden appearance in the British Legation, having come by way of the Chinese City through the high Tartar City Wall by the Water Gate to the south of the Legations. A patrol under an officer entered first. Close behind the General followed his escort of sixty Indian Troopers and after them came the 1st Sikhs and the 7th Rajputs. The siege was raised. But the besieged were not content to be lookers on now their rescuers had arrived. They instantly assumed the offensive. The Russians and Americans advanced to the Chien-Men Gate and let in the 1st Sikhs and Hong Kong Artillery, the British Marines and Volunteers under Captain Poole sallied out and occupied the carriage park, the Japanese and Italians cleared the enemy out of the Fu, while the Germans attacked their opponents and drove them back to the Hata-Men Gate, capturing guns and prisoners.

Little more remains to be told. The Allied troops continued to pour into the city from various quarters, among the arrivals on the 15th being a Royal Marine Battalion of 250[2] men under Major Luke attached to the Naval Brigade. This battalion was pushed on through the City to the relief of the Pei-Tang Cathedral where the priests, many of their Chinese converts and a small guard of French and Italian bluejackets had been holding out in desperate straits. But it was found that the Japanese troops had already effected this. In conclusion the following quotation from Sir Claude MacDonald's report bears eloquent witness to the worth of the Royal Marine Guard.

"They were exposed," wrote Sir Claude, "day and night, for two months, to the most arduous, irksome and responsible duties, which they fulfilled with a cheerful alacrity and with a courage and endurance which excited the admiration of everybody. Their bearing under fire was quite excellent, and could not have been surpassed by the best veteran soldiers. During the entire siege I did not observe the slightest signs of liquor in any of the men, neither was a case reported to me, and this though the facility for obtaining drink was great. To sum up, the general good conduct, soldierly bearing, and steadiness under fire of the men of the detachment was worthy of the highest traditions of the British Army and the Corps to which they belong."

"This high state of excellence was undoubtedly in a great measure due to the Officers and Non-Commissioned Officers. Captain Strouts was an excellent soldier and a gallant gentleman. He was killed in the defence of the Legation on the 16th July, and his loss was to me, and to the defence generally, irreparable. Had Captain Strouts lived, I should certainly have recommended him to the Lords of the Admiralty, through your Excellency, for promotion or for the Distinguished Service Order."

---

1 The eastern gate of the Tartar City to the north-east of the Legations.
2 The apparent discrepancy between this number and the 300 mentioned in the previous chapter is due to several men having been left to guard communications.

This generous tribute to the Royal Marines' invaluable services was echoed by Dr. Morrison, the "Times" Correspondent and by many others who wrote, publicly or privately, accounts of the siege. Captain Wray, who had succeeded Captain Strouts in Command of the Royal Marine Guard, was honoured by the following telegram from H.M. Queen Victoria :—

"I thank God that you and those under your command are rescued from your perilous situation. With my people I have waited with the deepest anxiety for the good news of your safety, and a happy termination of your heroic and prolonged defence. I grieve for the losses and sufferings experienced by the besieged."

(Signed) V.R.I.

The Lords Commissioners of the Admiralty also wired :—

"Board of Admiralty send their heartfelt congratulations on your rescue. They have felt intense anxiety as to your safety. Your countrymen are proud of your heroic defence."[1]

Here we may leave both the Siege of the Peking Legations[2] and also the story of the war services of the Corps of Royal Marines. Though many years had elapsed since Lord St. Vincent's famous eulogy of its valuable qualities, the Peking detachment justified his estimate; and that their comrades and successors will continue to do the same, no-one who knows the Marines and their intense *esprit de corps* will doubt for a single moment.

NOTES.

NOTE I.—RANDOM CHINESE FIRE.

"June 27th.—The men, however, seemed for the most part to fire quite at random, and storms of bullets flew high over our heads. It was curious to speculate where they all went : one would naturally suppose that scores of innocent people in the city must have been hit by stray shots. There were many conjectures as to the cause of this ridiculous waste of ammunition. One, mentioned by Dr. Morrison in his account of the siege in the "Times," was that the soldiers wanted to kill, or rather frighten away, the devils which protected the Legations, just as they fire off crackers to drive away evil spirits at any festival or leave-taking. Another theory, started, I believe, by Dr. Coltman, was much more worldly minded. It was that the soldiers emptied their cartridges in order to sell the brass cases. It was said that, when first the troops were supplied with foreign weapons and ammunition, they used to empty the powder out of their cartridges for the same purpose, and the practice became so universal that it had to be made a capital offence. But the refutation of this theory lay on the surface, the ground outside the Legation barricades being littered with cartridge-cases, which the Chinese had not taken the trouble to carry away. A most interesting solution was suggested by Mr. Cockburn. He said that in 1881 when China seemed to be on the eve of war with Russia, Gordon wrote a memorandum advising the Chinese how to meet the foreigners. He told them in that paper to avoid meeting the enemy in the open, but to worry them night and day, especially by making as much noise as possible at night, in order to keep them continually on the strain, for he said that the demoralisation produced by anxiety and want of rest would be of greater service to the Chinese than many victories."

Fr. "The Siege of the Pekin Legations," by Revd. Roland Allen, M.A. (Smith, Elder & Co., 1901).

---

1 *Vide* Note III. List of casualties.
2 The British Ensign that the Royal Marines kept flying over the British Legation was presented by Sir Claude MacDonald to Queen Victoria. It bears witness to the severity of the attack in 75 bullet-holes, while the Staff was struck 16 times.

NOTE II.—GUNS ON THE IMPERIAL CITY WALL.

July 5th—"At mid-day the sentries in the upper story of the Students' Library and Quarters reported the enemy at work amongst the yellow tiles on the top of the Imperial City Wall, which is distant some 200 yards from the North Wall of the Legation. At first it seemed as if they were loop-holing it for musketry, but by means of field-glasses through the foliage of the trees two guns could be plainly made out. How the enemy had succeeded in getting them up to their position it was difficult to ascertain, for the wall was over twenty feet high, and only some three feet thick. After the siege was over these batteries were found to consist of very elaborate gun-platforms, 20 feet by 16 feet, made of scaffolding strong enough to hold guns of a much heavier calibre than those actually used. They could accommodate from thirty to forty men, and were made of timbers 9 inches in diameter, some 700 to 800 being employed to make each battery. Ramps 12 feet broad led up to the platforms. A small gallery supported by scaffolding ran along to right and left of the batteries just below the yellow-tiled coping on the top of the wall. This gallery was loop-holed for musketry. The place where the guns stood was roofed over as a protection from sun and rain. The iron doors mentioned (to close the embrasures for the guns) were found in the battery after the relieving force arrived. They consisted of folding doors on hinges of wrought iron half-an-inch thick, but had been pierced over and over again by our rifle fire, and the left battery had a hole through its door as if made with a punch. This was the work of the Italian gun."—Sir C. MacDonald's Official Account.

NOTE III.—CASUALTIES IN THE ROYAL MARINE DETACHMENT AT PEKING.

KILLED : *Captain* B. M. Strouts ; *Ptes.* A. Scadding and C. W. Philips.

WOUNDED.—*Captains* L. S. T. Halliday and E. Wray.
Sergeant J. E. Preston.
Corporals W. Gregory and J. Gowney.
Lance-Corporals A. Sparkes and T. R. Allen.
Privates.—G. Sawyer, A. D. Tickner, J. Heap, A. E. Westbrook, W. G. Roe, A. T. Layton, G. Goddard, Wm. Horne, K. King, W. Hayden, W. T. Woodward, A. Webster, J. Buckler, J. Deane, G. Lister.

ROYAL MARINES MANNING THE "INTERNATIONAL GUN."
Alias "Betsy," *alias* "Boxer Bill," *alias* "Empress Dowager," *alias* "Long Claude."

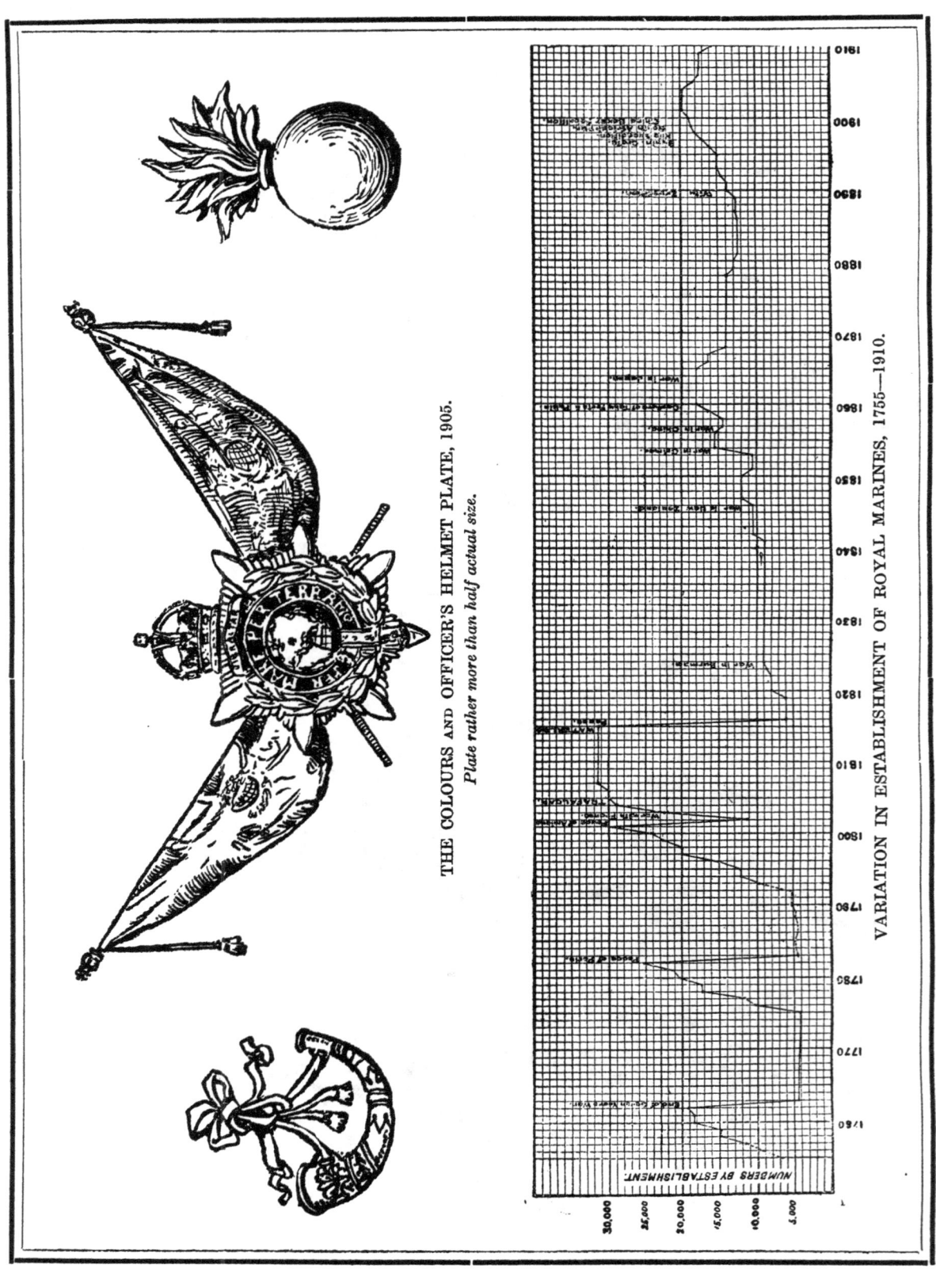

THE COLOURS AND OFFICER'S HELMET PLATE, 1905.
Plate rather more than half actual size.

VARIATION IN ESTABLISHMENT OF ROYAL MARINES, 1755—1910.

FORTON BARRACKS.

Chapter XXXVIII.

PRESENT ORGANISATION AND EQUIPMENT OF THE ROYAL MARINES.

"Their record is Second to None. I have been with them on Active Service, on Police Service, in Daily Routine and in Gales of Wind—I have had them with me everywhere, and I tell you there is nothing like the Royal Marines."
—*Admiral Lord Charles Beresford, 30th June,* 1909.

N.B.—This Chapter was written before the Great War broke out in 1914.

WITH the defence of the Peking Legations and their relief, the story of the War Services of the Corps of Royal Marines is brought to a conclusion. Since that time the nation has not had to call upon the Navy and Marines to take their share in hostilities of any importance or magnitude. There have been, as at all times in the past, and as there ever will be in the future, various small coastal operations in out-of-the-way parts of the world in which, though the fighting has been on a very small scale, both Bluejackets and Marines have been able to shew the stuff they are made of, and have "talked to them 'eathen Kings," and wild Arab chieftains in the self-same language that their ancestors used. But broadly speaking, the last ten years have been years of peace, though how long that peace will last no man can say. With every European nation armed "cap-à-pie," and Navies springing up like crops of "Dragon's Teeth,"[1] in quarters in

---

[1] The simile is taken from the Classical Myth of Cadmus who slew the Dragon that guarded the Well of Dirce in Bœtia He sowed the monsters teeth, and from these sprang up the Spartans. Some of the teeth which he did not sow came into the possession of Æertes, King of Colchis, and one of the tasks which he set Jason was to sow these and slay the Crops of armed warriors that grew from them.

which in the days of Nelson not a single war-ship harboured, a spark only is needed to bring on a sudden and wide-spread conflagration. Nor are the more important of these new Navies to be compared with those with which our greatest Naval hero and his officers and men fought so victoriously. The French Navy had been utterly demoralised by Republican doctrines which were fatal to discipline, and its commanders and its men further reduced in fighting efficiency by general orders to reserve themselves and their ships for the attack of our commerce rather than run undue risks in attacking our men-of-war. The Spanish Navy, was if anything, still more inferior in fighting value. What was more, our own Officers and Men knew all this, and acted on their knowledge. Our Naval Commanders, though always ready to tackle a superior number or force, by no means ignored the tactical principle of concentrating a superior force against that of the enemy, whenever possible, which was pretty often, thanks to the great numerical superiority of our men-of-war at that period. In the war of the immediate future we shall not have all these advantages. We do not appear likely to have many more ships than our possible opponents, and it is probable that there is hardly a Navy in Europe whose crews are not better disciplined and trained to warfare than were Nelson's opponents —bravely as they fought. Already before a shot has been fired, we have found it necessary to abandon the outworks of our Naval frontier and to concentrate round the Keep, and recall many ships to home waters from more distant seas.

But to return to the Corps of Royal Marines. We have recounted its past services, and in this, the concluding Chapter, it may be of interest to give some account of its present organisation and duties, a subject on which "the man in the street" knows very much less than he should, and not infrequently nothing at all. Those who have read the preceding chapters will agree that a Corps which has done so much for its country ought to be better understood by its countrymen. At the present time (1913) the Corps has a strength of 18,000 Officers, Non-commissioned Officers and Men. Those Marines who are not serving afloat are quartered in Barracks at Chatham, Portsmouth and Plymouth. The Royal Marine Artillery Barracks is at Eastney, to the East of Portsmouth. Those of the Royal Marine Light Infantry are at Chatham, just outside the Dockyard, at Gosport, on the Western side of Portsmouth Harbour, and at Stonehouse, between Plymouth and Devonport. In addition there is a large Depot Barracks at Walmer[1] to which all Recruits are sent for their preliminary training and instruction.

The Royal Marine Corps has the honour of having His Most Gracious Majesty, King George V, as its Colonel-in-Chief. His Majesty accepted this position when Prince of Wales, upon the decease of Prince Alfred of Saxe-Coburg-Gotha (who was appointed Colonel-in-Chief in recognition of the services of the Royal Marines in the Egyptian Campaign of 1882), and on succeeding to the Crown was graciously pleased to honour the Corps by remaining at its head.

The senior executive Officer of the Royal Marines at the present time is the Deputy-Adjutant-General,[2] Sir William Charles Nicholls, K.C.B., of the Royal

---

[1] Established in 1861. In this year there was proposal to raise a Battalion of Volunteer Marines six companies strong. The First Lord of the Admiralty was to be Colonel, one company was to be in London, the others on the coast. In times of emergency they were to be called up to do duty in Guardships or "Marine Fortresses," and might then volunteer to do duty as Marines on board ships and at "not more than ten miles" from the British Coast.

[2] This appointment was first established 19 July, 1825. Since writing the officer holding this appointment has been made Adjutant-General R.M.

Marine Artillery, who is attached to the Admiralty and through whom its orders and instructions are conveyed to the Corps. There are other General Officers on the Active List, both of the Artillery and Light Infantry Branches of the Corps, but unfortunately no General Officers' commands for them. This was recognised in the "New Scheme" introduced by Lord Selborne in 1902; but while regretting the fact, it brought forward no panacea to remedy this state of affairs.

Each Division[1] of the Royal Marines is under the command of a Colonel-Commandant,[2] as is also the Depôt. Each has another full Colonel as Second in Command, known as the Colonel-Second-Commandant. His duties unless the Commandant is away, are principally connected with the Clothing and Finance of the Division. He checks the Paymaster's, Barrack-Master's and the three Quarter-Master's Accounts daily, and personally supervises the fitting of the uniform made by the Master Tailor for the N.C.O's and Men. He is also President of the Officers' Mess. It should be explained, for the information of the uninitiated, that the Barrack-Master, who is an officer on the retired list, has charge of the Barracks generally, its furniture and fittings, repairs and maintenance, and is responsible for the supply of coal and certain other stores. He also is "ex-officio" supervisor of the Men's Recreation Room and Library.

The 1st Quarter-Master is responsible for the arms, musical instruments, cloth (for the use of the Master-Tailor), uniform clothing (after it is made up and before issue), accoutrements, Regimental necessaries, etc., and is in charge of the tailors and armourers. He is "ex-officio" secretary and treasurer of the Divisional Canteen, which, it may be remarked in passing, is a considerable business concern, having a big annual turn-over, and is managed entirely in the Division.

The 2nd Quarter-Master is responsible for all stores connected with the Instructional Batteries for the teaching and practice of Naval Gunnery, the Magazines, Regimental transport, Boats, Fire Engines, etc.

The 3rd Quarter-Master is responsible for the quartering of Officers and Men, and unoccupied rooms. He superintends the cutting up, weighing and issuing of rations, and of forage to the horses used for Transport and general Regimental purposes. He is also responsible that they are properly groomed and that Wagons, Stables (including those for the Mounted Officers chargers), and Harness are in good order. He is also in charge of the Pioneers and of the Sanitation of the Barracks.

From the description of the duties of these officers, some idea of the interior economy of a Royal Marine Division may be gained, though all this is only as it were, the "house-keeping part."

Next to the 2nd Commandant come the Lieutenant-Colonels, several of whom are, on account of seniority, Brevet-Colonels in the Army. These Officers' ordinary duties are the drill and tactical instruction of the "Battalion" which means as many men as can be spared from "house-keeping" and gunnery instruction—on one or two days in the week, the inspection of all men embarking, and disembarking, and of their kits, the instruction of the Officers in various branches of military knowledge, and to see that the routine duties of the Division are strictly carried out.

---

1 *i.e.*, the officers and men quartered in the various barracks which have been enumerated.
2 In 1913 Commandants were made temporary Brigadier-Generals, but later on reverted to their old title.

The Lieut.-Colonel who is in charge of the "Field Training" has the duty of supervising the detachments[1] which are formed one after the other, for the purpose of being trained by the Captains or Subalterns told off to take charge of them during a three weeks' course in out-post duty, bridging, entrenching, and many other duties in the field.

There are not, as a rule, more than two or at the most three, majors in Barracks for ordinary Parade Duty, the greater number being employed afloat, every Flagship carrying a Major of Marines to take charge of the battalion formed from the Marines of the squadron when landed.

There are generally three Majors on the Staff of the Division; the Gunnery Instructor, the Drafting Officer and the Instructor of Musketry.[2] The Gunnery Instructor, with the Assistant Instructor (a Subaltern), and a staff of N.C.O. Instructors, is responsible for the training of Officers and Men in Naval Gunnery. The instruction is carried out in closed and roofed sheds or "Batteries" which are built for the purpose at each Barracks and which inside are, as far as possible, fitted up like a ship, and equipped with Cannon and Machine guns of all sorts and sizes. Besides Gunnery, the men under instruction are taught Knotting and Splicing, and Boat-pulling.

The Drafting Officer has an office with several clerks, and his business is to keep the Sea Service Rosters of the N.C.O's and Men, tell off drafts as required for embarkation, and have everything cut and dried for immediate mobilisation.

Another office and staff of clerks is allocated to the Staff Officer, usually a Major, who takes charge of all the Colonel Commandant's Official Correspondence, prepares the Daily Divisional Orders for his signature and assists him in a great number of matters of all kinds.[3]

This brings us, in order of seniority, to the Captains, who are of course, in charge of Companies, as in every other Corps. There are eight parade Companies at each Division, but as there is a great demand for Officers of the rank of Captain afloat, to command the detachments embarked, some of the eight are generally commanded by Subalterns. As many of these have a good many years service, they are perfectly well qualified to carry out this duty, but the great drawback to the Company system in the Royal Marines is that instead of an officer remaining in charge of a Company for a long period in which he gets to know his men, and they get to know him, officers and men are incessantly changing.[4]

Coming finally to the Subalterns, we have, first and foremost, the Adjutant. He may be a Captain but is always appointed to the post as a Lieutenant. He is practically responsible for the Infantry drill of the Division, is constantly consulted personally by the Commandant with regard to matters relative to drill and Infantry instruction, and receives orders from him direct. Another and a most important part of the Adjutant's Duties is the instruction of young Officers on joining, not only in Drill, but in the customs and etiquette of the Service. He is also enjoined

---

[1] In other Regiments this Field Training is carried out by companies, which are struck off duty in turn for this purpose. This cannot be carried out in the Royal Marines as the Officers and Men of a Company are constantly changing.
[2] As evidence of the excellence of the Musketry Instruction, it may be mentioned that the Instructional Staff of the School of Musketry for the Army, at Hythe, in the year 1906 had no less than nine Royal Marines in it—1 officer and 8 N.C.Os.
[3] This officer is now termed the "Brigade-Major."
[4] Since writing there has been a great and beneficial change in this arrangement. Captains are now appointed to Companies definitely for twelve months, as well as a proportion of Subalterns, this realising greatly for increased efficiency. This arrangement was constantly suggested by the author when serving.

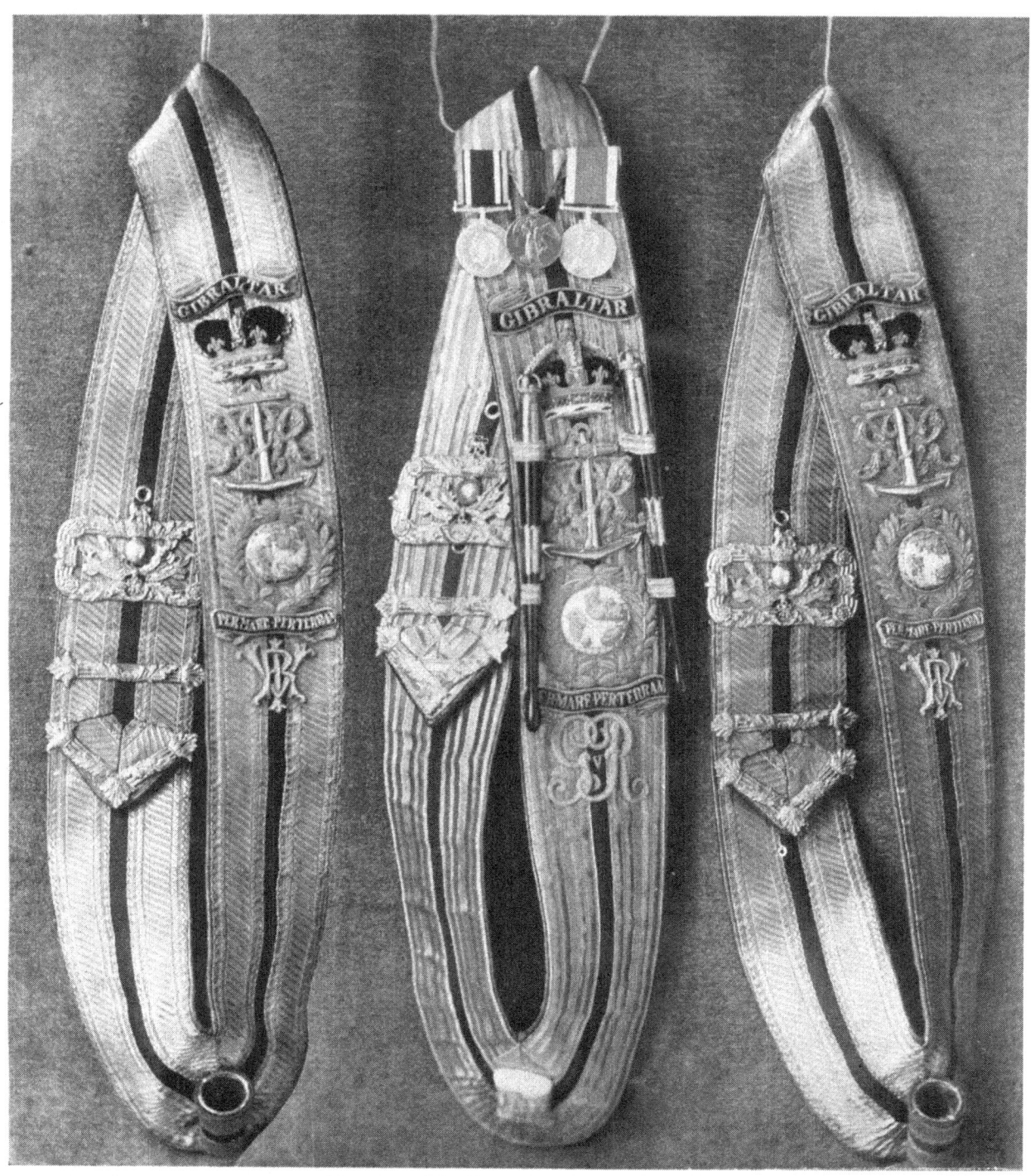

COLOUR BELTS AND DRUM-MAJOR'S BELT.
CHATHAM DIVISION.

to pay particular attention to the dress, military appearance and behaviour of Non-Commissioned Officers and Men.

The Subalterns, generally, have to assist the Captains of the Companies to which they are attached, and one is told off daily as "Subaltern of the Day," who carries out various necessary routine duties and inspections. From the foregoing short description of the duties of the various Officers and Departments some general idea will be gleaned of the scale on which things are done at a Marine Headquarters, which may be regarded as a home and a training establishment combined. A man who joins the Marines has a home, a linesman has none. After his eight or nine months at the Walmer Depôt where the recruit is initiated into the mysteries of Infantry Drill and Musketry, and put through a short course of Field Training, he goes for his final finish as a soldier to one or other of the Marine Barracks that have been enumerated. Here also he learns the Naval Gunnery which adds so much to his value afloat. From thenceforth that station is his home.[1] "He may be sent away to sea for a couple of years, but when he comes back he goes straight to his own head-quarters station, to his own home. He will probably, as a mere matter of routine, be assigned quarters in the actual block of buildings he formerly occupied, while if he has any special affection for the particular room in which he formerly slept and messed, he will only have to wait a few weeks before he can get a place in it. The advantages of this 'homing' system are even more apparent when a man marries. A linesman's wife is liable to be dragged all over the country; the Marine's wife remains at her husband's headquarters. And his home is permanent in two senses: in point of time as well as in point of place. When once the Marine has been accepted as a Recruit he knows that if he does his duty he has a permanent career before him. He enlists, in the first instance for twelve years. At the end of that time if something good turns up in the way of civil employment he is free to take his discharge. If, on the other hand, he wishes to stay on he may re-enlist for a further period of nine years, and when that second period has expired will become entitled to a pension."[2]

Although removed from the jurisdiction and command of the Colonel-Commandant when embarked under the pennant, the Marine is still affiliated to his own Headquarters. Various returns are rendered there by the Officers commanding detachments and his uniform clothing is supplied from there as it becomes due.

The Tailoring department has been merely referred to in connection with the duties of the Colonel Second Commandant. Not only is the whole uniform clothing of the Division with the exception of caps and helmets, made there in the Barracks, which includes that of the men belonging to it who are away at sea, but nowadays when the bluejackets seems to have lost the art of making his own clothes on which he used justly to pride himself, a great deal of seamen's clothing is made there also. The Boots and Leggings are also made in Barracks by the Master-Shoemaker and his men. In fact the Marine Division is to a great extent a self-supporting institution.

---

[1] And yet in 1833 some foolish person, actually proposed that the four Divisions should change round annually. Portsmouth Division to Chatham, etc., etc. "From being in Divisions" says a writer in the "United Service Journal," May, 1833 —"They enjoy certain comforts which the Line do not, but *they* never had them. If the Marines are available at a moment's notice, what more does the country require? By moving them from pillar to post it is likely they may be made ineffective; it is therefore to be hoped that the Admiralty will not attend to the *opinion* of any meddling person, etc."

[2] "Daily Graphic," 8th January, 1898.

But in assessing the strength of the Royal Marines in the annual estimates, all men constantly employed as tailors, shoemakers, etc., ought really to be reckoned as supernumeraries, if the Corps is to be in a thoroughly effective condition, able to embark fully trained men, have enough men at head-quarters to carry out battalion work and instruction and to enable men disembarked to amply revise all Gunnery and Infantry Drills and Instruction before re-embarkation.

No account of the Marine Divisions would be complete without some reference to their splendid Bands, which are probably much better known to the general public than any other part of the Corps. Each Division and the Depôt has a Brass and a String Band which ranks among the ten or a dozen best Bands in the Army. The Band of the Portsmouth Division has the distinction of wearing a small silver Prince of Wales feathers on the lower point of the star of its helmet-plate, granted in honour of its having accompanied the late King Edward VII, when Prince of Wales, on his tour to India in 1875-6. Similarly the Chatham Band wears a small silver York Rose from having provided music for our present Gracious Monarch when he, as Duke of York, made a tour of the Colonies in the *Ophir* in 1901. The Band of the Royal Marine Artillery, which went with his Majesty to the famous Durbar of 1911, in like manner wears a silver Royal Cypher and Crown. It may be noted in this connection that this branch of the Corps had the honour of supplying a Bodyguard of 100 picked men and three officers on the same occasion. Each gunner was six feet in height.[1]

Silver
Prince of Wales Feathers,
Portsmouth.

Royal Monogram R.M.A

SPECIAL BAND BADGES.

Silver
York Rose,
Chatham.

The Royal Marine Bands, at the present time, wear uniforms of the same colour as the rest of their branch of the Corps, and except for a little gold lace they are not much more ornamental than those of the gunners and privates. Formerly, however, the Marine Bandsmen were dressed in somewhat striking costumes, some of which are shewn in a coloured illustration.

---

[1] *Vide* Note I.

While on the subject of the Royal Marine Bands[1] it may be stated that the present official "March Past" of the Royal Marines is "A Life on the Ocean Wave." Previously, though nothing official was laid down, the usual Quick March played was "The British Grenadiers," possibly on account of the Marines having generally been considered Fusileers in all but in name, and Fusileers having a certain affinity with Grenadiers, and always marching past to this tune.

The Royal Marine Artillery used to march past to "The Soldiers' Chorus" in "Faust." According to Mr. Arrol, a former Bandmaster of the Portsmouth Division, who joined the Corps in 1824, the march from "Le Prophete" was generally used for the march past at that Division at the beginning of the reign of Queen Victoria, the air being a favourite one of the Prince Consort's. When it was decided to have a regulation "March Past" for the whole Corps it was proposed to adopt "Rule Britannia" for the purpose, but the Officers of the 9th Norfolk Regiment protested so strongly against the suggestion, pointing out that ever since Queen Anne had granted them the figure of "Britannia" as their Regimental Badge, they had always marched past to this tune, that the idea was given up and "A Life on the Ocean Wave"[2] became the recognised "March Past" for both the Royal Marines and the Royal Navy. This has now for many years invariably been played, but for some time after it was introduced it was ignored, in one at least of the Divisions, in favour of "The Dark Blue Sea."

The "March Past" naturally brings to mind the Colours, of which each Division has a pair. Those carried by the yellow-coated Marines of the Restoration have been already described.[3] Unfortunately there appears to be no record of those carried by the Marine Regiments at Gibraltar, but that they were carried we know from the fact that before landing the Prince of Hesse D'Armstadt arranged with Sir George Rooke that if he suspended the attack by day he would signal the fact to him by "extending all the colours." Those carried by the ten Marine Regiments of 1739-48 have been described and illustrated.[4] An Admiralty letter of 24th October, 1760, with reference to the Battalion destined for "the expedition"—without doubt the Belleisle expedition—directs in a postscript "There are to be Colours sent to the Battalion." Whether this was an extra set, the various Divisions already having sets, does not appear, but as the account for making a single pair of colours is dated also "October 24th, 1760," it seems probable that this was a fourth set specially made for the Belleisle battalion.[5] The Plymouth Division was ordered on the 2nd February, 1775, to send their Colours "to Boston with the Marines," and informed that they would be replaced with new ones. These, in all probability, were similar to those sent to Belleisle which have been described in Vol. I. These colours were carried at Bunker's Hill.[6] We have no account of a ceremonial presentation of any of these colours, but a set seems to have been "presented" at Constantinople in 1799 to the Marines destined to take part in the defence of Acre.[7] Plymouth Division asked for new colours in May, 1801, and they were of course changed on the Corps being made Royal in 1802.

---

1 *Vide* Note II. 2 *Vide* Note III. 3 Vol. I, p. 15. Plate facing p. 16.
4 Vol. I, p. 88. Sketch p. 100. Plates facing pp. 74, 80. 5 Vol. I, p. 113. 6 Vol. I, p. 157. Note.
7 I cannot now the find the reference, but certainly read an account of this quite recently.—C.F.

It is recorded that "a set of colours" was presented to the Royal Marine Battalion that went to Lisbon under the command of Major Richard Williams, R.M.A., in 1810, the presentation being made by the British Ambassador in Roscio Square.[1]

What these colours were like is not certain, but in the account of the presentation of the new set of colours bearing for the first time the "Globe" and the Cypher of George IV to the Portsmouth Division by the H.R.H. the Duke of Clarence (afterwards William IV), on 27th October, 1827, the "old colours" are referred to as follows:—

"The Royal Marines saluted the *old colours*, which being dropped, were not again raised."[2] According to another account a "Crown" was the only device on the old colours, which seem to have been supplied, without any ceremony, by the Navy Board in 1810 or 1811. With regard to the Badges on the new colours it is stated that when the device for them was submitted to George IV a long list of actions in which the Corps had distinguished itself was laid before him. It was found impossible to make a selection small enough to be emblazoned on the Colours in the usual way, and this determined His Majesty to direct that in lieu, the "Globe[3] encircled with the Laurel"[4] should be the distinguishing badge as the most appropriate emblem of a Corps whose duties carried them to all parts of the Globe, in every quarter of which they had earned laurels by their valour and good conduct. The King's Cypher was given, as H.R.H. explained at the presentation, as a "most peculiar and honourably distinctive badge," and "further that it might be known to posterity that King George IV had bestowed on them such an honourable mark of his approbation, His Majesty had directed that whatever King or Queen of Great Britain they might thereafter serve under, though the cypher of the reigning monarch must, of course, appear in their standards, still, in those of the Royal Marines, the cypher of George IV was for ever to remain.[5] Fresh colours were presented to the four Divisions in 1858, but they differed in many respects from those bestowed by George IV. But the old colours, presented by George IV were retained at Plymouth and taken to Japan and Mexico by the Battalions that went to those countries in the 'Sixties. They are still in the Plymouth Mess.

The instructions given by George IV were carried out when a new set of Colours was presented to the Portsmouth Division by the late Queen Victoria on 22nd August, 1894, on which occasion Her Majesty said:—

"They carry on them the Badge of my uncle, King George IV, and the motto defining your services by land and sea. I am confident they will always be safe and honoured in your keeping."[6]

The Cypher in question appears entwined with the Anchor on the Regimental Colour, Queen Victoria's monogram, "V.R.I." being placed at the corners of the Colour. The Anchor on the Queen's Colour has Her Majesty's monogram in combination with it.

---

1 Vol. I, p. 290.   2 An account printed by W. Woodward on the Hard Portsea in 1827.   3 *Vide* Note IV.
4 The Laurel Wreath had, it may be remembered, been previously granted for the gallantry of the Corps at Belleisle in 1761 and appears encircling the Anchor of the front plates of the forage caps worn by the Grenadier Companies at Bunker's Hill, 1775.
5 H.R.H. the Duke of Clarence presented similar sets of colours in the same year to the Chatham Division, 26th September, Woolwich, 10th October, and Plymouth, 21st December.
6 Similar stands of colours were presented by H.R.H. the Duke of Saxe-Coburg and Gotha to the Chatham Division on 22nd June, 1896, and to the Plymouth Division on the 3rd of July in the same year.

QUEEN VICTORIA PRESENTING NEW COLOURS TO THE PORTSMOUTH DIVISION OF THE ROYAL MARINE LIGHT INFANTRY AT OSBORNE, 22ND AUGUST, 1894,

The "Blue Marines" like other Artillery Corps, do not carry colours. The full dress uniform of the Royal Marine Artillery is blue with a wide red stripe down the trousers. The single-breasted tunic is edged all round with red piping and has a red collar bound with yellow cord. The skirts behind have a "slash" with three large buttons and edged with red piping. The collar-badge is a yellow grenade. The shoulder straps are of square yellow cord, and on each sleeve is a long "crow's foot" with an "eye" at the top embroidered in yellow cord. The buttons bear a laurel wreath surrounding a garter inscribed "Royal Marine Artillery." In their centre is a foul anchor with a small grenade on either side. As head-dress a white Helmet is worn surmounted with a ball and having an eight-pointed star in front with a crown at the top. Below the Crown on a Scroll is the word "Gibraltar." On the bottom point of the star is a small Foul Anchor. Laurel branches spring from either side of this to meet the Scroll at the top. In the centre of the plate is the Globe surrounded with a garter on which is the motto "Per Mare Per Terram."

The Royal Marine Light Infantry wear exactly the same Helmet and Plate. Their trousers have a narrow red welt instead of a stripe. The single-breasted Tunic is red, piped down the front edges with white. The skirts are closed behind with two back slashes, with three large regimental buttons on each. The slashes and back of the skirt are edged with white piping. The collar is of blue cloth with a very narrow white piping between it and the red cloth of the coat. The shoulder straps are blue edged with white piping and having the "Globe and Laurel" embroidered on them in white. The cuffs are round, of blue cloth with white piping between them and the rest of the sleeve, and having in front a slash of blue cloth with three points edged with white piping. There is no piping where the slash is sewn into the forearm seam. On each slash are three large Regimental Buttons placed on patches of white cloth beginning at the forearm seam and finishing in a triangle with a narrow light of blue between the button and the seam. The buttons are surrounded by a "Laurel Wreath." Inside the wreath "Royal Marine Light Infantry" appears on a garter and in the centre is the "Foul Anchor" surmounted by a Crown. The Officers' full-dress uniform conforms generally to the details given, but is laced with gold lace, has gold shoulder cords and gold embroidered "Grenade" and "Globe and Laurel" collar badges. The Globes are silver as are those in the Helmet-plates which are surrounded by a garter of blue enamel as a background to the motto. Blue Frock Coats double-breasted are worn as a second dress.

Both Corps have a second frock made of blue cloth with no facings or ornamentation, that of the one Corps only distinguished from the other by the buttons, a brass R.M.A. or R.M.L.I. on the shoulder straps and the collar badge, a brass "Grenade" or "Globe and Laurel." The undress Caps are of the type known as "Brodricks," the R.M.A. having the "Grenade" as a badge and the R.M.L.I. the "Globe and Laurel" surmounted by a "Bugle." As has been mentioned elsewhere both Corps have a blue serge frock or tunic, for drill and service. It is like the blue cloth frock but looser and well provided with pockets. The Great Coat is dark grey like that worn in the Army before the advent of khaki. Plain suits of white Russian duck are supplied for wear in hot climates and coarse duck jumpers for fatigue work.[1]

---
[1] *Vide* Notes V and VI.

With this necessarily inadequate account of the present organisation and equipment of the Corps of Royal Marines the record of their services by flood and field reaches its last page. As indicated by the proud badge of the "Great Globe itself" our "Sea-Soldiers" have, since 1664, fought in nearly all countries, seas and climates, and their present representatives can look back on a long line of ancestors of whose deeds and loyalty they have every reason to be proud. May those deeds and that fine loyalty never be forgotten while the British Flag flies over the Seven Seas and their coasts where Britain's Sea-Soldiers have fought and fallen. In the beautiful words of Felicia Hemans:

" The warlike of the isles,
The men of field and wave,
Are not the rocks their funeral piles,
The seas and shores their grave ?
Go stranger track the deep,
Free, free the white sail spread !
Wave may not foam, nor wild wind sweep,
Where rest not England's dead."

NOTES.

NOTE I.—HIS MAJESTY'S MARINE GUARD IN THE *MEDINA*.

The Hon. John Fortescue who accompanied their Majesties to India in the *Medina* makes the following remarks about the detachment of Royal Marines which went out as the King's Bodyguard.

There was a great games competition between the crew, officers and passengers, especially in what was known as the Spar and Pillow Fight; the combatants being seated astride on a spar armed with pillows. They were not allowed to touch each other with either hand.

" Lord Annaly after a strenuous conflict was defeated but not disgraced by Lord Shaftesbury; Captain Godfrey Faussett vanquished a bluejacket, but was overthrown by the Fleet Surgeon, a most dangerous opponent. Soon it became apparent that Major Phillips of the Royal Marine Artillery, a gentleman of Herculanean strength, and not less skilled in parrying with his left hand, than in striking with his right, was superior to all rivals; and after three battles, which can only be described as Homeric, he finally swept the Fleet Surgeon's legs from under him, and was hailed as victor by the officers. A private of his Corps won the same distinction among the men. . . . . . . Nearly every prize fell to the Marines; and in truth the Marine is a wonderful person. The press is fond of holding up the Bluejacket as a handy man, but in these days the epithet should be transferred to the Marines. On 1st December, the last day of the voyage out, there was a concert on board. The suite could produce in Lord Shaftesbury a trained singer who naturally eclipsed all other performers; but, setting him aside, the Marines had matters all their own way. One of them was a sufficiently accomplished vocalist to be accompanied by the Band, while several others played an astonishing number of instruments, and played them in tune. The credit of the Bluejackets was mainly saved by the proficiency, in a sister art, of Mr. Staples, the boatswain, who danced a hornpipe quite admirably."—Fr. "Narrative of the Visit to India of their Majesties George V and Queen Mary," by Hon. John Fortescue, 1912.

NOTE II.—NAVAL BANDSMEN.

The Royal Marine Divisional Bands do not embark even when a Battalion is sent from Headquarters. But Bands are carried on board most men-of-war of any size, and these Naval Bandsmen are now affiliated to the Corps of Royal Marines and called officially Marine Bandsmen. Formerly they were practically "nobody's children" on board ship. Some years ago they were uniformed in blue coats braided with white which, with the little round caps they wore on the side of the head, gained them the nickname of the "Hamoaze Hussars." It was a most inappropriate nautical uniform and was changed to a plain blue dress with a peaked cap which was the acme of ugliness. All this was changed when they were handed over to the Marines for training and discipline a few years back, and to quote the "New Scheme" Memorandum of 1902, "the policy of attaching the naval bandsmen to the Royal Marines has been attended with all the advantages expected of it, and both as regards musical performance, discipline and general smartness and efficiency, the Marine Bands compare very favourably with the bands under the old system." They are now systematically trained at the Royal Naval School of Music at Eastney, which is under the command of a Major of the Royal Marines, are enlisted and sworn in like Marine soldiers, wear a neat military uniform not unlike that of the R.M.A., but with a peaked red-banded cap in undress when the helmet is not worn, and when on board ship are under the special command of the Officer of Marines, just like the rest of his detachment. This ensures a smartness of appearance and care of their musical instruments and clothing which was, as a rule, conspicuously absent in the old Naval bands, for the simple reason that no officer was officially responsible for them.

Bandsmen have been carried afloat from a very early period. The "Trumpeter" was an important personage in Mediaeval and Tudor days on board our men-of-war. Indeed in most illustrated M.S. that have pictures of shipping in the Middle Ages the trumpeters are well in evidence. The Sieur de Joinville in describing the galley of the Count of Jaffa at the landing of St. Louis in Egypt in 1248 says :—"And as they came on the galley looked to be some flying creature, with such spirit did the rowers spin it along ; or rather with the rustle of flags and the roar of its nacaires (a species of kettle drum) and drums and Saracen Horns, you might have taken it for a rushing bolt of Heaven."

I am unable to say at what date Ship's Bands were first officially recognised in the British Navy, but I have in my possession a lithographed portrait, apparently published by John Richards, the Purser of the ship—of "John Maholt, Native of Berlin. Minstrel on board His Majesty's Ship *Victory*, 1824." It would appear from this that "Minstrel" was a recognised rating.

NOTE III.—"A LIFE ON THE OCEAN WAVE."

The composer of the Royal Marines' present March Past was Mr. Henry Russell, father of the well-known novelist Mr. Clarke Russell, and composer of "Cheer, Boys Cheer," "The Old Arm Chair," and other popular songs. Mr. Henry Russell in answer to a letter of enquiry from Mr. Geo. Miller, the Bandmaster of the Portsmouth Division, wrote :—"' A Life on the Ocean Wave ' was composed by me some sixty years ago whilst in America. The origin of the song emanated from Epps Sargent, the poet, walking with me on the Battery, New York, watching the ships in harbour. The scene before him gave him an idea which induced him to write the words. I set them to music, and the song ultimately became one of the most popular in England and America."[1]

The following additional particulars as to the above "March Past" are taken from Mr. Russell's book of reminiscences published in 1895 and entitled "Cheer, Boys, Cheer ":—

"'Epps Sargent . . . . had long owed me a song. . . . . His walk and my song were completed together, and Sargent went to the office of our mutual friend, George P. Morris, and wrote out the words. ' This is not a song at all,' said Morris, after reading it—' it will not do for music.' A few days later I met Sargent and asked him for the song. He told me very dolefully what Morris had said, but I insisted on seeing the manuscript. We then went into a Broadway music store kept by a mutual friend, and were invited into a back room where there was a capital piano. I hummed an air or two, ran my fingers over the keys, then stopped, feeling baffled ; suddenly an idea struck me, I began to hum a melody that seemed to be floating through my brain, and presently touching the keys with a confident exclamation, that bright little air rang out which is so well known as ' A Life on the Ocean Wave.' It at once became a favourite and met with an enormous sale both in England and America.

" Prior to 1883 (?) each Division had its own march, and even these often changed, as new commandants often introduced new marches," says a writer in *The Regiment* (2nd Feb., 1901), and goes on to say, "About that period, though we cannot find the exact date, the D.A.G., R.M., called upon the Bandmaster of each Division to arrange a march, if possible, on a Naval Song. Mr. Kappey, Mr. Winterbottom, Mr. Kreyer and Mr. Fröhnert each submitted a march. Mr. Kappey had selected ' A Life on the Ocean Wave ' and tacked on a phrase of another Naval song, ' The Sea, the Sea,' for the purpose of completing its artistic construction. On trial, Mr. Kappey's arrangement was selected and ordered to be played as the Regimental March of the R.M.L.I."

Personally, I do not think that the above statement is correct as regards date since to the best of my recollection "A Life on the Ocean Wave" was played as March Past at the Portsmouth Division when I joined it in the Autumn of 1879.

NOTE IV.—THE BADGE OF THE "GLOBE."

Though a unique Military Badge—except that it is now worn by the United States Marine Corps—it may be of interest to note that the "Globe" has been adopted as a Badge by various Royal and distinguished personages

---
[1] Fr. "The Globe and Laurel," September, 1897.

at different periods, though at the present day it has been appropriated as a trade mark by all kinds of Commercial undertakings and institutions. It enters, by the way, very largely into the decoration of the magnificent new Dock and Harbour Board Offices at Liverpool, and inside the hall under the central dome the Globe and wreaths, apparently of Laurel, are combined in a really striking and artistic way.

Going back to antiquity, we find according to Guillim's well-known work on Heraldry, published in 1724, that the shield of "that famous and valliant Grecian Captain, Achilles," was decorated with a Silver Globe on a golden field, "beautified and replenished with a manifold variety of celestial bodies environing the terrestrial Globe." So that if we accept this story we wear our silver Globe in distinguished classical company. What purports to be a representation of this shield appears in the " Gentleman's Magazine," of September, 1749. The weak point of the "yarn"— may I say, its "Achilles heel"—is the fact that, whether or no this " valliant Captain " had any real existence, our histories tell us that the world was not discovered to be spherical till the end of the Middle Ages. There is another remark made by Guillim with regard to the Globe, which is obviously incontrovertible, and that is that a sphere is "the most perfect figure in existence." So here is another honourable signification of the special Badge of the Royal Marines. According to Kennet's " Antiquities of Rome " (1785) the Emperor Augustus used as a standard a Globe fastened to the head of a spear, " in token of the conquest of the whole world." And in a quaint old book published in 1623 entitled " The Theater of Honour and Knighthood," by Andrew Favine, we find the following reference to the use of the Globe as a badge by the Roman Emperors : "And the same Emperors (Constantine the Great and his successors) carried the Globe also on the days of their Pompes and Solemnities, to make it publiquely known that by their belief in the wholesome sign of the Crosse they were Lords in the Earth, which the Globe represented by his rotundity, and in their faith by the Crosse ; on the tree whereon Jesus Christ was nailed, to deliver the World from Eternall Death, according as it is written by Suidas."

Coming to more modern times, it may be noted that the Globe forms part of the Crest of about sixty English families, and that it was awarded in combination of with the device of a ship in full sail, to Sir Francis Drake, in commemoration of his Voyage round the World. It is curious, too, that in a contemporary engraving of Queen Elizabeth on her way to St. Paul's to return thanks for the defeat of the Spanish Armada, what looks like a Globe surrounded with a Laurel Wreath is the principal decoration on the Canopy of the triumphal car on which she is seated.

Whether or no this decoration was actually a Globe, it is certain that Philip II of Spain, the organiser of the Armada, had adopted it as a Royal Badge with the motto " *Cum Jove*." Martin I., King of Aragon, in 1396, chose as a Badge, the figure of a Winged Victory standing on a Globe, with the motto " *Non in tenebris* "—" Not in darkness," meaning probably that his was a light not to be " hidden under a bushel." Another Spanish ruler, Joan of Castile (1555), assumed the Globe as a device, in this case with a peacock with tail extended standing on it, the accompanying motto being " *Omnia Vanitas* "—"All is vanity." Emmanuel King of Portugal (1495-1521) also chose the Globe as his distinguishing badge as being emblematic of the voyages and discoveries made by his subjects during his reign, together with the motto, " *Primus circumdedisti me*."—" Thou hast first encompassed me."

Nor was the Globe device confined to the Iberian peninsula. It appears on the foremost banner of the Austrian Knights at Sempach (1386) in a woodcut made early in the 16th Century.

The magnificent palace built at Rome by Rierio Rafferlio, Cardinal San Giorgio, in the 16th Century is decorated in every part with his especial device of a Globe surmounted by a helmet with the motto, " *Hic Opus* "—" This is my work."

Francis II of France assumed as one of his Royal Badges a Dolphin with a Globe encircled with the Diamond Ring which was an insignia of the Medici family. In the middle of the device were branches of palm and olive. The motto was " *Regam patris virtutibus* "—" I will rule (the world) with my father's virtues."

The Globe seems to have long remained a French device, for among a list of standards and colours captured at Blenheim (1704) we find :—1 Standard, Amien silk, in a Globe, embroidered with silver and gold, an eagle black and gold, taking its flight with Thunder darted to it." Motto : Audentior.

" 2 Colours, white and blue cheque, with a Globe painted in the middle."

" 1 Colour, blue with a Globe in the centre, and four coronets of cyphers in the four corners ; a wavy pyle border of blue."

Even at the present day a Globe with a laurel wreath and colour is the device in the French Medaille Coloniale.

The Globe as worn by the United States Marines differs from our own in that it represents the Western Hemisphere instead of the Eastern. It may or may not have been suggested by that worn by the Royal British Marines, but it is noteworthy that the device of a Globe is supposed to have been placed upon an American flag as far back as 1737, for in a French book on Flags published in that year we see illustrated a " pavilion de Nouvelle

Lieutenants & Colour Sergts. Clr. Sergt. R.M.A. Gunner R.M.A. Drummer R.M.L.I. Corpl. R.M.L.I. Commandant & Lieut. R.M.L.I.
R.M.L.I. (Review Order). (Review Order). (Marching Order). (Review Order). Brigadier General Undress
Major R.M.L.I. Captain R.M.L.I. Captain R.M.A. Major R.M.L.I. (Review Order). (White Cap Cover).
(Review Order). (Review Order). (In Frock Coat). (In Frock Coat).

UNIFORMS. ROYAL MARINES. 1914.

PRESENT ORGANISATION AND EQUIPMENT

Angleterre en Amerique." This is a blue flag having on a white canton the Cross of St. George, and in the first quarter of the canton a Globe—an allusion to America—the New World.

In conclusion it may be remarked that though no other Regiment or Corps in the British Service has the especial Badge of " the Great Globe itself," a Terrestrial Globe forms a portion of the Badge of the Manchester Regiment, which in 1881 received permission to wear the Arms of the City of Manchester on its Caps and Collars. These Arms were granted the city in 1842 and the crest which surmounts them is the "Terrestrial Globe, semé (i.e., 'sprinkled') with Bees." It is evident that in this case the Globe has no military significance as a distinction of honour, but merely symbolises the world-wide business of "Cottonopolis."

Further instances might be quoted, but enough has been said to prove that the " Globe " is not only a distinctive, honourable, and appropriate badge for the Corps whose motto is " Per Mare, per Terram," but also one that may claim to have a most distinguished history.

NOTE V.—PECULIARITIES IN MARINE UNIFORMS.

It is characteristic of good soldiers to cherish any little peculiarity of uniform or equipment which differentiates their own Regiment or Corps from others. The black silk " Flash " worn by the Officers of the Welsh Fusileers, and which is a survival of the bow with which all Officers' wigs were formerly tied at the back, is a well-known case in point. The R.M.L.I. retained the six buttons and slashes at the back of the tunic for several years after they had been done away with in other Infantry Regiments, and prized them accordingly, but quite recently they have become universal again. There are still one or two differences which are much appreciated. One is the return to the slashed cuff. Then the Drummers' "Looping Lace," is different to that of other Regiments. The Guards have blue Fleur-de-lis on theirs, the Line have red Crowns, while the Marines have a blue star-shaped ornament on the Drummers' lace which is popularly supposed to represent the White Rose of York because of their descent from the Duke of York's Maritime Regiment. Personally I do not believe this. Possibly the device on it may represent the Brunswick Star, though certain ribald persons have professed to see in it a representation of a "Turtle" as emblematical of the amphibious nature of the Corps.

There is a little custom which, I believe, is peculiar to the Corps, although it may possibly survive in other Regiments. It is that of the N.C.O's and Privates wearing a piece of crape over the third button of the Tunic or Frock when in mourning. In the King's Regulations for the Army there is no reference to this, but merely the order for Officers and Warrant-Officers to wear crape on their left arms. The Mourning Button in former days was a usual custom in the Army—among officers at any rate. In Hamilton's " History of the Grenadier Guards " we find an order issued on 26th November, 1737 on the death of King George II to the following effect :—

" Every Officer to have a scarlet coat buttoned on the waist with a *mourning button*, and faced with black cloth, no buttons on the sleeves or pockets ; black cloth waistcoats and breeches ; plain hats with crape hat-bands ; mourning swords and buckles. To get crape for their sashes, to be all got ready by Sunday seven-night, the 4th of December." Many other references can be found to " mourning buttons " in the 18th century.

NOTE VI.—UNIFORM OF THE ROYAL MARINES, 1881-1914.

1881. (CHATHAM), 14th January.—The Lds. Commrs. of the Admiralty have been pleased to approve of Corps Badges (Grenades for R.M.A. and Globes and Laurel for R.M.L.I.) being worn on Tunics and Mess Jackets by Officers R.M. The Badge is to be worn at each end of the collar $\frac{3}{8}$ of an inch from the inner point of the gold lace or braid and to rest on the inner edge of the lower row of braid.
(CHATHAM), 18th March.—The Chevrons of N.C.O's to be worn on the Right arm only. Good Conduct Badges will be worn on the Left arm below the elbow with their points upwards. (From 23rd April next).
(CHATHAM), 12th December. In accordance with Queen's Regulations, 1881, the Subaltern of the Day will in future at Mess, wear the Jacket hooked up, and will wear a sword.

1886. (CHATHAM), 2nd August.—Officers when parading in Marching Order will wear laced boots of as similar a pattern as possible to those worn by the men.

1887. (CHATHAM), 10th September. Kid Gloves are not to be worn by Officers on Parade.

1891. (CHATHAM), 7th March.—From 23rd April next, Armourer, Provost, Cook and Hospital Sergeants to be clothed and equipped as Staff-Sergeants. To wear Three-bar Chevrons below the elbow, point upwards. Armourer Sergeant to wear Badge of Hammer and Pincers (in Gold) on Tunic and Frock.

(CHATHAM), 11th July.—Newly Commissioned Officers on joining a Light Infantry Division Royal Marines will provide themselves with Buff instead of White Enamelled Sword-belts.

(CHATHAM), 29th July.—It is notified for general information that the authorised shape of the peak of the Helmet is Round, not Pointed. (*N.B.—This order continued to be more honoured in the breach than in the observance.*)

1895. Lee-Metford Magazine Rifle Mark II issued.

1896. (CHATHAM), 19th June.—Alterations in Dress and Equipment. Officers—(1) Garments and Articles about to become obsolete may be worn till 31st December, 1898; (2) Gold-laced Trousers or Overalls will be worn on State occasions and at Levees only. (3) Field-Service Cap of Austrian pattern to be worn. (4) The Sword Belt will be worn underneath the Red Patrol Jacket. *N.B.—This jacket not long introduced was of red serge with blue cloth collar, cuffs and shoulder-straps, very similar to the Kersey Frock worn by the Rank and File. There was no lace or piping. The Corps badge in metal was worn on the collar and metal badges of rank on the shoulder-straps*). Brown leather Gloves worn with this Jacket. (5) The Sash will only be worn with the Tunic and on Orderly Duty. (6) Field-Service Cap will be worn in Drill Order.

Warrant Officers, N.C.O's and Men.—W.O's and Sergeants will carry the Great Coat "*en banderole*" over left shoulder. Sergeants will only wear the Sash in Review Order, on Orderly Room duty and Walking Out. Officers New Swords, straight blade, steel hilt.

(CHATHAM), 24th June.—Officers will wear Gold laced Trousers in Full Dress at Balls.

(CHATHAM), 29th June.—Officers who may be about to provide themselves with a new Mess Jacket should defer procuring it until the question of pattern, now under consideration, is settled.

1897. (CHATHAM), 17th March.—Gold laced Trousers are not to be worn by Officers R.M.L.I. in Mess Dress. (*N.B.—Except at the Plymouth Division, these had not been generally worn with Mess Dress except sometimes on Guest Nights and at Balls*).

(CHATHAM), 10th April.—White Cap Covers ordered to be worn with the Field Service Cap by the R.M.A. as well as the R.M.L.I. (previously the former had been given a White Forage Cap upon embarkation).

(CHATHAM), 4th May.—Staff-Sergeants to wear the Army pattern Field Service Cap, with Globe, Laurel and Bugle the same as issued to Sergeants.

1902. (R.M. OFFICE CIRCULAR No. 2253/02), 17th April.—1—The Buff Pouch Belt for R.M.A., the Full Dress Sash and Belt for R.M.L.I., and Buff Sword Knot, Brass Spurs and Sabretache are abolished, as also Buff Sword Belts except as provided in para. 10. Gold laced Trousers are not to be worn, pending further orders, excepting by Officers R.M.A. in Full Dress.

2.—Colonels Commandant and 2nd Commandant will wear their Regimental Mess Dress, Tunic, Frock Coat, Great Coat, Sword Belt, Pouch Belt, Pouch and Sword, and will use their Regimental Horse Furniture—otherwise as at present. (*N.B.—These Officers had previously worn Staff Uniform*).

3.—The present Patrol Jacket for R.M.A. and Red Serge Frock for R.M.L.I. is abolished and replaced by a Frock-Coat.

4.—The present Forage and Field Service Caps are abolished and replaced by a new pattern Cap.

5.—With the Frock Coat the R.M.A. will wear the Full Dress Sword, Belt and Sword Knot, but no Pouch, or Cross Belt.

6.—The R.M.L.I. will in future wear a Silk Net Sash round the waist of the Tunic or Frock Coat. A webb-Sword-belt, with present Full-Dress Slings, will be worn under the Sash outside the Tunic or Frock Coat. The Gold Sword Knot will be worn in this dress.

7.—The present pattern of Tunic Cuff for R.M.L.I. is altered to the old pattern Slash Cuff for all ranks, and the Collar is altered for Colonels Commandant and Second Commandant.

8.—The Sam Browne Belts are in future to be worn with the Blue Serge Frock on occasions on which the Sword and Buff Belts have hitherto been worn, except as provided in para. 9.

9.—On board ship, for boat work, and on such other occasions as ordered, a plain web Sword Belt with two plain Brown Leather Sword Slings, with a plain Square Brass Buckle on each may be worn with the Blue Serge Frock.

PRESENT ORGANISATION AND EQUIPMENT

10.—Paras. 1, 4, 6, 8 and 9 will take effect forthwith. Paras. 2, 3, 5 and 7 will take effect from 1st January, 1906, or sooner if new articles are required. Officers in possession of serviceable tunics should have their cuffs altered as soon as possible. The Buff Sword Belt will continue to be worn with the R.M.A. Patrol Jacket and the R.M.L.I. Red Serge Frock while those garments are worn in lieu of the new Frock Coat.

11.—Any Officer appearing at Court after the 21st inst should appear in the revised uniform.

12.—New patterns can be seen or described on application at the R.M. Office.

(CHATHAM), Grant of White Rose (Silver) to be worn on Helmet and Forage Cap of Band Chatham Division in commemoration of being with H.R.H. the Duke of York on his Colonial Tour.

1905. (CHATHAM).—Abolition of Scarlet Kersey and introduction of Blue Frock for R.M.L.I. Blue Helmet abolished. White Helmet made uniform for both home and foreign service.

1910. (CHATHAM).—Introduction of Short M.L. Rifle and long Bayonet. Also woven web equipment.

1912. (CHATHAM).—Special Badge for Helmet and Forage Cap granted to R.M.A. Band in commemoration of T.M. King George and Queen Mary's Visit to India in H.M.S. *Medina*. Gilt grenade on which is mounted Royal Cypher, G.R.V. and Crown in silver surrounded by a gilt laurel wreath and he Cypher G.R.V. in ilver on Helmets Plate, over anchor and below Globe.

Introduction of Wolseley pattern White Helmet.

COLOUR-SERGEANT'S ARM BADGE R.M.L.I.
(*Actual Size*). Gold and Silver Embroidery.

APPENDIX E.

THE "HORSE MARINES."

"There are few terms in the English language which admit of so many varied interpretations as 'Horse Marine.' The majority will probably protest that it is merely the ordinary jocular term applied to those whose duty requires them to serve on sea and on land—the Royal Marines in much the same sense that the term 'Naval Mounted Horse' was applied to the bluejackets employed at the Royal Military Tournament at Islington a few years back, when they took on the cavalry at wrestling on horseback.

It would be absurd to urge that there is no reasonable foundation for this version of the term. In ordinary nautical significance no doubt it does imply "an awkward person."[1] It may be termed a popular form of paradox. The idea of one whose mètier is the deck of a ship bestriding an unaccustomed steed, or the cavalry-man with his spurs and tight clothing trying to keep his feet on the deck of a rolling and pitching vessel, presents an incongruity which, to many minds, is pleasing, not to say amusing to contemplate.

"In Farmer and Henley's 'Slang and Its Monologues,' the explanation is 'a mythical corps very commonly cited in jokes and quizzed on the innocent.' The late Admiral Smyth, in his 'Sailor's Handbook,' explains the term as implying 'an awkward lubberly person afloat, one out of place, a landsman afloat.' Dr. Ogilvie in his 'Imperial Dictionary,' adopts the same meaning, adding 'as a cavalry force would be in a sea-fight,' and in Murray's 'New English Dictionary' a similar interpretation is given. The term has, of course, for years past, been jocularly applied to the field, or mounted officers of the Corps of Royal Marines, but it is a feeble effort at fun. The Royal Marine Artillery and the Royal Marine Light Infantry boast, and with good reason, that, as their proud motto, 'Per Mare, per Terram' implies, they serve both on sea and on land when duty calls; and when on shore their field officers are mounted as in every regiment in the service, so that a 'horse-marine' is no more of a rara-avis on Southsea Common or at Walmer than a mounted lifeguardsman is at Whitehall."

Possibly the expression may have originated with some of the officers appointed to the Marines at the creation of the present Corps in 1755. These were selected either from the active or half-pay lists of all kinds of regiments, including cavalry ones. Those from the latter may have found themselves so very much "at sea" as to have grumbled sufficiently to earn a special soubriquet. This is, of course, a pure guess, but in a pamphlet written by a Captain of Marines in 1757,[2] who at this time had already left the Corps, he growls tremendously at the disillusions that await "the Marine Captain, when first promoted from his lieutenancy in a marching regiment, or a cornetcy of Dragoons, who, perhaps, never was before on board a man-of-war."

But as a matter of fact, joking apart, the "horse-marine" is not entirely a mythical and fictitious personage. In the Naval War with the Dutch in the reign of Charles II the Life Guards supplied a detachment of 200 men to do duty as Marines on board the Fleet.

The 11th Light Dragoons, now better known as the 17th Lancers, the "Death or Glory Boys," were for many a year known as the "Horse Marines" in consequence of a squadron having been embarked as Marines on board H.M.S. *Hermione* in the fighting in the West Indies in 1795. Again when the *Jason* of Boston was captured by the *Surprise* of 28 guns in 1779 she was found to have on board no less than 31 troopers who had served in the British Cavalry under General Burgoyne and who were now acting as American Marines.

On the other hand there have been many instances of Marines acting as mounted troops. During the conquest of Java in 1811, 180 Marines as well as 50 Seamen, were mounted for the purpose of making a forced march to Carang Sambang, and a relay of horses was prepared for them half way. What these warriors had to say at the end of their journey is not recorded. Again, according to an old Marine, who served in the Crimean War, "The only Marines landed for duty on shore (when the Army effected its disembarkation at Old Fort) were those landed at Eupatoria, some ten miles north of the Army with a lagoon between them. These were placed under the command of one Captain Brock, who converted the said Marines into Horse Marines, for the purpose of decoying the Cossacks under his guns."

In the early sixties a specially selected detachment of the Royal Marines was sent out from England to form a mounted Guard and Escort to Sir Rutherford Alcock, the British minister in Japan; and in 1864 a party of H.M.S. *Challenger's* Marines were landed at St. Vincent in the West Indies and mounted on horse-back to assist the authorities in putting down an insurrection of the negroes. It is said that these "Horse Marines" proved themselves a very efficient and useful force.

Later on, in the Egyptian War of 1882, several Marines were allowed to join the Mounted Infantry Corps, which was recruited from the various Regiments present, and did effective service; while at Suakin a year or two later a large number of them, led by their own officers, performed most efficiently the role of Mounted Infantry.

Again in December, 1913, and January, 1914, when H.M.S. *Lancaster* landed twenty-four Marines and ten Seamen in British Honduras, in order to capture or drive out the Mexican General Brito who was organising a raid into Mexico through this British Colony and Guatemala, eight of the former were mounted and did excellent work. They did not, however, succeed in rounding up the elusive general, who considering discretion the better part of valour, hurriedly cleared out on the approach of the landing party.

Cavalry Officers who became Marines in 1755 have already been mentioned and a few cases of the converse are on record. The first is that of Lieutenant Graham of the Marines, who, in 1744, was serving on board H.M.S. *Lion*, and so distinguished himself in the action which that ship fought with the French ship *Elizabet* that he "not only gained the approbation of 'My Lords,' but through their instrumentality was rewarded with a troop in the 4th Dragoons. Here is another case. A newspaper paragraph dated 14th May, 1814 states that "Lieutenant John Balkeney, of the Royal Marines, made his escape from Verdun some time since, but falling in with a regiment of Cossacks, he was entrusted with the charge of a company, at the head of which in one of the many renconnitres, in which he was engaged on the advance of the allied troops he was unfortunately killed." The next instance is rather a peculiar one. It is to be found in the "War Office Gazette" of March 15th 1831, which announces "15th King's

---

[1] Article in the "Globe." [2] *Vide* p. 129, Vol. I.

From an old Coloured Print.

APPENDIX E.

Hussars, Second Lieutenant Dennis Browne from half-pay, Royal Marines, to be Riding Master and Cornet." This really does seem an extraordinary appointment. More recently there have been many officers of the Royal Marines who have joined Indian Cavalry Regiments, notably Lieutenant (afterwards Major-General) C. V. F. Townshend, well-known as the defender of Chitral in 1895. "A very early mention of this interesting arm of the service," says the writer of the article in the "Globe" from which we have already quoted, "is found in Moliere's 'Les Precieuses Ridicules,' 1659. In Scene XII Le Vicomte de Jodelet says to Mademoiselles Madelon and Cathos, who are listening 'auribus erectis': 'Notre connaissance s'est faite a l'armée; et la premiere fois que nous nous vîmes il commandait un regiment de cavalerie sur les galeres de Malte.' To which Le Marquis de Mascareille replies: 'Il est vrai; mais vous etiez pourtant dans l'emploi avant que j'y fusse; et je me souviens que je n'étais que petit officier encore, que vous commandiez deux mille chevaux.' Someone has suggested the origin of the sobriquet in the word 'hawser,' by sailors called a 'Hawse.' 'Marines to the hawse; Bluejackets aloft,' would not sound strange to the nautical ear. It is suggested that when Marines first manned the hawse it would not entail any great energy of wit to play upon the word and give these fine fellows a name which seems to puzzle the learned in these days. Others recall the Sea-Horse and the Horse Fish or Hippocampus, that odd little fish with a head like that of a horse. Then there are the Horse-Marines or marine horse, the fabulous animals constituting Neptune's team.[1] And, more serious still, a note in the *London Gazette* of 1705—a publication not generally associated with humour—'On a Torse a Demy Horse-Marine.'

"Some forty-five years ago, at the Quarter Sessions held at Kirton-in-Lindsey, in Lincolnshire, the late Mr. Frederick Flowers, afterwards Police Magistrate at Bow Street, was examining a witness, who, on being asked the nature of his occupation, described himself as a 'horse-marine' much to the amusement of the Court. A further series of questions elicited the fact that the witness belonged to the class described in 'book English' as haulers, whose occupation it is to drag barges up and down canals with the aid of horses which are sometimes ridden by the hauler, but more commonly led by the bridle along what is called the 'hauling trod.' It may be added that the men who drove the quadrupeds whose painful duty it was to pull the 'fly-boats' upon the Regent's Canal were known as 'Horse-Marines.'"

Though admittedly far-fetched, I should like, in conclusion, to suggest another derivation of "Horse Marine." When the present Corps was formed in 1755 it wore cloth sugar-loaf caps *like those of the Grenadier Companies and the Fusileers* of that day.[2] According to the Army Dress Regulations of 1751 the fronts of these were made the same colour as the Regimental facings. Immediately over the forehead was a turn-up or flap of red cloth surrounded by the Grenadier motto "*Nec Aspera Terrent*," and ornamented with the "White Horse of Hanover." The Regimental Badge was on the cap above the flap. It is quite possible, if not probable, that the Marine caps conformed to these regulations, so that the newly formed Corps wore a horse on their caps in the place where their predecessors —the ten Marine Regiments of 1740-48—who also wore a high-fronted cloth cap of a somewhat different shape, —wore a Garter Star. May not this badge have gained them the name of "Horse-Marines" among their ship-mates, many or most of whom would remember the older Marines who did not wear the "White Horse?"

R.M.A.

R.M.L.I.

Sabretasches, Mounted Officers, 1872-1902.

---

[1] These are shewn in the medal struck in commemoration of the Taking of Gibraltar in 1704, so are again connected with the Marine Corps.—*Vide* p. 45, Vol. 1.
[2] *Vide* p. 112, Vol. I.

APPENDIX F.

SUPPLEMENTARY
CHRONOLOGICAL LIST
OF THE WAR AND OTHER SERVICES
OF THE
ROYAL MARINE CORPS
AND ITS PREDECESSORS
1665 to 1910

NOTE.—This List is intended to fill in—to some extent—the gaps in the History of the Corps which the general scheme of the work has necessitated between the Chapters and to form a General Record of its Principal and Some Other Services "*Per Mare, per Terram.*"

The List does not pretend to complete the record of the *whole* of its services, for space forbids a complete enumeration of the innumerable Single Ship Actions, Coastal Raids and other minor operations in which the Royal Marines have shared, although several which could not well be embodied in the main portion of the work are here noticed.

But if it is borne in mind that—except between 1713 and 1739—none of these took place without there being a proportion of Marines present, any good chronological list of the Services of the Royal Navy will supply the deficiency.

Some of the Expeditions and Operations, for which room could not be found elsewhere are here recorded, and mention is made of many well-known Battles in which the Marines have fought shoulder to shoulder with their Bluejacket shipmates, or with the Soldiers of the Army. These, in most cases, have not been previously referred to, because no account of the Sea-Soldiers' special part in them has been available—or at best, a very meagre one.

		Vol. Page
1665.	SEA-FIGHT WITH THE DUTCH OFF LOWESTOFT. 3rd June.	I, 11
1666.	PRINCE RUPERT'S VICTORY OVER THE DUTCH. 1st to 4th June. The four days' fight.	
1667.	THE *PARADOX* AND A FRENCH FLY-BOAT. — May.	

"The *Paradox* carrying over a Company of the Duke of York's yellow coates to Guernsey had a hot dispute with a French fly-boat of 14 guns, and drove her on the French coast."—"The *Paradox* had 100 soldiers besides their owne Company, and they plyed their small shot lustily—1 of them was killed and 6 wounded."—Edye, *Hist. R.M. Forces.*

1667.	DUTCH REPULSED FROM LANDGUARD FORT. 2nd July.	I, 19
1672.	BATTLE OF SOLE BAY. 28th May.	I, 21, 31
1673.	CAPTURE OF ST. HELENA. 15th May.	
1674.	BATTLE OF ENTZHEIM. 4th October.	I, 22

The ex-Marines in Churchill's Regiment probably participated also in the Battles of SINZHEIM (16th June), and TURCKHEIM (5th January, 1675), though not particularly mentioned as forming part of the English contingent which so ably assisted Turenne against the Imperialists. At the first named battle, when the enemy's cavalry had driven Turenne's first line back upon his second, the British Infantry "poured in such a furious fire on the enemy that they were unable to stand against it, and began to retire." Under cover of this fire the French Cavalry rallied and were able to make head against the enemy. Later on the French first line was again broken in several places, but the British fire was so effective as to prevent the enemy's Cuirassiers from passing through the gaps which had been made. At TURCKHEIM,

"THE KNIGHTS OF THE WAVE."

"No peace, alas, the world may know, and on the scroll of fame,
'By Sea and Land,' that gallant band, has deeper carved its name.
On Santa Maura's rocky isle their conquering bayonets sweep,
And Navarino's Bay shall sing the Soldiers of the Deep;
Amid Crimea's dreary snows thick lie the valiant slain;
On Abyssinia's uplands wild, on China's teeming plain,
The desert sand, the torrid veldt, the Red Sea's burning shore;
In every clime, on every sea, has fought that Noble Corps."—*Lionel Jervis.*

APPENDIX F.

where the enemy held a strong position with their left on Colmar and their right on the River Fecht, opposite the village of Turckheim, and with their front covered by the Canal de Loeglbach, Turenne, having deployed the whole of his Cavalry, moved away to the left under cover of this deployment, and screened by the winter mists and the forests of bare vinyard poles on the hillsides, crossed the Fecht with the Infantry, and launched his attack from the village of Turckheim upon the enemy's right. He had to recross the river and storm a strong entrenchment held by the enemy in the Cemetery of St. Siphorien at the junction of the river and canal, but after heavy fighting he threw in the British battalions and the Gardes Francaises who " poured in ' tous a la fois ' such a terrible fire that the enemy began to give way, and, the fire being redoubled, the Allied Infantry could stand it no longer and fled."—*Hist. du Vicomte de Turenne.* By the Abbé Raguenet. 1744.

		Vol. Page

1680. FIGHTING AT TANGIERS. 20th September. — I, 24

1690. CAPTURE OF ST. CHRISTOPHER'S. 21st June.

" June 19th.—In this action we had, killed and wounded, about 130 men, and Captain Keigwin, a sea-commander, who was appointed Colonel of the Marine Regiment (which consisted of about 230 seamen) was shot through the thigh, of which wound he died before he could be carried on board, and Captain Brisbane, who acted as 1st Captain to the Marines, receiving a shot through the body, expired next morning on board the *Bristol.*—*Burchett.*

The " Marine Regiment," which according to another account published in 1691, " was a detachment out of the frigates," 400 strong, would seem to be what we should now call a " Naval Brigade," but on the other hand, one would hardly expect the men to be called " Marines." Probably both seamen and Marines acted together as they have constantly done on later occasions. Captain Keigwin though here called a " sea-commander," had a commission in a Marine Regiment (Rev. Baring-Gould—*Cornish Oddities and Strange Events*). But this, in those days, would not debar him from a Naval Command, it was rather a reason for giving it him. He took part in the Capture of St. Helena as " commander of our land forces."

BATTLE OF BEACHY HEAD. 30th June. — I, 25

SIEGE AND CAPTURE OF CORK. 22nd to 28th September. — I, 26

TAKING OF KINSALE. 15th October.

" 2,000 Mariners " (? Marines) present.—(*Hist. M.S. Com.* Le Fleming).

1692. BATTLE OF BARFLEUR. 19th to 24th May.

1693. ATTACK ON ST. MALO. 16th to 20th October.

6 Officers, 25 Sergeants and 250 Marines specially embarked for this Service, including the Grenadier Company.

1694. ATTACK ON BREST. 8th June.

" No sooner was the *Monk* come within range of the enemy's mortars, but the enemy began to fling their bombs at her from the Point des Fillettes, and the Western Point of Camaret Bay ; insomuch that when she came within three-quarters of a mile of the Latter one of the bombs broke just over her, and a great piece of it striking through the Poop and two Decks more, flew out again into the Water, near one of the Stern Ports, and killed two of the Marquis's (Caermarthen) Marine Company and wounded a third, who stood close by him on the Poop."—*A Compleat History of Europe,* 1676 *to* 1697. London. 1698.

BOMBARDMENT OF HAVRE DE GRACE. 15th June.

BOMBARDMENT OF DIEPPE. 12th July.

BOMBARDMENT OF DUNKIRK. 12th and 13th September.

1695. FIGHT OFF MESSINA. 27th January.

Captain James Killigrew, a Captain in the 1st Marines, then in command of the *Plymouth,* 60 guns, defeats the French ships *Content,* 60 guns, and *Trident,* 52 guns. He was killed in the action, and buried at Messina with military honours.

1696. ISLAND OF GROY.

700 Soldiers and Marines were landed here and burnt twenty villages. It was intended to attempt a landing on Belleisle at this time, but the Admiral abandoned it " since he had but 240 of Colonel Norcutt's men," while the enemy had 25 companies of the Regiment of Picardy and 3,000 armed islanders.—*Burchett.*

1702. ATTACK ON THE TREASURE SHIPS AT VIGO. 11th and 12th October. — I, 36

1703. GUADELOUPE. 7th March.

" Colonel Codrington, Governor of H.M. Leeward Islands, came with the Land Forces under his command, on board a Squadron of H.M. Ships, with divers Privateers, and other Vessels, before Guadeloupa, receiving several Shot from the Shoar, tho' without doing any other Mischief than killing one Man, and wounding a Boy.

" The Colonel stood off till the 10th, waiting for the *Maidstone* and the small Vessels that carried the Provision and Ammunition. Upon the 12th, Colonel Byam, with his own Regiment, and 200 of Colonel Whetham's Men, landed by Break of Day at a Place called Les Petits Inhabitants, where they met with some Opposition, but soon constrain'd the Enemy to retire. About nine in the Morning, Colonel Whetham landed in a Bay to the Northward of a Town called Les Bayliffs, where he met with a vigorous Resistance of all the Enemie's Forces, posted in very good and advantageous Breastworks, plying the English with their great and small Shot; yet, notwithstanding all their Fire, the English marched up to their Entrenchments, with their Muskets shoulder'd, not firing at them a Shot, until they could lay the Muzzles of their Guns upon the Enemies Breast-works. Here the English had three Captains kill'd before they could make themselves Masters of the Enemies Entrenchments; which they did about Noon, and in an Hour after of La Bayliffe, and of the Jacobines Church, which the Enemy had fortified, and Ten Pieces of their Cannon.

"About 2 the English took a Platform with Three Pieces of Cannon, and the *Marine Regiment* attack'd the Jacobine Plantation and Breast-Work all along the Jacobines River, which the Enemy quitted upon the Firing of Two Volleys only of small Shot upon them. The next Day the English possess'd themselves of the great Town, called Basse Terre, where they continu'd some time, sending out Parties to burn and destroy the Enemies Houses, Works, Sugar-Canes, and Provisions thereabouts, and when the Messenger came away, they were laying Siege to the Fort or Castle of the same place. But after all their Endeavours, not being able to master the main Fort or Castle, which is both naturally and artificially very strong, they were at length forced to quit the whole Island."—*Compleat Hist. of Europe for* 1703.

1703. LANDING AT ALTHEA. 31st August.

"The whole Fleet came in sight of Althea" (it had come to obtain water), "and the *Flamborough* was sent close to the shore to cover the descent of their Regiments of Marines, who landed without any manner of confusion, and were actually drawn up in Battalia on the shore, before half the Fleet was come to an anchor. Brigdr.-Genl. Seymour landed with the 1st Detachment, and gave such orders that a more orderly descent could not have been made in an enemy's country. This done they formed a camp, and the Spaniards seeing them offer no injury, brought plenty of all provisions, for which they paid them ready money."—*A Compleat History of Europe.*

1704. CAPTURE OF GIBRALTAR. 24th July.   I, 38

SEA FIGHT OFF MALAGA. 13th August.   I, 45

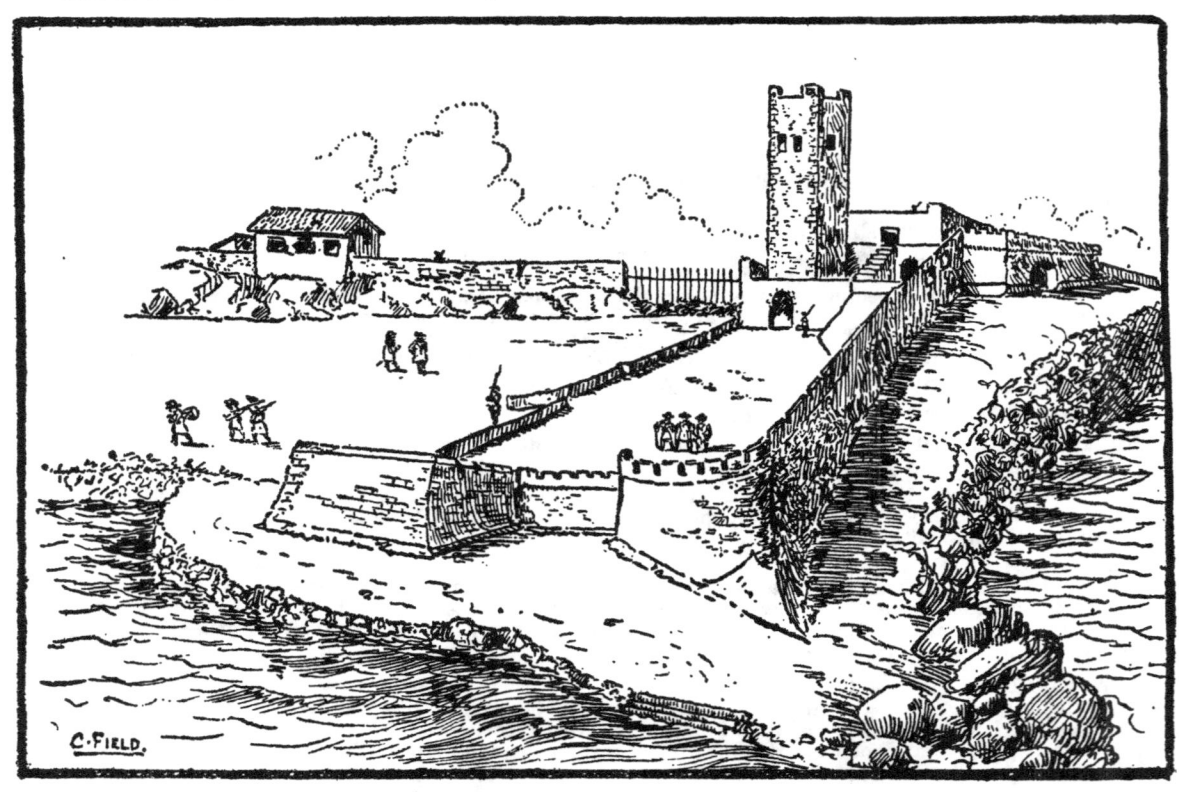

THE FORT COVERING THE NEW MOLE, GIBRALTAR.

From a Drawing in the Official Report drawn up by Lopez de Ayala and Luis Bravo in 1627. Brit. Mus. Addl. MS. 15152

THE SIEGE OF GIBRALTAR, 1704.

Contemporary German Print.

APPENDIX F.

1704-5. DEFENCE OF GIBRALTAR. 9th October to 18th April.

Vol. Page
I, 48, 322

In the "History of Gibraltar," by James Bell (1845), the writer seems to rely principally upon the account of Padre Juan Romero de Figueroa, Curate of the Church of St. Mary, Gibraltar, for his story of the capture of the Rock by the British and its subsequent defence. A few extracts may be of interest as shewing how things appeared to the enemy and also for some statements which seem somewhat at variance with those of our own contemporary writers.

"On the 1st of August (*new style*) this formidable expedition (Rooke's Fleet) appeared in the Bay, at the bottom of which, near *Punta Mala*, 3,000 or 4,000 men were landed without delay, creating alarm and consternation throughout the district." ... "The enemy, convinced that it was in vain to expect the garrison to surrender, placed their fleet in line of battle, consisting of thirty ships and some bomb-vessels; and on the 4th August, 1704, at 5 o'clock in the morning, commenced an incessant and most horrible fire, which lasted six hours, during which time thirty thousand balls were thrown into the town.... The consternation of the inhabitants was only equalled by the danger to which they were exposed." ... "Both the Moles were attacked with vigour, and, although the New Mole was defended with great valour, 100 sailors landed from their boats and possessed themselves of the Fort contiguous. The greater force, however, was directed against the Old Mole, and Don Bartolome Castano, its commandant, seeing that resistance was vain, resolved to abandon it; giving orders to blow up Fort Leandro that protected it: and this was so well accomplished, that seven of the enemy's launches were destroyed, and 300 troops, including many officers, were either killed or wounded by the explosion." This is very different to our accounts (*Vide* pp. 40, 41, Vol. I). After a summary of the terms of surrender the Padre continues :—" Such was the capitulation dictated by the Prince; and the conditions were less severe than might have been expected, considering the immense force of the enemy. The Imperial Standard was without delay raised on the wall, and the Archduke Charles proclaimed King of Spain and owner of the city."

"The English, however, violently resisted, and hoisting their own Standard, they proclaimed Queen Anne, in whose name they declared they took possession of Gibraltar, and which was confirmed by the subsequent Treaty of London, surrendering to England, together with this place both Ceuta and Minorca."

"Gibraltar, now in the hands of the English, was for the twelfth time to undergo a siege. Numerous Spanish generals of renown hastened to the scene of action. The Count of Tolosa landed twenty pieces of artillery, with the necessary ammunition, and many of the inhabitants returned to lend their aid, in the hope of recovering their lost possessions. The English garrison consisted of about 3,000 men, including many vagabonds from the provinces, and deserters from the Spanish Army. The Governor caused some redoubts to be constructed; the elevation overlooking Land Port to be crowned with twenty pieces of cannon, and a tower to be fortified that commanded the Spanish Camp; the inundation was formed, as at present, to narrow the approach to the garrison."

The Padre's story of the Forlorn Hope led by Susarte the goatherd up the back of the Rock to St. Michael's Cave tallies pretty closely with the English accounts of the episode. He adds, however, that the guide and "a few others" contrived to get back to the Spanish Camp "to express their indignation at being deserted on so trying an occasion."

It is interesting to learn from this Spanish writer that after the abandonment of the siege, "The hopes and expectations of the old inhabitants, being thus altogether frustrated, they dispersed themselves among the vinyards, farmhouses and cottages in the neighbourhood," where on 21st May, 1706, they received orders from the Royal Council ordering them to assemble in some place they might select in order that they might be reorganised as a civic community. "The spot where is now the town of San Roque was fixed upon by common consent as the centre of the jurisdiction under the new arrangement." The Government, "named for them a special Chief Magistrate or Corregidor in 1716, conferring the honour on Don Bernardo Dias de Isla, together, as declared in the Royal Patent, with a Council, Tribunals, Officers, and *Gentlemen of the City of Gibraltar*. The result was the re-establishment of the City of Gibraltar in San Roque, being in a central part of its district, and the congregating there of its inhabitants, by whom affairs were conducted as formerly."

1705. CAPTURE OF ALICANT. 29th July.	I, 62
TAKING OF CARTHAGENA. 12th July.	I, 62
1706. SIEGE OF BARCELONA. 12th August.	I, 60
CAPTURE OF MAJORCA. 14th September.	I, 64

KEY TO CONTEMPORARY ENGRAVING OF THE SIEGE OF GIBRALTAR.

This quaint old print is from a broadsheet published at Nuremburg, and is mendaciously called "A accurate and truthful representation."

1. The City of Gibraltar.
2. The Castle of Gibraltar.
3. Spanish Attack.
4. French Attack.
5. English and Dutch Reinforcements.
6. Watch Tower on a high mountain from which one can see as far as 30 miles out to sea.
7. Other Towers from which to observe hostile ships.
8. The Harbour.

		Vol. Page
1706.	DEFENCE OF BARCELONA. 23rd March to 30th April.	I, 62, 323
1707.	BATTLE OF ST. ESTEVAN. 15th January.	I, 63, 323, 324
	THE VAR. 28th June.	I, 64

"The Enemy had entrenched themselves very strongly on the other Side of the Var, a River that was a league distant from Nice, by extending their Works above Four Miles from the Shore, and these Intrenchments were guarded by 6 Battalions of Foot, and 800 Horse ; while Lt.-General Dillon, an Irishman, was marching with all Expedition to reinforce them with 12 fresh Battalions." ...... "Sir Cloudsley Shovel commanded 4 British Men-of-War, and one Dutch, to sail into the Mouth of the Var, attended by 600 Seamen and Marines in open Boats, under the conduct of Sir John Norris. The Men-of-War came within Musket-shot of the Enemy's Works, which lay so expos'd to our Fire, that their Cavalry and many of their Foot gave way. The Admiral himself follow'd Sir John Norris to the Place of Action, and observing the Disorder of the Enemy, commanded him to put to Land, and flank them in their Intrenchments. His Men advanc'd in such an undaunted manner, and seem'd so intrepid and fearless, by tossing up their Hats in the Air, and their loud Halloo's that the Enemy had not Courage enough to stay for them, but fearing to be surrounded, fled from their Works and retir'd with great Precipitation" (Seamen and Marines left in possession of works).—*Compleat History of Europe.*

	DEFENCE OF LERIDA. Sept.	I, 63, 324
1708.	CAPTURE OF CAGLIARI. 2nd August.	I, 64
	CAPTURE OF PORT MAHON. 18th September.	I, 64
1709.	DEFENCE OF ALICANT. December to 7th April,	I, 62
1710.	LANDING AT CETTE AND OCCUPATION OF AGDE. 13th to 14th July.	I, 64
	CAPTURE OF ANNAPOLIS ROYAL. 1st October.	I, 65
1741.	ATTACK ON CARTHAGENA. 9th March to 16th May.	I, 71
1743.	OCCUPATION OF THE ISLAND OF RATTAN. 23rd August.	I, 89
1744.	MATTHEW'S ENGAGEMENT OFF TOULON. 11th February.	
	VILLEFRANCHE. 9th—11th April.	

Detachments of the 3rd, 4th, 7th and 9th Marines were landed to assist the Sardinians to defend their lines against the French and Spaniards. Detachments were also landed from the 2nd, 7th, 10th, 29th and 45th of the Line who were serving as Marines on board the Fleet. The Detachments of the Royal Artillery from the Bomb vessels had been landed some days previously but had all been captured in the early hours of the 9th.

1745.	ACTION BETWEEN THE *LION* AND THE *ELIZABETH*. 9th July.	I, 128
	CAPTURE OF LOUISBURG. 17th June.	
	Naval Brigade, 800 Marines and Seamen.	
1746.	ORKNEY ISLANDS. 20th May to 3 September.	

Captain Benj. Moodie sent with Detachment to Orkneys, by Admiral Smith, S.N.O. Coast of Scotland "in search of Rebels, and to secure those islands, pursuant to H.R.H. the Duke's Orders."

EXPEDITION AGAINST L'ORIENT. September 20th to 30th.

160 Marines left at landing place at Quimperlé Bay, remainder with three 3-pounder guns under Colonel Holmes, marched with the rest of the Army on L'Orient. Seamen and Marines afterwards brought up two 12-pounders and furnace for red-hot shot. 7 Marines were drowned during re-embarkation.

1747.	ANSON'S DEFEAT OF THE FRENCH FLEET OFF FINISTERRE. 3rd May.	
	GOUDHURST. 8th August.	

An officer and 20 Marines ordered from Maidstone to Goudhurst to protect it from a threatened attack by Smugglers.

	SIEGE OF PONDICHERRY. 8th August to September.	I, 93
	(880 Marines present).	
	HAWKE'S VICTORY OVER THE FRENCH OFF FINISTERRE. 14th October.	
1748.	ADMIRAL KNOWLES' VICTORY OFF HAVANNAH. 1st October.	
1756.	DEFENCE OF FORT ST. PHILIP. MINORCA. 8th May to 28th June.	

Marines present—1 Captain, 2 Subalterns, 4 Sergeants, 2 Drummers, 97 Privates (effective), and 7 sick. Total 110. One of Admiral Byng's excuses at his trial for not relieving the garrison was that his Marines had been taken from him at Portsmouth, and the 7th Fusileers embarked *in their place*, instead of *in addition* to them, and that therefore he could not spare this Battalion for duty on shore. During the siege " a young Lieutenant of Marines lost both his legs by a chain shot. In this miserable and helpless condition he was conveyed to England, and a memorial of his case presented to the Admiralty in order to obtain some additional consideration to the narrow stipend of half-pay. Major Mason, a friend, had the poor fellow conducted to Court on a public day in his uniform, where, posted in the guard-room, and supported by two brother officers, he cried out as King George II was passing to the Drawing Room, 'Behold, great Sire, a man who cannot bend his knee to you, he having lost both in your service.' The King, struck no less by the singularity of this address than by the melancholy object before him, stopped and hastily demanded what had been done for him. 'Half-pay,' replied the Lieutenant, 'an please your Majesty.' 'Fie, fie, on't,' said the King, shaking his head; 'but let me see you again next Levée day.' The Lieutenant did not fail to appear at the place of assignation, where he received from the immediate hands of Royalty £500 ready money, and an appointment of £200 a year, to be paid quarterly, as long as he lived." History has not preserved the name of this recipient of the King's generosity and kindness.

1757. FORREST'S ACTION WITH DE KERSAINT OFF CAPE FRANCOIS. 21st October.
1758. CAPTURE OF FORT LOUIS, SENEGAL. 2nd May.
   Major Monson and 310 Marines present.

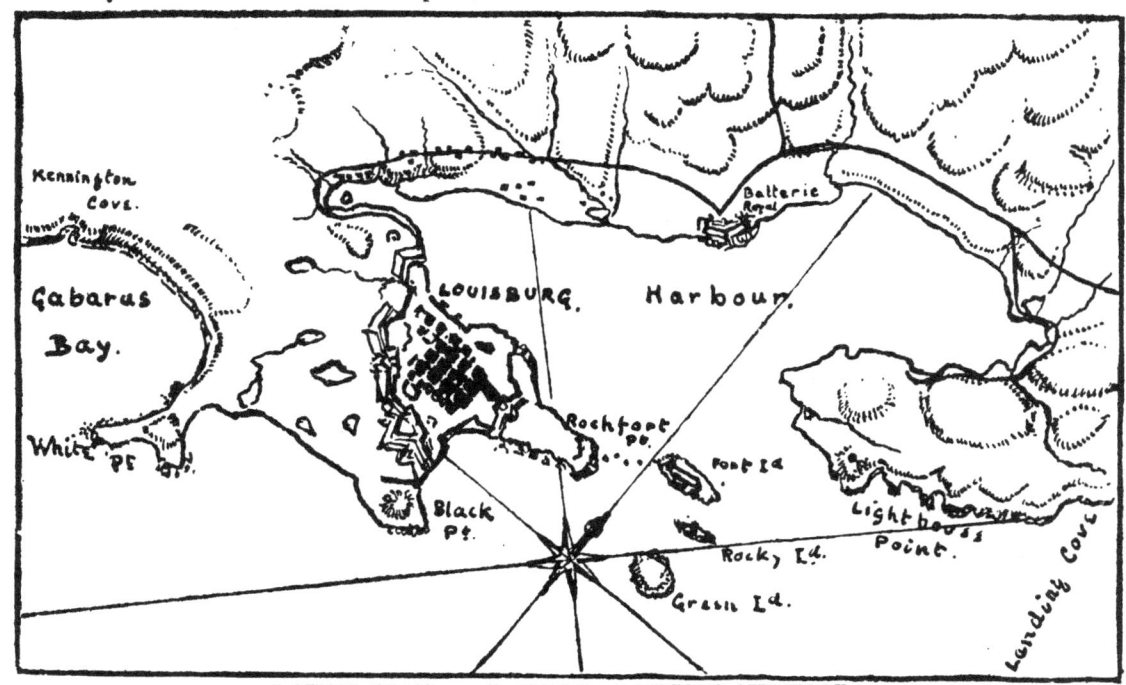

ROUGH PLAN OF LOUISBURG NEIGHBOURHOOD.

SIEGE OF LOUISBOURG. 25th June to 26th July.
   Sunday, 25th June.—500 Marines landed and took post at Kennington Cove. ("A place which is a great care to the Army.")
Admiral the Hon. E. Boscawen to Captain Arthur Tooker Collins, of the Marines.
   Sir,
      I propose to land your company to-morrow, you are to join Brigadr. Wolfe, therefore not to come in their coats, but cropped hats, short jackets, etc., thirty-six rounds of ammunition, and a blanket each man rolled up on their backs. They are to bring only their provision for to-morrow, bring four flints a man, if any of your arms are bad, take the ship's arms, you may bring your knapsacks and haversacks. I write this to you as I know Capt. Buckle is not on board. I shall be on board early.
         I am Sir your
                              very humble servant
If Capt. Buckle returns before I do shew him this letter."[1]   E. BOSCAWEN.
   Sunday, 2nd July.—100 Marines sent on shore and joined General Wolfe's Army.
   Wednesday, 5th July.—*General Orders.*—As soon as it is dark the Highlanders are to draw the 2 light 6 pounders and place them in a battery prepared for them upon the right of the redan. One of the Artillery and some Marines are to serve these 2 pieces, and their ammunition is to be deposited in the redan. The Cohorn Mortars are not to play any more at the shipping, but the 5 Royals may be employ'd a day or two in the redoubt constructed by Anstruthers and the Marines. . . . . The Marines are to do duty with the Corps of Artillery, by that means they will be able to keep their own batteries in constant repair.
   Saturday, 15th July.—A Sergeant of Marines taken prisoner by our Light Infantry, he was at some distance from his post without arms.

---
[1] This letter is not in the "Journal" but from an original in the possession of the Rev. J. Trelawny-Ross, of Ham, Devonshire, a descendant of Capt. Collins.

Tuesday, 25th July.—The *Prudente* set on fire and the *Bienfaisant* towed off to the North-east Harbour by the boats of the Fleet which carried in about 450 men, Seamen, Marines, etc., commanded by Captains Laforey and Balfour, boarded the ships without opposition from them, but from the town, who, having the service, fir'd grape and musketry, did not kill above seven and wounded as many. The *Prudente* being on ground oblig'd to set fire to her, eleven officers, mostly Marines and about 122 sailors out of the two were made prisoners."—Fr. an M.S., *Journal of the Siege of Louisbourg*, by Lieut. W. A. Gordon, 40th Regiment.

The following is a letter from Capt. Collins to his wife :—

Camp before Louisbourg,
July 27th, 1758.

"I have had the honour to command a party of Marines on shore under Gen. Wolfe, who has always been in the hottest fire and the nearest advanced to the Enemy; and the cannon balls play'd very fast on us for three weeks, yet they could do nothing more than come what the World calls very near me.

"I was three weeks and three days without pulling my clothes off, or getting any sleep but on boards, and never more than two hours at a time; sometimes 48 hours without any sleep; and notwithstanding this may appear hardships, yet I never had my health better the whole time. I needn't tell you much about the Siege; the public papers will give you that fully. We took the Town, destroyed 5 Ships of the Line of Battle, and made all in the Town Prisoners of War. . . . . We have done such brave deeds that England ought to be proud of such sons of Liberty, and think better of us than they have hitherto done. I believe most of us were determined to conquer or die."

EXPEDITION TO CHERBOURG. 15th August to 27th September.
DEFENCE OF MADRAS. 12th December to 16th February, 1759.   II, 108
1759. TAKING OF GOREE. 28th December.

"Mr. Keppel sent a party of Marines ashore, taking possession of the Fort, hoisted the British Colours, and finished the ceremony by 3 loud huzzas from the battlements of the citadel and Castle of St. Michael."

CAPTURE OF GUADELOUPE. 1st May.
BOSCAWEN'S VICTORY OVER THE FRENCH OFF LAGOS. 18th August.

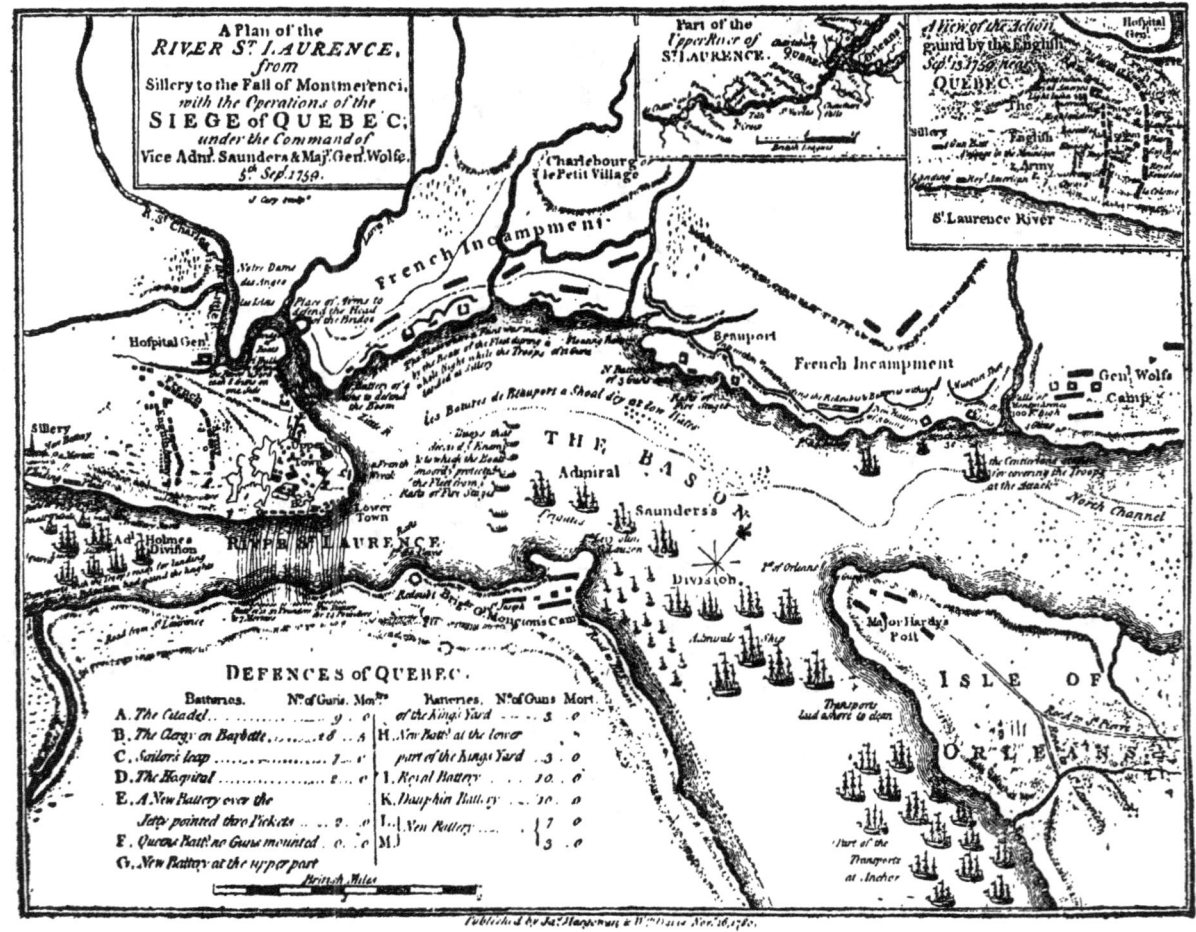

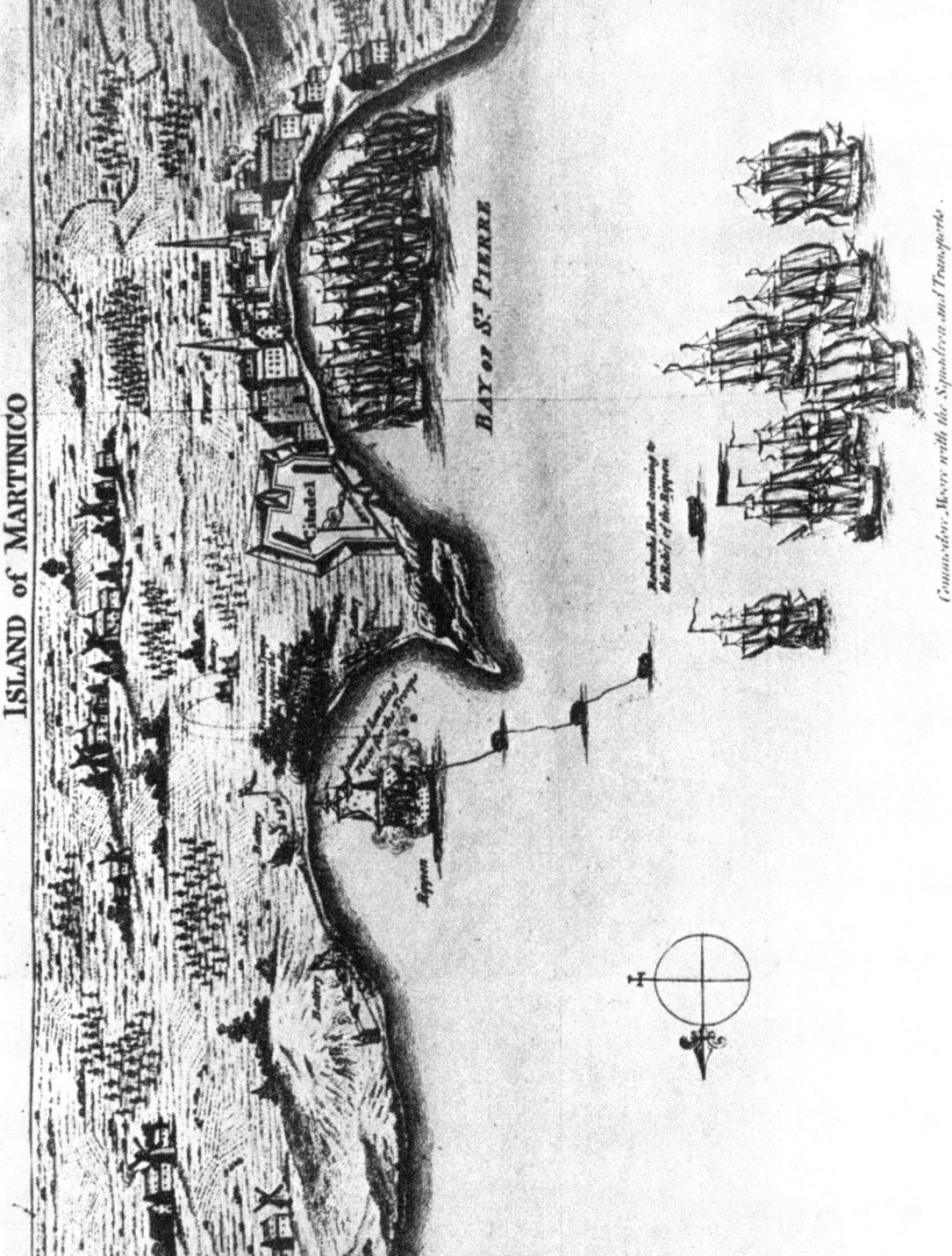

APPENDIX F.

Vol. Page

1759. TAKING OF QUEBEC. 12th September.

A Battalion of 24 Officers, 1 Surgeon, 21 Sergeants, 16 Drummers and 540 Rank and File was embarked at Portsmouth to take part in the Expedition against Quebec. During the operations the Marines were encamped at Point Levi on the South side of the St. Lawrence, but on the 26th July, two companies of them were sent over to General Wolfe's Camp, at Montmorenci, as a reinforcement. Afterwards "600 men of the Marines and (Major) Hardy's Corps" were sent over to defend the Island of Orleans in the middle of the River between Montmorenci and Point Levi. Some of these must have been sent from the ships as the Battalion was only 540 strong, or possibly, this was entirely a "ship battalion." When the real attack on Quebec took place the line-of-battleships which lay in the river below Quebec made a demonstration in front of the French lines to the N.E. of the City in order to divert attention from the landing at Sillery to the West of Quebec. They stood in as close to the shore as the depth of water would allow, lowered their boats and filled them with Marines to deceive the enemy into expecting a landing at this point.

1760. CAPTURE OF CARICAL, EAST INDIES. 5th April.

Major Monson and 300 Marines.

PONDICHERRY. 16th January.   II, 108

422 Marines.

1761. TAKING OF BELLEISLE. 8th April to 7th June.

Badge of the "Laurel Wreath" gained on this occasion.   I, 101

1762. CAPTURE OF REDOUBTS ON MORNE TORTENSON, MARTINIQUE. 16th February.

The Marines of the Expedition had previously landed and with the aid of a few seamen captured a Fort at Grand Ance, and held it till relieved by a Line Battalion. Landing again with the rest of the Army in Cas de Navires Bay, the Marines formed in two Battalions of 450 men each, took part in the three days' fighting which resulted in the capture of the Redoubts on Morne Tortenson, Morne Garnier, and the attack on the Citadel of Port Royal. On the fall of this place the Marines of the fleet, with 500 seamen were landed, and the whole Island of Martinique submitted to the British Crown.

CAPTURE OF THE *HERMOINE*, SPANISH TREASURE SHIP. 21st May.

This ship, the net proceeds of whose cargo realised no less than £519,705 1s. 6d., was taken off Cadiz by the 28-gun Frigate *Active* and 18-gun Sloop *Favourite*. The share of each Private Marine amounted to £484.

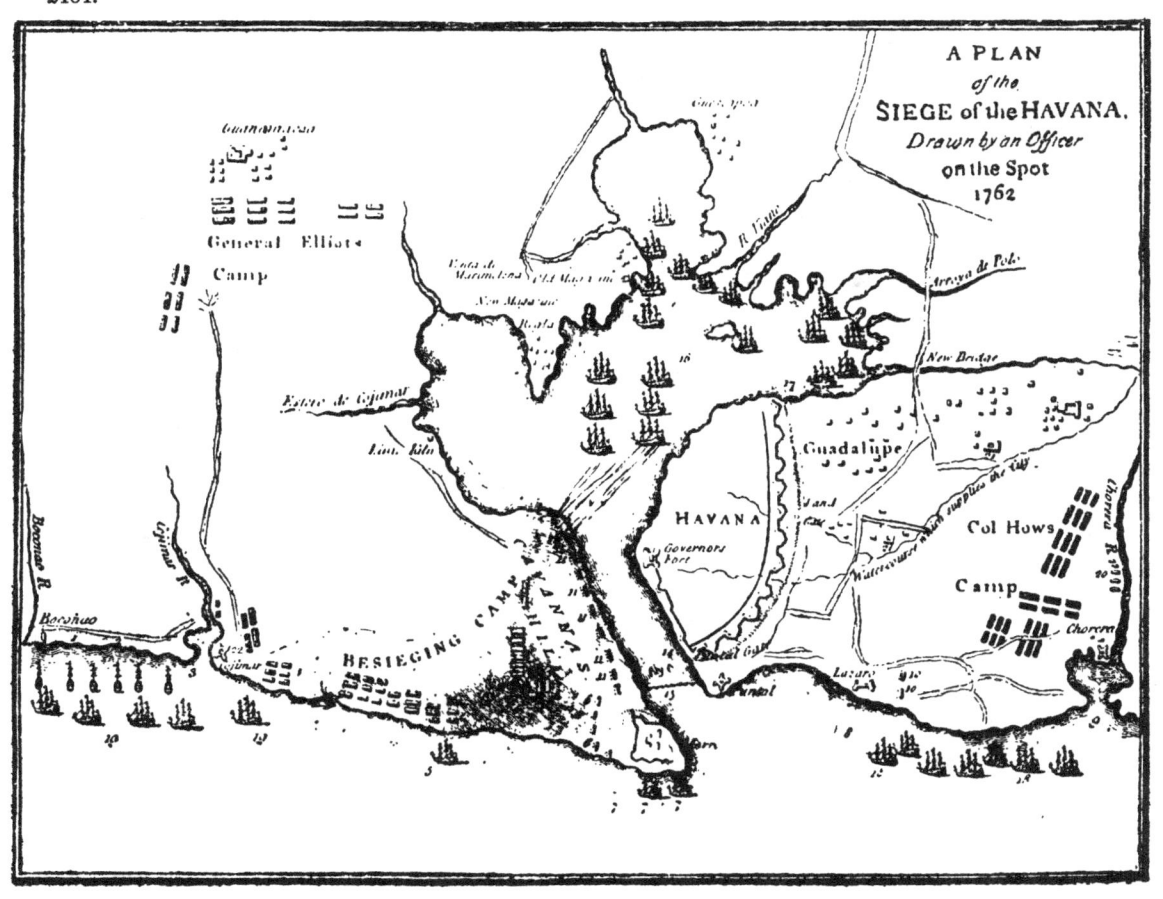

1762. SIEGE AND CAPTURE OF HAVANNAH. 7th June to 13th August.

On the 7th June the Marines were placed in the boats and made a feint of landing 4 miles to the Westward of the City, while the remainder of the Army effected its disembarkation without opposition between the Rivers Boca Nao and Coximar some way to the Eastward. Being checked at the latter River by a castle at its mouth, the Army halted while the *Dragon* stood in and silenced its guns in about an hour, after which her Marines went on shore and took possession of it. On the evening of the 10th the Marines were in the boats again while the *Belleisle, Cerberus, Bonetta, Mercury* and *Lurcher* bombarded the Castle of Chorea at the entrance to the River of that name on the East side of the City. The Castle and adjoining batteries were taken on the 11th, and "a part of the Marines landed for its security."

At this time the Marines, who were about 800 strong, were formed into two Battalions and placed under the command of Majors Campbell and Collins. On the 15th June they were landed and encamped near Chorea under the command of Colonel Hon. William Howe. The main attack was directed against the Morro Castle—the Citadel of Havannah—which occupied a high and steep rock on the East side of the entrance to the harbour. For a long time it defied all the effortsof the beseiegrs while disease decimated their ranks. On the 5th and 6th July it was found necessary to draw on the Marines for reinforcements, and during these two days 400 of them were transferred to the trenches in front of the Morro. A portion of them at any rate were employed in the mining operations which were very difficult to carry out on account of an immense ditch cut in the solid rock, 80 feet deep and 40 wide. But on the 20th July the miners—totally uncovered—managed to cross the ditch by a narrow ridge of rock which had been left to cover it towards the sea, and soon buried themselves in the wall. On the 30th of the month the mines were sprung, breaching the wall and partially filling in the ditch, and the British stormers soon made themselves masters of the Citadel. Its fall was very shortly followed by that of Havannah itself, and the Marines, who, it is reported, "had proved very serviceable," were re-embarked. Much booty fell to the victors including a great deal of gold and silver specie, which on arrival in London was conducted to the Tower in eleven waggons, each guarded by 4 Marines and surmounted by a Union Jack flying above a Spanish Ensign. Each Private Soldier's Prize Money amounted to £4 1s. 8d. The total amount was £368,092 11s. 6d.

CAPTURE OF MANILLA. 5th October.

A small military expedition under the command of Colonel Sir William Draper carried in a squadron under Admiral Cornish anchored in Manilla Bay on the 23rd September.

The Admiral contributed 500 Seamen and "270 good Marines"—300 by some accounts—to the landing force. After sending in an ineffectual summons to the town, and reconnoitring the coast, no time was lost in commencing operations. A proper spot, two miles to the Southward of Manilla, having been selected for the debarkation, the 79th Regiment, all the Marines and Artillery, with a howitzer and a few field-pieces, were placed in the boats which were formed in 3 divisions, under the sterns of 3 frigates which had been detailed to cover the landing. Numbers of Spanish Indians had assembled on the shore to dispute our landing, the men-of-war opened fire, which compelled them to retire. In spite of a violent surf which dashed many of the boats to pieces and wetted and injured the muskets, the troops effected their landing, and during the night of the 24th succeeded in establishing themselves in a village called Malata, little more than a mile from the enemy's works. The day following a detachment was pushed forward to occupy Fort Polverista which had been abandoned by the enemy, while Major Monson with the Marines advanced and took possession of the Hermita Church which was close to the city and of considerable strategical importance. Moreover, the rainy season having set in, it was necessary to get under effective cover. This point was further reinforced by the 79th Regiment. The Marines garrisoned Forts Polverista and that at Malata which protected the line of communication with the squadron and to guard the stores and heavy artillery. "They, from the good conduct and example of their Officers, behaved very well, and were of great use upon all occasions."

The port of Cavite, with other dependencies of Manilla were included in the capitulation, and Captain Champion with 100 Marines and a party of Sepoys were sent as garrison to the former. Our total loss upon this brilliant service was 4 Officers, 1 Sergeant and 25 Privates killed; 1 Lieutenant drowned; 6 Officers, 3 Sergeants and 102 Rank and File wounded. Among the first were 5 Marines, while Lieutenant Spearing and 6 Private Marines were wounded. During these operations Captain Richard Bishop of the Marines so distinguished himself by his bravery and professional knowledge that Sir William Draper appointed him Governor of the town of Cavite. While holding this appointment he met with an adventure which all but cost him his life, and which is thus related:—

"At this time there was in the neighbourhood a Malay of extraordinary bulk and strength, and of most ferocious disposition, who had formerly worked in the Dockyard, but had deserted, and having collected nearly a hundred men of like character with himself, committed every species of lawless violence on the persons and property of the peaceful inhabitants. For the apprehension of this man Captain Bishop had long offered considerable rewards, but without effect, when one day riding out with a brother officer, attended by about forty men, he saw this desperado armed with a carbine, a brace of pistols, a scymeter and a dagger, issue out of a wood at a short distance, at the head of his troop. Instigated by a sudden emotion of resentment, Bishop determined to inflict on this man the just punishment of his offences. But being himself without weapons, he borrowed a pistol from the holsters of the officer who accompanied him. Thus provided he galloped up to the Malay, and presented the pistol at his head. The Malay and his followers, confounded at the bold act of a single man, offered no resistance. The pistol missed fire, on which Bishop, striking the Malay with a violent blow on the head, knocked him off his horse; in the meanwhile the English troop, hastening to the assistance of their leader, and concluding him to be

THE TAKING OF HAVANNAH, 1762. From a Print after D. Serres

"The attacking and taking of the Castle and Batteries of Chooree and the landing of all His Majestsy's Marines.

APPENDIX F.

                                                                                                    Vol. Page

fully able to cope with his fallen antagonist, pursued the banditti, who immediately fled, and both parties were soon out of sight. All this was the work of only a few seconds, during which Bishop seeing the Malay stunned on the ground, alighted in order to secure him, or, if necessary, to kill him with one of his own weapons. No sooner, however, was he off his horse than the Malay was on his feet and began a desperate struggle with his rash assailant. It was the business of the former merely to employ his own offensive weapons, the latter had the double necessity of defeating their use and of applying them to his own advantage. The Malay was singularly strong and active, and inured to hard labour, and of exerting himself in his native climate; the Englishman of much less muscular force, and that reduced by long privations and by the influence of excessive heat, but the disparity was in a considerable degree compensated by the energy of an invincible mind. This contest for life continued for almost an hour, when at length Bishop, almost fainting from fatigue, was thrown on his back, and the Malay, kneeling on him drew his dagger and with all his force aimed at his breast the fatal blow. At that moment, Bishop, exerting his last remains of strength, with both hands averted the point of the dagger as it descended, and changing its direction, drove it upwards into the throat of the Malay, who immediately fell down dead upon him. Bishop, unable to walk, crawled on his hands and knees to his horse, which he found grazing at a distance of a quarter of a mile, near the spot where the contest began. He mounted him with difficulty, and was soon afterwards happily joined by his friends who had chased their opponents into some dangerous passes, and returned, not without solicitude for the fate of their commander whom they had so long left."

1764. BATTLE OF BUXAR. 23rd October.   II, 112

"Silver Medal presented to Captain Ewing (of the Marines) for wound received at Bunker's Hill."

A copy is at the Victoria and Albert Museum. Captain Ewing's name is not in the list of Officers of the Battalion published in Orders of 20th May, 1775, but he must either have joined them later, or been landed from a ship.

1775. BATTLE OF BUNKER'S HILL. 17th June.   I, 154

1776. LONG ISLAND. 27th August.

In this action 1 Officer and 20 Marine Grenadiers were captured from having mistaken the blue uniforms of the Americans for those of the Hessians. There were 2 Battalions of Marines totalling 1172 men in General Howe's Army at New York this year.

MARTHA'S VINYARD. — November.

"The *Diamond*, Captain Fielding, having been driven by the weather into Martha's Vinyard, sent a boat ashore with a flag of truce. The inhabitants suffered the boat to come within gun-shot, and then fired upon her—one man was wounded. To punish this treachery the *Diamond's* Marines were landed, and at once attacked and routed a party of the enemy, though strongly posted on a hill and sheltered by rocks and bushes, from behind which they kept up a brisk fire. One Marine was killed and one wounded, while the rebels lost 4 killed and many wounded. The Marines then set fire to their houses and barns and brought off as many oxen, sheep and poultry as they could."—*Beatson's M. & N. Memoirs.*

"These are Highland Pistols very elaborately engraved and ornamented. They were taken from Pitcairn's Horse and given to Israel Putnam, who carried them throughout the war."

| | | Vol. | Page |

1777. CAPTURE OF PHILADELPHIA. 26th September.

The two Marine Grenadier Companies present with the rest of the Grenadiers belonging to the Army. During the advance on the city the U.S. rebel frigate *Delaware* ran aground and was taken possession of by a Company of Marines under Captain Avarne.

1778. CAPTURE OF BORDEN TOWN AND DESTRUCTION OF REBEL SHIPPING. 7th May.

Carried out by the Light Infantry of the Army under Major Hon. John Maitland, of the Marines. Presumably, therefore, the two Marine Light Infantry Companies were present.

1779. DEFENCE OF SAVANNAH. 9th October.

The seamen and Marines were landed from the men-of-war present to assist in the defence against the French and Americans. The latter were attached to the Grenadier Company of the 60th Regiment, and occupied a position on the right of the line of entrenchments. When the final assault on the works by the French had almost succeeded but had been checked by the fire of the seamen's guns, the Marines, with the Grenadiers of the 60th, made such a furious counter-attack on a redoubt which had been taken by the enemy that they were driven out in an instant and a general offensive being assumed by the garrison, the enemy's attack totally failed and they shortly afterwards abandoned the siege.

STORMING OF OMOA. 17th October.

An expedition, consisting of detachments of the Loyal Irish, the Marines of the *Charon*, *Pomona*, *Lowestoffe* and *Porcupine* frigates, and 250 armed slaves, 500 men in all, commanded by Captain Dalrymple, sailed from Truxillo Bay on 10th October, and arrived at Porto Cavallo Bay on the 11th. In the evening of the 10th, the troops were landed, and marched with the intention of attacking Port Omoa (Honduras) that night; but the roads proved so intricate and rugged that they did not arrive until after daybreak. After a short halt they again moved forward, but still had to encounter passes and defiles similar to those which had obstructed their night march, having to skirmish with Indians as they advanced. Learning from some prisoners that the enemy were drawn up in position to resist their attack, it was arranged that the Marines and the Loyal Irish should force the pass in column, and then advance rapidly, supported by the reserve. The defile was instantly carried, and the Spaniards, after a scattering discharge of musketry, fled, some to the forts, others to the woods, and the town. From the heights on which the troops now stood there was a full view of the fort, situated about half-a-mile distant from Port Omoa, at the bottom of the hills; and as the enemy kept firing from the town, Captain Dalrymple was under the necessity of destroying the place. While it was in flames the squadron came into the bay and endeavoured to get into position to batter the fort, the land forces seconding their efforts; but the latter were unable to effect very much owing to the scaling ladders not arriving in time. The *Lowestoffe* got aground and both she and the *Charon* suffered severely from the enemy's fire. But it was determined to continue the attack, and at 3 in the morning of the 20th the storming party, 150 strong, was in position for the assault. It was arranged in four parallel columns, four guides at the head of each, two of the columns consisting of Seamen and two of Marines with a few Loyal Irish. Upon an agreed signal from the *Charon* that she was under way, and would attack in twenty minutes the columns of assault moved off covered by the fire of the shipping, It was now 4 a.m. The Spaniards did not observe the movement but concentrated their fire upon the squadron and the guns which had been placed in battery on the hills. In profound silence, with trailed arms, the English approached the enemy's sentries undiscovered, but suddenly their drums beat to arms.

The ladders being quickly planted against the wall, 28 feet in height, surmounted by a battery of 5 guns, the seamen rapidly ascended, and being reinforced by the Marines, the Spaniards fled to the casemates, while about a hundred escaped by a sallyport. The Governor and the officers then delivered up their swords to Captain Dalrymple, and the garrison, with the register ships in port, surrendered.

1780. RODNEY'S VICTORY OFF ST. VINCENT. 12th April.

CAPTURE OF LA CAPRICIEUSE BY PRUDENTE AND LICORNE. 4th July.   I, 140

FIGHT BETWEEN THE *FLORA* AND THE *NYMPHE*. 10th August.   I, 140

1781. ACTION OFF THE DOGGER BANK. 5th August.

TAKING OF NEGAPATAM. 29th October to 11th November.

On the 21st October, 3,200 of the Honble. East India Company's troops were at Nagore and Vice-Admiral Sir Edward Hughes landed the Marines of the squadron 443 strong, and the next day 827 seamen with four 24-pounders, twelve 18-pounders, two 12-pounders, two 10-inch and six 5½-inch mortars. The Marines who, on landing immediately joined the land forces, " co-operated to the utmost; and during the siege of Negapatam, were unrivalled in their gallantry, as well as performing most important services, in landing with the utmost difficulty and danger, through the surf, guns and mortars for the batteries on shore."—*Hist. 1st Madras European Regiment.*

1781-2. DEFENCE OF FORT ST. PHILIP, MINORCA. 19th August to 4th February.

430 Marines present.

"A small corps of Marines and Sailors belonging to such of His Majesty's ships as chanced to be here when the Spaniards blocked up the Harbour, were of great service during the siege; and being more accustomed to live on salted provisions, they kept their health much better than the other troops in the garrison did."—Beatson's *M. & N. Memoirs.*

THE FRENCH REPUBLICANS STORM FORT MULGRAVE, TOULON.
Lithograph by Raffet.

APPENDIX F.

Vol. Page

One of the charges against General Murray the Governor of the Island, when called to account for its loss, was that in order to make out that he had a garrison weaker than it really was, he suppressed in his report to the Secretary of State " the mention of the Marine Corps, which alone consisted of 430 fit for duty, with 125 Artillery men, besides Greeks, Algerines and Corsicans." Lieutenants Davis and Crew, 3 Sergeants and 54 Privates were killed in this defence, and Captain Harman and Lieutenant Hodges were wounded.

1782. CAPTURE OF TRINCOMALEE. 11th January.   II, 114

LORD RODNEY'S ACTION OFF DOMINICA. 12th April.

HUGHES' ACTIONS WITH SUFFREN OFF CEYLON. 17th February, 12th April, 6th July, 3rd Sept.   I, 140

RELIEF OF GIBRALTAR. 11th October.

1783. TAKING OF NEW PROVIDENCE (NASSAU), BAHAMAS.

1788. MARINES LAND AT PORT JACKSON AND FOUND SYDNEY, N.S.W. 26th January.   I, 175

1793. CAPTURE OF TOBAGO. 15th April.

The British force included Major Richard Bright, 1 Lieutenant, 2 Sergeants, 1 Drummer and 27 Private Marines, out of the 400 men of which it was composed. Fort Castries was carried by storm and the island submitted.

FIGHT BETWEEN THE *BOSTON* AND *L'EMBUSCADE*. 31st July.   I, 319

OPERATIONS AT TOULON. 15th August to 18th December.

Lord Hood with a squadron of 21 sail of the line and several frigates entered the harbour of Toulon on 15th August, and in response to his proclamations offering assistance to the well disposed inhabitants against the tyranny of the Republican faction which had seized the reins of Government, the loyalists handed over the town into his keeping. He landed 1,500 troops and a number of Marines under Captain Richard Bidlake near Fort la Malgue. The latter occupied this fort which stood on a hill between the Little and the Great Road, while Fort Mulgrave was situated on the tongue of land continued from this hill into the harbour. A Spanish fleet soon afterwards arrived with reinforcements, and on the 31st August the allied British and Spaniards marched out and defeated a Republican detachment near Ollicules. The Marines of the Fleet were dispersed over the various forts and lines of defence, which soon came under fire from the enemy's batteries, the number of the besiegers increasing day after day. Fighting continued until December, when the increasing pressure of the enemy rendered the evacuation of the town inevitable. One of the most brilliant events of the siege was the defence of a redoubt by Lieutenant Thomas Naylor of the Marines with 120 men, mostly of his own Corps. A French column, 2,000 strong, covered by a fog attempted to surprise the redoubt in the early morning, but the garrison was on the alert, and Naylor, ordering his men to reserve their fire until the Republicans were at close quarters and then to fire by platoons, succeeded in killing or wounding nearly a quarter of their numbers and eventually repulsing their attack. Fort Mulgrave, known as the " Little Gibraltar," and other forts fell one after another into the hands of the enemy, and at 10 p.m., on 18th December, the defence was restricted to the town and the Fort of La Malgue, which were held while the French men-of-war in harbour and the magazines were burnt and blown up, and the loyalists to the number of nearly 15,000 men, women and children embarked on board the fleet to save them from the bloodthirsty Republicans.

There was a curious sequel to the evacuation of Toulon. Ignorant of the withdrawal of the British force, H.M.S. *Juno*, coming from Malta, arrived off Toulon at 10 p.m., on 11th January, 1794. She had no pilot on board, and made her way in as best she could. Her captain was somewhat surprised to see none of our ships in the outer harbour, though the lights of several vessels were visible further in. Presently a brig at anchor loomed up through the darkness, and as the *Juno* passed a voice hailed her but the hail was not understood, and supposed to be " What ship is that ? " Upon making answer, the crew of the brig was heard to cry " Viva," and as the *Juno* crossed her stern a voice from her called out distinctly, " Luff ! " The helm was at once put a-lee, but the *Juno* grounded. The boats were hoisted out to warp her off. A sudden flaw of wind drove her astern, the anchor was let go, but as she swung to it she touched again aft. While the boats and sail-trimmers were at work to get her off again, a boat came out from the shore, and running alongside, two officers and a party of seamen came on board and informed the Captain—Sir Samuel Hood—that it was the regulation of the port and the Commanding Officers' orders that the ship should go to another branch of the harbour to perform quarantine. " Where is Lord Hood's Flagship ? " asked the Captain. The reply he received aroused suspicion, and it was then discovered that the visitors were Frenchmen. All pretence was dropped. " Soyez tranquille," said the visitors, " les Anglais sont des braves gens, nous les traitons bien ; l'Amiral Anglais est parti il y a quelque temps." It was a terrible trap, but just then a puff of wind came down the harbour, and " I believe, Sir," said the 3rd Lieutenant, " we shall be able to fetch out if we can only get her under sail." Thereupon it was " every man to his station " to get sail upon the ship. The Frenchmen drew their cutlasses, but the Marines seizing the boarding pikes from their racks charged and drove the unwelcome visitors below, where they were disarmed. The cable was cut, way was got on the ship, and in spite of a heavy fire opened upon her from the batteries and forts on shore, the *Juno* succeeded in making her way out to sea without the loss of a man.

1794. CAPTURE OF MARTINIQUE AND ATTACK ON GUADELOUPE. 5th February and 11th April.

Captain T. Oldfield and Marines of the Squadron. In storming the works at St. Nicholas Mole, Oldfield was the first to enter and struck down the enemy's colours.

	Vol. Page

1794. SIR J. B. WARREN'S ACTION OFF GUERNSEY. 23rd April.

LORD HOWE'S VICTORY. "THE GLORIOUS FIRST OF JUNE." 1st June.

The accompanying engraving of this hard-fought engagement, in which, by the way, the 29th Regiment shared with the Seamen and Marines of the Fleet the honours of the day, is of interest from the original having been published in the same year. The following extracts from an account by an officer who served in the battle, and wrote immediately afterwards, give a vivid description of the scene illustrated:—"The sinking of the *Vengeur* was one of the most awful sights ever beheld. This ship and the *Brunswick* by some means got on board each other. The *Brunswick* lost her mizzen-mast before she got clear; but left her enemy a wreck of horrible ruin. She carried her masts and yards, every one, away; tore her decks and sides to pieces, and left her sinking. She went to the bottom at about a quarter-past six, and I saw her sinking, fast, but gradually. After the loss of her mizzen-mast, main-top mast, and rigging cut to pieces, the French hoisted an English Jack, and called for quarter, but the *Brunswick*, having all her boats shot to pieces, could not board the enemy, and was obliged to let her go down, and all on board perished.

The most obstinate conflict, however, was between the *Defence*, of 74 guns, Captain J. Gambier, and the *Jacobin*, of 110 guns. They were in close action for upwards of three hours, at the expiration of which time the *Jacobin* went to the bottom; and the *Defence* was become so totally unmanageable as to be obliged to be towed out of the line by the *Phaeton* frigate. The *Jacobin* lay without masts or helm, and wearing round by the force of the water, which rapidly entering shot holes, and running over her her galleries, she quickly sunk. Yet so invincible was the spirit of her crew, that they actually fought their upper-deck guns when the water was running in at the lower deck ports. It seems that they had previously agreed never to strike, and nailed their colours to the staff, which were flying when she went down. Those on the upper-deck even to a man, refused to be taken into a cutter; and when the water had gained the place they stood upon, they took off their hats and gave three cheers, universally crying out, "*Vive la Republique! Vive la Liberté!*" This is corroborated in a letter from a seaman on board the *Queen*, reproduced in "Naval Yarns," by W. H. Long. "The *Mutius Scaevola* was one of the best-fought ships belonging to the French in this action. She was engaged with the *Orion* for five hours, during one of which the men could be picked off the guns with pistols. The Captain of the *Mutius Scaevola* was a man of most undaunted courage. During the action he ran twenty of his men through their bodies for attempting to desert their quarters. He was easily distinguished by a large *bonnet rouge*, ornamented round the bottom with gold fringe. He had only one arm; but whether the other was shot off during the action, has not been ascertained."

The whole of the colours, except the white ensign, of the *Marlborough* having been shot away, she was fired into by several English ships, the French ensign having also a white fly. When this, too, went, Appleford, one of the crew, stripped off the red jacket of a Marine who had been killed, stuck it on a boarding pike, exclaiming, "The British colours shall never be dowsed where I am!" The cartridges on board the French ships were mostly made of the fine painted church music used in the cathedrals, and, of the *preuves de noblesse* of the principal families, many hundred years old, and illuminated with their genealogical trees. The Convention had decreed the application of the archives of nobility to this purpose.

1795. *BLANCHE* CAPTURES THE *PIQUE*. 5th January.

"The Marines under Lieut. Richardson keeping up so well-directed and constant a fire, that not a man could appear on the forecastle till she struck."—*Official Report*.

MARINES AT QUIBERON. 25th June.

300 Marines present.

HOTHAM'S ACTION OFF HYERES. 14th March.

BRIDPORT'S VICTORY OFF L'ORIENT. 23rd June.

CAPTURE OF THE CAPE OF GOOD HOPE. 7th August to 16th September.

On the 7th 350 Marines landed under Major Hill and took part in the battle of Muizenburg, receiving the commendation of Major-General Craig "for their steadiness and resolution" upon this occasion. The advanced guard of the 78th, supported by the Marines, drove the Dutch from their position on the heights, and on the 8th repelled a counter-attack supported by artillery. In a subsequent unsuccessful assault upon a strong position of the enemy, during which a lagoon had to be crossed, "the Marines under Major Hill displayed an equal degree of steady resolution upon the occasion" crossing the water under a heavy fire from the Dutch without returning a shot.

1796. CAPTURE OF AMBOYNA AND BANDA NIERA. 16th February and 8th March.

STORMING OF BATTERIES AT HERQUI. 17th March.   I, 277

CAPTURE OF THE ISLAND OF ST. LUCIA. 27th April.

320 Marines present. "The Conduct of the Marines upon this, as upon all other occasions, was perfectly correct."—*Official Report*.

H.M.S. *GLATTON* ENGAGES A FRENCH SQUADRON. 15th July. (*Date in p. 140 is incorrect*).   I, 140

1797. BATTLE OF CAPE ST. VINCENT. 14th August.

1 Major, 1 Lieut., 1 Sergt., and 5 Rank and File killed; 21 wounded.

BOMBARDMENT OF CADIZ. 3rd to 5th July.

THE GLORIOUS 1st OF JUNE, 1794.   From an Engraving in the "Britannic Magazine." Published immediately after the battle.

APPENDIX F.

Vol. Page

1797 ATTACK ON SANTA CRUZ. 25th July.
  2 Lieuts., 1 Sergt., 16 Privates killed; 15 Privates wounded, many drowned.
  BATTLE OF CAMPERDOWN. 11th October.   I, 142
  21 Privates killed, 2 Captains, 5 Lieuts., 1 Sergt., and 49 Privates wounded. When Admiral Winter, the Dutch Admiral, was brought on board the *Venerable*, he went to the cabin of Lieutenant G. G. Chambers of the Marines, who had just suffered amputation of both his legs. As the Admiral leaned over the wounded officer, he said, "Your wounds are heavy, Sir, and your sufferings great, but you have that within," laying his hand upon his breast, "that will enable you to sustain it." He paused a few minutes, the tears glistening in his eyes; when he mournfully said, "How happy should I be, Sir, to be as you now are, if I had been the victor, and had seen my fleet conveying the British prizes into the Texel!"

1798. DEFENCE OF THE ISLANDS OF ST. MARCOU. 7th May.   I, 212
  BATTLE OF THE NILE. 1st August.
  1 Capt., Lieut., 1 Lieut., 46 Privates killed; 3 Capts (1 mortally), 1 Lieut., 48 Privates wounded.   I, 142
  WARREN'S VICTORY OFF IRELAND. 12th to 14th October.
  Capt. R. Williams of the Marines having lowered a boat took possession of the French ship *La Hoche* with 50 officers of rank on board going to join the rebel forces in Ireland and also the notorious Wolf Tone, at whose subsequent trial in Dublin he was a principal witness. A pair of large engravings of this action were published by an Officer of Marines, who was present in H.M.S. *Canada*.
  MALTA. October.
  300 Marines served on shore during the blockade of Valetta under Major Weir who raised an efficient Regiment of Maltese. Castle of Gozo occupied by Captain J. Creswell and detachment Marines.
  REDUCTION OF MINORCA. 7th to 14th November.
  Captain Minto with Marines of H.M.S. *Centaur* and *Leviathan*.

1799. SALERNO. February.
  Marines of *Zealous* assist Neapolitans to repulse 3,000 French troops.
  DEFENCE OF ACRE. March to May.   I, 215
  CUTTING OUT OF *LA SELVA*. 6th June.   I, 143
  NAPLES. SIEGE OF FORT ST. ELMO. 11th July.
  800 Marines present under Col. Strickland.
  TAKING OF CAPUA AND GAETA. 29th July and 4th August.
  DEFENCE OF LEMMERTOWN, WEST FRIESLAND. 11th October.
  The garrison consisted of 157 Seamen and Marines. At 5 a.m. a small advance party of French and Batavians attempted to storm the North Battery. They were entrapped between two fires, surrounded by the seamen armed with pikes and surrendered. The main body of the enemy 670 strong, soon after assaulted the village but after a sharp fight of four hours and a half were driven off with a loss of 5 killed and 11 wounded. They were pursued by the Marines but escaped by destroying a bridge, during which operation the fire of the Marines cost them an additional 18 killed and 20 wounded. The Officers of Marines present were 1st Lieut. Marmaduke Wybourn and 2nd Lieuts. J. Howell, Jas. Higginson and Rd. Gardner.

1800. MALTA. 4th September.
  A Battalion of Marines occupy Valetta after its surrender on this date.
  FERROL. 25th August.
  During the abortive attack on this place by an expedition under Lieut.-General Sir James Pultney, Lieuts. Jasper Farmar and George Richards with their detachments landed and stormed a battery of 6 guns which commanded the landing place selected for the Army.

1801. EGYPT. BATTLE OF ABOUKIR. 13th March.
  The British Army, 7,000 strong, effected its disembarkation at Aboukir on the 8th March, defeating the French force opposed to it. In this engagement, Lieut. E. Bailie of the Marines was attached to the 27th Foot. The Marine detachments of about 30 ships were formed into a Battalion just over 600 strong (all ranks), and landed on the 12th March. This Battalion was attached to the 3rd Brigade under Lord Cavan, as were the 50th and 79th Regiments. It was at once paraded under a blazing sun, and after 2 or 3 hours one half-battalion was set to fill sand-bags for the batteries, while the other heavily laden with muskets and knapsacks of the working party advanced for a considerable distance through sand in which the men often sank knee-deep. Some hours later, at 7 in the evening, it was rejoined by the other half-battalion and the whole were ordered to march and join the rest of the Army, then about 15 miles distant. After the hard day's work the battalion had put in under a broiling Eastern sun it reached its destination at one in the morning of the 13th, a fine marching record for men whose service had been on ship-board up to the day before.

At 5 a.m. the troops were under arms, and the British advanced in two lines with the object of turning the French flank. To counter this the French descended from the hills on which they had been posted and attacked the leading brigades. The engagement becoming general the Marines, owing to the narrowness of the peninsula upon which the fighting was taking place, were somewhat crowded in their ranks by the battalions on their right and left, and it was at this crisis, owing to their too great eagerness to get to close quarters with the enemy, that they suffered severe loss. Both officers and men greatly distinguished themselves, and charged the French so repeatedly and with such determination and gallantry that they earned for themselves the cognomen of "The Bulldogs of the Army." The battalion was under the command of Colonel Walter Smith, and in Sir Ralph Abercrombie's Orders of the Day following, he was asked to accept the thanks of the General for himself and his battalion "for their gallant conduct in the course of the service of yesterday."

The same day the Marines marched to Aboukir, and when Aboukir Castle surrendered on the 18th after some days' bombardment, they were again thanked in orders for their assistance and detailed as its garrison. Two days later the Marines were relieved by the 92nd Regiment and joined Major-General Erye Coote's Brigade before Alexandria. This city capitulated on 2nd September, the Marines re-embarking on the 5th, on which day their Brigadier—Major-General Finch—issued the following farewell order :—

'Major-General Finch, in taking leave of Lieut.-Col. Smith and the Marines under his command, requests him to accept his warmest thanks for the order, regularity, zeal and attention that have uniformly marked their conduct during the period he had the honour of commanding the First Brigade ; and he shall be happy on all occasions, to bear testimony to their merit in the correct performance of their duty, in every respect, which has come under his observation."

H.M.S. *TRENT* AT HAVRE DE GRACE. 3rd April.   I, 234
     Bravery of Lieut. Tait of the Marines. (This officer has been thought to have been the original of Sir Walter Scott's "Captain Clutterbuck.").

OFF ALGEZIRAS. 6th July.   I, 235
     Heroism of Lieut. J. D. Williams of H.M.S. *Hannibal*.

ATTACK ON THE BOULOGNE FLOTILLA. August 15th and 16th.   I, 236

CAPTURE OF THE SPANISH SHIP *NEPTUNE* AND OTHERS AT CORUNNA. 20th August.
     Lieutenant Mark Anthony Gerrard of the Marines of H.M.S. *Fishguard* was a volunteer in this cutting out affair effected under the guns of the Corunna batteries. He was presented with a sabre and belt by his shipmates "in memory of the action with *L'Immortalite*, on 20th October, 1798, the boarding expeditions at the Saintes, Penmarcks, Quimper, Noirmoutier, St. Matthieu, St. Andero, and Corunna, in which he served as a Volunteer and bore so distinguished a part."

DEFENCE OF PORTO FERRAJO. 14th September to 25th March, 1802.
     Lieut. Lawrence and the detachment of H.M.S. *Pearl* served with the garrison. "This little force by its constancy and courage, ever set the best of examples, and its men were always foremost on service, and stood their posts and their guns when the Tuscan and other foreign troops gave way. They were most useful in preparing shells, mounting and transporting cannon and in repairing their carriages, as well as in constructing works. Their knowledge of gunnery . . . and their ambition to gain honour for their Corps and themselves induced them to live in their batteries, and the little sleep they got was alongside their cannon." Colonel Airey who commanded the British garrison having applied to Admiral Sir J. Warren for his co-operation in an attack upon some French batteries which shut up the port, 449 Marines under Captain John Richardson and a division of 240 seamen were landed just after daybreak on September 14th. They were joined by a detachment of Swiss troops and a party of Tuscans. The Maltese Corps raised and commanded by Major Weir of the Marines was also engaged on this occasion. At the beginning of the attack on the batteries on the right of the Bay, Captain Long, R.N., was killed while gallantly leading his men. "A suspension of arms was maintained while his body was borne with military honours to the grave." After this remarkable pause in hostilities, Lieutenant Campbell of the Marines instantly charged, drove the French into a narrow pass, where, his further advance was checked by the arrival of French reinforcements, and he had to fall back on the garrison. Meanwhile on the other side of the Bay several of the batteries were destroyed by the British together with a large quantity of ammunition, after which the arrival of a very superior force of the enemy compelled a retreat to the boats.

1802. MUTINY OF THE 8TH WEST INDIA REGIMENT AT DOMINICA. April.
     The "Naval Chronicle" of 1802 gives an interesting account of the gallantry of a small party of Marines in the suppression of a revolt in the West Indies, and of some special acts of personal bravery of those engaged. It says :—"A very dangerous insurrection of the 8th West India Regiment in the Island of Dominica, marked by circumstances of the most shocking barbarity, was checked in its immediate effects, in part, by English Marines. It fortunately occurred, when those murderous revolters first shewed their spirit, that H.M.S. *Magnificent* was at anchor in Prince Rupert's Bay. Some shots, from the lower Carbetta, which went over her, was the first symptom of mutiny on the shore, and it was soon confirmed by intelligence that the blacks had risen in arms, and had assassinated a number of their officers. Captain Gifford tendered his services to the president of the island who, conceiving it to be only the prelude, gladly accepted the offer. Lieut. O'Neale[1] volunteered the duty of disembarkation, and he felt it a difficult task to restrain the ardour of the whole party of Marines to follow him." "But his number was confined to 2 Sergeants, 2 Corporals, and 30 Privates, with which he put off from the ship just at dawn on the morn-

---

[1] This Officer had been promoted from Sergeant in 1798 for detecting a conspiracy of some United Irishmen on board H.M.S. *Caesar*.

APPENDIX F.

Vol. Page

ing of the 10th of April. Observing the rebels advancing rapidly to the beach, he anticipated their object, quickly effected a landing, and took post on a hill, after the exchange of some scattered shots. Opposed to nearly 500 blacks, whom he kept at bay during the day, reinforcements became necessary, and he was further strengthened by two successive detachments of Marines under Lieutenants Lambert and Hawkins. Upon this rising ground, those brave fellows, not exceeding sixty-six, gave refuge to many officers who fled from the ferocious hands of the mutineers. They were afterwards joined by some Colonial Militia, who were little calculated, from the mixed nature of their arms, to oppose a resolute enemy. The dispositions of Lieutenant Lambert through the night, aided by the counsels of Mr. O'Neale, were those of a good officer. The native troops gave way to slumber. His outposts were, therefore, confined to his faithful companions, and all his energies were derived from his own brethren. Incessant rains had nearly rendered all their ammunition useless.

On the following day the Marines were ordered to Grand Ance, in order to protect the inhabitants, and through that night were posted in the swamps to prevent the escape of the blacks from Fort Shirley. Many of our men had been 56 hours on shore amid the greatest privations, having had nothing to eat but raw salt beef and biscuit. The stagnated smell from their position pointed out the necessity of obtaining some other refreshment to recruit nature, and to avert disease. A Marine of the party, overhearing the discussion amongst his officers, nobly said, "I will go to the village and bring them—I know I must go and repass the enemy's fire, but my life is not mine, it is at the constant command of His Majesty's service." He accordingly performed this duty, and escaped unhurt. Bread was distributed and brandy administered, in scanty portions, through the night by the officers, who exhorted the men to keep up their spirits. The feelings of the brave are ever reciprocal in acts of kindness. One and all they exclaimed "We wish to add another laurel to our Corps! We will follow you wherever you go!" The mud collected by the rains had, in the course of marching, deprived many of them of their shoes, which could not be remedied but from the ship. Frequent flags of truce had passed between General Johnstone and the Fort. Mr. Roberts, an officer of Engineers, requested to storm it, if the mutineers would not surrender the barrier, provided the Marines accompanied him, who, to a man, volunteered, saying, 'We don't mind shoes, we can fight without them.'

"The Marines, united with the detachments from the Royal Scotch and 68th Regiments, marched into the Fort upon the 13th, and drew up in front of the Black Corps, which presented arms to the troops, having three of their own officers as prisoners placed between their colours. General Johnstone was obeyed by them in his orders to 'Shoulder,' 'Order' and 'Ground' their arms; but on being ordered to step three paces in front the cry was 'No.' They instantly resumed them, and fired a volley; this was returned, and was followed up with a charge of bayonets, which broke their ranks, and dispersed the mutineers in every direction. The greater part fled up the outer Cabaret, keeping up a fire until they reached the rocks, down which many precipitated themselves; and those who could afterwards crawl from the bottom were exposed to a discharge of grape and canister from the *Magnificent*.

"John Budd, private Marine, distinguished himself most signally during the pursuit. He was attacked singly by four black grenadiers, one of whom he killed with his first fire, wounded another while coolly awaiting a return from the other two, reloaded his musket, with which he shot a third, and bayoneted the fourth; afterwards turning to him who was wounded, he closed his destinies, and, throwing the remains of the whole of them over the rocks, finished his exploit by saying, 'This is the way I shall serve all traitors.'"

1803. LIEUTENANT NICHOLS, R.M., CUTS OUT THE *ALBION*. 5th November.   I, 238

BOATS OF *BLENHEIM* AT MARTINIQUE. 16th November.
    Lieut. G. Beatty and 60 Marines storm Fort Dunkirk protecting the harbour of Marin, while the seamen cut out *L'Harmonie*, French privateer.

STORMING OF A BATTERY AT PETITE ANCE D'ARLETTE, MARTINIQUE. 26th November.
    Captain Acheson Crozier, Lieut. W. Walker and Marines of H.M.S. *Centaur*, carried 9-gun battery of 24-pounders. Lieut. Walker received a sword of honour and £100 from the Patriotic Fund.

1804. ATTACK ON CURACAO. 3rd January to 25th March.
    Lieut. Nicholls and 199 Marines belonging to H.M.S. *Hercule, Blanche, Pique* and *Gipsy* present. Fort Piscadoro was stormed and French troops driven under the guns of Fort Republique by the Seamen and Marines of these ships.

CUTTING OUT OF *LA CONCEPTION*. 27th May.   I, 248

CAPTURE OF THREE SPANISH TREASURE SHIPS OFF CADIZ. 5th October.
    The Captain, Officers and Crew of H.M.S. *Lively*, one of the ships engaged in the capture, subscribed £50 for Thomas Tough, a Marine who lost his arm in the engagement in testimony of their admiration of his "brave and meritorious conduct in the action."

1805. OFF FINISTERRE. SIR ROBERT CALDER'S ACTION. 22nd July.

PHOENIX and *DIDON*. 10th August.   I, 239

BATTLE OF TRAFALGAR. 21st October.   I, 250
    3,600 Marines present.

SIR RICHARD STRACHAN'S VICTORY IN THE BAY OF BISCAY. 4th November.

1806. CAPTURE OF THE CAPE OF GOOD HOPE. 7th January.
    Capt. A. McKenzie and 400 Marines present.

	Vol. Page
1806. SIR ROBERT DUCKWORTH'S ACTION OFF ST. DOMINGO. 6th February.	

    TAKING OF CAPRI. 12th May.   I, 277

    H.M.S. *POMPÉE* CAPTURES CONVOY AT SEALIA. 23rd May.   I, 278

    TAKING OF BUENOS AYRES. 27th June.
        Major Alezr. McKenzie and 340 Marines present.

    BOATS OF H.M.S. *MELPOMONE* TAKE A FRENCH SETEE. 4th July. ("April," p. 241, is incorrect).   I, 241

1807. CAPTURE OF CURACOA. 1st January.
    The Royal Marines of H.M.S. *Arethusa* land and storm Fort Amsterdam.

    STORMING OF MONTE VIDEO. 3rd February.
        800 Royal Marines present.

    FORCING OF THE DARDANELLES AND TAKING OF FORT PESQUIES. February.
        During the fighting with the Turkish Fleet on this occasion Fort Pesquies, on the point of that name, mounting 31 guns, fired heavily on the British squadron, and continued its fire after the Turkish ships had been run ashore or captured. The beach too, was crowded with armed men, and the *Pompée* having fired a few shells to disperse them, her Marines loaded and brought off a Green Standard. Lieutenant Nichols of the Marines brought off the flag of the Capitan Pasha from the 40 gun frigate on which it flew and which he set on fire in accordance with his orders. He then entered Fort Pesquies, spiked the guns and set the gabions in a blaze.

    H.M.S. *HYDRA* ATTACKS BEGUR, CATALONIA. 7th August.   I, 278

    BOMBARDMENT OF COPENHAGEN. August and September.
        Royal Marines landed 5th September.

1808. OCCUPATION OF MARIE GALANTE. 3rd March.
    400 Royal Marines left as garrison under Capt. Chas. Tyldesley. Heavy mortality from disease, the Barracks being in a swamp.

    DESTRUCTION OF BATTERIES AND SMALL CRAFT AT VIVERO. 13th March.
        Detachment Royal Marines of H.M.S. *Emerald*, under Lieuts. G. Meech and J. Husband. The latter received a Sword of Honour from the Patriotic Fund.

    H.M.S. *MELPOMONE* AND DANISH GUNBOATS. 23rd May.   I, 243

    RAIDS ON THE FRENCH AND SPANISH COAST. 24th July and later dates.
        Lieut. J. Ryves Hore performed an extraordinary series of raids on the French and Spanish coasts during this summer. Landing from H.M.S. *Imperieuse*—a 38-gun frigate commanded by Lord Cochrane—he took part in the destruction of many coastal batteries and roads near Barcelona in order to hamper the movements of the French Army in Catalonia. On 31st July he and his detachment seized and occupied the Castle of Mongal which completely commanded a pass on the road from Barcelona to Gerona, then besieged by the French. To preserve the Frenchmen he found in the Castle from the fury of the Spaniards, Hore had to escort his prisoners to the point of embarkation, after having blown up the Castle in such a way as to completely block the road. During the latter part of August he was constantly engaged in raiding the enemy's posts "with varying opposition, but with unvaried success," says an official letter of 28th September, "the newly constructed semaphoric telegraphs which are of the utmost consequence to the safety of the numerous convoys that pass along the coast of France at Bourdique, La Pinede, St. Maguire, Frontignan, Canet and Fay have been blown up and completely demolished, together with their telegraph houses, fourteen barracks of gens-d'armes, one battery and the strong tower on the Lake of Frontignan." These operations had the effect of drawing off about 2,000 French troops from the important fortress of Figueras to defend their coastal communications.

    FIGUERAS. July.
        A strong detachment of Royal Marines under Captain G. Lewis was landed at this place in July to secure the landing place for the British Army under Sir Arthur Wellesley. The Portuguese flag was hoisted which hundreds flocked to enroll beneath and the post was held till the arrival of General Anstruther's Brigade on the 19th August.

    ATTACK ON CONVOY AT NOLI. 1st August.   I, 279

    H.M.S. *AMETHYST* CAPTURES *THETIS*. 10th November.   I, 242

    DEFENCE OF FORT TRINIDAD-ROSAS. 15th November to 5th December.   I, 220

1809. TAKING OF CAYENNE. 7th to 14th January.
    Lieut. J. Read mortally wounded in leading the assault on Port Dimant.

    FIGHT BETWEEN H.M.S. *PROSERPINE* AND TWO FRENCH FRIGATES OFF TOULON. 28th February.
        Heroism of a Private of Marines.   I, 246

    CORUNNA. 17th and 18th January.
        Detachment Royal Marines of H.M.S. *Resolution* landed to destroy the batteries commanding the harbour. Officers and Men received the thanks of both Houses of Parliament for this service, but did not get the Army Medal and Clasp.

APPENDIX F.

	Vol. Page
1809. ATTACK ON THE FRENCH FLOTILLA IN THE BASQUE ROADS. 13th April.	I, 245
CAPTURE OF THE ISLAND OF ANHOLT. 18th May.	I, 226

Lieut. E. Nichols and 120 Royal Marines.

VIGO. 7th June.
"The Forts at Vigo were occupied by 60 stragglers from Sir John Moore's army, aided by some seamen and Royal Marines" (Napier). This day the Marines of H.M.S. *Lively* garrisoned the Castle of Vigo.

CAPTURE OF RUSSIAN BATTERIES AT HANGO. 19th June.

CAPTURE OF FORT LOUIS, SENEGAL. 8th to 13th July.
Lieut. Lewis B. Reeves, Royal Marines, and 50 Privates took part in the little expedition despatched from the garrison of Goree under Major Maxwell The little force—only 210 strong in all—was being badly pressed after landing, when the enemy's attack was broken by a bayonet charge delivered by the Marines, and on the 13th Fort Louis capitulated with its garrison of 400 men. The Marines were left to occupy the fort for 7 months, during which time nearly half of them succumbed to the climate.

CAPTURE OF A FORT AT BREMERLE, CUXHAVEN. 27th July.
A detachment of Royal Marines under Lieut. John Benson, R.M., was landed at Ritzbuttle to cover the destruction of the Fort and its guns, and to intercept the advance of any French troops. The Marines advanced as far as Bremerdike and Gersendoz, a distance of 28 miles.

BOMBARDMENT OF FLUSHING. 13th August. I, 245

OCCUPATION OF FORT VEER, WALCHEREN. 30th August.
Captain F. Liardet and 700 Royal Marines.

REDUCTION OF THE ISLE OF BOURBON. 21st September.
Lieut. Cottal, 6 officers and 130 Royal Marines landed near Point du Galet, together with 100 seamen, 200 of the 56th Regiment and 168 Bombay Sappers. The objective of this force was to destroy the batteries protecting the harbour of St. Paul and to take out the shipping. Five batteries were surprised and destroyed and a quantity of shipping, including two men-of-war, captured or destroyed.

STORMING OF RAS-EL-KHYMA. 13th November.
The detachments Royal Marines of H.M.S. *La Chiffone* and *Caroline* were landed under Colonel Smith in command of troops to attack the pirate stronghold of Ras-el-Khyma in the Persian Gulf. After a short bombardment a landing was effected on the south side of the town which was burnt and the enemy driven out. Lieut. T. Drury commanded the Marines. Three Marines obtained booty amounting to 4,500 gold Mohurs (£7,650).

1810. BESIGLIO. 18th January.
Castle stormed and held while ships were cut out. "The Royal Marines were led on with their usual gallantry by Lieut. Moore whom I have had frequent occasion to mention for his bravery and conduct." (*Official Report*).

STORMING OF BATTERIES AT BAIE MAHUT, GUADELOUPE. 21st January.
Lieut. Shillibeer and 30 Royal Marines served in a boat expedition which was sent in at dusk to cut out a brig protected by two batteries. She was boarded and taken under a heavy fire. The Marines and Seamen then waded ashore, the water reaching to their waists. On landing they at once dashed forward and drove the enemy from the nearest battery, and closing with the bayonet the Marines compelled them to abandon a position they had taken up in rear of a brick breastwork. Having thrown a 24-pounder over the cliff and buried 6 howitzers in the sand, the party renewed their advance and stormed a second battery of three 24-pounders protected by a ditch all round. After destroying the guard-house and spiking the guns, two vessels were burnt and the brig brought out. "The gallant manner in which Lieutenant Shillibeer led the Royal Marines to the charge, as well as their steady discipline in keeping possession of the heights while the Seamen were destroying the batteries," were specially mentioned in the Official Report. On February 6th, Vieux Fort, Guadeloupe, was stormed by the Royal Marines under Captain C. Abbott.

DEFENCE OF THE FORT OF MATAGORDA, NEAR CADIZ. 27th January to 22nd March.
This small Fort, not more than a hundred yards square, with no ditch and no bomb-proofs, was held for nearly two months by a little garrison of 25 Royal Marines, 25 Seamen (from H.M.S. *Invincible*), 25 Royal Artillerymen and 67 N.C.O.'s and Privates of the 94th Regiment under Captain MacLean.[1] The Fort was close to the French lines at the Trocadero. "A Spanish 74 and a Flotilla had co-operated in the resistance till daybreak on the 21st of March, but then a hissing shower of heated shot made them cut their cables and run under the walls of Cadiz, while the fire of 48 guns and mortars of the largest size was turned on the Fort, whose feeble parapet vanished before that crashing flight of metal, leaving only the naked rampart and undaunted hearts of the garrison for defence. The men fell fast and the enemy shot so quick and close, that a staff bearing the Spanish flag was broken six times in an hour; the colours were then fastened to the angle of the work itself, but unwillingly by the men, especially the sailors, all calling out to hoist the British ensign and attributing the slaughter to their fighting under a foreign flag! Thirty hours this tempest lasted, and 64 men out of 140 had fallen, when Graham (the General in command in Cadiz) finding a diversion he had projected impracticable, sent boats to carry off the survivors."—*Napier's Peninsular War.*

---

1 Spelt "Maclaine" in some accounts. He belonged to the 94th Regiment—not the 78th as stated by Sergt. Rees below.

1810.   Sergeant Thomas Rees, of the Plymouth Division Royal Marines, in his *Journal of Voyages and Travels* (published posthumously in 1822) gives the following account of this heroic defence. He was then serving on board H.M.S. *Temeraire*, off Cadiz:—

"On the 17th of April,[1] several sailors and Marines were ordered to Fort Matagorda, the only one which was left on that side of Spain. The command was given to Captain MacLean, of the 78th Regiment. There were in it 9 guns and 80 men, which were so divided, that half engaged for two hours at a time, and were then relieved by the others. In this way we went on till nearly all our powder and shot were expended, and we had nothing to make signal with; for the staff had been shot through five times in one day. But the Captain sent a boat off to Cadiz for some shot, when the Spaniards returned for answer, that they did not choose to supply us with any more; for as the French had got so much of the country, they might as well have that also. And oh! what a passion on hearing this did Captain MacLean get into! throwing his hat on the ground, and stamping on it for very madness, to think that they had been day and night fighting for them, and this was all the thanks we got for it.

This little Fort was of great importance, for it commanded the whole harbour; and although we lost several men, yet they were immediately replaced, and the wounded also removed, by means of boats, which was easily done, the Fort being erected on the very edge of the water. The enemy could not have held out much longer. We must have got the better had we not been so basely refused a supply by the Spaniards. It was a great vexation to us to be obliged to abandon it, which we did in the afternoon of the 5th of July; and we then had the mortification to behold the French march into it. Before we left it we had taken care to spike the guns and break the carriages; yet notwithstanding this, the enemy found means, on the following morning, to fire red-hot shot and shells; so that the ships were obliged to cut their cables and lie further out. But their fire set fire to the *San Paulo*, a Spanish ship of 80 guns, and we went on board to help to extinguish it, which was more than they deserved; for if they had only sent us the supply we wanted, nothing of this would have happened. Another consequence was, as we knew it would be, that our boats could not go to water without the danger of being sunk, or the men killed; for although Cadiz is so fine a city, it is destitute of springs of water."

The Royal Marines in Matagorda were under Lieut. Kenyon Stevens Parker, and lost 2 killed and 10 wounded.

AMBOYNA CAPTURED. 17th February.
Royal Marines of H.M.S. *Cornwallis*, *Dover*, and *Samarang* formed part of the small force of 401 seamen, Marines, Artillery and detachment of the Madras European Regiment which effected this capture against formidable fortifications manned by very superior numbers.

ATTACK ON SANTA MAURA. 22nd March.
The troops landed for the attack of this place had to advance over a narrow isthmus defended by two redoubts behind which was an entrenchment, mounting 4 guns, and having a wet ditch and an abbatis in front which extended to the sea on either side. It was manned by 500 troops. The British force consisted of 240 Royal Marines from H.M.S. *Montague*, *Magnificent* and *Belle Poule* under the command of Captain Snowe—who formed the centre of the attacking line—160 men of De Rolls' Regiment placed on the right, 216 men of the Calabrian Free Corps on the left, with 100 men of the same corps in reserve in rear of each flank. Brigadier-General Oswald of the Calabrian Corps was the senior officer present. The line advanced on the redoubts covered by the fire of the *Leonidas* frigate, and carried them at the point of the bayonet, after which it advanced "left in front" on the entrenchments. At the first discharge from these the Calabrians threw themselves down and could not be got to advance in spite of every effort to rally them, and "the indignant treatment they received from the Marines," says Nicholas. The latter, cheering, marched over their bodies, scrambled through the abbatis and drove the enemy out of their entrenchments at the bayonet's point, pursuing them until recalled to garrison the redoubts previously captured. Brigadier General Oswald the next day issued an order in which he referred to the "great gallantry displayed" by the stormers and stated that "the intrepid manner in which the Royal Marines performed that service claims the highest admiration." Siege was then laid to the citadel which, after an outwork had been taken, capitulated. The Marines lost 6 men killed, Captain Snowe and 16 men severely and Lieutenant Morrison and 5 men slightly wounded.

CONVOY CUT OUT AT GROA. 29th June.   I, 280
CAPTURE OF ISLE DE LA PASSE. 13th August.
Marines of *Nereide*, *Sirius* and *Staunch*.

THREE BRIGS CUT OUT AT POINT DU CHÉ. 27th September.
The boats of H.M.S. *Caledonia* and *Valliant* were sent to destroy three French brigs lying under the protection of a battery at Point du Ché near La Rochelle. Five officers and 130 men of the Royal Marines were landed at half-past two in the morning in order to capture the battery. As the boats pulled in to attack the brigs they were discovered and fire opened upon them. "Lieutenant Little of the Royal Marine Artillery," says the Official despatch, "immediately on landing pushed forward with the bayonet to the assault, supported by Captain McLachlan's division, with Lieutenant Coulter, both of the Royal Marines, and Lieutenant Couche with a separate detachment, and succeeded in carrying the battery and spiking all the guns. Lieutenant Little, in a personal encounter with one of the enemy, when in the act of wrestling his musket from him, received the contents in his hand, which was so much shattered in consequence as to render amputation necessary." After the capture of the redoubt a French force advanced

---

[1] It will be observed that Sergt. Rees' dates are quite wrong, but his story is not less interesting on that account.

APPENDIX F.

from the village, but was checked by the fire of the Marines and one of the boats. They then brought up two field-pieces to take the Marines in flank, but they instantly charged them with the bayonet, and captured the guns. Meanwhile the boats carried out the destruction of the brigs, and the detachment of Marines was re-embarked in perfect order. Lieutenant Little received a reward from the Patriotic Fund, a pension for wounds of £70 a year and an appointment at the Woolwich Division.

CAPTURE OF MAURITIUS. 3rd December.

A Battalion of Royal Marines from the men-of-war present served with the Army under Major-General Hon. John Abercromby, who reported that "The Battalion of the Royal Marines, under the command of Captain Liardet, supported the reputation of this distinguished Corps."

DESTRUCTION OF ARMED AND OTHER VESSELS AT PALAMOS. 13th December.

The Marines of the *Kent, Ajax* and *Cambrian*, 250 in number, were landed and having occupied the enemy's batteries without much resistance, the seamen brought out most of the shipping. But in retiring through the town to re-embark they were attacked and lost 12 killed, 22 wounded, and 43 missing.

SPAIN AND PORTUGAL.   I, 289

In addition to the services of the Royal Marine Battalions already mentioned; it should be said that the 3rd or innermost line of the series of defences famous as the Lines of Torres Vedras was occupied by the Royal Marines. This interior line extended from Passo d'Arcos, on the Tagus, to the Tower of Junquerra on the coast; and within it, near Fort St. Julian, was an entrenched camp occupied by the Royal Marines. In the Autumn of this year, at the suggestion of the Duke of Wellington, Admiral Berkeley in command of the British squadron in the Tagus, formed a Naval Brigade of 500 Royal Marines, and the same number of seamen. Captain Lawford, R.N., of the *Impetueux* was in command. There were nine Captains of Marines in the Brigade and as many subalterns as could be spared, "leaving only one to each Ship of the Line." There was also, of course, a proportion of Naval Officers. The Brigade seems to have marched up the left bank of the Tagus, on which there was an armed British flotilla, to Almeirim, a place nearly opposite to Santarem where Marshal Massena was building and assembling boats with which to cross the river, probably with a view of outflanking the Lines of Torres Vedras. The right of the first line rested on the Tagus at Alhandra, some miles further down. Attempts were made to destroy some of Massena's boats which were drawn up on the beach by gun-fire, but with little result. Captain Ross, R.M., seems to have been the senior Officer of Marines in the Brigade. Meanwhile, a Battalion of Marines—referred to by Napier "as a superb body of Marines"—had been despatched from England, and upon its arrival the seamen were recalled to their ships as "their Lordships cannot approve of the landing the seamen of the Fleet." It was this Battalion that held the third of the Torres Vedras Lines, as mentioned above. Lieut. Ashmore, Royal Marines, who was on picquet near Santarem, on the night of Massena's retreat from the Lines of Torres Vedras, was the first to report the enemy's movement.

1811. CUTTING OUT OF VESSELS AT ORTONA. 12th February.   I, 281

BATTLE OF BAROSSA AND THE NEXT DAY'S OPERATIONS. 5th and 6th March.

The Royal Marines co-operated in the Battle of Barossa on the 5th March by storming the enemy's batteries at the mouth of the Guadelete; they were brigaded with two Spanish Regiments and ordered to destroy the batteries, which they did, but the French coming down in force they were obliged to re-embark under heavy fire. A detachment under Captain G. Nicholson 300 strong was sent to destroy a battery at Rota, which they blew up after spiking the guns. On 6th March parties of Royal Marines and Seamen were landed between Rota and Catalina. A 4-gun redoubt near Santa Maria was stormed by a detachment under Capt. P. Fottrell, Royal Marines, and with the exception of the Fort at Catalina which was too strong to be attempted by a coup-de-main, all the coast defences between Santa Maria and Rota were dismantled and their guns spiked.

HOSTE'S VICTORY OFF LISSA. 13th March.

DEFENCE OF ANHOLT. 27th March.   I, 226

It may be remarked that in the account of Captain J. W. Maurice, R.N., who commanded at Anholt, in O'Byrne's Naval Biography, the Royal Marines are not even mentioned as forming the garrison, while it says that "*he* rendered his name for ever famous by the brilliant manner in which he defeated an attempt made to reduce it (Anholt) by a Danish flotilla and army, etc., etc."

CUTTING OUT OF 26 VESSELS AT PORTO DEL INFRESCHI. 21st July.   I, 282

CUTTING OUT OF 28 VESSELS AT RAGOSNIZA, DALMATIA. 27th July.

CONQUEST OF JAVA. August and September.

A Battalion of Royal Marines under the command of Brevet-Major F. Liardet was landed to reinforce the Army under Sir Samuel Achmuty. Batavia having been occupied without resistance, the British advanced against the Dutch Army which was entrenched at Meester Cornelis, about 9 miles from the city. After some days fighting an assault was ordered under the command of General Gillespie. The men detailed for this were 250 of the Royal Marine Battalion, the Grenadiers of the 78th and two companies of the 89th Regiment. The troops moved forward at midnight on the 25th August, and after a desperate struggle, in which the Royal Marines bore a most distinguished part, carried all before them. 257 officers including 3 Generals and 5,000 men were made prisoners and more than 1,000 were found dead in the works. After the battle Sir Samuel Achmuty thus addressed the battalion: "I have halted you to express my high opinion of the zeal and gallantry displayed by the Royal Marines, who were attached to the advance under General Gillespie in the action of the 25th. I cannot sufficiently express my gratitude for their exemplary good conduct. I beg you therefore to accept my warmest thanks, and to communicate the same to the officers and men under your command." On 31st August an expedition was sent to Cheribon to intercept the retreat of the Dutch General Jansens from Meester Cornelis. As it would have taken too long to embark troops for this purpose, the *Nisus, President, Phoebe* and *Hesper* were sent round and landed their Marines together with the detachment belonging to H.M.S. *Lion*, amounting to 180 men in all, who were under the command of Captain Welchman, Royal Marines. The Fort at Cheribon surrendered and was occupied by Captain Welchman and his Marines, but on the news arriving of the approach of 350 of the enemy's Infantry and the same number of Cavalry from Buitzenburg, the Marine garrison was relieved by a detachment of seamen in order that it might be free to assume the offensive.

The Marines and fifty seamen were therefore mounted on horseback, and under the command of Captain Welchman, Royal Marines, were pushed forward by forced marches to attack a Fort at Carang Sambang, about 35 miles off in the interior of the island. This small advanced force was supported by a body of troops under the command of Colonel Wood. Captain Welchman captured 22 chests of money at Bongas, about half-way to Carang Sambang, which were sent back by Colonel Wood, and pushing on met a Dutch Officer with a flag of truce proposing the surrender of Carang Sambang. A great quantity of stores was taken at this place including coffee to the value of 250,000 Spanish dollars, as well as a large number of prisoners. The Marines were now re-embarked and the *Nisus* and *Phoebe*, moving along the coast, landed them successively at Panca and Taggal, both of which places were taken. Samarang, Gressie, and Sourabaya were occupied shortly afterwards, the main body of the Marines being under the command of Captain Bunce who had become senior officer present by the death of Major Liardet from dysentery. Lieutenant White, Royal Marines, of the *Minden* who, with his detachment and a party of the 14th Regiment had been landed to keep open communications with Pangorah and to procure supplies for the squadron, was sharply attacked by a considerable body of the enemy with two guns. After 15 minutes' fighting they were driven off, but just as reinforcements were arriving from the 14th and 89th Regiments they renewed the attack in greater force. They were again defeated with some loss. Captain E. W. Hoare, R.N., of the *Minden*, in making his official report of this affair wrote : " I feel it my duty to report the conduct of Captain Robert White of the Royal Marines, who commanded at the first attack, assisted by two officers of the 14th Regiment. I was astonished at the bravery and coolness displayed by those officers and their men." The reduction of the neighbouring island of Madura was effected by the seamen and Marines of H.M.S. *Drake* and *Phaeton*, although the native troops had been strengthened by the landing of a French force. Effecting a landing under cover of the darkness, the small British force advanced on the Fort of Samanap, the capital of the island, in two columns, each consisting of 60 bayonets (presumably Marines) and 20 pikemen. The Marine detachment of the *Hussar* acted as a reserve. The fort was taken by a sudden rush just before daybreak. A spirited battle with a very superior force followed as soon as it was light in which the resolution and superior tactics of the British secured them the victory. Lieutenant Roch, Royal Marines, was twice speared by the native pikemen while wresting the colours from a French officer, whom he slew in the contest. The conquest of Java was now complete and the captors were rewarded by the distribution of prize money to the value of the property taken which amounted to no less than a million sterling.

		Vol.	Page
1812.	STORMING OF A BATTERY AT ISLE VERTE, NEAR CIOTAT. 1st June. Marines of the *Furieuse* and *Menelaus*.		
	CAPTURE OF FORT LEQUERTIO AND DESTRUCTION OF BATTERIES ON THE NORTH COAST OF SPAIN. June to October.	I,	290
	ACTION AT LUNGUILLIA AND ALLASSIO. 27th June.	I,	283
	OPERATIONS AT CADIZ. 28th August. Heroism of gunner John Collard.	I,	247
	ATTACK ON MITTAU, RIGA. 29th September. Royal Marines of H.M.S. *Aboukir* and *Ranger*.		
1813.	CAPTURE OF THE ISLAND OF AGUSTA. 3rd February. Marines and Seamen of the *Apollo*, 35th Regiment, and Artillery.		
	FRENCH TOWN, CHESAPEAKE TAKEN. 28th April. Captains Wyburn and Carter with 150 Royal Marines.		
	MORGION. 2nd May. Captain Ennis and party of Royal Marines from H.M.S. *Undaunted* and *Volontaire* blow up battery and capture six laden vessels.		
	THE FIGHT BETWEEN THE *SHANNON* AND *CHESAPEAKE*. 1st June.		
	FORT SAN FELIPPE DE BALAGUER. 3rd to 8th June.		

A small but important fort garrisoned by 100 men situated upon an isolated rock in the very gorge of a pass and blocking the only carriage way between Tortoza and Tarragona. Five men-of-war and two battalions were detailed for its attack. Guns and mortars were landed from the ships and with great difficulty placed in position on the mountain sides. Earth for the batteries had to be brought up from below and water was only obtainable from the ships, the landing place being a mile and a half distant from the scene of operations. The surrender of the fortress was due to the fire of a couple of 8-inch mortars worked

APPENDIX F.

                                                                                                           Vol. Page

by Lieut. H. James, R.M.A., which exploded a magazine. He and his party belonged to the *Stromboli* bomb-vessel. After capture a garrison of Royal Marines under Captain E. Baillie was placed in San Felippe.

BATTLE OF HAMPTON.   25th June.   I, 291

FIUME.   3rd July.

    The detachment Royal Marines of H.M.S. *Milford* took and spiked the guns of a battery, took possession of a fort and hoisted the British colours. On advancing through the town they were much annoyed by the fire of a field piece and by musketry from the windows, but headed by 2nd Lieuts. S. Lloyd and E. Nepean they pushed the French troops—about 350 strong—before them till they came to a square. Here the enemy made a stand but were dispersed by the fire of the carronades in the ships' boats. Nine guns were captured, 90 vessels taken or destroyed, 59 guns disabled and two magazines burnt.

BORDIGHERO.   19th July.   I, 283

ROVIGNO.   2nd August.

    The Royal Marines of H.M.S. *Eagle* and *Bacchante* under Lieuts. C. Holmes, W. Haig and S. Lloyd took part in the capture of 14 merchantmen and 10 gunboats lying in this harbour protected by 100 troops and 2 field guns. The Royal Marines charged the guns with the bayonet and captured and destroyed them.

STORMING OF CASSIS.   18th August.   I, 284

PORT D'ANGO.   5th October.

    Convoy destroyed. Royal Marines storm battery.

MARINELLO (near Civita Vecchia).   14th October.

    Boats of *Furieuse* cut out convoy, Royal Marines storm battery.

BATTLE OF LEIPZIG.   16th, 17th and 18th October.

    Detachment Royal Marine Artillery.   I, 265

TRIESTE.   5th to 29th October.

    Detachment Royal Marines with 2 guns.

STORMING OF BATTERIES AT PORT NOUVELLE.   9th November.   I, 285

THE HAGUE.   29th November.

    " On the 28th November, four English men-of-war appeared off Scheveningen, Captain Baker immediately landed from the *Cumberland* and proceeded to the Hague. . . . . In order to dispel the general anxiety he ordered as many Marines to be landed from the *Cumberland* and *Princess Caroline* as could be spared without endangering the safety of those vessels. Accordingly on the following day (29th) 200 Marines were disembarked. The people were overjoyed at their arrival; the women embraced them as their deliverers; the men welcomed them with eagerness and delight, and contested for the satisfaction of having an Englishman billeted at their house."—*A Narrative of the late Revolution in Holland.* G. W. Chad, 1814.

LEGHORN.   11th to 15th December.   I, 286

1814. OPERATIONS IN SOUTH BEVELAND.   4th January.   I, 297

      LERICI (near Spezzia).   25th March.

        Royal Marines of H.M.S. *Edinburgh* and *Swallow* land capture the castle.

      COLE MILL, CANANDA.   13th March.   I, 294

      GENOA.   13th to 17th April.

        Co-operating with the Anglo-Italian Army in its attack on this place, the Royal Marines of the British Squadron were, on the morning of 17th April, embarked in boats " ready to land if occasion required." While the troops were engaged with the enemy, the guns of the British flotilla kept up such a tremendous fire that the French gunners were driven from their guns in the shore batteries. This enabled the Royal Marines and Seamen to storm them with but little loss, and to turn their guns against the town.

      OSWEGO.   5th May.   I, 295

      LEONARD'S TOWN.   18th July.   I, 298

      YOCOMICO.   3rd August.   I, 299

      CAEN RIVER.   7th August.   I, 299

      BATTLE OF BLADENSBURG.   24th August.   I, 300

      HAMPDEN.   3rd September.

        Stormed by Seamen and Royal Marines. U.S.S. *Adams* burnt and vessels destroyed at Bangor.

      FIGHT BEFORE BALTIMORE.   12th September.   I, 300

      CAPTURE OF AMERICAN FLOTILLA ON LAKE BORGNE.   13th and 14th December.

        Lieut. J. Uniacke, Royal Marines, was wounded and specially distinguished himself upon this occasion. He was mentioned in despatches, received a reward from the Patriotic Fund and a Pension of £70 a year for wounds.

332 BRITAIN'S SEA-SOLDIERS

Vol. Page

1815. BATTLE OF NEW ORLEANS. 8th January.   I, 306

CAPTURE OF POINT A PITRE. 12th January.   I, 301

NAPLES. 21st May.
Royal Marines landed 500 strong to occupy Forts St. Elmo and d'Uovo on its surrender by the French.

MARSEILLES. 14th July.
500 Royal Marines landed under Brevet-Major H. Cox co-operated with the Army under Sir Hudson Lowe in the occupation of the city.

FRENCH CONVOY CUT OUT AT CORIGEOU. 18th to 19th July.
On the 15th July, the frigates *Rhin*, *Menelaus* and *Havannah*, with the *Fly* and *Ferret* brigs, and the schooner *Sealark* chased a French convoy into the Bay of Corigeou about eighteen miles from Brest. The boats left the squadron at 10 p.m. on the 18th, and "came to a grapnel under a range of rocks about a quarter of a mile from the shore." Here they lay till the moon went down, finally effecting a landing, undiscovered, at 2·45 a.m. on the 19th. The Marines of the *Menelaus*, 45 Rank and File, formed the advanced guard under Lieut. A. Burton, R.M., the main body consisting of 120 Marines under Lieutenants Bunce and Hurdle, and 80 seamen, was commanded by Captain Malcolm, R.N., of the *Rhin*. Having stormed the two batteries which protected the anchorage, the brigs were able to enter and bring out the convoy.

This little affair is of some interest as being the last of the numerous cutting-out expeditions in which the Marines played such an important part during the long war with France, and also because it is the only one of which I have been able to obtain a plan of the operations made by an officer of the Corps who was present.

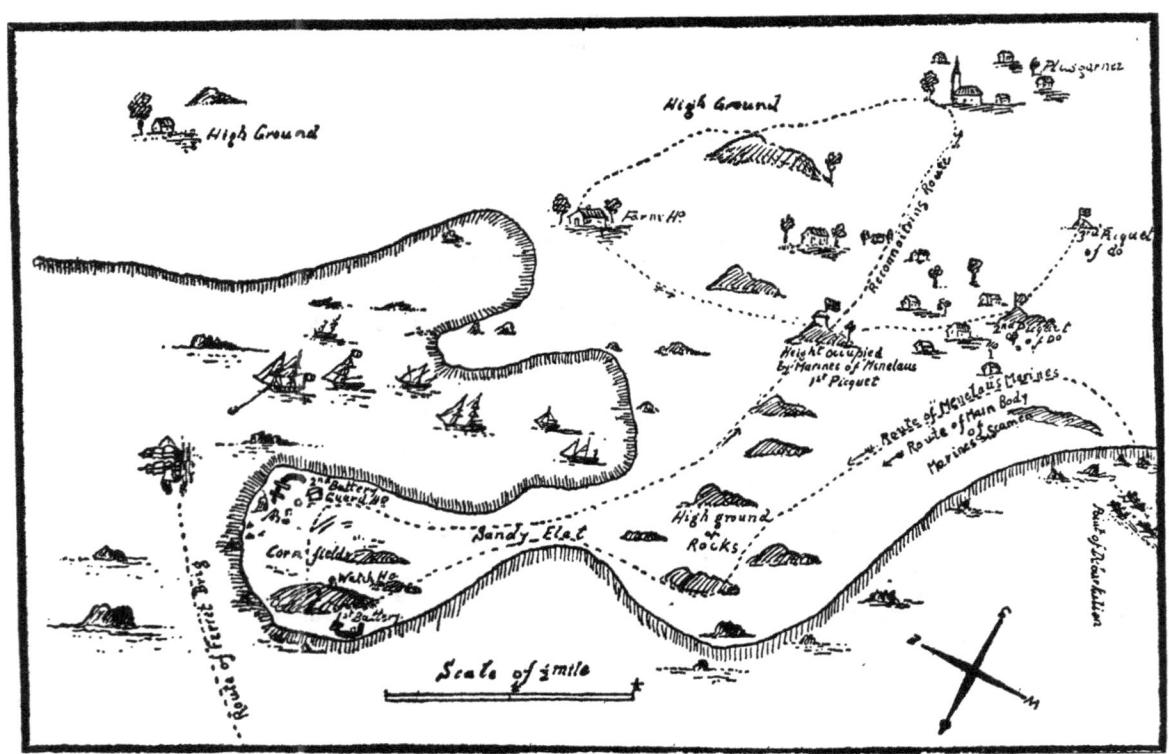

Plan made by Lieut. A. Burton, R.M., of the Cutting Out Operations at Corigeou.

1816. BOMBARDMENT OF ALGIERS. 27th August.   II, 12
The following is from the MS. Journal of General F. W. Whinyates, R.E., published in the R.E. Journal of 1st February, 1881 :—" On the 9th August, arrived at Gibraltar, after 13 days passage. Whilst at Gibraltar the Marines of the Fleet, about 100, were formed into two Battalions, to be commanded by Majors Vallack and Collins of the Royal Marines. It was intended that the Company of Royal Sappers and Miners should land with them at Algiers, and each Sapper and Miner was to carry two hand-grenades and a piece of slow-match in his haversack, besides his musket and ammunition.

APPENDIX F.

Vol. Page

1816. The Marines were to land without any encumbrances, with 60 rounds of ammunition, and a proportion of small rockets was to be distributed among them for throwing into the casemates, and four steady men from each Division were to be selected to carry rockets and storming poles. It was intended to have stormed the Mole opposite the *Queen Charlotte*, but it was the difficulty of communicating with her and getting the Sappers and Miners off again, that prevented Lord Exmouth's ordering it."

1820. STORMING OF FORTS AT MOCHA. 4th to 20th December.
Royal Marines and Seamen of H.M.S. *Topaze*.

1824. ISLE OF PINES. March and April.
Destruction and capture of a gang of pirates who made this island their headquarters and had murdered a lieutenant and some men belonging to a British man-of-war. Lieut. Beadon, Royal Marines, was on this island about two months, performing most arduous duty, marching from 5 to 10 miles daily through the jungle in search of the pirates. Eventually with 15 Royal Marines he ran them to earth, dispersed and captured the survivors who were executed at Jamaica. On the first 3 days only about 70 seamen with their officers assisted in the search.

ASHANTEE. May and June.
Seamen and Marines from the Squadron assisted in the defence of Cape Coast Castle. Lieut. W. O. Aitcheson, R.M.A., was killed here after greatly distinguishing himself and doing great service with a 6-pounder gun.

1824-6. OPERATIONS IN BURMAH.
Royal Marines and Seamen from the East Indian Squadron assisted in this campaign.

1827. BATTLE OF NAVARINO. 20th October. (*Date below plate is incorrect*).   II, 15

1828-9. TAKING OF THE CASTLE OF MOREA (or RHION) AND SIEGE OF PATRAS.
A few Royal Marines, Artillery and Infantry, and some bomb-vessels co-operated with the French Army in these operations. Lieut. Logan, R.M.A., mainly caused the surrender of the Castle by blowing up the principal magazine for which he received the Legion of Honour.

1831. MAINTENANCE OF ORDER, NEWCASTLE. April.
"On Wednesday week, a Detachment of 80 Marines and 3 Subalterns under the command of Major Mitchell, sailed from Portsmouth for this port (Newcastle), on account of disturbances among the colliers. The vessel, towed by a steamer, sailed in less than an hour after the orders were received."—Contemporary Newspaper, of 28th April, 1831.

LOYALTY AND DETERMINATION OF PTE. GEO. HIGHAM.
"Whilst the *Medina* steam-vessel was stationed on the coast of Africa in the year 1831 a boat containing a midshipman, 9 seamen and a Marine was despatched on service; and on ascending a river, the crew became so mutinous, that the officer was under the necessity of using violent measures, and ran one of them through the body. This so exasperated the others, that they determined to throw the midshipman overboard, and were attempting to put their threat into execution when the Marine, named George Hyam or Higham, with great firmness stood between them, and declared he would shoot the first man who dared to lay his hand upon the officer, and bayonet the next who might venture to approach him. This determined act of courage so overawed the sailors that they desisted in their murderous intention, and the midshipman, thus nobly supported, was enabled to maintain his authority and rejoin his ship in safety."—((Nicholas—*Hist. Record R.M. Forces.*)

1832-4. BATTALION ROYAL MARINES KEEPING ORDER IN IRELAND.
Mention of this was omitted in Chapter XXX.

1835. BATTALION OF ROYAL MARINES IN PORTUGAL.
"On Thursday morning, at 6 o'clock, 3 officers and 200 Rank and File of the Royal Marines and 5 officers and 90 Gunners R.M.A. embarked on board H.M.S. *Talavera* and *Britannia*, left Portsmouth for Plymouth where they were joined by 7 officers and 200 Rank and File from that Division and the *Romney* troopship. They took with them 4 guns and a Brigade of Rockets. Never did a finer body of men quit the shores of England. They have orders to join Admiral Parker, and it is said Don Miguel will very soon be made acquainted with the object of their mission. The Portsmouth contingent was to be transferred to the *Romney* at Plymouth and the Plymouth one to embark for passage in H.M.S. *Caledonia*.—(Contemporary Newspaper, 30th May).

1836. BATTLE OF AMETZA. 6th June.   II, 30

1837.—BATTLE OF HERNANI. 16th March.   II, 35

1838. PRESCOT, CANADA. 12th and 13th March.
Lieut. O. A. Parker, Royal Marines, and 30 Privates Royal Marines, formed part of the force of 300 Infantry and 40 Militia Cavalry which, under the command of Col. Young, K.H., engaged and defeated a body of 800 Americans and Canadian insurgents, who with 3 guns had entrenched themselves near the village of Prescot on Lake Ontario. The village was defended by a few men of the 83rd Regiment, 30 of the Royal Marines, and such of the Glengarry Militia as had had time to collect. The American force after landing had taken up a position in which they were protected by the walls of an orchard, from behind which they kept up a galling fire upon the advancing Marines, while the latter pushed on, firing as objects offered. In this position of affairs, Lance-Corporal James Hunn, Royal Marines, who was on the

right of the British line, ran forward and jumped over the wall which covered the American sharpshooters, and found himself on their extreme left, and almost in contact with six or seven of them, who were separated from their main body by another wall running perpendicular to that which covered their front. These men were either loading or in the act of firing at the advancing Marines when Hunn leaped the wall, and were so intent on their occupation that they did not notice Hunn until he was on them ; so that he was able to close with them, and was seen by his commanding officers to bayonet three one after the other before they had time to load their pieces and fire. A fourth man, whose piece was loaded, turned and fired, and his ball struck the swell of Hunn's musket, where it was grasped by the left hand, which it passed through, destroying the second finger ; while at the same time the musket was driven so violently against his stomach as for a moment to suspend his breath. Recovering himself, however, he fired effectively at the enemy, now in full retreat ; but his disabled hand prevented his again loading, and he was most unwillingly obliged to give up any further share in the glory of the day, after having thus accounted for four of the enemy.

Captain Sandon, in his official despatch, says : " It may appear invidious to particularise any one man of the small band of Marines engaged, where all have shone so conspicuous ; but I trust I may stand excused for naming James Hunn, acting corporal, a young man twenty years of age, who, in the melée with the rebels, was seen by his officer and companions to beat back seven of the pirates, three of whom fell dead before him, and although at this time having his left hand shattered by a rifle-ball, he still continued the unequal contest. I feelingly hope such a noble example of bravery and devotion will plead my excuse for urging you to move the Lords Commissioners of the Admiralty to bestow promotion and a medal upon this valiant young soldier. He is in every way fit to become an officer."

Hunn was in consequence promoted to the rank of Sergeant without passing through the intermediate grade of corporal. The poor fellow died a year or two after, a victim to yellow fever, while serving in the *Arab* on the coast of Africa.'—Fr. *Deeds of Naval Daring*, Giffard, 1852.

		Vol. Page
1839.	CAPTURE OF ADEN. 19th January.	
	Lieut. Ayles and Royal Marines of *Volage* and *Cruiser* served with combined force that effected capture of this place.	
1840.	CAPTURE OF CHUSAN. 5th July.	II, 54
	ATTACK ON THE CASTLE OF GEBAIL, SYRIA. 12th September.	II, 45
	CAPTURE OF CAIFFA. 17th September.	II, 48
	ATTACK ON TORTOSA. 20th September.	II, 47
	STORMING OF SIDON. 26th September.	II, 49
	BOMBARDMENT OF ST. JEAN D'ACRE. 3rd November.	II, 51
1841.	TAKING OF CHUENPEE. 7th January.	II, 56
	OCCUPATION OF HONG-KONG. 26th January.	
	STORMING OF THE BATTERIES AT ANUNGHOY. 26th February.	II, 58
	STORMING OF MACAO PASSAGE FORT. 13th March.	II, 60
	ACTION NEAR CANTON. 24th May.	II, 62
	TAKING OF AMOY. 26th August.	II, 64
	ASSAULT AND CAPTURE OF TING-HAE. 1st October.	II, 65
	ASSAULT AND CAPTURE OF CHING-HAE. 10th October.	II, 65
	OCCUPATION OF NING-PO. 13th October.	II, 66
1842.	TAKING OF TSE-KEE. 15th March.	II, 67
	TAKING OF CHA-POO. 18th May.	II, 68
	CAPTURE OF WOO-SUNG. 16th June.	II, 69
	CAPTURE OF CHIN-KEANG-FOO. 21st July.	II, 70
1844.	HEROISM OF PTE. DRAKE, R.M., IN A MUTINY.	

The Brazilian slaver *Romeo Primero* was captured off Cape Lopez by H.M.S. *Waterwitch* and *Racer* somewhere about the middle of 1844. Commander Mansfield, R.N., 3 Seamen, a Private Marine named Drake, and 1 Krooman were put on board her as a prize crew in order to navigate her to St. Helena. On the night of the second or third day after parting company with the men-of-war, the Brazilian crew, four of whom were left on board, attempted to re-take the vessel. Some accident having happened to the topgallant halliards, the only two seamen who were on deck were ordered by Commander Mansfield to go aloft and repair the damage, he himself taking the wheel. Drake, the remaining seaman, and the Krooman had the watch below, and were fast asleep in their hammocks. The four Brazilians, on the alert to sieze the first favourable opportunity, took instant advantage of the temporary isolation of Commander Mansfield, and opened the attack by possessing themselves of Drake's musket, which one of them fired at the British officer, who fell, stunned by a severe wound in the head, which tore off a piece of his skull. In the meantime another of them stole below, and having mortally wounded the seaman who lay asleep in his hammock, was proceeding to despatch Drake. But the Marine, feeling a peculiar sensation about his throat, awoke, and raising his arm, diverted the murderer's knife, but not without receiving a deep and severe wound above the collar-bone. Without for a moment losing his presence of mind, he flung himself out of his hammock, and wrenching the knife from the murderer's hands, plunged it into the ruffian's stomach with such furious energy and hearty good-will that he felt the point of it grate against the spine. He then seized the man's cutlass and seeing that his officer was down, gallantly rushed to his rescue, regardless of the blood that poured profusely from the wound in his neck. Standing over the Commander's body he fought so well in resisting the attacks of the three remaining Brazilians, that by the time the two seamen had got down from aloft to his assistance he had killed one and wounded the two others who fled precipitately below, fairly terrified at the indomitable valour and fierce overpowering energy of their gallant opponent. Drake fainted from loss of blood as soon as they disappeared, and did not recover consciousness for a whole week. After several months in hospital Drake made a good recovery from his wounds, went afloat again and three years later was back in England and laid up with sickness in Haslar Hospital. Then, at length his heroism was recognised and the Admiralty on 7th June, 1848, directed that he should be "immediately and specially promoted to the rank of Corporal, and that this order be read at the head of each of the Divisions of Royal Marines." Moreover, on the 14th of the following month, he was ordered to be further promoted to Sergeant, and to Colour-Sergeant nine months later. In 1850 he was appointed to the *Birkenhead*, and was one of the survivors when she was wrecked on 26th January, 1852. Drake saw service in the Baltic, Crimea and China, leaving the Service in 1864. He died in 1905 after 28 years service as an attendant at Westminster Abbey. An excellent account of this gallant Marine illustrated by two portraits is to be found in "A Deathless Story, or the *Birkenhead* and its Heroes," published by Messrs. Hutchinson and Co., in 1906.

1845. NEW ZEALAND. STORMING OF HEKE'S PAH AT OKAIHU. 8th May.
Royal Marines of *Hazard* and *North Star* present.

BORNEO. 19th August.
Operations against the pirates of Borneo by the Royal Navy had been in progress for two or three years. On 19th August : the pirate stronghold of Malludu defended by 100 men and two forts armed with 12 heavy guns was attacked and destroyed by the boats of the *Agincourt* and 7 other vessels. Captain Hawkins, Royal Marines, 4 Lieutenants, 8 Sergeants, 8 Corporals, 3 Fifers and 178 Privates were present.

FIGHT AT OBLIGADO.

SOUTH AMERICA. PUENTE OBLIGADO. 20th November.
Brevet-Major R. Leonard with the Marines of the Squadron was landed for the protection of British interests during the Siege of Monte Video by the Argentines, and remained there from 1843 to 1847. At the destruction of the Batteries erected by General Rosas at Puente Obligado by the combined British and French squadrons on 20th November, Captain F. Hurdle landed with 145 Royal Marines and drove back the enemy from their position covering the batteries at the point of the bayonet. 180 Seamen who had been specially trained as Light Infantry by Lieutenant J. E. W. Lawrence of the Royal Marine Artillery drove them out of a wood they held at the same time. To facilitate the passage of a convoy

past the Batteries of San Lorenzo, Lieut. C. L. Barnard, R.M.A., with 12 gunners, Lieut. Mackinnon, R.N., the Boatswain and pilot of the *Alecto* and 11 Seamen with 4 rocket tubes lay concealed for three days on a small island close under their guns. When the moment came for the convoy and their escorting gun vessels to pass the batteries, the R.M.A. and Seamen manned their rocket tubes. Lieut. Barnard planted the British flag "under the nose of the enemy," and by the well aimed and heavy discharge of rockets the passage of the convoy was made possible. In the evening the Marines of the Squadron under Captain Hurdle, R.M., and 4 Subalterns were landed and supported by the bluejacket small arm men, stormed the batteries and spiked the guns.

1846. STORMING OF RUAPEKAPEKA. 31st December to 11th January, 1846.
  Royal Marines of ships on N.Z. Station.
1848. STORMING OF FORT SERAPAQUI, NICARAGUA RIVER. 12th February.
  Lieut. R. Boyle, R.M., and 30 Royal Marines from *Alarm* and *Vixen* were present.
  ROYAL MARINE BATTALION IN SOUTH OF IRELAND. — II, 182
1851. TAKING OF LAGOS. 26th to 27th December.
  By boats of *Bloodhound* and *Tartar*, Lieuts. J. W. C. Williams, R.M., and E. McArthur, R.M.A., were present with 27 R.M.A. and 47 Royal Marines.
1852. SECOND BURMESE WAR.
  Royal Marines of the Squadron which co-operated with the Army participated in the operations.
1854. BOMBARDMENT OF ODESSA. 22nd April. — II, 91
  ATTACK ON BOMARSUND. 8th to 16 August. — II, 81
  BATTLE OF BALAKLAVA. 25th October. — II, 94
  BATTLE OF INKERMAN. 5th November. — II, 98
    Corporal Littlejohns gains V.C.
  SEBASTOPOL. 5th June. — II, 103
    Br. Wilkinson, R.M.A. gains the V.C.
  ATTACK ON VIBORG. 13th July. — II, 89
    Lieut. Dowell,, R.M.A. gains V.C.
1855. BOMBARDMENT OF SVEABORG. 9th August. — II, 89
  BOMBARDMENT OF KINBURN. 17th October. — II, 104
1856. DESTRUCTION OF BARRIER FORTS, CANTON. 24th October. — II, 125
  STORMING OF CANTON. 29th October. — II, 126
  CAPTURE OF THE BOGUE FORTS. 12th and 13th November. — II, 126
1857. BATTLE OF ESCAPE CREEK. 25th May. — II, 128
  BATTLE OF FATSHAN CREEK. 1st June. — II, 128
  RELIEF OF LUCKNOW. 17th November. — II, 117
  BOMBARDMENT OF CANTON AND CAPTURE OF FORT LIN. 28th December. — II. 130
  ASSAULT AND CAPTURE OF CANTON. 29th December. — II, 130
1858. CAPTURE OF FORT AT HANDIPORE. 17th February.
  BATTLE OF PHOOLPORE. 26th February.
  FORT BETWA. 2nd March.
    Lieut. Pym and Detachment *Pearl*.
  CAPTURE OF THE PEIHO FORTS. 21st May. — II, 139
  BATTLE AT WHITE CLOUD MOUNTAIN NEAR CANTON. 2nd and 3rd June. — II, 135
  ACTION AT HURRYAH, INDIA. 18th June.
  TAKING OF NAN-TOW. 11th August. — II, 136
  RELIEF OF BHANSI. 14th September. — II, 124
1859. CAPTURE OF SHEK-TSENG. 8th January. — II, 138
  ATTACK ON THE PEIHO FORTS. 25th June. — II, 139
1859-1872. THE ISLAND OF SAN JUAN.
  In 1855, as it seemed impossible for Canada and the United States to settle definitely to which this island belonged, a provisional agreement was made under which it was jointly occupied by a small garrison from each nation. In 1859, however, General Harney, the C.O. in Washington Territory largely reinforced the American contingent and made an unqualified declaration that the Island belonged to the United States. This brought a British squadron on the scene which, after some negotiations between the British and United States Governments, was withdrawn on the understanding that the joint occupation by small bodies of troops should be continued for the present. General Harning was removed from his

APPENDIX F.

command in 1860, and for the next twelve years the British Government was represented by a detachment of the Royal Marines, its first commanding officer being Capt. Geo. Bazalgette. The British and American detachments continued on terms of good fellowship until their two Governments decided to have the question of the ownership of the Island arbitrated upon by the German Emperor, who on 21st October,

BLOCK-HOUSE, SAN JUAN.

R.M. CAMP, SAN JUAN.

1872, decided in favour of the United States. The Royal Marine Detachment, then commanded by Capt. W. A. Delacombe, evacuated the Island on the 22nd of the following month. The old block-house erected by the Royal Marines to protect their camp on the shore was still standing in 1905 and was still a source of much interest to tourists. The sites of both the British and American camps are now marked by marble and granite columns with suitable inscriptions.

		Vol.	Page
1860.	FIGHT AT PUKITAKANERI, NEW ZEALAND. 27th June.		
	STORMING OF THE PEIHO FORTS. 21st August.	II,	141
	FIGHT AT CHANG-KIA-WAN. 18th September.	II,	143
	FIGHT AT TUNG CHOW. 21st September.	II,	143
	TAKING OF PEKIN. 13th October.		
1861.	SABA, GAMBIA. 21st February.		
	PORTO NOVO, LAGOS. 25th February.		
	Royal Marines and Seamen of H.M.S. *Brune, Bloodhound* and *Alecto*.		

1861-2. ROYAL MARINE BATTALION IN MEXICO.

England, France and Spain sent a combined Expedition to demand guarantees for the safety of their subjects living in Mexico, and to urge their claims to the repayment of money borrowed by the Mexican Government, which had recently suspended payment. The British Contingent consisted of 4 Officers and 63 Gunners, R.M.A., and 28 Officers and 669 N.C.Os. and Privates R.M.L.I. Lieut.-Col. S. N. Lowder, R.M.L.I., was in command. On January 8th, 1862, the combined expedition consisting of 600 Spanish and 2,600 French troops besides the British Marines landed and occupied Vera Cruz. The French had already 5,600 men in Mexico, and their claims on the Mexican Government became so extortionate that the British and Spanish Governments withdrew their troops on receiving a promise of repayment of the sums their countries had advanced, and the Royal Marine Battalion returned home disappointed in its expectation of seeing active service.

1863.	BOMBARDMENT OF KAGOSHIMA, JAPAN. 15th August.	II,	146
	CAPTURE OF RANGARIRI PAH, NEW ZEALAND. 20th November.		
1864.	MAORIES DEFEATED AT TA AWAMUTA. 22nd February.		
	ATTACK ON THE GATE PAH, TAURANGA. 29th April.		
	ACTION WITH THE JAPANESE AT SIMONOSEKI. 5th and 6th September.	II,	148
	Lieut.-Col. Suther and 2 Battalions Royal Marines present.		
1868.	ROYAL MARINE BATTALION ON SPECIAL SERVICE IN IRELAND.	II,	183
	Lieut.-Col. John H. Stewart in command. From 3rd January.		
	CAPTURE OF MAGDALA. 13th April.		
	Detachments *Dryad* and *Satelite*.		
1873.	DEFENCE OF ELMINA, GOLD COAST. 13th June.	II,	152
	Lieut.-Col. Festing, R.M.A., and 110 R.M.A. and R.M.L.I.		
	BATTLE OF ABRAKAMPRA. 5th November.	II,	155

		Vol. Page
1874.	CAPTURE OF BORUBASSIE. 29th January.	II, 158
	Lieut. Crosbie, R.M.L.I., and 70 Royal Marines present.	
	BATTLE OF AMOAFUL. 31st January.	II, 158
	FIGHT AT BEQUAH. 1st February.	II, 159

Lieut. Crosbie, R.M.L.I. and 70 Royal Marines present.

In moving that the thanks of the House of Lords should be given to various officers employed in the Ashantee Campaign, the Duke of Richmond said: " Of Colonel Festing I would speak with the highest praise. His despatches describing the operations which he himself conducted speak with natural modesty of his own achievements; but no one can read those despatches without realising the fact that the greatest possible thanks and praise are due to him and those who acted under him (cheers). . . . . The Marines maintained their ancient *prestige* (cheers) and from the moment they landed shewed that it was not without reason they bore the motto ' Per Mare, per Terram.' " (Cheers).

1875. OPERATIONS AT PASSIR SALA, PERAK. 2nd November.

1876. OPERATIONS AT RATHALMA, PERAK. 21st January.

1879. WAR IN ZULULAND.

The Royal Marine detachments of the *Shah*, *Boadicea* and *Tenedos* were present at the Battle of Gingelovo and the Relief of Ekowe, with Captains Philips and Dowding, R.M.L.I. A Battalion of Royal Marines was sent out from England to South Africa and landed under the command of Lieut.-Col. Bland Hunt, R.M.L.I., but arrived on 7th July, too late to take part in the war and returned home on 24th July.

1880-1882.	BATTALION ON SPECIAL SERVICE IN SOUTH OF IRELAND.	II, 183
	Lieut.-Col. Maskery, R.M.L.I., and afterwards Col. H. S. Jones, R.M.L.I., in command.	
1882.	BOMBARDMENT OF ALEXANDRIA. 11th July.	II, 167
	ACTION AT MALLAHA JUNCTION. 5th August.	II, 168
	Lieut.-Col. Tuson and 1st Battalion Royal Marines and R.M.A.	
	ACTION AT TEL-ELMAHUTA. 25th August.	II, 170
	FIRST BATTLE OF KASSASSIN. 28th August.	II, 171
	SECOND BATTLE OF KASSASSIN. 9th September.	II, 172
	BATTLE OF TEL-EL-KEBIR. 13th September.	II, 173

Lieut.-Col. H. B. Tuson and Battalion R.M.A. and Lieut.-Col. H. S. Jones and Battalion R.M.L.I. were present at the above four actions.

1882-3.	DETACHMENT ON SPECIAL SERVICE IN DUBLIN. 3rd December to 1st June.	II, 184

Major Noble, R.M.A., Captains H. H. Morgan and C. P. Boyd Hamilton, R.M.L.I., and 200 selected Royal Marines dressed in plain clothes.

1884.	BATTLE OF EL-TEB. 29th February.	II, 191
	BATTLE OF TAMAII. 13th March.	II, 193

Lieut.-Col. Ozzard and Royal Marine Battalion.
Battalion on Police Duty in Skye, Lieut.-Col. Munro, R.M.L.I., in command.

1885.	BATTLES OF ABU KLEA AND ABU KRU. 17th and 19th January.	II, 206 and 210

Captain W. H. Pöe, Lieuts. H. S. Neville White and C. V. F. Townshend, R.M.L.I., and the Royal Marine Company of the Guards Camel Regiment.

	BATTLE OF HASHEEN. 20th March.	II, 200
	BATTLE OF TOFREK. 22nd March.	II, 202

McNeill's Zareeba.

1886. BATTALION ON POLICE DUTY IN TIREE.
Col. Heriot, R.M.L.I., in command.

1894. OPERATIONS ON THE GAMBIA. February and March.

Early in the year an expedition organised by Captain Gamble, R.N. of H.M.S. *Raleigh* against a chieftain named Fodi Sillah who had made himself troublesome to the British settlements on the Gambia River, was ambushed and cut up. Lieut. Hervey, R.M.L.I., 2 Naval Officers and 10 Men were killed and 40 wounded. On the 22nd February a punitive force of 50 Royal Marines, 50 men of the West India Regiment, and 1 gun under the command of Lieut.-Col. Corbet, R.M.L.I., attacked and destroyed a stockade at Sukutta, after which a position was taken up and entrenched at Subaji to protect the frontier of British Kombo. Here, on the 26th, Col. Corbet was attacked by 1,500 Mandigoes, who he defeated and drove back across the border. On 1st March having been reinforced by 50 more Marines and 10 West Indians he took up another entrenched position at Isswang, and on the 5th having been further reinforced by seamen and others to a total strength of 500 men, marched to relieve Major Madden, R.A., who with 200 men of the West India Regiment was entrenched at Busumbula. The following day Col. Corbet returned to Sabaji with the greater portion of his command. Having re-embarked with the Royal Marines he went round with the squadron consisting of the *Alecto*, *Satelite*, *Magpie* and *Widgeon* to the town of Gunjur, and after it had been subjected to a two days' bombardment, landed with his men and with 270 seamen and a portion of the 1st West India Regiment destroyed the place. This operation brought the fighting to a close.

1895. SACRIFICE ISLAND, BRASS RIVER. August.
Major Denny and Detachment West Africa Regiment.

BUSH FIGHTING AT BENIN.

APPENDIX F.

Vol. Page

1896. CRETE. January to June.
The Island being in a very unsettled state on account of an insurrection against the Turkish Government, an international Gendarmerie was formed and Major Bor, R.M.A., was appointed to organise and command it in January, 1897. He resigned this position in March, and took command of the European troops holding the fort of Izzedin during the insurrection. During the insurrection, too, Major C. G. Brittan, R.M.L.I., with Lieuts. P. Molloy and F. A. Nelson was landed with 100 N.C.O's and men from the *Rodney*, *Revenge* and *Barfleur* to assist in the occupation of Canea by the European Powers and remained there for five weeks.

1897. THE BENIN EXPEDITION. 10th February to 20th February.
The massacre of a peaceful mission which had been despatched to the capital of Benin led to the formation of an expedition with orders to capture Benin city, depose the king and punish the murderers. Rear-Admiral Rawson, who flew his Flag in the *St. George* as Commander in Chief on the Cape Station, was in command. The forces at his disposal consisted of 5 Companies of Houssas under Lieut.-Col. Bruce Hamilton, 100 native scouts, his own Naval Brigade of Seamen and Marines, a detachment of 3 Officers and 100 R.M.L.I., under Captain Byrne, R.M.L.I., and Lieut. F. L. Diblee and 20 gunners, R.M.A. (known as the "Marine Battalion"), and the Seamen and Marines from the *Theseus* and *Forte* detached from the Mediterranean Fleet. On 10th February a base was formed at Warrigi and by the day following the whole force was on shore. On the 13th there was a sharp skirmish at Oglobo but the enemy were driven off. As the expedition advanced it was constantly fired upon from the thick bush. The Marine Battalion arrived at the front on the 15th and encamped at a place known as the "Cross Roads." The day following a selected force marched in the direction of Benin City. The Marine Battalion was the largest unit. With it marched the Marine detachment of the *Theseus*, two companies of Bluejackets and a demolition and rocket party of 20 men. The weather was intensely hot and the bush thick, so that the day's march ended at Ogagi, only 5 miles having been covered. A start was made the next morning at 4-30 a.m., and in the afternoon the column bivouacked at Awoko, where it was shortly afterwards attacked by the natives, who were repulsed by a heavy rifle fire. At daybreak on the 18th the column started off to attack the city which was now close at hand. Though fired at continually from the bush there were but few casualties and no serious opposition was encountered until a wide open road leading directly to the city was reached. The bush on either side was very thick and all along the road the enemy had collected in great numbers. Several guns opened fire on the British loaded with all manner of scrap iron but were fired at too high an elevation to occasion much damage. The fire at this point was very hot and two gunners of the R.M.A. were killed, and Captain Byrne, Private Varndell and Samuels, R.M.L.I. fell dangerously wounded. Ptes. Hooper and Palmer, though badly hurt, after being bound with a field-dressing continued to advance with the firing line. A Naval Warrant Officer, a Petty Officer and 3 Seamen were also wounded. The 2 Maxim Guns accompanied the column, and the rocket-tubes made a very effective reply to the fire of the enemy, and when four pieces of ordnance placed on the ground so as to command the road came into sight, their gunners were driven off by a hail of bullets. Admiral Rawson at once gave the order, " Now men, before they load again, charge." Bugler Allen, R.M.L.I., sounded the "Charge," and Marines, Bluejackets and Houssas, with fixed bayonets and a ringing cheer rushed over the guns and into the city driving all before them. The "Halt" was sounded and the victors poured a withering "independent" fire into the fleeing masses of their sable enemies. The king escaped but was hunted down and captured a few weeks later. It was found that he had not been directly responsible for the massacre which the expedition had set out to avenge, but two of the fetish chiefs out of six who were proved to have instigated it were executed. Of the other four, one had died, two committed suicide and the last was captured and executed two years later. In the meanwhile the victorious expedition had returned to the coast, Captain Byrne, who had gallantly led and commanded the Royal Marines, gave his life for his country, as his wound proved a mortal one. He was brought to England, but died on the 24th of March in St. Thomas' Hospital.

1898. OPERATIONS ON THE NILE.   II, 214
Capt. Oldfield and N.C.Os Royal Marine Artillery.
ATTACK ON BRITISH FORCES AT CANDIA. 6th September.
A sudden attack was made by Moslem fanatics on the small force of the Highland Light Infantry quartered in Candia on 6th September. Aided by what Royal Marines and Seamen could be spared from the *Hazard*, torpedo gunboat, which lay in the harbour, a desperate fight went on for four hours against hordes of Bashi-Bazouks, who found excellent cover in the houses of the town. The main attack was directed against the hospital, which was defended with the greatest gallantry by doctors, nurses and patients. The Royal Medical Corps especially distinguished itself. But the hospital had eventually to be evacuated and the little handful of British —3 or 4 companies of infantry and a few sappers—were driven to bay on the ramparts at the corner of the town. H.M.S. *Camperdown* at the time of the fighting was lying in Suda Bay, sixty miles off, but thanks to the bravery and resource of Lieut. Kennedy of the Royal Engineers a wire got through to her asking for immediate succour. The *Camperdown* sailed the same evening for Candia, all preparations for putting a force on shore being made on the way round. She anchored off the town early the following morning and at once landed a detachment of Royal Marines under the command of Major W. P. Drury, R.M.L.I.—about 60 in number. A heavy surf was running and all hands got thoroughly drenched during the difficult process of landing on the beach a little way outside the town walls ; as the town being in the hands of the Turkish mob no disembarkation was possible in the harbour. Access to the beleaguered Highlanders was obtained by means of a convenient sallyport in the walls. In the afternoon the remainder of the Royal Marines from the *Camperdown* and 40 men from the *Astrea* also got on shore—a welcome reinforcement. Two or three days of heavy work in

patrolling and erecting improvised defences on the ramparts followed, but the British were not again attacked, thanks, probably to the menacing appearance of the *Camperdown*, and the dread of her big guns. Soon, too, French, Italian and Russian troops from other parts of the Island began to march in, and with the arrival of a British Battalion from Malta, all fear of further disturbances was at an end, and the *Camperdown's* detachment, which had arrived so opportunely, was able to return on board.

The conduct of the little detachment of Royal Marines belonging to the torpedo-gunboat *Hazard* on this occasion was worthy of the best traditions of their Corps. Captain Vaughan Lewes then in command of the *Hazard* thus wrote of them to a senior officer of the Corps:—

"I must write and tell you of the magnificent behaviour of my little detachment at Candia, September 6th, 1898. Sergeant Bunn and 8 men landed with the first party, and I was told by Colonel Reid of the H.L.I. that undoubtedly they saved his life by their firm behaviour and discipline. When I landed with the second lot of bluejackets, in my boat 2 men were killed and 2 wounded. I was grazed on the head, and the men with me had their clothes in ribbons—this out of 8 all told—as we landed. The sight that met me I wouldn't have lost for worlds, it is impressed on my brain. Those nine men, as stiff as on my deck, and as steady at the ready as if there wasn't a bullet anywhere about, with a set determination that I shall never forget doing their very best to cover my poor fellows landing to the rescue. It was a grand sight, and throughout our imminent position for four hours, those men with mine stood their ground under their sergeant, watching every loop-hole, seeing none of the enemy except by chance, and put body into my young fellows—ordinary seamen, who followed. This grand sight we saw on landing *all* doing splendidly. I am as proud of those nine as if they were a whole battalion, and they, all but one, Priestner (who did magnificently) belong to your Division. We were in a very tight hole finally; being burnt out on the left flank, murderous fire on right flank and front, and the devils were digging us out in rear, and the men knew that unless help came, we were done for, and yet not one failed me."

		Vol. Page
1899.	BELMONT, SOUTH AFRICA. 23rd November.	II, 236
	Major Plumbe and 213 Royal Marines.	
	BATTLE OF GRASPAN. 25th November.	II, 239
	Major Plumbe killed. Captain Marchant, R.M.L.I., brings the Naval Brigade out of action.	
1900.	BATTLE OF PAARDEBURG. 18th to 27th February.	II, 244
	Majors Urmston and Marchant and 160 Royal Marines.	
	BATTLE OF POPLAR GROVE. 7th March.	II, 244
	Major Urmston and Detachment Royal Marines.	
	VIET RIVER. 5th May.	
	Major S. P. Peile and 70 men.	
	ZAND RIVER. 10th May.	
	Major S. P. Peile and 80 men.	
	BATTLE OF DIAMOND HILL. 12th June.	
	Major Peile and 60 Royal Marines.	
	CAPTURE OF MILITARY COLLEGE, TIEN-TSIN. 17th June.	II, 255
	COMMENCEMENT OF SIEGE OF PEKIN LEGATIONS. 20th June.	II, 278
	CAPTURE OF HSI-KU ARSENAL. 22nd June.	II, 257
	Major Johnstone and 180 Royal Marines.	
	RELIEF OF TIEN-TSIN. 23rd June.	II, 259
	SORTIE FROM PEKIN LEGATIONS. 24th June.	II, 280
	Captain Halliday, R.M.L.I., gains the V.C.	
	RELIEF OF ADMIRAL SEYMOUR'S COLUMN AT HSI-KU ARSENAL. 25th June.	II, 259
	CAPTURE OF THE PEI-TSANG ARSENAL. 27th June.	II, 260
	CAPTURE OF THE NATIVE CITY OF TIEN-TSIN. 14th July.	II, 264, 267
	BATTLE OF PEIT-SANG. 5th August.	II, 266
	RELIEF OF THE PEKIN LEGATIONS. 14th August.	II, 289
	BATTLE AT BELFAST, SOUTH AFRICA. 26th August.	II, 246
	DEFENCE OF LADYBRAND. 5th September.	II, 247
	Major F. White, R.M.L.I.	
1902-3.	BLOCKADE OF THE VENEZUELAN COAST. 20th December to 14th February.	
	Royal Marines in *Ariadne, Charybdis, Tribune, Retribution* and *Indefatigable*.	
1904.	STORMING OF ILLIG, SOMALI COAST. 21st April.	
	Major Kennedy, R.M.L.I., and 51 Royal Marines served in the Naval Brigade from the *Hyacinth, Fox* and *Mohawk*. 125 men of the 1st Hants were also present.	
1910.	FIGHT AT DABAI, PERSIAN GULF. 24th December.	
	In pursuance of the duty of putting down "gun-running" a party of 4 Officers and 79 Petty and N.C.Os and men including Major Heriot and Lieut. Brewer, R.M.L.I., and 33 Marines were landed from H.M.S. *Hyacinth*, Flag-ship on the East Indian Station, under Captain Dick, R.N., the Flag Captain, to search for arms in two suspected houses at some distance apart. After arms had been found by Major Heriot, fire was opened from the houses on the search parties and on the men left on the beach. Major Heriot entrenched himself on the beach and after a sharp skirmish the guns of the *Hyacinth* put an end to the attack. The Royal Marines lost Sergt. Capon killed and 4 Privates wounded.	

ADDITIONAL ADDENDA TO VOL I.

CHAPTER II.

"GENESIS OF THE ADMIRAL'S REGIMENT."

The following paragraph from "England under the Stuarts," by Mr. G. M. Trevelyan (page 354) is somewhat corroborative of the suggestion I have made on page 17, Vol. I as to a probable reason for the establishment af the "Admiral's Regiment."

"There were in fact three elements among the Captains of the Restoration Navy. First, ignorant and incompetent young men of fashion who had begged or bought commissions at Whitehall. Secondly, the 'Tarpaulins' or old sea-dogs who lived and died at sea and knew the management of a ship in all weathers, and on every coast. These two classes were mutually exclusive. But there was a third class, whose existence has sometimes been overlooked in history, perhaps because it is merged with the Tarpaulins at one end and the favourites at the other. This third class consisted of men who had seen Military Service on land, but who adapted themselves to Sea Warfare, and helped the Tarpaulins to fight the battles and evolve the traditions of the English Navy."

The writer quotes Mahan and Corbet as his authorities for the above assertion and many officers, at any rate, of the Admiral's Regiment certainly belonged to the third class he mentions.

CHAPTER IX.

SEA KIT OF MARINES WHEN EMBARKED, 1702-3.

	£	s.	d.
A Bed, Blanket and Pillow	0	16	0
2 Speckl'd Shirts and Cravats	0	9	0
2 Pair of Shoes	0	7	0
2 Pair of Hose	0	2	6
2 Pound of Tobacco	0	3	0
A Knapsack	0	1	0
A Pair of Spatter-Dashes	0	4	0
A Frying Pan and Kettle to 6 Men	0	0	8
A Chest among 6 Men	0	1	8
	£2	4	10

These items were to be provided by the Officers upon embarkation and the cost to be refunded by stoppages from the Soldiers' Sea Pay *upon their return home.*

Vide Record Office, W.O.55, 1810.—"A Scheme for maintaining a Body of Marines" (*circ.* 1725).

CHAPTER IX.

CLOTHING AND DUTIES OF MARINES WHEN EMBARKED, 1740-46.

A Committee to consider the Payment, Recruiting and Mustering of H.M..'s Land Forces and Marines was formed in 1746, and the following extracts from their Report are of interest. Captain *John Murray* of Cochran's Marines referring to a detachment of 70 men "belonging to different companies" which he had commanded in the West Indies (apparently on board the *Prince of Orange* which was wrecked "in the late hurricane at Jamaica") said that of these "only 22 came home with him" and that these "had all the Cloaths due to them, when they came to Quarters; that when the men went out, they were supplied with Slops; and were afterwards furnished with what they wanted, by the Purser; but that they had had no Cloathing (presumably regimental uniform.—C.F.), except that which had been delivered to them in *November* before their going to Sea; nor was any sent to them during the time they were out, which was Two Years and Five months. And the Witness added, That he never knew an Instance of extraordinary Cloathing being sent to the Marines, except for a Detachment of Colonel *Lowther's* Regiment, with Admiral *Davers*; which Favour was obtained by means of the Colonel's Intimacy with the Admiral.

The Witness further said, That by Slops is meant all Necessaries for the Cloathing of the Men, except the outside Apparel; besides which Necessaries, when they go to Sea, they have regimental Frocks, and Caps, made of coarse Cloth, provided for them, which they pay for out of their Subsistence; and that they are fed as the Ship's Company is, and do Duty upon Deck; but that he never knew them put to the Guns; and he added, That the Men are frequently prevailed upon by the Petty-Officers on board, and others, to make Wills in their Favour, and that a Sergeant belonging to this Regiment, being detected, was lately broke for this Practice. Being further examined he said, That the Marine Officers are not allowed to take Servants on board the Ships with them, there being no Provision for them; but that the Officers generally employ one of the Marines to attend them, which, the Witness said, is no Hindrance to the Service, they doing Duty on board; and that, in the West Indies, by General Wentworth's Orders, every Officer's Servant went upon Duty, only when his Master went; but if the Officers were absent, the Men did Duty in Turn."

This Witness and others spoke as to the difficulty of making out correct Muster Rolls and returns on account of the mixing up of men of different regiments in the same ship and from the practice of some Captains, of transferring Marines to other ships without any reference to the Marine Officer, if there was one on board.

Lieut.-Col. *Sewell* of the Duke of Bolton's Regiment said that he had been a Captain in Jeffrey's Marines till the previous October, and that in his opinion "the Marines should be regularly borne on board the Ship's Books, distinguished from the Seamen, and mustered with the Ship's Company; and that they were so mustered, and borne, on board the *Leopard*, when the Witness commanded them; but that they are often borne promiscuously with the Seamen; and that sometimes the Captain of a Ship will not permit the Marine Officer to inspect the Ship's Books, to see if his Men are regularly entered.

That the Marines on board the said Ship were employed upon Deck; but that no Orders were given to them to furl the Sails, tho' they did it voluntarily, at the Witness's Desire; the Reason of which was, that the Men might be of Use, after they are discharged from this Service.

Being asked, whether any Men were allowed to the Colonels by the Captains of this Regiment (*i.e.*, imaginary men, in order that the Colonel might draw their pay.—C.F.), he said, That, from June, 1741, during the Remainder of the Time he continued in the Regiment, he allowed about 6d. per Diem to the Agent; which Money, he supposed, was given to the Colonel.

Being further examined, he said, That the Cloathing for this Regiment was regularly sent down to Quarters; and that, when the Men came home, all the Cloathing due was delivered to them: That he had seen the whole Cloathing given to them, tho' he has heard that a Sum of Money is sometimes offered, in lieu of Part of it; but that he does not know, whether this is a Fact, nor what the Sum offered is; but has heard, that the usual Price given is a Guinea, or 25s."

Whether due to this Committee's investigations or not, it is somewhat of a coincidence that Colonel Jeffreys was "broke for false Musters" at Minorca in the same year (1746), and it is probable that its report induced the Admiralty to put the whole 10 Marine Regiments into the same Uniform in May of the year following. (*Vide* pp. 87 and 88, Vol. I).

CHAPTER XI.

UNIFORM. FIRST APPEARANCE OF THE ROUND HAT.

The following should have appeared on page 169, Vol. I, prior to the Order dated Boston, Dec. 19th, 1775.

1775 (Boston), July 4th.—The C.O. desires the Officers would appear uniformly dressed on duty with the men, and each Officer immediately to provide himself with a Jacket and a Round Hat with a Silver Band.

It seems probable that the cocked hat, comparatively small up to the middle of the century, was becoming too large and unwieldy for service, in the infantry at any rate. At the Siege of Louisburg we find "cropped hats" referred to (*Vide* Appendix "F"). This probably meant that the cocked hats were to have the greater part of their brims cut off instead of being turned up on three sides. This gives us the prototype of the Round Hat now ordered to be worn by officers and which remained the active service head-dress for Officers in the Army until the brim was removed altogether and the cap or cylindrical shako became uniform for the infantry in all ranks. The Marines, however, adopted the Round Hat for all ranks about the same time and retained it till the large crowned shako—copied from the French—superseded both hat and cap.

CHAPTER XVII.

SIR JAMES SAUMAREZ' PROPOSAL TO ESTABLISH A CORPS OF ROYAL MARINE ARTLLIERY IN 1796.

Orion, St. Helens' Roads,
30th December, 1796.

MY LORD,

I have had it in contemplation for some time past, to' lay before your Lordships the enclosed plan for the establishment of a Marine Artillery for the service of the Navy, but was prevented from doing it by the late prospect of a peace; at present, as the haughtiness of our enemies seems to have removed that desirable object to a distant period, and as a further augmentation to our forces may in consequence take place, it may not appear unseasonable.

If it has the good fortune to meet with your Lordship's approbation, I shall think myself amply recompensed for the time I have bestowed upon it.

I have the honour to be,
My Lord,
Your Lordship's most obedient
And very humble servant,
JAMES SAUMAREZ.

A PLAN FOR FORMING A CORPS OF ARTILLERY FOR HIS MAJESTY'S NAVAL SERVICE.

"In consequence of the present great increase of the Royal Navy, it becomes from time to time necessary to augment proportionably that very useful body of men, the Marines—but that very respectable corps would be rendered of far greater importance to the service were they trained up and exercised in the management of the great guns; for which purpose it is humbly submitted, that a division be established at either Woolwich or Deptford, to be composed of drafts from the divisions of Portsmouth, Plymouth and Chatham, in order to be instructed in the exercise and use of artillery; and thereby become expert gunners when ordered to be embarked on board His Majesty's ships: their numbers to consist of one man to every four guns in each line of battleship, which would compose about one-third of their present complement. In addition to which two companies should be quartered at the other three divisions, to complete such vacancies as occasionally would occur on board the Fleet.

"The great utility of this corps must appear obvious when it is considered that the only person supposed to be qualified and experienced in gunnery on board His Majesty's ships is the gunner, who, too often ignorant of his own duty, is totally unable to instruct others. In the quarter bills of most ships, it is well known that a very small proportion of the Marines are reserved for musketry, the greater part being in general divided on the different batteries. With what advantage would they not go to their quarters, after having been well practised and exercised as artillery-men; and how soon would not the rest of the ship's company become also expert gunners in emulating their example

"These men would also be found particularly useful on expeditions abroad, in landing or making a descent on the enemy's coast, when a well-served artillery is often of the greatest importance.

"The officers might be appointed from the other divisions, and should consist of those who, from their age and services, were incapable of being engaged in actual duty; they would here find a comfortable asylum during life; and end their days in the service of their country.

"The expenses incurred by this establishment would be inconsiderable, and no doubt can be entertained of its proving a lasting advantage to His Majesty's service, and adding strength to the great bulwark of this country —the Royal Navy.

"JAMES SAUMAREZ, *Orion*.

"The Right Honourable Earl Spencer, &c., &c., &c."

Admiralty,
2nd January, 1797.

DEAR SIR,

"I hazard a line in the uncertainty whether you may not have sailed before this reaches Portsmouth, to thank you for your paper on the establishment of a Corps of Artillery for the Naval Service. The idea is one which I have often heard discussed, and in many points of view a very good one; but I fear that there would be so many difficulties in point of official arrangements to overcome in carrying it into execution, that no very sanguine hopes can be entertained of its succeeding.

"It is, however, a subject well worthy of attention, and which, at a less pressing moment, it may perhaps be worth while to renew.

"I am,
"Dear Sir.
"With great regard,
"Your very obedient humble servant,
"SPENCER.

"To Sir James Saumarez."

SOME FURTHER INSTANCES OF SLOW PROMOTION.

The terrible slowness of Promotion under which Officers of the Marines suffered as indicated in this Chapter and in Note IV at the end of it does not seem to have been mitigated until the Order in Council of 13th November, 1858, provided for the compulsory retirement of Colonels Commandant at the age of 60, and even afterwards, especially following on the reduction of the Woolwich Division in 1869, Promotion was anything but rapid. But in 1845 the following was the state of the 75 Captains at the head of the list:—

2 had held Commissions for 43 years.				3 had held Commissions for 36 years.			
8	do.	do.	42 do.	6	do.	do.	35 do.
10	do.	do.	41 do.	8	do.	do.	34 do.
7	do.	do.	40 do.	3	do.	do.	33 do.
3	do.	do.	39 do.	5	do.	do.	32 do.
8	do.	do.	38 do.	—			
12	do.	do.	37 do.	75			

In 1849 there were two 2nd Commandants, aged respectively 67 and 68! In 1850 ten Captains were recommended for full pay retirement, their ages ranging from 61 to 52, and service from 41 to 36 years!

In January of that year the ages and services of the three senior Captains and Brevet-Majors were as follows:

Age.	Full Pay.	Half Pay	Total
58	35	9½	44½ Years.
61	35	9	44 do.
61	35	11	46 do.

The above reveals a dreadful state of affairs likely to promote neither efficiency nor enthusiasm for the National Service.

A

Aboukir, Battle of, *II.* 323.
Abrakrampa, Battle of, *II.* 155-6.
Abu Klea, Battle of, *II.* 206.
Abu Kru, Battle of (or Gubat), *II.* 211.
Abuses in bestowal of Commissions, *I.* 271.
Abuses, Naval, *I.* 27.
Accounts of The Manchester Marines, *I.* 320.
Acre, Bombardment of, *II.* 51.
Acre, Defence of, *I.* 215.
Aden, Capture of, *II.* 334.
Advantages of permanent Barracks, *II.* 296.
Advertising for a Commission, *I.* 271.
"Advice to Sea Lieutenants," *I.* 130.
Agusta, Island of, captured, *II.* 330.
Albion, Nichols cuts out the, *I.* 238.
Alexandria, Bombardment of and Occupation, *II.* 166.
Alexandria, Complement of the, *I.* 4.
Algerine frigate burnt by Lt. Woolridge, R.M.A., *II.* 13.
...... Pirates, *II.* 9.
Algiers, Bombardment of, *II.* 12, 332.
...... British and Dutch Squadrons at, *II.* 12.
Alicant, the Rock of, *I.* 62.
Allowances and Pay, *I.* 70, 110, 134.
Almanza, Battle of, *I.* 64.
Aloft, Officers of Marines going. *I,* 234.
Althea, Landing at, *I.* 312; *II.* 321.
Amboyna captured, *II.* 328.
American Marines, Good comrades, *II.* 282.
American Marines at Alexandria, *II.* 167.
.... at Pekin, *II.* 265 *et seq*
American Militia, *I.* 151, 163.
.... Rebellion, *I.* 148 *et seq*.
.... Troops, *I.* 65, 88.
.... Uniform, 1775, *I.* 164.
Ametza, Battle of, *II.* 30.
Ametzegana, Attack on, *II.* 35.
Amoaful, Battle of, *II.* 158.
Amoy, Capture of, *II.* 64.
Annapolis Royal, Expedition against, *I.* 65.
Anglesey, The Marquis of, on the Royal Marines, *II.* 53.
Anholt, Capture of and Defence, *I.* 226; *II.* 329.
Anson's Marine Detachments, *I.* 74, 312.
...... Voyage, *I.* 90, 119.

Arabi Pasha, *II.* 165.
Archduke Charles of Austria, *I.* 36, 42, 313.
Arms and Appointments, Munitions, &c.
 Arms and Appointments in 1842, *II.* 230.
 Arms, Bells of, *I.* 88.
 Arm Chests, *I.* 121, 133.
 Arm Racks, *I.* 121.
 Arms, Ward Room, *I.* 121.
 Ballistae, *I.* 5.
 Bayonets, *I.* 25, 113, 126, 164; *II.* 7, 192.
 Bells of Arms, *I.* 88.
 Belts, Various, *I.* 73, 113, 126, 164. *II.* 21, 22, 23, 25, 74.
 Bows, *II.* 139, 144.
 Canteens, *II.* 75, 164, 223, 224.
 Carcases, *I.* 40; *II.* 13.
 Cartouche Boxes (*Vide also Pouches*), *I.* 25.
 Chandeliers, *I.* 51.
 Chests, Arm, *I.* 121, 133.
 Drakes, *I.* 19.
 Drums, *I.* 25, 88, 121, 126, 148.
 Equipment, *I.* 15, 25, 33, 123; *II.* 162, 163, 222.
 Fascines, *I.* 80.
 Firelocks, *I.* 15, 16, 25, 28, 70, 121, 126, 163, 189; *II.* 106, 159.
 Flints, *I.* 126.
 Fusil or Fuzee, *I.* 16, 104, 113, 114, 128, 267; *II.* 106.
 " Granador" Pouches, *I.* 25.
 Grenades, *I.* 19, 23, 27, 54, 83, 222, 321.
 Halberds, or Halberts, *I.* 33, 104, 121, 126; *II.* 22, 75.
 Half-pikes, *I.* 33.
 Hammers (Soft), *I.* 125.
 Hatches, or Hatchets, *I.* 25, 41.
 Jags, *II.* 212.
 Jingalls (or Gingalls), *II.* 72.
 Knapsacks, *I.* 113, 169; *II.* 77, 163, 224.
 Matchlocks, *I.* 28, 44; *II.* 106.
 Muskets, *II.* 24, 75, 230.
 Muzzle-Stoppers, *II.* 160.
 Partizans, or Pertuisans, *I.* 33.
 Partridge, *I.* 80.
 Percussion Muskets, *II.* 64, 159.
 Pikes, *I.* 16, 25, 29, 104; *II.* 75, 106.
 Pistols, *I.* 200; *II.* 18. 319,
 Pouches, *I.* 73, 113, 126, 169; *II.* 22, 76, 77, 161, 163, 166, 222, 230, 282.
 Rammers, *I.* 73, 125.
 Rifles { Mimic, *II.* 101, 121.
  Enfield, *II.* 156, 162.
  Snider, *II.* 162.
  Martini-Henry, *II.* 164, 282.
  Lee-Metford, *II.* 306.
 Scabbards, *II.* 77, 159, 162.
 Slings, Musket or Rifle, *I.* 113.
 Spontoons, *I.* 104.
 Swords, *I.* 114, 164; *II.* 22, 23, 75, 77.
 Trebuchets, *I.* 6.
 Valise Equipment, *II.* 163.
 Ward Room Arms, *I.* 121.
Arms for the defence of the Admiralty, *I.* 189.
Army, Interchange with the, *I.* 128, 132, 174.
Army and Navy Gazette, Correspondence in the, *II.* 227.
Ashantee War, *II.* 151, 333, 337.
.... Colonel Festing in the, *II.* 152, 337.
Atbara, Battle of the, *II.* 217.
Atcherley, Captain, receives surrender of Admiral Villeneuve, *I.* 256.
Australia, Marines found Commonwealth, 170 *et seq*.
.... Expedition organised, *I.* 172.
.... Marines in "First Fleet" *I.* 172.
.... Streets &c. called after officers of the Marines, *I.* 175, 184.
.... Later services of Marines in, *I.* 186.

B

" Babies in arms," *I.* 272.
Badge of Romano-British Marines, *I.* 1.
Bagnold, Capt. T., his high angle gun, *I.* 258.

INDEX

Baker Pasha defeated at El Teb, *II*. 190.
Balaguer, Fort St. Philip de, taken, *II*. 330.
Balaklava, fighting at, *II*. 94, 95, 96, 97.
.... occupied, *II*. 92.
.... Royal Marines at, *II*. 93.
Ballad, "The Manchester Marine," *I*. 318.
Baltic, The, *II*. 80.
.... Unsatisfactory campaign in the, *II*. 80.
Bands, The R.M., Badges, Uniform, &c., *II*. 297.
Bandsmen, Naval, *II*. 301.
Bank Notes, Eating, *II*. 229.
"Baraguay Bobs,"*II*. 82.
Barbary Pirates, Ammunition supplied to, *II*. 21.
Barcelona, *I*. 61, 62, 63, 324.
Barracks, Royal Marine, Various, *II*. 293.
Barrier Forts, Capture of the, *II*. 125.
Barossa, Battle of, *II*. 320.
Bartleman, Capt., his musket-lock cover, *I*. 258.
Basque Roads, the Attack on, *I*. 245.
Basse-Terre, Attack on, *I*. 137.
Bayonet Exercise, The, *II*. 7, 8.
Beaconsfield, Lord, on the R.M., *I*. i.
Beatty, Lieut. (now Earl Beatty), *II*. 216, 217.
Beckman, Sir Martin, *I*. 34, 42.
Begur, Operations at, *I*. 278.
Belleisle Expedition, The, *I*. 101.
Belmont, Fighting at, *II*. 236.
Benin Expedition, The, *II*. 339.
Beresford, Lord Charles, on the Royal Marines. *II*. 293.
Berselem, Skirmish at, *I*. 297.
Besiglio, Operations at, *II*. 327.
Betwa Fort taken, *II*. 336.
Beyrout, Bombardment of, *II*. 47.
Bhansi, Relief of, *II*. 121, 122, 123, 124.
Bishop, Mathew, Adventures of, at Malaga, *I*. 46, 47.
.... at Gibraltar, *I*. 51, 52, 56.
Bishop, Captain R., and the Malay, *II*. 318.
Bishop of Winchester, supplies Marines to ships, *I*. 6.
Blackheath, Sea Soldiers mustered on, *I*. 8.
Black Marines, *I*. 302, 303.
Black Sea, and Crimea, The, *II*. 91.
Bladensburg, Battle of, *I*. 300.
Blanche captures *Pique*, *II*. 322.
Bligh, Capt. R.N., and Governor of New South Wales, *I*. 179, 180.
Block-ships, *II*. 80.
"Blue Colonelcies," *I*. 132, 173.
Blue Marines, Uniform of the, *II*. 300.
Boats, R.M., Officers in charge of, *I*. 248.
Bocca Tigris, Forts Captured, *II*. 58, 59.
Bomarsund, Attack on, *II*. 82, 83, 84, 85, 86.
Bomb-Ketches or Bomb Vessels, *I*. 39, 66, 102, 106, 220, 222, 274; *II*. 13.
Borden Town, Capture of, *II*. 320.
Bordighero, Operations at, *I*. 284.
Borneo, Operations against Pirates of, *II*. 335.
Boston, Evacuation of, *I*. 162.
...... Marine Battalions in, *I*. 152 et seq
...... Position and Surroundings of, *I*. 149, 154.
Boulogne Flotilla, Attack on the, *I*. 235, 236.
Bounties, Recruiting, *I*. 72, 290, 317, 319.
Bourbon, Isle of, taken, *II*. 327.
Bows and Arrows, Chinese, *II*. 139, 144.
Bowyer, Fort, Attack on, *I*. 304.
Boxers, The, *II*. 250.
.... Dress of, *II*. 279.
.... Massacre by, *II*. 276.
.... Proclamation by, *II*. 275.
.... Punishment of, *II*. 277.
.... Their Standards, *II*. 287.
Bravery, Instances of, Individual, &c.—
Brown, Pte. J., *I*. 294.
Budd, Pte. J., *II*. 325.
Coryton, Lieut. J. R., *I*. 243.

Collard, Gr. J., *I*. 247.
Covey, Pte., *I*. 142.
Dowell, Lieut. G. D., *II*. 89.
Drake, Pte., *II*. 334.
Evans, Lieut. H. L., *II*. 140.
Gillespie, Capt. A., *II*. 14.
Halliday, Capt. L. S. T., *II*. 280.
Hewett, Lieut. J., *I*. 296.
Higham, Pte. G., *II*. 333.
Hill, Pte., *II*. 17.
Hunn, Corpl. J., *II*. 333.
Jones, Lieut. W. F. C., *II*. 243.
Langston, Lieut. J., *I*. 236.
Milligan, Sergt., *I*. 241.
Nicolls, Lieut. E., *I*. 249.
Philips, Lieut. M., *I*. 144.
Preston, Sergt. J. E., *II*. 287.
Prettyjohns, Corpl. J., *II*. 99.
Roch, Lieut., *II*. 330.
Tait, Lieut., *I*. 234.
Tickner, Pte. A. D., *II*. 283.
Wemyss, Capt. J., *I*. 255.
Wilkinson, Bombr. T., *II*. 103.
Williams, Lieut. J. D., *I*. 235.
Wilson, Capt. J., *II*. 14.
Wolridge, Lieut. S. A. R., *II*. 297.
Wood, Sergt.-Major, *II*. 140.
A Private at Cassis, *I*. 286.
A Private at Navarino, *II*. 17.
A Corporal at Trafalgar, *I*. 255.
A Private of the *Proserpine*, *I*. 246.
A Private of the *Success*, *I*. 143.
Four Privates of the *Wager*, *I*. 312.
Bromerie, Capture of Fort at, *II*. 326.
Brest, Attack on, *II*. 311.
Brigadier-Generals, Commandants made, *II*. 294.
British Marines in Roman Fleet, *I*. 1, 2.
Buenos Ayres, Capture of, *II*. 326.
"Bulldogs of the Army," *II*. 324.
Bunker's Hill, Battle of, *I*. 150, 166.
.... Howe's dispositions for, *I*. 165.
.... Account of, in "Lionel Lincoln, *I*. 165.
Burmah, *II*. 333, 336.
Butes-Carles, The, *I*. 5.
Buxar, Battle of, *II*. 112.
Byng, Admiral, at Gibraltar, *I*. 38.

C

Cabins to be allotted to Marine Officers, *I*. 130.
Camel Regiment, The Guards', R.M. Company of, *II*. 206, 212, 213.
Cadiz, *I*. 36; *II*. 327.
Campbell, Col., John of Glenlyon, *I*. 139, 146.
Camperdown, Battle of, *II*. 323.
Cagliari, Capture of, *I*. 64.
Canada, R. Marines in, *I*. 293.
Candia, Royal Marines at, *II*. 339.
Canteens, *II*. 294.
Canton, Operations at, *II*. 60, 62, 63, 73, 126, 130, 131, 134.
Cape of Good Hope, taking of the, *II*. 322, 325.
Cape St. Vincent, Battle of, *II*. 322.
Capri, Capture of, *I*. 277.
Carical taken, *II*. 317.
Carlists, Attack repulsed by Royal Marines, *II*. 38, 39.
Carlist War, of 1836-37. Its causes, &c., *II*. 27.
Carruthers, Capt., *I*. 107, 110, 114.
Carthagena (Spain), Major Hedges at, *I*. 62.

Cassis, Operations at, *I*. 285.
Cave, St. Michael's, *I*. 45, 49.
Cawnpore, The lesson of, *II*. 269.
Cette, Landing at, *I*. 64.
Chan-kia-wan, Battle of, *II*. 143.
Chapoo, Taking of, *II*. 69.
Chesapeake, Royal Marine Battalion in the, *I*. 291, 296, 298.
China, Royal Marines land, 1840, *II*. 56.
China, Royal Marine Brigade leaves for, in 1857, *II*. 129.
Chinese attack the lorcha *Arrow*, *II*. 125.
Chinese Imperial Troops, Uniform of, *II*. 279.
...... Random Fire, *II*. 290.
...... Gun Platforms, *II*. 291.
...... and Royal Marine Guard, *II*. 72.
...... Tea Party, Royal Marines at, *II*. 144.
...... War of 1840, Outbreak of, *II*. 54.
Ching-hae, Capture of, *II*. 65, 66.
Chuen-pee, Capture of, *II*. 56, 57, 58.
Churchills, Commissions held by the, *I*. 17, 22.
Clarence, Duke of, *I*. 34, 267, 274.
Clarke, Lieut., His narrative of Bunker's Hill, *I*. 157, 158, 159.
Clarke's Island, *I*. 175.
Classiarii, Soldiers for Sea Service, *I*. 1, 2.
.... Discontent of, *I*. 5.
Clothing, Economics in, at Sea, *I*. 123, 124; *II*. 223, 225.
Cobden Dyke, Defence of, *I*. 297.
Cole Mill, defence of, *I*. 293, 294.
Cochrane, Adml. Sir A., on the R.M., *I*. 300.
Collins Street, Melbourne and Hobart, *I*. 184.
Colonel-in-Chief, H.M. King George V., *II*. 293.
Colours, The, *I*. 15, 18, 22, 24, 32, 88, 100, 113, 157, 291; *II*. 73, 298.
...... Presentation of, *I*. 34, 290; *II*. 300.
...... New Union, first flown at Almanza, *I*. 64.
...... of Manchester Marines, *I*. 317.
...... American, captured by Royal Marines, *I*. 292.
Commission, Advertising for a, *I*. 271.
Commissions in the Royal Marines, Regulations for, *I*. 273.
Commonwealth, Soldiers of the, serving afloat, *I*. 11, 12, 321.
Companies below strength on the Pay Rolls, *I*. 311.
Company of Infantry, Composition of, in 1678, *I*. 16.
.... System, its drawbacks, *II*. 295.
Complements of Marines carried in ships of the Ancients, *I*. 2, 4.
.... Henry VIII's ships, *I*. 8.
.... In the time of Queen Elizabeth, *I*. 12.
.... of Officers of Marines embarked 1695, *I*. 32.
.... at end of 19th Century, *II*. 226.
Conan Doyle on the Royal Marines, *II*. 243.
Concord, Expedition to, *I*. 149, 163.
Conscientious Objector, a, *I*. 168.
Convicts, *I*. 171, 172, 174, 175.
Cook, Death of Captain, *I*. 144.
Coolie Corps, Chinese, *II*. 141.
Corigeou, Operations at, *II*. 332.
Cork, Siege of, *I*. 25, 26.
Corporal, former meaning of the word, *I*. 10.
Corresponding Societies, The, *I*. 201, 210.
Corunna, *II*. 324, 326.
Coteau du Lac, 2nd R.M. Battalion at, *I*. 293, 296.
Count of the Saxon Shore, The, *I*. 5.
Cracherode, Colonel Mordaunt, &c., *I*. 90, 312.
Craney Island, Repulse at, *I*. 291.
Crete, *II*. 338.
Crimea, Disembarkation in the, *II*. 92.
...... Position of the Allies before Sebastopol, *II*. 96.

INDEX

Cromwell's Army, *I*. 11-23.
.... Gibraltar project, *I*. 42, 52, 58.
.... Soldiers in Action afloat, *I*. 11, 12, 321.
Cronstadt, a Bugbear, *II*. 81.
Crystler's Farm, Battle of, *I*. 293.
Cubitt, Private Charles, Magnanimity of, *I*. 199.
Cumberland Island, *I*. 301, 302, 303.
Curaçao, Attack on, *II*. 325.
.... Taking of, *II*. 326.
"Curse of Glencoe, The," *I*. 146.
Cutting Out Expeditions, nature of, *I*. 237.
Cuxhaven, Operations at, *II*. 326.

D

Daimios, The Japanese, *II*. 147.
Dalrymple, Col. Campbell, proposes Marine Artillery, 1761, *I*. 261.
Damages awarded Officers and Soldiers, *I*. 316.
Darbai (Persian Gulf), fight at, *II*. 340.
Dardanelles, Forcing of the, *II*. 326.
"Dash" R.M. Battalion dog at Hernani, *II*. 37.
Davy, Colonel, his Pictorial Proclamation to Tasmanians, *I*. 184.
Dawes Point, Sydney, *I*. 175, 186.
Death of Captain Adair, *I*. 255.
.... Lieut. Langton, *I*. 236, 237.
.... Captain Lloyd, *II*. 267.
.... Admiral Nelson, *I*. 255.
.... Major Plumbe, *II*. 242.
.... Captain Senior, *II*. 242.
.... Captain Strangways, *I*. 141.
.... Captain Strouts, *II*. 287, 289.
.... Major Uniacke, *II*. 71.
.... Lieut. Williams, *I*. 235.
Dee, Dr. John, his proposals for Sea-Soldiers, *I*. 9.
Deputy-Adjutant General, Appointment first instituted, *II*. 293.
Detachments, Royal Marines, Reductions in, *II*. 226.
Dice, Throwing for Execution, *I*. 41, 44.
Difference between a Marine and a Land Soldier, *I*. 308.
Dilkes, Admiral, *I*. 49.
Disbandment of Marine Regiments, *I*. 68, 323.
Discipline Afloat in 1665, *I*. 32.
Discipline, Dibdin, on, *II*. 78.
Divisions, The Four, *I*. 269, 270.
D'Jounie Bay, Landing at, *II*. 43.
.... Camp at, *II*. 44.
Doig, Captain, His attempt to reach Tien-tsin, *II*. 266.
Domness, Attack on, *II*. 87.
Dongola, Bombardment of, *II*. 215.
Douglas, Major, Letter on his services, *I*. 232.
Dowell, Lieut., gains the V.C., *II*. 89.
Doyle, Sir Conan, on the Royal Marines, *II*. 243.
"Dragon's Teeth," *II*. 292.
Drill and Exercises, *I*. 14, 27, 28.
Dromons, *I*. 5.
Drums and Fifes, *I*. 32.
"Dumphies," The, *II*. 138.
Dundas, Fort occupied, *I*. 186.
Durango Decree, the, *II*. 40.
Dutch attack on Landguard Fort, *I*. 19.
Duties of Sea-Soldiers Afloat, *I*. 10, 26, 30, 32, 122, 248; *II*. 221, 224, 227, 228, 230, 232, 341.
Duties of Officers of Marines at Headquarters, *II*. 294.

E

Eastney, *I*. 269.
Eating Bank Notes, *II*. 224.
"Egypt for the Egyptians," *II*. 165.
El Magfar, Fighting at, *II*. 170.
El Teb, Battle of, *II*. 191.
Elizabethan period in the Navy, *I*. 9.
Enemy, a generous, *I*. 236.
"Enforced Idleness," *II*. 227.
Ensigns flown at Trafalgar, *I*. 254.
Entzheim (or Molsheim), Battle of, *I*. 22.
Epibati, Ancient Grecian Marines, *I*. 2.
Escape Creek, Attack on junks in, *II*. 128.
Essamen, Fight at, *II*. 154.
Eureka Stockade, Fight at the, *I*. 186.
Europa, Chapel of St., *I*. 40.
Execution of Admiral Byng, *I*. 112; *II*. 111.
.... of Mutineers, *I*. 200; *II*. 111.
.... Unfortunate mistake at, *I*. 146.
.... Throwing Dice for, *I*. 41, 44.

F

Fatshan, Fight at, *II*. 128.
"Fearful Blue," the of the Marines, at Tel-el-Kebir, *II*. 174.
Female Marines, *I*. 94, 99, 100.
Fernyhough brothers, the, *I*. 246, 247.
Ferrol, Attack on, *II*. 323.
Festing, Col., at Elmina, *II*. 152.
.... Thanks of the House of Lords, *II*. 337.
Field Officers, R.M., deprived of command *I*. 136.
.... necessary to the service, *I*. 308.
Field Training, *II*. 295.
Figueras, Operations at, *II*. 326.
"Firelocks," i.e., Fusileers, *I*. 15.
Fireships, Explosion vessels and Torpedoes, *I*. 244.
"First Fleet," The, *I*. 172, 174.
First Shot in Crimean War fired by a Marine, *II*. 91.
First White Man born in Victoria, *I*. 181
Fiume, Operations at, *II*. 331.
Flag, the "Bloody," *II*. 209.
Flank Companies, *I*. 164, 165.
Flannel Shirts, Introduction of, *I*. 150.
Fleets fitted out by Marines, *I*. 27; *II*. 80.
Flotilla on American Lakes, *I*. 296.
Foreigners enlisted as Marines, *I*. 208, 209.
"Forlorn Hope," meaning and derivation of, *I*. 237, 247.
Formation, too close at Graspan, *II*. 243.
Forton in old times, *I*. 275.
Free State, Advance into the, *II*. 244.
French Marine Regiments, *I*. 29; *II*. 102, 124.
French ships mentioned, *vide* "Ships" French.
French Town, Chesapeake taken, *II*. 330.
Fresh water soldiers, *I*. 10, 11.
Friction between Naval Officers and Officers of Army, *I*. 262.
Frye, Lieut., Curious Case of, *I*. 315, 316.
Fuentarabia, Attack on, *II*. 33.
Fusileers, *I*. 25, 323; *II*. 106.
.... Marine Regiments referred to as, *I*. 323; *II*. 106.
Futtegurh, Battle of, *II*. 120.

G

Gallantry, *vide* Bravery—
Gambia, Operations on the, *II*. 338.
"Gants à Crispin," *I*. 33.
Gascoigne, Sir Bernard, His suggestions for a Marine Corps, *I*. 30.
Gebail, Repulse of attack on, *II*. 45.
General Officers, R.M., *II*. 294.
Genoa, Operations at, *II*. 331.
Gentlemen Adventurers, *I*. 11.
Gibraltar, Capture and Defence of. *I*. 34, 322.
.... Punch drunk at opening of Grand Battery, *I*. 322.
.... French Account of opening of the Siege, *I*. 321.
.... Spanish Account, *II*. 313.
Girona saved by the Marines, *I*. 324.
Globe, Badge of the, its Antiquity and Distinction, *II*. 303.
...... and Laurel, Bestowal of the Badge, *I*. 34; *II*. 299.
"Glorious First of June," The, *II*. 322.
Goree, Taking of, *II*. 316.
Goschen, Mr., on the R.M., *II*. 220.
Goudhurst, Smugglers threaten to attack, *II*. 314.
Gough, Sir Hugh, Letter to Major Ellis, R.M., *II*. 67.
"Granger's Wonderful Museum," *I*. 43.
Graspan, Battle of, *II*. 239.
Grenade Exercise in Marine Corps, *I*. 222.
Grenadiers, *I*. 23, 24, 25, 27, 36, 37, 43.
"Grenadiers' March," The, *I*. 36, 37, 43; *II*. 106.
Groa, Operations at, *I*. 280, 281.
Grog, *I*. 89.
Guard, H.M. Marine in the *Medina*, *II*. 301.
Guards and Sentries afloat, *II*. 224.
Guards, Foot, provide nucleus for Marines, 1740, *I*. 72.
Groy, Island of, Marines land, *II*. 311.
Guadeloupe, Attacks on, 1703 and 1794, *II*. 311, 321.
.... Batteries stormed at Baie Mahut, *II*. 327.
Gubat, or Abu Kru, Battle of, *II*. 211.
Gun, 4.7, the R.M.A's in South Africa, *II*. 245.
Gun, the "International," *II*. 286.
Gunboats, Danish, attach *Melpomone*, *I*. 243.
.... Egyptian, on the Nile, *II*. 211.
Gunners in 16th Century, *I*. 8, 12. 259, 260.
"Gunners of the Tower," or "Fraternity of Artillery," *I*. 259.
Gunnery, *I*. 27, 122, 138, 140, 245, 260, 261; *II*. 225, 231, 295, 341, 342.

H

Hague, The, R.M. at, *II*. 331.
Hamilton, Lord, *I*. 39.
Hammond, Sergeant, promoted for training Black Marines, *I*. 302.
"Hamoaze Hussars," the, *II*. 301.
Hampden, Taking of, *II*. 331.
Hampton, Attack on, *I*. 291.
"Handy Man," Epithet should be transferred to Royal Marine, *II*. 301.
Hasheen, Battle of, *II*. 200.
"Hatches," or Fighting Stages, *I*. 2, 4.
Havannah, Capture of, *II*. 318.
Hawes, Lieut., R.M., organises Japanese Marines, *II*. 150.
Hay, Lord John, Letter commending R.M. Battalion, *II*. 39.

INDEX

Hayes, Lieut., cuts out *Nisus*, *I*. 279.
Healthy state of Marines at Walcheren, *I*. 245.
Hereditary Cup Bearer to the King, *I*. 312.
Hermione, Prize Money for her capture, *II*. 317.
Hernani, Battle of, *II*. 35, 36, 37.
Hesse, Prince of, the, *I*. 34, 35, 38, 39, 41, 42, 45, 48, 49, 52, 54, 55, 56, 57, 60, 61, 62.
.... His lying in state *I*. 322.
"Hints to Young Marine Officers," *II*. 220.
Holland, 3rd R.M. Battalion at South Beveland, *I*. 297.
"Honours of War, The," *I*. 67.
Hopson, Vice-Admiral, *I*. 67.
"Horse Marines," The, *II*. 308.
How, Lieut. H., His conduct at Fort Trinidad, *I*. 222.
Hsi-Ku Arsenal, Storming and Defence of, *II*. 257.
Hun, Fine specimen of, a, *II*. 109.
Hunt, Lieut. H., at Cassis, *I*. 285.

I

Illig, Storming of, *II*. 340.
Ill-treatment of Officers by Mutineers, *I*. 196.
Ill-usage of Soldiers afloat, *I*. 16, 127, 134.
Independent Companies, *I*. 72, 90, 102, 111.
India, Marines in, *II*. 107.
Indian Marine Regiments, *II*. 124.
Inkerman, Battle of, *II*. 98, 100.
Ireland, Royal Marines in Dublin, *II*. 184.
.... Their useful work, *II*. 188.
.... landed for eviction duty, *II*. 183.
.... Marine service in *II*. 177.
.... Never a Nation, *II*. 178.
.... Phoenix Park Murders, *II*. 184.
.... Recruiting for R.M. in *II*. 179.
Irish Loyalist Volunteers, *II*. 179.
.... Marines of King James II., *I*. 31.
.... The, in Naval Mutinies, *II*. 180.
.... Marine Volunteer Corps, *II*. 180.
.... Revolutionary Propaganda in Marine Barracks, *II*. 180.
.... Recruits in 1796, *I*. 196.
Isle aux Noix, 1st R.M. Battalion at, *I*. 293.
Isle de la Passe taken, *II*. 328.
Isle of Pines, Pirates captured at the, *II*. 333.
Isle of Rattan, Marines quell Mutiny at, *I*. 89.
Ismalia occupied, *II*. 170.

J

Jacket, Marine's, as Colours, *II*. 322.
Jamaica, Marines sent to, *I*. 27.
Janizaries, *I*. 23.
Japan, Condition of in 1860, *II*. 145.
...... R.M. Battalion arrives in, *II*. 146.
.... leaves, *II*. 150.

Java, Conquest of, *II*. 124, 329.
"Jolly," Derivation of name, *I*. 18.
Jingalls (or Gingalls), *II*. 72.
"Jolly Roger," The, *I*. 209.
Journal of Carlist War, Lieut. Halliday's *II*. 29.
.... Operations in the Chesapeake, *I*. 298.

K

Kafr-Dwar, Reconnaissance towards, *II*. 168.
Kagoshima, Bombardment of, *II*. 146.
Kajwa, Action at, *II*. 117.
Kaowle, Battle of, *II*. 143.
Kassassin, 1st and 2nd Battles of, *II*. 171, 172.
Khartoum, General Gordon sent to, *II*. 196.
Kinburn, Expedition to, *II*. 104.
King William IV., Funeral of, *II*. 38.
.... His letter to Sir R. R. Williams, *I*. 267.
.... His Portraits at each Division, *I*. 274.
"King's Battalion," The, *II*. 111, 112, 113, 114.
"'King's' or Kent Division," the *II*. 174.
"King's Letter Boys," *I*. 17.
Kinsale, *II*. 311.
Kinsaile (or Kensall) captured, *I*. 299.
Kotka destroyed, *II*. 88.
Kwan, Admiral, killed by a Royal Marine, *II*. 59.

L

Lace, Marine, *I*. 12.
Ladé, Battle of, *I*. 4.
Lagos taken, *II*. 336.
Lake Borgne, Capture of American Flotilla, *II*. 331.
Lally, The Comte de, *II*. 108.
Lambert's Bay, *II*. 249.
Landguard Fort, Attack on, *I*. 19.
Landing Orders, *I*. 41, 126.
Lang-Fan, Admiral Seymour's Column at, *II*. 253.
"Laurel Wreath," the, *I*. 101, 103, 115.
Leake, Sir John, *I*. 46, 48.
Leandro, Fort, taken by Marines, *I*. 41.
.... Blown up according to Spanish account, *II*. 313.
Ledyard, John, Sergeant and explorer, *I*. 144, 147.
Leeward Islands, Expedition against the, *I*. 134.
Legation Guards leave for Pekin, *II*. 269.
Leghorn, Operations at, *I*. 286.
Legion, the British, *II*. 28.
.... and the Royal Marines *II*. 33, 40.
"Lembarii," supposed river Marines, *I*. 2.
Lemmertown, Defence of, *II*. 323.
Leonard's Town, Capture of, *I*. 298.
Lerici, Castle of, captured, *II*. 331.
Lerida, Defence of, *I*. 63, 324.
Lexington, Skirmish at, *I*. 150, 152.
Liability of Military Officers to Naval Court Martials, *I*. 262.

"Life on the Ocean Wave," Its origin, *II*. 302.
Light Infantry, Royal Marines created, *II*. 105.
Light Infantry Division, The, Marines attached to the, *II*. 98.
"Lion and Crown," The, *I*. 306.
Lisbon, Expedition to, *I*. 10.
.... Battalion at, *I*. 289; *II*. 329.
Liverpool Volunteers, serving with Nelson as Marines, *I*. 317.
Lofa, Skirmish at, *II*. 253.
Long Island, Battle of, *II*. 319.
Looping Lace, Drummers', *II*. 304.
Lord Exmouth's praise of the R.M. at Algiers, *II*. 14.
Lord High Admiral, the, *I*. 8, 14.
"Lord High Admiral's or Hants Division," *II*. 74.
L'Orient, Expedition against, *II*. 314.
Louisburg, Sieges of, 1745 and 1758, *II*. 314, 315.
Loyalty of the Marines, *I*. 187, 194, 199, 204, 207.
Lucknow, *Shannon's* Brigade at, *II*. 117, 121.
Lunguillia, Operations at, *I*. 282.

M

Macao, R. M. at, *II*. 55.
MacDonald, Sir Claude, on the R.M., *II*. 289.
MacKenzie, Colonel, Anecdote and Services of, *I*. 110.
McLeod, Colonel, Services of, *I*. 91.
McNeil's Zareba (or Tofrek), Fight at, *II*. 202.
Madras, Defence of, *II*. 108.
Mahdi, The, *II*. 189, 197.
.... his Tomb blown up, *II*. 219.
Maiden's Choice, Fight at, *I*. 301.
Maitland, Capt. the Hon. John, obtains allowances, etc., for the Marines equal to those of the Navy, *I*. 110.
.... Commands Light Infantry and Fraser Highlanders, *I*. 133.
Malaga, Battle of, *I*. 38, 46.
Malta, *II*. 323.
Manchester Marines, The, *I*. 317, 319.
Manilla, Expedition to, *II*. 108.
.... Conquest of, *II*. 318.
Manora, Bombardment of, *II*. 114.
Manual Exercise, The, *I*. 122.
March, The Grenadiers', *I*. 36, 37, 43; *II*. 106.
March Past, The, *II*. 298.
Marie Galante, Occupation of, *II*. 326.
Marine, A, becomes a King, *II*. 231.
Marine Complements on board ship, *I*. 4, 6, 8, 11, 12, 32, 133, 234; *II*. 226.
Marine Corps, Position and Status of, *I*. i, ii, 2, 26, 127, 128, 132, 173, 262, 271, 307; *II*. 227, 228, 341.
Marine Heights (Balaklava), *II*. 94.
Marine Messes Afloat, *I*. 201, 204; *II*. 229.
"Marine Officer, The," or Sketches of Service, *I*. 228.
Marine Store Room, The, *I*. 123; *II*. 221.
Marine Regiments—
The Duke of York and Albemarle's Maritime Regiment, *I*. 14.
Prince George of Denmark's, *I*. 25.
The Regiments of Lords Torrington and Pembroke, *I*. 25.
Brudenall's, Colt's, Seymour's and Mordaunt's, *I*. 27.
King James' Marine Regiment in France, *I*. 31.

348   INDEX

Marine Regiments—continued—
Prince Rupert's Marine Regiment, *I.* 32.
Saunderson's, Villier's, Fox's, Mordaunt's, Holt's, Seymour's and Shannon's, *I.* 35, 39.
The "Queen's Marines," *I.* 35.
Primrose's, Newton's, Molesworth's, Leigh's, Evans', Kane's and Stanwix, *I.* 38.
Will's, Goring's, Bor's and Churchill's, *I.* 39.
The Ten Marine Regiments of, 1740-1748, *I.* 72, 86, 87, 91; *II.* 314, 341.
Ambiguous position of, *I.* 70.
Attacks on, *I.* 27.
Breaking of, in 1713, *I.* 68, 69, 323.
Burchett on their usefulness, *I.* 321.
Services of, in Spain, in 1702-1714, *I.* 323.
"Marine Volunteer," The, *I.* 118, 120.
Marines, Augmentation of, in 1760, *I.* 102.
...... King's Speech on the, *I.* 71.
...... placed on the Right of the Army, *I.* 108.
...... and Seamen in the past, *I.* 287.
...... Parliamentary Views on the, 1740, *I.* 306.
"Marine's Lament, The," *I.* 275.
Marinello, Operations at, *II.* 331.
Marseilles, Occupation of, *II.* 332.
Martha's Vinyard, Marines at, *II.* 319.
Martinique, *I.* 136; *II.* 317, 321.
.... H.M.S. *Blenheim* at, *II.* 325.
.... Storming Batteries at Petite Anse d'Arlette, *II.* 325.
Master Gunner of England, *I.* 259.
Matagorda, Fort, Defence of, *II.* 327.
Matchlock, Dangers of the, *I.* 44.
Matrimony on Paying Off, *I.* 99.
Matrosses, *I.* 68, 70.
Mauritius taken, *II.* 329.
Medal for Conspicuous Gallantry awarded, *II.* 287.
"Mediterranean, Sheere's Discourse concerning the," *I.* 42.
Mehemet Ali, *II.* 42.
Melstedt, Major (Danish Army), Death of, *I.* 232.
Messina, Sea Fight off, *II.* 311.
Mexico, R.M. Battalion in, *II.* 337.
Middle Ages, Sea Soldiers in the, *I.* 5.
Milligan, Sergeant, exploit of, *I.* 241.
"Military Treatise on Discipline of Marine Forces when at Sea," *I.* 120.
"Military Memoirs of Four Brothers," *I.* 249.
Militia, Royal London, the, *I.* 18.
Mines, *I.* 82, 91.
Minorca, Defence of Fort St. Philip, *II.* 314, 320.
.... Reduction of, *II.* 323.
Mocha taken, *II.* 333.
Monument Hill, Engagement at, *II.* 246.
Morea, Castle of (or Rhion), taken, *II.* 333.
Morgion, Operations at, *II.* 330.
Mortar Vessels at Sebastopol, Good work of R.M.A., *II.* 104.
.... Sweaborg, *II.* 90.
Mossel Bay, Royal Marines at, *II.* 249.
Mudge, Capt. Zachery, R.N., His treatment of "Fighting Nicholls," *I.* 239.
Musketry, *I.* 119, 120; *II.* 223.
.... Efficiency of Marines in action afloat, *I.* 122, 140, 240, 256.
.... Instruction, *I.* 153; *II.* 295.
Mutiny of Will's Marines, *I.* 68, 70, 323.
.... Garrison of Quebec, *I.* 188.
.... Athol Highlanders, *I.* 188.
.... Western Fencibles, *I.* 188.
.... New South Wales Corps, *I.* 180.
.... Fingall Regiment, *I.* 194.
.... at Gibraltar, *I.* 188.
.... attempted at Plymouth, *I.* 199.
.... of 8th West India Regiment, *II.* 324.
.... Indian, *II.* 115.
.... of 9th Native Infantry, *II.* 111.

Mutiny on board H.M.S. *Chesterfield, Namur, Ganges, Janus, Proselyte, I.* 190.
.... *Culloden, I.* 191.
.... *Beaulieu, I.* 192.
.... *London, I.* 195, 199, 200.
.... *Hermione, I.* 199.
.... *Impeteux, Danae, I.* 204.
.... *Thunder, I.* 205.
.... *Gibraltar, I.* 206.
.... *Excellent, I.* 207.
.... the *Romeo Primero, Slaver, II.* 334.
.... S.S. *Milwaukee II.* 249.
.... described by Captain Basil Hall, R.N., *I.* 207.
Mutinies, the Great Naval of 1797, 1802, *I.* 187.
.... Hesitation of Naval Authorities to call on the Marines, *I.* 193.

Names of Marines mentioned—
1—**Officers**—
Abbot, *I.* 67.
Abbott, *II.* 327.
Abercrombie, *I*, 133.
Adair, *I.* 67, 250, 255.
Adair, C. W., *II.* 148, 149.
Adair, T., *I.* 306.
Agnew, *I.* 87.
Airey, *II.* 204.
Aitcheson, W. O., *II.* 333.
Alexander, *II.* 96.
Alnutt, *II.* 155.
Anderson, *I.* 263; *II.* 17.
Anderson, A., *II.* 51.
Armstrong, H. G. B., *II.* 254.
Ashmore, *II.* 329.
Aslett, *II.* 39, 95.
Aston, G. G., *II.* 247.
Atcherley, *I.* 256.
Atkinson, R. G., *I.* 227.
Avarne, T., *I.* 159; *II.* 320.
Ayles, *II.* 334.
Baile, J., *I.* 286, 287.
Bailie, E., *I.* 323, 331.
Baldchild, G. E., *II.* 225.
Baldwin, F., *II.* 196.
Balkeney, J., *II.* 308.
Ball, N., *I.* 32.
Banks, *I.* 140.
Barclay, *I.* 241, 263, 264.
Barnard, C. L., *II.* 336.
Bartleman, J., *I.* 258, 297.
Barton, S., *I.* 294, 323.
Baxter, *II.* 14.
Bazalgette, G., *II.* 337.
Beadon, *II.* 333.
Beattie, or Beatty, *II.* 67.
Beatty, *I.* 218; *II.* 325.
Beauclerk, Lord G., *I.* 87.
Bell, H., *II.* 74.
Bell, *II.* 17.
Benson, J., *II.* 327.
Berry, J., *I.* 32.
Beyts, *II.* 259.
Blake, *II.* 132.
Bland, *I.* 248.
Blumberg, *I.* ii.
Blyth, *II.* 97.
Bidlake, R., *II.* 321.
Bishop, R., *II.* 318, 319.
Bisset, *II.* 106.
Bisset, J. P., *II.* 13, 14, 15.
Bor, *I.* 38, 39, 41, 49, 51, 54, 57, 61, 69.
Bor, J. H., *I.* 38; *II.* 338.
Bowater, *I.* 200.
Boyd-Hamilton, *II.* 184, 186.
Boyle, *II.* 128, 336.
Brattle, *I.* 280.
Brewer, *I.* 340.
Bright, R., *II.* 321.
Brisbane, A., *I.* 159.
Brittan, C. G., *I*, ii; *II.* 338.
Brittan, E. P., *II.* 193, 194.
Browne, D., *II.* 309.
Brown, L., *II.* 286.
Brudenall, T., *I.* 27.
Buckland, *I.* 265.
Bunce, *I.* 278; *II.* 330, 332.
Burton, *I.* 215; *II.* 332.

Bury, *II.* 37.
Butler, J., *I.* 319.
Byam, *II.* 116.
Byng, *I.* 87.
Byrne, *II.* 338, 339.
Caermarthen, Marquis of, *I.* 27, 32; *II.* 311.
Caldwell, R. K., *II.* 83.
Campbell, A., *I.* 159.
Campbell, J., *I.* 172.
Campbell, *I.* 263, 265.
Campbell, of Glenlyon, *I.* 139, 146, 147.
Campbell, *II.* 318, 324.
Carden, P. R., *I.* 286, 287.
Carruthers, W., *I.* 107, 110, 114.
Carter, *II.* 330.
Casiau, *I.* 36.
Caulfield, *I.* 89.
Chamberlaine, T., *I.* 32.
Chambers, G. C., *II.* 323.
Chambers, *I.* 107.
Champion, *II.* 318.
Channer, H., *I.* ii.
Chaundy, *I.* 138.
Chudleigh, S., *I.* 159.
Churchill, G., *I.* 17, 87.
Clapperton, *II.* 30, 32.
Clark, J. R., M.A., *II.* 247.
Clarke, *I.* 157, 158, 159, 161, 163, 164, 166.
Clements, *I.* 301, 302.
Cochran, *II.* 80.
Cochrane, J., *I.* 76, 78, 79, 87; *II.* 341.
Coffin, R. P., *II.* 169.
Cole, N., *I.* 248.
Collins, *II.* 332.
Collins A. T., *I.* 102, 105, 111, 147, 165, 175; *II.* 179, 315, 318.
Collins, D., *I.* 111, 173, 175, 176, 178, 179, 180, 181, 182, 183, 188.
Collins, W., *I.* 172.
Colt, H. D., *I.* 27.
Columb, J. C. R., *I.* 263.
Colwell, G. H. T., *II.* 190, 193, 195.
Cook, *II.* 132.
Cooke, J., *I.* 279.
Corbet, A. D., *II.* 338.
Cornwall, H., *I.* 87.
Coryton, J. R., *I.* 243.
Cottal, *II.* 327.
Cotter, F. G., *II.* 202.
Cotterell, J., *I.* 87.
Couche, *II.* 328.
Coulter, *II.* 328.
Cox, S., *I.* 286.
Cox, H., *II.* 332.
Cracherode, M., *I.* 90, 312.
Crease, J. F., *II.* 154.
Cresswell, J., *I.* 172; *II.* 323.
Crew, *II.* 321.
Crooden, *I.* 64, 90.
Crosbie, A. B., *I.* 158; *II.* 337.
Crozier, A., *I.* 306; *II.* 325.
Curle, *I.* 138.
Daniell, S., *I.* 76, 79, 87, 91.
Danby, The Earl of, *I.* 32.
Larrell, N., *I.* 19, 20, 21, 30.
David, G. F., *II.* 218.
Davidson, J., *I.* 63, 68.
Davidson, *I.* 143.
Davis, *I.* 274, 286; *II.* 321.
Davy, T., *I.* 172.
Davy, *I.* 184.
Dawes, W., *I.* 173, 176.
Deane, R. B., *I.* 158.
De Courcy, *II.* 158, 199.
Delacombe, B. J., *I.* 286.
Delacombe, W., *II.* 136, 337.
Denmark, Prince G. of, *I.* 34, 35.
Denny, R., *II.* 338.
D'Esterre, *I.* 196.
Diblee, F. L., *II.* 338.
Digby, *I.* 17.
Digby, *II.* 109.
Doig, *II.* 259, 266.
Douglas, C., *I.* 72, 76, 87.
Douglas, *I.* 217, 219, 220, 232; *II.* 51.
Dowding, T. W., *I.* 186; *II.* 337.
Dowell, G. D., *II.* 89.
Doyley, H., *I.* 133.

INDEX

List of Officers mentioned continued—

Drake, H. D., *I.* 186.
Drury, T., *II.* 327.
Drury, W. P., *II.* 339.
Dutton, *I.* 159.
Duncombe, J., *I.* 87.
Dupuis, *II.* 36.
Dyer, J., *I.* 159.
Dyer, T. W. P., *II.* 267.
Eden, F. M., *II.* 169.
Edye, L., *I.* i, ii.
Elliott, N. B., *I.* i.
Elliott, G., *I.* 306 ; *II.* 68.
Elliott, H., *I.* 306.
Ellis, *II.* 55, 56, 57, 62, 63, 64, 114.
Ellis, S., *I.* 159.
Ennis, *II.* 330.
Ensor, *I.* 214.
Evans, H., *II.* 141.
Evans, L., *II.* 140.
Ewing, *II.* 319.
Faden, *II.* 8.
Faddy, W., *I.* 172.
Farmer, J., *II.* 323.
Fawtry, J., *I.* 24.
Fegan, C., *II.* 44, 47.
Fernyhough, H., *I.* 249.
Fernyhough, G., *I.* 249.
Fernyhough, R., *I.* 245, 249.
Festing, F. W., *II.* 152, 153, 155, 158, 337.
Fischer, N. J., *I.* 230.
Fisher, *I.* 54, 55.
Fitz-James, H., Duke of Albemarle, *I.* 31.
Fleming, *I.* 75.
Flight, *I.* 203.
Foley, *I.* 281.
Foote, *II.* 136.
Forshall, *I.* 206.
Fottrell, P., *II.* 329.
Fox, *I.* 35, 39, 41, 49.
Frampton, C., *II.* 173.
Frazer, R., *I.* 87.
French, A. H., *II.* 246.
Frye, *I.* 316.
Furzer, J., *I.* 173.
Gardiner, F., *I.* 159.
Gardiner, R., *I.* 136, 139, 140.
Gardner, R., *II.* 323.
Garmston, *II.* 304.
Gascoyne, *II.* 142, 143.
Gascoigne, H. B., *I.* 241, 242.
Gatliff, A. F., *II.* 247.
Gerrard, M. A., *II.* 324.
Gilbert, R., *I.* 265.
Gillespie, A., *I.* 194, 195 ; *II.* 14.
Gillespie, N. J., *I.* 220.
Gillespie, *II.* 58, 59.
Gooch, *I.* 73.
Gordon, *I.* 133.
Gordon (Bey), *II.* 218, 219.
Graham, F., *II.* 83.
Graham, S. J., *II.* 169.
Graham, W., *I.* 128.
Grant, J., *I.* 76, 83, 84, 87, 91.
Grant, P., *I.* 279.
Gray, *II.* 116, 117, 120, 121.
Griffiths, J. H., *I.* 168, 306.
Gunn, G., *I.* 286.
Hadden, *I.* 115.
Haig, S., *II.* 331.
Hailes, *I.* ii.
Hall, W., *I.* 141.
Halliday, L. S. T., *I.* ii, *II.* 29, 269, 270, 274, 275, 276, 277, 280, 281, 288, 291.
Halliday, F. A., *II.* 29, 30, 31, 32, 33.
Hambley, A. J. B., *II.* 68.
Hamilton, *I.* 96, 312.
Hanlon, J., *I.* 279.
Hanmore (or Hanmer), W., *I.* 83, 87.
Harman, *II.* 321.
Harrison, J., *I.* 298.
Harrison, R. S., *I.* 97.
Hawes, A. G. S., *II.* 150.
Hawkins, *II.* 325, 335.
Hawley, C. O., *II.* 83.
Hayes, M., *II.* 93.
Hayes, R., *I.* 199, 278, 279.

Hearle, P., *I.* ii ; *II.* 158.
Hedges, R., *I.* 62.
Henry, R., *I.* 227 ; *II.* 13.
Hepburn, D., *I.* 107, 110.
Herbert, Hon. W., *I.* 87.
Heriot, A. H. J., *II.* 338.
Heriot, G. M., *II.* 340.
Hervey, *II.* 338.
Hewes, J., *I.* 287.
Hewett, J., *I.* 296.
Hewitt, C. C., *II.* 70.
Hicks, J. S., *I.* ii.
Higgins, *I.* 133.
Higginson, *II.* 323.
Hill, *II.* 322.
Hill, J. G., *I.* 286.
Hobbs, F. M. B., *II.* 219.
Hocker, *II.* 129, 131.
Hockin, C. F., *II.* 50.
Hodges, *II.* 321.
Holland, N. C., *II.* 14.
Holmes, C., *II.* 331.
Holmes, H., *I.* 87 ; *II.* 314.
Holloway, *II.* 129, 130, 131, 132, 135, 138.
Holt, H., *I.* 35.
Holtaway, *I.* 229, 296.
Hood, C. H., *II.* 297.
Hopkins, *II.* 95, 98, 99, 100.
Hore, *I.* 283, 284.
Hore, J. R., *I.* 223 ; *II.* 326.
How, T., *I.* 220, 222, 223.
Howell, J., *II.* 323.
Hughes, *I.* 91.
Hunt, B., *II.* 337.
Hunt, H., *I.* 285.
Hurdle, T., *II.* 18, 93, 95, 103.
Husband, J., *II.* 326.
Hutchinson, A. R. H., *II.* 247.
Inglis, *II.* 140.
Irving, *I.* 91.
James, F., *II.* 13.
James, H., *II.* 330.
Jeffreys, J., *I.* 87 ; *II.* 342.
Jekyll, *II.* 204.
Jewers, F., *I.* 234.
Jolley, N. K., *I.* ii.
Jolliffe, *I.* 96.
Jones, H. S., *II.* 175, 183.
Jones, W. T. C., *II.* 235, 243.
Johnson, *I.* 150.
Johnston, G., *I.* 172, 177, 179, 180.
Johnstone, D., *I.* 159, 207.
Johnstone, J., *I.* 172.
Johnstone, J. R., *II.* 253, 254, 255, 258, 260.
Jordan, J., *I.* 87.
Jumper, W., *I.* 35, 40.
Kappey, M., *II.* 303.
Keightley, G., *I.* 87.
Keigwin, *II.* 311.
Kellow, R., *I.* 172.
Kendall, *I.* 242.
Kennedy, C. H., *II.* 340.
Killigrew, J., *II.* 311.
H.M. King George V., *II.* 293, 297, 306.
Kreyer, M., *II.* 303.
Laforey, J., *I.* 87.
Lambert, *II.* 325.
Lambrick, *I.* 115.
Langley, C. G., *II.* 29, 30, 31, 32, 38.
Langston, J., *I.* 236, 237.
Laurie, *I.* 296.
Lawlor, *I.* 248.
Lawrence, *I.* 223 ; *II.* 90, 324, 335.
Lawrence, H., *I.* 38, 41.
Lawrie, F. B. A., *II.* 256, 263, 267.
Layton, A. T., *II.* 281, 291.
Lees, J. (Manchester M.), *I.* 317, 319.
Legge, W., *I.* 19.
Le Grand, F. G., *II.* 169.
Lemon, *II.* 116, 129, 136, 138, 139, 140.
Leonard, R., *II.* 44, 335.
Lewis, G., *I.* 296, 297, 298, 300, 301, 302 ; *II.* 326.
Liardet, F., *II.* 327, 329.
Lillington, *I.* 27.
Little, *II.* 328.

Lloyd, *II.* 265, 266.
Lloyd, S., *II.* 331.
Logan, G., *I.* 159.
Logan, *II.* 33, 333.
Long, J., *I.* 87.
Long, *I.* 173.
Lord, E., *I.* 182.
Lowder, *II.* 87.
Lowder, S. N., *II.* 337.
Lowther, A., *I.* 72, 81, 87.
Luke, E. V., *II.* 175, 254, 259, 266, 287.
Lye, *II.* 148.
Lynch, *I.* 294.
Lyttleton, C. (or Littleton), *I.* 19, 21, 23.
MacAdam, *I.* 282.
McCallum, *I.* 214, 215.
McArthur, E., *II.* 336.
McArthur, J., *I.* 186.
McCausland, E. L., *II.* 175.
MacDonald, A., *I.* 141.
MacIntire, J., *I.* 118, 121, 123, 124, 125, 126, 234.
MacKenzie, *I.* 102, 105, 110, 133.
MacKenzie, A., *II.* 325, 326.
McKinnon, W., *I.* 275.
McLachlan, *II.* 328.
MacLeod, *I.* 78, 91.
McLeux, *II.* 95.
Maclurcan, J. L. R., *II.* 203.
Maitland, Hon. J., *I.* 110, 133 ; *II.* 320.
Malcolm, J., *I.* 291, 295, 298, 300, 302, 303.
March, *II.* 99, 100, 141.
Marchant, A. E., *II.* 199, 203, 234, 236, 238, 240, 241, 242, 243, 244, 246, 247.
Marjoribanks, *I.* 91.
Markham, *I.* 69.
Marriott, R. A., *II.* 212.
Marshall, *II.* 5, 7.
Mascall, J. R., *I.* 275.
Maskerry, *II.* 183.
Mason, J., *I.* 70.
Matthew, G. E., *II.* 218, 219.
Maughan, *I.* 214.
Maule, J., *II.* 13.
Maxwell, T., *I.* 258 ; *II.* 327.
Maxwell, E. R., *II.* 55, 62.
Mayne (Manchester M.), *I.* 320.
Mears, *I.* 281.
Medlicott, *I.* 91.
Meech, G., *II.* 326.
Mercer, D., *I.* 150.
Meredith, J., *I.* 186.
Middleton, *I.* 147.
Middleteton, C., *I.* 22.
Miller, *II.* 17.
Miller, G. J., *II.* 303.
Milrea, *I.* 140.
Minheer, *I.* 140.
Minto, *II.* 323.
Mitchell, T., *I.* 25, 286.
Mitchell, *II.* 333.
Molloy, P., *II.* 338.
Monson, *II.* 315, 317, 318.
Moodie, B., *II.* 314.
Moore, *I.* 280, 281 ; *II.* 327.
Moore, T. C., *II.* 17, 21, 94.
Moore (or Morton), *I.* 91.
Morgan, *II.* 184, 186.
Morgan, R. H., *II.* 244.
Morrison, *I.* 172.
Morrison, *II.* 328.
Morrison, A., *II.* 49.
Mordaunt, H., *I.* 27, 35.
Morton, Hon. D., *I.* 72, 87.
Mullins, G. J. H., *I.* ii ; *II.* 247, 256, 262, 263, 264.
Munro, G., *II.* 338.
Murray, *I.* 78.
Murray, J., *I.* 105 ; *II.* 341.
Naylor, T., *II.* 321.
Nelson, F. A., *II.* 247, 338.
Nepean, E., *II.* 331.
Neville-White, H. S., *I.* ii ; *II.* 206, 212.
Nicolls, E., *I.* 227, 231, 237, 238, 239, 248, 249, 303, 304, 306 ; *II.* 325, 326, 327.

List of Officers mentioned continued—
Nicholas, J. H., *I.* 193, 217, 218, 226, 250, 251.
Nicholls, W. C., *II.* 293.
Nicholson, G., *II.* 329.
Nicholson, J., *I.* 220.
Noble, *II.* 184, 186.
Norcutt, *I.* 27; *II.* 311.
Oats, *I.* 278.
O'Grady, *II.* 136.
Oldfield, H., *I.* 232; *II.* 214, 215, 218, 219.
Oldfield, J. H. R., *I.* 232.
Oldfield, T., *I.* 142, 143, 217, 218, 221, 232; *II.* 2, 51, 321.
O'Loghlan, T., *I.* 73, 118, 119, 120, 122, 123, 124, 127, 128, 133, 234.
O'Neale, *II.* 324.
Ord, *II.* 86.
Orr, *II.* 114.
O'Sullivan, N. D., *I.* ii.
Owen, J., *I.* 252, 257, 283; *II.* 28, 29, 32, 35, 36, 37, 38.
Ozzard, *II.* 338.
Paris, A., *II.* 247, 248.
Parke, *I.* 292, 293; *II.* 38, 41.
Parker, *II.* 140.
Parkes, C. A., *II.* 333.
Parkes, K. S., *II.* 328.
Patterson, R. O., *I.* ii.
Pattoun, G., *I.* 220.
Payne, *I.* 242.
Pearce, *I.* 145, 146.
Pearce, C. W., *I.* 275.
Pearson, A. C., *II.* 206, 212.
Peile, S. P., *II.* 247, 248, 340.
Pemberton, *I.* 312.
Pembroke, Earl of, *I.* 25.
Pengelly, E., *I.* 278.
Penrose, *II.* 124, 132.
Peterborough, Earl of, *I.* 60, 61.
Philips, J., *II.* 337.
Phillips, M., *I.* 144, 145.
Phillips, P., *II.* 302.
Pickard, J., *II.* 55.
Pierce, *I.* 140.
Pitcairn, *I.* 149, 150, 151, 157, 158, 159, 160, 166, 167.
Pitcairn, W., *I.* 158.
Pleydell, *I.* 240.
Plumbe, J. H., *II.* 234, 235, 241, 242, 243.
Prynne, *II.* 143.
Poe, W. H., *II.* 206, 212.
Poe, W. S., *II.* 244.
Portlock-Dadson, W., ii; *I.* 257; *II.* 80, 83, 84, 99, 100, 132.
Poulden, G., *I.* 220.
Pownall, T., *I.* 63.
Powlett, C., *I.* 87.
Poyntz, W. H., *II.* 130, 133, 135, 139, 147.
Pratt, *II.* 33.
Prideaux, *I.* 91.
Pym, *II.* 96, 121, 336.
Rabon, *I.* 133.
Ragg, *I.* 159.
Raikes, G. L., *II.* 244, 245.
Rea, H., *I.* 279, 286, 287.
Read, J., *II.* 326.
Reading, *I.* 65.
Reeves, L. B., *II.* 327.
Reeves, R., *I.* 32.
Renwick, J., *I.* 279.
Rice, *II.* 241.
Richards, *II.* 150.
Richards, G., *II.* 323.
Richardson, *II.* 322.
Richardson, C. N., *II.* 324.
Rivers, J. J. C., *I.* 286.
Roberts, *I.* 138.
Roberts, *II.* 97.
Robertson, *II.* 247.
Robinson, *I.* 91.
Robinson, C., *II.* 45, 46.
Robinson, W., *I.* 72, 81, 87.
Robyns, *I.* 302.
Roch, *II.* 330.
Rodney, A., *I.* 61.
Rokeby, *II.* 136.

Rooke, G., *I.* 17, 18, 34, 36, 39, 41, 42, 43, 44, 45, 46, 47, 48, 49, 53, 54, 55, 56, 57, 60.
Roscarrock, E., *I.* 19.
Ross, R., *I.* 173, 177, 178.
Ross, *II.* 329.
Ruel, J. G., *I.* 279.
Rycaut, *I.* 136.
Sanderson, T., *I.* 35.
Sandford, *I.* 298.
Saunders, F. J., *II.* 235, 236, 238, 240, 243, 244.
Savage, J. B., *I.* 143, 273, 274.
Savage, *II.* 36.
Saxe-Coburg, Gotha, Prince Alfred of, *II.* 293, 299.
Sayer, *II.* 86.
Schomberg, *II.* 90, 129, 227.
Senior, *II.* 235, 237, 238, 239, 240, 242, 243.
Sewell, *II.* 341.
Seymour, W., *I.* 27, 35.
Seymour, *II.* 312.
Shairp, J. N., *I.* 172.
Shanks, *I.* 234.
Shannon, Viscount, *I.* 35, 37.
Shea, J., *I.* 172.
Shea, R., *I.* 159.
Shillibeer, *II.* 327.
Short, *I.* 59.
Shovell, C., *I.* 27, 47.
Simms, *I.* 195, 209.
Slessor, H., *I.* 218, 219.
Smith, F. T., *II.* 109.
Smith, J. S., *I.* 205.
Smith, W., *II.* 324.
Smithwick, R., *II.* 6.
Snowe, *II.* 328.
Sowle, R., *I.* 87.
Spalding, *II.* 204.
Spearing, *II.* 318.
Spratt, M., *II.* 131.
Stanners, *I.* 278.
Steele, *I.* 240.
Steele, R., *I.* ii, 228; *II.* 28, 32, 34, 36, 38.
Stevens, *I.* 293.
Stevens, A., *II.* 18.
Stevens, J. H., *II.* 12, 17.
Stewart, J. H., *II.* 183.
Stirling, *II.* 116, 117, 121.
Stockley, H. H. F., *II.* 248.
Story, J., *I.* 32.
Strangways, H. L., *I.* 141.
Stransham, A. B., *II.* 20, 60, 62.
Strickland, R., *I.* 32; *II.* 323.
Strong, H. H., *I.* 168, 174.
Strouts, B. M., *II.* 269, 271, 274, 276, 279, 281, 287, 288, 289, 290, 291.
Studdert, *II.* 115.
Sturgeon, *II.* 20.
Suther, C. G., *II.* 146, 148, 149, 150.
Swale, *II.* 126.
Tait, *I.* 234; *II.* 324.
Tench, W., *I.* 172, 174, 175, 206.
Thompson, *I.* 91.
Timmins, T., *I.* 157, 172, 258.
Timpson, *II.* 95.
Timson, *I.* 186.
Torrens, *I.* 228, 230, 231.
Torrington, Earl of, *I.* 25.
Tothill, J., *I.* 275.
Townsend, *I.* 26.
Townshend, C. V. F., *I.* 133, 163; *II.* 200, 212, 219.
Travers, J. C., *II.* 129, 135, 141, 142.
Trollope, *I.* 197.
Trotman, C. N., *I.* ii.
Tucker, *II.* 171, 173.
Tupman, A. J., *I.* ii; *II.* 248.
Turnbull *I.* 229.
Tuson, H. B., *II.* 169, 193.
Tyldesley, *II.* 326.
Uniacke, J., *II.* 71, 331.
Urmston, A. B., *II.* 244, 340.
Urquhart, J., *II.* 220.
Vallack, J., *II.* 15, 332.
Vaughan, R., *I.* 31.
Villiers, G., *I.* 35.

Walker, *I.* 164.
Walker, W., *II.* 43, 44, 52, 325.
Wall, H., *I.* 222.
Waller, J., *I.* 156, 157.
Walsh, *II.* 129, 136.
Wardell, *II.* 173, 174.
Washington, *I.* 78.
Watson, H., *I.* 91.
Weir, *II.* 323, 324.
Welchman, *II.* 330.
Wemyss, J., *I.* 255.
Wemyss, M., *II.* 107, 109, 110, 111, 112, 114.
Wemyss, *II.* 90.
Wesley, *II.* 104.
Whalley, *I.* 133.
Whitcombe, J., *II.* 56, 59, 64, 67.
White, *I.* 109.
White, F., *II.* 247.
White, F. J., *II.* 38, 41, 56, 64.
White, R., *II.* 330.
Whitfoord, *I.* 130, 131.
Whiting, G. W., *II.* 63.
Williams, J., *II.* 107.
Williams, J. D., *I.* 235.
Williams, J. W. C., *II.* 336.
Williams, R., *I.* 193, 264, 266, 267, 270, 289, 290, 292, 293, 294, 295, 296, 301, 302, 303, 317; *II.* 14, 180, 299, 323.
Williamson, *I.* 186.
Wills, C., *I.* 43, 63, 68, 323, 324.
Wilson, D., *I.* 197.
Wilson, J., *I.* 168; *II.* 14.
Wilson, L. O., *II.* 242, 244, 245.
Winter, D., *I.* 70.
Winterbottom, *II.* 303.
Wolfe, E., *I.* 72, 81, 87.
Wolfe, J., *I.* 75.
Wolridge, S. A. R., *I.* 297; *II.* 13.
Wolridge, *I.* 140, 148.
Worth, *I.* 265.
Wray, E., *I.* ii; *II.* 269, 271, 274, 275, 277.
Wrey, C., *I.* 19.
Wright, *II.* 15.
Wright, J., *I.* 109.
Wright, W. A. G., *I.* 186.
Wybourn, M., *II.* 323, 330.
Wyegate, *I.* 95, 96.
Wylock, *I.* 44, 49, 50.
Wynyard, S., *I.* 72, 75, 78, 81, 83, 87.
York, Duke of, *I.* 15, 22, 24, 28, 43.
Young, G., *I.* 236.

2.—OTHER RANKS.

Allen, *II.* 339.
Allen, T. R., *II.* 282, 291.
Anderson, *II.* 204.
Baddeley, *II.* 241, 242.
Barton, W., *I.* 192.
Baughan, T., *II.* 87.
Beaumont, W., *II.* 232.
Beer, R., *II.* 66.
Bennet, *II.* 56.
Billinge, W., *II.* 57, 58.
Boyce, *II.* 231.
Brabazon, *II.* 14.
Branham, *I.* 200, 201.
Brown, J., *II.* 294.
Buckler, J., *II.* 291.
Budd, J., *II.* 325.
Bunn, *II.* 339.
Burroughs, *II.* 246.
Bush, *I.* 279.
Butler, *II.* 121, 122.
Campbell, J., *I.* 51, 58.
Capon, *II.* 340.
Coffee, *I.* 200, 201.
Coleman, S., *II.* 231.
Collard, *I.* 247.
Collins, H., *II.* 87.
Cooper, *II.* 256.
Covey, *I.* 142.
Cubitt, *I.* 197.
Deane, J., *II.* 291.
Derry, H., *II.* 56, 73, 115.
Douglas, A., *I.* 99.
Drake, *II.* 334.
Dyson, *II.* 243.

INDEX

Other Ranks continued—
Eagles, *II*. 204, 213.
Field, G. H., *II*. 232.
Fisher, J., *II*. 91.
Freeman, H., *II*. 241.
Gangell, *I*. 182.
Gilborn, A., *I*. 201.
Goddard, G., *II*. 291.
Gowney, J., *II*. 282, 283, 291.
Gregory, W., *II*. 270, 277, 281, 283, 284, 291.
Hammond, *I*. 202.
Head, *II*. 117.
Heans, W., *I*. 206.
Henderson, *I*. 214.
Hicks, *II*. 255.
Higham, G., *II*. 333.
Hill, *II*. 73.
Hill, *II*. 17.
Hook, J., *I*. 204.
Hooper, *II*. 339.
Hunn, J., *II*. 333.
Jays, W., *II*. 66.
Jeffries, *II*. 232.
Jenvey, *II*. 217.
Johnson, *II*. 241.
Jordan, *II*. 100.
Keen, *I*. 198.
King, K., *II*. 291.
Knight, *II*. 56.
Lambert, *II*. 219.
Ledyard, J., *I*. 144, 147.
Lee, *I*. 199, 200, 201.
Lister, G., *II*. 291.
Lye, *II*. 231, 256.
Lyne, *II*. 126.
MacGinnis, *I*. 200.
Marley, G. T., *II*. 215, 216.
Marr, *II*. 256.
Martin, W. H., *II*. 213.
Maton, *II*. 231.
Maynard, *II*. 219.
Milligan, *I*. 241.
Mitchell, *II*. 203.
Murphy, *II*. 278, 281.
Nicol, E. J., *II*. 231.
O'Gorham, *II*. 4.
Oliver, H. A., *II*. 232.
O'Neale, *I*. 201.
Packwood, *I*. 242.
Palmer, *II*. 339.
Parker, T., *II*. 66.
Peek, *II*. 262.
Philips, C. W., *II*. 291.
Polter, *II*. 14.
Preston, *II*. 276, 287, 291.
Prettyjohns, J., *II*. 99, 100.
Rann, W. H., *II*. 232.
Ranner, L., *II*. 234.
Rees, T., *I*. 243 ; *II*. 328.
Richards, *II*. 99.
Rigsby, *II*. 241.
Robinson, *II*. 255.
Roe, W. G., *II*. 291.
Russell, *II*. 216.
Salisbury, *I*. 279.
Samuels, *II*. 338.
Sawyer, G., *II*. 281, 291.
Scadding, A., *II*. 279, 291.
Sutchings, R., *II*. 232.
Secker, *I*. 253.
Segar, G., *I*. 36.
Sheppard, *II*. 271.
Snell, H., *I*. 93 to 100 ; *II*. 107.
Sparkes, A., *II*. 291.
Spicer, G., *II*. 232.
Stanton, *II*. 203.
Sullivan, P., *II*. 99.
Sudbury, J., *II*. 2, 3, 4.
Sweet, J., *I*. 201.
Symons, J., *II*. 51.
Thorne, *I*. 181.
Thornton, *I*. 204.
Tickner, *II*. 283, 291.
Tough, T., *II*. 325.
Turner, N., *II*. 96, 98, 100.
Varndell, *II*. 338.
Ward, J. E., *II*. 232.
Watts, G., *II*. 66.
Westbrook, A. E., *II*. 291.

Wilkinson, T., *II*. 103.
Wilson, *II*. 15.
Windsor, R. W., *II*. 232.
Witney, H., *I*. 99.
Wood, *II*. 140.
Nantow, Attack on, *II*. 136.
Napier, Sir Chas., at Cronstadt, *II*. 81.
Napier, General Sir C. J., on the R.M.A., *I*. 259.
Naples, *II*. 323, 332.
Napoleon Buonaparte, *I*. 215.
.... On board H.M.S. *Bellerophon*, *II*. 4.
.... Said to have asked for Commission in British Marines, *II*. 1.
.... reported suitable for a Naval Officer, *II*. 2.
.... Wounded by Sergeant of Marines, *II*. 5.
.... Goes on board H.M.S. *Superb*, *II*. 6.
.... and Capt. Beatty, R.M., *II*. 7.
.... and Royal Marines of H.M.S. *Undaunted*, *II*. 4.
Nathan Brooks, his " General and Compleat List Military," *I*. 33.
Naval Brigades, *I*. 10, 24, 26 ; *II*. 61-67-68-116 *et seq*, 135 *et seq*, 148-149-158-208, 233 *et seq*, 259-329.
.... Guards, *II*. 74.
.... Gunnery School, *I*. 263.
.... Officers appropriate highest Marine Ranks and Pay, *I*. 132, 173.
.... " Should be gentlemen " (Nelson), *I*. 17.
.... Supply of, *I*. 17.
" Naval Sketch Book, The," Author's opinion of R. Marines, *I*. 276.
Navarino, Battle of. What led to it, *II*. 15.
.... Lieut. Hurdle's account of, *II*. 18.
.... Sir Anthony Stransham's account of, *II*. 20.
Navies, Foreign, Now and in Nelson's time, *II*. 293.
Navigation, Marines said to have been instructed in, *I*. 310.
Negapatam, Capture of, *II*. 320.
Nelson carried below by three Marines, *I*. 255.
Nelson's Pocket Knife, *I*. 255.
" Nelson's Revenge," *I*. 258.
Newcastle, disturbance at, *II*. 333.
New Orleans, Attack on, *I*. 306.
" New Scheme, The," (Lord Cawdor's), *II*. 243, 294, 302.
New South Wales Corps, The, *I*. 177.
New York Marine Artillery Company, *I*. 261.
New Zealand, Engagements in, *II*. 335, 336, 337.
Nicholas, Lieut. Paul Harris, R.M., *I*.
Nicholls, " Fighting," made Governor of Anholt, *I*. 227.
.... His services, *I*. 248.
.... and his Indian Levies, *I*. 303.
.... in Pensacola and the Gulf, *I*. 304.
Nile, Battle of the, *I*. 142 ; *II*. 323.
.... Expedition, Start of the, for Khartoum, *II*. 206.
.... Operations on the, 1896, *II*. 214.
.... Gunboats, *II*. 214, 215, 216.
Ningpo evacuated, *II*. 68.
Noli, Operations at, *I*. 278.
Nominy, Destruction of, *I*. 299.
" No Popery," *I*. 10.
Norfolk Island, *I*. 176, 178.
Norfolk Regiment and " Rule Brittania," *II*. 298.
Nugent, Lord, *I*. 39, 41-321.

O

Obligado, Operations at, *II*. 335.
Odessa, Bombardment of, *II*. 91.
Officers for Marine Regiments of 1740, *I*. 72.
.... Royal Marine for Special Duty in South Africa, *II*. 247.
.... R. Marine, Position and Status afloat, *I*. 27, 70, 127, 128, 129, 130.
Oldfield, Major T., at the Nile, *I*. 142.
.... at Acre, *I*. 217.
.... Services of, *I*. 231.
Omdurman, Fall of, *II*. 218.
Omoa, Storming of, *II*. 320.
" Order of Battle " at Boston, *I*. 161, 168.
Order in Council of 1664, establishing Maritime Regiment, *II*. 15.
Orders, Divisional, etc. *I*. 164, 169, 208 ; *II*. 21, 74, 159, 305.
Orders, Marine, when embarked (1742), *I*. 133.
Orders for Rooke's Expedition, *I*. 36.
Orkney Islands, *II*. 311.
Ormond, Duke of, *I*. 36.
Ornagacuan (or Kornet Sherouan), Skirmish at, *II*. 47.
Ortona, Operations at, *I*. 281.
Osman Digna, *II*. 190, 193.
Oswego, Capture of, by 2nd Battalion R.M., *I*. 295.
Owen, Lieut. J. R. M., takes possession of *Argonauta*, *I*. 253, 257.

P

Palamos, Operations at, *II*. 329.
Palmerston, Lord, on the R.M., *II*. 42.
Parker the Mutineer, *I*. 191, 196, 197, 198.
Passages, R.M. occupy, *II*. 30.
Patna, Storm of, *II*. 109.
Patriotic Fund, The, *I*. 242, 248, 279, 288.
Patrouski, March to, *II*. 105.
Pay and Allowances, *I*. 184, 194 ; *II*. 222.
Paying Off, Disturbances on, *II*. 224, 231.
Pearl's Brigade, The, *II*. 121, 336.
Peh-Tang, Landing at, *II*. 141.
Pei-ho Forts, Description of the, *II*. 141.
.... Abortive attack on the, *II*. 139.
.... Capture of the, *II*. 142, 255, 278.
Pekin, Description of, *II*. 271.
Pekin Legations, " Carving Knife Brigade The," *II*. 274.
.... Commencement of the Siege of the *II*. 278.
.... Conduct of the R. Marines, *II*. 289.
.... Description of the, *II*. 272.
.... Guns available, *II*. 275.
.... Regular Fighting Men available, *II*. 274.
.... Relief of the, *II*. 289.
Pembroke, Earl of, Marine Regiment of the, *I*. 25.
Percy, Earl, thanks the Marines, *I*. 162.
Peterborough, The Earl of, *I*. 60, 61, 62.
Philadelphia, Capture of, *II*. 320.
Philip, Capt. Arthur, R.N., Organises Australian Expedition, *I*. 171.
Phoenix and *Didon*, Fight between the, *I*. 239.
Pianosa, Operations at, *I*. 279.
Pink, a, *I*. 47, 96.
Pirates, Barbary, *I*. 11 ; *II*. 9.
.... English, *I*. 11.
.... at Isle at Pines, *II*. 333.
.... Northern, *I*. 5.
.... Borneo, *II*. 335.
Pitcairn's Island, *I*. 166.

Pleydell, Lieut., Letter from Capt. Baker, R.N., *I.* 240.
Pocock, Rev. Thos., Journal of the, *I.* 38.
Point du Ché, Operations at the, *II.* 328.
Point Pitre, Attack on Fort at, *I.* 301.
Police Duty, Marines employed on, *I.* 191.
Pondicherry, Attacks on, *I.* 93, 96, 111; *II.* 108, 317.
Port d'Ango, Operations at, *II.* 331.
"Port and Starboard," *I.* 138, 253.
Port Essington, R.M. Detachment at, *I.* 186.
Port Mahon taken, *I.* 324.
Port La Nouvelle, Operations at, *I.* 285.
Port Moresby, Annexation of, *I.* 186.
Port Philip, Marines at, *I.* 181.
Port Royal, Attack on, *I.* 136.
Port Spergui, Operations at, *I.* 277.
Port Said, Occupation of, *II.* 169.
Portmore, Lord, *I.* 37.
Porto del Infreschi, Operations at, *I.* 282.
Porto Ferrajo, Defence of. *II.* 324.
Portraits of King William IV., *I.* 274.
Portugal, Battalion R.M. in, *I.* 289; *II.* 329, 333.
Prescot (Canada), Fighting at, *II.* 333.
Presentation of Colours, *I.* 34, 290; *II.* 298.
Presentiment of Death (Lt. Bisset), *II.* 14.
.... (Capt. Stevens), *II.* 17.
Preston Pans, Battle of, *I.* 131.
Pretoria, Action near, *II.* 245.
Prettyjohns, Corporal, wins the V.C., *II.* 99.
"Princess Victoria's, or Essex Division," *II.* 74.
Privateers, Marines serving in, *I.* 132.
Privileges in the City of London held by R. Marines, *I.* 18.
Prize Money, *I.* 90, 319; *II.* 317, 318, 327.
Promotion, Slowness of, in R. Marines, *I.* 270, 275; *II.* 343.
Promotions for Algiers, *II.* 15.
.... for Loyalty, *I.* 192, 198, 201, 204, 205.
Proposal to "Change round" the Marine Divisions, *II.* 296.
Prussian Regulations, The, *I.* 119.
"Punch, Mr. on the R.M." *II.* 167, 189, 268.
Punishments, *I.* 41.

Q

Quarters, First of the Admiral's Regiment, *I.* 18.
Quarter-Gunners, *I.* 261.
Quebec, Failure of Expedition against, *I.* 68.
.... Taking of, *II.* 317.
Queen Anne's Marines stated to be still in America, in 1740, *I.* 310.
"Queen's, or Devon Division, The," *II.* 74.
Queen Victoria, Accession of, *II.* 38.
"Queen's Marines, The," *I.* 35-54.
Quiberon, Expedition to, *II.* 322.

R

Raids and Landing Parties, Instructions for, *I.* 126.
Raids, by Lieut. Hore on the French and Spanish Coasts, *II.* 326.
Ras-el-Khymer destroyed, *II.* 327.

Rations, *I.* 68.
Reasons for formation of the Admiral's Regiment, *I.* 16; *II.* 341.
Rebellions, Irish, *II.* 180, 182.
Recruiting, Difficulties of, *I.* 16; *II.* 179.
Red Coats first adopted by the Marines, *I.* 25.
Red Marines, The, Their present uniform, *II.* 300.
Regiment, Nomenclature of, *I.* 25.
"Regiment, The, of the Sea," *II.* 54.
Regiments at Gibraltar, *I.* 43.
Regiments mentioned—
N.B.—The Regimental numbers in this list do not necessarily refer to the regiments bearing them at the present day, especially where mentioned in the first half of the work. Many of these bearing numbers higher than about 40, have been so often disbanded and raised again at later dates in quite different quarters, that they cannot be identified with those bearing the same number in the 19th and 20th Centuries. Those referred to in Volume II. however may be generally considered to be those of to-day.
Cavalry—
Horse Guards, *I.* 14, 38.
Household Cavalry, *II.* 170, 171, 206.
2nd Scots Greys, *II.* 274.
5th Lancers, *II.* 190.
10th Hussars, *II.* 190.
15th Hussars, *II.* 199, 309.
17th Lancers, *II.* 308.
19th Hussars, *II.* 190, 206, 212.
21st Lancers, *II.* 218.
Wiltshire Yeomanry, *II.* 247.
Royal Artillery, *I.* 74, 82, 153, 168, 295; *II.* 28, 59, 61, 97, 126, 130, 143, 158, 170, 171, 175, 191, 193, 199, 217, 229, 236, 240, 248, 315, 318, 321, 327, 338.
Royal Engineers, *II.* 28, 81, 136, 138, 140, 142, 147, 158, 168, 199, 218, 219, 229, 332.
Infantry—
Guards' Camel Regiment, *II.* 206, 208, 210, 211.
Grenadier Guards (1st Gds.), *I.* 18, 21, 22, 33, 72; *II.* 171, 174, 175, 199, 201, 203, 237, 239, 240, 305.
Coldstream Guards, *I.* 14, 25, 29, 37, 72; *II.* 171, 174, 175, 199, 201, 203, 237, 239, 240, 305.
Scots Guards, *I.* 72; *II.* 171, 174, 175, 199, 201, 203, 237, 238, 239, 240, 305.
1st Foot (Royals), *I.* 14; *II.* 138, 325.
2nd Foot (Queen's), *I.* 15, 37; *II.* 143, 314.
3rd Foot (Buffs), *I.* 15, 18, 37, 110; 4th Foot, *I.* 15, 35, 54, 137, 150, 163, 168, 300.
5th Foot, *I.* 166, 168; *II.* 237, 240, 248.
6th Foot, *I.* 37, 94; *II.* 217.
7th Foot (Fusileers), *I.* 29; *II.* 219, 314.
9th Foot, *I.* 102; *II.* 299.
10th Foot, *I.* 149, 168; *II.* 217, 314.
13th Foot, *I.* 294; *II.* 123, 124.
14th Foot, *II.* 330.
15th Foot, *I.* 74, 188; *II.* 274.
18th Foot (Royal Irish), *I.* 158, 161, 166, 168; *II.* 55, 56, 61, 62, 63, 65, 66, 67, 68, 170, 172, 175.
19th Foot, *I.* 102, 105, 110.
20th Foot, *II.* 147.
21st Foot (Royal Scots Fusileers), *I.* 102, 103, 300.
22nd Foot, *I.* 160, 168.
23rd Foot (R. Welsh Fusileers), 150, 168; *II.* 158, 159, 256, 259, 265, 305.
24th Foot, *I.* 74.

26th Foot (Cameronians), *II.* 55, 56, 64.
27th Foot (Enniskillings), *I.* 188, *II.* 323.
29th Foot, *I.* 27; *II.* 247, 314, 322.
30th Foot, *I.* 35, 102, 107, 108.
31st Foot, *I.* 35, 36.
32nd Foot, *I.* 35, 36; *II.* 168, 171, 172.
34th Foot, *I.* 74, 134.
36th Foot, *I.* 74.
37th Foot, *I.* 102, 104.
38th Foot, *I.* 159, 161, 166, 168; *I.* 168, 274.
40th Foot, *I.* 168.
42nd Foot, *I.* 135, 137, 139; *II.* 158, 159, 190, 194, 195.
43rd Foot, *I.* 161, 166, 168.
44th Foot, *I.* 168, 300.
45th Foot, *I.* 168; *II.* 314.
47th Foot, *I.* 158, 166, 168; *II.* 240, 248.
49th Foot, *I.* 150; *II.* 55, 56, 61, 62, 63, 66, 67, 68, 142, 199, 200, 201, 202, 203.
50th Foot, *II.* 170, 172, 323.
51st Foot, *I.* 166.
52nd Foot, *I.* 159, 168.
53rd Foot, *II.* 117, 120, 199, 200, 219.
55th Foot, *II.* 65, 71.
56th Foot, *II.* 327.
58th Foot, *II.* 237, 240.
59th Foot *I.* 161 168; *II.* 126, 130, 132, 135.
60th Foot, *I.* 188; *II.* 168, 171, 173, 191, 193, 196, 320.
61st Foot, *I.* 192, 104.
63rd Foot, *I.* 168; *II.* 305.
65th Foot, *II.* 191, 193, 194, 195.
66th Foot, *II.* 235.
67th Foot, *I.* 102; *II.* 7, 142, 143, 147.
68th Foot, *I.* 188; *II.* 325.
69th Foot, *I.* 102, 108.
70th Foot, *II.* 199.
71st Foot, *II.* 28, 279, 339.
72nd Foot, *I.* 319; *II.* 172, 217.
75th Foot, *II.* 191, 193.
76th Foot, *I.* 108.
77th Foot, *I.* 188.
78th Foot, *II.* 322, 328.
79th Foot, *II.* 108, 217, 318, 323.
81st Foot, *I.* 188.
83rd Foot, *II.* 333.
84th Foot, *II.* 109, 170, 171, 172, 190.
85th Foot, *I.* 102, 300, 306.
86th Foot, *II.* 235.
88th Foot, *I.* 166; *II.* 101.
89th Foot, *II.* 108, 191, 193, 329, 330.
90th Foot, *I.* 102, 108.
92nd Foot, *II.* 324.
93rd Foot, *II.* 118, 119.
94th Foot, *II.* 327.
95th Foot, *II.* 158.
99th Foot, *II.* 143.
102nd Foot, *I.* 291; *II.* 247.
105th Foot, *II.* 237, 239, 240, 242.
Royal Army Medical Corps, *II.* 339.
Regiments known by their Colonel's Names—
Cavalry—
Burgoyne's Light Horse, *I.* 104, 106.
Foot—
Anstruther's (58th Foot), *II.* 315.
Barrymore's (13th Foot), *I.* 43, 54.
Beauclerk's (19th Foot).
Bellair's (2nd Foot).
Bolton's *II.* 341.
Boscawen's (75th Foot).
Churchill's (In French pay), *I.* 22; *II.* 310.
Churchill's (3rd Foot).
Columbine's (6th Foot).
Colville's (69th Foot).
Coote's (84th Foot), *II.* 108.
Crauford's (85th Foot).
Cromwell's Own, *I.* 12.

INDEX

Regiments known by their Colonel's Names continued—
De Rolls (Swiss), *II.* 328.
De Watteville's (German), *I.* 295, 296.
Donegall's, *I.* 43.
Draper's (79th Foot), *II.* 108.
Dumbarton's (1st Foot).
Erskine's (67th Foot).
Farringdon's (29th Foot). *I.* 27.
Fingall, *I.* 194.
*Fox's (32nd Foot).
Goff's, *II.* 11, 12, 321.
Grey's (61st Foot).
Guise's (6th Foot).
*Holt's, *I.* 35, 36.
Hotham's, *I.* 62.
Ingoldsby's *I.* 11, 12, 321.
Lambert's (67th Foot).
Loudon's (37th Foot).
*Mordaunt's, *I.* 35.
Morgan's (90th Foot).
Mountjoy's, *I.* 43.
Ruffane's (76th Foot).
*Saunderson's (30th Foot).
*Shannon's, *I.* 35.
Stuart's (37th Foot).
Sybourg's, *I.* 62.
Trelawney's, *I.* 38.
Tryawly's, *I.* 63.
*Villier's (31st Foot).
Waldegrave's *I.* 316.
Whitmore's (9th Foot).
N.B.—Where no page number is given refer to page given opposite the Regimental number. In the case of those marked by an asterisk (*) reference may also be made to "Marine Regiments."

Colonial and Various—
Australasia—
New South Wales "Bushmen," *II.* 247.
New South Wales Contingent, *II.* 204.
New Zealand Contingent, *II.* 248.
Calabrian Free Corps, *II.* 328.
Canada—
Canadian Chasseurs, *I.* 291.
Canadian Fencibles, *I.* 294.
Canadian Voltigeurs, *I.* 294.
Glengarry Light Infantry, *I.* 295, 296.
Glengarry Militia, *II.* 333.
10th Veteran Battalion (?), *I.* 294.
Cape Coast—
Cape Coast Volunteers, *II.* 152.
The Cape—
Rhodesian Field Force, *II.* 247.
China—
Chinese Regiment, *II.* 265.
Hong-Kong Artillery, *II.* 289.
Hong-Kong Regiment (Sikhs), *II.* 262, 264, 265.
Tien-tsin Volunteers, *II.* 255.
Egypt—
1st Egyptian Battalion, *II.* 219.
12th Egyptian Battalion, *II.* 219.
14th Soudanese Battalion, *II.* 219.
Ireland—
Cork Boyne Volunteers, *II.* 179.
Cork True Blues, *II.* 179.
Loyal Irish, *II.* 320.
Loyal Marine Volunteers, *II.* 182.
Sea Fencibles, *II.* 180, 182.
West Indies—
1st West India Regiment, *II.* 338.
2nd West India Regiment, *I.* 303; *II.* 153, 157.
8th West India Regiment, *II.* 324.
India—
Bengal Volunteers, *II.* 55, 56, 61, 62.
9th Bengal Cavalry, *II.* 199, 201.
Bengal Yeomanry Cavalry, *II.* 122.
Bombay Sappers *II.* 327.
Central Indian Horse, *II.* 219.
East India Co's Grenadiers, *II.* 110, 111, 112.
East India Co's Hussars, *II.* 110, 111.
Madras Artillery *II.* 55, 61, 71.
Madras European Regiment, *II.* 328.
Madras Sappers, *II.* 55, 199.

Marine Battalion, *II.* 124; V. 121st Pioneers.
Probyn's Horse, *II.* 143.
Purgunnah Battalion, *II.* 109.
1st Sikhs, *II.* 289.
4th Sikh Rifles, *II.* 118.
6th Native Infantry, *II.* 110, 111.
7th Rajputs, *II.* 289.
9th Native Infantry, *II.* 110, 111.
12th Madras Native Infantry, *II.* 136.
15th Native Infantry, *II.* 110.
15th Sikhs, *II.* 199.
17th Native Infantry, *II.* 199.
20th or Marine Regiment, *II.* 124.
28th Native Infantry, *II.* 199.
38th Madras Native Infantry, *II.* 130.
57th Madras Native Infantry, *II.* 54, 56, 57, 61, 62, 63, 71.
65th Bengal Native Infantry, *II.* 134, 138.
69th Punjabis, *II.* 124.
70th Bengal Native Infantry, *II.* 134, 136.
121st Pioneers, V. Marine Battalion.
N.B.—The Regimental numbers in the above list do not necessarily bear any relation to the Regiments to which they belong at the present day. They refer merely to the number borne by the regiment at the dates on which it is mentioned on the page referred to.

Foreign Regiments—
America (United States)—
1st U.S. Riflemen, *I.* 301.
68th Regiment, *I.* 292.
85th Regiment, *I.* 292.
9th Infantry, *II.* 264, 265.
Marines, *II.* 265, 277, 282, 283, 284, 303, 304, 308.
Austria—
Marines, *II.* 50.
Rocketeers, *II.* 47.
Denmark—
1st Jutland Infantry, *I.* 227.
2nd Jutland Rangers, *I.* 227.
1st Jutland Sharpshooters, *I.* 227.
France—
Anjou, Le Regiment d', *I.* 29.
Amiral, Le Regiment (Vermandois), *I.* 29.
Berwick's, *I.* 32.
Bigorre, Regiment de, *I.* 105.
Chasseurs de Vincennes, *II.* 85.
Clare's, *I.* 31.
Compagnies Franches de la Marine, *I.* 29.
Corps Royal d'Infanterie de Marine, *I.* 19.
Franco-Algerine Legion, *II.* 28.
†Fitzgerald's, *I.* 31.
Infanterie de la Marine, *II.* 124, 274.
Lorraine, Le Regiment de, *II.* 108.
Lee's, *I.* 31.
Marine Regiment, *II.* 108.
Royal Marine, *I.* 29.
Royal Vaisseaux, *I.* 16, 29.
Nixe, Le Regiment du, *I.* 108.
†O'Donnell's, *I.* 31.
Picardie, Le Regiment de, *II.* 311.
Pondicherry, Le Regiment de, *II.* 108.
†Queen's Regiment of Foot Guards, *I.* 31.
†Royal Body Guard, *I.* 31.
†Royal Regiment of Foot Guards, *I.* 31.
Swiss Marines, *I.* 29.
Vielle Marine, *I.* 16, 29.
Zouaves, *II.* 97.
5th Regiment, *I.* 280.
51st Regiment, *II.* 85.
81st Regiment, *I.* 280.
88th Regiment, *I.* 32.
102nd Regiment, *II.* 142, 143.
†These regiments were Irish regiments which accompanied James II to France and took service with the French Army.

Germany—
Imperial Guard, *II.* 274.
3rd Marine Battalion, *II.* 274, 277, 283, 286.
Japan—
Marines, *II.* 150, 274, 277, 284.
Russia—
9th East Siberian Rifles, *II.* 274.
Spain—
Athlone, *I.* 31.
Ultonia, *I.* 224.
2nd Infantry, *II.* 29.
Marines, *II.* 29.
Princessa Regiment, *II.* 35.
British Legion—
Queen's Own Lancers, *II.* 28.
Reina Isabel's Lancers, *II.* 28.
1st Infantry, *II.* 28.
2nd English, *II.* 28.
3rd Westminster Grenadiers, *II.* 28.
4th Queen's Own Fusileers, *II.* 28.
5th Scotch (or Highland) Light Infantry, *II.* 28.
6th Scotch Grenadiers, *II.* 28, 36.
7th Irish Light Infantry, *II.* 28.
8th Highlanders, *II.* 28.
9th Irish, *II.* 28, 35.
10th Munster Light Infantry, *II.* 28, 33.
Turkey—
The Chifflic Regiment, *I.* 219.
Remarkable Escapes of Capt. G. Elliott and Lieut. H. Elliott, *I.* 306.
"Remembrance, The," *I.* 36.
Report on the Marines by Admiral Keppel, *I.* 115.
Rescue of a Company, 37th Madras N.I. by R.M., *II.* 63.
"Retenue de poupe," *I.* 6.
Review on Hounslow Heath, 1678, *I.* 23.
.... Putney Heath, 1684, *I.* 14.
Rifle Legion, Proposed R.M., *II.* 41.
Rifles, Martini-Henry, used at Pekin, *II.* 282.
Rifleman and Russian, Fight between, *II.* 102.
Rockets, Chinese, *II.* 130.
Roman Marines, Relic of, *I.* 1.
Rooke, Admiral Sir Geo., Anecdote of, *I.* 18.
Roshensalm Fort destroyed, *II.* 88.
Routine for Marines when afloat, 1782, *I.* 122.
Rovigno, Operations at, *II.* 331.
Royal Engineers flogged by order of a Commodore, *II.* 28.
Royal Marine Artillery, *I.* 259, 265, 289, 292, 297; *II.* 13, 35, 84, 90, 104, 135, 171, 214, 245.
Russian War, 1854-1855, R.M. Battalions in the, *II.* 79.

S

Saints, Wooden at Gibraltar, Anecdote of, *I.* 42.
St. Christopher's taken, *II.* 311.
St. Domingo, Operations at, *I.* 243.
St. Estevan, Battle of, *I.* 63, 106, 323.
St. Helena taken, *II.* 310.
St. Malo attacked, *II.* 311.
St. Lazar, Assault on, *I.* 81, 92.
St. Lucia, Capture of, *II.* 322.
St. Marcou, Defence of, *I.* 212.
Salamis, Battle of, *I.* 4.
Salerno, Operations at, *II.* 323.
San Juan, Occupation of, *II.* 136, 336.
Santa Cruz, Attack on, *II.* 323.
Santa Maura, Fighting at, *II.* 328.
Sardinia surrendered, *I.* 324.

Saumarez, Sir James, His congratulations on Anholt, *I.* 230.
.... His proposals for Marine Artillery, *II.* 342.
Savage, Sir John Boscawen, His Commissions, *I.* 273.
Savannah, Defence of, *II.* 320.
Saxon Shore, The Count of the, *I.* 5.
Scaling Ladder taken at Landguard Fort, *I.* 21.
Scalping, *I.* 152, 163.
Scheldt, Forcing of the, *I.* 246.
Scotswoman at Balaklava, Fable of the, *II.* 100.
"Sea Crab Engine, The,", *I.* 37.
Sea Fight, Duties of Marines in a, *I.* 121.
Sea-Kit (*Vide* also Uniform, Clothing, etc.), *I.* 123; *II.* 223, 225, 341.
Sea-Lion killed by Lieut. Hamilton, *I.* 313.
Sea-Service of Marines at beginning of 19th century, *I.* 251.
Sea Service, Regiments for, *I.* 35.
Sea Soldiers disappear from James I Navy, *I.* 11.
.... in Henry VIII Navy, *I.* 8.
Sealia, Operations at, *I.* 278.
Seamen, Characteristics of, *I.* 4, 30, 32, 287.
........, Poor quality of Recruits in 1854, *II.* 80.
........, Marine Regiments as a Nursery for, *I.* 26.
Secunderabagh, Assault on the, *II.* 118.
Senegal, Capture of Fort Louis, *II.* 315, 327.
Serapaqui, Storming of Fort at, *II.* 336.
"Serious Considerations on the War in Europe" (1706), *I.* 41.
"Seven Men of Moidart, The," *I.* 128.
Seymour, Admiral, His expedition towards Pekin, *II.* 252.
Shah Najif, The, Attack on the, *II.* 118.
Shaluf, Battle of, *II.* 169.
Shannon's Brigade, Pte. H. Derry's Account of, *II.* 116.
Shannon's Gunners trained by the R.M.A. *II.* 115.
Shek-Tseng, Attack on, *II.* 138.
Shendy, Fighting at, *II.* 217.
Shield of Achilles, *II.* 304.
.... Classiarii, *I.* 2.
"Ship, The, Fort," at Passages, *II.* 31.
Ship of Earl Godwin, Her complement of Soldiers, *I.* 5.
...... Large, of Ptolemy Philopater, *I.* 4.

Ships, Men-of-War, British—
Aboukir, *II.* 330.
Achille, *I.* 251.
Achilles, *I.* 102, 103.
Active, *I.* 146, 280, 281; *II.* 317.
Adamant, *I.* 197, 213, 214.
Agamemnon, *I.* 197; *II.* 93.
Agincourt, *II.* 335.
Aibates (?*Achates*), *I.* 12.
Aide, *I.* 12.
Ajax, *II.* 80, 329.
Alacrity, *II.* 256.
Alarm, *II.* 336.
Albion, *II.* 14, 17, 18, 20.
Alecto, *II.* 336, 337, 338.
Alexandra *II.* 167, 170, 190.
Algerine, *II.* 114, 269.
Alligator, *II.* 54.
America, *I.* 283, 286, 287.
Amphion, *I.* 280.
Anholt, *I.* 228, 230.
Anne, *I.* 25.
Antelope, *I.* 12, 31.
Apollo, *II.* 330.
Arab, *II.* 334.
Archangel, *I.* 27.
Ardent, *I.* 198, 243.
Arethusa, *II.* 326.
Argo, *II.* 106, 109.
Argonaut, *I.* 198.
Argus, *II.* 152, 154.
Ariadne, *II.* 340.
Aristocrat, *I.* 277.
Armada, *I.* 283, 284.
Arrogant, *II.* 88, 89.
Asia, *II.* 16, 17, 18, 20.
Assurance, *I.* 189, 321.
Athenian, *I.* 278.
Auckland, *II.* 70.
Aurora, *II.* 254.

Bacchante, *II.* 331.
Badger, *II.* 212, 214.
Barfleur, *II.* 254, 256, 338.
Barke of Bullen, *I.* 12.
Barracouta, *II.* 152, 249.
Beaulieu, *I.* 199.
Beelzebub, *II.* 13.
Belleisle, *I.* 250, 257; *II.* 318.
Belle Poule, *II.* 328.
Bellerophon, *I.* 234, 255; *II.* 1, 2, 3, 6, 7, 8, 232.
Benbow, *I.* 270; *II.* 47.
Berwick, *I.* 139.
Blanche, *I.* 238, 239; *II.* 322, 325.
Blenheim, *II.* 59, 64, 66, 67, 80, 325.
Blonde, *II.* 64, 70, 71.
Bloodhound, *II.* 336, 337.
Boadicea, *II.* 337.
Bonaventure, *I.* 12.
Bonetta, *II.* 318.
Boston, *II.* 318, 319.
Bounty, *I.* 179.
Boyne, *II.* 39.
Bridgwater, *II.* 108.
Bristol, *I.* 137, 138.
Britannia, *II.* 228, 333.
Briton, *II.* 196.
Brune, *II.* 337.
Brunswick, *II.* 322.
Bull, *I.* 12.

Caesar, *I.* 201; *II.* 231.
Caledonia, *I.* 285; *II.* 328, 333.
Calliope, *II.* 72, 73.
Cambrian, *II.* 20, 329.
Camperdown, *II.* 323, 339.
Canada, *II.* 323.
Caroline, *II.* 327.
Carysfort, *II.* 45, 46, 47, 48, 169, 170.
Castor, *I.* 205; *II.* 29, 30, 32, 43, 48.
Cephalus, *I.* 282.
Centaur, *II.* 323, 325.
Centurion, *I.* 63, 74, 162, 312; *II.* 251, 253, 264.
Cerberus, *I.* 280, 281; *II.* 318.
Challenger, *II.* 308.
Charon, *I.* 304; *II.* 320.
Charwell, *I.* 295.
Charybdis, *II.* 340.
Chatham, *I.* 162.
Chesterfield, *I.* 190.
Chiffone, La, *II.* 327.
Christopher, *I.* 7.
Clio, *II.* 70.
Clyde, *I.* 198.
Colombine, *II.* 70.
Commonwealth, *II.* 232.
Conqueror, *I.* 256, 257; *II.* 146, 147, 148.
Conquest, *I.* 248.
Conway, *II.* 54.
Cornwall, *I.* 297.
Cornwallis, *II.* 67, 70, 71, 328.
Coromandel, *II.* 128, 143, 150.
Cossack, *II.* 88.
Cruiser, *II.* 334.
Culloden, *I.* 191.
Curacoa, *I.* 282.
Cumberland, *II.* 331.
Cyclops, *II.* 45, 46, 49, 50.
Danae, *I.* 204.
Dartmouth, *II.* 16.
Decoy, *II.* 152, 154.
Defence, *II.* 322.
Defiance, *II.* 230.
Deptford, *I.* 44.
Diadem, *I.* 262; *II.* 231.
Diamond, *I.* 277; *II.* 319.
Dictator, *I.* 198.
Dido, *II.* 43, 45.
Diomed, *I.* 291.
Discovery, *I.* 144.
Dolphin, *II.* 199.
Doris, *II.* 234, 235.

Dorsetshire, *I.* 81.
Dover, *II.* 328.
Dragon, *I.* 65, 102, 103; *II.* 318.
Drake, *II.* 330.
Dreadnought, *I.* 12.
Driver, *II.* 81.
Druid, *II.* 55, 72, 152.
Dryad, *II.* 337.
Duke of Wellington, *II.* 87.
Eagle, *I.* 277; *II.* 331.
Eclair, *I.* 282, 283.
Edgar, *I.* 68.
Edinburgh, *I.* 287; *II.* 80, 331.
Electra, *I.* 186.
Elizabeth, *I.* 12, 32, 128.
Eltham, *I.* 96.
Emerald, *II.* 326.
Encounter, *II.* 127.
Endeavour, *I.* 122.
Endymion, *II.* 251.
Escort, *I.* 102.
Espiegle, *I.* 186.
Espoir, *I.* 284.
Essex, *I.* 102.
Etna, *I.* 102.
Euryalus, *II.* 196, 231.
Eurydice, *I.* 213.
Excellent, *I.* 207, 220, 222, 263, 267, 273; *II.* 80.
Exmouth, *II.* 232.
Fairfax, *I.* 321.
Falmouth, *I.* 65.
Fame, *I.* 222.
Faulcon, *I.* 12.
Favourite, *I.* 12.
Ferret, *II.* 332.
Firebrand, *II.* 92.
Firedrake, *I.* 102.
Fishguard, *II.* 324.
Flamborough, *II.* 312.
Flora, *I.* 140.
Fly, *II.* 332.
Foresight, *I.* 12.
Forte, *II.* 338.
Fortune, *I.* 17.
Fox, *I.* 291; *II.* 73, 340.
Furieuse, *II.* 330, 331.
Furious, *II.* 91.
Furnace, *I.* 102.
Fury, *II.* 13.
Gabriel Royal, *I.* 8.
Ganges, *I.* 190.
Garland, *I.* 39.
Genoa, *II.* 18, 19, 20.
George, *I.* 12.
Gibraltar, *I.* 206.
Gipsy, *II.* 325.
Glasgow, *II.* 20.
Glatton, *I.* 140, 141.
Glendower, *II.* 226.
Gorgon, *II.* 45, 49.
Goliath, *I.* 236; *II.* 231.
Grampus, *I.* 198.
Great Barke, *I.* 8.
Guardian, *I.* 178.
Hampshire, *I.* 44.
Hampton Court, *I.* 111.
Handmayd, *I.* 12.
Hannibal, *II.* 235.
Harry Grace a Dieu, *I.* 8.
Hart, *I.* 189.
Haughty, *II.* 128.
Havannah, *II.* 332.
Hazard, *II.* 335, 339.
Hecla, *II.* 13, 82, 84.
Henry Imperial, *I.* 8.
Hercule, *II.* 325.
Hercules, *I.* 208.
Hermes, *I.* 304.
Hermione, *I.* 199; *II.* 308.
Hesper, *II.* 330.
Hibernia, *II.* 8.
Hindustan, *II.* 231.
Hogue, *II.* 80.
Holmes, *II.* 38, 44.
Hope, *I.* 12.
Hound, *I.* 247, 263.
Hussar, *II.* 330.
Hyacinth, *II.* 54, 55, 58, 340.
Hydra, *I.* 278; *II.* 49.

INDEX

Ships, Men-of-War, British—*continued*—
Illustrious, II. 231.
Imperieuse, I. 223, 245, 282; II. 81, 326.
Impetueux, I. 204; II. 329.
Indefatigable, II. 340.
Indomitable, II. 232.
Infernal, I. 102; II. 13, 14.
Invincible, II. 327.
Iris, I. 198; II. 108, 169.
James Watt, II. 81.
Janus, I. 190, 191.
Jennet, I. 8.
Jhesus of Lubeck, I. 8.
Juno, II. 321.
Katherine, I. 26, 32.
Katoomba, II. 247.
Kent, I. 206, 279; II. 329.
King Alfred, II. 231, 232.
Larne, II. 55.
Lancaster, II. 308.
Lavinia, I. 246.
Leander, II. 13, 14.
Lennox, I. 20.
Leonidas, II. 328.
Leopard, I. 199; II. 341.
Leviathan, I. 256, 282; II. 323.
Liberty, I. 277.
Licorne, I. 140.
Lightening, II. 84.
Lion, I. 128, 188; II. 308.
Lively, I. 154, 161; II. 325, 327.
Liverpool, II. 109, 110.
London, I. 32, 38, 193, 203, 208, 209, 210.
Lord Nelson, II. 232.
Lowestoft, II. 320.
Loyall Katherine, I. 32.
Lucifer, I. 222, 223, 226.
Lurcher, I. 318.
Lynn, I. 111.
Lyon, I. 12, 136, 138.
Madagascar, II. 59, 60, 72.
Magicienne, I. 122; II. 88, 89.
Magnet, I. 295.
Magnificent, I. 290; II. 231, 324, 328.
Magpie, II. 338.
Maidstone, II. 311.
Malta, I. 206.
Marlborough, I. 202, 203, 292; II. 322.
Mars, I. 234.
Mary Rose, I. 8.
Matthew, I. 8.
Meander, II. 186.
Mediator, I. 196.
Medusa, I. 290; II. 70.
Medina, II. 333.
Medway, II. 107, 109.
Meleager, I. 248.
Melpomene, I. 241, 243, 244.
Melville, II. 57.
Menelaus, II. 330, 332.
Mercury, II. 318.
Meteor, I. 220, 223, 226.
Milford, II. 331.
Minden, I. 234; II. 330.
Minerva, II. 57.
Modeste, II. 60, 64, 70, 71.
Mohawk, II. 340.
Monarch, II. 169, 234.
Monk, II. 311.
Monmouth, I. 140, 198.
Montagu, I. 297, 298; II. 328.
Montreal, I. 295.
Mosquito, II. 170.
Myrmidon, II. 3.
Naiad, II. 249.
Namur, I. 190.
Nankin, II. 126.
Nelson, II. 126.
Nemesis, II. 57, 59, 73.
Nereide, II. 328.
Newark, I. 190.
Niagara, I. 295.
Nicholas of the Tower, I. 259.
Niobe, II. 248.
Nisus, II. 229.
Nonsuch, I. 44.
Norfolk, I. 78.

North Star, II. 29, 335.
Northumberland, II. 1, 3, 4, 6, 7.
Nymphe, I. 140.
Odin, II. 82.
Orestes, I. 213.
Orion, II. 169, 170; II. 342.
Orlando, II. 251, 254, 255, 269.
Panther, I. 139.
Paradox, II. 310.
Pearl, II. 32, 115, 116, 121, 324, 336.
Pembroke, II. 185.
Penelope, II. 84.
Perseus, II. 148, 150.
Peter, I. 8.
Phaeton, II. 322, 330.
Philip and Marye, I. 12.
Philomel, II. 17, 244.
Phoebe, II. 330.
Phoenix, I. 239, 240; II. 29, 41.
Pique, II. 25, 43, 48, 325.
Plegethon, II. 130.
Plymouth, II. 311.
Polyphemus, I. 254.
Pomona, II. 320.
Pompée, I. 201, 278; II. 326.
Porcupine, I. 276, 279; II. 320.
Powerful, II. 43, 234, 235, 245.
President, II. 330.
Primrose, I. 12.
Prince, I. 44.
Prince of Orange, I. 102; II. 341.
Prince Regent, I. 295.
Princess Caroline, II. 331.
Princess Charlotte, I. 295; II. 45.
Princess Royal, I. 205; II. 81, 231.
Proselyte, I. 190.
Proserpine, I. 246.
Prudente, I. 140.
Pultusk, I. 280.
Queen, I. 234; II. 57.
Queen Charlotte, I. 192, 193, 198; II. 12, 13, 333.
Racer, II. 334.
Rainbow, I. 321.
Raleigh, II. 338.
Ramillies, I. 130.
Ranelagh, II. 38.
Ranger, I. 198; II. 330.
Redwing, II. 284, 285.
Reformation, I. 188.
Renown, II. 139, 162.
Repulse, I. 198.
Resolution, I. 206; II. 326.
Restoration, I. 44, 70.
Retribution, II. 340.
Revenge, I. 245; II. 338.
Rhadamanthus, II. 182.
Rhin, II. 332.
Rippon, I. 136, 137, 138, 140.
Robust, I. 193.
Rodney, II. 43, 338.
Roebuck, I. 137, 139.
Romolus, I. 202, 291.
Rota, I. 303.
Royalist, II. 29, 32.
Royal Charles, I. 32.
Royal James, I. 21.
Royal Katherine, I. 26, 32.
Royal Sovereign, I. 193, 251.
Royal William, I. 32, 120.
Ruby, I. 31, 321; II. 88, 89.
Russell, I. 78.
Saint David, I. 44.
Saint Fiorenzo, I. 198.
Saint George, II. 338.
Saint Jean d'Acre, II. 80, 81.
Salamander, II. 30.
Samarang, II. 328.
Samson, II. 92.
Sandfly, I. 212.
Sandwich, I. 102, 196, 198.
Satellite, II. 337, 338.
Seagull, II. 152, 170.
Sealark, II. 332.
Seine, I. 141, 248.
Shah, II. 337.
Shannon, II. 115, 116, 183, 330.
Sheldrake, I. 229.
Shrewsbury, I. 78.
Sirius, I. 178; II. 328.

Slaney, II. 3.
Snake, II. 144.
Southampton, I. 102, 205.
Sparkler, I. 215.
Speaker, I. 321; II. 10.
Standard, II. 226, 227.
Star, I. 295.
Statira, I. 245.
Staunch, II. 328.
Stromboli, I. 78; II. 49, 331.
Success, I. 143.
Superb, I. 102; II. 5, 6, 15.
Surprise, II. 308.
Surveillante, I. 290.
Swallow, I. 12, 95; II. 331.
Swiftsure, I. 12, 102, 188.
Sybille, II. 126.
Tagus, II. 12.
Talavera, II. 333.
Tartar, I. 6, 47, 96, 229, 230; II. 336.
Temeraire, I. 102, 205, 243, 244; II. 328.
Tenedos, II. 337.
Termagant, II. 86.
Terrible, II. 234, 235, 247, 256, 259, 260, 261, 262, 263, 264.
Thalia, I. 203.
Thames, I. 282.
Theseus, I. 148, 216, 217, 218; II. 338.
Thetis, I. 242.
Thomas of the Tower, I. 259.
Thunder, I. 205.
Thunderer, II. 49, 50.
Tiger, I. 10, 12.
Tigre, I. 216, 217, 218, 232.
Tonnant, I. 256, 298; II. 4.
Topaze, II. 232, 333.
Torbay, I. 37, 102.
Trent, I. 234.
Tribune, II. 340.
Triumph, I. 8, 12.
Truelove, I. 20.
Tweed, II. 28, 32.
Undaunted, I. 284, 285, 286; II. 330.
Valiant, I. 102; II. 328.
Valorous, II. 82, 84, 185.
Vanguard, I. 32, 188.
Venerable, I. 142, 197; II. 323.
Vengeance, I. 206.
Vesuvius, II. 92.
Victorious, II. 231.
Victory, I. 12, 251, 255, 257; II. 231.
Ville de Paris, I. 201, 202, 203, 204.
Vixen, II. 336.
Volage, II. 54, 334.
Volontaire, II. 330.
Wager, I. 312, 313, 314.
Warspite, I. 258.
Wasp, II. 43, 49.
Waterwitch, II. 334.
Wellesley, II. 54, 55, 64, 66, 67, 72, 73, 114, 230.
White Bear, I. 12.
Widgeon, II. 338.
Windsor Castle, I. 206.
Woolwich, I. 137, 139.
York, II. 109, 110.
Zealous, I. 142; II. 323.
Zebra, II. 47, 48.

Ships, Men-of-War, Foreign—

American (U.S.)—
Adams, II. 331.
Chesapeake, II. 330.
Delaware, II. 320.
Jason, II. 308.
Austrian—
Guerriera, II. 49, 50.
Dutch—
Van Trump, I. 321.
Egyptian—
Fatteh, II. 216, 219.
Kailar, II. 219.
Melik, II. 219.
Metemneh, II. 215.
Nasir, II. 216.
Tamai, II. 215.

Ships, Foreign, continued—
French—
  Albion, I. 238, 239, 249.
  Aquilon, I. 245.
  Bienfaisant, II. 316.
  Bucentaur, I. 250, 254, 256, 257.
  Calcutta, I. 245.
  Capricieuse, La, I. 140.
  Columbe, La, I. 205.
  Content, II. 311.
  Didon, II. 239, 240.
  Doutelle, I. 128.
  Duchayla, II. 139.
  Elizabeth, I. 128.
  Embuscade, I. 318, 319.
  Etourdie, I. 277.
  Fouguex, I. 256.
  Guerrier, I. 142.
  Hoche, II. 323.
  Harmonie, II. 325.
  Imortalite, II. 324.
  Jacobin, II. 322.
  Majesteux, I. 246.
  Mutius Scœvola, II. 322.
  Naturaliste, I. 179.
  Neptune, I. 254.
  Nisus, I. 279.
  Nymphe, I. 140.
  Orient, I. 142.
  Pique, II. 322.
  Pomone, I. 239.
  Prince Eugene, I. 278.
  Prudente, II. 316.
  Redoubtable, I. 255, 256, 257.
  Sceptre, I. 84.
  Sirene, II. 16.
  Spartiate, I. 142.
  Tonnant, I. 142.
  Tonnere, I. 245.
  Trident, II. 311.
  Vengeance, I. 141.
  Vengeur, II. 322.
  Victoire, I. 215.
  Vigilante, I. 279.
  Warsaw, I. 245.
Italian—
  Volpe, II. 249.
Spanish—
  Africa, I. 80, 84.
  Algeciras, I. 256.
  Argonauta, I. 257.
  Carlos, I. 80, 84.
  Conception, I. 248.
  Covadonga, Neustra Senora de, I. 63.
  Galicia, I. 80, 84.
  Hermoine, II. 317.
  Neptune, II. 324.
  Rayo, I. 249.
  Reyna, II. 30.
  San Agustin, I. 256.
  San Carlos, I. 146.
  San Paulo, II. 328.
  San Philip, I. 80.
  Santissima Trinidada, I. 250, 255.
  Selva, La, I. 143.
Turkish—
  Gulsefide, II. 49.
Privateers—
  Duke, I. 132.
  Mentor, I. 118, 124.
  Resolution, I. 99.
Naval Transports—
  Euphrates, II. 70.
  Himalaya, II. 158.
  Tamar, II. 158, 166, 170.
Ships, Mercantile—
  Adelaide, II. 129.
  Alexander, I. 172.
  Ambriz, II. 153.
  Atlantic, I. 178.
  Betsy Cains, II. 265.
  Birkenhead, II. 325.
  Brune, I. 298.
  Carnatic, I. 118–124.
  Calcutta, I. 180, 181, 182; II. 126.
  Ceylon, I. 296, 303.
  Charlotte, I. 172.
  Dacca, II. 169, 170.
  Diadem, I. 290.

Diana, I. 158.
Friendship, I. 172, 175.
Gorgon, I. 178.
Grand Duchess of Russia, I. 162.
Imperador, II. 129.
Imperatrice, II. 129.
Lady Nelson, I. 182.
Lady Penrhyn, I. 174.
Medina, II. 302, 307.
Melpomone, I. 298.
Milwaukee, II. 249.
Moor, II. 235.
Nerissa, II. 170.
Ocean, I. 108, 181, 182.
Ophir, II. 297.
Prince of Wales, I. 172.
Rachel, II. 236.
Regulus, I. 301.
Resistance, II. 182.
Romeo Primero, II. 334.
Romney, II. 333.
Roshina, II. 170.
Roslin Castle, II. 235.
Royal Tar, II. 28.
Scarborough, I. 174.
Security, (Prison ship), I. 208.
Somerset, I. 149.
Supply, I. 178.
Three Brothers, I. 75.
Utopia, II. 196.
Ships, newly commissioned, fitted out by R. M., I. 268; II. 80.
Shoe-making Department, II. 297.
Sidon, Bombardment and Capture of, II. 49.
Signal, Nelson's Famous I. 252.
Simonoseki, Bombardment of, II. 148.
.... Storming of Stockade at, II. 149.
Simons Town, R.M. Battalion leaves, II. 234.
Sinzheim, Battle of, II. 310.
Skelton, Sir Bevil, I. 21.
Sluys, Battle of, I. 7.
Smith, Sir Sidney, R.N., on Death of Major Oldfield, I. 217.
.... His costume, I. 220.
Snell, Hannah, The story of, I. 93.
Sole Bay, Battle of, I. 21, 31.
Somerset, Cape York, Detachment R.M. at, I. 186.
Soudan, Evacuation of the, II. 204.
Spain, North Coast of, R.M. on the, I. 290; II. 28.
.... War of Succession in, I. 36.
Spanish system of ship manning, I. 11, 13.
Standard of height in 1740, I. 72.
Status of Seamen, according to Juvenal, I. 4.
Steele, Sir Robert, R.M.A. His account of Anholt, I. 228.
Stink-pots, II. 73.
Store Room, The Marine, I. 123; II. 221.
Storm, Great, at Balaklava, II. 102.
Strength of R.M. Corps in 1913, II. 293.
Suakin, Occupation of, II. 190.
.... Defences of, II. 197.
Sudbury, Pte. John, "His List of Nepolane Buonaparte," II. 3.
Suggestions for formation of Marine Corps, by Dr. John Dee, I. 9.
.... By Sir Bernard Gascoigne, I. 30.
.... By Col. Campbell Dalrymple (for R.M.A.), I. 261.
.... By Sir James Saumarez, II. 342.
.... Volunteer Marine Corps, II. 294.
Sujah Dowla, II. 108.
"Sun, The Glorious, of York," I. 15.
Surgeon, Pte. R.M. receives pay as, I. 301.
Sweaborg, Bombardment of, II. 89.
Swords, Presentation, I. 230, 235, 279; II. 325, 326.
Syria, British Fleet sent to, II. 42.
...... R. Marines in, II. 44.

T

Tailoring Department, II. 294, 296.
Taku Forts, Bombarded and taken, II. 255.
Tamai, Battle of, II. 193.
Tangiers, Defence of, I. 24.
.... Uniform at, I. 33.
"Tarpaulins or Tarpawlins," I. 17; II. 341.
Tasmania, Settlement in, I. 182.
.... Colonel Collins made Governor of, I. 182.
.... Colonel Davey made Governor of, I. 184.
"Tawney" Coats, I. 15.
Taylor, Captain Silas, Report on work of Marines, I. 19.
Tel-el-Kebir, Night march on, II. 173.
.... Battle of, II. 174.
.... Comet at, II. 176.
Tench, Captain, His literary work, I. 174.
Thetis and Amethyst, Fight between the, I. 242.
Tien-tsin, Fighting at, II. 255, 260, 265, 267.
.... Railway Station, R.M., Again at in 1901, II. 267.
.... Unrest at, II. 254.
Timmins, Captain, Promoted to Major for Trafalgar, I. 258.
Tinghae, Capture of, II. 55, 65, 141.
Tiree, R.M. Battalion at, II. 338.
Tobago, Capture of, II. 321.
Tofrek, Battle of (McNeil's Zareba), II. 202.
Tong-ku, Allies land at, II. 251.
Torres Vedras, Lines of, II. 329.
Torrington, The Earl of, His Marine Regiment, I. 25.
Tortosa, Repulse at, II. 47.
Toulon, Operations at, II. 320.
.... Escape of H.M.S. Juno, II. 320.
"Tour," of Embarkation Duty first laid down, I. 136.
Townshend, Major-General C. V. F., Services of, II. 219.
Trafalgar, Battle of R. Marines at, I. 250.
Trained Bands, The, I. 15, 17, 38.
Traitors at Gibraltar, I. 54.
Treasure Ships Captured, I. 63, 124, 319; II. 317, 325.
Treaty signed by Lieut. Pearce of the Marines, I. 145.
Trenches before Sebastopol, In the, II. 100.
Trieste, Occupation of, II. 331.
Trincomalee, Capture of, II. 114.
Trinidad, Fort, Defence of, II. 220.
"Trumpeter, The," II. 302.
Tsee-Kee, Capture of, II. 67.
Tung-Chow, R.M. occupy gate of, II. 143.
Turckheim, Battle of, II. 310.
Turkish Fleet at Navarino, The, II. 16.
Turks, Form of prayer against the, II. 10.
.... versus Roman Catholics, II. 21.
.... a "Turk prisoner" at Carthagena, I. 82, 91.
.... at Acre, I. 217.
Turnbull, Lieut., His drawing of action .... at Anholt, I. 229.
Tweebosch, Defeat at, II. 248.
Tyre taken, II. 48.

INDEX

U

Uniform Clothing, &c.
Badges, Band, *II.* 164.
Badges, Company Sergeants, *II.* 24, 78.
Badges of Rank, *II.* 23, 24, 77, 161, 162, 163, 164.
Badges, Regimental, *I.* 87, 88, 101, 112, 268, 306; *II.* 22, 23, 76, 77, 106, 161, 164, 221.
Baldrics, *I.* 33.
Balls (for Shakos), *II.* 76, 77, 90, 162.
Boots (Officers), *I.* 114, 168; *II.* 22, 23, 24, 74, 76, 163.
Breeches, *I.* 14, 73, 90, 112, 114, 124, 164, 169; *II.* 21, 74, 75.
Busbies, *I.* 268; *II.* 164.
Buttons, Regimental, *I.* 88, 114, 169; *II.* 22, 75.
.... Mourning, *II.* 305.
Caps, Grenadier, *I.* 23, 33, 35, 36, 43, 57, 71, 73, 87, 88, 106, 112, 115, 123, 124, 125, 164, 165; *II.* 106, 162.
...... Light Infantry, *I.* 164, 165; *II.* 21, 22.
...... (*i.e.*, Shakoes or Chacos), *II.* 23, 24, 74, 75, 76.
...... Sea, *I.* 118, 123.
...... Surtout (?), *II.* 75.
...... Undress, or Forage, *I.* 123, 266; *II.* 22, 25, 75, 76, 77, 78, 79, 85, 160, 163, 164, 230, 231 232.
Chevrons, *II.* 23, 77, 160, 161, 162.
Cloaks, Officers', *II.* 76, 162.
Clothing, Care of, *I.* 123, 124; *II.* 222.
.... Cost of, *I.* 12; *II.* 22.
.... Issue of, *II.* 162, 225.
.... Overdue, *I.* 300.
Coats (Including Coatees)—
...... Blue, *I.* 25, 33, 263, 264, 266, 268; *II.* 268.
...... Frock (*Vide* " Frock Coats ").
...... Great (*Vide* "Great Coats ").
...... Red, *I.* ii, 11, 15, 16, 25, 31, 36, 73, 88, 106, 113, 164, 165, 169, 321; *II.* 21, 22, 23, 24, 53, 74.
...... Sea Green, *I.* 2.
...... " Tawney," *I.* 15, 16.
...... White, *I.* 12, 29; *II.* 25.
...... Yellow, *I.* 14, 15, 88; *II.* 310.
Cockades, *I.* 125, 266, 318; *II.* 41.
Corselets (*Vide* Gorgets).
Crape, *II.* 74, 76, 160.
Crescents, *II.* 221, 229.
Epaulettes (including " Wings,"), *I.* 114, 134, 165, 250; *II.* 22, 23, 24, 75, 76, 159.
Facings, *I.* 14, 25, 29, 33, 36, 73, 88, 106, 114.; *II.* 22, 23, 161, 222.
Feathers, *II.* 22, 23, 25, 75, 76, 77.
Frock Coats, *II.* 77, 161, 162.
Gaiters (*Vide* Leggings).
Garters, *I.* 164, 169; *II.* 21.
Gloves, *I.* 33, 113; *II.* 77, 231.
Gorgets, *I.* 33, 114, 169, 187, 276; *II.* 22, 75, 76.
Great Coats, *II.* 22, 24, 162, 166.
Hair, *I.* 114, 125, 164, 169; *II.* 22, 23, 24.
Hats, *I.* 33, 113, 114, 123, 164, 165, 169, 233, 249; *II.* 22, 23, 24, 25, 41.
Helmets, *II.* 106, 164, 166, 282.
Jackets, *I.* 113, 123, 249, 264; *II.* 21, 22, 24, 41, 74, 75.
.... Shell, *II.* 75, 77, 78, 161, 162, 222, 225, 230.
.... Mess (*Vide* Mess Jacket).
.... Patrol (*Vide* Patrol Jacket).
Jumpers, *II.* 222, 225.
Lace, *I.* 14, 71, 87, 88, 112, 165, 268, 306; *II.* 22, 23, 24, 41, 77, 160, 161, 162.
Leggings, *I.* 73, 123, 164, 169; *II.* 22, 77, 162.
Mess Jackets, *II.* 163.

Moustaches, *II.* 160.
Pantaloons, *II.* 22, 23, 24, 74, 163.
Patrol Jackets, *II.* 162, 163, 164.
Plate, Hat, Shako, Helmet, *I.* 266, *II.* 24, 40, 41, 53, 54, 74, 76, 188, 204.
Plate, Shoulder-Belt, *I.* 306; *II.* 22, 23, 24, 53, 78, 90, 177, 232, 249.
Plumes, *II.* 78, 106, 161, 162.
Ribband, Cap, *I.* 318.
Roses and Ribbands for Gorgets, *I.* 169; *I.* 21, 22, 76.
Sabretasches, *II.* 163, 309.
Saddlery and Saddle Cloths, *II.* 75.
Sash, *I.* 33, 114, 164, 268; *II.* 22, 23, 77, 78, 106, 159, 163.
Shakoes (or Chacos), *II.* 13, 40, 73, 90, 106, 107, 160, 162, 163, 164, 221.
Shirts, *I.* 113, 114, 123, 150, 169; *II.* 23, 230.
Shoes, *I.* 114, 123; *II.* 22.
Shoulder Knots, *I.* 33, 88, 113, 114; *II.* 23.
Shoulder Scales, *II.* 78, 79, 229.
Shoulder Straps, *II.* 76, 77, 221.
Spatterdashes, *I.* 114, 124.
Steel-bound Hats, *I.* 249.
Stocks, *I.* 169; *II.* 75.
Stockings, *I.* 14, 113, 114, 123; *II.* 75, 76, 223, 230.
Stripes, Defaulters, *II.* 75, 160.
...... Trouser, *II.* 160, 161, 163.
Trousers, *I.* 88; *II.* 22, 23, 24, 74, ... 160, 161, 163, 222.
Tufts, *I.* 124, 165, 266, 268; *II.* 22, 25, 75, 76.
Tunics, *II.* 160, 161, 162, 164.
.... Khaki, *II.* 226, 234, 282.
.... Blue Serge, *II.* 162, 166, 174, 225.
Uniform, Tropical, *I.* 33; *II.* 25, 162, 164, 230, a.
Waistcoats, *I.* 88, 112, 114, 124, 164, *II.* 21, 22, 23, 24, 163, 222, 225.
Vide also " Orders Divisional,"
" United Irishmen, The," *I.* 192, 199, 201, 210.
Unpopularity of Service afloat, *I.* 5, 16.
Urimea, Crossing of the, *II.* 30.
Utrecht, Peace of, *I.* 68, 71.

V

Value of Marines afloat, *I.* 26, 32, 321.
Vancouver Island, R.M. at, *II.* 136, 336.
Von Kettler, Baron, Murder of, *II.* 278.
Var, French entrenchments on the, stormed, *I.* 64; *II.* 314.
Various positions held by Officers of Admiral's Regiment, *I.* 16, 27.
Vaughan, Capt. Roger, Terrible Fate of, *I.* 31.
Venezuelan Blockade, *II.* 340.
Vernon, Admiral, *I.* 73, 82, 86, 90.
Veterans, Gibraltar, *I.* 57.
Via Reggio, Operations at, *I.* 286.
Viborg, Attack on, *II.* 88.
Victoria Crosses gained by R.M., *II.* 79.
Victoria Cross, Captain Halliday gains the, *II.* 280.
.... Lieutenant Dowell, *II.* 89.
.... Corporal Prettyjohns, *II.* 99.
.... Bombardier Wilkinson, *II.* 103.
Victoria, Queen, Her telegram to Capt. Wray, *II.* 290.
Vigo, Operations at, *I.* 36; *II.* 327.
Villadarias, The Marquis of, *I.* 47, 48, 49-56, 322.

Villefranche, Marines engaged at, *II.* 314.
Vincent, Lord St., and the Marines, *I.* 201, 210.
.... on the Marines, *I.* 187.
Virginia, Colony of, Marines go there in 1676, *I.* 22.
" Viva Marines," the " usual toast in Catalonia," *I.* 324.
Vivero, Operations at, *II.* 326.
Volunteers, British Royal North, *I.* 161.
.... Loyal American Associations, *I.* 161.
.... Loyal Irish, *I.* 161, 167; *II.* 179, 182.
.... Proposed Royal Marine, *II.* 293.

W

Walcheren, Fort Veer, occupied, *II.* 327.
Walfisch Bay, R.M. at, *II.* 248.
Waller, Lieut. J., His letter describing Bunker's Hill, *I.* 156.
War of the Succession in Spain, *I.* 36.
Ward Room Arms, *I.* 121.
"Warlike, The, of the Isles," *II.* 301.
Warren's Victory off Ireland, *II.* 323.
Washing and Cleanliness, *I.* 135.
Washington (? Lawrence), *I.* 78.
.... George, *I.* 89.
Washington, Capture of, *I.* 300.
Watch, Marine Officers keeping, *II.* 232.
Wei-Hai-Wei R.M. Detachment ordered to Pekin, *II.* 269.
White Cloud Mountain, Battle of the, *II.* 135.
White, Lieut. F., His capture by Carlists, *II.* 38, 41.
Whitford (or Whitfurd) of Ballochmyle, *I.* 130.
Whittaker, Capt. R. N., *I.* 39.
Wilkinson, Bombr., wins V.C., *II.* 103.
Wolfe, General James, *I.* 75.
Wood and Water, *I.* 44.
Woosung, Fighting at, *II.* 70.
Wright, Capt. John, commended by Gen. Hodgson, *I.* 109.

Y

Yang, Gallant Chinese General, *II.* 67.
" Yellow-Coats," *I.* 14, 23.
.... Drive off French Fly Boat, *II.* 310.
Yokahama, R.M. Battalion at, *II.* 146.
Young Pretender, The, Orders to search for, *I.* 111.
.... escapes from H.M.S. *Lion*, *I.* 128.

Z

Zululand, R. Marines in, *II.* 337.